THE
MAX BRAND
COMPANION

''Max Brand''

THE
MAX BRAND
COMPANION

EDITED BY
Jon Tuska and Vicki Piekarski
Darrell C. Richardson, Consulting Editor

GREENWOOD PRESS
Westport, Connecticut • London

Library of Congress Cataloging-in-Publication Data

The Max Brand companion / edited by Jon Tuska, Vicki Piekarski ;
  Darrell C. Richardson, consulting editor.
     p. cm.
    Includes bibliographical references (p.) and index.
    ISBN 0–313–29750–9 (alk. paper)
    1. Brand, Max, 1892–1944. 2. Western stories—History and
criticism. 3. Authors, American—20th century—Biography.
  I. Tuska, Jon. II. Piekarski, Vicki.
  PS3511.A87Z77   1996
  813'.52—dc20   96–18207
  [B]

British Library Cataloguing in Publication Data is available.

Library of Congress Catalog Card Number: 96–18207
ISBN: 0–313–29750–9

First published in 1996

Greenwood Press, 88 Post Road West, Westport, CT 06881
An imprint of Greenwood Publishing Group, Inc.

Printed in the United States of America

The paper used in this book complies with the
Permanent Paper Standard issued by the National
Information Standards Organization (Z39.48–1984).

10 9 8 7 6 5 4 3 2 1

For Robert and Jane Easton

CONTENTS

Photo essays follow pages 140 and 281

INTRODUCTION

Jon Tuska

At the time Vicki and I were preparing the first edition of the ENCYCLOPEDIA OF FRONTIER AND WESTERN FICTION (McGraw-Hill, 1983), I had read only two books by Frederick Faust who wrote as Max Brand, BLOOD ON THE TRAIL (Dodd, Mead, 1957) and DESTRY RIDES AGAIN (Dodd, Mead, 1930). Vicki had never read anything by this author. Accordingly, we engaged a contributor to do the entry on Frederick Faust. But we were dissatisfied with that entry and also in a quandary because the finished text was due at the publisher. In desperation I read Robert Easton's biography, MAX BRAND: THE BIG ''WESTERNER'' (University of Oklahoma Press, 1970), and fashioned the Faust entry as best I could, relying heavily on biographical details and Easton's critical assessments.

When we began the preliminary work of preparing the second edition of the ENCYCLOPEDIA, I decided to include Faust among those authors whose entries I would do. Now it is not possible in doing such an entry to read every book an author has written, especially one as prolific as Faust, but I did select somewhat at random fifty of his Western novels and fifty of his short novels and stories published in magazines. What I discovered, once I had concluded my reading, was one of the most extraordinary literary artists in American letters.

It is perhaps worth noting that when Vicki and I undertook to prepare the first edition of the ENCYCLOPEDIA, I had read under ten novels in the field and Vicki had read fewer than that. Our first years in Oregon, from 1978 through 1982, we literally read Western fiction morning, noon, and night, consuming thousands of books and stories. Since we had each selected different authors, we confined our reading principally to those authors whose entries we were doing and would discuss the books each other had read in order to share the experience and eliminate the necessity of both of us having to read the same stories. Virtually all of the fiction I had read prior to 1978 was confined to the Greek and Latin classics, as well as modern German, French, British, Italian, Russian, and American literature. Other than an occasional detective story or science fiction opus, I had virtually no exposure to popular fiction. What critical judgments I formed for my entries in the ENCYCLOPEDIA were against this background of classical literature, both from antiquity and the post–Middle Ages, and Western stories by the authors whom I had read. Faust seemed readily to belong in this company as one of the foremost authors not only of the Western story but of literary fiction in general.

It wasn't until we founded Golden West Literary Agency and Frederick Faust became an estate client in June 1992 that Vicki became deeply involved with reading his fiction, especially the stories for our various anthologies and novels and story collections either published in our Five Star Westerns program, Circle Ⓥ Westerns, or by other publishers where we had to prepare the texts from Faust's original manuscripts. Vicki came to share my enthusiasm for Faust's work, and we were in agreement that what was most remarkable about him wasn't how much he wrote but how fine is so much of what he wrote. In even a minor story there is, notwithstanding occasional flaws, always something that stays with a reader and makes the experience of having read the story memorable.

Frederick Faust, no matter under what *nom de plume* he may have been published at a given moment, is always eminently readable and accessible. For some academic scholars these qualities are often considered to be handicaps and compromise an author's claim to literary significance. The resulting debates are endless, as have been the efforts to demonstrate why Henry James wrote on a higher plane than Jack London, as presumably Dostoyevsky has more claim to greatness than Turgenev, Austen than Dickens, Flaubert than Balzac, Thomas Mann than Hermann Hesse—and so it goes. I find all such ranking wearisome and not really meaningful. Ultimately, all any author has to give a reader is himself or herself. If he or she is able to create characters who amuse, interest, and involve us, he or she has fulfilled their compact with the reader which, in Prospero's words in "The Tempest," is primarily to please.

Depending on your sensibility, you may derive as much pleasure from reading Jane Austen as from reading Charles Dickens and feel no compulsion whatsoever to rank one over the other. Moreover, while pundits in the literary establishment resent the fact, it is nonetheless true that those authors whom posterity has continued to read have usually been among the most popular and widely read authors of their day. In the case of Frederick Faust, his posthumous popularity with the reading public has exceeded anything he experienced during his lifetime, as popular as he always was with readers. In the spring and fall publishing seasons of 1996, Frederick Faust, who died in 1944, published no fewer than thirteen titles that are first time in book form, in some cases published for the first time anywhere. I cannot think of another author in literary history about whom such a claim can be made.

THE MAX BRAND COMPANION has been designed for the reader interested in this author who wrote as Max Brand. It is divided conveniently into three general sections: Biography and Tributes that tell us about the man as well as the author; Bibliographies that chart the publication history of Faust's work as well as derivations of that work in other media such as motion pictures, annotated bibliographies of critical commentaries about Faust and his work, and (albeit slightly more arcane) the joys of collecting first editions of Faust's work; and finally Belles Lettres and Literary Criticism that present characteristic works by Faust himself indicative of the scope and depth of his imagination and mastery, and critical essays and articles about individual aspects of his work by a variety of critics, scholars, and fellow authors. There has been no attempt to arrive at a consensus of opinion on critical matters; rather our objective has been to present varying viewpoints in the spirit of a symposium where many ideas and interpretations are equally admitted into the discussion.

The headnotes which appear throughout this book are intended primarily to define or introduce what follows. Those interested in learning more about some of the individual contributors beyond what is stated in the headnotes will find this information in About the Editors and Contributors. Citations to serials, short novels, short stories, and published books by Frederick Faust under various pen names are not dated since all of this information can be found in the chapter Frederick Faust: A Bibliography. In every case, however, the texts cited are those closest to the author's original manuscripts where editorial intervention has been at a minimum. Hence, the serial ''Black Jack'' will be cited rather than the Dodd, Mead abridgment, which excised nearly 25,000 words from Faust's original. It should be stressed that all of the texts of Faust's works are now appearing in authentic or, in some cases, restored editions. Reference to these authentic texts is made variously throughout this companion, and it is recommended that the reader seek Faust's work in such editions. A case in point is the tetralogy concerning Thunder Moon that the University of Nebraska Press published in fall 1996 in texts derived directly from Faust's typescripts as opposed to the bowdlerized three-book series issued earlier by Dodd, Mead. In the Five Star Westerns series from Thorndike Press, four new Max Brand Western titles are scheduled to appear annually. In the majority of cases where Faust's original titles are known, these too are being restored to his works. In future editions of the Faust Bibliography, such restored titles, as well as authentic editions, will be duly noted. At present in the Bibliography abridged or bowdlerized texts have been indicated where these have occurred.

Ultimately this book is designed to serve many needs and fulfill many desires, the least of which would not be making some semblance of order out of the work of an author with nearly 600 appearances in periodicals and 900 different copyrights to his name. If, in the process, all of the contributors collectively, as well as the editors, manage to win greater critical recognition and appreciation for Frederick Faust, who has enriched so many lives with his imperishable stories, it will in a sense be a small repayment for the many hours of pleasure he has brought to legions of readers for now hard on seventy-five years.

BIOGRAPHY AND TRIBUTES

DESTRY AND DIONYSUS

Martha Bacon

During the 1930s, when the Fausts lived in Florence, Leonard Bacon and his family were close neighbors. Their eldest daughter, Martha, was Jane Faust's constant companion, and in this evocative memoir Martha Bacon recalls those years. When she wrote this essay, she was working as an associate editor for the Atlantic Monthly, *where it first appeared. It was also the first attempt to deal with Frederick Faust on a dual level, as a pulp writer and as a poet.*

It was a fine spring night. The stars hung like almond blossoms over Florence, shedding a scent and a lyric over the turgid Arno; above the Torre del Gallo, Jupiter hung like a sword. The professor of astronomy invited me to the pedestal.

"Shut one eye and look and you will see three moons." There were indeed three moons. The astronomy professor continued with his disquisition. "We measure in units of distance called light-years. The light from that star took twenty-five years to reach you. You do not see the star to which I am pointing now, but only the light of it, which started on its way to the earth before you were born."

I must take my stand from that star and let the light take me back rather than forward, back to the moment at which the light started, and I find myself in Forte dei Marmi, on the coast of Liguria, below La Spezia. Between the sea stabbed with brilliant July sunlight and the garden full of zinnias, rooted in sand, are Faust and his daughter, Jane, come to pick us up for a swim.

He is a huge man, over six foot three; he is in his late thirties, and the look of his youth has left him; the hair is thinning on his massive head. His cold blue eyes are at war with the heated modeling of the jaw and lips. He is Michelangelo's man, the shoulders big, the limbs well cut, the hands heavy with stub fingers. Jane resembles him as the lion cub resembles her sire. Her thick hair burns like brass in the sunlight; her blade-like twelve-year-old body stands ready to pierce the sea.

Faust, Jane, my sisters Helen and Alice, Bigboy, the Faust's Newfoundland, Celia, our Sealyham, and Piero, who is anybody's big socialist cat, run across the baking sands, giving a wide berth to the hornet-haunted clumps of sage, to the sea. Piero stops before we get to the beach to hunt for lizards; Bigboy splashes in first of all; Celia, torn between love of people and hatred of water, remains an agitated dot at the edge of the surf: "Come back, come back. You will all drown."

Faust has a project this summer; the stars are his project, and Forte dei Marmi is the place to pursue it. During a Mediterranean summer everything that is serious happens at night. In the early morning before the heat begins, we are in pursuit of music and art. At eleven we swim; at noon we eat figs and *prosciutto* and drink wine. The rest of the day we sleep under white nets to keep off the mosquitoes. At twilight we rise, as the evening primroses, taller on their long stalks than we are, open their yellow eyes to Arcturus in the west and to Capella coming over Carrara, escaping the shark's-tooth range by inches. The sand is cool now, and we have lit a bonfire on the beach. We are grouped around Faust who, with his worker's hands and scholar's lips, translates into his own terms the universe.

"Do you see that necklace of stars almost directly above you? That is called Corona. Those are not stars of the first magnitude. They are thousands of light-years away. There is Polaris. There is the Great Bear, the Little Bear, Io and her son. Later on in the year you will see Orion and the weeping Pleiades. There will be Sirius and there, invisible, will be the dark companion whose atomic substance outweighs our solar system." And the voice continues, impressing upon us the precise number of light-years at which we are standing off from Vega, whom we are approaching, as it happens, at a really nerve-wracking pace.

"Mother, Mother, the stars are going to fall on me!" It is astonishing that this holocaust, the sun, plagued by whirlwinds, constricted by earthquakes, hurling flaming gas a million miles into outer space, rises so punctually over Italy. Faust makes the stars real. Faust makes it possible to believe that time is what it is, a great ring of pure and endless light that comprehends the dinosaur, the drowned body of the author of "Prometheus Unbound," the undrowned bodies of the authors of POINT COUNTER POINT and THE FURIOSO who at this moment sit clasping their thin knees on the other side of the fire, their glasses gleaming like four stars, admonishing us dryly not to fall into the flames.

Faust makes the stars real. Our summer at Forte dei Marmi is over, and we are again in Florence. It is time for other realities. All Gaul is divided into three parts; the sum of the squares of the legs of a right-angle triangle is equal to the square of the hypotenuse—the minuet from *Don Giovanni*, Austrian tyranny, Papal tyranny, four wars of independence, and now the blue-jowled Duce who has brought prosperity and plumbing to the land of the Caesars. For Faust, however, there are three essential realities. "Repeat after me . . . Homer, Shakespeare, Dante, Æschlyus, yes, Sophocles, maybe, but no gentleman would read Euripides.''

Faust works furiously at the typewriter from early morning until late afternoon and rounds off the day with six sets of tennis before dinner. He is split by two necessities: what the public will read, and what he longs to write. The split is an agony, and he drinks to soothe it, until he cannot tell friend from foe. In a flood of unrecognizing anger he turns upon his butler, Elia, and catches him by the throat, pinning him over the balustrade while the Italian household alternately wrings its hands and marvels. It is midnight or after, and my father is summoned from across the garden. My father is subject to unpredictable spasms of common sense.

"Hullo, Faust. Drop that butler."

Faust drops the butler, who is all unrestrained gratitude, and the two gentlemen retire to the library to get even more drunk, as gentlemen will, to read Æschylus and to talk of daughters.

"There's just one thing about Jane, the thing we begin with. Jane is perfect. Jane is my daughter. I have no mother, but I have a daughter, Jane."

The mother is a memory. In 1900 her son, Frederick Schiller Faust, is a child eight years old, sitting in a carriage with his father and half-brother, Wolfgang Goethe Faust. They are driving home from the graveyard on the outskirts of the California town where the mother has just been buried. Schiller Faust chooses this moment to tell his father that he doesn't believe in God. He is soundly and instantly thrashed for this impropriety by the fierce German immigrant whose passion for the classics of his native land has led him to name his sons magnificently but not to do much else for them.

The future looks dark for young Schiller Faust. He is bound out to a neighboring farmer, pitches hay, feeds the hogs, and sleeps in a barn, getting what schooling he may when his master will let him. Yet in this life of brutalizing labor he acquires a passion for poetry, reading it by sunlight, by moonlight, by candlelight, memorizing it when he can't find the time to read it, and filling his voracious need by writing it. His head ringing with poetry, he gets through high school, grows to an enormous size, and blunders into the University of California. He studies Greek, becomes a brilliant student. He shakes the academic dust from his sandals and makes his way to New York and there becomes for the nonce a subway guard, so poorly paid, so hungry, that he staves off his pangs by snatching discarded sandwiches from the trash barrel. At the outbreak of the First World War he joins the Canadian army but finds it unchallenging and deserts at a moment when desertion can well mean the firing squad. But the gods are with him and lead him safely through the Maine woods and back to California.

The war is ended, and he becomes a husband and father and a writer. He is perhaps one of the most successful writers of the twentieth century. For Schiller Faust is Max Brand; he is also Evan Evans, Frank Austin, George Owen Baxter, Lee Bolt, Walter C. Butler, George Challis, Martin Dexter, Evin Evan, John

Frederick, Frederick Frost, Dennis Lawton, David Manning, Peter Henry Morland, Hugh Owen, Nicholas Silver, and Frederick Faust. On subways, in trains, on boats, in lighthouse stations, in doctors' offices, people while away the time reading the novels that he grinds out every afternoon between two and five. They are Westerns and hairy-chested popular tales with good workmanlike plots, written in clean, serviceable prose that whips a story from the gate to the finish line without a pause.

He writes for a fortune and gets it. Alive in him like a nerve is the instinct for poetry. He spends long painful mornings, not wooing his muse, but ravishing her. But she resists, and though he masters tennis and Greek and makes success his slave, the muse evades him.

He lives like a medieval prince in his Florentine villa. His swimming pool and tennis court are the envy of the petty aristocracy for miles around. He runs a pack of Newfoundlands and keeps the stars in sight with a telescope on his terrace. He has a weak heart which threatens momentarily to kill him; and against the advice of a battery of doctors he puts the heart in its place by drinking deep, playing tennis like a champion, driving an Isotta-Fraschini a hundred kilometers an hour through the Rhone valley, and keeping a work schedule that would murder a stevedore. He argues that the heart is a muscle and should be exercised. He loves his family and tyrannizes. He wants your happiness, wants to arrange it for you. He marries you, delivers you, buries you, thrashes a daughter, dries her tears, charms the women, and sees what the boys in the back room will have. And the novels are stacked like cordwood in the offices of Brandt & Brandt. He writes them faster than they can be printed. Faust is a one-man factory.

And in 1931 Basil Blackwell brings out in a limited edition a small volume (eighty-nine pages) called DIONYSUS IN HADES. In elevated and measured iambics, irregularly rhymed, Faust tells his own myth, the story of wine and hope and a hard journey and a lost woman.

Accompanied by Silenus and a rout of dancing satyrs and bacchantes, Dionysus descends into Hell, where he pleads with Persephone to restore to him his mother, Semele. He is permitted to see Semele, but Pluto warns him that it is not in his power to free her. He must go to Prometheus for help. Dionysus continues his journey through nether Hell and comes at length to the Titan, who from the midst of his torments tells him that Zeus has been defeated. The god has denied to men the gift of immortality, but Prometheus has brought them the illusion of hope and Dionysus has brought them the illusion of wine, and out of these two illusions comes the everlasting life of mortals. Dionysus learns that Semele may live only if he will surrender her to forgetfulness. He therefore leads her to Lethe, where she drinks and is recreated in Heaven as Thyone, the goddess of rapture, and Dionysus returns to the island of Cos, "to the beautiful and blind life on earth."

It is not poetry for our time. The diction is lofty and Parnassian, smooth as cream, and there is not a line in it whose reference would be obscure to a citizen of the Age of Pericles. He has whipped the verse into submission, and only occasionally the elegiac outcry that he seeks splits the boundaries that he has descried for himself.

He fears not contemporary literature; neither regards he Metro-Goldwyn-Mayer. But Hollywood gets him. Although he has sworn by the nine gods that he will never live in California and that he will never work for the movies, he does both. He goes to M-G-M at the usual hyperbolic figure to do a series called "Young Dr. Kildare."

His big movie is DESTRY RIDES AGAIN (Universal, 1939). In a cloud of dust and a pounding of hoofs it stars young James Stewart and brings Marlene Dietrich back to the screen, superb in flounces and long black stockings, half strumpet, half angel, to sing in her throaty Berlin voice against the saloon and prairie backdrop that is the temple of American myth. Faust is after all a myth-maker, and the despised medium serves him better than he knows. Destry and Brandy roar through the film, Centaur and Bacchante, and the Stetson hat and the ruffled petticoat are as classic in their own way as the helmet and the chiton. It is a *succes fou* with the fans, and the critics are chanting yet.

As it has been in Florence, so is it in California. The talk still teems with Homer and the house with people, some of whom are a pretty far cry from Ilium. Faust drinks with Irish poets, polo players, physicists, and movie stars, and plots stories—he keeps a few acquaintances for the special purpose of bouncing plots off them, as he puts it. He supports promising artists and once promising drunks and anyone who touches him for a loan or a job or both. He plays the horses at Santa Anita, staking long shots across the board, obscure neutral-colored geldings with vague names like King Pharamond and Bubbling Boy who pay fourteen to one and win. His generosity is equal only to his output, and those who benefit from him far outnumber his pen names. He writes po-etry—Dionysus drives him to it, and the mornings are sacred to poetry. He is outrageous, ungovernable, adorable. He loves and hates and strikes the board and has an opinion on every subject—Rembrandt, Bach, and Einstein. "You can have Mozart, but no Brahms and no Keats."

He hasn't forgotten the stars. He keeps the telescope on the roof of the Bur-lingame Avenue house with which to order their courses. Between rushes of Dr. Kildare he is teaching Morris, the butler, the science of astronomy.

"Do you remember that star I showed you last night? The bright one?"

"Yes, Doctor Faust."

"That's Venus. Go out and see if she's still there."

Morris returns. "She's still there, Mister Faust."

"Good." He arises from the table and goes to her, returning presently to tell us that all is well with Venus.

At Santa Maria Infante it is over. He struggles for a year to get into the war and finally goes as a correspondent for *Harper's* to cover the Italian campaign in May of 1944. What his weak heart cannot do, a German mortar shell does.

The light from the star has reached us now, and we find ourselves in the presence of the dark companion.

> Among the ruins, I also breathed the past
> And the sweet clover, I without a name
> Where Dionysus sat, until at last
> Sorrow, not for the Greeks, upon me came.

THE LETTERS OF
FREDERICK FAUST

William A. Bloodworth, Jr.

Raised in near poverty and orphaned at an early age, blessed with literary talent, trapped by his own desire for success in a career as a writer of pulp magazine stories, earner of incredible numbers of dollars from those stories, troubled by his abuse of alcohol, afflicted with a weak heart in an oversize body, haunted by even more oversize dreams, preferring to live in an Italian villa while writing American Westerns, gaining fame afterward as a Hollywood writer, driven by a desire to experience war, and killed as a correspondent on an Italian battlefield in 1944, Frederick Faust led a life of drama, intensity, and interest. The most significant feature of that life was his own personality.

Unfortunately, it would seem, his life and personality are absent from his published work. The stories of Max Brand—or anything else that Faust published—do not bring his experiences to life or even to light except in obscure ways. He was not interested in writing for publication about himself or his experiences. Unlike many other writers in the twentieth century who took the self as the primary subject of art and expression, Faust's genius lay in the presentation of highly imaginative stories whose characters seldom resembled their author. Even as a student at the University of California, where he gained fame as the best of a group of very good undergraduate writers, his own experiences hardly ever became the subject of his poetry, prose, or drama. Such a lack of interest in using his life as the substance of literature turned out to be a fortunate trait for him, however, when he later became a writer of stories. Producing thousands of words per day and dozens of serials, stories, and novels per year meant that he could not be a single writer. Having to be not only Max Brand but also George Owen Baxter, David Manning, et al. meant that he could not bare his life as Frederick Faust to the public even if he had wanted to do so. It was lucky for him that he had no such desire.

It was less lucky for the reading public. Since Faust chose not to write about himself, the "life" of Max Brand (and the presumed lives of the other Faust pseudonyms) was a matter of guesswork during his lifetime. As one of his obituaries observed, he was a "mystery man" of American letters. Since his death he has become less a mystery, thanks especially to Robert Easton's 1970 biography and, to a lesser extent, my own 1993 book. It is now possible for readers and scholars to read Max Brand novels—and anything else written by Faust—with some reliable knowledge of the author's life. But the flavor and texture of his life are impossible to capture in biography. It needs Faust's own telling of it. Fortunately, Faust was almost as prolific a writer of personal letters as he was of pulp fiction. Brevity was not a distinguishing feature of his expression in print, in person, or in correspondence. He was a man of words, a person compelled to write or speak. Moreover, the personal reticence that distinguishes his published work is absent from his letters. They not only document his life, but they provide a full measure of his personality.

His letters are important also for a second reason: they are interesting. They sparkle with wit and humor; they sometimes bulge with sentimentality and pretense; they often allude to serious problems of health and personal relations; and they seldom miss an opportunity to express an opinion.

Most of Faust's existing letters are in the Faust Papers at the Bancroft Library of the University of California at Berkeley. Dorothy Faust, his wife, was careful to keep most of the letters she received from him—and she received them in large numbers whenever he was away from home. These letters were passed on to other members of the family, especially Faust's daughter Jane and her husband, Robert Easton, who have placed them in the Bancroft Library. There are also many Faust letters in the Papers of Robert L. Davis at the New York Public Library and of Leonard Bacon at the Beinecke Library of Yale University. Other Faust letters will turn up elsewhere; Faust's acquaintances were always blessed with letters from him.

The selections from letters here are provided through the generous permission of Robert and Jane Easton. For the most part, they have not been quoted in previously published works on Faust. I present them in chronological order as statements from various stages in Faust's life and career.

LEAVING CALIFORNIA

In May 1915 the University of California refused to grant Faust a degree; he was then twenty-three years old. The ostensible reason for this action was his failure to attend classes in his senior year, during which he chose simply to take course examinations. He and others believed that the real reason for the university's action was President Benjamin Ide Wheeler's displeasure with Faust's writings as editor of a campus humor magazine in which he criticized the president. Faust had been a prolific undergraduate poet and one of the best-known members of the class of 1915. Following his misadventures with President Wheeler, Faust planned that summer with a close college friend, George Winthrop ("Dixie") Fish, to join the nationalist movement in British India. On August 2 Faust wrote a long letter to Thomas Downey, with whom he had lived while attending high school in Modesto, illustrating his early romantic cast of mind and sense of personal mission, neither of which would ever leave him entirely any more than did his literary idealism.

Dear Mr. Downey,

It has been a very long time since I have seen you. . . . I can see now that, if I had taken your advice, I would have graduated without trouble. It was my own stubbornness and my own insane bluntness and pride in an interview with President Wheeler which ruined my chance after the diploma was already signed and ready for my hands. Still on the whole I value that talk with President Wheeler more than a signed piece of paper. I think I told a few straight truths which he heard then for the first time in his life. But the fact remains that the very self assertion which you tried to drill out of me in high school is the thing which spoiled an opportunity for graduation. As things stand now, I could not receive a diploma if I studied here ten years, unless Benjamin Ide should die—fortunate event! Yet I wish you could have taught me the lesson! But we young men are blind. We live in the world of possibility and keep our eyes turned from the world of fact. We expect life to be what we wish it to be; and ah, the bitterness of the time when we realize our limits, so often self-created walls to our own progress—when we know that we can reach only so far, that we can grasp only so much.

I am entering that period now. My boyhood is past, and a man's work and a man's way is before me. All that has gone before is nothing—is a dream, but here is reality, and how am I prepared to work with it? Illy enough, but I have caught up a creed: that if a man works simply and sincerely, seeing that he always avoids cruelty and cowardice, he will achieve that which may not be large but which will be lasting; because he will work with eternal material. I think that every individual possesses in himself that which is worth expression—surely that of which there never has been and never will be a duplicate. Therefore, if he can be sure that he is healthy, normal, and real; if his heaven is not a book-made heaven; if his hell is not a remembered hell; if he does not substitute twisted sensations for the beauty of truth nor mistake the howling of the jackal for the singing of an angel, then I think that with this sense of self reality he can walk straight on and find at the end of the road that he has climbed *up*. And I think, too, that there is something in hard, hard work for its own sake. Do you remember that poem of Browning's, ''The Grammarian's Funeral?'' Do you remember how his pupils carry out that ruined old body whose life has gone to the service of—*grammar?* Ay, but that man had given his soul to it. So, when they carry him out, they look about for the right place to bury him and, looking up, see the mountain tops and say: ''There's the appropriate country. . . . He's for the morning!'' And so they march out—''Our master—famous, calm, and dead, borne on our shoulders.'' And they say as they go on with that wretched, withered

corpse, "He was a man born with thy face and throat, lyric Apollo!"
(God, what a line!) And finally they reach the mountain-top and lay down
the body, and the poem ends somewhat in this wise: "Leave him here,
loftily lying, still loftier than the world suspects—living and dying!"

There's my Bible—if I can have any, and I wouldn't change it for the
New Testament and the Old. And hasn't some such belief been your creed,
too, all these years? I like to think so, for it helps me to remember you,
tenderly always, and . . . reverently, too. Surely a man has done well who
in his own lifetime can give even one human being such a memory. You
have helped me in the past; the thought of you will help me in the future
to fight harder and fight cleaner—but always to fight.

I think I shall never see you again. My work takes me to Japan and
then to India. It's a glorious opening—I shall have a chance to do real
work, and my hands are tensed and ready for it. What I have done in the
past has been bad enough. There is much of the past two years that I
would like to rub from my memory like chalk from a blackboard. But
since I cannot forget, I can at least keep my past from influencing my
future. I must do that for I have much to do. I am engaged to marry a
beautiful girl—I think her beauty goes clear through to the soul—and it
is hard to work a way for two. But after all it's a glorious hardship. After
some four years in India I go to Egypt, and after a year or more there my
work takes me into Europe where I shall probably remain indefinitely. So
for you and me this is the parting of the ways, and as we part I want to
thank you with all my soul for all the kindness you have shown me, and
all the tender care, not only to me but to how many hundreds of young
men and young women. They may not realize it now, but the time will
come when they shall feel toward you as I feel. God bless you now and
always.

Affectionately,
Schiller

*"Schiller" was his boyhood name. To many friends at Berkeley he had become
"Heinie," an oblique tribute to his Germanic heritage. Since Faust had been
a prolific student poet at Berkeley, the "work" to which he referred was almost
certainly poetry. As things turned out, he did not become the poet he yearned
to be, nor did he ever get to Japan or India. He and Dixie Fish made it only
to Hawaii, where Faust worked for a few months as a reporter. Soon both
young men grew eager to join the war in Europe, took a tramp steamer to
Vancouver, and enlisted in the Canadian Army. All the while Faust was writing
to Dorothy Schillig, the young woman he had left behind in California.*

Honolulu
September 15th, 1915
Dear Dorothy,

I'm glad you took that few moments off and admired yourself, sweetheart, because it must be a mighty pleasant thing to have such a sight look out at you every time you stand in front of the mirror. I'm sure that, if I were a woman and beautiful, I would camp in front of a glass all day and visit the photographer's at night. You bet I would. Don't be afraid of your looks. I think beauty must go through to the soul. I worship it in a woman so much that I can't think that it is merely a quality of the body. It must be something more. How can a woman be beautiful without wanting to make her soul harmonious with her appearance and give the whole an even tone of loveliness? I know that every fine looking woman must. They may be weak minds—I think that most of them are, as far as I can make out, but morally aren't they a pretty fine lot—Maupassant to the contrary?

Damn these French writers with their eternal insistence upon the material facts of living and of flesh. Never read Zola if you love me or yourself. And consign Maupassant to the devil and have done. Rather pick up your filthy old Rabelais than either of those writers. They're bad all through and no mistake. He's an out and out sort of a fellow who calls a spade a spade, but I'm afraid that he's a little too filthy for any modern woman. No one's education is complete without having read him, but it's better for a woman's education to remain incomplete, I suspect.

Heinie

He often wrote about the future.

Vancouver
December 26, 1915
Dear Dorothy,

But although most things seem uncertain, and most of all myself, there still remain two things to love, poetry and you, dearest. At least we have passed beyond the stages of quavering sentiment and hysterical rhetoric that burns out so-called love more quickly than anything in the world. After all, however beautiful your character, I am glad that to me you will always be a woman and not an abstraction. . . . [O]ur acquaintance so far is like the first rough drafts of the poem I have now written in parts; our married life will be like the work on the body of the poem, the growth of the characters, the polishing of the lines, the plotting of every detail of action, the wearinesses, the disappointments, but after all something done. So it will be when we are dead that perhaps our lives will stand for something, that toward the end we can look back and say: In this and in that this union has meant a giving and a taking; it has been a fair interchange; we are both better and stronger *realities* in a real world, just as I pray I may after many years look back upon a poem completed and not perfect but still containing living characters almost in the flesh, and sorrows, and happinesses, and above all the purging hurt of a great tragedy which other men shall read and understand after me.

This is my conception of our married life. A life of work.

Heinie

NEW YORK, BOB DAVIS, AND PULP FICTION

The romantic sentiments of 1915 soon gave way to the stress of distance, Faust's unsuccessful efforts to join the war in Europe, and—by the fall of 1916—his struggle to make a living in New York City. It was in New York that he eventually opened a door into a field of writing that he had never before considered: stories for pulp magazines.

He had left the Canadian Army and gone to stay in the city, where he lived at the Bowery YMCA. Hoping to establish himself as a poet, he published only two poems (though one was in The Century, *edited by Stephen Vincent Benét). Then, upon the recommendation of a friend, he went to the office of Robert H. Davis, an editor at the Frank A. Munsey Company. Munsey published magazines, including* The Argosy *and* All-Story Weekly.

Davis asked Faust to try his hand at a story and was amazed at the results, for which he paid good money and launched the young man on a career in prose. Over the next twenty-five years Bob Davis became more than Faust's editor. He became a mentor, a good friend, and, in some respects, a surrogate father. The letters between the editor and the writer, not always limited to matters of magazine fiction, are gems of witty expression and, from Davis, excellent advice. Even at the beginning of the relationship Faust's extra-literary behavior was a subject for discussion.

January 30 [1917]
Dear Sir,

An apology is surely owing to you so here goes for it. If I had realized how drunk I was yesterday afternoon, I would not have called on you at all. But King Alcohol steals on a fellow by such gradual degrees that I often can't tell when he has the upper hand. That's the way it was yesterday.

After I left you, I found all my memories of our interview so extremely hazy that I knew I must have been pretty drunk. It's damned humiliating, and I'm mighty apologetic on account of it. In the first place it was discourteous for me to appear in your office in that condition. In the second place it was mighty poor business.

Hope I didn't talk absolutely like a fool. I incline toward that when the rum gets into my brain.

Yours,
Frederick Faust

Davis replied two weeks later with good advice.

February 14th, 1917

My dear Faust:

Have yours of the 30th. Spoken like a man.

Now I am going to be equally frank with you. I have one aversion— *yes, that's it.*

I regard you as a man of tremendous potentialities. With a few short strides you can bridge the chasm between yourself and fame and take a high place among the writing men of this generation. Notwithstanding the trip is a short one, it is on a tight rope. Now, Mr. Blondin, watch your step. Look across Niagara, not at it, no matter how loudly it roars in your ears. In the meantime I am yours with high praise.

Drop in and see me about "The Homecoming of Lazy Purdue." I think in this type of man you have got the proper hero for a novel.

Very sincerely yours,
Robert H. Davis

More typical of the Faust-Davis correspondence was the discussion of possible stories. In his early years as a magazine writer Faust had a tendency to propose stories that were highly melodramatic. Davis offered good, hard-nosed advice that served as a corrective to Faust's youthful enthusiasms for plot and character. One of the most revealing early exchanges of opinion occurred in April 1917, when Faust proposed a story to be called "The Longest Way Home." It was to be the tale of an oppressed bookkeeper in a small town who murders and robs the heartless man for whom he works, flees with his money to New York City, falls in love with a beautiful prostitute named Madame Dechane, who "if she has a heart she does not know it," awakens in her a better self "which she never knew existed," and lives blissfully with her for several days in a small suburban house. Soon overcome by fear of losing Madame Dechane once his stolen money runs out, and ignorant of the fact that she has "enough money for them both to live quietly on," he commits suicide. Faust wrote passionately to Davis about the story.

April 4, 1917

Dear Mr. Davis,

I cannot finish the story which I mentioned to you earlier in the day at once. The more I think it over and the longer I work upon it the more it seems to me to expand to the size of a truly significant piece of fiction. . . . I am certain that I can make this into a book which you will be glad to publish in your magazine, as certain as I am that there is not a heaven or a hell.

Can I see you at once and talk this over? I have never been so eager for anything in my life. . . . I cannot wait to get at this thing with the sanction of your experience to lend assurance to my enthusiasm. Work is no matter to me now. Time is no object. I will give day and night to this work.

Here I have a man who will strike at the heart of every laborer who is ruled by schedule and yet a man who has the delicacy of perceptions and the fineness of instincts which will make him significant to the most casual and time-wearied literary critic. . . . In New York he comes across Madame Dechane and falls madly in love with her. I see her as her picture had been painted by Rembrandt, a glorious woman, hair as red as the sea at sunset and gray green eyes that go violet when the lashes shadow them. . . .

Now this plot, as I know, is morbid in the extreme. I also know that you prefer novels of happy action only. But in any case the core of a good plot is here, I think. . . . The play is upon a man who has been held down by convention and the necessity of breadwinning and a woman who has been constricted in her life by artifice and mock emotion. They meet, tear away the foolish bonds that hold them, and become a man and a woman mad for each other. The particulars of the action which I have outlined do not matter. Young men like myself are apt to frame their thoughts in a black border. Perhaps it would be better for the man to be guiltless of murder and for the woman to be innocent. Perhaps it would be better to place a happy ending at the close which could be done easily enough. I leave this to your discretion, confident that in this plot I have the germ of a truly big story. At least the characters and the major incidents live for me, and I am confident that I can make them live for others.

Yours,

Frederick Faust

Apparently Faust went ahead with the writing of the story at his usual astonishing speed. Twelve days later Davis indicated that not only had he read a draft of the entire story, but he also received comments on it from other editors at Munsey. He did not mince words.

April 16th, 1917

My dear Faust:

Why the hell don't you write a story that means something? Here in "The Longest Way Home" you put good love, good English, good drama, but when the end has come, the reader says, with justice, to what good? . . . It's a story without a moral, without a purpose, and in my opinion a waste of time and space. Of course, somebody will print it. Probably the *Smart Set* will be mighty glad to have it; but, if I could hurl the English language as well as you do and could do so much honest work in twenty-four hours, I would sit down for forty-eight hours and write a story that everybody wanted to read, and having once read, could not forget. And I would make for myself a name in this country that would lift me out of the short rut onto the broad highway which leads to fame.

Damn you, Faust, it's a crime for you to throw your fine genius overboard in this manner. Come in and talk with me about a rational story and get back to work on the earth. Can the bronze hair, the violet eyes, and the hectic flush.

Yours as ever,
Robert H. Davis

The melodrama in some of the plots that Faust proposed to Davis resembled the melodramas of his own experiences, especially those connected to his relationship with Dorothy Schillig. Faust had not seen Dorothy since his departure in the summer of 1915. After his impassioned letters late that year, she had grown weary of waiting for him and made plans to marry a hometown lawyer. Learning of this, Faust gathered together his earnings from Bob Davis, sold a story to Thomas Ince in Hollywood, took off on the train for California, convinced Dorothy and her parents that he was deserving of her affection, and married her in Yuba City on May 29, 1917, his twenty-fifth birthday. Shortly before the wedding he wrote the following letter to his editor.

May 23rd, 1917
Dear Mr. Davis,

Tuesday is the day of the wedding. I think I telegraphed to you that we would leave for New York the same day. We go by the Sunset Limited, train 102, to New Orleans. Then we take a boat to New York. Arrive there June seventh.

Ridiculously happy. The world seems to be mine. Get married on my birthday and I think my twenty-fifth year will be the best of my life. Of course she's the finest girl in the world. I think you'll agree with me when you see her.

I've been struggling through the first installment of the "Sword Lover" [an adventure serial that would be published six months later], but I find that writing fiction is a rather prosaic game just now. However, I shall have the thing done by the end of the week. I sent the girl away to her home so that I could have these few days for the writing. I think you will rather like the story the way it opens out. Colin Ornald [the hero] promises to be a great guy.

I won't say how grateful I am to you for seeing me through with this marriage game. I realize that I would probably never have been in a position to marry if I hadn't hooked up with you. As it is, the future looks pretty bright to me, and I think I can do a lot better work than I have in the past when I hit New York with a wife. There was too much excitement and too much booze before. I'm going to cut all that out. It's not much to do for a girl, and I want to give her the squarest deal in the world. Since leaving New York, I haven't hit the liquor except for a glass of wine with the girl herself. I thought you would agree that that was all right, and I hope you won't consider it an infringement of the promise I gave you just before I left.

Very gratefully

Frederick Faust

This short letter is rich in references, of course: romance, writing, future happiness, and booze. The reference to "The Sword Lover" marks Faust's turn as a writer to stories of adventure and a significant shift in his writing career. One June 23, exactly one month after this letter, a story of his would appear for the first time under the byline of Max Brand. The next month the first serialized Max Brand novel, "Fate's Honeymoon," began its run in a Munsey magazine. It was set in the West. "The Sword Lover" was set in eighteenth-century West Virginia. Under his editor's urgings, Faust was moving away from city stories of romance and deception. He had come, as Davis requested, "back to work on the earth." By the next year he was working hard—and, for him, unusually long—on a novel that he was calling "Whistling Dan." It would eventually be published as "The Untamed," his first major western novel, appearing initially as an All-Story Weekly *serial and immediately afterward as a book from G. P. Putnam's. His first reference to it in a letter to Davis was in early 1918. By then Bob Davis was no longer "Mr. Davis," and the "Max" at the end of the letter was in honor of his increasingly famous pseudonym.*

February 17, 1918
Dear Chief,

The first chunk of Whistling Dan ought to be in your hands on Wednesday. Sorry I have been so long about it.

I don't like Whistling Dan as a title. Chief, this is the story of an atavism, a terrible fighter. I think, when he learns of his almost weird power through his first fight, the blood lust should go to his head like wine. He should be in a perpetual struggle to hold himself back from violence. He will be like a wild animal which suddenly learns it is stronger than its keepers. Perhaps the following title is overdone or too melodramatic. Nevertheless I suggest: THE LONE WOLF (because Dan will feel himself shut off from the rest of mankind by his peculiar nature) or WINE OF POWER. Neither of these titles is exactly what I want, but I think something along the line of these will suit better than WHISTLING DAN.

However, you can tell better when you get the first chunk of the story. I think you will find it a thriller.

Yours,

Max

Of course, Bob Davis, who spurred Faust to write three sequels to the original "Whistling Dan" story, was not the only recipient of Faust letters during these years. Faust stayed in contact with many friends from his Berkeley days. In June 1918, for instance, he wrote a long letter to Sid Howard, then an aviator

in France, telling him of his hospitalization to have an enlarged testicle re-
moved and his renewed expectation to enter the war.

June 17, 1918
Dear Sid,

I had to postpone enlisting again [due to the operation]. It's getting to
be an old story. . . . My heart is not broken. No, from present indications
there will be plenty of Germans left, no matter how late I arrive in France.

It seems that the swine can't be beaten. We watch the maps and see
that they are gnawing their way slowly and surely into the heart of France
(and not so damned slowly at that). All the genius for war and all the
driving power seems to be on their side. The U. S. may contribute a lot
of man-power, but I doubt if we send over any astonishing generals. . . .
The United States has never produced a military genius. . . . Think of our
country going into this war, Sid, with a college professor to run it! He
has a high amperage but a low voltage. He makes a lot of buzzing, but
his lifting power seems to be nil. . . .

For my part I'll admit that the war no longer gives me the thrill it used
to. . . . It may come back, but at present I really care deeply for nothing
save art. Don't laugh yourself to death. I mean what I say. *A-R-T!* In spite
of the labors of Max Brand . . . I've got the colors nailed to the mast. You
can take it any way you want to. I'm just as extreme as you can possibly
imagine me at the worst. I think, for instance, that a single good piece of
music is more important than the outcome of this entire war. . . . I know,
for instance, that I had rather write a single good sonnet (even a passable
one) than command a victorious army. When I say art with capitals, I
don't mean that I know a hell of a lot about it . . . but I'm going to learn
more. . . .

This is a long way of telling you that, when I get into the Army, I'll
try to be a man, but all the time I'll wish that I were back banging a
typewriter or sharpening pencils.

Adíos,
Heinie

Two days later Faust also wrote to Dixie Fish, with whom he had traveled to
Hawaii and Canada. Fish would remain his close friend for life, ultimately
serving (after Fish became a famous New York urologist) as the model for
Doctor Kildare. Again Faust commented on his operation, the war, and his
writing.

June 19, 1918
438 W. 116 Street
New York City
Dear Dix:

I have just left the hospital where I had my left testicle removed. . . . It may be another month before I'll be fit to enlist . . . but before long I'll be in uniform. . . .

I still grind away at the typewriter with a little more success than formerly—not in making much more money, but in turning out junk that I'm not quite so ashamed of. The prose is slowly improving, though I'll never be anything better than a hack writer in that line. . . . The poor old "Tristan" poem is also done at last, after some three years of work. It is now only about 4,500 lines long, instead of the 12,000 it occupied after the second revision. It think it is greatly improved, but still it's a great disappointment, and I'll never set the world afire with it. The day of blank verse seems to have passed, but it took me a long time to realize it.

Wish you could see Jane. She's beginning to smile and crow, which is wonderful for a two-months baby. Dorothy sends her love.

Adíos

Heinie

The operation was a success, and Faust soon enlisted in the U.S. Army, only to be stationed at Camp Humphreys, Virginia, for the duration of the war. He wrote Dorothy almost every day, and Bob Davis almost as frequently. His letters to Dorothy were mixtures of love, news, and the business of writing.

August 12, 1918
Dorothy dear,

This is right at the end of a long and excruciatingly hot day during which we have drilled steadily in squad formations—stupid stuff but better than pick and shovel work.

And when I reached my tent I found two letters waiting for me. . . . It makes me sad to know you miss me, and still I'm glad at the same time. If you *didn't* miss me, why I'd simply take French leave and go up to New York to find out what was wrong. Don't you dare ever stop missing me, young lady. As for me I've confessed so often I'm ashamed, and yet I have one more confession to make. Do you remember how I used to talk over plots with you? Well, I have been turning over the scenario of The Wild Geese [working title for a sequel to "The Untamed"] and getting some really bully stuff, but every time I get an idea, I stop and look around for someone to tell it to. It doesn't seem worth while until someone has listened to it. . . . So I've been going around with a peculiar vacant feeling—a *need* of something. Well, do you see what it means? Oh, Duch, never a man since the world began has been so chained to a woman as I am. I need you to be happy. I need you to love, and I need you for my *work.*

Dorothy, are you laughing? You little Vixen, have you seen how I have grown into the habit of leaning on you more & more from day to day? It's a fact. All those sessions of talk have had their effect, and now my

Dorothy dear is a staff I must lean on for support. It must be terrible to have a husband so dependent. I'll try my best to break the habit, but it's your own fault for being such an old dear. I'm just living from day to day now for the time when I'll get that furlough. Duch, what a reunion we'll have! . . .

Good bye,
Heinie

Faust produced prose for Davis the entire time at Camp Humphreys, even while surviving an attack of flu. As he neared the end of his life in uniform, he knew—or had been told repeatedly by Davis—that he needed to concentrate on Westerns. The people at Munsey well knew Zane Grey's success in that category, and Faust was certainly willing to follow suit, in his own way.

December 20th, 1918
Dear Chief,

That note of yours rather put me in place. . . .

In the meantime I'm passing many words of bull about a serious-minded young man out West who can shoot the hell out of a needle with a revolver at a distance of one thousand yards, ride a wild mustang standing up, eat a couple of sheriffs before breakfast, and then complain that life is getting dull and in general act in a way to make the kitchen mechanics sit up late and forget dinner time. Some dirty dog stole forty pages of the manuscript the other day. I hope it gives him indigestion and a nightmare. The part he stole contained three murders and a love scene. So you see I'm keeping up to average.

Yours as usual,
Max

By early 1919, with THE UNTAMED *in print as the first Max Brand book and selling well, Faust was riding high in the Western market. Davis even sent him to Texas in February and March to absorb local color. At times, however, Faust still slipped back into his urban melodrama mode, as he did in April when he proposed to Davis an idea for a novel to be entitled "Lady," about a young woman who grows up with underworld types in New York City. Writing to Faust in California (where he and Dorothy were staying for several months with her mother and father), Davis once again let his young writer know what he thought about such ideas.*

April 17, 1919
Dear Max:

This letter is belated because I have been ill. All right now. . . .

Concerning "Lady" personally I do not like this story a little bit. There is nothing in it that will do your reputation a bit of good. I think the situation of a child growing up in the society of four crooks and reaching mature beauty without the coincident disaster is pure tommyrot. . . .

If you haven't discovered that your forte is the West, and that the public want your books about the West, and that you have got the most magnificent flying start any Western writer ever had, the Lord knows I don't wish to persuade you from rushing pell-mell to perdition through plots of the "Lady" type. It is like a great singer coming out and whistling for an encore or a violinist playing the jew's harp in an east-side barroom. You see I am doing my best, Max, to give you some suggestion of my mood. I admit this, that you are the only living man who could write the story of "Lady" and get away with it. All my objections, when I see the manuscript, might be overcome. It is a thousand to one shot that it will be a readable story. . . . I haven't any suggestions to make on the scenario. I don't like it. Don't like the theme and don't like to see you writing stories of that type. . . .

I enclose a copy of a review from the evening *Post.* A man who can get this kind of applause for his Western fiction (without ever having really been west) ought to see the handwriting on the wall. In my opinion THE UNTAMED has made a sensation. "Bluebeard" [working title of another Western] will make another. "Children of the Night" [an urban melodrama] is a [S]wiss cheese and "Lady" is a stench in an alley.

The sequel to THE UNTAMED is a sure shot for 30,000. When you get back from the West and I can get my hooks on you, I shall feel a good deal better.

Yours to the bone,
Bob

The letter had its intended effect.

April 21st, 1919
Yuba City, California
Dear Chief,

Your letter and enclosures have just reached me. Your opinion of "Lady" is a staggering blow. For several months I've been turning the yarn over in my head, and it has been my hope that with that idea I could put something across with a shade of a literary tang to it as well as a rather unusual human-interest story. Your letter has put me thoroughly up in the air. I know, of course, that you are journalistically wiser than any man in the United States, and as a rule I accept your criticisms as final from the jump. In the present case, however, your opinion leaves me such a heartache that I have to sit down and digest the bad tidings for a while. Now, I suppose that no writer is a very good critic of his own work, and I certainly shall not pose as an exception to any rule. So I'll turn what you say over in my mind and will try honestly to abide by your decision. I quite realize that there is a field for my Western junk as long as I have you to put the jazz in it. But, Chief, why shouldn't we keep two strings for our bow, because one of them is so apt to break? And why can't we work at two opposing extremes? A man who lives on one article of food is apt to get constipated. A man who keeps turning out one atmosphere is apt to get the same way. I wonder if it wouldn't be wise if we turned some attention to the other side of things where men do not pull six-guns, etc., and where the raising of an eyebrow has sometimes the effect of a cannon shot?

In short, if I find that I can throw "Lady" into the junk heap, I'll do so; but, if the idea keeps bothering me as a "might have been," I'll write it to keep it off my mind—and no disrespect to your opinion. [Editors' Note: Faust later was able to use this plot in his King Charlie stories for Street & Smith's *Western Story Magazine* where the orphaned heroine, Louise Alison Dora Young, known as Lady, is raised by four thieves without any "coincident disaster" for her.]

You must not think, Chief, that anything you say irritates me. After all, the only sort of criticism that has the whip-sting is the shrugged shoulder and the implied sneer. A man can stand almost anything but scorn, and as long as your guns blaze right in my face, I'll take all the straight from shoulder swats and keep coming back for more. I think that you and I have been unusually honest with each other so far, and for Christ's sake let's not abandon that policy.

I am enclosing the statement connected with the sale of THE UN-TAMED. I suppose you are right and that the yarn is making a hit. At least, if we can believe papers like the Brooklyn *Daily Eagle* and the *Evening Post,* which are both, I understand, representative of the best journalism. I wonder, however, what the *New York Times* had to say, or did it say anything at all, or simply class us among the "also rans"? I'm much surprised to think that THE UNTAMED got across. And now I'm determined to hit 'em in the eye with the next thing we get out—"The Wild Geese." If THE UNTAMED will do, "The Wild Geese" will get their goats. I'm sure of it.

Yours,
Max

Following the advice of Davis, Faust began turning out thousands of words of Western fiction each day. By 1921, however, most of his Western work had begun going to another editor, Frank E. Blackwell, of the new and highly successful Western Story Magazine, *which eventually published over 300 Faust serials and novelettes. Bob Davis continued to serve as Faust's agent for other outlets and as his friend. As the relationship developed, their letters were not limited to pulp fiction.*

January 23rd, 1923
Dear Chief,

Thank you very much for the Æschylus. I have looked at the script, and that is all. I am barely through with the ANABASIS and ready to tackle Homer; but, although Homer is the greatest, he is not the hardest. He's many miles to leeward of that position. People to whom Homer is as simple as Mother Goose put on their oilskins and their tarpaulin hats and get ready for a storm when they tackle Æschylus. No, Chief, that old boy is still three years away from me. I have two years of work on Homer, and then I'll approach the dramatic poets by the easiest end, which is Euripides, and pass on to our friend Æschylus at the last. So you see, Chief, though I appreciate your kindness down to the ends of my toes, your gesture is a little too quick.

As for Alexander Harvey, I suppose he wants to see me in order to chat with me about Greek literature. If you gave him the impression that I dashed through a play of Æschylus while drinking my tea in the morning, he probably was impressed. Anybody would be. But, since I am only worming my way over the threshold of the house, so to speak, I don't think I'll see Alexander Harvey just yet. Besides, he's a critic, isn't he? And to quote from his favorite Æschylus, a critic makes me "smell blood."

The top of the day to you, Chief, and here's your book back again.

As ever,
Max Faust

ITALY

For several years Faust wanted to do more than study Greek literature in the original language. He wanted to live in Europe. In late 1921, at the age of twenty-nine, he had suffered a serious heart attack, for which he blamed, in part, the pace of life in New York City. He moved his family, including the couple's two very young children, Jane and John, out of the city soon after and then began making plans to move to Italy. Adele Downey Tillson, the daughter of Thomas Downey, had been Faust's classmate at Modesto High School and the University of California.

Katonah, New York
December 29th, 1924
Dear Adele,

Christmas is such a homesick time of the year that Dorothy and I have been talking about California a great deal. I suppose that there is a California fever as well as a desert fever that never gets out of the blood; and California means all the more to me because in three or four months we expect to leave this country for an indefinite period—perhaps six months, perhaps six years. I rather suspect that it will be closer to six years. . . .

As you will see from the address, we have left New York and are living in Westchester County about forty-five miles from the city, which keeps us near enough for shopping and fun and yet gives us enough space to raise dogs, God bless them! We have discovered that zero weather is not so dreadful if one gets out in it and doesn't stay inside, shivering. Dorothy had a nervous breakdown last spring which we could attribute to nothing but the damned excitement of the big town, so we are done with it forever. We are all very well and foolishly happy in the country, and we trust that everything is contentment with you and your people. . . .

By the grace of God I'm breaking away from the rotten pulp-paper magazines and have a blank verse play which I think will be produced before many months.

All good wishes for the New Year.

Schiller Faust

The blank verse play, "Rimini," was never produced. By the next summer the Fausts were in Europe, starting in Great Britain. As always Faust stayed in contact with old college friends, including Chandler ("Chappie") Barton, a would-be writer.

July 30th, 1925
Portree, Skye, Scotland
Dear Chappie,

I pity you, you poor simp, and commend a course in comic supplements before you advance to a criticism of serious art. Back to Krazy Kat, Comrade.

When I said "human beauty," I meant the beauty of the human form, etc. and what is most sea-sick of all is idealization of human beauty. Very true that Da Vinci did not paint creatures of this world, so much the worse for him. Nobody gives a damn what a painter can imagine in ideal fields. If he wants to do that, let him work in stone. There is left to your true artist in paint only the interpretation of *facts* and *characters.* And that is why portrait painting is the greatest field, because it imposes on the artist the greatest restrictions. In a medium so free as paint there *must* be stringent restrictions, and the audience must feel them, just as lyric verse, which is so light, so easy and so free cannot amount to a damn unless it is frozen into a rigid form. . . .

Michelangelo is a great guy, I suppose, but he couldn't forget anatomy any more than Rubens could forget fat. Look at Michelangelo's David, which is close to his top notch, I suppose. There is something wrong with it. That head is turned too much, and the cords of the neck stand out too much. He has carved a young man rather than a young god. And stone ought to do gods, not men. As for his paintings, I want to get to Italy and see them in the bulk, but I'll wager that you'll find that Michelangelo was a man who could do almost anything that he wanted to do. The trouble was that his *taste* was wrong. He was in a period that was becoming decadent. He lacked the simplicity that goes with surety, and the surety that goes with simplicity. He wasn't pure. When he puts a beard on a statue, he does better, but even his Moses does not stick inside the limits of what stone should do. The face is too violent.

(I thank Jesus this letter is not for publication!!!)

We are sitting up here in the island with the most interesting name in the world, admiring its fogs and mists and wondering how folk live here in the winter. But to somebody some place I suppose that this is a bright and southern land. Just now we are in the biggest town on the island (pop. 2,000) and eating the first good food that we have found here. My serious occupation is teaching my family to play catch and jump rope, and in my spare moments I am doing ten thousand words a day, because Blackwell [of *Western Story Magazine*] recently refused a story. How that poor bum can continue to absorb this junk I cannot tell, but he still does it!

Heinie

One of Faust's most admired friends was Leonard Bacon, who had been his literature professor at Berkeley and who would later win a Pulitzer Prize for poetry. Bacon had earlier been introduced to, and sought assistance from an English psychoanalyst named H. G. Baynes, a leading disciple of Carl Jung.

c/o Guaranty Trust Co.
50 Pall Mall, London
Sept. 16, 1925
Dear Leonard,

It was very fine to see you for those three days and now I can understand why you seemed so awfully fit. I have been seeing your friend Baynes and am beginning to understand a few of the things that he has to say about extr[o]verts & introverts, etc. It appears that I belong to the second category, and I suppose that is why you and I disagree about most things. This fellow Baynes is a grand chap. I don't know him well, but I hope to know him better. He is as clean as a whip and so damned keen that he gets a man's drift before a sentence is half spoken. I think he is going to untie some of the knots in the rusty old machine that has to serve me in the place of a brain.

I have taken the liberty of asking my agent to send you a copy of my play ["Rimini"] and I shall wait for your opinion in much anxiety. I know that I need not remind you that I don't mind hard hits. You may lay the axe at the root of the tree.

We have not budged from London, which is very pleasant in this early autumn weather. But I begin to discover that, though the English may excel us in many things, their theatre is just as stupid as ours and just as perverted. (I know that you will not agree.)

We'll soon be adrift on the continent in search of a home, and I hope that you will pick out the same town that we choose.

Will you remember us both to your wife?

Affectionately yours,
Frederick Faust

Bacon indeed provided a "hard hit," accusing Faust of trying to mimic Shakespeare.

September 30th, 1925
Care of Guaranty Trust Company
50 Pall Mall, London
Dear Leonard,

Your letter about the play hits the sore point, I suppose. Two or three other people have said things which were faintly to the same effect, but now that you come out into the open and hit from the shoulder, it jars a bit of sense into me about "Rimini." Of course, I am awfully glad that you liked the lines, here and there, but as Mr. Aristotle said a long time ago, bad verse may ruin a good play, but good verse can never redeem a bad play. At least, he intended to say that.

"Rimini" is now at such a sufficient distance that it is no longer the pound of flesh nearest my heart. Your letter, I suppose, only took off a leg or two. But I am not much in doubt that the members will grow again. Every one of us who writes possesses an enormous egotism and, though someone occasionally steps upon our faces, we are soon up and about again, shouting our convictions forth in blank verse or something worse. Not that your criticisms were anything savage in their nature, but they ring the bell in me. . . .

Yes, you are quite right on the whole, and on the whole what you say probably errs only on the side of kindness. I am surprised to find that I can admit this without bitterness. But I think I can attribute that to the influence of Baynes. I believe that he is going to show me how to put together the scrambled fragments of my life and make something out of them that will be worthwhile. He is a fine fellow, but as a literary critic he is not worth a damn. He read "Rimini," for instance, and did not see through it at all. I felt quite important for a day or two, after he had finished it, but after that your letter came and removed the illusion. There is nothing on this green earth that is so good for a man as destructive criticism. Thank you for your letter. It makes me see how easy it is to bamboozle oneself unless one has friends who refuse to be bamboozled. . . .

Affectionately yours,
Frederick Faust

*By 1926 the Fausts were in Italy, some impressions of which Faust offered to
Dixie Fish late that year in an undated letter. By then Fish was practicing
medicine in New York City. The malady mentioned in the letter was Faust's
heart problem.*

Villa Pazzi
Arcetri
Florence
Dear Dix,

You see by this address that we are living in a villa near Florence. A
villa is a place with a pleasant outside and a lousy inside. Dorothy picked
this dive, and she done us dirt. There are fifty windows—one looking
south! And a great junk collector used to live here and has left most of
his shop behind. . . .

We like Florence a lot, though we've been spending most of our time
getting settled, and though the English and American colony seems to be
a lousy set of bums. But after all, what are people? One can only hope
for two or three friends in the world, and the rest are simply to be looked
at. What?

It's a healthy damned country, Dix. All the family are in fine shape,
and I'm so well that I can play tennis hard for two hours without bad
effects. Exercise seems to be the great cure for my malady. . . .

Heinie

*In 1927 the Fausts moved into a better villa, rented from Arthur Acton in
Florence. It was to be their residence for ten years. But as he told Leonard
Bacon, Faust often had travel on his mind.*

Villa negli Ulivi
83 Via dei Bruni
Florence, Italy
November 26th, 1927
Dear Leonard,

You are quite right. Nothing in your letter hits so hard as that about
our judgments. . . . Our thinking seems a mess and yet I don't know how
one can live without thinking unless one takes the viewpoint of a friend
of mine who lives by only one commandment: ''Nothing has anything to
do with anything else!''

. . . In the spring I hope to go to British East Africa and shoot big game. I know nothing about shooting except for a few rounds out of Army rifles. But I hope to learn. . . .

Yours as ever,
Frederick Faust

Carl Brandt, of Brandt and Brandt literary agency, became Faust's agent in 1925. By 1932 Faust's traditional pulp magazine markets were beginning to fail, along with his income. Much of his correspondence with Brandt and with Frank Blackwell had to do with the writing and selling of prose. Faust, never free of debt no matter what his earnings were, always wanted to publish as many words as possible at the highest rate per word.

83 Via dei Bruni
Florence
April 6th, 1932
Dear Brandt,

I failed to take up the point of length in writing to you about the new arrangements. You say that Blackwell will take seven or eight serials of 70,000 words or better. Usually he takes 80,000 words per serial. You say 25,000 words for novelettes, but usually he takes 30,000. Will you make sure? Twenty novelettes at 30,000 is 600,000; 8 serials at 80,000 is 640,000. That makes 1,240,000 words for a year. Will you bear down on that point to make sure?

As far as I'm concerned, I don't mind a bust with anybody. For the first time in eleven years I have found a dope that keeps my rotten heart from going crazy—digitaline and quinine, if you want to know the mystery—and I now can work at least twice as hard as I ever did before, and three or four times as hard in a pinch.

Be sure to let me know about shorts for hard paper [short stories for ''slick'' magazines], and what sort of stuff, if any, you think I should fire in that direction. What about gangster material? Do the papers still print that bunk? I know a great deal about the lousy booze, a good lot about gangsters, and I have plenty of background, bought and paid for.

Yours,
F. Faust

Faust continued to be concerned about his earning power, especially when Blackwell cut his word rate.

La Dime
Giverny, Eure
France
July 30th, 1932
Dear Brandt,

Thank you for your long letter and for the advice you give me about writing to Blackwell. No doubt that you are right, in a sense. But I cannot kiss the foot that has kicked me.

Instead, I have written to him at long length, not telling him that he has stabbed me in the back and twisted the knife in the wound, but telling him all my reasons for thinking that he has done so, asking him definitely if he has made the refusals on the basis of the value of the manuscripts, or if he has been influenced by malice and hostility. . . . I ask him to cable me whether he wants me to continue, or to stop after getting my letter.

My trip to New York [to see Blackwell and Brandt] was a fool's trip, and I begin to see that the only way, as I suspected long ago, to get on with editors, is never to appear before their eyes. I got a great deal of good advice from you and Blackwell, a great deal of constructive criticism which is going to help me in the future. But in personal contact there is something about me that irritates people and always has irritated them. My only out is to live like a hermit, which is the sort of a life I lead in Europe.

Brandt, can you find *no* editor with a magazine, no matter how small, who would like to take my output, or a great part of it? . . . Outside of Blackwell, is there any other market for 25,000-word novelettes?

I note that you are too strapped to make any advances whatever. Naturally I cannot get advances from Blackwell. I would rather starve than ask for one. I am living on borrowed money now, and that money already is used up. I don't doubt that you are making every effort, and this is certainly the sink or swim moment with me. I shall try more short stories, not revising the old ones as yet, but attempting new ones.

Yours truly,
Frederick Faust

While Faust was assaulting the pulp markets with renewed efforts, producing more fiction than ever before, he continued to think about poetry. The mention of Dionysus in the following letter to Dixie Fish is a reference to his privately printed epic poem, "Dionysus in Hades" (1931).

83 Via dei Bruni
Florence
February 27th, 1933
Dear Dixie,

I am glad that Oppenheimer [a mutual acquaintance in New York] got something out of Dionysus. I am just beginning to see that it needed a hell of a lot more polishing than I gave it. . . . The discovery of that sort of verse was new to me. And the result was that I frequently was singing a tune in a wordless sort of way. Dorothy—she seems to be, along with you, about the best friend I have—laid down the law a month ago and swore that, even if we had to go to the poorhouse and rot, I had to start writing verse and write it every day. So I started. I asked her what I should write about and she said: "Oh, anything. Write about land talking to man. Earth talking to man." That idea stuck in my mind. I began to hash it over. Then I hit on this. When the Olympians had their great war with the Titans, they called on the hundred-handed monsters, Cottus, Gyges, and Briareus, to help them. The hundred-handed helped to subdue the Titans and were rewarded by being made jailers in Tartarus. A very neat Greek gift. Well, I was all boiled up about . . . this idea: that Briareus rises out of the sea, a monster. Because the Greeks probably got their conception of the hundred-handed from the octopus. And in the middle of the night Briareus speaks to his mother Earth (Asia, in my poem) complaining about the pain of his eternal existence in which there is only one day worthy of remembering, and that was the day when he heard the call from Olympus and rose out of the sea and saw the beauty of the Gods and won their battle for them. But afterward, because their need of him was no longer as great as their horror, their disgust exiled him from Olympus and sent him to hide himself in the sea. The reply of Earth is that he needs only patience, that all life is short, that she herself was only yesterday a fiery mist, condensing, and that tomorrow she will be fiery mist again. But that nothing that has been is ever lost.

I hope this makes some sense to you, and I think that I am handling it in verse that is far stronger than that of Dionysus. . . .

The world looks better to me, speaking from a selfish viewpoint, because I've begun to sell lots of prose and write lots of verse. The two things, by the way, generally go together. . . .

Heinie

What Faust did not often write about was the unhappiness that Dorothy felt. His hopes for the future usually conquered any worries about her.

[Florence]
August 22nd, 1934
Dear Dix,

Concerning expense, perhaps I did not tell you in my last letter that things are opening up very wide for me, and that Blackwell is now buying as of old. Something has happened. I won't know what until I get to New York. But as soon as my rate is boosted, I'll be on easy street again. The avoidance of debts, hereafter, will be my chief concern, and once we are in the clear, ten years will drop from the shoulders of Dorothy. . . .

All is going very well, young feller. The only actual burden at this moment is the nervous condition of Dorothy, but that will clear up the instant we get on the boat. The entanglements with the past are what annoy her, not fear of the future, and once we are away, with everything in the course of easy settlement here in Florence, we'll be driving into a new future and, perhaps, into a new life. We may wind up, inside a year, at any place from Singapore to Maine, and if Dorothy will bring to this time of uncertainty a bit of the sense of adventure, we'll be a very happy pair. . . .

Heinie

The immediate future turned out not to be especially new.

[Florence]
January 19th, 1935
Dear Dixie,

There is no important news. I'm writing no verse, and therefore life is a tasteless, dull affair. I'd like to murder a millionaire and line my pockets with so much leisure that I could afford to work twelve hours a day at what I want to do, but I seem to be condemned indefinitely to the treadmill. On the highest plane of all, there is not very much to be said for marriage, at least for marriage which the man takes in an important sense. . . . It isn't Dorothy's fault; it's simply that the combination proved too engrossing. And then such things as vanity about the physical aspects of living are always apt to obsess a man who is born into the sort of poverty that I rubbed elbows with for so many years. It produces the cheapest sort of megalomania. There has to be a big house, a big automobile, etc. . . . The only proper marriage is between a man and his work. . . .

Heinie

Literature, however, always gave Faust some pleasure, even in his letters to his urologist friend.

83 Via dei Bruni
Florence
February 15th, 1935
Dear Dixie,

The immense extravagances of Shakespeare probably are what keep you from reading him more; it's hard to leap up to his plane at the end of a day's work. That's why youngsters ought to read good books. Later on, they have no time. You might find it interesting to pick out a play and read it in the Variorum, where you will find a disagreeable folio text but a flood of notes on every possible question. Best of all, read a good text like the Cambridge one and use the Variorum only for notes. I suggest this because the leisurely prose pace at which one goes through the Variorum is more like the newspaper reading which is the bulk of our American reading. You will be picking up, in this way, a great deal of information about Shakespeare plus a good deal of the poetry itself. Don't try to force yourself to enjoy every line of Shakespeare. Half of his lines are not worth enjoying. Many of his entire acts are balderdash of the most worthless sort. Wait placidly and see how often he will knock at your door by his own weight of hand and not by your invitation. If you get a copy that you can mark, all the better. A year after the start it would amuse you to go back over your marks and see how much you have changed your mind. . . .

You can't find better reading than Froissart. When you tackle Malory again, read the first three books and then skip directly to the last three. After that, if your appetite is aroused, go through the rest. Some of the dullest books contain some of the finest passages. The treatment of the Tristram story is the worst possible, but it has gloriously high points. In Monstrelet you will be disappointed, but not in Joinville, if you like chronicles.

This is written in a professorial tone for which I apologize; but it saves time to be absolute. . . .

Heinie

To Dixie he also wrote about his old problem of alcohol.

[Florence]
August 16th, 1936
Dear Dixie,

I feel happier than ever before, and quieter. Perhaps beating the booze to death is the main element in the new feeling. . . . Just now I am full of things to do. . . . Sometimes the fiction writing makes me grind my teeth a little, but not more than a fellow should do who has to earn his living by the sweat of his brow. What I wonder now is if I can maintain the same happiness even in America, if I keep the booze under control? Why not?

Heinie

By 1936, with war building in Europe, Faust knew that he would have to move his family to the United States. Carl Brandt and Brandt's associate, Collier ("Collie") Young, contacted studios in Hollywood the next year to find regular work for Faust. Apparently there were some questions about the identity of Max Brand. Faust was in New York at the time.

[New York]
[April 1937]
Dear Collie,

About the eloquent description of the life and events of Max Brand, I don't know what to say. Carl has some stuff about that fellow Brand. For my own part, I never knew him well and never liked what I knew about him. I've seen him smoke a cigar with sensitive females in the room. I've seen him groggy with liquor and disgusting even to a strong male stomach.

Some people say that he's a Jew. I don't know. The name sounds Jewish, don't you think? Someone who ought to know told me that he'd never been west of the Rockies and that all of his tales of violent action should go with dreams of wish-fulfillment. I shouldn't be a bit surprised if the fellow is a case for a psychoanalyst. Note the ''anal'' in ''analyst.''

Yours,

Heinie

Faust's facetious tone hid the unhappiness he often felt in 1937. His pulp markets were largely gone, along with his earning power. He was working hard but not happily to produce stories for slick magazines. He knew he had to leave Italy, which he loved. His heart continued to give him trouble. So did booze. Dorothy suffered from depression. And he had begun an affair with a younger American woman. He was not immune to self-pity.

[Florence]

June 27th, 1937

Dear Carl [Brandt],

If I send you a cable saying: ''Call me home,'' please sit down and compose a brief masterpiece naming half a dozen reasons why I should return at once. Don't ask me home. Command me back.

Don't ask me why I may want to be called home. The truth is that I'm damned unhappy. God, God, why shouldn't mature men get rid of fancies?

It's better than I make it out. No one is resting an elbow on my liver . . . but the glory is gone from Italy, and for weeks I've been gritting my teeth until my jaws ache.

Call me a bastard. I am one. But try to understand. I'm damned wretched. I'm as lonesome as a hound dog on a December day when he hears the horn of the other dog's master blowing, and no corn meal to eat in the home trough.

Besides, I'm dissatisfied with everything I'm doing. Listen, Carl, the only guy that ever had a right to write ''Of Mice and Men,'' without a let-down ending, is Heinie Faust. Why the hell can't I do something? Why can't I see you and talk about something except cheese to fit the *Collier's* market? I'm sick. I don't like life. All I want to do is to write verse which makes everybody else sicker than I am. Just now, I think I'm writing better than Milton. Which means that I need a brain doctor. The verse seems so *damned* good, and I know that nobody will read it.

I want to sit in a small room and write and write and take advice. Also I want something else which is nobody's business. I want to work like hell and spend almost all the money on friends and family. But I seem to want something else. Am I a lousy son of a bitch? Of course I am. This world isn't funny at all. It's just hell. I ought to be able to make a hell of a lot of money writing words that I esteem, but all I can do is to make money writing words that I despise with my whole soul and guts.

Make me a simple guy, Carl. Make me like one of the lousy bastards who do so well in the *Sat. Eve. Post.* I beg your God-damned pardon. I want to be simplified and efficient. And my marrow-bones ache like hell for something that's four thousand miles from Italy, and Giotto, and Brunelesch, and what have you. Maybe if Italian wine were better, I would be better, but why the hell should one poor guy have such a talent for being unhappy???? Can you teach me how to be happy, you big fat bum? I'll work like hell if you can. I want to be a good guy, but God how good the other fellow's pasture lands seem, how smooth and green and kind under the rain. I want to talk to Carol [Brandt]. To hell with men. They don't mean anything. I wish to Christ that I had white hair. Then I'd be all right. I'm not old fast enough. That's the fact. Wait for my cable, but when it comes, send the answer fast and strong, strong, strong.

Dear old man, lots of real love to you, and regards to Collie, who has the makings of even a better guy than you suspect.

Heinie

─────────────── *HOLLYWOOD* ───────────────

In 1938 Faust became a Hollywood writer, working first for M-G-M, then for other studios. In the beginning he was excited at the prospects, telling Carl Brandt that the studios "might welcome new blood, even forty-five-year-old new blood." He had put his affair aside and was trying once again to stay away from liquor. He began his work for the studios in March before his family joined him.

Beverly Hills Hotel
Beverly Hills, CA
March 26th, 1938
Dearest [Dorothy],

There is only time for a very brief note. To say, in the first place, that nothing has started as yet, and that, having rushed out here at full speed, I shall see nobody of the slightest importance until Monday morning, at which time I shall be tossed on the M-G-M lot. In the Selznick office . . . the office itself has the plain dignity of a bank. Selznick is one of the names of mystery and wonder out here. . . .

I feel strangely calm and assured, for some silly reason. Last night I slept eight unbroken hours. And that is the result of being on the wagon, I suppose. And perhaps this perfect California air, not too brisk and not too narcotic, is having its effect in part. When I really get on my toes, I expect to be quite a different man from the nervous idiot you've been living with for some time. . . .

I thank God daily for sobriety. I now have once a day a glass of sherry on a compote; it is more a flavor than a drink and it does not make me want more. I now am certain that I shall not be beaten by liquor again so long as I live. . . .

Good bye for the moment, my lamb.

Heinie

The story of Faust in Hollywood is the stuff of legends. From the beginning, as the following letter from Collier Young to Carl Brandt illustrates, it was obvious that Faust was to be a challenge for the studios, and for himself. The reference to Kildare is to Dr. Kildare, whom Faust had created as the hero of two magazine stories.

May 5, 1938
Dear Carl,

Eddie Knopf [of M-G-M and brother of publisher Alfred A. Knopf] and myself, a week or so ago, tentatively discussed a deal [in which] Heinie, whether he is working for the studio or not, would then receive $1,750 every time Metro uses the character Kildare. . . .

Heinie, as you will imagine, is alternately wildly excited about working for pictures and alternately depressed. He is certainly an agency handful, but one that I'm glad to cope with because of my real fondness for the unbreakable Max Brand.

One of the typically screwy ideas he got in his head last week . . . was going to the help and support of a local Richard Whitney out here, an old school chum, and who stands on the brink of failure and disaster. Heinie wanted to hand $10,000 into the pot immediately. And . . . he wanted to do it without consulting me, because the whole affair was so confidential. He went down to Eddie Knopf's office and offered to sell immediately ten, twenty or even thirty of his titles outright for $10,000, Eddie called me up and asked me what manner of man Mr. Faust was and told me about this insane proposition. I went to see Eddie, and we agreed I better beard Mr. Faust in his den and see if I couldn't cool him down. This I did and minced no words in calling Heinie a lot of names with real emphasis. I told him doing this was not fair to Dorothy or his children, as he was virtually selling his estate. I told him that Knopf refused to make such a deal. He then begged me to go to several other studios which I would not do.

In writing Heinie I suggest you do not mention this, as he is now pretty much ashamed of himself, and it has all been settled anyway. As usual, Heinie is the leading sucker for anybody who happens to be down on his luck. . . . I think he is also running a night school for broken-down writers or dilettantes, which seem to cluster around him. . . .

You should be surprised by none of this anyway. He's just the same old Heinie, as you can readily see. . . .

It is like Heinie to stop, in midair, and think up a story for Joan Crawford, then the next minute he is planning to do a story involving the life of Offenbach, and God knows what else. But right now I'm happy to tell you it is KILDARE, and nothing but KILDARE. . . .

I think this covers the case of Frederick Faust. One thing we should be thankful for, he is very strictly on the wagon, and I've never seen him quite so fit.

Yours,
Collie

When Dorothy and his children joined Faust, things looked up for the family. But Dorothy's unhappiness continued, and Hollywood was a difficult setting for her husband. For one thing, he was not able to stay on the wagon. But he often tried to convince himself that all the bad times were past and the best days lay ahead. As usual, no matter how serious his personal problems were, he took pleasure from and sought relief in his correspondence with other writers. Grace Flandrau, a writer from Minnesota whom Faust met through Carl Brandt, was the recipient of many letters from Hollywood.

[1941]
Dear Grace:

Your letter made the whole St. Paul environment rush about my ears and eyes. I can't write a letter about it, but I must send a note. Once more I press California on your attention. The beauty lies not so much in the climate as in the newness. This is the farthest outpost west. The wind that blows here from the sea comes clear from China, the oldest wind on the newest land. The newness provides an odd charm, since nothing matters. That is to say, there is no human expression anywhere near one. The [European] Continent is soothing, to me, because the strata of life are laid on like the rings of growth around a Sequoia. . . . The sense in Europe of the many crowding generations is beautiful to me, and I am carried along on a river of existence; whereas here in our own country that river of existence seems to me always pouring over a great brink into darkness, into emptiness. . . . Peace such as I've never known in America comes to me in Europe. I think I may have told you how, returning once to Italy from New York, I noticed that the peasants working in the twilight fields were the color of the earth; and an ocean of peace rose up around me.

California offers none of these things, but its ideal emptiness makes one turn straight back to the old countries. Serious conversation almost offends the air of California. A brainless, dreaming peace is its ideal product. Nothing matters very much except that oranges are ripening in the sun, and the petunias never have been so lovely. . . .

Heinie

In 1938 the Fausts had bought a house at 317 Burlingame, in Brentwood. Although he was often dissatisfied with studio work and unable to get out of *debt in spite of the high earnings he enjoyed (his basic salary for M-G-M was $1,250 a week), Faust sporadically took an interest in gardening and other domestic projects. He continued to struggle with alcohol, however. The following letter was written in September, 1941, to Dorothy, who had gone on vacation with her mother.*

Saturday morning
Dearest old dear,

Your letter from the Columbia Gorge Hotel came this morning, only one day on the way, and it is a blessing to hear from you. . . .

You speak sadly about unhappiness at 317, but you must not feel that way. The habit of drink is the basis of all my trouble, and my trouble is the base of all of your nervousness. The present regime is working perfectly. And I begin for the first time in my life to feel that I have brought liquor down to a proper basis. It is now six days since I've had a drink during the day, and I've averaged—to give you details—two bottles a night in bed. In the meantime I've stopped sleeping pills. The total result is some irritability and some instability—that is, a tendency to look around for something better than typewriting to do. Nevertheless the work has been turning out, and better than before. At the beginning of the week my brain was very foggy, so foggy that, as it has cleared, I realize in what an alcoholic twilight I had been living. Already I am a hundred per cent more efficient than before. And now even in six days I begin to have a revulsion against the effects of drink.

I must say that people are easier for me to take when I have a few drinks but, though conversations may be carried along more easily at the start with some alcoholic help, they usually don't finish so well, and every third or fourth time I drink so much that I go overboard and undo all the good effects. Undoubtedly just now I'm impatient and hasty and apt to judge people harshly, but this will pass, I'm sure. If not, I'd rather be a bit ugly at times than inefficient all the time.

What I want you to feel is that you have not been to blame for unhappy details at home. That unhappiness has actually grown less and less. But still I have done enough drinking to trouble you, because the drinking causes less work, and worse work, and that creates the financial difficulties, and besides it gives me the horrible knowledge that I'm not doing what I ought to do in verse, etc. And this knowledge reacts upon you, until we both feel that we are living on a treadmill instead of climbing the hill that gives the good view.

In spite of these things, you must try to see that we are broadening the basis of our happiness. 317 Burlingame is more and more important and somehow through the garden I feel that we're in touch with an immense reality of living, more than we ever were before. . . .

A sober life *always* has made me do the good work before, and it will now but, instead of a semi-hysterical outpouring of pulp stories on the one hand and forced verse on the other, perhaps I now can begin to work more truly, more slowly and surely to better ends. As for the moving pictures, I'm sufficiently established, I hope, so that I'll continue to get good work to do. . . .

Darling, I have filled this letter with talk about myself because I know that our troubles—constantly diminishing from a very bad high a couple of years ago—have been based on my shortcomings. Let me show you a better Heinie and in no time at all I'll show you a Dorothy who no longer has sleepless nights or nerves or a discontent with servants, or a brooding over household burdens. There will *be* no burdens, and we will sit down to salad and cheese and fruit and a glass of wine more happily than to a feast. . . .

So often I have attempted this same reform, and so often it has broken on the rocks that I know you will doubt this change in me. I let myself keep doubting, too; there is more strength to act when one does not waste all of one's strength on the rigid determination of the will. Too hard a grasp makes for brittleness and an easy break. Let me only say that this week has been amazingly easy—and I'm only now beginning to harvest the results.

Please be happy and at ease while you're away and trust that, when you come back, you will find the household moving on oiled bearings and a Heinie who can show you something worthwhile. I'm not driving myself suddenly to commence a full schedule. . . . Eventually, and long before you return, I hope to be pushing out a steady flow of what we know I should do. . . .

This letter has grown long, but I wish it could go on forever, because now as I finish I am saying good bye for a moment. Dearest, dearest, be calm and patient and keep a good, bright hope. And remember that virtue *can* be learned, even by

                                                                    Heinie

When the United States entered the war after Pearl Harbor, Faust grew desperate to find some way for him to see the conflict first hand. He had missed the First World War entirely. There is some reason to believe that Faust wanted to go to war because he wanted to escape his situation in Hollywood. He begged Carl Brandt for help.

[March 1942]
Dear Carl,

I begin really to choke with desire to get to one of the fronts. You remember we talked a bit about it. You thought some magazine might be willing to send me.

How could it be wangled? What magazine would assure me of enough income to make it possible to take the chance?—I mean, with income taxes and family support still going on here in California. What magazine could assure me of even *half* of the necessities, so that I could gamble on the other half? Would the Hearst people take me in mind?, do you think? Hearst is the Beast of the Ages, of course, but rather strike a stroke for a bad master in a good cause than strike no strokes at all. In the meantime things are happening from Bataan to Australia to Mandalay to Iran to Krakhov to Smolensk to Leningrad to England to Gibraltar to Sicily to Egypt. . . . Oh, my God! And here sit I at 317 Burlingame Avenue!!!!!!!

Is this pure selfishness on my part? Might I not be able to write war fiction? Might I not even be able to do straight war reporting that would be worth the reading? But fiction can be made to see truer, less propagandized, than any amount of communiques from the fronts.

A wild flier at a chance—suppose young Doctor Kildare were actively placed with a medical unit on one of the fronts. Is there not a world audience that would listen to him and wait for his adventures????????

Things go on very well with the Western screenplay. At last I have a producer who is *totally* happy with my work. It may lead to anything. But it could not lead to anything half so lovely as the noise of honestly hostile aircraft in the sky, or the chance to duck noises that come much closer home than airplanes.

Let me have your mind on all of this. I seem to be writing to you constantly and you, poor Carl, have other things to think about, of course. But find me a corner of your time when you can. I ache with an immense emptiness to sock somebody with the butt of a gun, or with a few thousand words below the belt.

Heinie

ITALY AGAIN

Ultimately Faust was successful. He wangled an assignment as a war correspondent for Harper's *Magazine. It was his hope and intention, for the first time in his literary career, to write from the direct observation of experience. He wanted to tell the story of ordinary American soldiers.*

Faust left for his Harper's *assignment in February 1944. By May he was back in Italy, thirty miles north of Naples, assigned to the 88th Infantry Division of the U. S. Fifth Army. As he observed the troops, he awaited news of the birth of his second grandchild back in California. On the night of May 11th, two weeks before his fifty-second birthday, he was killed by German mortar fire.*

His last letter had been written the day before. Appropriately, it was to Dorothy.

May 10th.

Dearest Dorothy,

Yesterday I had a flight in a little observation plane—a queer little box that took off at a mere fifty miles an hour and couldn't go faster than eighty in the air. However, it got me across some vital territory and gave me a look at the German towns that lie up a valley with big hills (mountains, we call them) piled up on all sides. We had smoke pots at work along our river to cover the bridges with a screen, and they set up a great level mist that looked like water, an inlet from the sea, when we were well off from it with the sun coming down at a good slant. The ground the troops will advance over, from the air, looked quite smooth, just a pleasant excursion and not a very big one, at that. We flew back and forth on the edge of the ack-ack zone and then back to the air field. It was such a perfect evening that I got the pilot to cruise about for a while, low over the fields. There was a road, a perfect white, marble white, with its dust on the bushes along the way, and we flew above that just fast enough to keep a good wind in the face. There isn't any reason that this countryside should seem more beautiful than a thousand others except that it's Italian, but the word makes the difference. Italian houses, particularly when the war has broken away the date-marks, and Italian streams always going the longest way round, and even the sea and the sky are Italian. To nearly all the men, the part the Italian people have played in the war, and the absence of any hard liquor worth drinking, and the badness of most of the wine, and the distance of language between them and the women, makes our soldiers detest the land and most of the people in it. But nothing takes away the old magic from me. Here and there the boys come to me, besides, with stories of individual families who have been warm and charming and amazingly liberal, and these tales make me very happy. But on the whole there is very little human contact for the boys, and they hate the whole business.

There's nothing for them to spend money on, and that's the hardest part of the curse. It really seems that they hardly care what they get; they merely want to spend every cent in their pockets, and then they come back with a feeling of relief, as though the natural happy state of man is complete poverty. (I think that's a state we soon may inherit, all of us.) But in the meantime it's very queer to have no chance to buy anything. I'd like to have wine, of course, but I can't find anyone who will sell it. The boys wangle some of it in exchange for cigarettes, soap, and other small things that mean more than money to the Italians. I've told you a bit about this before, but the strangeness of it remains fresh and odd all the time. The youngsters won't let me pay; therefore I tell them that I don't like the wine; and the result is a state of high aridity that carries on for days and weeks at a time. I can't say that this virtue lightens my old feet.

Speaking of age and change, I notice that the hands of most of these young men who have done labor are what my hands used to be at their age—thick-fingered and bent up a little crookedly at the wrists. Even the smallest of them usually have big, competent hands. And even the smallest seem capable of slogging along uphill under the burden of heavy packs, with their weapons and all.

Now that battle is not far from them, supposedly, it's curious to see how little they change. They're just a little more tense, but they don't sit around and brood. They don't sit in corners with their thoughts, but every man carries on about as always. They do a little bit of battle-planning, but on the whole their subjects of conversation are about as usual. I share a room now with the supply sergeant, and as you can imagine I see a drift of soldiers constantly coming through—because now that action is not far away every man needs some one bit of equipment desperately. And the chatter that I hear is the aimless, witless mental wandering that I used to hear on the porch of the crossroads store when I was a boy on the farm.

It's amazing how little the idle talk matters, particularly since I know what lies ahead for them. A man who may be about to die, and not for a crime, stands in a high light and has a lot of overtones that aren't hard to appreciate. The majority of these boys expect a very hard fight. They appreciate the combat qualities of the Germans, and they realize they are attacking a naturally strong position. They hope they will win, but there is no logic that convinces them they will be successful. The mysterious and very beautiful truth is that they want to do their duty, make a good, hard fight of it, and then have the war end for them—through death, through wounds, or through victory. I have talked to so many of them, now—best of all I've been silently in the corners of rooms while they were talking—that I'm confident this is the average feeling of these green troops, who have been hardened by little more actual contact than mere patrols, big or small. This is more than I expected to find, of course. I came hoping that I'd find our American boys better than the sour reports we've heard about our spiritless Army, with its head in a sack, stuck in the Italian mud; but I didn't dream that I'd run into this simple and elevated attitude. A rather blind attitude, you may say, and perhaps I have to agree but, when men are not defending their native soil, they lack something that the Russians have—they are less wolfish and savage and of course they don't see the reason for fighting so clearly. Dimly, but deeply, these men see that Hitlerism cannot be permitted to exist in the same world with our own ideas, and without passion, really without hate, they are willing to go out and die, doing the things their officers tell them to do. Of course the battle has not yet been fought, but I have a growing conviction that they will be real soldiers and that I can write with honesty about them a book that their families and perhaps other Americans will be glad to read.

After this, old darling, let me never have to grub merely for money—

let's try really to make the work true and honest all the way through, even if we take in a meager income. I know you want it; I know it's an idea I've given more lip service to than true conviction. But now this may make the turning point.

After all, I shall not be going with Company L during the first hours but with another outfit in another battalion that will have a clearer view of the stuff; afterward I'll come back to my own boys and go on out with them.

There are tons of things that I would write except that they're already in my notes. And other tons, of course, are censorable. I want you to know that Italy as always is giving up beautiful weather and warm nights— which means a great deal to the boys who will be out there fighting.

I have to turn this off. Give my love to everybody. No matter what is happening, just now there's one part of me that never stops thinking of you, particularly of the first, breathless days. I suppose that's natural. STILL NO NEWS ABOUT THE BABY. No news at all, in fact.

Heinie

A SKETCH OF MY LIFE

Frederick Faust

Always, Faust avoided publicity. During the whole of his twenty-seven-year professional career he did not grant a single interview to the news media. Beyond the circle of his family and friends, he remained a very private man, instructing his agent to refuse all editorial requests for photos or personal data. He made one exception to this rule in 1933. His friend, Harper and Brother's president, Cass Canfield, wanted to publicize their "new" writer, Evan Evans, and asked Faust if he would be willing to provide a brief self-portrait. From Italy Faust replied:

> *If you want to say that I have been a tramp, it would be true. At least, I've worked my way around a good part of the world. You can say that I have worked on farms and ranches, that I've followed the sea in some fair weather and a great deal of foul, that bronchos have heaved me into the air and slammed soft parts of me on hard parts of the Sierra Nevada, that I've broken scythes on the stones of Maine hayfields, that I've learned more from beer than from books, that I've wandered from Honolulu to Wadi Halfa, that I started on my own at thirteen and learned how to take it on the chin early and late. You can say all of these things and they will all be true, and they may turn out to be the sort of things that readers of "Evan Evans" will expect to hear about him. I am forty-one years old, married, three children, and come from the West.*

Faust met Dorothy Schillig, a campus beauty, at an English Club dance in Berkeley when she was nineteen and Faust was twenty-two. They were married three years later on May 29, 1917. Their first child, Jane, was born on March 29, 1918. Jane later married Robert Easton and raised four daughters of her own. A son, John Frederick Faust, was born to the Fausts on November 2, 1919. John became a teacher in Florence, Italy and was principal of an Amer-

ican school there in 1950. He died in 1989. Faust's third child, Judith, was born on February 3, 1928, and lived in Florence from 1950. She worked as an Italian translator, never married, but had one daughter. She died in 1985. Dorothy Faust died in 1960 in California.

"A Sketch of My Life" was written as a letter to Jane Faust in the fall of 1939. Jane had turned twenty-one and wished to know more about her father's early life. Faust obliged with a long letter. This autobiographical letter, reprinted in its entirety for the first time, is remarkable in its candor and emotional intensity. It remains one of the finest examples of Faust's prose, revealing much of his pain and passion.

Your letter waited for me at the office this morning and gave me a shock of tragic emotion—I mean that sense of fear and pity and suffering about which Aristotle speaks. I sit down to answer it still shuddering, but I feel that I must try to offer you, as nearly as I can, a due to the Heinie mystery, if there *is* any due. I wanted so much to have at least one real talk with you while I was in New York, but the necessary hours never were on hand, and I must try to do this by writing.

The fact, briefly, seems to be that so far as male-female love is concerned there only has been space in me for one great passion. Only one, and never-to-be-repeated. In 1915 I saw your mother, loved her at first sight, and kept on loving her so that I thought it would never end and that it was made out of the strange stuff that composes heaven, or our thoughts of it. We were married after a long separation during which she had become engaged to another man, but since our marriage I don't think she's ever looked away from me toward anyone else, at least not for more than a glance, so that there have been since the marriage twenty-two years of faithfulness on her part. There is also a natural and very feminine sweetness and softness, and there are powerful instincts that make her love her children. I don't need to add up the qualities of your mother. You know that she is a lady and that there is a light that shines in her; even the most gross of men and women see the radiance in some part. However, the fact is that what I thought was the eternal passion gradually sickened in me and began to die. It never will entirely die. I can assure you, I never would dream of marrying another woman, and my hope is that she never will know the change that has taken place in me; but the truth is that for many years it has been impossible for me to feel toward her as I did in the beginning. I feel, savagely, that marriage is a job and that I'll stick to it, and that home *has* about it something sacred. I say that even while this letter may begin to undermine for you the sense of that holiness.

I don't want to make this letter a defense of myself. I would rather write it as a testimony, which you can weigh and to which you can assign values impersonally; and yet before I'm through I'm sure that I *shall* be defending myself.

Now I must go back toward the beginning and, repeating many things that

I've told you before, try to sketch in, rapidly, the picture of my life. You know that I started in great poverty, that my mother died when I was eight, almost unknown to me, and that my father was a passionate man with a good deal of brain but also with an unhappy talent for acting parts and giving them a certain German false sentimentality; I loved him a great deal, but I kept seeing through the sham until I almost wished that I could be blind and accept him as he wanted me to accept him. In this way something hard, cold, critical was born in me— or perhaps it existed from the first, in the child of parents whose added ages reached ninety years. I grew up tall, gangling, crushed with shame because of dodged bills at local stores, learning to withdraw from children of my age, thrown utterly into a world of books and daydreaming, daydreaming, daydreaming. So a barrier began to be formed between me and my fellows. At the nineteen different schools I attended there were always the series of fistfights until I had found my place, and I went for years with a swollen and scarred face because the fights at one school had hardly healed before I had to begin them again in another. All of this, you see, was forcing me thousands of miles away from normalcy in my human relations.

Then came the death of my father when I was thirteen and life on wretched farms in central California among people who would not and could not talk the language I wanted to hear. By the time I was ten, I had written enough to know that I wanted to write more and at about the same time a sense of high destiny (laugh a lot, Janie, because laughter is in place here) overcame me once and for all. It never has left me from that day to this, in spite of all that I'm to relate to you now. But in the dimness of that life I passed through agonies so real that all pain, since then, has seemed rather unimportant. I wanted to have a chance at what seemed to me important living, thinking, and being. That want has never left me.

Now I leave the ranches and go to high school. It makes no change whatever. I work in the country, walk to the school, never make a friend among the schoolboys, never even shake hands with a girl of the right sort. In the meantime there is the drudging hard labor to pay for my way, and so all things conspire to remove me farther and farther from real human contacts, so you see that I am becoming more and more stiff, rigidly stiff, and living completely inside myself. I begin to write little compositions, verse, none of it really good but enough to rather astonish the pupils and the teachers in a small country high school. At last I go on to college. I am the "good boy" who makes his way and is conscious of his virtues. At nineteen I have had my first drink, but drink is no problem. I live in college exactly as I lived in high school. And then on the strength of contributions to college magazines I'm elected to the English Club as a sophomore, which opened the door to me, forced people to consider me just a little, and enabled me to talk a bit with boys and girls who could at least understand what I had to say, no matter how bitterly they disagreed. Suddenly I began to drink with them; all the dark walls fell down; I am in the midst of glorious, shining noble humanity. The free winds blew on me for the first time. People listen to me rave. They scratch their chins. They're not used to hearing about men, women, historical events, what is poetry, what is prose, what is true beauty, wherein lies honor, glory, and what is the essential mystery of man, the God in him. However, they *do* listen a little, and I discover that, if I underexpress myself in slang, swear a great deal, and drink a great deal more, a great many things that they would pay no attention to now become worth listening to. So I drink, swear, and talk down. I am now the outstanding drunk in the college; I am also the best known of the campus writers; the honor societies all open their doors; I feel that I am understood, loved, and out rushes, in exchange, all of the penned up and unexpressed love of twenty-one years of solitary living and thinking. It is a glorious riot. At last on the crest of the wave I meet Dorothy, love her at a glance, become engaged after three meetings.

There is no doubt in me that the future will be magnificent. I have written well enough to astonish the college; I shall go on to write well enough to astonish the world. In the meantime there is the silly little old world itself, so filled with glorious men and women. I rush off, having failed to graduate because I'm not "morally fit to represent the college," toward India. I take Dixie along. In Hawaii I learned that my friends I was to join in India are being charged by the British. That doesn't matter. There's the jolly old World War coming along. I take a ship to Vancouver to join the Canadian army. But it takes too long, hanging around Vancouver and waiting to get across. Somehow I must get over there, kill a few Germans, return to America with a wound or two which will secure my quick return, marry Dorothy, and then settle down to a long life, perhaps as a college teacher, but spending exhaustless hours writing magnificent poetry and living contentedly in some cottage on perhaps two hundred dollars a month. There will be time to study, teach, have children, help my wife with the dishes and the heavy cleaning, and still pour in three hours a day on the verse. This calm, hard life I must hurry into. I desert my regiment, rejoin another farther east in Canada. The regiment is stalled in a Nova Scotia camp and seems destined never to sail. I desert again and come down on foot through New Brunswick into Maine, work on farms, pass coal to get to New York by sea, walk into the English consulate, ask how I can get across to the English army, am considered a German spy, get back to the street, find a job working in a subway at William and Beekman streets, write some verse for magazines, sell some, begin story writing after a starvation period, marry on the first money after a trip to California (to get Dorothy away from the other man), and suddenly I'm started on the life I've been waiting for???

No, not at all. Poetry is not important, but money. So I hack at silly stories. Make more money, hunt vainly to find that magnificent mirage of humanity which first dawned on me when I was in college. There is still no one to talk to. I read poetry to my wife and put her asleep. There are no friends to whom I can talk. I find a few eccentrics and argue with them. But life is empty, or thinner than an eggshell. I write in the spare hours a long poem. When it is completed, it is junk. I lose all faith in myself. The war has come along. I am refused, physically unfit, have an operation that finally makes me fit, join the army, get flu in the camp, and from the flu get a bad heart. But all of this is nothing compared to the inside story, which is one of an aspiration that has gone wrong, and the blind fumbling to find somewhere that Attic environment of people devoted to some purpose of beauty. Instead, I find a Schoolcraft and a Leonard Bacon. My own aspiration seems more and more childish. At home I keep turning to a wife who is puzzled by what I have to say, then weary of the repetition, engaged in child-bearing and rearing, unwilling to use the hands of her mind, unwilling at last to make any effort, physical or mental. I have on the bus-top our celebrated scene in which she definitely says that she will continue to lead her own life regardless of what I want. Whether it's French, piano, the reading of better books, or close attention to the raising of children and their education, she will *not* make the effort.

I say to myself, then, that I have made a frightful mistake and married the spoiled darling of the bourgeoisie, the pet of the small town who has been spoiled by favor. I think long, dark thoughts for months. But there are the children growing up. I think, by degrees, that I've grown accustomed to Dorothy and tell myself that this is what is to be expected from an American wife. I try to write better stuff. The habit of doing pulp has corrupted whatever little talents I have; I try to do verse again, slowly, like a child learning to walk again. I have a thousand new ideas. I throw them at my friends; it is as though I had flung rocks at them. They are angry. They consider me a hopeless drunk with a failing brain. I still drink more and more. The heart crashes; the doctor lets me go to Europe to die. At last in Italy I begin to find that beauty of which I had dreamed but in which I never had lived. It is not the supreme, the Grecian beauty, but it is actual; it is a fact that outweighs everything I have known before. It is 1926; I am thirty-four years old; it is not too late to make a new start; a new education is beginning; Dante enters my life like a great man; I try a new kind of verse, closer to the language of the streets, a poem about the voyage of a sailing ship; but always there is an increasing demand for money. I now need to make seventy thousand dollars a year simply to keep my mouth and nose above water.

The first enthusiasm for Europe dies away in Dorothy as it grows stronger in me. In the house is Monty with the children. The children, discovered in the winter of 1925 by me, begin to be overwhelmingly important. Although my life is a wreck and a failure, perhaps I can show them a light to the right path. I insist on overseeing their education, am bitterly opposed in everything by Dorothy and friends; the burden of learning foreign languages plus school work makes them lag. They seem more stupid than their companions. Perhaps I'm entirely wrong about this as I seem to have been about everything else. But I begin to find a great and increasing interest and a comfort as deep as the soul in Janie. She is not beautiful; she is not quick or clever; but I think I see in her the springing of a root of profound human rightness and reality. I begin to cling to her and my moments with her.

It is 1930. A summer in Bavaria, I lend money to a friend ($5000) and work like a crazy man to write extra stuff to cover the advance; things are more dull and hopeless between me and my family than ever before. I begin to think that John is a helplessly weak character; Judy is a tough little brute. I come back ahead of the others to Florence. The garden is dry and burned. Even Italy, which always had been a blessing, seems a curse; I start adding up my days and telling myself that I never have written anything worthwhile and never shall. I am thirty-eight. I have nothing to give the world or it would have been given before. I meet a rather low type of woman. There is no sign of affection but simply a sort of physical excitement. I go off with her to Rome. It is like the falling of fetters. To my amazement, I feel no shame. I look back with surprise and see that it is the first time I have stepped off the straight road in thirteen years.

My defection is discovered. Extraordinary hell breaks loose in the home. I can't guess it, but this is the beginning of a new period in my life. If my wife has loved me before, it has been only placidly. Now there is a jealous frenzy. I plan a new poem, a direct return to the interests of my boyhood. I sit down one morning and begin to write. I get out nineteen lines absolutely different from anything I have ever done before. In a crazy delirium of joy I know that I have found, at last, my style. In this delirium I write the rest of the poem. It is a hodgepodge, unplanned and unconstructed. It is not good, though I still think so for a year or so. However, it is the first real writing I ever have done. I go to Greece and walk into a golden mist of joy. It seems that I have, at last, touched an electric core of existence. Even God cannot feel more happiness than comes to me, at times. But there is more and more perturbation at home. Since I left Dorothy once, it is expected that I shall leave her again. There are frightful scenes if I even stay out late at night. Suddenly I discover, with a profound shock of surprise, that it is almost better to be alone than to be with her; to be alone with my notebooks begins to be my real life, other than my life with you and John, which grows rapidly in importance. You go to Switzerland to school. Suddenly you wake up, just as I had waked up a few years before. In your letters I have an entrancing glimpse of the birth of a bright soul into the world. *That* part of my work, insofar as it has been mine, is not wasted. It is real. It is true.

I begin to maul away at the idea of a long poem to express something, I hardly know what, that is aching in my heart to come out into the light, something about all mankind. Finances grow harder and straighter. I come to New York. I meet Mary [Hand Churchill, daughter of Justice Learned Hand]. She is alone, tormented by her loneliness, unable to find in the world the least food of happiness, unable to give, unable to take, only on speaking terms with people or with events, but distinguished by her hunger. She speaks badly; she can't write a line without filling it full of dashes; and yet there is something about her that attracts me instantly and powerfully. I make a sudden dead set at her. She fights back furiously. I bear down. She begins to open her mind, and I find in it a passionate desire for good and beauty that amazes me. Compared with life with Dorothy, this is real excitement. Love? No, it probably has no relation whatever with what I felt for Dorothy during the first dozen years. But from the beginning of time men have looked for women they could love and women they could talk to. This is at last someone I can talk to. So I talk. There is a tremendous resistance, a horror at the thought that she might disgrace her family, a growing unhappiness because of that. Then I go away. Letters follow me that seem to come from a different person. She is writing with eloquence, and all the darkness seems to have been swept away from her. Have I had a hand in it? It seems that I have, and that is still more exciting.

As for telling her the truth about what I feel, why try to talk to a tornado? That is what she has become. She is struggling toward a life which will give her a husband and more children, but she keeps putting off eligible men. Am I ruining her chances for future happiness? I begin to cudgel myself with this thought. Sometimes I wish to God that I never had seen her, except that she is proof that there is an essential fire at the heart of every human being and that miracles of expression are possible if they are properly encouraged.

Dorothy discovers that something is wrong; she hardly knows what, but she suspects the worst. A long hell begins, culminating with last winter. Since then we've been working up from the bottom. Things are better at home now than for years, and yet it seems mere surface living to me, to tell you the truth. Thank God that the drink has been at last, suddenly, put in its place. Is it true that I must arrive at everything suddenly, never by degrees? Do I have to be ploughed up in some way before the brain opens and functions? I go off to Rome and come back with a new style of verse. I meet Mary, and my long poem begins suddenly to grow clear; I know that what I want to say is that there is no deity but a partial God in every man, and that men in groups can express that godhead.

I go back East. I see Mary again. She seems a squat, ugly little thing. But there *is* some spark of the divine fire in her. Some reality comes from her as a gift to the trees she looks at, the men she speaks to. Still, I half wish that I'd never seen her. What she sees in me is not the truth. But *is* there any truth in me? Am I not and shall I not always be ready to pay anything for the sake of coming in touch with such reality as she has to offer? How can I explain this to her without breaking her heart? How can I tell her that the thing she thinks is in me did, actually, die those many years ago in Italy? I cannot tell her that. Some good has been planted and is growing in her. For God's sake, let it grow.

Dearest Janie, the one creature in the world on whom I can look with calm joy is you. How easy it is for a father to love a daughter! As for my other problems, I must expect time to diminish them, tarnish them, if you will.

I started this letter in the hope that I could tell you exactly how I feel at the moment; I have wound up with a confused narrative which I'm more than half sure I should not send, except that you always understand everything I say and lend it something out of your own charity. Chiefly I'm sick that you've been wounded. Remember always that there are two fundamental bedrocks to my life: my family and my work. There are a few other things. Mary is one of them.

But they are not essentials. I shudder at the thought of telling her how inessential she is.

Does this clear up anything for you??? How damnable is the lie that I act with Mary, or rather the lie that I assent to? At any rate, this letter will tell you something. Burn it, for heaven's sake, as soon as you've read it.

Don't throw Mary away. She loves you with a devotion and a fire of which how many people in all the world are capable? She is growing like a weed in importance and in mind. It has been almost proven that when I draw away from her, as I tried to do and did do for so many months this year, her mind stops; her life lies fallow; she falls into the old confusion and makes meaningless gestures toward life. There is something like murder in such a thing.

On the other hand there is a great deal of honesty, true devotion and kindness, wonderful possibilities of tenderness and understanding in her, otherwise I never would dream of letting her come close to the soul I prize most in the world, which is the spirit of my sweet girl, my dear Janie.

I felt you were disappointed in me and depressed by me when I was with you in New York. I guessed at the reason, and your letter makes it more clear.

Remember, first and last, that the clear, high life is the only life for you; learn by my failures, at least. You are not cursed by the strangeness and pain of my early life. You are a tree that has grown straight and never must bend, no matter what wind blows on it.

Remember, still last of all, that I love you and must help you to happiness.

D[addy]. H[einie].

THE UNIVERSITY YEARS

Harvey Roney

Faust's years at the University of California in Berkeley were important in his life for they marked a transition from lonely introvert into campus rebel, from a promising high school writer to a brilliant college scholar. Harvey Roney here recalls his friendship with Faust in an affecting memoir. Roney and Faust remained friends through the decades that followed their university years, and, when a committee was formed for a twenty-fifth reunion of the Class of 1915 at the Fairmont Hotel in San Francisco in November 1940, both Faust and Roney were chosen to serve. A full circle had been closed.

The first time I saw Fred Faust was on Wednesday night before the 1912 Stanford game. That night twenty sophomores had assembled quietly in the Eucalyptus Grove back of the Greek Theatre on blind orders from the upper classmen. The plan was a dark secret: we were to invade the Stanford campus, burn the Cardinal rally bonfire ahead of time, paint the statues blue, and imprint our college marks generally around the Farm.

Faust moved among the crowd, provoking the spirit of do or die. His deep voice rumbled in the darkness, and soon we were all galvanized to his plan. We knew as time went on, and in the months and years later when we worked with him in the daylight and in the prosaic endeavors of publishing *The Pelican, The Occident,* and *The Daily Californian,* that here we were with a man who always moved forward without regard of risk. Here was a man who "pressed on toward the goal" which his clear blue eyes could see, a goal which to most of us was not really visible at all.

When Faust came to Berkeley, he seemed removed entirely from the accepted pattern of 1911 freshmen; as fraternity material he didn't dress right; he didn't look right; he didn't seem to belong at all. However, there he was, and the first two years he kept to himself and his work. He entered more courses than any three men could handle, lived in a garret room and made his way as a reader in English, very nearly starved at times, learned to drink gin straight, and improved his born talent to write good verse. He made the mistake of registering in many subjects which couldn't hold his interest, then instead of formally withdrawing from these courses he simply stalked out.

Shortly after the Stanford invasion was successfully disposed of, Faust and I struck up a friendship. From the beginning it was close and understanding. In the small world of campus activity I thought I knew my way around, and I knew Faust had brains, so we teamed up for the high endeavor.

As early as his junior year he was something of a star. He wrote splendid prose and better verse, won essay prizes for students who had money (instead of ability) by writing their papers for them, edited *The Pelican,* the humorous weekly, wrote, jointly with Sidney Howard, the *Junior Farce* and the *Senior Extravaganza,* and won the Emily Cook Chamberlain prize in 1914, a national honor. As Senior Week approached, Faust was looked upon as the most illustrious man to be graduated, but such was not to be. During the closing months of that year he rebelled openly at the established standards, chided in verse, prose, cartoon, and speech what seemed to him a superficial campus world. He criticized the president of the university, as well as others of importance, when it appeared necessary to shade thinking into a realistic channel. The faculty regarded his independence with antagonism, and his degree was in jeopardy.

Most of those who were proud to know him a year before no longer hung about. "Dixie" Fish, Sid Howard, and I were among the few still sufficiently reckless not to fear being seen with him. We did our best to make the necessary concessions to the officially injured feelings before commencement week. We argued with him for two days and two nights, hoping to prepare him for a friendly interview with President Wheeler. The early morning interview came about and, although we thought we had the situation in hand, he simply told Dr. Wheeler how little his college degree actually meant to him. Therefore graduation was denied on the technical grounds of unexcused absences despite the fact that his scholarship record in the courses he actually attended may have justified him to be medalist and to be elected Phi Beta Kappa.

I received my degree following several incidents of suspense; Sid Howard got his six months later; and Dixie Fish was granted his in '17. Doc Smithson, a professor who took up the cudgels for Faust in a session of the Academic Senate at that time, suffered loss of position among his fellows. Benjamin Ide Wheeler, two years later, told me that no man with whom he had had an argument in all the years of his service as head of a great university so provoked the calm of his serene, accepted way as Faust did. Dr. Wheeler was a prominent figure among teachers. He was Theodore Roosevelt's choice for an exchange educator to represent American university teaching in Germany from 1909 to 1911. He made an important reputation on the Continent at that time. He was not a man easily moved by the erratic impulses of young blades. However,

Faust certainly hurled a monkey wrench into the wheels of his composed philosophy.

The president translated the shock of his early-morning interview with Faust, "the man of action," as the text for his commencement address at the ceremonies in the Greek Theatre a few days later. Faust sat in a misty sun on one of the top ledges of the stone pit and heard his own "action" outlook on life described as that of a man who eventually would step along with his eyes in the mud. Below him twelve hundred "real" students, robed sedately in black, graduated in the official manner. To his right and to his left sat the mothers and fathers, proud to know their sons and daughters were so bountifully blessed with the philosophy of idealism. Of course, the brief speech of the president was skillful and no direct references connected it with the man he had in mind. I knew, so did Howard, the meaning behind his words. In later years the president confirmed it.

It seems friends and family and joyous graduates always troop off in the merriment of the hour. A college town is a lonesome, ashen place when the festivities of commencement day are over. I, too, was alone with no beaming parents there to spirit me away. Faust and I sat on a nearby doorstep to watch the crowd depart. That night, as the sun was setting on his college career, Faust decided to strike out for some place far away.

I heard from him in Oahu; he lived in Honolulu for several months, writing sports on a local paper there. In the following year a ship, bound for Liverpool via Vancouver, found him aboard. At last he was really pointed toward the war; it still was only 1916. However, the ship went no farther than Vancouver, and Faust enlisted there in a Canadian unit "ready" to entrain for embarkation overseas. The brigade went on to Gallipoli, but Faust's regiment was detached and held in the Northwest. Of course he had done much scribbling in spare moments and, when he finally developed sufficient courage to desert, he left behind him in the rush of the moment these writings, as well as his razor and socks.

Of course, Faust was brought back; he got as far south as Victoria. He was returned in irons as the penalty was death, and his was a German name. The colonel saw the things he had written as his effects were examined in preparation of the evidence of his trial. The writings hit the "old man" in a vulnerable spot, and he gave Faust the privilege of buying a discharge.

Next, he turned up in the American Legion, in Nova Scotia. Political implications were such that this outfit seemed destined never to reach the front. However, desertion held no forebodings to Heinie Faust. He chose a particularly dark night while a blizzard wrapped the border. He struck out on foot, cutting his uniform into bits as he went to leave no trail, replacing shoes and uniform with a pair of rubber-soled shoes, blue overalls, a sateen shirt, and a cap which he had brought with him. As a breather he cut timber in the Maine woods, hurried on to New York City without trying for a change in costume since word had reached him that he should apply at once to the John Hays Hammond headquarters then enlisting volunteers for ambulance service in France. But he was rejected. His German name may have had something to do with it.

He slept in a Bowery mission, swept the tracks in the subway until his earnings bought him suit, shoes, and hat; then he secured a job as a porter at Wanamaker's. More food and daylight and soon he was banging on the doors of the editors. It wasn't long until old Bob Davis of *Munsey's* took him in hand and showed him the way to pay dirt in Grub Street.

America was soon in the war, and for Faust it meant another enlistment as that seemed the best way to get to France in a hurry. He finally found a draft board and a promise of Class A enlistment, but then the medicos said no, and Faust went in for repairs on his own time and at his own expense. Once again he crashed the draft board and was promised an assignment to the first contingent bound for France. However, he ended up in the middle of the night in a half-completed Engineers' cantonment at Camp Humphreys, Virginia. The main job was stump pulling, and there Heinie Faust labored out the duration of that war, carving his initials with a pick in Virginia clay, "stickier and redder than any clay in the world."

During the dreary Camp Humphreys days I wrote Faust a reminder of our congenial friendship on the Berkeley campus and under the date of October 18, 1918 I received a reply which I quote in part:

What you wrote about college hit me where I live. Alma Mater has disclaimed me in the eyes of the world and kicked me through the door and let me go bouncing down the marble steps on my rear end and so out into the cold, cold world. . . . However there's no one who keeps a tenderer regard for our old university days than I do.

What I think back to are the days when I was a desperately lonely freshman, wandering about the streets of Berkeley, past the open doors of the fraternity and sorority houses, and watching the noise and the light pour out, and wondering how people could be so happy.

The university was a grand and solemn institution to me then, and I was a very reverent frosh, for almost a whole semester. And the tang of that first reverence has never quite left me. And something like love for the old U.C. comes back and takes me by the throat more times than I am willing to tell you.

I suppose I deserved, as you have pointed out, all that I got, though what I got still stings as Dad's switch used to sting. But it's damned stimulating, old-timer, and I suppose you will smile when I tell you that I shall judge of my success or failure in the world according as I can make U.C. proud to have me as an alumnus. But there are things, Harvey, which sound too self-concerned when they are written in black and white. Some day I shall tell them to you over some of the best whiskey New York can produce.

FAUST'S MILITARY INTERLUDE

Gilbert J. McLennan

At twenty-four Faust was seeking what his fictional characters would later term "the bright face of danger." War was romantic, glorious, the stuff of myth to him. Gilbert McLennan, who later became a rancher in the Colorado Rockies, was there to record what happened when Faust was shipped off for Toronto.

Frederick Faust came to Toronto, Canada, and joined what came to be called the "American Foreign Legion" or the 97th Canadian Battalion in the early months of 1916. The Legion was a unique outfit, being composed of Americans who were, to quote the then current phrase, "not too proud to fight." We were 1,200 strong at most times, and ranks were filled with a motley of U.S. cavalry, Leathernecks, U.S. sailors, old Spanish American veterans, U.S. infantrymen, merchant seamen, and all manner of other soldiers of fortune, all come up for the love of adventure. Most of them came in the uniform of their stateside units, and it was a common sight in those days to see the legion parading of a Sunday, marching down Yonge Street, Toronto, with a great many of the boys dressed in United States uniforms topped by a Canadian greatcoat.

Fred Faust and I were members of the same Machine Gun Section, on the same team, together with Don Blanding, and a boy from Kentucky called Kennedy, and one Freddie Fayling from heaven knows where. I have a photo of the team with Faust at the gun. Don Blanding turned out to be a soldier of fortune, artist, traveler, and poet.

Both Fred and Don were greatly impressed with our captain, Tracy Richardson. Tracy was an incredible character. A buddy of Jack London's, he accompanied the writer on several jaunts, particularly THE CRUISE OF THE SNARK. TR was our idol, and we were his "chosen people." We had to pass a stiff appraisal from TR before we were allowed to qualify as members of "Tracy's Boys."

TR was one time a rebel general under Pancho Villa and in later Mexican brawls, and his stories, told us around a campfire, were like another form of A THOUSAND AND ONE NIGHTS. Tracy had been over to France with the original Princess Pats and was wounded and sent back home. Then the 97th started forming in Toronto by members of the American Club. I was in Montana at the time. I came up to Calgary, joined the American Legion there, and went off to Toronto, meeting TR. Then Fred Faust drifted in, with dozens and dozens of others from all over the world. Fred Fayling was an old cowpuncher and general hobo who bummed about with Faust quite a bit. We used to go down to Hall's Harbour in Nova Scotia on fishing trips and have lobster feasts on the beach. I had been range-riding in Canada and in Montana and had my own tales to tell at that time.

We spent the winter in Toronto in training and most times, when the team was not working, Fred and Don used to sit on the lake front or in High Park with their notebooks, always scribbling! We used to joke and say that Fred might be an enemy spy taking notes on us, for he was a typical Germanic type and with the close-cut army hair-do he sure looked the part. Actually, Fred was a good chap, though he was generally quiet and reticent, usually going off by himself when not on duty or on parades and marches. But when he was in barracks, in the old Machinery Building of the Canadian National Exhibition Grounds, Toronto, our quarters during the winter of 1915–16, Fred, together with the gang, joined in the fun, practical jokes, and general kidding and raised his deep voice in the songs from time to time.

The legion suffered a prolonged stay in Nova Scotia, bogged down due to political red tape. Faust was getting more and more frustrated. From Kentville, Nova Scotia, Fred took the alternative given us by the C.O. and "went over the hill" to join another unit. A boy, Cousins, from Nashville, went with him. Kennedy, his other pal, stayed with us and, when we finally got shipped overseas in the fall of 1916, he was killed on Vimy. I myself was wounded on Vimy and invalided back to Canada in 1918, the year I turned twenty-four. I lost complete track of Faust.

Around 1935, when I was in England doing Art Direction for Alexander Korda and other film companies, I received a letter from Tracy Richardson, telling me that he was in New York and had just had a guest to dinner by the name of Max Brand. Tracy revealed that Max Brand, the famous writer of Westerns, was in fact our old pal, Fred. This was a real shock to me. I'd never connected the two names.

Richardson was on his postwar travels then, and it may be that TR, Fred, and Don combined forces for a while. I was unable to join them due to my war disability. Then, in 1944, I read with great sadness of Fred's death in Italy.

A man is remembered by his works, and we are fortunate that Max Brand, or Fred as I knew him, left us much to remember him by.

BOHEMIAN DAYS ON GRUB STREET

John Schoolcraft

John Schoolcraft was one of several of Faust's classmates at the University of California who became lifelong friends. He met Faust in 1911 and was a year ahead of him at the university. Like Faust, Schoolcraft wanted to become a professional writer. He was later to claim that Faust helped him achieve this goal. After Faust's death in 1944, Schoolcraft began gathering materials for a book he wanted to call THE FABULOUS FAUST: HIS LIFE AND LETTERS. The book was never published in its completed form, but parts of it have been incorporated into this essay, especially edited by William F. Nolan. It details the period when Faust and Schoolcraft labored together in New York at the outset of their careers, when their literal survival depended on penny-a-word pulp sales.

My first impression was that of everyone who met him—one of great height. Actually, Faust was not exceptionally tall at six feet three, but he seemed taller because of a rather longish neck, and a very erect carriage.

We found ourselves living near one another in that fall of 1911 and met occasionally between classes to drink beer in one of the many excellent German beer halls then in existence. Through these meetings our likes and dislikes came to light and to some extent began to match up. I became aware of his passionate interest in Malory's MORTE D'ARTHUR, a love which had its beginnings in his first reading and which lasted throughout his life. This love of the Arthurian legends was an asset in his great career as a writer of Western stories.

Faust had no money when he came to college and in his early years was no stranger to physical hunger. At one time he was working from four in the afternoon to midnight in the Railway Express office in San Francisco; after coming back to Berkeley, he would sit up until all hours, working on his verse.

At one time he was actually testing to see what the minimum was in sleep that he needed to keep going. He was annoyed to find that he had to have *some* sleep in order to get along, but he reduced it to the absolute minimum.

Faust was a great talker, but he was also a great listener. I went away from our meetings elated and feeling a little larger than my normal self. Other people, after talking with him, have felt the same. Perhaps it was just a habit of blarney natural to a family in which there was a strong Irish strain (on his mother's side) and carried by Faust to an excess which was characteristic of most things he did. Deeper than that, he seemed always to feel an urgent need to find people who were abler and more knowledgeable than himself. Since these were hard to come by, he created them out of the materials which came to hand. Or, as a friend expressed it, Faust was always finding stores of wit and knowledge in his friends which they just didn't possess.

It was through his younger brother, Tom, that the nickname ''Heinie'' became attached to Faust. In his childhood he had generally been known as Schiller, or ''Schil,'' also as Big Gloom, Flying Dutchman, Silent Guy, Pash Poet, and Long Drink. Tom began calling him ''Heinie-blitz,'' a nonsense nickname with, perhaps, some vague Katzenjammer Kids association. Faust sometimes referred to himself as ''the skinny Irishman with the German name,'' and on balance it does seem as if he were more Gaelic than Teutonic.

Faust's English teacher at the university, Leonard Bacon, never used the nickname. Faust and Bacon were to become as close as men could be; they were neighbors in Florence for many years, played tennis, fought out exhausting games of chess, saw their children grow up together, and met in towering arguments on poetic matters. (It is not on record that either made much of a dent in the other's point of view.) Yet an odd trace of formality, derived perhaps from teacher/student days, persisted between them. Bacon always addressed Faust as ''Fred,'' instead of ''Heinie,'' and Faust always signed his letters ''Frederick Faust,'' instead of using the cheery ''*Adíos,* Heinie,'' with which he usually closed his communications.

The race for campus honors was very keen, and these honors Faust reaped in good measure in his later college years. But he never forgot the ''also rans'' and, accordingly, wrote this poem which stands on the flyleaf of the *Blue and Gold* [the University of California Annual]:

You who turn these pages through shall find
That the small covers of this book enfold
Some record of the few whose hands were bold;
They wrought the given and the unassigned.

Yield them the triumph willingly, ay, bind
New wreaths about them for the withered old;
And spell their names in letterings of gold,
The athlete and the leader of the mind.

> Yet still remember us who have remained
> Unknown, and felt it glorious to be
> An undistinguishable unit in the throng.
>
> Remember us whose actions are unnamed,
> It was our cheer made sweet the victory,
> And in defeat we sang the last great song.

After commencement week in 1915 I did not see Faust for almost a year and a half. To be specific, it was in September, 1916, and the place was New York City. By then Heinie had adventured his way around a good part of the globe, including Hawaii, western Canada, eastern Canada, and New York. We had kept in touch by correspondence.

Thus it came about that we sat in Busy Jack's in the autumn of 1916, eating a fifteen-cent meal and picking up the endless threads of talk which we had begun to spin while in college. He wore an outfit purchased at a second-hand store in Skid Row for the sum of three dollars: a coat much too small and bleached to a light mouse color, a pair of trousers ending at his shoe-tops, and a black sateen shirt, no tie. He was submitting a great deal of verse to the magazines and not selling any of it.

But within a year, Faust *was* selling short fiction to Bob Davis at *Munsey's.* We were quite highbrow in those days and writing for the pulps was a side issue which we did not take seriously. Our artistic drive was elsewhere—Faust's in his verse and mine in gloomy, realistic stories which, thank God, nobody would publish. I don't think that in all his young dreams of a future Faust ever pictured himself as one of the world's great writers of popular stories.

It is my impression that ''Mr. Cinderella'' was the first piece to open Faust's eyes to the possibilities of a future in prose fiction, which he had always scorned. It was also the first yarn that he wrote beyond short-story length, and the first that brought him any ''substantial'' sum of money (at a penny a word, a bit over $100).

It is improbable that Faust, after that sale to Davis, had any conception of the flood of words that lay ahead. In fact he said later that, after finishing a story in those beginning days, his mind was a complete blank, and he felt that he would never come up with another plot. We saw a great deal of each other, and we talked shop constantly. When one was stuck on a story, the other came to his assistance. Faust always gave a great deal more than he received in these exchanges, but it wasn't an entirely one-sided affair. He drew quite a lot on his friends—not for ideas, of which he had a supply that constantly renewed itself from some mysterious source, but for local color and for bits of everyday observation which are useful in creating a situation or shaping a character. There are quite a few of us around who are happy to think we had some small part in stoking the atomic furnace known as Faust.

As soon as money began to come in, he took a room at 129 East 63rd Street, in a brownstone operated as a rooming house by a Mrs. Murphy, fresh from the

Old Country. As Faust told it, she'd come in and stand with her hands wrapped in her apron, wondering how this poor young man could spend such long hours at his typewriter.

"The Double Crown," on which Faust used the pen name John Frederick and I used the pseudonym Peter Ward, was our only attempt at actual collaboration. For this historical Faust compounded John Frederick out of our first two names. It was the second in a long series of pseudonyms which he eventually evolved. I took the "Ward" from Ben Ward, a young illustrator who shared the working quarters set up in a back bedroom at Mrs. Murphy's. (He later became well known in the advertising field.)

This serial, for *Argosy,* was written in the winter of 1917–1918, from cold as well as hunger. The war was on, and there was no coal in New York. Water spilled on the floor of the apartment in which we lived, froze, and stayed frozen for weeks. I well remember walking up Broadway on New Year's Day, 1918, with the thermometer at eight below zero and a wind coming out of the north as cold as the heart of Frank A. Munsey himself. As I recall, my contribution to "The Double Crown" was the original remark out of which the story grew, the title, and a few of the chapters. They could be identified by their anemic tone. I received $300 as my share of the proceeds. I thought at the time that I was being grossly overpaid.

An eating place which we patronized quite frequently was Joe's Restaurant on Third Avenue. A three-course dinner could be had for twenty-five cents, and the chicken dinner (the most expensive) was forty-five cents. I suppose that the cooks and waiters of that time are probably all in heaven, serving even more nutritious meals at even lower prices. Certainly none of them could have had any idea that the tall, rather solemn young man who ate there would turn out to be one of the writing geniuses of all time.

Heinie had no bank account and, after cashing checks into hundreds of dollars, would roam New York with the side pockets of his coat stuffed with bills. Prime dinners in good restaurants, huge tips to waiters and hat-check girls, debts paid off, books bought, loans and gifts to friends in need, the money went about as fast as it came in, as it always had before, and as it did throughout Faust's life.

Heinie turned to Westerns quite by accident. He had written a story called "The Homecoming of Lazy Purdue," and Davis got excited about it. "I think in this type of man you have the proper hero," he told Faust. It was printed as "The Adopted Son," in October, 1917, and became his first real Western. Then, of course, his first novel in the genre was THE UNTAMED. He continued to write in the field for the simple reason that there was a market to be filled—for him a very easy market. Thus, he made himself an important figure in our most American kind of writing, a definite current in the great stream of world literature. He was writing in the vein of our own saga—the westward movement of Americans.

Of course, verse was Heinie's prime passion, and it was a great pity that he was driven by his demon to choose his themes not only from ancient sources but sources which had already been mined by the world's greatest writers. He was trying to set up milestones where milestones had already been placed. Literary taste (for good or ill) had passed those milestones, and the public is seldom in a mood to go back and examine freshly placed markers in the same area.

His death in 1944 sent a shock wave through us all. It was as if a favorite player had been struck down in some great stadium game. Below, on the playing field, was the team: Faust's family and friends, a group closely attached by a deep warmth of feeling. In the boxes and choice seats on the fifty-yard line were the others who had known him, who'd been flattered by his friendship, however brief. And in the great stands, stretching back to the horizon, were the myriads who had known him only through his writings. But to the lips of all came the same hushed cry, because each was, in his or her degree, attached to this remarkable American. But when the full story of his death was known, there were many who felt that in spite of the dreams of ''turning a new corner and climbing on a higher stair,'' this was how Faust would have wanted it.

In 1923 I dedicated my novel, THE BIRD OF PASSAGE, to Frederick Faust. The dedication—''May God love me as I love a straightforward man''—expresses my feeling about him, early and late.

MORE ON FREDERICK FAUST

John Schoolcraft, compiled by Darrell C. Richardson

For a number of years John L. Schoolcraft was thought to be another pseudonym of Frederick Faust. In fact, in my earliest bibliography of his works I listed John L. Schoolcraft and Peter Ward as two of his noms des plumes. *His only published book,* THE BIRD OF PASSAGE *(Grosset & Dunlap, 1923), was dedicated to F. S. Faust. Some early Faust appearances in* Argosy *were coauthored by J. L. Schoolcraft and Peter Ward. After the first issue of* The Fabulous Faust Fanzine *was published with this information, Dorothy Faust sent a copy to Schoolcraft. He promptly wrote an article about his early friendship with Faust and set us straight about the pseudonym. Schoolcraft was a great friend of Fred Faust and kept up with him and his family through the years. In this article he reveals how Faust got his pen name "Max Brand" and the origin of the "John Frederick" pseudonym. Mr. Schoolcraft and I became good friends, and we corresponded regularly for several years.*

D.C.R.

I am sorry to pull the rug out from under those who have been cherishing THE BIRD OF PASSAGE as a rare Faust item, but the fact is that it was written by me at Scarsdale, New York, during the spring of 1922. I am sure of this because I was married in June of that year on the proceeds. An excellent investment.

I have been so absorbed in business during the past twenty-three years that I cannot be exactly sure as to what happened back there in the innocent 'Twenties. I probably have a record somewhere of all the stories I wrote and of where they were published, but I would not know where to lay my hands on it. Any stories appearing over my own name or over the name of Peter Ward were written by me. I recognize all of the titles except one—"The Undying Flame." That rings no bell whatever but, if it has my name on it or the name of Peter Ward, it's my baby. Neither do I remember having had a story printed in *Flynn's Detective*

Fiction Weekly. I remember the "Hearing Eye" yarn well enough, but I was under the impression I had sold it to Bob Davis for *All-Story Weekly*. It may be that Davis bought it for *All-Story* and then shifted publication to *Flynn's*. I remember that he was engaged at one time in starting a detective magazine, and this was probably it.

I cannot agree that Faust revised and rewrote my stuff until it was pure Faust. There was absolutely nothing of this kind. If either had laid hands of that kind on the other's work, there would have been murder in Grub Street. We were close friends. We saw a great deal of each other, and we talked shop constantly. It is flattering to be thought of as one facet of his amazing genius, but what I don't understand is how anyone could mistake my polite memoranda for his full-blooded yarns. I hope you will make it clear to your readers that he did *not* write a book and then dedicate it to himself. This misapprehension arose from the fact that I (supposedly one of his pen names) dedicated THE BIRD OF PASSAGE to him. Such a maneuver would be for him entirely out of character, because there was no one who was less egotistical about himself or about his work than Fred Faust.

The matter of pen names came about very simply. In one office at the Munsey factory sat genial Bob Davis, editing *All-Story*. Down the hall was another office in which sat earnest Robert Simpson, editing *Argosy*. (Simpson was, by the way, a very good writer; his "Grey Charteris" is well worth reading.) Davis had a genius for turning up new writers, and I think was annoyed to have Simpson quietly kidnap them for work on *Argosy*. There was considerable rivalry between the two magazines, but it was all right to work for both provided different pen names were used. Faust, of course, used the name Max Brand with his very first story [actually his third story for a commercial magazine] because he wished to save his own name for his verse. Max Brand was invented by a friend who had a theory that a *nom de plume* should have a two-syllable punch and that the vowel sound should be the same in both parts of the name. When it came to writing for *Argosy,* Faust was obliged to cast around for another name and compounded John Frederick out of our two first monikers.

It is my impression that "Mr. Cinderella" . . . was the first tale that brought him any substantial sum of money. It is easy to reckon how much he received for it; all that is necessary is to count the number of words and multiply that by one cent. A cent a word was the regular Munsey rate for a beginning writer. "Mr. Cinderella" will always be associated in my mind with baked beans. At the time it was written I was a graduate student of Yale and had come down to New York for a few days during vacation. Faust was living on upper Broadway at that time, sharing an apartment with a remarkable Californian who had been flying a plane for [Pancho] Villa during the Mexican civil wars and had been shot down by the primitive means of rifle fire from the ground. All of us were hard up and every cent spent for food had to bring its full return in nutriment. There was a corner restaurant which supplied a very large plate of beans for fifteen cents, and the consequence was that we ate beans three times a day. I believe that it was at my suggestion that the story ended happily instead of tragically, as the author had planned. Faust said in later years that this change was what sold the story and what started him on his fiction career. This is ridiculous, of course, but it does show how a pair of friends, in the throes of early writing, exchanged ideas.

FICTIONAL AUTHOR "PORTRAITS" OF FREDERICK FAUST'S PERSONAE, FROM STREET & SMITH'S *WESTERN STORY MAGAZINE*

THE ROUND-UP
unsigned by F. E. Blackwell in
Western Story Magazine (September 2, 1922)

A good gun is a good gun; there's no denyin' of that, and we all like to have 'em. But, after all, in nine hundred ninety-nine cases out of a thousand, it is the man behind the gun that counts. Remember old Natty Bumppo, in the LEATHERSTOCKING TALES, and that famous muzzle-loading rifle of his? And we know of many a good shot today who uses a shootin' iron whose replica has been out of the catalogues for a generation.

Now it's just like this, folks. There's a dictionary—in fact, there are several of 'em—and they are filled with the finest lot of ammunition that could be imagined. Don't know whether it's hundreds of thousands or millions of 'em, but there are an awful lot of words in those dictionaries. And for typewriters, there's a dozen makes with all kinds of labor-savin' contraptions on 'em.

So there you are, word-ammunition and word-guns, but, lordy, Harry! What a difference it does make who shoots 'em off through the keys of those little black pianos. It is kind of interestin', don't you think, to peek into the lives of some of the folks that mixes those words up to make 'em so all-fired entertainin' for us all—the men behind the guns, as it were?

One of the best and most popular shooters of Western story words is George Owen Baxter. We have known George only since we bought his first story for the magazine, though he had been writing for a little while before that; but it was only the other day that we got a peek at the real George, the inside George. The outside George is big and husky, well over six feet, and built in proportion.

He has a long, easy, get-there stride; but the thing that's most notable about him is his eyes—big, dreamy, blue eyes. They seem to be lookin' over and beyond, out yonder, nearly all the time. He gets everything you say and all that, but it seems like he's lookin' 'way off out West.

It was in a little restaurant in New York, down on the East Side, that he opened up—and he sure does seem sort of pent up in this man's town—and told us something about himself. Bein' as he's not here tonight, because we don't want to embarrass him, we thought you'd like to hear what we learned about him.

Just thirteen when his father died out in California, George saw it was up to him to get victuals and shelter for himself at once. He did it pronto, goin' to work on a big ranch. Bein' as how he looked about sixteen instead of thirteen, they handed out the work according; but the grub was there, and the sleep was there, and George stuck, goin' to school in the winter time, until by and by he went to high school down to the town, working at odd jobs around, then back on the ranch again in the summer. This same he kept doin' through college, gettin' out just about the time that the big war started. We hadn't gone in it yet, so he up and beat his way to Canada and enlisted. He got in, but, when they came to pick and choose as to who was goin' overseas, they found some little trouble with George, only a minor defect that needed a little cuttin' to make him all right.

Well, bein' as he had put in about eight months in the Canadian army, George moseyed down into the U.S.A. along the eastern coast, thinkin' as how Uncle Sam might need him. He sure did, and, as the little cuttin' operation was pulled off successful, they were glad to take him. But the cards were stacked against George. Down South he got the influenza, and he got it bad, so that that old necessary blood-pumpin' organ is kind of crimped for life. And that put the kibosh on George fightin' for his country.

But George had always had a hankerin' to write, to write about the country that gave him work and chuck and a place to sleep and an education. At first, like it is in most trades and professions, he couldn't just mix the ammunition right; it got clogged in the barrel or something. And for a time he worked in the basement of a department store. He was choppin' tickets in the subway when his first yarn went over, and it went over big.

He is only twenty-six—just think of that!—and he is *there*; he has *arrived*. But he is not satisfied, though he has arrived. He is going to arrive a whole lot more, because, fortunately for him, he ain't stuck onto himself, which means he is going forward, always forward, and never back.

George is out West again in California. A good yarn came in from him this morning. You will read it by and by. We think you will reckon it is extra good. No doubt the air out there is most helpful to mixin' ammunition.

So that's the man behind that gun. Keep a-watchin' him, and keep a tally of his score, because he's goin' to shoot straighter and farther and bigger and better all the time. We know, because he is that kind, the kind that grows.

THE ROUND-UP
unsigned by F. E. Blackwell in
Western Story Magazine (September 15, 1923)

You have read the opening installment of "Wooden Guns," which begins in serial form in this issue. We say this with assurance, for we don't expect for one minute that any of you are goin' to turn to the Old Man's efforts first. Our feelin's ain't hurt one single drib about it. It's right and proper that folks should do the big and interestin' things first off, and then gather around the fire and chat and talk things over.

Wish we were a picture-book magazine for lots of reasons, but mostly because we would like to show you what our authors look like. Perhaps we're unduly partial to our authors because all of them have been so loyal and untiring in their efforts to aid us in making *Western Story Magazine* such a big success, but we think they are a dandy-looking lot.

Take Max Brand. My, but he's a fine, upstandin' boy. If you want to see a typical product of the West, just cast your glance on Max. And watch out that your glance doesn't become six feet, for Max is the kind who "fills your eye." He's way over six feet, but built so nice, got such good conformation, as we horsemen say, you don't realize how tall he is till you see him standin' with other big men.

California can be proud of this boy, for his youth was spent in that state, and he didn't live in cities or towns, or even villages. It was ranches that claimed him for their own until he was twenty.

Bein' so big and strong, always lookin' several years older than he really was, Max at twelve was doin' work a boy of sixteen would find it all he could do to handle, and it's always been that way with the big fellow. Without sayin' anything about it, not doin' it in a way that might attract attention, he just naturally takes hold, and with a will, to the heavy end of things, no matter what they be.

One thing, though, Max isn't good at, and that's talkin'. No, sirs, and ladies, when it comes to conversation, Max is sure weak. He's got all gifts the gods can hand out, save one, the gift of gab. If you're alone with him, and he likes you, you may get a little more than yes and no answers, by puttin' questions; but in a crowd, say, he might just as well be a hitchin' post, for all the noise he makes. But speakin' of hitchin' posts, there isn't a better one of the human kind than Max to tie to.

It's Max's eyes that sure get you most. Pale blue, they are, and with a look in 'em that comes when the person as owns 'em has spent much time alone in the open places. Max looks at you—yes, he's a straight looker, but with a look that seems to go through, past you, and way, way out yonder.

Gosh all hemlock, hope you all haven't got tired with our talkin' so much about one of our children. But those of you who are parents will understand just how proud we feel, and, when we get to praisin' our authors up, we act jest like proud parents and can't seem to tell when it's time to stop.

But it was about the new serial we had intended to speak, and now there is so little time left. When Max brought "Wooden Guns" to our desk, we up and asked him point-blank, before we even looked at the title, if he thought the story was a good one.

"Don't know," he said. "Author can't judge his own work, but I'll say this much, had more pleasure doin' it than any story I ever wrote." Max would say nothing more; we made all the noise during the rest of the interview.

Well, you've read the first installment, and you have only that much to go by, but we have read the whole yarn, and we say and declare that "Wooden Guns" is the best thing Max Brand has ever done. Kind of bad thing, perhaps, to go to praisin' up a thing that way, might tend to set folks ag'in' the story, but not this one we think, for—gosh hang it!—if we know our business, just one little part of our business, "Wooden Guns" deserves all the praise we can give it, and then some more.

Excuse us, if we've gone too far, please.

THE ROUND-UP
unsigned by F. E. Blackwell in
Western Story Magazine (February 9, 1924)

Well, boys and girls, old and young, middle and between, how be ye?

Nice night, nice night, but quite some sharp. Stir up that fire, cowboy, stir up that fire. A couple of you lads had better go down to the river bottom yander, and fetch up some more wood. There, that's better.

Say, folks, anybody would think we were goin' in the pup business. First comes along Max Brand, with: "Oh, boss, seein' as how you used to raise bull terriers, will ye help me get a good pup?"

Well, it was our busy day, but when anyone comes along and asks us in an admirin' manner if we will be so kind as to help 'em pick out a pup or a hoss, well, we jest then got busier business to do than sit around an office.

"We're with ye, Max," says we, picking up our coat, and at the same time turnin' over the ranch to the help with one sweepin' gesture of an arm what was trying to get into a perworse sleeve.

Now Max, he's stayin' in town for a few months, so as to be near the Old Man and The Round-Up, him sayin' as how he could thus get a better idea as to what's wanted.

We didn't bother with no elevator, and gettin' down to the street we trails a sea-goin' hack and heads for Coney Island.

"It's winter," yells Max. "What ye headin' for that place for?"

"Friend er mine," we answers over the top of the noise made by our hack and all the other hacks, and the trolley cars and the trucks and the elevated roads and subways and the voices of all the other guys as if tryin' to make theyselves heard.

Now, folks, get this "friend-er-mine" stuff.

Down in Coney Island we meets up with my "friend." We put 'im in quotes 'cause he *used* to be our friend. He ain't no more.

"Has my 'friend' got a bull terrier pup?" Most certainly, yes. Will he sell 'im? Well, he sure does hate to part with that pup, particularly as the family is so stuck on 'im. But bein' as how Max is a friend of mine—Max still *is,* but I don't know why—he'll part with that pup for just one hundred and twenty-five dollars, and no less. Max, he sure is stuck on that pup, and he was, two ways, as you all will presently see. And this used-to-was friend er mine was hep.

On the square, we'll tell The Round-Up, it was sure one fine pup; tail set nice and low, close coupled, great head. Honest, we don't know as we ever sot eyes on a nicer pup.

Max, he pays the money. We bundles the pup into the back and starts for Max's home. My business ranch bein' on the way, Max drops me off, we likin' to look in and see how much copy the folks has mangled while we was buyin' that pup, us goin' along being necessary to give *expert* advice, yer understand.

So Max, he goes along home, and we goes up to the office. And if there ain't [Kenneth] Perkins sittin' a-waitin' for us; Perkins—he havin' just stopped off on his way to California, after makin' a little visit down East.

"What can we do for you?" we asks in that kind er set-up way a feller puts on after he's been asked for advice and guidance in such an important matter, and has given 'em.

"Say, we're all broke up," says Perkins. "You know that wire-haired fox terrier we was always cartin' 'round with us, the wife and I? Well, he went an et some pizen, and died. Nothin' to do but we must have another, and right away. Know where?"

"You sure have come to the right man," we answers, in a kind er proud-like way. "Come on." And down the stairs we go, hop another hack, and head to the hills of Harlem, we havin' a particular "friend" as raises fox terrier pups up in *that* direction.

Well, Perkins gets his pup. And it's a dandy, ye can take our word for it. Price, one hundred and fifty dollars. Little fancy, we'll say, but Perkins is sure particular about pints on a pup, even more so than Max.

Perkins goes home, and so do we, and plumb tired we are too.

Next mornin', that same bein' yesterday, we're a little late showin' up at the office, seein' as we'd been chasin' pups most of the day before.

"Perkins and Max Brand is both on the wire to-once," pipes up the help, so soon as we opens the door.

We picks up the receiver, and there they both were, our central girl knowin' 'em to be friends, has put 'em on the same wire, so as they could talk a spell till we come in. It's a nice habit she has.

"Hello," we says. "Let Perkins speak first."

"He's got stole," cries Perkins. Cries is right, too, for he was pretty near doin' it, at that.

"What?"

"Yes. I lets him out of the hack, when it pulls up in front of my house, and the pup makes a break for the middle of the street. A taxi comes along . . . door opens, and a guy scoops him up. Good bye pup! Say, I thought your friend said that dog was trained to mind?"

"!!!!! ???? !!!! ???? !!!!" All this to try to give ye the remotest idea of Max tryin' to butt inter the tale of woe Perkins is givin' me. At last I gets:

"Deaf, STONE DEAF, I'm tellin' ye. S-T-O-N-E DEAF! The PUP! Can't *ye* hear, either. THE PUP'S STONE DEAF!"

Spare me the necessity of handin' out further details. Suffice it to say that the gent in Harlem refused to give Perkins another pup, sayin' a guy as doesn't know how to hold onto a pup he's just paid one hundred and fifty cold smackers for, don't deserve to own one. As to my "friend" in Coney Island, he'd moved when Max and I went back there. We're still lookin' for him. That pup is sure stone deaf, but he's got a fine nose, and may happen-chance we'll fetch up with my "friend" through that pup's scentin' him out.

Any of you want some advice on the pints of a dog and where to get a good one? If you do, step right up, we're always glad to oblige, when it comes to helpin' pick out a pup or a hoss!

What, no one here as wants our help in er little matter of this kind? Say, our feelin's is hurt. And we're goin' to turn in right this very instant, pronto now.

FAMOUS WESTERN STORY WRITERS
GEORGE OWEN BAXTER
by D. C. Hubbard in
—————— *Western Story Magazine* (April 28, 1928) ——————

Although George Owen Baxter's father was a wealthy ranch owner in southern California, George himself was shown no favoritism when it came to riding or roping or herding cattle. He was obliged to work as the other ranchmen worked for his father, and his graduation from an eastern college didn't signify that he was to be made boss of an outfit the day he arrived home.

George understood the spirit which made his father treat him in the way he did. The first time he fell off a horse was when he was but ten years old. He picked himself up lamely and brushing the dust from his eyes saw his father standing a few feet away, motionless, making no effort to help him, and not even asking if he were hurt. Several of the ranch hands were looking on, wondering what would happen. "Look after your horse, George," said his father coldly. At that moment Mrs. Baxter appeared in the doorway of the house. The boy wanted to rush to her comforting arms, where he knew sympathy lay. But there stood his father, grim and terrible, and about him lounged the bunkhouse boys ready to laugh or to applaud, whichever way the wind blew. Something within the child's breast rose with a mighty pride, the pride of his father and his father's father, those fearless pioneers of the early days. He forced back the lump which was rising in his throat, turned and ran limping after his horse. "That was the moment I became a man," says George Owen Baxter himself. And now that he has sons of his own, he knows it was no easy task for his father to be severe with him in those days.

To his mother Mr. Baxter owes his early education. She had been a school-teacher and had received his father, James Baxter, as a pupil, although he was two years her senior, and later married him and went to live on the big ranch. Before her son was a year old she amused him by the hour by reciting poetry to him; he could not understand it, of course, but the soft rhythm of her voice instilled in him a love for poetry which he never completely outgrew. Her library, although small, had been chosen with thought and deliberation, and her only son grew up with a thirst for reading.

At college he was dubbed "the cowboy kid." It so happened that he was the only real Westerner in his class, that is, from beyond the Rockies. Had it not been for this eastern training, Baxter might never have taken to writing. Ashamed as he was of it, there was no denying the fact that he was terribly homesick for the rolling plains, the night rides under the stars, and the rough, kindly cowboys of his father's ranch. To ease this longing, he began writing little sketches of his early life, some of them true, some of them fancy. He was shy with girls, but on paper his romantic instincts soared. Soon he became a regular contributor to the college paper. Later, friends urged him to send something to the magazines which published Western fiction. While the school paper was loyal to the young writer, the magazines returned his efforts as regularly as he mailed them.

Then came the day when George received a telegram that his father had been hurt in a stampede and was not expected to live. It was the last semester, and this news meant that college would close without him. That night he should have spent studying for the finals. He could not get a train until the next day. There was no use studying for examinations he would not be able to take, and he must get his mind off the tragedy which awaited at his journey's end. So he started to write a story about the world he loved and knew most about. All night he wrote, scattering the pages on the floor as they slipped out of the machine until the room resembled a snowstorm. In the morning the call came announcing breakfast, but it was ignored. Ten minutes before the train was due, the tired author gathered up his sheets of typewritten paper and hastily scribbled on a envelope, "Buck, please send to *Western Story Magazine,* New York. Cowboy Kid." Buck was his roommate, who had spent the night before cramming for the next day's exams. The wheels of the westbound train were already turning as Baxter swung aboard.

Two weeks later Baxter sat reading to his convalescent father in the familiar and dearly beloved ranch house. A cloud of dust rolling in the window announced the arrival of the mail man. Baxter says that no thrill—if men will admit they ever have thrills—ever was quite the same as the one he felt when he opened an envelope addressed to him from New York. The words that accompanied the enclosed check are as clear to him today as if it were yesterday that he had received it. "We liked your story. Won't you please send us some more?" Baxter needed no further urging than that. He wrote so steadily for the next six months that his mother felt she was sorry she had ever taught him to read. But, of course, she did not mean just that, for she was inordinately proud of him.

Such sudden and steady appliance to the typewriter, and the worry of his father's illness, coming on top of a strenuous four years at college, taxed Baxter's strong physique. At the first hint of a cough, his father bought him an outfit and sent him off to spend his days and nights in the open, to wander wherever he pleased, but with the injunction not to come home until he was a man again. The stern, relentless parent put the typewriter under lock and key.

So off the young author went to regain his health and strength. For nearly a year he traveled about, getting jobs, meeting all sorts of men, rangers, hobos, prospectors, always on the alert for a new and interesting face with a tale to tell of struggle and desire.

Satisfied at last that his father would approve of his condition, he returned home, his head packed with ideas and color for more stories. The father gave him one long, earnest, scrutinizing look, then silently handed him the key to the cupboard which held the magic typewriter, magic because it wove his dream characters into living persons and appeased a yearning that only written expression could satisfy.

Even now, George Owen Baxter tramps off alone for a few months every year to refresh himself both in body and spirit, and with his own hand locks the typewriter away in the cupboard to await his return from a trip into new and promising fields of observation.

Most of his stories which have appeared in *Western Story Magazine* have been published in book form, some of the most successful being "Free Range Lanning," "The Shadow of Silver Tip," "Train's Trust," and "The Whispering Outlaw."

FAMOUS WESTERN STORY WRITERS
MAX BRAND
by D. C. Hubbard in
Western Story Magazine (June 2, 1928)

By the time our pony had brought us to the Ranch Cross B we were mighty tired. Jogging along for twenty miles through a hot, dusty day was tough on us, since we haven't been traveling much in that style for the past three or four years.

The object of our search, Max Brand, had gone to Ore City, forty miles away, and would be back "in a day or two." Never saw anything like it out on those ranches. Time means nothing to them. Well, we can remember the day when time meant little or nothing to us, too, but that was before we had a taste of the East, where everybody moves in double-quick haste.

The boys took us in just as if we had all been pals together all our lives, and what a grand, old supper they gave us! Browned potatoes, spare ribs—well, what's the use—it only makes us wish we were back with the boys again instead of sitting at our old workbench telling you about one of your favorite authors, Max Brand.

After supper the gang took us out to sit under some trees a short distance from the ranch house where it was cooler and a fine view of the sunset could be had, while we smoked pipes and cigarettes and talked. Just wish we had time to tell you about some of the thrillers those boys go through, but we know you'd rather hear what they had to say about their leader and boss, Max Brand.

Brand, they said, is one of the whitest men they had ever worked for. A tall, wiry, lean individual, with snapping blue eyes, he holds the respect and admiration of every cowpuncher he comes in contact with, and hasn't a real, serious enemy. Of course, it would be unnatural if there weren't a few who did not envy this fellow enough to begrudge him his position and popularity, but there are evidently very few who do not feel it an honor to be on equal footing with him. Born and raised on the range, Max Brand at an early age showed great resourcefulness and courage. One of the cowpunchers had known him since he was a tiny lad, and told us about one time when Max was ten years old. He was riding to town with his two aunts, both very stout ladies from the East, who were paying a short visit to their brother. It was a spring day and the team which drew the light wagon was feeling frisky, but young Brand thought there was no danger, since both aunts knew how to drive.

On the way to town the off horse took fright at something, probably a snake suddenly darting across the road, and broke into a run, pulling his teammate into a gallop equal to his own. The aunt who was driving became frightened when the reins were snatched from her hands by a mighty swish of the horse's tail. They both screamed—which did not help calm the runaway team. Little Max, sitting between them, looked from one white face to the other and then made his decision. He leaped over the dashboard, made his way along the pole, and climbed on the back of the off horse. The light buckboard was swinging and swaying, and an approaching sharp curve would in short order shape the destinies of the two horses, one boy, and two aunts. But the off horse was Max's own saddle horse, and the moment the animal felt the boy on his back, regardless of the harness and trailing carriage, he slowed down. Taking the check rein in his hands, the boy quieted Ginger until his gallop slowed to a safe trot, and his mate obligingly matched his stride. All this happened before the dangerous curve was reached.

At the end of the story the cowpuncher slapped his thigh soundly. ''I'm tellin' you, *hombre,* them two ladies came back to the house with faces as white as chalk, and them faces *stayed* white all the time they was here, which was two weeks longer." The rest of the boys laughed. One of them nudged us and whispered: "Every time Sam tells that story, them ladies' faces stay white longer. In a few years he'll have it forever."

Max's father, it seems, was restless, moving from one ranch to another every two or three years, so that Max lived in eight different states before he was twenty-one. In the meantime he went to college in California and graduated. At that time he took a trip East, intending to get a job doing newspaper work, as he felt he would like to become a writer, and everyone told him that that was the best way to start. But Max, from the time he was very small, was quick to make decisions, which no doubt saved his own neck as well as the necks of others. It also got him into a few unpleasant scrapes. A quick mind usually means a quick temper, and although the boys at the Ranch Cross B would not admit it to us, Max himself, when he showed up two days later, acknowledged it freely.

But to go back to his trip to the East in search of a newspaper job. Max arrived in New York on a Monday morning. It was his first visit to a big city. He gazed at the buildings and at the people hurrying in endless procession. After walking half a block from the Grand Central Station, Max made up his mind with one of those lightning twists for which he was famous. Going back to the ticket window, he leaned forward confidentially to the clerk. "When's the next train back to Chicago, *hombre*?" he asked. A few hours later Max Brand, the would-be newspaper reporter, was speeding on his way across the continent. "New York's all right," he told the boys, "but it's too far away, and besides, there're plenty of folks there already."

So in a small western town which gave Max all the elbow room he needed, he made his entrance into the newspaper world and from that time onward for four years he worked steadily at the business of writing until he began to sell a few short stories to various papers and later to magazines. Among many which have graced the pages of *Western Story Magazine* are: "The City in the Sky," "The Silver Stork," "Pleasant Jim," and "Weakling of the Wild."

Mr. Brand was rather bashful when we insisted upon having a picture of him, but finally he dug one up from among a great pile of half-finished manuscripts. "'Tisn't good," he apologized. "The sun was shining in my eyes." We agree that it isn't a very good picture of Mr. Brand, but we felt you readers could set some idea of what this popular author looks like, and some time perhaps he may have another picture taken that will bring out his best features. But looks don't count much with the Western boys, whether they are authors or cowboys. It is how a man holds up his end and carries on that places him at the head or the end of the list. And Max Brand is one who without doubt is in the front line of worthwhile men of today.

FAMOUS WESTERN STORY WRITERS
DAVID MANNING
by D. C. Hubbard in
——————— *Western Story Magazine* (June 16, 1928) ———————

Out of the wind-blown, sun-baked Mojave desert furiously rode the anxious-eyed father of David Manning. His boy, the idol of his heart, his very breath and being, hovered between life and death. Only a doctor could save him, and then only if he could be procured quickly.

Perspiration made irregular streaks down the sand-covered face and mingled with still more sand upon the shirt of the breathless man who pounded excitedly upon the door of Doctor Snell. It was said by some that Doctor Snell was only a veterinary who had become sufficiently interested in human ailments to act the part of physician. Whether this was true or not, his name was always spoken with reverence, for in the fifteen years of his stay at Marble City he had never lost a patient.

Fortunately, Doctor Snell was sitting in his stuffy office that day and was surprised from his reverie by the frantic clamor at his door. A powerfully built man he was, slow of movement, but every move counted—there were no useless flourishes.

"Come," panted the man in the doorway.

Doctor Snell did not ask whether it was to man or horse. It made little difference to him. He paid small attention to medicine anyway. Hot water, bandages, massages, proper food, and rest, he believed, would cure almost anything.

Up to the time of Doctor Snell's visit to the ranch fifteen miles distant from Marble City, David Manning was a pampered, only child, who had managed to live through seven years in spite of candy, cake, hot bread, and indulgences of all kinds granted by an over-anxious father and a doting mother, to say nothing of various aunts, uncles, and cousins who did their share to spoil him.

That was how David Manning began life. It was Doctor Snell who made the family see their folly, and who set the child on the road to health and strength. And David outdid everyone's expectations. He was truly a wonder child, for he developed into a strong athletic youth, equaled by no one for miles around in skill and strength. At the country school he attended he was leader in his classes. There was danger of his becoming an idol, but somehow he survived having his head turned.

After David learned as much as the teacher who taught in the little frame schoolhouse could impart, he decided to travel and make his own way. So for over ten years he trapped, prospected, mined a little, and roved through nearly every state in the Union, going as far east as Massachusetts.

It was while he was in the East that Manning, barely past twenty, discovered that he had just fifteen cents to live on and no job in sight. To him, this was more terrifying than any saloon brawl he had ever witnessed, or being lost in the woods which was filled with wild animals; more awful than staggering across deserts in the scorching sun searching for water.

Wondering how to get out of his plight, he noticed that a large building he was approaching was a newspaper office. Boldly the lad walked in, and found that a copy boy was needed immediately. What more could he ask? He jumped at the opportunity and applied for the job. The pay was small, but his enthusiasm made up for this deficiency. It was not long before his integrity and aptness won him the job of reporter. From this position he went steadily forward. Occasionally the call of the rangeland gripped him and it was all he could do to stick to his post. Then one day it did get him, and back to the West he made his way.

Manning's next job was on a western newspaper. One of the columnists failed to put in an appearance one morning, and Manning was given a try-out. It was a column about western and desert life, which he knew thoroughly, and this knowledge, coupled with a growing ability to write, made the job a permanent one.

One day, after Manning had been running the newspaper column for a year and a half, he was seized with the old wanderlust. It was dry and hot, and everyone sweltered in the city heat, listlessly watching the thermometer rise and scanning a sky that promised no rain. The city editor was unusually cross; everyone's nerves seemed to be on edge. Manning's western and desert column had always gone through without comment. This day it had been sent back to him by the editor, who had scrawled across it, "Not enough western atmosphere." He had chosen the wrong moment to object. Manning smiled and wrote something beneath the editorial criticism. With a yawn, he stretched himself to the length of five foot three and slowly rose to his feet. When the copy boy read what Manning had written under the boss's signature, he dropped the paper on the editor's desk and beat a hasty retreat. It was well he did so. Manning had already strolled out of the office when the editor read the following words: "Going out to get some western atmosphere. Won't be back."

In the country he loved, Manning sat down before the secondhand typewriter he had purchased on the way. There he began to write stories. They were not accepted immediately, but publishers and magazine editors showed interest in his work. Then he began to sell regularly. The West doesn't "get" him any more, for he lives right in it, breathing the air and spirit of the country, living and reliving the romantic splendor of it all.

HEINIE

Carl Brandt

Carl Brandt of Brandt and Brandt literary agency became Faust's agent in 1925.

He had a heart too large for his body, even if he was bigger than average. It worked so hard and put in so much overtime for other people, it kept him from being able to do the things he most wished to do.

Heinie loved horses—and he was not allowed to ride. He wanted to take part in games which were hard physical contests, and it was his part either to sit and watch or pat balls softly over the net. He desired desperately to live gustily, with color in every action and background. But his unsafe heart condemned him to inaction, except the vicarious living he got from the tales he wrote. He broke out at times. There was too full a head of steam always up in his boilers to make him a good patient, but he paid for these lapses a dozen times over.

In the twenty odd years that I have known him, there has never been a time when he was not supporting at least one lame duck.

"Carl," he'd say to me, "you've got to send $67.50 every two weeks to Johnny Doe. God, man, there is someone who *really* can write. If I had what he's got, I'd not be the pulp paper hack I am. He'll reach the stars."

I'd sigh and reflect that it was his money, not mine. Then I'd wheedle Heinie into showing me some of this new protégé's work. Frequently, it would be hopeless, and backed by other opinions I would eventually separate the *soi-disant* artist from the payroll. But Heinie never lost heart and soon he would find another budding genius. Other charities I could not, and would not disturb. People who had been kind to Heinie in his early days always could dash in when the need came. Several thousand dollars of Heinie's money went to an associate editor who had been kind to Heinie when the pulp man became an invalid. It only ended with this man's death.

Heinie was a classicist and a romantic. A few years ago, the only things published under his own name were some poems in heroic pentameter, peopled with obscure heroes of mythology, and his version in verse of the Paolo and Francesca legend. He had a beautiful speaking voice and read poetry musically with passion and conviction. I would sit and listen to him read his own lines. Drugged by the spell of his voice, at three in the morning, I'd be convinced that the verse was great. But in the next day's cold white light, reading made it clear how personal a thing his poetry was and little of it was publishable.

All the years I worked with him, and for several before that, Heinie would write between 1,750,000 and 2,000,000 words a year—and 99% of it was published. He appeared in every sort and class of magazine, from the pulps to *Harper's* was his range, with *The Saturday Evening Post, Collier's, Ladies' Home Journal, The American Magazine,* and *Cosmopolitan* as way stations. No matter how simple a concept might be—and it had to be that to be a successful pulp yarn—there would be a passage of such beauty that it would make your senses tingle. His rate of payment from the pulps was the biggest anyone received. Some years as many as ten new books by him would appear under perhaps six pseudonyms. Max Brand was, possibly, his best-known pen name and it was chiefly identified with Western stories. George Owen Baxter, George Challis, Evan Evans, W. C. Butler were others. But I can settle the John Schoolcraft controversy, for I met and talked with him. He was *not* another Faust pen name.

His yarns were, and are, translated into all the languages of the world. No other client of mine has ever had such a far-flung world market. Yet Heinie was indifferent to it all. He insisted that I must sign all the contracts as his attorney, and he never wanted to see copies of the printed books that resulted from these contracts. Also, he refused to have small payments sent to him. So a precedent grew into a fixed habit. I'd gather together a lot of old receipts in a special account that I, with a feeble attempt at whimsy, called the Squirrel Fund. When there was a sizable sum collected, I would tell him the Squirrel Fund could let him have $1,000 or $3,000 or $5,000 or whatever. Over the years I think he made himself believe that this was not his own money; that the squirrels, i.e., our office, who had harvested the acorns, really owned it. When he wanted to do something very much which did not come under his ordinary financing, he'd wire almost apologetically and ask if the Squirrel Fund could afford to send him $750 or $1,000. Rarely would he ask for more. His hospitality stemmed directly from the examples of the Golden Age of Italy. He was as munificent as Lorenzo di Medici. Anyone who tried to pay for anything when Heinie was in the party had a fight on his hands. He loved salads and fine wine and cheese with ripe pears. He knew food—from Voisin's best to the simplest Italian peasant dish—and he made you know it too when you were with him. For many years he had a villa in Florence. It was probably the only house he ever lived in that he loved completely. It is my ill fortune that I never saw it or this modern Lorenzo in what was to him his most nearly perfect background. Even so, from what he told me of it, it made clear to me his love of Italy—the Italy of the Renaissance—so that I could understand his passionate determination to go overseas. It is indicative that he had no desire to go to any war theatre except Italy. He felt that in some way, and somehow once he was there, it would be revealed to him how his contribution could be made.

He loved Italy, but he was passionate about America. His overloaded heart had taken on as extra baggage all the boys of this country who were giving their lives so that a decent world should continue. He felt, rather than knew, that there was a job for him to do with them.

I believe, the night of the day when I learned he had fallen at the side of our attacking troops, that the revelation had come to him; that, in his eyes, his mission was clearly defined, and that he went forward, happy and confident, to its successful completion. And it is indication of the great heart of the man we loved that since his death no one, ever to my knowledge, has ever said, "Poor Heinie." It always has been "Poor us." Ours is the grievous loss. Heinie went as he uniquely would have written it: it was the only fitting climax to the romance that was his life.

FREDERICK FAUST: AN APPRECIATION

Walter Morris Hart

Walter Morris Hart, a professor in the English Department at the University of California at Berkeley, was a former teacher of Faust's, a longtime friend, and a correspondent. This memoir was to be included in John L. Schoolcraft's biography but has not otherwise been published.

On that night of May eleventh, "it was quiet and peaceful . . . the stars were out. . . . It was warm and clear . . . the jasmine hung heavy in the air." Surely, for him, the scent of jasmine called up a picture of the villa in the hills up toward Fiesole, approached through a mass of winding lanes with high walls on either side, its front all covered with that vine; before it, the terrace with its carved stone table and balustrade, where one looked down through the cypress-guarded paths, across the little valley, and up to the hills beyond; long rows of olives with grape vines festooned from gray tree to tree, the yellow wheat between. To the southward, down the valley, a glimpse of the perfect lines of Brunelleschi's dull red dome and the bell tower Giotto raised, hinted of the charm and magic of Florence.

For ten years that was Heinie's home. There, I believe, he was happiest; and there he was most himself. Primarily, it was a place of escape, a place for long hours of writing; but friends who had the privilege of seeing him there will remember it always as a place where a perfect partnership created a boundless hospitality, an atmosphere of austere devotion to work, and opportunity and occasion for delightful talk. For, next to work, Heinie believed that talk was the best thing in the world. Many an evening, in his library or out on the terrace under the stars, he and his friends outwatched the Bear and could not believe the absurd tale told by the clock when at last they heard its insistent note. He liked to look back upon such an evening: "Such happiness does not come into a life very often, for there was a fine exchange among all of us, all brains were working, everyone was making a profit. It was possible to leave the door open when one walked out with an idea. There was no cheap arguing to make points, but so much good honest discussion which is the breath of life.''

"All brains were working"—Heinie stimulated the talk, never sought to dominate it. In those last days at Santa Maria Infante the young soldiers noticed that "he didn't talk much, but he listened a lot." At the villa he "kept the door open." And so it was that the talk for all who engaged in it was, in that setting, singularly free, spontaneous, unconsidered and uncalculated; ideas expressed as they came into the mind, not as reasoned opinions to be maintained, rejected, or accepted. He himself professed to delight "perhaps most of all in being checked at so many places, so that my neck is broken only a few times during an evening."

He begot that same attitude in others. He never tried to smash the ball and win the point. He made a swift return, which was not necessarily out of one's reach. He delighted in a good stroke, his own or another's, yet not in the stroke merely for himself but rather as it contributed to the game. And he played the game in the amateur spirit, not to win but for its own sake. However, the word *game* is misleading; his interest was always intensely serious. "Being scribblers," he wrote to Professor [Leon] Richardson, "to talk of the mere mechanics of scribbling will set our brains on fire, and burning brains are the only ones that are worth a damn, even if they give off more smoke than heat."

What he liked was "to sit down in conference in which one could handle real metal and hammer it into real forms—or real question marks at least." And indeed it was likely to end, for the moment, in question marks rather than in final shapes; often he was "in part remembering what he once thought and in part trying to strike forward into something new." Doubtless he agreed with Lessing in preferring "the ever-restless search after truth" to the possession of all truth itself.

Unfortunately, I kept no record of that handling of real metal, but letters that followed or preceded it dealt with the same material and in much the same fashion. For in them he wrote as he talked, freely and spontaneously; as I re-read them now I hear his voice, see his attitude and gestures. Like his talk, they do not set forth reasoned conclusions; they were written, sometimes, when everything was "cloudy and unreal"; they attempt rather "to strike forward into something new." They let one know what he was thinking about and thus help one to know the kind of man he was. They help; those that he wrote to me give a glimpse naturally not of the whole man but only of a part. We have it on excellent authority that the meanest of God's creatures has two soul-sides. Heinie had many. He was built on the grand scale. Those soldiers of the second platoon at Santa Maria Infante thought that he was the biggest man they had ever known. They liked him, as all who knew him liked him. He was a man of many friends; these friends were men of all sorts and conditions; and to them all he could speak with ease and opportunity. To them he gave generously out of the abundance of his own personality—sympathy, counsel, and, at need, material aid.

And yet for his life's sake, he found a "certain grimness" to be "not really selfish but absolutely necessary. I begin to feel that except for a half-a-dozen persons I should like to keep the world at a great distance, and see my other friends once a year, then with great cordiality and a hungry need of seeing them which would make the entire relation real."

"In our country," he wrote in 1936, "the days are short because we begin with certain social obligations instead of with certain obligations to work. I know, now, that every man needs a considerable percentage of time spent in absolute solitude. By solitude, I don't mean the chance to read the words of somebody else, but an interval during which there is nothing but one's own thought to contemplate. Narrative ideas come out of conversation (or out of legend), but the emotion and the inward seeing, which are the breath, flesh, and bone of art, are born out of silence. I feel certain about it, and I feel certain that it is impossible for a man to be sufficiently alone in America unless he turns himself into a freak and lives on top of a hill surrounded by barbed-wire fences." Even in Florence, however, visitors came his way, and occasionally "those damnable depth-bombs, letters of introduction."

Later he came to feel the need of solitude, of loneliness, for reasons more intimate and more profound. In 1941 he wrote, as part of a poem on which he was then at work:

> Yet as the stars that seem to cloud the night
> Are recluse in the void, their companies
> Afar dispersed in never-ending flight,
> So the cold spirit to the silences
> Retires apart, received by destiny
> And bound unto the unalterable course.

"All of this on the way to a sort of theorem which more and more haunts me, that out of our essential loneliness springs love, which is in effect a knowledge of the distance that separates us from one another, and the need being so great produces that higher self, conscience, God, or companion, which never speaks to us except of the high beauty and the pure truth. So that the strong man must search out loneliness, live with it and love it, and out of that contemplation there comes a re-seeing of life and an easier ascent, or habit of ascent. . . . In the final conception there is something that for me has been a great healer of pain. I don't pretend that it is new. I hope it is *not* true. The comfort would seem more real if it were old."

He felt excited by a phrase of Santayana's concerning Dante's Paolo and Francesca: "Love itself dreams of something more than mere possession." "I would enlarge, or rather vary, the expression. 'Life to be shared in a varied world' may not be the full statement. Is it not rather that love is the mutual contemplation of a third object, which becomes real as its beauty, strength, etc., is revealed to the lovers? But far above love is there not the divine conversation that exists, at times, in the mind of the individual when he is totally alone, totally at rest, except that the mind and spirit are on wings together?''

''Divine conversation,'' one imagines, was continual with Heinie, alone or in the company of others. Often, we may be sure, not infrequent for all his reluctance to read the words of others, it was concerned with a matter of perennial interest to him—the appreciation of brief passages of great poetry. ''Every phrase,'' he maintained, ''even every word of real poetry can be known by its authentic wings, or by its alcoholic taste, if that makes better sense.'' He admitted that he might be wrong, but he said, characteristically, ''I feel very strongly about it.'' ''It doesn't require a special talent to find [the great lines] any more than it requires sharp eyes to see lighthouses unless a fog of modern prejudices lies around the reader. I don't find in myself any special blessing whatever except that my interest never has been in modern writers of verse and therefore their fashions of thought and emotion (because, of course, there are fashions of emotion) have not blinded me. Given a century or two of elbow room, I feel that any reader of the poetry of the past can find the beautiful moments because, once more, they shine by their own power, they are dynamos which never stop running, the only instances of perpetual motion. . . . Great lines hit me in the brain and the heart at the same time and give me a special happiness and that feeling of ascent about which we have spoken.'' Again, ''God knows I am not scholar enough to speak easily of the Greek. But after five years of interrupted study, when Homer still cost me an hour for every twenty lines, it seemed to me that the great lines always came off the page for me. And in a sense is it not true that great lines must be universals, otherwise they are not truly great?''

Tenable or not, this position has immense value for the man who holds it, particularly if, with regard to details, he holds it with a tenacity and vehemence like Heinie's. And certainly it makes for the most lively, profitable, and stimulating discussion. None who takes part in it is likely to be convinced that what he admires is not worthy of admiration. Each in attempting to prove his case will find new evidence to support it and so find an increased delight in the lines in question. And each will be happy to adopt as his own some of the other's favorites. One who talked with Heinie was likely to be the chief gleaner in this way.

He thought it ''not foolish to write down what we have found that is beautiful and attempt to collate it in some way that will show kinships here and there.'' So far he was willing to go; but he thought it ''as foolish to try to define poetry as it is to try to define the taste of a wine.'' However, he could not agree with Housman when he said: ''Poetry is not the thing said but the way of saying it.'' For Heinie, poetry was ''the mystical blending of sense and rhythm. . . . Rhyme, metre, even measure can be taken from the lines and still there remains an effect of poetry, if in the first place we give it the full attention and ardor and reverence of a collected mind and spirit." "Emotion and the inward seeing . . . are the breath, flesh, and bone of art." He found "an element of truth" in Leonard Bacon's view that poetry is "utterance delivered under special tension"—Wordsworthian "recollection in tranquillity" was not his way, which was rather the "spontaneous overflow of powerful feelings."

Poetry, in his view, should be simple, should be intelligible. Commenting on his own "Dionysus," he says that "a poem that has to be explained is not a good poem." Since poetry "deals so much with pictures it stands rather to reason that we want the pictures as clear as possible, and I contend that the highest masters are extremely clear in their imagery: witness Homer, Dante, and Shakespeare, where the keys of the pictures are sometimes obscure but, once mastered, nearly all of it pours straight into the realm of reason and good sense."

Homer, Dante, Shakespeare—these were for him the highest masters; to these we should add Milton, whom he chose to follow as his master in the writing of "Dionysus," Chaucer, in whom he took a special delight, and the popular ballads: "There are the ballads for one thing; and for another thing there are more ballads, and still more ballads. The fake eeriness of Blake, or his honest spirit if it *is* honest, are stuff and tripe to me compared with some of the ghostly effects of the ballads." As to the Romantic poets, "their taste is, after all, delicate rather than strong, and diluted wine if it be wine at all." The modern writers of verse did not interest him.

The Greek poets, though read largely in translation, meant most to him. And for his own verse Greek myths provided subject matter that seemed "so much more vital and *modern* than anything else I can think of." He wished that he could find a reasoned and logical defense of such themes; "it isn't really a preference for them, but a lack of all others." He had a keen sense of "the perfect Greek beauty"; the "savage directness and force of the early dynastic art" of Egypt was important for him, but "desert and river can't offer the background of Greek mountains and the Greek sea."

Manifestly, he had come to feel the ancient Greeks as his contemporaries. The reception accorded his "Dionysus" was inevitable: "Among people I know, very few men or women of my own age or younger have had much to say about it, but older readers have liked it, so far as I know, without exception, and some of them so extravagantly, that they have made me feel out of breath."

For the "Dionysus" he had taken Milton as his master. He delighted in the "delirious long cadences . . . of 'Lycidas,' or the opening of the third book, which seems to me so majestic and so ethereal that God is almost visible through his works." In the use of rhyme his model was the sonnet to Lady Margaret Ley. "I am never tired," he wrote to Professor Richardson, "of running the first lines of that sonnet ['which is a glorious thing'] through my mind. So I thought that I would take [Milton] as my master and try to follow him, no matter at how great a distance, burying rhyme most of the time so that the eye would find it more often than the ear, but yet keeping it present all the while so that I could sometimes bring it to the surface in complete, even and end-

stopt couplets at that.'' Absence of rhyme, in the ''Dionysus,'' was not inten-
tional, but the result only of failure to find the rhyming word. ''Blank verse,
for narrative purposes . . . is too unornamented.'' Only Milton succeeds.

Commenting on Housman's praise of

> Though love repine and reason chafe,
> There came a voice without reply,
> 'Tis man's perdition to be safe
> When for the truth he ought to die.

he says: ''I think [this stanza] is a good reason for poets in English to avoid
the four-foot line, particularly in this form where one feels the rapid hammers
beating out the rhymes, ding-dong, ding-dong.'' In contrast, there is his characteristic praise of ''Hark! Hark! The lark,'' which no man alive can read ''without having his heart leap like the bird in the song, just as no man can read the
last word of that line without prolonging it like the bird singing in the air,
because already we're up there in the region of the rising sun, until we return
for an instant to the winking Mary-buds and then to his lady sweet who will
herself arise, arise, arise.''

It is evident that Heinie's interest was consistently in short poems or in brief
passages in longer ones. I do not remember that he ever spoke with enthusiasm—or indeed spoke at all—of the architecture, of the plan of the whole of
''Paradise Lost'' or the ''Odyssey'' or the ''Divine Comedy.'' Of the ''Dionysus'' he writes (I quote once more from the letter to Professor Richardson):
''I am ashamed to say that I didn't know exactly where I was going, except
that I wanted to get Dionysus into Hades. . . . Dionysus was outside of Dis before I thought of ringing in Prometheus.'' And of a long poem on which he was
at work in recent years: ''Even the narrative doesn't interest me so much as the
mere excuse to write verse and have some sort of nail to hang it on.''

The ''narrative point'' of the ''Dionysus''—the underlying if not the unifying
idea—is ''the deification of our life as men and on earth; . . . the only punish-
ment that the condemned souls in Hades feel is their loss of the earth, not of
any heaven, and beside that sense of loss all their tortures are not worth mentioning.'' ''That is to say, our goal ought to be our own mortality, and not a
turning of our backs upon it.'' Hence the significance of the story of Prometheus,
profound, beautiful, dramatic, in that he ''was sure of nothing but the pain that
would collect.'' And even ''more people'' are worth considering when ''one
adopts the attitude that all experience is worthwhile.''

Mortal pleasure and pain! Heinie knew both and was intensely sensitive to
both, in his own experience and in a lively sympathy with the experience of
other persons, real or imagined. Pleasure he found chiefly, I believe, in family
life, though of that, naturally, he said little; after that, mainly in work—that is,
in the writing of verse, but also occasionally in his more ambitious fiction,
stories that he published under his own name, and sometimes in passages in the

Westerns; then perhaps in talk, yet also in "the divine conversation that exists, at times, in the mind of the individual when he is totally alone," "the emotion and the inward seeing which are the breath, flesh, and bone of art"; then, in reading the poetry he loved, and indeed in art in all its forms, whether "fine or applied." I have not known a better man with whom to view his own or another's garden, or to listen to a Bach record, or to see old pictures in Florence, or the Parthenon in the moon's eclipse; or with whom to dine—he was learned in exotic cookery, and I have heard him, informed not by his eye but by his palate alone, say to a *sommelier:* "I ordered the 1928; this is the '29"; and, "Now you have opened the second bottle." In a word, Heinie had a rare zest for life.

Yet no one who knew him would describe his life as a life of pleasure, or think of him as a popular writer enjoying the fruits of his vast success. There was pain in plenty as well as pleasure, the common human lot. He thought of a friend as suffering more than the normal share "of this pain that we all must feed on." The intensity of sympathy, in this instance, was characteristic; keen sense of the sufferings of others was always a source of pain for him. But chiefly, I believe, it came from his own conflicts, conflicts of interests and activities, conflicts within himself, as of the yearning for solitude with the yearning for talk with friends. Most trying must have been the conflict of Frederick Faust with Max Brand.

A man of letters, unless he inherits a fortune, has to earn his living: he may be soldier, ambassador, controller of customs, clerk of the King's works, like Chaucer; theatre employee and actor, like Shakespeare; clerk in the East India House, like Lamb; apothecary's apprentice, like Keats; clerk of the Board of Trade, like Austin Dobson; stockbroker, like Edmund Clarence Stedman; professor of English Literature, like Quiller-Couch, Longfellow, William Vaughan Moody, and the American Robert Herrick. Where the gainful occupation requires much time and energy and comes closest to his vocation—to the way of life to which he is divinely called and for which he feels a special fitness—then the conflict is most bitter, an internecine strife more keenly felt than war with an alien enemy. With Heinie, both interests called for creative writing, narrative—the good, gripping tale for its own sake in the one case, merely a nail to hang verse on in the other. Frederick Faust yearned with all the intensity of his intense nature to give himself to the writing of verse. When he could not do so, he felt that he was being starved for the lack of it.

He was, he once said, half Irish; and indeed much in Matthew Arnold's characterization of the Celt suggests Heinie: "An organization quick to feel impressions, and feeling them very strongly; a lively personality therefore, keenly sensitive to joy and sorrow." He was half Irish, yet he had to exercise, through the years, as Max Brand, all the drive and resolution and all the steadiness and patience of the "creeping Saxon." The amount of his production alone is evidence that he did so. Wherever he was, he maintained his program of so many hours a day at the typewriter. Up at the villa, or in much solitude as he contrived in New Canaan, was best for that. But any place had to be made to serve. Crossing the Atlantic, a Western begun in New York harbor was sent back from Gibraltar to the publishers; and, in Greece, each day of long driving and intense sight-seeing was followed by a day's labor at the typewriter.

About 1932 it appeared that the Depression had stimulated the brain of the pulp-reader; it became necessary to turn out words that had a meaning and weight of their own, words that went somewhere. He had now and again to spend bitter months in New York, "because the writing of fiction is very largely a shrewd game of business rather than the practice of an art. Each magazine has its own peculiar editorial policy, and, if one fails to hit that bull's-eye, one may miss every other target. One does not sit down simply to write a good gripping yarn but to write a yarn for one peculiar group of editors. . . . I have revised a single story as much as five times; and I have revised a serial three times throughout, and still remain uncertain about the sale. It is a keen, quick, rather bitter struggle. I have to be quick on my feet and hit hard with both hands, or I'll lose the decision." "My God, why should finances be such a pain, such a knife twisting around in the insides of us? However, if I can make a go of the slick paper markets—and not make a god of it—we may find health, wealth, and happiness all at a stroke."

He regarded his Westerns with scorn or indifference. He quite literally never read them. His wife corrected errors in the typing, then sent them off to the publishers, who were responsible for all proof-reading. Yet, for all his desire to put them out of his mind, there are passages in them that might well have given him pleasure—admirably written descriptions, witty dialogue in the racy vernacular of a perfectly plausible West, passages of psychological insight, and shrewd comments on life based manifestly on his own experience and expressing his own views in "words that meant something."

"He told us," writes Sergeant Jack Delaney, his "name was Frederick Faust. It didn't mean much to us. He told us also that he wrote under the name of Max Brand and, when we heard that name, we felt as though we'd known him a long time for there wasn't a man of us who hadn't read his stuff when we were younger." (They may well recur to his stuff when they are older. The one room in General Eisenhower's "circus wagon was littered with an odd assortment of Wild West yarns and psychological novels," and he was found, early on the morning of D-Day, awaiting the first word of the invasion, "in bed propped up behind a Wild West novel." On one of our battle ships the radioman, who was that morning monitoring German military stations, was "reading a Western thriller as he twiddled his dials.")

It is fair to assume that most of the men of our Armed Forces had read Max Brand. Fortunate were those who had done so in the impressionable period of youth. It may seem a far cry from Max Brand to Trollope—who, however, is said to be the favorite author of General Montgomery—but it was Trollope who reminded his readers that "a vast proportion of the teaching of the day—comes from novels which are in the hands of all readers''; and it is the business of the novelist to ''make virtue alluring and vice ugly.'' Vice certainly is ugly in the villains of Max Brand's Westerns; their blackness is lamentably complete. But certainly the heroes are by no means virtue personified; they have conspicuous imperfections; but they are sound at heart, and they charm by their courage, their audacity, their coolness, their habit of looking before they leap, their impossible but not improbable gun play, their hard riding. Who shall say to what extent our soldiers owe these qualities to the Max Brand whom they had all read when they were younger? Only the Brand heroes' love of fair play—''Fill your hand,'' says the hero to the villain whom he will not shoot down unarmed—only this trait would place a man at a disadvantage before unscrupulous foes. And something is to be said for the sharp distinction, now in disfavor, between white and black. There is so much good in the worst of us and so much bad in the best of us—no doubt—but still there is a worst and there is a best.

Even in the Westerns, then, there is something of that ''essential humanity,'' which came to seem to Heinie ''the most beautiful of all conceptions, entailing an acceptance of our mortality and not a revolt against it, so that the brevity of our lives is not something to fill us with ache and horror. . . . This is the secret, I once thought, that Prometheus stole from heaven. He could return and tell humanity that of all things death is the most beautiful; but, if this were known, humanity would rush at once to extinguish itself, embracing its greatest gift.'' Later, he went on with this thought, though only, as he said, ''fumbling and in the dark'': ''My feeling (out of which a thought may come) is that there is no death; which in fact is an old thought of mine to the effect that at any given moment man is not apt to be expressly happy, but from the past the mind inherits, by force of nature, chiefly happy memories, and for the future there is hope; so that, even if our conception is without a God, it is impossible for one to *feel* the reality of death or the certainty of any period to existence, however easy it may be to rationalize on the subject.''

''Of all things death is the most beautiful.'' ''It is impossible for one to *feel* the reality of death.'' Something of all this was doubtless in his mind at Santa Maria Infante. He wanted to know how men ''felt when they were pinned down by mortar fire or machine guns—what they thought of, what their reactions were.'' By his own feelings he would know theirs. He insisted on going up with the advance scouts; he was well aware, he said, of the possibility that he might get killed out there. (Yet still, one imagines, it was impossible for him to *feel* the reality of death.)

''I'm twice a grandfather, and these men are just kids. They're not staying back. I guess if they can take it—I can. . . . ''I've lived a pretty full life and, if it's my time to go tonight, I'm ready to go.''

He was one of the first to be hit, a shell fragment in the chest. ''We went for him but he told us to take care of two boys near him. 'They're worse off than I am,' he said. 'I feel pretty good.' "

Sir Philip Sidney, we may be sure, was far from Heinie's thoughts. Yet his words are in that great tradition: "thy necessity is greater than mine." Inevitably, in a like situation, a similar spirit finds expression in similar words.

A FAREWELL TO MAX BRAND

Steve Fisher

When Faust came to work for Warner Bros. in the early 1940s, he met fellow studio writer Steve Fisher. As veterans from magazine writing now working in the film industry, they had much in common. Fisher would publish twenty novels, mostly crime fiction, including his best-known work, I WAKE UP SCREAMING (Dodd, Mead, 1941), as well as writing seventy-five screenplays and over two hundred television scripts. He was a highly emotional man with a deep capacity for friendship.

His real name was Frederick Faust. He wrote stories under it, too, some of his best stories, and his best were very great. He created Dr. Kildare, of magazine and movie fame; he wrote DESTRY RIDES AGAIN, and his last screenplay for the studio where I worked was the Errol Flynn film, UNCERTAIN GLORY (Warner, 1944). He lived in Italy for years, and loved Italy; he traveled the world, and in his obituary the papers said: "He was one of the last true soldiers-of-fortune—a globe-trotting writer with worlds of information at his fingertips." They said, too, that he was "a man of mystery," and, reflecting back, I guess he was. Millions of readers loved him, and he was one of the anointed—a "writer's writer" as well. But only a few knew him intimately, and you never heard anything about what he was like in person, or how he lived—except for an anecdote once in a while from Jack Byrne at the time when he was editing *Argosy.* Byrne would refer to him by his nickname, "Heinie," but his voice was one of admiration, and I think awe. Yet the actual, living Max Brand you never really saw. He was legend.

I remember that now, very well: those years in New York, when I idolized his work. One of his *Saturday Evening Post* stories, "Johnny Come Lately," I read so many times I almost knew it by heart. No one knew anything about the author. So I consider it a privilege that I learned to know him so well in Hollywood. He was a very dear friend—an immense man, with an immense capacity for work, and an immense heart and soul, and the most extravagantly generous person I have ever known.

It was in my office at Warner Bros. that his mission to Italy started. I was working on an Army picture and a Colonel Nee, from Washington, was a sort of technical advisor to me for a few days. Heinie met him in my office. Then one afternoon . . . remember, old boy, remember Heinie? . . . how you sat there, your long legs crossed, leaning back on the red divan, one eye squinting, looking thoughtfully at Colonel Nee, and then saying, finally: "You know what I'd like to do, Colonel? I'd like to go to the Front. I'd like to travel with a company of doughboys. I'd like to eat with them, sleep beside them, sit down nights and talk to them. I'd like to fight with them, go with them into action . . . and then write a book which would be the story of that one company."

That was your idea, Heinie, your mood of the moment, as you sat there, your hair tousled, your suit looking like you'd slept in it. You had, I think; you'd just taken a nap. You were almost fifty-two, and it was a reckless thought, more of a dream than an idea, really. But you lived on dreams and by them. You walked the stars as no other man I have ever known. Warner was paying you $3,000 a week to go to the Front? I'm afraid I smiled to myself. I never thought you'd actually do it, you fabulous so-and-so! The magic you had, though! You even talked like a poem. You were a good man. A decent man. None of your characters was ever any different, either! They were all as fabulous and as magic and as eloquent as you. Adventure and heart and music. That's the way your prose read. It is difficult to imagine anyone in actual life who is like that. But you were.

Heinie told me a great deal about himself. But only when I asked. First let me stop for this—the picture of him doing it is so clear—he used to write at the studio, sitting in his shirt sleeves, his immense legs straddling a small coffee table, pounding on a portable typewriter. His office was a mess—there'd be paper all over everywhere. But no matter how absorbed he was in what he was writing, when you opened the door to peek in, he'd immediately stop, push back the coffee table, look up smiling and say: "How's it go, Steve? Here, boy, sit down and tell me about it." And if you tried to back out, saying you'd catch him when he wasn't busy, he'd refuse to hear it. He'd insist that you stay and discuss with him whatever it was you wanted to discuss—and it was always something you wanted, *your* problem—nothing that could benefit him in the least. He is the only writer I have ever known who would drop everything—deliberately and unselfishly interrupt his own train of thought for a friend.

I am sure that, if it were not for him, I'd never have written my last novel. I was doing the story as a picture and had only "talked" of developing it as a book, too, the way writers talk sometimes, needling themselves. But Heinie pounced on the idea. He saw in it powerful things that had never remotely occurred to me. He said it was an opportunity to write with my guts, the way

I should. He hounded and tormented me to start the book, then came in every day to see how many pages I'd done. It was published, and I sold it in addition as a serial, but I don't think Heinie liked it. I could never have come up to the expectations he had for me.

He did almost the same thing for Frank Gruber. Frank had a detective character named Johnny Fletcher, and one Saturday afternoon Heinie plotted out an entire Johnny Fletcher novel for him. It was always you Heinie talked about. It was always you who was being helped. It was one-sided, lopsided, whole-hearted generosity. He would accept no help on his own work. The most he ever said about his stories was once, about one thing: "Junk. Sheer junk. Gibberish." Yet when he talked stories (and when he wrote them, too, never fear) he was a wild man, tender and passionate and fierce, and his ideas soared!

He told us once that he wrote fourteen pages every day of his life. Sometimes he wrote much more (one day at the studio he wrote fifty pages before lunch), but never less than fourteen pages. One afternoon he scribbled off a little scrap of a sonnet, which he had composed just that minute. It was beautiful. I carried it for months in my wallet—the corner off the back of a menu—and I would like to include it here. But now, now that he is dead, I can't find it.

Heinie was a highly literate man. In a class with Aldous Huxley. He could talk intelligently on any subject—history, religion, war, life, death, and love. I don't think he knew what hatred was. I am not saying this to eulogize. I swear that it's true. He loved, did Heinie.

He had a peculiar habit, though. I've heard that professors sometimes do it. His power of concentration was intense—especially when he was walking. Often, his mind miles away, he would walk past you on the sidewalk looking stonily ahead, so absorbed that, if you said hello, he didn't hear you. You'd have to call his name. But one writer, upon bidding Heinie "Good morning" and getting no response, felt it was a personal slight. He was an extremely sensitive guy and began to form a hatred for him. He told people that Faust was a "snob." Heinie heard about it and one day walked into the writer's office.

The writer was bent over his desk, working, and, when he didn't look up, that was the well-known signal we have that means: "Lay off, I'm hot on something . . . don't want to lose the thought. Come back later." The whole thing unspoken. Heinie never practiced it himself, though he knew very well what it meant. But now he paid no attention. He leaned over the desk, affectionately put his two big hands on either side of the writer's face, and lifted up his head. He said: "Listen, you son of a bitch, I hear you hate me." Under the writer's protestations he hauled him out of there, off the lot, and across the street to a bar where he stood him two quick drinks. I saw them when they returned. They were arm in arm—pals. That's Heinie. It's him a thousand times.

In the earlier days he wrote for the pulps at five cents a word. (The rest of us were averaging a cent and a half a word top rates.) He was king of the pulps, the biggest and best and most famous writer of all. But he never talked of any of his work and didn't even vaguely remember "Johnny Come Lately," the story I'd thought was so wonderful. Once he entered my office as I was telling a group about one of his serials, "Six Golden Angels," and, when he heard what the conversation was, he turned and walked out, and refused to come back.

It was in 1938 he came to Hollywood. Of this town he is said to have told Carl Brandt: "I like it because I can get all of my work done in the morning and have the entire afternoon to write poetry."

If Heinie were here right now, he'd be making wry faces at me for trying to write this. "You've got a nerve," he'd say affectionately. "What the hell do you know about me?" And it's true. I don't really know anything about him. He was a man of mystery. Moral, idealistic, a poet and a dreamer. Of tremendous energy, and tremendous emotion. When he spoke of his love for Dorothy, his wife, and this was frequently, he'd make tears come to your eyes. "I'm the meanest guy in the world . . . and she's put up with me all these years." His love for his children was great, too: Judy Faust, in boarding school, a big girl, like her father, and very pretty—I saw her once or twice when she picked him up after work—his son, John, in the Army, and Jane, a married daughter in Santa Barbara.

I have used the word *affectionate* twice, and this makes the third time. Heinie *was* affectionate. He had a great love and a great spirit and a great, beautiful talent. It is trite to say but true, that he made millions of people laugh and millions cry, and all of them loved him. He was truly a great man. The literary critics may never know how great—that book of Italy and the front lines—he had in him power and depth and beauty he'd never even tapped. And now he's been killed in action. Frederick Faust and Max Brand are dead.

So say good bye, say good bye to the most gallant, poetic, romantic characters that ever walked across the pages of fiction. Say good bye to all the singing prose, and all of the hours he gave you, and all the pleasure, for the song is done now, and the music has stopped.

Heinie gave you his heart, and it was a very good and bold and generous heart. No man, I am sure, has ever given more.

MY FATHER

Jane Faust Easton

Jane Faust Easton is the eldest daughter of Frederick and Dorothy Faust. Much about her life growing up can be found in her book, MEMORIES OF THE '20S AND '30S: GROWING UP IN FLORENCE, NEW YORK, AND LOS ANGELES, first privately published and now being expanded for trade publication. What follows was written especially for this collection.

He seldom mentioned his Irish-German ancestry and then only in the most casual way. "My ancestors liked schnapps and came over on the *Berengaria*." In truth, his father had fought in the Civil War on the Northern side a good many years before the *Berengaria* put to sea. His father and mother were from the Iowa-Illinois region. It was her first marriage, his third. Pop had a full brother and sister in California who died before we were grown.

Mum's genealogy was better defined, at least on her mother's side. They were Greeleys from Maine, related to Horace Greeley, and owned a farm in the Sacramento Valley near Yuba City. Mum recalled happy days on the farm with her grandparents. She had always been lovely to look at and in college was considered the belle of the campus with her high color and long blonde hair. Daddy was very proud of her looks and insisted on spending a great deal of money on her clothes.

In 1922, when I was four, we lived in a long, narrow apartment in New York City. Daddy had an office in the Woolworth Building where, he told us solemnly, he "made shoes." I had no idea until years later that he was a writer.

I was a little afraid of him. He was so powerful, so intense.

Bob Davis, Daddy's editor at the Munsey Company, sometimes stopped at our apartment on his way home. Coming in, he brought the excitement of the street and of the great buildings I knew existed out there and the great things that were being done in the grown-up world. Bob was a big jovial man, very fond of Mother and Daddy. He smoked strong cigars and reeked of them—and made a great fuss over me and kept hard candy for me in one pocket of his tweed coat.

In 1925 we went to England so that Daddy could be treated for his heart trouble by an eminent cardiologist, and then to the south of France so that he might find peace and quiet in which to write and regain his health. Nearby at Antibes were the Gerald Murphys whom we would know later, but we led no social life nor did Daddy involve himself with the new ideas in painting and music or writing that were being expressed in Paris by Picasso, Stravinsky, Gertrude Stein, and others. He wrote his popular stories "to make shoes" and devoted his serious effort to his rhymed, or blank verse, poetry on classical subjects. At Menton he began studying Greek so that he could read Homer in the original, Italian so that he could read Dante.

In 1927 we moved into the Villa negli Ulivi, 83 Via dei Bruni on the Fiesole, or north slope, of the Arno overlooking Florence. Daddy had rented the villa from Arthur Acton who lived across the narrow lane up the hill in his palatial Villa La Pietra. During the summer our new villa had been renovated at Pop's expense. A large living room was added and above it a master bedroom, dressing room, bath, and terrace—and above them a large study with fireplace. In all, it made a three-story addition. A winding outside staircase led to the roof, which we eventually used for a telescope and sun bathing. Daddy gave us regular astronomy lessons.

The villa was originally a fifteenth-century farm house and over the years had been gradually enlarged. It was simple, attractive, shaped like a rectangle. Inside it was spacious and pleasing. Its floors were of red tiles that were polished daily. In the living room Mum placed oriental rugs in front of the couches (brought from America with us, along with boxes of books and twenty-one steamer trunks of belongings), and there were attractive lamps and tables. Before reaching the living room, however, you entered a large welcoming hall with stairway winding up. The dining room, to the left, was a deconsecrated chapel. To the right was a small sitting room, known as the "cocktail room." Beyond was a large music room with an oak floor for dancing and, beyond that, the new L-shaped living room with large windows, French doors opening onto the garden and gravel drive, and built-in bookcases on all available wall space. A small courtyard at the far end of the entrance hall had a fountain. Vines kept it cool for lunch in summer.

On the left of the dining room was a large butler's pantry and the big kitchen where Ugo, our chef in his tall white hat, ordered the second cook about, then a large servants' dining hall and storage room. On the second floor were five bedrooms and baths and a cheerful sitting room, or *salottino*. On the third floor were servants' rooms and a huge general workroom where the ironing was done. John and I also had a playroom up there, where my dolls' house and his trains and many other toys were kept.

Giulia, and her husband, Elia, the head butler, were our chief retainers, and they ran the villa. Our garden was full of flowering plants as was the house: gardenias, azaleas, hydrangea. Climbing star-jasmine covered the front of it. On summer mornings, when Giulia came in at 7:30 to open my shutters, the fragrance of jasmine blew in. Even today the odor of jasmine reminds me of the villa and my young years.

Below the garden and the dwarf lemon trees in terra cotta pots was the *podere,* open fields worked by the peasants, or *contadini* as we called them. There were grape vines, olive trees, and crops such as wheat and barley. Also at the bottom of the garden were the swimming pool and tennis court, which Daddy had built. A lovely rose arbor along one side of the pool provided shade for stone benches. A load of sand was brought in by truck and spread out to make a ''beach'' for sunbathing. The cypress-bordered path down to the pool, its trees planted by Pop, became one of the most cherished features of our garden.

After candlelit dinners with Mum and Pop, we moved into the living room and read aloud a Shakespeare play—each taking a part. Pop insisted we read carefully and correctly, and there were tears and scenes when I made a mistake or read badly. John was always an excellent reader. Pop explained lines, shouted over the good ones, taught us the difference between the best and the poorest passages and in all ways formed our taste. He was very good with children in a rather autocratic way, but he never talked down to us and could tell wonderful stories. Whenever he talked, things came alive.

Daddy and I talked all one afternoon about Napoleon. He admired him greatly and knew his campaigns by heart, down to the position of every man and gun, it seemed. Above all, he admired Napoleon's power and brains and his sheer achievement. Grand achievements always fascinated Daddy, but I had no idea he was achieving anything grand himself. He never read to us or allowed us to read any of his money-making prose fiction. We knew he produced enormous quantities of it, but we sensed that he felt it was unimportant compared to his poetry. He thought of himself as a poet, so we did too. Read aloud in his powerful deep voice, his poetry always sounded impressive. In those years I thought him the most wonderful man in the world.

Daddy was keen on schedules. He was acutely aware of time. It was how he managed to get so much work done. Even without a watch he could tell time to within one or two minutes' accuracy, day or night. ''Now what about this fifteen minutes between 7:30 and 7:45,'' he would say, ''what are you doing then?'' We had tennis lessons, swimming lessons, piano lessons, singing lessons, fencing lessons, dancing lessons. Daddy could never understand that we needed free time. Even on Sundays the tennis pro, a German, would arrive at 8:00 A.M. chauffeured by Olimpio in the DeSoto town car. Sometimes Olimpio used our four-door Isotta-Fraschini touring car, but usually it was reserved for Daddy— who drove it to the terror of all his passengers and many pedestrians!

Across the garden on the opposite side of the valley was the Villa Emilia where the Leonard Bacons, old friends of Daddy, lived for several years. Martha, their eldest daughter, became one of my closest friends, and we played together on holidays and attended birthday parties. Leonard was a poet, and he and Daddy spent many hours discussing poetry or playing chess.

I don't think we resented Mum's concentration on Pop rather than on us, but still we wanted a stronger, more authoritative mother. She spent much time days upstairs on the couch in Pop's enormous study that looked out over the Duomo and the city in one direction and over the *podere* and garden in the other. She talked plot with him for hours while he paced the floor, and she read proof on all his manuscripts and made corrections in her large hand. Sometimes she read aloud to him after lunch so he could fall asleep, stretched out on the study sofa. Her voice was beautifully modulated, and she learned to read with a minimum of effort. Often during the night when Pop woke with a nightmare (caused by his heart trouble), she would patiently read aloud until he dropped off again. She could keep this up for two or three hours, knowing that, when she stopped, he woke immediately.

In fact she *was* tired a great deal of the time because she was always looking after him, terribly worried lest he have another heart attack (and he did have them repeatedly), knowing that he was always overworking and pushing himself into deadlines and too many typewritten pages a day. As we grew older, she told us of the strain it was to "live with such a tempestuous giant of a man."

She watched and worried and saw the debts pile up and the many people dependent on Pop increase in number and needs. His largesse was staggering— out of scale, like nearly everything else he did. All who asked for his help— and they were numerous—received it and usually got more than they deserved, or he could afford.

Pop couldn't resist playing the lavish host. It may have had something to do with the deprivations of his youth, but I think it was a completely natural trait. He was by nature one of those who give and give. Casual visitors would drop by and remain in our guest room for days or weeks. Pop stuck to his work schedule: mornings in his study writing verse, afternoons (and sometimes evenings also) writing his prose stories. He was never called to the phone until after luncheon at 1:00.

Often he poured a glass of vermouth before sitting down to table and strolled with it in hand in the garden with Mum or Elia, noting with his powerful interest the growth of vines, gardenias, roses, hedges, bulbs, and outlining grand new plans for planting and landscaping. Or he might go to the aviary on the terrace on the second floor to watch his canaries and listen to them sing. He had installed it so that he, and we, could have their singing close around us, and Giulia fed them weeds and grass from the garden to supplement their diet of bird seed.

Mother's chief anxiety continued to be Daddy's health and his tendency to overdrink. His frequent over indulgences resulted in Dr. Ancona's or Dr. Giglioli's (stout and genial, he had once treated Henry James) arriving to see how his heart was standing the strain he subjected it to, and sometimes he was ordered to stay in bed a day. Against the doctors' orders (all his doctors prescribed rest for bad hearts), Pop formulated his own regime of strenuous exercise. He played tennis (singles or doubles) with Leonard Bacon or other friends nearly every day that weather permitted and sweated in the most copious manner I have ever seen. "The heart is a muscle," he insisted. "Like any other muscle, it needs exercise to remain healthy." Such statements were heresy in those days, if accepted doctrine now. I caddied for him and became a good thrower of tennis balls and improved my own game by playing against him. He would go up to the house afterward with his English flannels literally soaking wet, mopping his brow with a towel. Sometimes, smiling roguishly, he would say that the climb up the slope from the court was too hard on his heart and would tell Elia to drive him up on his motorcycle, Pop riding astride behind him, to the consternation and delight of the laboring *contadini* in nearby fields. "Nothing in moderation" could well be described as his motto. He threw himself unsparingly into everything he did.

Even during trips to Greece, Egypt, and motoring through Italy, France, or Spain, there was always the daily stint at the typewriter, coupled with proofreading, discussion of plot, the sending and receiving of urgent business cables, and the usual silent—and sometimes not so silent—prayer from all of us that he would not drink too much that night and go on a real spree.

I think Mum felt she was incapable of being the ideal wife for him, though she adored her Heinie and tried her best to fend off unnecessary guests, money seekers, etc., and to keep him well while he pursued his amazing schedule of work. Perhaps any woman would have proved inadequate to the demands placed on her by his giant energies and needs.

We were always short of money. Later I understood better the worried look on Mum's face in those years when the crates of beautifully bound books would arrive from London—books Pop had bought there and had bound with no thought of expense—Shakespeare, Chaucer, Milton, Malory, the Greek tragedians, the Oxford English Dictionary. "Feel this!" he would say as we opened the boxes in the evening after dinner and took out the volumes, their leather and parchment covers shining so handsomely. "Isn't this wonderful! Look here!" And so on far into the night while Mother's face grew longer not just from weariness but also at the thought of the bill. One invoice alone amounted to $10,000. But Daddy loved them and did not care. He had given blood for them. They were all his—his best beloved and most admired authors, poets mostly, bound and processed in the finest packaging he could give them.

Leaving the villa in the late summer of 1938, after eleven years there, was one of the hardest blows of Pop's life. He loved every tree and plant in the garden, the rose pergola by the pool, the tennis court he had built, the cypress avenue he had planted, the gardenias in the small "Dorothy's garden," the ampelopsis vine he watched climb and cover the walls of his addition to the villa. The thousands of books had to be packed in cases. Items of furniture were to be shipped also. Mother had sent over a list of chests, tables, chairs, beds, linens, and trays she wanted. It was very depressing and tiring work and soul searing for Pop as well as for John and me.

Pop never confessed his despair at leaving his villa, but war clouds were gathering, and I'm sure he knew our life there was over. He did reiterate: "I will come back to die here . . . in Italy!"

John and Judy sailed separately. Pop and I would join them in the house at 317 Burlingame Avenue, Los Angeles—near Santa Monica, between the U.C.L.A. campus and the sea—that Mother had bought and was fixing over. Mum greeted us at the new house. It was a two-story white stucco Spanish-style with red-tile roof, set in dense green shrubbery, attractive from the outside, and Mother could always make the interior of a house charming. By removing partitions, putting mirrors on walls to enlarge rooms, and using our old furniture with new slipcovers and a few Italian tables, lamps, and old chests that had been shipped from Florence, she contrived to make this home both charming and livable.

Its garden was small but attractive. A front lawn was surrounded by a tall fence on which grew a thick cover of Burmese Ivy. The ivy had enormous green leaves which shielded us almost completely from the street. Burlingame Avenue was lined with lovely large pepper trees and was attractive and comparatively quiet.

Off our living room, through French doors at the back, was a porch with pots of flowers, also a small reflecting pool set in a red brick walk, a small lawn, and surrounding flower beds, all protected from our neighbors on that side by a tall cypress hedge. Mother had added a study for Pop upstairs off their bedroom with a staircase leading down to this back garden. There were only two other bedrooms and baths. Eventually the maid's room and bath downstairs off the kitchen was remodeled into a guest room; there were by that time no live-in servants because of wartime labor shortages.

We had very little contact with the entertainment world. Although he mixed easily with them and was evidently accepted, Pop rarely brought home the producers, agents, directors, or actors he met at the studios. He believed his private life should be kept very private and separate.

There were many times when Mother and I were ready for dinner, and it was after six, and Pop was late getting home from the studio. We listened for the Buick and became more and more worried. When he was late, it almost always meant he had stopped at a bar and would have had too much to drink or had gone to lunch at Musso and Frank's and been talking and drinking all afternoon. In either case he was likely to have an accident driving while "under the influence" and was a constant source of anxiety to us. But as usual he bore a charmed life. When he finally appeared, he would be bleary eyed, his eternal gray suit rumpled, his tie undone, his color pale—but safe.

Our problem would be to get him to eat dinner, stop drinking as much as possible, and to entertain him so that he didn't decide to go out again to meet a friend and continue partying. There were many long nights when he didn't return till dawn, and Mother lay awake worrying about his heart and general condition.

We often called Dr. Eikenberry to come and listen to his heart. Eikenberry would give him a shot to make him sleep a few hours. His recuperative powers always amazed me. He could rise after three hours' sleep—his old charming, tender self, remorseful, ready to go "on the wagon" again, and ready for work. This pattern repeated itself at intervals and exhausted Mother more than it did Daddy.

Life at 317 Burlingame Avenue became a kind of hell, and I was torn between my suffering parents, loving them both; and they increasingly turned to me as the one who could keep peace between them—the one who symbolized their earlier devotion and, perhaps, a reconciliation that yet might be. Pop had fallen in love with another woman several years earlier, and this added to the little hell in which we now lived with his being constantly torn between her and his loyalty to Mum. Mum was torn between her loyalty to him and her sense of betrayal. It was a miserable time for all of us.

Pop complicated it by terrible fights with Judy who refused to be intimidated by him and refused to cry when she was young and he spanked her. When he had had too much to drink, he told her she was much like him—and had re-bellious unregenerate tendencies for wrongdoing. These scenes may have dam-aged her psyche irreparably. They certainly clouded her later relationship with Pop and her memory of him.

The great success of his Kildare films was little more to him than a source of income. He was often in a state of despair over what he considered his failure as a poet, and the mess he was making of his personal and family life, but his natural optimism carried him through. Somehow he *would* meet the next dead-line, pound out the screenplay, mail the story off to the editor, carry on. He still believed he would write great poetry.

In looking back, I think Daddy spent his happiest hours in Italy. The whole purpose for our living in Florence was to satisfy his hunger for beautiful things, to find peace and quiet and health for his work and, to such a degree as was possible for him, he found what he wanted.

There are so many fragments of him that I can still remember, and yet they are all really parts of a whole person. I remember him lying in bed while re-covering from a heart attack, pale as a ghost, his portable typewriter propped on his belly, saying: "I have to work twice as hard to catch up." Pop listened to his heart regularly with a stethoscope he kept by his bed. He would instruct Mum or me or John or Judy to listen to "the old ticker"—and would joke about it with us. This may have been his way of dealing with his heart prob-lem—bringing it out into the open and talking about it, making it a kind of adversary in a game in which we all were players. He thought he would die young because of his frail heart and the intensity with which he lived.

He had the knack of making an occasion something special, whatever it ac-tually was. He loved perfume and was continually buying it as a present for

Mum and me. He had an aversion, never explained, to using an apostrophe to show possession and never used it in his writing that I know of. Similarly he never used a period when writing longhand, always a small x.

He nearly drove us crazy by encouraging people to write who had little or no talent. I can think of only one or two who succeeded, out of literally dozens who took up his time, energy, money, and faith. He had poor judgment in certain areas. Pop loved magicians like Houdini, perhaps because they shared his view that the seemingly impossible was in fact possible and that illusion is at the heart of life.

My father never urged me to go to college. A college girl wasn't his idea of what a woman should be. Rather, he saw my role as a homemaker and partner who could and should nurture a man in his life and work, and this fitted nicely with my own ideas. Mother, however, wanted me to go to college—without telling me she thought I might find a husband there, as most girls hoped to do those days in the 1930s. Pop thought that Prince Charming would appear before me like magic when the time was ripe, like the Prince to Miranda in ''The Tempest.''

He was keen on games of all kinds, and he saw life as a kind of great game. He drove cars like he caught trains and planes and like he lived, in a mad dash with only split seconds between him and disaster. We children were so shielded by his strength, his courage, his powerful convictions that it became very difficult for us to assert ourselves, be independent of his all-embracing, sometimes tyrannical love. Perhaps his greatest legacy to me was his faith in life, his insistence—often repeated—that life could be beautiful, good, heroic, and happy.

FREDERICK FAUST AS I KNEW HIM

Robert Easton

Robert Easton came to know Frederick Faust while he was courting Jane Faust whom he subsequently married.

I first met him one Sunday in August, 1939, at his home at 317 Burlingame Avenue in Brentwood, an upscale enclave on Los Angeles's West Side. His oldest daughter, Jane, asked me to lunch there. I was a budding journalist of twenty-four, Los Angeles editor for the San Francisco–based *Coast Magazine*. Frederick Faust was forty-seven and in his prime as person and writer. At first sight he seemed enormous. Actually he stood about six feet three and weighed maybe two hundred and twenty, large for those days, but he gave such an impression of power and intensity that he seemed much larger, and a sternly lined face and remarkably deep voice added to this impression.

As he greeted me with cordial courtesy and evaluated me with a large and uncompromisingly cool eye, the mixture of good and harm in his face startled me. "Here's a man capable of anything," I thought; and those impressions of size, power, sternness and ambivalence continued during the years that I knew him. Jane also introduced me to her mother, one of the most attractive women I'd ever met. Dorothy Faust's gentle femininity seemed an ideal counterpart to her husband's forceful masculinity, and they seemed to have a close and mutually supportive relationship.

I had no idea of Faust's professional achievements, though Jane had told me he was a writer and was working for the movie studios. I had no idea he thought of himself as a poet and had published two books of poetry under his own name and some hundred and thirty novels under various pen names, mainly Max Brand, creating such popular characters as Destry and Dr. Kildare. I'd never knowingly seen any of the many movies based on his novels or magazine stories.

I was aware that he'd lived with his family in Europe for a number of years, chiefly in Florence, and to that I attributed his cultured accent and sophisticated manner. I learned later that he greatly admired England and the English and had sent two of his three children to school there. I thought him charming and interesting but had no inkling of what was to come.

Not long after our first meeting, when I brought Jane home from a date at his prescribed hour of 11:00 P.M., her father peremptorily, if affectionately, dismissed her upstairs to bed and haled me into a comfortable, book-lined living room where a silver tray with glasses and several bottles of Pabst Blue Ribbon beer were set on a coffee table before a welcoming fire and where a small, dark-haired, nearly bald man not a great deal younger than Faust—but wearing an old blue-serge suit and an open-throat white shirt like Faust's—was sitting in one of several large, chintz-covered armchairs. He was Faust's secretary, Francis Gallagher, a would-be playwright and former secretary to the playwright, Philip Barry, author of ''Philadelphia Story'' and other stage successes who had, I learned later, recommended him to Faust.

Faust and Gallagher had evidently been deep in conversation, lubricated by the beer, and it soon continued, and I began hearing talk led by Faust such as I'd never heard before. The subject was not him or his work but me and mine and Gallagher and his. Faust had learned from Jane of my ambition to write fiction and promptly encouraged me to show him my stories and eventually spent hours with me discussing them and literature and life generally. Gallagher was writing—with, I gathered, much help from Faust—a play about Van Gogh, and our talk touched on Van Gogh and his tragic and marvelous life and took off from there into what seemed boundless realms of thought. I'd recently graduated in English from Harvard and had read a good deal before and since and thought I was fairly well educated but now realized I'd only been scratching the surface. Suffusing them with his passionate enthusiasm, Faust made Homer, Dante, Shakespeare, Plato, Napoleon, Herodotus, Kant, Copernicus, Jesus and their worlds become actual presences—as he did, in due time and with the help of my questioning, his own experiences ranging from an orphaned boyhood working on San Joaquin Valley farms and ranches, to college at Berkeley, to itinerant newspaper reporting in Hawaii, soldiering in Canada, starving as an aspiring writer in New York, and so on, though always modest to the point of reticence about his own achievements. While working on ranches, he'd learned to swear eloquently and still larded his talk with what he regarded as unprofane profanity, ''bastard,'' ''son of a bitch,'' ''Jesus Christ''—but never any four-letter obscenities as they were then known. I never heard him tell a dirty story. He'd traveled very widely—Egypt, Greece, Spain among other places, as well as England, France, Italy, Germany, and many parts of the United States—and this, too, entered his talk.

Most encouraging and flattering to me, he made me feel increasingly important, potentially on a par not only with him but with the world's greats and worthy to be received by them all. I found myself thinking and speaking as if inspired. Later I learned it was his habit to treat others—and not just aspiring writers—in this way. It was his method of encouraging human potential and acting as advocate for the greatness he identified with so strongly. Time flew by. I noticed a strange light at the window and realized it was daylight. Gallagher had long since disappeared. Faust sent me home feeling exhilarated and transformed, resolved to become a great writer, laden with books he insisted I read: Thucydides' HISTORY OF THE PELOPONNESIAN WAR, the poetry of Theocritus— "light but worthwhile," Benjamin Franklin's AUTOBIOGRAPHY—"the best non-fiction written in America," Arthur Waley's translation of A HUNDRED AND SEVENTY CHINESE POEMS, and Fabre's LIFE OF THE ANT, among others.

When I reached my three-dollar-a-week room in a shabby downtown rooming house, I was too excited to sleep and resumed work immediately on one of several stories I hoped to publish. Jane later told me that after two hours' sleep her father had gone to his screenwriting job at M-G-M where he was developing his Dr. Kildare stories for a series of movies featuring Lionel Barrymore and Lew Ayres. I wondered how often he stayed up talking all night and where his apparently boundless energy came from. Like Cortez in Keats's poem, viewing the Pacific for the first time, I felt something mighty and marvelous had swum into my ken.

When Faust worked at home, it was usually on the second floor of his unpretentious, Mediterranean-style house in a corner room with a southern exposure and many windows that could be opened to give him the fresh air he craved. I didn't realize at first that he suffered from feelings of suffocation due to heart trouble. While working, he sat in an easy-chair with broad wooden arms, his old Underwood upright typewriter on an adjustable stand in front of him, and pecked away rapidly with two fingers. The many volumes of the ENGLISH DICTIONARY, expensively bound in leather, were shelved within reach and also handy were an unabridged Webster's, collegiate and rhyming dictionaries, a thesaurus, and a number of freshly sharpened yellow pencils.

I once worked at his invitation for several weeks in the room with him, using the new 1942 Royal Portable he'd given me, a duplicate of one he'd just purchased to keep up with the latest technology. On mine I typed those stories he encouraged me to write and which he helped, with typical generosity, to sell through his New York agent, Carl Brandt, first to *The Atlantic* and then to Viking Press to become my first book, THE HAPPY MAN. Though we were only a few feet apart as our machines clicked away, we were so lost in our work most of the time that we were unaware of each other, though occasionally we would interrupt for a question or to share a thought.

Once he exclaimed—"Listen to this!"—and began gently turning the pages of the dictionary he was holding. "Hear that sound? Suppose you waked in the dark, thinking you were alone, and heard that?" He was imagining a mystery story in which the whispery turning of the pages of a book might play a part. He regularly noted and jotted down such minutiae, often in the notebook he usually carried, and used them in his writing. While working with him, I felt his physical and imaginative excitement communicate itself to me. He seemed to throw himself into his writing as if actually experiencing it.

Little actualities, like the sound of a turning page, seemed to interest him as much as grand abstractions, and he could discourse as eloquently on potting petunias as on the immortality of the soul or on best methods of walking, running, breathing, seeing, thinking. "If you want to see a thing clearly in a dim light," he advised me, "look just to one side of it, not directly at it," adding that this could be helpful with ideas, too. Human potential of all kinds fascinated him, perhaps because impoverished orphanhood and early ill health (he had been sickly and threatened with tuberculosis) plus his later heart trouble (atrial fibrillation) had forced him to think long and hard about what he could do or be. He liked to quote from "Hamlet" what he called Shakespeare's greatest prose passage, beginning: "What a piece of work is a man!" He told me more than once: "There is a giant asleep in each of us and, when that giant wakes, miracles can happen." He seemed to be speaking from personal experience and to be convinced that human potential was unlimited and that all we needed to do to transcend limits was to make up our minds that we could.

After dinner he and I and Jane and her mother and Jane's fourteen-year-old sister, Judy, would gather in the book-lined living room, and Faust would read aloud what I had written and what he had written during the day, and we would all join in criticizing it. These were truly frank and helpful working sessions. Then Faust might read aloud from "Iliad" or "Odyssey" or HUCKLEBERRY FINN or the Scottish-English border ballads, or we might all join in reading a Shakespeare play, each taking a part. It was not only good entertainment but highly educational and often inspiring as Faust led us in debating which lines of poetry were great and which not and why. This regimen of reading aloud after dinner often continued when other visitors were present and seemed to arise naturally out of the order of things, and Faust seemed to spark and guide as if born to it.

Greatness fascinated him, as I've suggested. He liked to make lists of the greatest poems, plays, novels, prize fighters, tennis players, generals, kings, queens, greatest peoples at any given time in history, greatest painters, sculptors, composers, philosophers, scientists, and so forth and get you to argue pro and con with him about them. Though this tended to marginalize many deserving candidates, its net effect was to fix his attention and yours on the highest and best. Here is a reading list he made for Jane and me in 1942 as minimal for a knowledge of world literature. It begins with a generic entry, "Proverbs and Fables of All the World," and then continues with authors nation by nation.

Greece: Homer, Sappho, Pindar, Herodotus, Æschylus, Sophocles, Thucydides, Aristophanes, Xenophon's "Memorabilia," Theocritus, Lucian

Italy: Dante

Spain: Cervantes

France: Villon, Rabelais, Montaigne, Molière

Germany: Goethe, Heine—selected lyrics

Russia: Tolstoy, Dostoyevsky

China: Tu Fu, Po Chin, Li Po

England: Chaucer, Malory, Spenser, Shakespeare, Bacon, the King James translation of the Bible, Milton, Addison, Steele, Swift, Fielding, Boswell

His favorite poets, in addition to Homer and Shakespeare, were Sappho, Dante, Chaucer, and Milton after whose "Paradise Lost" he had patterned an epic of his own about a mythic descent to hell. His favorite playwrights were Æschylus, Sophocles, Aristophanes, and Shakespeare; his favorite novels were "Odyssey" (though written in verse, he considered it a novel because of its complexity and unity and was emphatic that Homer should be read in the original, as he read him, or in prose translation because no poetic reconstruction could do justice to the original), GARGANTUA AND PANTAGRUEL, DON QUIXOTE, TOM JONES, WAR AND PEACE, and THE ADVENTURES OF HUCKLEBERRY FINN. His favorite historians were Herodotus, Thucydides, Livy, and Froissart, his favorite painters, Leonardo and Rembrandt, and his favorite composers, J. S. Bach and Mozart. When teased about not being modern, he replied: "Since modernity is impossible, what choice have I?" He thought the twentieth century a dark time because it was not an age of poetry but of prose, of materialism, and of political dictatorship at odds with the poetic spirit and the spirit of greatness he idolized.

Though he admired some of Hemingway, he had little or no use for contemporary prose fiction, believing it was preoccupied with the ugly and down-beat. "There is not one admirable character in THE GREAT GATSBY," he pointed out to me and described how he had flung Sinclair Lewis's novel, MAIN STREET, across the room in disgust after reading a few chapters "because it's so damned ugly and narrow. It is usually the people who have strawberries and cream for breakfast who talk about the need for 'realism' in writing. Most of us have enough realism in our daily lives." He believed that only great poetry like Shakespeare's could place the down-side and the up-side of life in proper perspective and portray the seamy and sublime in true context. "Poetry is the only form for serious literary expression," he insisted dogmatically. He professed no interest in writing so-called serious fiction, though, when he did write it, in stories such as "The Wedding Guest" and "A Special Occasion"—both published in *Harper's* under his own name—he did so very well. In fact in the latter he dealt frankly with the down-beat and seamy in his own life, for he is clearly its thinly disguised protagonist, a failing architect who once had great promise but is now into alcohol, a mistress, and suicidal feelings of despair.

He never mentioned his prose in my hearing except to belittle it as inconsequential, and Jane told me he forbade her and her brother and sister to read it.

Yet, when I read a copy of his 1940 story collection, WINE ON THE DESERT, inscribed to Jane and me, I was struck by how good much of it was, particularly those stories just mentioned and "Our Daily Bread" and "Wine on the Desert"—now to be found with others in THE COLLECTED STORIES OF MAX BRAND which Jane and I recently edited. Together with his poetry and such Western novels as THE GARDEN OF EDEN and DESTRY RIDES AGAIN, such historical ones as THE BAIT AND THE TRAP, and his spy trilogy, SECRET AGENT NUMBER ONE, SPY MEETS SPY, and THE BAMBOO WHISTLE, they showed me the extraordinary writer he was, but, when I tried to compliment him on his prose, he waved me off. "I write prose to pay the bills!" He clearly wanted to be thought of as poet which was how he thought of himself, but, I gathered, perhaps he thought more highly of his prose than he let on.

He never discussed his screenwriting in my hearing and had a low opinion of American movies generally, his favorites being the European GRAND IL-LUSION and MAYERLING. They were in part what brought him to Hollywood under the illusion he might have a hand in films like them. "We live by illu-sions," he said more than once and cited the illusory "The Tempest" as Shake-speare's corroboration of this. It was probably his favorite play. He believed that we live by the illusion that we are important, by the illusion that there is a God, a heaven, and so forth, and thus create our realities much as in imagining a story. I think this belief was at the heart of his storytelling. As a lonely, sickly, highly sensitive boy, he'd had to create his own reality in order to escape the realities of his surroundings "until," as he told me, "my daydreams became more real than what was actually around me."

He considered himself fortunate to have escaped his humble origins, some-times describing them pejoratively as "the ruck of mediocrity," but he never forgot them or the friends or relatives who'd helped him escape and in return helped put several of their children through college. Yet he could be as ambiv-alent about humble origins as about most other things, one moment denigrating, the next moment praising. I heard him do this about whites, blacks, Mexicans, Chinese, Japanese, and American Indians, Catholics, Jews, Muslims, French, Germans, Irish, and Italians, and about the human race generally. He was noth-ing if not consistent in his ambivalence and could take any position and defend it convincingly, much as he could create many kinds of characters in his stories. He was, however, consistently sympathetic to underdogs, perhaps because he'd been one. He dealt with them perceptively in many of his stories such as "Out-cast Breed" and in such novels as CLUNG, which feature respectively an Amer-ican Indian of mixed blood and a Caucasian who thinks he's Chinese. Similarly in "Master and Man," a short novel from 1924, the hero is a Negro, perhaps the earliest in Western fiction. Though he could mingle with and write for the elite, he remained a populist at heart, writing and identifying primarily for and with the ordinary people he liked to think he sprang from.

His friends and acquaintances, when I knew him, ranged from bartenders and truck drivers to Aldous Huxley and Huxley's fellow Englishman and fellow screenwriter also poet, novelist, and biographer, Richard Aldington, the German novelist and Hollywood refugee, Thomas Mann, the Pulitzer Prize poet, Leonard Bacon, and Robert Millikan, head of the California Institute of Technology. He knew studio moguls such as Columbia executive, Harry Cohn, and professors at U.C.L.A. and Berkeley as well as his Japanese-American gardener, Sato, and the blacks, Morris and Ella Mae, who worked for him as butler-chauffeur and cook respectively. He seemed to treat them all with similar naturalness and courtesy. The Benét brothers, William Rose and Stephen Vincent, could be added as could former world's heavyweight boxing champion, Gene Tunney, tennis champion, Helen Wills, Faust's friend from Berkeley days and Pulitzer Prize–winning dramatist, Sidney Howard, who had recently written the screenplay for GONE WITH THE WIND (M-G-M, 1939). There were also prominent short-story writer, Grace Flandrau, as well as Henry Seidel Canby, founder of *The Saturday Review of Literature,* the publisher, Edward Dodd, of Dodd, Mead, and Robert A. Lovett, a Wall Street banker and later Undersecretary of War. Faust never gave me the impression of celebrity seeking or social climbing. He seemed rather to enjoy people for what they were, not for where they stood in the social hierarchy.

He told me that, when he first started writing, each story seemed the last he would ever find but little by little his story-finding faculty increased until he could spot them everywhere, "flying out of conversations, out of newspaper items, out of inversions of things as they are. Suppose the rich man suddenly loses his money, or the beggar suddenly acquires wealth? What tempts the just man to acts of injustice?" Or: "Read somebody else's story. Stop when you are half way through and imagine an ending for it. Fit in a new beginning, and there you are."

He had published no non-fiction professionally though he'd tried to, submitting essays on various subjects when at the height of his great success as a popular writer of fiction, but they found no takers. His forte was imaginative writing, "dreaming," as he called it. Yet this dreaming was based largely on his own experiences, internal and external, as one who knows his life story can readily tell, or on his reading the thousands of volumes in his library on nearly every subject imaginable. His favorite books were bound in expensive vellum, and there were facsimiles of original editions of Homer, Dante, Malory, Chaucer, and Shakespeare. Freud, Jung and Einstein could be found side by side with the Loeb Classical Library, the BOOK OF PIRATES, and the latest works on astronomy and biology. I got the impression that he took nothing less than all of life—past, present and future—as food for his mind and as subject matter for his writing, and I was not surprised later when I discovered he had authored a science fiction novel, THE SMOKING LAND, involving spaceships.

One of his essays that failed to find a publisher is revealing. It is titled "Steam—Leisure and Fiction." In it Faust finds a close connection between the leisure created by the industrial revolution and the rise of fictive prose as exemplified by Jane Austen, Scott, Dickens, Fielding, Tolstoy, and Proust, among others he praises. But no matter how well done, he finds prose fiction by nature incapable of dealing with "grave imaginative creation" such as found in the poetry of Shakespeare or Milton. Because of marketplace forces, current fiction focuses on pain and disillusion or on mere entertainment with a happy ending. This is what the public wants, and therefore what editors want. Faust then makes a rare reference to his own magazine fiction, lamenting that "the only real check upon it is that it be not too grave." This essay may have failed of publication because it amounts to a sweeping indictment of the current literary scene or because it is strangely flat, or both. Though he was thoroughly familiar with the essay form and very enthusiastically gave me two volumes of Montaigne to read, and though he admired Samuel Johnson and chuckled over E. B. White's *New Yorker* essays, his own were unconvincing. They lacked the authority he could bring to his imaginative work and the voice, which perhaps was present only when he was "dreaming," reaching into his unconscious for what was distinctively his own.

There is one exception, but a very dramatic one, to Faust's lack of success with non-fiction. In 1943, eager to make a contribution to the war effort, he began to write the story of the 212th Marine Fighter Squadron recently returned to El Toro Air Base near Los Angeles after distinguished service at Guadalcanal in the South Pacific where its pilots were among the first to engage the Japanese in sustained aerial combat. At a time when he was heavily pressed by other matters, Faust spent many hours interviewing members of the 212th, ground crew as well as pilots, and then spent many more hours turning his interview notes into narrative prose. He invited the young Marines to his home, became personally involved in their lives, identified with them strongly. Jane met a number of them while acting as hostess with her mother at Sunday lunches, and I did likewise when home on leave from the Army. Charming, cool, and modest in manner, much decorated, they seemed the ideal of American fighting men. So it was a bitter disappointment to Faust when his book failed to find a publisher. Fifty years later by an extraordinary combination of circumstances the manuscript, which had been lost and all but forgotten, resurfaced and with the help of veterans of the 212th was shaped by Jane and me into publishable form. FIGHTER SQUADRON AT GUADALCANAL was accepted in 1995 for publication by the Naval Institute Press.

One failed attempt at serious fiction which he labored at during much of the time that I knew him and which haunted him was an epic novel about the Civil War, tentatively titled WYCHERLY. Cass Canfield, head of Harper & Bros., one of his many publishers, was encouraging him, and he had done an immense amount of research for it as he did for many of his historical novels and for his Westerns as well, especially what I call his Indian Westerns, a group of twenty or more in which he portrayed the American Indian with striking power and sympathy. He felt personally involved with the Civil War because his father had fought on the Northern side and marched through Georgia with Sherman and because he greatly admired the Southern enlisted man along with such generals as Lee, Jackson, and Stuart. He knew all its major campaigns in detail as he knew those of Napoleon, Wellington, the Duke of Marlborough, Caesar, Alexander the Great, Hannibal, Epaminodas of Thebes, Frederick the Great, and others including those of leading generals in the Great War.

Warfare fascinated him. "Life is a battle," he said, and: "Man is a fighting animal." He felt that to believe otherwise was to miss a central reality. Yet there was nothing arrogant or jingoistic in his attitude. He'd fought his way up the ladder physically and mentally and was simply stating what he believed to be a fact. In the five or six thousand books in his library were several dozen on the Civil War and warfare generally, including volumes by Jomini, Von Clausewitz, and Mahan. He did most of his research himself, often typing or writing out notes on 8×5 cards, employing helpers such as Gallagher as need be. For technical help on his Kildare stories he relied on the family doctor, Kenneth Eikenberry, or on his old friend from college days, George Winthrop "Dixie" Fish, a New York surgeon whose experiences as intern served as a model for those of Kildare. Over the years he had amassed vast reference files on a variety of subjects including the French and American Revolutions as well as our Civil War. So it was a crushing blow when Canfield didn't care for the first hundred pages of WYCHERLY, and he had to postpone work on the project because of other demands on his time.

While publishing some of Faust's best Westerns and historical novels, Canfield suggested another project that failed. It was a running commentary on "The Tempest" in which Shakespeare's text would appear on the right-hand page and Faust's comments on the left. I was excited and flattered when Faust asked me to work with him, he writing to me his line-by-line comments on the play and I writing him mine. But I was surprised and disappointed when his written comments lacked the passionate conviction of his spoken ones. We hadn't finished Act I when the project got lost in the demands of war and his death. I felt he never found the time to give it the attention it required.

Faust showed little interest in contemporary poetry, although he praised Edwin Arlington Robinson for dealing with the Arthurian legends he was using in his own poetry. He believed in the fundamental importance of legend, myth, and fairy tale as basic transmitters of human culture and recommended them to me, explaining how he used them as plots for stories and poems or as a source of similes and metaphors. He insisted I read Frazer's treatise on mythology, THE GOLDEN BOUGH, and Andrew Lang's and others' collections of fairy tales.

To hear him read his own poetry or that of poets he admired was to be carried away by the emotion in his remarkably expressive voice. It could bring tears to your eyes as well as to his. But when I read his published epic, "Dionysus in Hades," to myself it was like eating nothing but cake. Though I couldn't tell him so, I found his marginal prose notes more readable—and more convincingly poetic—than his poetry. Despite its many fine passages, and some fine shorter poems, I think he labored too hard at his poetry, thought too much about it until it was for him like prayer and, like many formalized prayers, suffered from lack of spontaneity. He had little or no use for free verse, believing strict form essential for serious poetry, and for his Dionysus epic devised his own rhyme scheme based on Dante's *terza rima*. Though he could read Latin and Italian, as well as Greek, he usually read his ancient masters in translation and could quote them at length from memory. He identified with them so strongly that he sometimes seemed to be writing in the manner in which they wrote rather than in his own manner, and that, I think, is further reason much of his poetry seems to lack the originality which is not at all the case with his prose.

When I went to see him one afternoon to ask permission to marry his daughter, which was still customary, he promptly gave it, though not without some reservation which I sensed. He adored Jane, probably beyond anyone else, and felt that no man on earth would be good enough for her. He said she was in the "grip of wanting to have children," as he put it, and told me frankly that he'd brought her up to believe that "all men are sons of bitches where a woman is concerned" and that she should expect infidelities from her husband in accordance with the prevailing double standard which he advocated, though I did not. He was an absolute believer in true love, he said, and in enduring love and marriage, and in love at first sight as had happened between him and Dorothy. Then he added, over the next bottle of beer, that he'd been faithful to her for thirteen years, as if that were quite an achievement, but implied that he had strayed since, as I knew from Jane. I'd begun to notice friction between him and Dorothy, especially when with too-evident anxiety she tried to curb his drinking lest it bring on a heart attack. He usually had a cocktail or two before dinner, several glasses of wine with dinner, and brandy afterward followed by beer throughout the evening, not to mention drinks during the noon hour or after work with his studio friends. However, I never knew him to drink while working, nor did Jane. Since I'd known him he'd had one severe heart attack that kept him in bed a day or two, but I had no idea of the depth and complexity of Dorothy's anxiety or the nervous strain she was under—and he was under, thinking he might die at any moment. For more than twenty years she'd watched over him while, regardless of caution, over drinking, over smoking, over working, over spending, living as if each moment might be his last, he seemed to court an extinction that would leave her a widow and their children fatherless—not to mention his chronic debts. Then there was his infidelity while she remained entirely true to him.

"I'm a son of a bitch myself in many ways, Bob," he confided with the maudlin frankness that sometimes came over him when he was drinking. Even so, most men and women were attracted to him, though some were offended by his strong opinions and almost overpowering energy. He could be especially considerate and ingratiating toward older women, genuinely admiring them for the experience and wisdom they represented. To younger ones he could be a sex object. Carol Brandt, Carl's wife, expatiated to me at length on "Heinie's sex appeal—so masculine, yum, yum!" Like many old friends, she used his youthful nickname. At any rate, I knew Dorothy, feeling cruelly rejected by him, had tried to kill herself on two occasions not long before I came on scene by taking an overdose of sleeping pills. Faust steadfastly insisted he loved her and would never divorce her or grant her a divorce, at the same time insisting on his right to that double standard of sexual conduct he advocated. He claimed it to be what civilized people the world over adhered to, yet I gathered he was less than comfortable with his infidelities and with the pain they caused Dorothy and himself and their children.

While adhering to no formalized religion or philosophy, he had a strong moral sense and at the same time a strongly amoral one. "Beauty is the god I worship," he told me more than once, meaning beauty in a line of poetry, or a race horse, or a flower, or in any of its many forms, dark or light, satanic or saintly. The most memorable characters in his stories were often villains, rather like Satan in Milton's "Paradise Lost" or Iago in "Othello." He seemed to create them with inspired understanding and perhaps that is what I saw in his face the first day that we met, a presence that diminished as I knew him better but never quite disappeared. "God is the substance of pure thought," he said—or, as we might say today, "pure consciousness." I think it was his ambition to be completely aware, completely conscious, and to express everything he possibly could, however harsh or gentle, "bad" or "good," and this was what lay at the heart of his drive to talk and to write, to bear witness to what he found fascinating and in the largest sense divine. "Strength is beyond good or evil," he would say, perhaps paraphrasing Nietzsche, and clearly in his stories as in his conversation he admired strength beyond goodness or any other quality. Yet he said that the Sermon on the Mount "expresses an ecstasy of truth," and one of his major but unfinished poems dealt with Christ at Gethsemane. "Isn't it too bad we can't be like God and never grow tired?" he asked me. Yet in his relatively short writing life of about twenty-five years he produced more than anyone else on record for a comparable period, some twenty-five million published words. Three or four hours' sleep was all he needed, and all his heart trouble would allow. He was plagued by suffocation nightmares in which he was buried alive under loads of coal and regularly slept propped up by pillows and sometimes woke, crying out to Dorothy for help. He sometimes spoke of God as energy, or as light, and once read aloud to me the opening passages of the Gospel of St. John to that effect. Speaking of immortality, he said: "Good conversations never die. They have life somewhere. They are the food of the Deity, perhaps."

He loved talk, did in fact regard it as at the sacred heart of life. "In the beginning was the word, the idea," he would say, meaning not only the *logos,* or ultimate reality, but also the ordinary spoken word. He conducted conversations which were in fact two-man seminars on a regular basis with a retired head of the U.C.L.A. philosophy department, Charles Rieber, who lived not far away, and he made periodic trips to Berkeley to talk with another of his former teachers, also retired, Walter Morris Hart. He made notes on these conversations for use in his stories and poems and in his ongoing effort to understand life. Once he went to a Franciscan retreat house at Malibu for a weekend of discussion and meditation and likewise made notes for later use. "Only in transition, in the process of becoming, are we fully alive," he said. If he adhered to no religion or philosophy, Faust was one of the most religious and philosophically minded people I ever knew, and a sense of reverence for life was inherent in the modesty and courtesy with which he usually treated other people and life generally.

He enjoyed his work and liked to record the numbers of pages he produced in a day. "Work is my salvation," he said, and: "Work is a kind of prayer," and: "In our work we come closest to God." His record output for one day, so far as I know, was fifty-six typewritten pages of prose fiction, or approximately 20,000 publishable words. He sold ninety-nine percent of the fiction he wrote.

He liked to talk about the work habits of other fabulous producers such as Balzac and Dumas, and he said that through work we pay back the Creator for our existence. He usually worked seven days a week, doing poetry, or "verse" as he called it, in the morning whenever possible. By special arrangement he sometimes did studio work at home where he could do his other work, too, and by further special arrangement he retained magazine and book rights to most of his studio work, thus greatly increasing his income.

Though he concealed himself behind twenty money-making pen names so that he could have the privacy as well as the money with which to write poetry, his true identity had begun to leak out, and he was regarded by studio executives and fellow writers as a kind of prestidigitator. It was rumored that he employed a team of ghostwriters because one man could not produce so much so quickly. He never gave interviews and discouraged all forms of publicity, letting his agent or editors concoct largely imaginative biographical sketches for publicity purposes. Since this was an era when screenwriters were not considered very newsworthy, studio public relations people didn't bother him much. He never to my knowledge collaborated as screenwriter with Huxley, Aldington, or F. Scott Fitzgerald, though they were at M-G-M when he was. He was reticent about those he worked with. I didn't learn till years later that he had collaborated extensively at Warner Bros. with William Faulkner on a story based on the life of Charles De Gaulle that never reached the screen. He showed no interest in knowing movie stars though he went to tea with Myrna Loy when her then producer-husband, Arthur Hornblower, invited him and Dorothy. He also met Joan Fontaine, Brian Aherne, and others socially and entertained Gladys Cooper and her actor-husband, Philip Merivale, at dinner. He tried repeatedly to interest producers in his beloved Arthurian legends but found no takers. I'm sure he tried to interest them in "Iliad" and "Odyssey" too. It was the gods of the Olympian pantheon that inspired him most, as they had inspired his role model, Homer, and he worked them into his prose and poetry if not into his screen stories. When he chose a subject for his first epic poem, it was the mythic descent of Dionysus to the Underworld to visit the shade of his dead mother, Semele, a subject that might well have inspired Homer and did perhaps inspire the scene in "Odyssey" where Odysseus descends to the Underworld and sees the shade of his mother. Faust's loss of his own mother, when he was eight, must certainly have entered into the writing of his epic. While at times despairing over his failure to achieve widespread acceptance, if not greatness, as a poet, he had at least two more epic poems in hand when I knew him.

Giantism was apparently one of his characteristics. He liked things on large scale, and in fact there was nothing perceptibly small or mean spirited about him but rather a largeness and even a nobility about his everyday manner as well as his view of life. Politically he was, generally speaking, conservative, seeing little good in the Presidency since George Washington's time and considering Washington superior to Lincoln or any other President as person and leader. He admired Theodore Roosevelt but considered Franklin Roosevelt little more than a slick politician until FDR led the country out of the Depression and toward a war Faust thought just. Even so, he voted for Wendell Willkie in 1940 against FDR for a third term. Though he believed strongly in democracy, he feared it also represented a leveling process that threatened distinguished performance. He could admire both kings and beggars. Egalitarianism and elitism were constantly in conflict in him.

He liked animals almost as much as he liked people and at various times had raised white bull terriers and Newfoundlands, among others, and now had an Airedale named Cowboy whom he treated as if he were a human being. It was the same with horses. When his daughter, Judy, became interested in them, he revived his own interest which had begun with ranch and farm horses and continued to the riding ring in New York's Central Park, where for a time he rode regularly, and to Ireland where in County Kildare he broke his leg nursing an Irish jumper over a high barrier, and now to regularly watching the races at Santa Anita. Though he no longer rode himself, he encouraged Judy and her black gelding, Lonely, to take the high barriers at the Uplifters Polo Club not far from his home.

He was continually taking up new hobbies: photography, gardening, outdoor cooking, playing chess alone against his chess book. His generosity toward others was striking. "Five dollars can sometimes make all the difference," he said, having known what it is to be hungry and broke, and also what it is to be discouraged. I didn't realize till years later when I came to write my biography of him how much he must have been suffering during these years from disappointed hopes, high aspirations repeatedly crushed, and how valiantly he concealed his suffering with never a whimper, unless it was in soul-baring talks with Dorothy. He supported a platoon or two of financially needy relatives, would-be writers, old friends, hangers-on, and deadbeats, not only with money but with letters, phone calls, and other forms of moral support. Generosity seemed to be a compulsion with him. If not a natural part of his make-up, it was evidently part of his personal code. When he reached first for the luncheon or dinner check, as he usually managed to do, it seemed to be from good manners and genuine consideration for others, not ostentation or ego building. He was similarly generous with his time and literary advice, giving unstintingly to all who asked as if it were a matter of honor to do so and sometimes being taken advantage of by people who used him to further their interests at the studios or elsewhere. He was continually discovering talent in others, talent that often didn't exist in reality, and spending hours on them as he did on me, encouraging them to think of themselves as important writers. This may have been an aspect of his own aspiration, or it may have been simple generosity, or both. I have a copy of his 200–page manuscript entitled "Some Doubted," dealing with an imaginary three-way conversation between Jesus, Judas, and Pontius Pilate in which Judas plays the role of poet and skeptic, Pilate that of world-weary sophisticate, and Jesus his scriptural self. It began as a proposal by Faust to an old friend, Chandler Barton, an alcoholic whom he was supporting financially and housing in his villa at Menton on the French Riviera, just to keep Barton, a failed writer, busy and to give him hope; but, as usual in such cases, it ended with Faust's doing most of the work and most of the hoping. Barton appeared at 317 Burlingame Avenue while I was there, abandoned by most of his other friends, and Faust again housed him, fed him, and tried to find work for him.

While often despairing over the human race, Faust never gave up on its individuals, especially those he believed to be his responsibility. Where did his money go? He seemed to live comfortably but not lavishly. I think during the years that I knew him his money went largely into helping others, such as singing lessons for the daughter of his cleaning woman and into educating his children at expensive private schools where he thought they could get the best education possible. Dorothy was exquisitely dressed, true, but he wore one of three lightweight (for coolness) gray suits, day in day out. He drove an Oldsmobile four-door convertible several years old while Dorothy's car was an aging four-door Buick sedan. I know that he once loaned ten thousand dollars to a friend and never got it back. How many such loans there were I never learned.

He had a rich sense of humor, firmly based on the foibles and paradoxes of human nature, expressive too of what Melville called "the universal thump" we are all heir to. It plays throughout his writing, as it played throughout his daily life. "Anyone who can make people laugh should be pensioned for life," he said. He liked to laugh at himself and to tease others and delighted in Shakespeare's Falstaff scenes and the scene in HUCKLEBERRY FINN where the two scamps, The Duke and The Dauphin, come aboard the raft and for a while fool Huck and Jim with their imposture only to be exposed in the end. He admired the broad gusto of Rabelais as well as the sophisticated humor of P. G. Wodehouse's novels, *New Yorker* cartoons, and the Jewish humor of the Hyman Kaplan stories in the *New Yorker*. He read the funny papers regularly.

Faust had almost as many states of being as there were hours in the day.

Bringing Jane home late one night, I found him sitting up alone, listening to recordings of Bach and Mozart, tears streaming down his face at the beauty of what he was hearing and making notes. He also liked ragtime but thought jazz decadent and corruptive. He could be deeply moved by classical painting and sculpture, poring for hours with exclamations and moist eyes over his albums of Alinari prints of the Old Masters acquired during his Florence days. Time fascinated him, and he could tell it accurately without a wristwatch—he had had to give up wearing one because they stopped working after a few days, apparently de-magnetized by his personal magnetic field. The only other case of this sort I know is that of the English writer, Robert Graves, Faust's contemporary who like him was part Irish and part German and like him a poet and novelist. Faust could do complex mathematical problems in his head by what seemed instinct rather than thought. He told me that when a young boy mathematics had been opaque to him and then "one day it all became clear and simple."

During periods when he abstained entirely from drinking, he seemed his best self, keen, thoughtful, remarkably sensitive and considerate of others. Then he would fall off the wagon, as he put it, and overdo not only his drinking but other things. I think he drank to relax the enormous tension he was under and—or so he thought—to stimulate his imagination and conversation and to escape the sense of failure that dogged him. I never saw him drunk to the point of loss of control. He could smoke up to a pack of Chesterfields a day despite doctor's orders to the contrary and was continually making resolutions about reducing his smoking, his drinking, his spending of money, his seeing too many people he didn't really want to see, or about spending more time on his poetry, or being better toward Dorothy and his children. He could be as convincing in announcing such resolutions as with nearly everything he said or wrote.

He was good with children, treating them as equals, frequently spending large amounts of gratuitous time and energy on them as with older people. I once dined with a New York doctor, Carnes Weeks, who years before had invited Faust to his home on an occasional basis. Faust had formed such an ongoing friendship with the doctor's two young sons, based on reading and writing projects Faust suggested, that as grown men they were still talking about him. Yet with his own children he could be a tyrannical taskmaster, requiring them to memorize long passages from Shakespeare and other poets and recite them to him and prescribing such extracurricular activities as lessons in Greek, Latin, tennis, fencing, boxing, dancing, the piano, so that nearly every waking moment was filled. Still they felt mainly affection for him, realizing the strenuous program was intended for their own good. When drinking, however, he could be tactlessly frank and abusive toward them and antagonize them thoroughly. He thought that a boy should be totally exposed to experience, like Odysseus, and a girl totally protected, rather like Miranda in "The Tempest" who has never seen a young man until the moment her Prince Charming appears. As Jane said, it was part of the unreality or grand illusion he lived in.

He loved dancing, had attended performances of Pavlova and Martha Graham, and for years he and Dorothy had danced alone in their villas to the music of phonograph records after the children were in bed, but they did so no longer. He was fastidious about personal cleanliness, showering and changing at least once a day but took little interest in clothes and, when writing a short-sleeve "play," wore shirt and slacks, though he could don a tuxedo for social occasions. For Jane's and my wedding he wore white tie and tails. He was keenly interested in food and drink and had a wide knowledge of the culinary arts and of fine wines but ate little and rapidly, his favorite meal being an aged two-inch-thick steak done very rare. On the cook's day off he liked to prepare dinner himself, wearing a white apron, his copy of an Escoffier cook book open at his elbow. A favorite late-night snack in which I joined him more than once was eggs scrambled in brandy washed down with white wine. He could tell a fine French wine's vintage year by its taste.

He never complained in my hearing of his heart trouble, never expressed any form of self-pity, but played ferociously competitive tennis with me and others, though limiting himself to two sets of singles. Though afraid he might drop dead at any moment, he was outwardly fearless, and I think his precarious health had much to do with his drive to live as fully and produce as much writing as possible. He was an eloquent advocate of sweating as a way to remove bodily poisons and refresh the spirit, loved games and sports of all kinds: poker, at which he was expert, chess, likewise, crossword puzzles, golf, Ping-Pong, croquet, football as spectator, and perhaps boxing above all because of his close affinity with it in youth during the golden age of the sport when the Irish with whom he identified strongly were producing most of the champions and when he boxed, or fought barefisted, in school yards or improvised rings. He first achieved distinction as a freshman at Berkeley by defeating the sophomore champion in a boxing match at the annual freshman-sophomore smoker (later achieving distinction as prolific contributor to all undergraduate publications and as hell-raiser and campus leader), and in later life he regularly watched fights in New York and Los Angeles and regularly read sports news of all kinds in the newspapers. He knew boxing backwards and forwards and could recreate famous fights blow by blow.

I once took him to Jim Jeffries's "Barn" in the San Fernando Valley and introduced him to the former world's heavyweight champion who ran a school there in a former hay-barn for young fighters and served beer when the fights were on. I'd just done a feature on Jeffries for my magazine. Faust and the old champion got along famously at first, beers in hand as they recalled famous fights from the past, until Faust began giving Jeffries a blow-by-blow recollection of his fight with the prominent challenger, Tom Sharkey, and they disagreed over whether Jeffries had broken Sharkey's ribs in the eighteenth round or the nineteenth. They nearly came to blows until I extricated Faust from the presence of the snarling Jeffries who was beginning to lead with his famous left.

At about this time I had one of the disappointments of my life when Faust invited me to lunch at 317 Burlingame Avenue with Aldous Huxley, then one of the world's most prominent literary figures, but I couldn't go because of a scheduled visit to Lockheed Aircraft for a story I was doing. When I asked what they had talked about at lunch, Faust said: "Everything under the sun." Not long afterward Huxley invited Faust and Dorothy for a weekend with him and his wife, Maria, at their hideaway cabin in the high Mojave Desert near Pearblossom for more talk. Faust did not admire Huxley's fiction or poetry or philosophical writing but thought him a fine conversationalist, and they shared a love of Italy where Huxley, too, had lived for a number of years and where they had first met. Besides having earlier days in common and also current ones at M-G-M, Faust and Huxley shared the same editor at Harper & Bros., Gene Saxton, highly regarded by them both and adding a further common bond.

Faust had an unusually close relationship with his literary agent, Carl Brandt of the New York firm of Brandt & Brandt. He'd gone to Brandt in 1925 at the recommendation of Stephen Vincent Benét, a poet, novelist, and short story writer who like Faust depended largely on popular magazines for his income. Brandt had kept Faust's work appearing steadily in a variety of magazines while placing his books with half a dozen publishers and helping him earn as much as a hundred thousand dollars a year, or a million by today's values. Brandt also played the role of friend and confidant, discussing Faust's personal life as well as literary business with him in long letters and conversations, loaning him money, arranging for him to work in a room near Brandt's office at 101 Park Avenue when he was in New York, and sending out monthly checks, often grudgingly, to the many dependents Faust supported. Brandt strongly opposed his working for the movies, fearing screenwriting would take so much of his time he would lose his magazine and book markets as well as damage his talent. During his Hollywood years Faust did publish less, perhaps proving Brandt right, though he did produce two of his best short stories, "Honor Bright" and "The King" as well as the Kildare stories.

In addition to Brandt he had a Los Angeles–based movie agent, Collier Young, later a producer, who handled his affairs at the various studios including Columbia and RKO as well as M-G-M and Warner Bros. He had a business manager for his personal and household affairs who allowed him thirty dollars a week spending money out of a weekly income of $1,250 and up—while the manager embezzled hundreds for himself. Faust gave me the impression not so much of being careless but simply not caring about money and of being overly trusting of people. I think that trust was not naiveté but part of his belief in human beings. He preferred to think of them the way he wanted to think of them rather than as they were.

After Jane and I were married, we made our home in the little town of Rio Vista on the lower Sacramento River in the great Central Valley of California where Faust had grown up. I worked on a ranch as he had once done. When he visited us in what was nearly his first visit to his home turf since leaving it to go to college and out into the world, it was coming full circle. Before reaching us, he had stopped in the Modesto-Stockton area to see relatives and old friends, and there had been much celebrating as the local boy who'd made good returned home. By the time he reached us his heart was acting up, and he was pale and shaky. He was being driven in the open Oldsmobile by his butler-chauffeur, Morris, because, though he liked to drive himself, he was a terrible driver. You would put your heart in your mouth when you rode with him as he traveled at the highest possible speed with the narrowest margins of safety, apparently oblivious to all hazards. Dorothy had insisted that Morris drive him, declaring she could no longer stand either his drinking or his driving. Morris, a Texas Negro about thirty, had a rich store of folklore about blacks and whites that Faust induced him to share and made notes of, whether they were at home or on trips. Morris knew how to take care of him and make him comfortable. When I took him out to the ranch where I worked and introduced him to the young cowboy I worked with, Dynamite Carter, about a foot shorter than Faust, blue eyed and so bowlegged you could have driven a half-grown hog between his legs, they had a spirited conversation while standing in the barn, Dynamite not the least intimidated. Faust told me afterward: "That's the kind of fellow I used to work with on ranches."

The trip became a nostalgic reprise for him in several ways. One morning, when I was driving him along the Sacramento River, we passed a peach orchard in bloom, and he remarked how the trees were putting forth after having been pruned back and added thoughtfully: "I was like that," apparently remembering his less than privileged youth in this same region. Though he sometimes denigrated the valley, in the end he returned to it enjoyably with some comments to Jane and me on the circularities his return and our living there represented and the importance of the circle as a mythological symbol. There is an exhibit of Faust memorabilia at the McHenry Museum in his hometown of Modesto, and many of his personal papers and books are not far away at the Bancroft Library at the University of California, Berkeley, where he was denied a degree because of perceived misconduct as an undergraduate.

From the outbreak of the Second World War he was hoping to become involved, and this feeling grew compelling after the Japanese bombed Pearl Harbor. Many, including Dorothy, his children, and I, tried to dissuade him, but he was adamant. He'd missed the First World War through no fault of his own. So now he was determined to become involved.

Faust's first plan was to be dropped by parachute into the wilds of Yugoslavia and join the guerrilla forces of Drza Mihailovich who was leading the resistance against the German invaders. Negotiations were begun through Brandt and others with the Yugoslav government in exile in London, but they fell through. Next he tried to accompany a convoy of U.S. cargo ships bound for Murmansk in northern Russia. When that too fell through, he fastened on the idea of writing a book about our infantry, then bogged in the bitter winter campaign of 1943–44 in Italy and taking much criticism for being ineffective. He decided he would accompany an infantry platoon in combat, go through an entire campaign with it, and then write a book that would be the inside story of the infantry in action. Nothing like it had been done. It would be his unique contribution to the war effort. Along the way he would send dispatches and letters home for publication. Arrangements were made through Brandt and Cass Canfield for him to be accredited as a correspondent for *Harper's Magazine* and *The Infantry Journal*. No mention was made of his bad heart. He left 317 Burlingame Avenue in late February, 1944, abandoning the house to Dorothy, Judy, Jane, and our small daughter, Joan, and our soon-to-be-born Katherine. Faust's son, John, was also on his way overseas, and I was to follow. He'd had a stormy relationship with John. He had wanted him to be a man of action as well as a thinker, a kind of cross between Achilles and Plato, while John, handicapped by poor health, insisted on being a thinker and had done well at Harvard and later became a Fulbright scholar. Now they would be united in wartime service.

"War is the greatest challenge a man can face," Faust told me. He wanted to test himself in this one, and he hated Nazism and all it stood for. He was, furthermore, tired of sitting on the sidelines, as he put it, while others fought the war, and tired of his screenwriting work which brought him as much as two thousand dollars a week but did not satisfy his soul. And he was weary of what he called the mess he had made of life and wanted to get away from it even, I think, though it might cost him his life.

Although he had published two books of poetry and posthumously would publish two more, and though he had recently published a distinguished short poem in *Harper's* titled "Distance" in which he addressed the isolation in which we are all fixed from the moment we are born, he felt himself a failure as poet and person, believing he had failed his muse as he had failed his wife and others. Dorothy had a premonition she would never see him again as they said good bye. He left behind those two fine stories, "Honor Bright" and "The King," that would be published after his death and a fine war novel, "After April," in which he transformed current events into fiction.

Unsure where he would be sent, he carried a letter of introduction from Richard Aldington to the British novelist-scientist, C. P. Snow, then deeply involved in war work in London. He also had a letter from Robert Lovett at the War Department in Washington to General Ira Eaker, commander of Allied forces in the Mediterranean, and this finally enabled him to return to his beloved Italy.

Our last meeting a few days before he left was rather unsatisfactory yet in a way typical. He was over an hour late for dinner because of having a few drinks with fellow writers after work at Warner Bros., and his face and gray suit were in more than usual disarray when he finally arrived home. Dinner was painful because of Dorothy's and Jane's disapproval of his yet-once-again rather sodden condition and because of my—I thought hidden—anger. I was home on my last leave and looking forward to what might be our last talk. After dinner, when the two of us were alone by the fire, he said: "You're angry with me, aren't you?" and asked my forgiveness, which I promptly gave, and then we had a good if somewhat restrained conversation, each thinking of what might lie ahead. Both of us were intending to write about the war if we lived through it. Unspoken was the thought that we might not. Nevertheless, I felt his all-embracing energy and optimism and generosity permeate me and all the room, like the rising tide that lifts all boats, and again for a moment it seemed that life *might* be eternal, and good talk and thought *might* be the food of the Deity. His last words were about his faith in me and my writing and in Jane's and my marriage.

From Algiers he flew to Naples and wrote home: "Suddenly we were over hills that were big and brown in the sun with curving terraces carved out of their sides, and I knew that for the first time in almost six years I was looking at Italy again, and it made my heart jump." From the front line, the so-called Gustav Line established by German Field Marshal Kesselring in the mountainous country north of Naples, he wrote of the GIs he was with, an untried unit composed entirely of draftees. "Dimly, but deeply, these men see that Hitlerism cannot be permitted to exist in the same world with our ideas, and, without passion, really without hate, they are willing to go out and die, doing the things their officers tell them to do. Of course the battle has yet to be fought, but I have a growing conviction that they will be real soldiers, and that I can write about them a book that their families and perhaps other Americans will be glad to read." When Lieutenant Herbert Wadopian, commanding the platoon he was with, tried to dissuade him from accompanying its leading squads in the big attack, he said: "I'm twice a grandfather and these men are just kids. They're not staying back. I guess, if they can take it, I can. I've lived a pretty full life. If it's my time to go tonight, I'm ready to go."

He was killed the night of May 11 while accompanying the foremost elements of our 88th Infantry Division uphill through minefields and barbed wire against the German-held strongpoint of Santa Maria Infante. A mortar shell fragment struck him in the chest. While he lay wounded, a sergeant bent over him and asked if he were all right. "I'm fine," he said, "take care of the others," motioning to wounded lying near. When the stretcher-bearers found him, he was dead.

The Battle of Santa Maria Infante lasted sixty hours and cost hundreds of American casualties, but it helped break the Gustav Line and led to the capture of Rome and the eventual liberation of all Faust's beloved Italy. His end epitomized his life for me as did the fact that either on his person when he died or in his duffel bag back in camp—we don't know which because, like nearly everything else he had with him, it was lost—was the manuscript of his unfinished epic poem about Prometheus, the titan who befriended humankind by giving us the gift of fire.

His death was first announced nationwide by the popular radio commentator, Walter Winchell, then by all major U.S. newspapers, followed by a photograph and story in *Time* and other magazines. A few weeks later his serial, "After April," a moving love story of the Second World War, began running in *The*

Saturday Evening Post under his true name. (At the time appearing in the weekly *Post* was rather like appearing on network television today.) His work has continued to be read widely in many languages as new books based on previously published magazine material or on newly discovered manuscripts continue to appear. They have brought his total to 227 or an average of a new book every four months for the past seventy-five years. Sparkling through them is that poetry he tried to put into poetic form but which came out best in the prose he belittled.

One night, not long after his death, he appeared to me in a dream wearing his long brown trench coat and saying solemnly: "Some day we'll know, old man, some day we'll know."

As I look back, what strikes me most about him are his enthusiasm for life and his generosity of spirit. It sometimes seems his life was mainly a projection of his imagination, a grand illusion. He had wanted to escape poverty and obscurity, and he did. He had wanted to marry the girl he fell in love with at first sight, and he did. He had wanted children and a family life, and he had them. He had wanted to live in Europe and particularly in Florence, and he did. He had wanted to return to Italy and did so. He had wanted to die and be buried there, and he did. He had wanted to die in battle, and he did. He had wanted to be remembered as a poet and I think someday he will be, though not the poet he had in mind but perhaps a greater one. For, if his work in its many genres be taken as a whole, it is like a giant Shakespearean play, intermingling poetry and prose, offering something for everyone from whatever walk of life or ethnic group or intellectual orientation. Most remarkable of all, perhaps, his life makes a better story than any he wrote.

FREDERICK FAUST, SOLDIER

Herbert Wadopian

Learning of Faust's death on the battlefield in 1944, longtime friend George "Dixie" Fish immediately began to seek details. One of his contacts, Lieutenant Herbert Wadopian, who had led his platoon and Faust into the heart of war, was himself wounded and, after recuperating from combat for a year or so, made good on his pledge to describe Faust's last days. The narrative that follows is from Wadopian's reply to Fish from Martigues, France, on July 24, 1945, in which he recalled images of the conflict as well as of Faust's personality.

He merely introduced himself as Mr. Faust of *Harper's* and let it go at that. He never mentioned his more famous *nom de plume*—at least not to me. He was "discovered" by someone—and I don't think he denied being a celebrity—but he certainly didn't capitalize on it either. In all, I think he was with us a total of four days—certainly not more—but they were certainly four long days—and I'll tell you why later.

Faust came to us one afternoon (it must have been the 7th of May) when we were in a reserve position just (about a thousand yards) back of the line. I remember it very well for I was sitting out in front of the farmhouse we were using for company headquarters, and I had a good view of the very exposed trail that led to the rear. So I was the first to spot the figure slowly moving along the trail to take cover against the expected barrage that movement along the trail usually brought and mentally prepared the "ass-chewing" I was going to give the soldier—whoever he was. The barrage, miraculously, never materialized—and just as miraculously neither did the "ass-chewing." I don't know what it was—the unsoldierly look perhaps—but I couldn't get the words out to tell him how unappreciated (at the moment) he was.

We were all, of course, quite flattered to hear that a war correspondent had decided to attach himself to us for a few days. Names in print in the papers back home are certainly welcome to combat soldiers—they always feel that they are on the short end of the deal as far as publicity is concerned. So he was received with open arms. Everyone knew at the time that we were about to jump off in a big attack, but no one knew what day it would come off, so we thought we would have a few days in which to tell this big fellow of all the heroics we had performed at Cassino or somewhere, and he would write our names in our hometown papers. But the "big fellow" was not a newspaper man—and more, he wasn't particularly interested in how many patrols we had been on or how many Krauts we had killed. No, all he wanted to do was just hang around and be one of the "boys" for a few days.

His first request of the C.O. was that he be allowed to bunk down with the platoon that was to be the spearhead of the attack—and from then on he was "my baby," for it was my platoon that was to jump off first. So he came to live in my "hole"—portable typewriter and all.

That first afternoon I questioned him as to what he had been doing, and I learned that he had just come over from the States and had only been around for a coupla weeks—and most of that time had been spent with Company L of the same regiment (351st Infantry, 88th Infantry Division) which was just a bit over to our right. He spoke glowingly of Company L. He had grown quite fond of several of the men in Company L and planned to rejoin them in a few days after the attack jumped off. He was anxious to get out and meet my men and to get a picture of them before the attack, so that he would have something to compare them with during and after the attack.

I'm afraid I'll have to admit that Faust had a screwy conception of a battle—and no amount of talking could convince him that it was not like the movie versions, with long sweeping waves of men rushing out to meet the enemy. I tried to tell him that it was more like trying to watch a couple of moles fighting, as it was mostly all done on your belly. But he wanted to meet them anyway—and I took him around to each one of them—or rather I had them come to him. He seated himself on a log and put his portable on his knees and, looking over his shoulders, I could see that he put down the man's name and age, the job he did in the platoon and then a few notes about his appearance, his civilian back-ground, etc. Then, as each man left, Faust would turn to me and ask what kind of a soldier he was. For some reason he was particularly interested in the "bad" boys and asked for complete details in their criminal records—and he marked the name of each boy that I told him was a trouble-maker or a "no good from 'way back."

The evening in the company command post was quite a lively one with Faust around. We had five officers in the company and, as soon as it was dark, we would all gather at the command post for the evening's bull session. In the time we had been together we had talked about every subject we could dig an ar-gument out of, so the addition of "fresh meat" was welcome tonic to our discussions. Faust was a difficult man to argue with—he just knew too damn much about too many things. He fast became the company judge of all things in dispute, because he seemed to have the ready answer for the most difficult of questions. So it didn't take many nights for our bull-sessions to become lecture periods—with Faust doing the lecturing. I can't say that they were the most enjoyable lectures I've heard—for the circumstances were not amenable to enjoyment—but they are highly prized moments of my life.

The next morning we were briefed on the coming attack and were told the part we were to play. Everything was set—we were told everything except the day and hour of the attack. We knew, though, that we would have at least twenty-four hours to prepare, so we made the most of it. With a copy of the battle map Faust and I went up to the observation post on the line, and we spent several hours with the glasses while I picked out the route I planned to follow. It was, I believe, Faust's first time in an observation post, and he plied the Intelligence man on duty with many questions. He had a chance to see a few barrages being laid down whenever Jerry showed himself—and I laughingly reminded him of the time he had first come up to our company and had made himself a target—but I don't think he appreciated the humor of it.

The next days dragged themselves into nights, and we became jittery as we usually did before something big. It suddenly occurred to me that Faust was not making mention of going back to the rear where he belonged, and I asked him when he planned on going to the rear.

"I'm not going to the rear, Lieutenant, I'm going with you," he said simply—and I blew up. There was absolutely no good reason for a man of his age to be trying to keep up with a bunch of men the oldest of whom was half his age. I told him again and again that he could not see anything from that far forward—that, if he wanted to watch the attack, the best place would be at the observation post or on some other high hill—I brought up every argument that I could think of—and he still insisted on going. So I finally gave him a reluctant okay to come along. His most convincing argument was that he just *had* to go along, so that he could get the feel of being in battle—the feel of being shot at—the feel of hurting or being hurt. He said he couldn't write about these things unless he had really experienced them—so he talked me out of sending him back. I felt that, if I had said no, he would have gotten permission from some other officer—so, since I liked him, I might as well have him with me.

Then came the argument as to which element of the platoon he would ac-company. Actually, with a platoon it doesn't make a helluva lot of difference whether you are with the lead man or the tail man—for you all catch plenty of hell—but the law of averages gives the tail man a better chance than the lead man, so I insisted that he follow behind the platoon guide who brings up the rear—and this was very distasteful to Faust. He would have no other position than right behind the lead scout—and we had quite a battle on that point. We finally came to terms, and he allowed me to place him with the guide on the grounds that he might not get in the way—that was one argument he could not dispute!

One of the sergeants asked him one day if he wanted an arm—he could have his choice: pistol, rifle, or tommy-gun. I knew, of course, that the Geneva Convention wouldn't permit it, but I was greatly amused by Faust's reply. He told the sergeant that he would indeed like to take a shot or two at the enemy, but he was sure that, if he got close enough to Jerry to accurately shoot him, he'd be so close that a club would do the job. The sergeant thought that was funny, too—and the next morning he presented Faust with a cudgel that could be used to help in hiking up the hills—and Faust was deeply touched and told the boy so. The club was wrapped in adhesive tape on which someone had scribbled: "From the boys of Company E to Mr. Faust." It was the company joke for a day.

The night of May 11 was "it." The word was passed around just before dark that 2300 hours would be "H" hour, so we used the twilight hours to roll our packs, pick up our issue of atabrine, halazone, "D" and "K" rations, and get ready to take off. After dark we lay around and talked in whispers, trying to draw as much comfort as possible out of the fellow next to you—and I'll say now that I was fortunate in having a man like Faust around. He moved about, talking to the boys, and you could hear little ripples of laughter that followed his movement. He himself was as calm and collected as if it were a Sunday school picnic, and the men and I drew much courage from him.

The last cigarette time was up at 2045, for it was a fifteen-minute hike to the line of departure. This line (an imaginary line in front of which you set your jump-off) was about 300 yards north of the town of Minturno—and we were to head for the town of Santa Maria Infante with that stronghold as our immediate objective. We reached the line of departure precisely at 2300 and, as planned, all hell broke loose. In all my months of combat I had never seen a barrage like the one that we laid down that night—it was a continuous roar for thirty minutes that shook us almost as much as it must have shaken Jerry.

We followed closely behind the barrage to take advantage of the confusion it was causing, and things were going wonderfully well—until we reached the outskirts of Santa Maria—then Jerry started giving it to us. And it seemed to me that he gave us as much as we had given him, plus interest. Naturally, we were having casualties, and it wasn't long before we were pretty well disorganized and rather decimated. I halted the platoon for a moment to try to reorganize it, and of the forty-one men I had started out with I could find only twelve—and among the twelve was Faust. He was breathing very heavily and, though it was black night and I couldn't see him, I sensed that there was something wrong with him. I asked him if he had been hit, and he said he thought he had been hit in the chest because he felt rather numb there, and it was getting hard to breathe. I told him to lie down and take it easy as the medics were coming up right behind us, and they would take care of him, and I left him there as I returned to continue the attack.

I heard nothing more of him for several days, for after leaving him we fought our way into the town and were cut off for two days—then on the third day I picked up a couple of pieces myself and was taken to a hospital. I was a couple of beds away from Associated Pressman George Tucker and through him I learned that they had picked up Faust's body near Santa Maria and were burying him in the cemetery across the road from the hospital that day. I told Tucker to pay my respects to Faust for I was indeed sorry to see him go.

I am not sure whether Faust was killed by the shrapnel that he had been hit with when I last saw him or whether he was hit again later—for there was a terrific barrage laid down in the area after I left. The day and hour was, as close as I can figure, 0030 of 12 May 1944.

I hope that this letter answers the questions you've had in mind. If not, please don't hesitate to write me and ask them. I will answer them to the best of my ability—it's the least I can do for Frederick Faust, Soldier.

A HERO'S DEATH: NEW FACTS ON THE LAST HOURS OF FREDERICK FAUST

William F. Nolan

The ending of Frederick Faust's life could have been written by Max Brand. Like many other pulp stories, it was an awakening to heroic action and the facing of mortal danger beyond the call of necessity. That his death took place in the Italy he loved seems almost a poetic touch to the event, perhaps even the way that Hollywood would have chosen to portray it.

William A. Bloodworth, Jr.

A full half-century has passed since the death of Max Brand on a shell-pocked Italian hillside in May, 1944. On that fateful night, when war correspondent Faust charged forth with U.S. assault troops in the opening battle of the Italian Campaign against Hitler's "impenetrable" Gustav Line, enemy defenses were at their strongest. On the summit of the rocky high ground surrounding the village of Santa Maria Infante, not far north of Naples, the Germans were deeply entrenched behind mine fields and barbed wire, protected by heavy concrete pillboxes and grimly determined to halt the Allied advance. That decisive sixty-hour battle was one of the bloodiest of World War II.

There have been several published accounts of this fierce assault, and of Faust's part in it. We know that in the heat of action he was struck in the chest by a shell fragment. When the litter bearers started to carry him back to the line for medical treatment, he waved them away. "Those other wounded boys need help more than I do. Take them!" They did—and by the time they were able to get back to him, Faust was dead.

His unarmed charge into battle and his selfless act while lying wounded on the field are more than enough to establish his heroic credentials, but only now, all these long decades later, does the full story of his heroism emerge . . . from a freshly-discovered account by Arthur D. Posa who was there. That night, in May of '44, Posa was a sergeant with the U.S. Army's 88th Infantry Division. He had read several Max Brand books before the war and felt "honored" to meet Faust in person (who admitted he was Brand) just prior to the attack. "I warned him that it would be safer if he stayed close to the machine gunners, that they would be providing covering fire. He thanked me and said he'd do as I suggested." Posa lost track of Faust in the bloody conflict that followed, but after it finally ended he located a soldier who had been near Faust during the battle.

"He went with us in the first attack wave," the soldier told Posa. "But we didn't get very far before Jerry began pounding at us like crazy. Our regiment was pinned at the base of the slope under a killing mortar barrage, and I was laying down covering fire with my BAR [Browning Automatic Rifle]. Running low on ammo, I eased up and that was when I saw that Faust was wounded and bleeding. He was breathing hard. I told him to go back for medical aid, but he refused. 'You need more ammo,' he said, 'and I know where to get it.' Then he took off."

Despite his chest wound, Faust crawled out under a hail of enemy fire to some slain soldiers on the hill, taking bandoliers of ammunition from their bodies. Then he inched back to the BAR man. "I'll load. You keep firing," he said. "He stayed right next to me," the soldier said to Posa. "Kept loading and I kept shooting. Because of him, I was able to stay alive. I'll never forget him. He was a very brave man."

With this decisive battle won, the Fifth Army pushed on, city by city, village by village, up the long boot of Italy. Ironically, had Faust lived, he would have seen U.S. troops liberate his beloved villa in the hills above Florence as part of this same campaign.

Surely, though, he was there in spirit.

LETTERS OF ROBERT AND JANE EASTON FROM *LOVE AND WAR*

The letters that follow are taken from LOVE AND WAR: PEARL HARBOR THROUGH V-J DAY (University of Oklahoma Press, 1991) by Robert and Jane Easton. Married on September 24, 1940, when they were both very young, their marriage prospered through the years, an enduring romance of which Max Brand might dream but of which Frederick Faust himself was not able really to achieve in his own life. In large measure it has been due to the Eastons' belief in Frederick Faust's remarkable talent and their determination to heighten our awareness of it that so much of his considerable literary estate has been preserved to enrich new generations of readers.

Los Angeles
April 29, 1944
Dear sweet Mum gets so upset by little things, such as the letter from Pop yesterday. He is on the Italian front, having a fascinating time, he says, but barely mentioned he loved her and missed her and didn't make enough fuss over her so she was depressed and full of self-pity and suspicion that he had picked up some great love while she slaves away with numerous household details and dozens of grandchildren.

Women are odd creatures. One of the first rules all men should understand is that wives never take it for granted they are loved or adored; they insist on being told over and over. I am no better than the rest. I should expect the same from you, only you always tell me what I want to hear. If you didn't, I should mope as Mum did yesterday.

Of course, she's sure Pop will be killed any day. She is pathetic. I scarcely know what to say, and I do not feel that I can say: "I know what you are suffering." I do not think anyone can understand fully until one's own husband is in it too.

I have that ahead of me. But dear Mum is a mixture of going to pieces and being very brave. I have tried to make her laugh as much as possible and not let her become morbid, or be alone too much. She will go off this afternoon to "the farm," as she calls the vacant lot on Amalfi Drive, and the sunshine there helps as much as any words a human being can say.

I keep my thoughts on Pop a good deal too. But he is not my husband, and the difference is something incredible. No two human beings can ever be as close as man and wife, not a mother and child even. I fully see that now. I hope I shall be able to take the days serenely when you are in combat. Mum dreams of Pop at night and imagines he's calling for her. Oh God, how terrible is this war! Anyway, no matter what happens, if anything should, Pop will be happy, and he will go as he wanted to. How much better than a heart attack after a drinking bout! Mum realizes all this too.

Kentucky
May 16, 1944, Tuesday

I was in the orderly room when your telegram came. Connell said this morning he heard Winchell say something Sunday night about Pop's being wounded. So, when I saw the telegram, I guessed the truth. We don't get the metropolitan dailies, but I understand they've been carrying the news. Naturally, I called right away, inadequate as such calls are, but I wanted to hear your voice and you to hear mine.

You've been in my thoughts all day. The shock wears off me when I work. I only wish it were the same with you and Mum. Make it so if you can.

There is nothing, my heart tells me, that would please him more than to have us all busy and productive. As the good news comes from Italy, somehow I take it as *his* victory, and in a very real way it is and will be all our lives.

I cannot in the deepest sense feel badly. He died for a great cause, a cause he believed in. He said Hitlerism could not exist in the same world with our ideas. God, but my heart breaks with the loss, though. He had so much to give, always to give, and the world is so hungry.

Los Angeles
May 17, 1944, Wednesday

Now I know death is not final. I cannot believe Pop isn't very close to us all. We must try and live by and with the ideals he stood for. It is a large task, but we can stretch ourselves for his sake.

I am so thankful for so much: that he knew and loved my husband, that he saw his John become a fine man, that Judy came through the hard period with flying colors, that he held and adored his first grandchild. I am thankful that he died in the land which meant most to him, that it was a quick, clean death, surrounded by the lovely Italian hills and with the young men near him he admired. I can fairly see him as he must have been. I am thankful it was May which is always a lovely month, and the month of his wedding and birth. He had lived a rich, full life, Bob, and he was happy during a great deal of it. Now that there are only the good and beautiful things left of him, there is a kind of peace for us to grasp and understand and through which we may see him even more clearly.

This house is a mad rush. The telephone hasn't stopped ringing since Daddy's death was announced yesterday morning. It seems weeks ago, heavy weeks laden with a million things and a million words and thoughts intertwined. Telegrams and flowers keep pouring in. People come and go all day, and there are little children to look after and keep on schedule. I go about doing all I can, yet it seems so very little. I am not tired. I am very lonely in my deepest heart. There is only you now, darling. I felt that you and Pop stood for the same things and how rich I was to have you both. Now there is only you. The blow is lessened because you are strong and wise and you love and believe in the things he did. I cannot tell you how much this means to me. Thank God for giving you to us, to me especially.

Mother is wonderful and brave and terribly sad. There is little or nothing to say to her. She sees clearly that he died in the best way and that there are so many blessings to be thankful for. She talks of him constantly; she looks very beautiful; she is very weak in her body and very strong in her spirit. The first days will be totally unreal. Gradually she will feel worse, I think, before she can feel better. She says I must stay here with the children as long as you are away. It is the only thing to do. I do not know how I feel about it; I am too tired tonight to think much. But she wants me and clings to me, so I must just do what I can, small as it is.

There is no real comfort for her because a husband and wife are so close, the closest of all, and hers is taken away. There must forever be great voids in her. I'm glad the children are so fresh and lovely and such a joy to her and to us all. The terrible part is the little things; I cannot look at Katherine's tiny helplessness and realize that my dear, dear father never saw her. I don't even know whether he knew of her birth. When I see Joan and think of all the years that he would have adored her, it breaks my heart! He had so many happy days to come. But is it ever time for death? Who can say: "Yes, now I've had all I want from life!" He wanted so badly to live on a ranch near us and have hours in which to talk to you.

People from all over the country have volunteered to help in any way they can. Their kindness and love is incredible. Renzo, who feels he has lost his father and best friend, has done the marketing and fetched Mum's sedatives, and watered the garden. Aidan has come each evening after work and has written us such beautiful letters. Pinkey has been up too.

Everyone is utterly broken and incredibly sad and the loss hits us all. We are drawn together now. Sorrow is a purifier. I have had so little of it in my life that I'm trying to rise and feel the inner beauty of it. I keep seeing Daddy in such living moments, standing before the fireplace reading Shakespeare aloud to us . . . in his chair in the big room with a beer in hand . . . bending over the flowers in the garden he planted . . . all such recollections are very alive and precious. I would give anything in the world to be with you, but I am here where Mum needs me. Will you get a leave? I cannot face the fact that you may go over without my having a glimpse of you. And how terribly short a leave is! But I can't come to you now, not for months, and then I'm afraid you will be gone.

Judy comes tomorrow morning for a few days. We may have a memorial service in a little church Daddy liked, in Westwood. Everything seems vague and hard to plan. An hour seems a year. I have not said half of what I wanted to—but I must get to bed. I am strong, darling, but terribly tired now from a million little things. I have to take a sleeping pill these nights as I cannot quite let go enough to sleep.

Kentucky
May 20, 1944

Your letter nearly broke my heart but filled me right up again with pride and joy, that you are such a woman. I know Pop would be proud of you. He loved you, as you know, more than anything else on earth. These last days he has been closer to me than ever before. "How anyone so great could die?" is the question I keep asking myself. And the answer comes: "He did not die. Great things don't die unless we let them."

One point in your letter, Janie, I cannot agree with is the making of decisions now about the future. You see, we are all grief-stricken; we have lost something very precious and, when one has done that, one instantly strives to repossess what remains, to go back in memories, to cherish a house, a book, a certain bed of flowers, because it was beloved by the person who is gone. This is not right, however natural. Therefore let's not be too hasty in deciding that you and the babies will stay with Mum at 317 Burlingame Avenue indefinitely. Just now it seems right. I doubt this will be true later. Because Pop once lived there, because we knew him there, would he want us to go on living backward, so to speak, cherishing memories for years and years, making a memorial of a mere place, rather than go out as he was forever showing us how to do, and *live*! What is Mum to do for thirty years or more? Live on and help raise a second family in that house? I think she will not, in the end, want to.

I'm not suggesting you depart tomorrow for Santa Barbara, but I strongly suggest that sometime you do. You will know when it is best. I should not even mention it now. I should give Mum every care and con-

sideration, until the tide of this backward cherishing has ebbed, as it will—
and as we must make it ebb.

I wish I were there to help you carry the load. Regardless of any other
desires the well-being of Mum does come first; but I want it to be a true
well-being. To be that, plans for it must be laid now, with a long range
in view.

All my love again.

Los Angeles
May 21, 1944, Sunday Evening

I weep for Judy in my heart. Her loss is very great, because she is
sixteen and these are hard years, and she depended so on Pop (as we all
did as children) to guide her. She is wonderfully brave and has wept so
little and has not thought of herself at all. I am sending you her two letters
to Mum which she wrote from school because they are absolutely beautiful, and they will show you what a person she is, how mature.

Mother is very weepy and yet very wonderful, and I do admire her. I
don't think any of us realize Daddy is dead. That is the point, it's still
numbing. I am in a daze and we are all very tired. We've had days and
days of people and telephones and a million things to plan and decide.
I've been harassed because Joan caught a cold and decided that I was the
only person she wanted around her! It is very difficult to cope with a sick
child. However, she's better tonight, and the nurse is back to look after
Katherine, so we should get a little rest now.

When I see you I'll tell you about the memorial service. Many thoughts
occurred to me while we sat there. I scarcely could look at Mum. Her
face was beautiful with grief, and so moving and young. I hope we children and the grandchildren can make her feel that life still holds many
happy moments. I try to imagine what it would be like for me with you
gone. I've lived with that possibility in mind ever since we were married
(for we knew then that war was coming to us eventually, and I always
knew you'd go). I have thought about it from every angle. Daddy's death
makes me sure that death is not final. He seems so near to us, and I know
that I should feel even nearer you.

We will have to cut down here a lot, and I must give Mum a hundred
a month when we live on here (we, is me and the babes). Oh, I must see
you to talk it all over with. I shall start getting a ticket tomorrow for June
22nd. I hope to heavens you will still be there then! Judy thinks I should
go to you by all means. She says ''husbands always count first.'' I know
she's right. But because that is what I want to do I have a feeling I may
be shirking here. Your parents are also eager that I go.

Good night. I am tired. Sweet Judy is in her bed beside me. She is
absolutely tremendous. I think she is of Daddy's caliber. I love her very
much, and I want to make this summer a gay and happy time for her. I

have you, darling, but she has no husband. I wonder if I could ever have stood losing Pop at her age. I shudder to think what she is going through so bravely.

Bless you, my love. We go the road alone now. What a loss Daddy is, but I think he is happy.

RITORNO

Adriana Faust Bianchi

Adriana Faust Bianchi, the only daughter of Faust's youngest child, Judith, has spent much of her life in Italy, the only one of Faust's grandchildren to do so and to live in his beloved city of Florence. This proximity to the Villa negli Ulivi was to her advantage in the reminiscence that follows. She knew neither of her maternal grandparents when they were alive.

December, 1995

I often found myself trying to remember what and how I felt the day I visited Villa negli Ulivi long ago with Mamma Judy. It was a good twenty years ago, and I must've been about ten years old, if that. We entered the main gates of the property, and there was the grand villa, unfortunately closed to the public that day. Since the 1950s the villa has been an Olivetti property and is used as a school at the university level. Being a beautiful summer day, we asked a gardener if we could walk through the garden and, even though he looked rather suspiciously at us, he eventually uttered a "Yes." Naturally Mum didn't tell him she'd lived there as a child, as I think she felt a certain embarrassment at having had such a privileged childhood, compared to most other people.

I didn't quite believe she'd *really* lived there myself, and I was trying to understand why on earth we weren't *still* living there! As we walked, Mum was chatting non-stop to me, trying to make me enthusiastic about our visit, but I was very busy thinking how awfully unfair life was in the changes it brought. Somehow, just looking at the old beautiful photos hadn't been enough to make Mum's childhood real to me and seeing it all in front of me for the first time made me ask Mum if by any chance Lord Arthur Acton wouldn't simply be thrilled at the idea of renting the house to *us*! "Oh, darling, how funny you are," was the only reply I got as we drifted along that beautiful garden. By this time Mum was bouncing away so much at ease that it seemed as if she'd lived there up to the day before. All of a sudden I had the feeling that she wasn't really walking beside me in the 1970s but with God knows who in the 1930s.

Even if I was rather impressed by Mum's familiarity with the gorgeous garden, I still felt that the whole situation was too tragic for words until my attention was finally taken when we arrived at the empty D-shaped swimming pool. "Pop had it made in a D-shape in honor of Mum who was called Dorothy," Mamma Judy said. Now, this was romantic and, when we actually walked through it, I thought the visit wasn't that bad after all . . . you simply don't walk through empty pools every day! We had many photos at home of Mum, Aunt Jane, and Uncle John jumping in with their long legs and funny swimming suits and with their lovely big patient dog waiting "on land."

Mum's expression changed and her eyes flashed as she'd spotted some lovely tomato plants that had evidently been very jealously cared for by some nice, old *contadino* as they were full of juicy red tomatoes: "Rumble"—that, alas, was the unfortunate nickname she'd given me—"look, let's take some tomatoes home with us!" I barely had time to say, "Mamma," in as shocked a voice as I could manage than off she went, scrambled up the hill, gently took the tomatoes with her saintly expression that she was so good at putting on when up to mischief and then, giggling away, she started running full speed back to the villa. I certainly had never seen *that* side of Mum before, but I'm sure she'd done it hundreds of times as a child.

That is as much as I remember of that long-ago visit, but I did feel the urge to go back the other day. I thought that maybe at thirty my impressions would be a little less materialistic (I was wrong!!), and I was also very curious to see the inside of the villa. Not wanting to have anything to do with the suspicious gardener again, I phoned beforehand and talked to a nice Mr. Rapaccini, manager of the Olivetti School at the villa. He was very curious, I think, to meet a relative of the man who maybe is the symbol of the villa, having added on many parts to the original building and having lived there for so many years.

Needless to say I was a little scared about my own visit to the Villa negli Ulivi. I knew that all kinds of emotions would go through me, but being sure that, after all, they'd be positive ones, I was very keen to begin the experience, and I arrived at the appointment a good half hour early. I parked my car (especially cleaned for the occasion!) beside at least another ten in the graveled parking place which was carefully indicated by at least three ugly parking signs. The old garage is still standing, and I tried to imagine the beautiful DeSoto and Isotta-Franschini convertible standing there.

I walked toward the villa and rang the bell of a beautiful iron and glass door and entered the hall. I stopped aghast as straight ahead of me stood Coca-Cola, coffee, and snack machines. I quickly closed my eyes in disgust, nearly ran over a poor little student, and entered the secretary's office which once must have been the sitting room. I asked for Mr. Rapaccini and started studying the room. One could still appreciate its beauty even if partially ruined by all the files, phones, desks, and computers. A prefabricated wall had been erected to make the huge room into two smaller ones. I'm sure that, if the room could, it would be shouting: "Please give me back my original glory. I don't like all this confusion!"

Mr. Rapaccini arrived: "So, you are Mister Faust's granddaughter . . . come, this must've been him!" We walked up to a marble column in the entry hall and there, still very visible, were black marks all the way up. I recognized them immediately as the marks Grandfather had made to measure the children because my mother used the same technique, and our house was always full of dots all over the walls! I would've loved to have stared at the column all day long, but Mr. Rapaccini was already asking me what in particular I'd like to see. "Well, everything please!" was my quick reply. So off we went through the old kitchens, the old courtyard where they ate in the summer, now covered and turned into an office, the lovely old music room, and the fifteenth-century dining room. We climbed the beautiful stone staircase leading up to the old bedrooms which now seemed all the same as they'd become classrooms and offices. Files and people smoking all over the place, and all I kept thinking was how could I possibly get any kind of special feeling from all these impersonal rooms. I was beginning to feel a little disappointed when we started climbing a lovely wooden staircase, and, once we reached the top and looked into the room, I held my breath. It was miraculously empty of people; it had no ugly files, machines, or smoke but had been left in peace as a quiet studying room. The bookcases are still there, the fireplace, the huge windows overlooking beautiful Florence, and a grand wooden table. Granddad's study had managed to keep its own special dignity, and I could almost see him sitting there with his typewriter, writing away at all times of the day. I tried to picture Aunt Jane and my grandmother reading aloud until he feel asleep, exhausted.

Looking out of the enormous windows onto the olive trees, vineyards, and Florence, I had the incredible wish to see it as he saw it all those years ago. The countryside must've been so much more green and without the dozens of modern buildings that had popped up after World War II. I would even have adored being a fly for one day to see what a typical day was like for my family, hear their voices, their steps, their laughter. But we don't have the gift to go back in time, so of course I didn't see him, but I certainly *felt* him there. That study was probably the place he loved most, and I'm sure that I'm not the only one to feel there is something special about it. The fact that the room was left intact must mean that a great person, as he was, has the capacity to lend a kind of unique and respectful atmosphere to a place, and that is what he'd done. You simply *can't* ruin a room like that! I was tempted to ask Mr. Rapaccini if I could sit there a few hours and write this piece. I felt a sudden urge to write everything down, but courage failed me, and I'm still kicking myself for it! Seeing that room made me feel much more light hearted, and I didn't really care too much any more if the rest of the house didn't give out any feeling about who'd lived there so long ago. It's inevitable nowadays for a big house to lose part of its personality by turning it into a school or what else . . . but in any case much better than seeing it tumbling down. The study has survived miraculously and that seems enough to me.

Descending the stairs I heard a few creaking sounds from the steps, and I immediately remembered a story of how Mum, with her old friend, Francesca, would love creeping up the steps, trying to spy on Granddad. The creaking sounds would give them away, and a thunderous and deep voice would say: ''Who's there?!'' At that the girls would fly down the staircase again and hide in the camphor-smelling closets just under the study. I felt like looking in the closets to check if they still smelled of camphor, but I was sure Mr. Rapaccini would think I was completely batty.

Preferring to walk through the garden by myself, I thanked the manager and slowly started toward my old friend, the pool. Some of the rose bushes by the house are still there, the cypresses on the path that had been planted back then are now nice and tall, and I even found a little pond where once Mum had been caught, at the charming age of three to six, cutting up a poor live little red fish. When the horrified baby-sitter found her and screamed—''Judy, what are you doing?''—Mum looked up and without changing expression said: ''Chat up, Kitty.'' I loved that story and often asked Mum to tell it to me.

Walking, I felt that everything was precious to me there, even the smallest of stones on which I kept slipping, risking my neck a few times! In front of me, at the bottom of the hill, was the pool, still very empty and with a few more cracks but still beautiful to me. I looked up the hill, but I didn't manage to spot the poor tomato plant which probably had never recovered from that far-away summer.

I wished very much that Aunt Jane could've been there with me, but I definitely didn't feel alone, and I could honestly have stayed for hours. I peeped around some bushes and found the tennis court with a net still hanging, all broken . . . I could once again easily have given a few years of my life to be able to go back in time!

The gardeners are keeping the grounds as tidy as possible and, even though it's not as perfect as it was, I'm sure that my grandparents are happy with what the villa is being used for. Granddad would've loved the idea of students living there, I'm sure.

Faust with his mother, Elizabeth Uriel Faust, in Seattle, 1892.

Staff of *The Occident*, University of California, Berkeley, 1915. Faust back row center.

Dorothy Schillig Faust, New York, 1918.

Frederick Faust in army fatigues at Camp Humphries, Virginia, 1918.

Faust with Jane and John in 1923 at 340 West 86th Street, New York.

In September 1924, the Faust family moved to this house, owned by playwright Clyde Fitch, situated on a 200-acre estate at Katonah, New York.

Faust with his favorite bull terrier, Tige, at the Villa Pazzi, Florence, 1926.

The lane leading from the pool and tennis court through the garden at Villa negli Ulivi, 83 Via dei Bruni, Florence.

The swimming pool and dressing room at Villa negli Ulivi when Faust lived there.

Faust's study at Villa negli Ulivi.

HORSE (Bones)

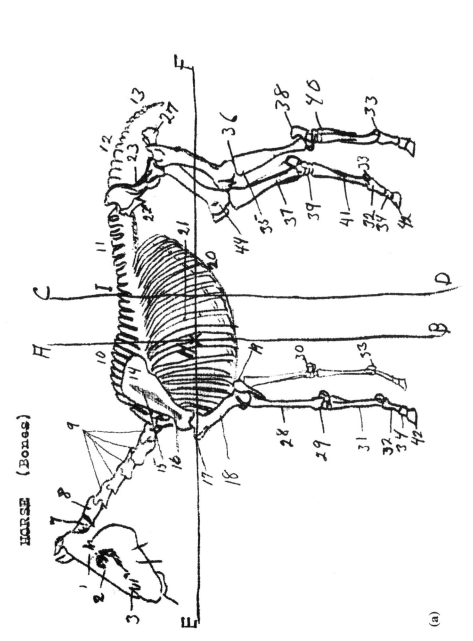

Faust's detailed drawings of the skeleton (a) and hoof (b) of a horse.

(a)

(a)   HORSE (Bones, 1)

1. zygomatic arch
2. eye cavity
3. face bones
4. incisor teeth
5. molar teeth
6. lower jaw
7. Atlas (1st vert. of neck)
8. Axis (2nd " ")
9. cervical vertebrae (5)
10. spinal processes of back
11. dorsal & lumbar vertebrae
12. sacrum
13. tail bones
14. shoulder blades
15. acromion process
16. hollow shoulder (tendon)
17. upper end of arm bone or
18.   humerus

33. sesamoid bone
34. small pastern "
35. upper end of leg
36. stifle joint
37. leg bone or tibia
38. point of hock
39. hock joint
40. long of ... or astragalus bone
41. cannon or metatarsal bone
42. coffin bone
43. fetlock joint
44. pastern or stifle bone
45. fibula

19. elbow bone
20. cartilages of ribs
21. ribs
22. haunch
23. haunch...trochanter
24. great trochanter
25. knuckle "
26. thigh bone
27. ischium
28. radius or fore arm bone
29. carpal : three bones
30 Trapezium
31 cannon bone "
32 pastern "

(b)

A = wall or crust
B = sole
C = frog
D = The sensitive sole
e = coronary band
f = sensitive frog
g = small or lower pastern bone
H = great or upper "   "   "
J = flexor tendon
K = coffin bone

L = sensitive laminae
LL = Insensitive "
M = Inferior sesamoid ligament
N = extensor tendon
O = coffin bone

Two line drawings from Street & Smith's *Western Story Magazine* of popular authors Max Brand and George Owen Baxter (both Faust pseudonyms).

MAX BRAND

GEORGE OWEN BAXTER

Faust takes a noontime break with Jane and her dog, Beppina, at Villa negli Ulivi, 1931.

The Faust family (l. to r. Faust, Dorothy, Jane, John, and Judith in the foreground) at Bedford Cottage, Katonah, New York, 1933.

Faust in the rear garden at 317 Burlingame Avenue, Los Angeles, 1940.

Faust and his daughter Judith at the horse races at Santa Anita, 1942.

Frederick Faust holding his first granddaughter, Joan Easton, 1943. This was the last photograph taken of him.

IN GRATEFUL MEMORY OF

𝔐𝔯. 𝔉𝔯𝔢𝔡𝔢𝔯𝔦𝔠𝔨 𝔉𝔞𝔲𝔰𝔱,

WHO DIED IN THE SERVICE OF HIS COUNTRY ~~AT~~

𝔦𝔫 𝔱𝔥𝔢 𝔐𝔢𝔡𝔦𝔱𝔢𝔯𝔯𝔞𝔫𝔢𝔞𝔫 𝔄𝔯𝔢𝔞, 𝔐𝔞𝔶 12, 1944.

HE STANDS IN THE UNBROKEN LINE OF PATRIOTS WHO HAVE DARED TO DIE

THAT FREEDOM MIGHT LIVE, AND GROW, AND INCREASE ITS BLESSINGS.

FREEDOM LIVES, AND THROUGH IT, HE LIVES—

IN A WAY THAT HUMBLES THE UNDERTAKINGS OF MOST MEN

Franklin D. Roosevelt

PRESIDENT OF THE UNITED STATES OF AMERICA

A commendation, signed by President Franklin D. Roosevelt, upon the occasion of Frederick Faust's receiving the Purple Heart for "military merit and for wounds received in action."

THE UNITED STATES OF AMERICA

TO ALL WHO SHALL SEE THESE PRESENTS, GREETING:

THIS IS TO CERTIFY THAT

**THE PRESIDENT OF THE UNITED STATES OF AMERICA
PURSUANT TO AUTHORITY VESTED IN HIM BY CONGRESS
HAS AWARDED THE**

PURPLE HEART

ESTABLISHED BY GENERAL GEORGE WASHINGTON
AT NEWBURGH, NEW YORK, AUGUST 7, 1782

TO

Mr. Frederick Faust,

FOR MILITARY MERIT AND FOR WOUNDS RECEIVED
IN ACTION

resulting in his death May 12, 1944.

GIVEN UNDER MY HAND IN THE CITY OF WASHINGTON
THIS   5th   DAY OF   February   19 45

OFFICIAL:

_____
THE ADJUTANT GENERAL

_____
SECRETARY OF WAR

BIBLIOGRAPHIES

FREDERICK FAUST: A BIBLIOGRAPHY

The first attempt to produce a bibliography of the published works of Frederick Faust was compiled by Darrell C. Richardson, appearing in his book, MAX BRAND: THE MAN AND HIS WORK (Fantasy Publishing, 1952). The following bibliography is an expansion of the Richardson bibliography and has been significantly augmented by the unpublished indexes prepared by William J. Clark, Robert Easton's bibliography in his MAX BRAND: THE BIG "WESTERNER" (University of Oklahoma Press, 1970), William F. Nolan's bibliography in his MAX BRAND: WESTERN GIANT (Bowling Green University Popular Press, 1985), the accumulated sales slips of Brandt & Brandt Literary Agency, and the combined copyright and assignment records from all magazine and book publishers of the works of Frederick Faust subsequently assembled by and in possession of Golden West Literary Agency.

Pen names used professionally by Frederick Faust are given as Austin (Frank Austin), Baxter (George Owen Baxter), Bolt (Lee Bolt), Brand (Max Brand), Butler (Walter C. Butler), Challis (George Challis), Dawson (Peter Dawson), Dexter (Martin Dexter), Evan (Evin Evan), Evans (Evan Evans), Frederick (John Frederick), Frost (Frederick Frost), Lawton (Dennis Lawton), Manning (David Manning), M.B. (Max Brand), Morland (Peter Henry Morland), Owen (Hugh Owen), Silver (Nicholas Silver). The name Henry Uriel was used by Faust during his lifetime, but he was never published under it. It was used as the byline for his poem, "The West Wind," appearing in The Fabulous Faust Fanzine, Vol. 2, no. 2, dated December 1948. It is derived from his mother's maiden name. With this addition the total list of pseudonyms comes to nineteen.

Faust's first published work of any kind appeared in his high school annual and was bylined Schiller Faust. Thereafter in high school and college he used variations of his full name or initials, finally preferring Frederick Faust. School and college bylines are given as "Faust" or variations of his initials, with one exception. Between January 13 and April 23, 1915, during the last semester of his senior year, Faust wrote some twenty-three satirical columns for The Daily Californian *bylined "Little Bobbie."*

*The bibliography is divided into three parts. The first part chronologically lists all Faust's published work other than those in books. The next part lists his books alphabetically. Finally, the third part lists his books chronologically. Due to word counts made by the late William J. Clark and others since, it is possible to indicate if a book version has been abridged from the serial version. Where this has occurred, it is noted by the word {**abridged**} following the book title. In virtually all cases now of new book editions of Faust's work, his original typescripts or the unabridged magazine versions are being used as the basis for the texts. In some cases the same applies to short novels such as "The Strange Ride of Perry Woodstock" which was cut 10,000 words when it first appeared in* Dime Western *(March 1933) under the title, "Death Rides Behind." Faust's original version of this story, with his title restored, has since been collected in* THE BIG BOOK OF WESTERN ACTION STORIES *(Barricade Books, 1995) edited by Jon Tuska. All of Faust's work appearing in book editions published in Five Star Westerns by Thorndike Press, crime stories published by St. Martin's Press, Black Horse Westerns published by Robert Hale, Ltd., and books published by the University of Nebraska Press adhere as closely as possible to Frederick Faust's original versions. Abridgments and other instances of editorial intervention in Faust's work are being systematically withdrawn by Golden West Literary Agency as publishing licenses expire, and the original versions are being published in their place. Since there is sufficient material by Frederick Faust not yet published in book form to fill an additional one hundred volumes, this bibliography will continue to expand and require periodic updating.*

CHRONOLOGICAL LIST OF PUBLISHED WORK: *Periodical Fiction and* ——————————— *Nonfiction, Plays, and Poems* —————————

[Short story = 1,000–20,000 words; short novel = 20,000–40,000 words; book length = 40,000+ words]

1910

June	*The Sycamore*	The King Is Dead (short story) (Modesto H. S. annual)	Faust

1911

June	*The Sycamore*	The Fate of Llewellyn Cadmon (short story)	Faust
June	*The Sycamore*	The Magic Draught (poem)	Faust
June	*The Sycamore*	The Three Arts (poem)	Faust
June	*The Sycamore*	I Am the Emperor (humor)	F.S.
June	*The Sycamore*	The Paragon (poem)	F.S.F.

1912

Jan.	*The Occident*	A Sea Call (poem) (University of California, Berkeley, literary magazine)	Faust
Mar.	*The California Pelican*	The Days of Yore (poem) (University of California, Berkeley, literary magazine)	Faust
Apr.	*The Occident*	Wordsworth (poem)	Faust
Apr.	*The Occident*	Hastings (poem)	Faust
Aug.	*The California Pelican*	Miss Boston Recites "Break, Break, Break!" (poem) (with L. K. Newfield)	F.S.F.
Aug.	*The California Pelican*	The Raven (poem)	F.S.F.
Aug.	*The California Pelican*	Requiescat (poem)	F.S.F.
Oct.	*The Occident*	Oscar Wilde (essay)	Faust
Nov.	*The California Pelican*	When (poem)	F.F.
Nov.	*The Occident*	Guenevere (poem)	Faust
Dec.	*The California Pelican*	Dedication Day (poem)	F.F.
Dec.	*The Occident*	The Bards (poem)	Faust
Dec.	*The Occident*	Night Songs (poem)	Faust

1913

Jan.	*The California Pelican*	Brass Tacks (poem)	F.S.F.
Jan.	*The Occident*	The Holy Grail (poem)	Faust
Mar.	*The California Pelican*	The Baseball Bat (poem)	F.S.F.
Mar.	*The California Pelican*	Calls to Glory (poem)	F.S.F.
Mar.	*The Occident*	The Rule (poem)	Faust
Mar.	*The Occident*	Scotch for Four (poem)	Faust
Mar.	*The Occident*	Bjornsen (poem)	Faust
Apr.	*The Occident*	Judgment (poem)	Faust
Apr.	*The Occident*	Stradivarius (poem)	Faust
Apr.	*The Occident*	As If Inquiring What Their Grief Might Mean (poem)	Faust
Sep.	*The California Pelican*	Parting (poem)	F.F.
Sep.	*The California Pelican*	Strange (poem)	F.F.
Sep.	*The California Pelican*	Sartor Resartus (humor)	F.S.F.
Sep.	*The California Pelican*	Psalm of the Knife (poem)	F.F.
Sep.	*The California Pelican*	The Co-ed's Summer (poem)	F.F.

Sep.	*The Occident*	Brother John (play)	Faust
Sep.	*The Occident*	Jude the Obscure (essay)	Faust
Sep.	*The Occident*	Palomides (poem)	Faust
Oct.	*The California Pelican*	The Fall Guy (poem)	F.F.
Oct.	*The California Pelican*	Pride (poem)	F.F.
Oct.	*The Occident*	At Forty (poem)	Faust
Oct.	*The Occident*	The House of Rulaki (short story)	Faust
Nov.	*The California Pelican*	A Ringer (poem)	F.F.
Nov.	*The California Pelican*	On the Origin of ''Damn'' (humor)	F.F.
Nov.	*The Occident*	Foscari (poem)	Faust
Nov. 28		Jeanette's Way (Junior Farce Play) (with Sidney Coe Howard)	Faust
Dec.	*The California Pelican*	Ode to a Beer Opener (poem)	F.F.
Dec.	*The California Pelican*	How It Really Happened (humor)	F.F.
Dec.	*The Occident*	Ulysses and Circe (poem)	Faust
Dec.	*The Occident*	''Strange Things Are Found'' (poem)	Faust

1914

Jan.	*The Occident*	What Will You Do? (poem)	Faust
Feb.	*The Occident*	The Glove (poem)	Faust
Mar.	*The Occident*	In the Fairy Dell (poem)	Faust
Mar.	*The Occident*	Ingeborge (poem)	Faust
Mar.	*The Occident*	The English Club Plays (criticism)	Faust
Apr.	*The Occident*	Song to Mars (poem)	Faust
Apr.	*The Occident*	Missolonghi (poem)	Faust
Apr.	*The Occident*	The Phantasy (poem)	Faust
July	*University of California Chronicle*	One of Cleopatra's Nights (poem) (Emily Cook Chamberlain Prize for 1914)	Faust
Sep.	*The California Pelican*	College Spirit (editorial)	unsigned
Sep.	*The Occident*	College Sonnets (21 poems)	Faust
Sep.	*The Occident*	To Arthur Ryder (poem)	F.F.
Oct.	*The California Pelican*	Bond Issue (editorial)	unsigned

Oct.	*The Occident*	The Sonnet (poem)	Faust
Oct.	*The Occident*	Philosophical Fulminations (poem)	Faust
Oct.	*The Occident*	Dawn (poem)	F.F.
Oct.	*The Occident*	The Night (poem)	F.F.
Nov.	*The California Pelican*	Women's Organization (editorial)	unsigned
Nov.	*The Occident*	Campus Moralists (essay)	Faust
Dec.	*The Occident*	Fools All (play)	Faust
Dec.	*The California Pelican*	The Common Law (essay)	Faust

1915

Jan.	*The California Pelican*	Dream University (editorial)	unsigned
Jan. 13	*The Daily Californian*	A Little More of Little Bobbie (23 humor pieces: 1/13/15–4/23/15)	Little Bobbie
Feb.	*The California Pelican*	Morality (editorial)	unsigned
Feb.	*The Occident*	Orpheus and Eurydice (poem)	Faust
Mar.	*The California Pelican*	Antiquity (editorial)	unsigned
Mar.	*The California Pelican*	R.O.T.C. (editorial)	unsigned
Apr.	*The California Pelican*	Our Crew Is Not Winning (editorial)	unsigned
May	*The California Pelican*	Nostalgia (editorial)	unsigned
May	*The Occident*	The Long Road (poem)	F.F.
May	*The Occident*	To Sleep (poem)	F.F.
May	*The Occident*	Meeting (poem)	F.F.
May	*The Occident*	The Amulet (poem)	Faust
May 8		Fiat Lux (Senior Extravaganza Play) (with Sidney C. Howard)	Faust
June	*The Blue and Gold*	Dedication poem in college annual	Faust
June	*The Blue and Gold*	Senior Election (poem)	Faust
June	*The Blue and Gold*	Defense of Guenevere (poem)	F.S.F.
Sep. 4	*Honolulu Star-Bulletin*	In Memoriam (poem)	F.S.F
Nov.	*The Occident*	I Dreamed That Death Came to Me (poem)	F.F.
Dec.	*The Occident*	The Ride to Camelot (poem)	F.F.

1916

Jan.	*The Occident*	The Black Cross (poem)	F.F.
June	*The Blue and Gold*	Julius Caesar Is Slain (humor)	Faust
Dec. 11	*The Bang*	The Wonderful Maid (poem) (five-cent poetry pamphlet)	Faust

1917

Feb.	*The Century Magazine*	The Secret (poem)	Faust
Mar. 31	*All-Story Weekly*	Convalescence (short story)	Faust
Apr. 28	*All-Story Weekly*	The Gambler and the Stake (short story)	Faust
June 23	*All-Story Weekly*	Mr. Cinderella (short story)	Brand
July 14	*All-Story Weekly*	Fate's Honeymoon (5-pt. serial: 7/14/17–8/11/17)	Brand
Aug. 4	*All-Story Weekly*	Your Country Needs You (short story)	Faust
Sep.	*The Occident*	Odysseus' Gift of Wine (poem)	F.F.
Sep.	*The Occident*	The Nightingale (poem) (with John L. Schoolcraft)	Faust
Sep. 15	*All-Story Weekly*	The Sole Survivor (short story)	Brand
Sep. 22	*All-Story Weekly*	Dragon Teeth (poem)	Brand
Oct.	*The Occident*	Bed-Time (poem)	Faust
Oct. 6	*All-Story Weekly*	One Glass of Wine (short novel)	Brand
Oct. 27	*All-Story Weekly*	The Adopted Son (short story)	Brand
Nov. 10	*Argosy*	The Sword Lover (7-pt. serial: 11/10/17–12/22/17)	Brand

1918

Jan.	*Railroad Man's Magazine*	Red Lights Turn Green (poem)	Brand
Feb. 23	*All-Story Weekly*	Who Am I? (6-pt. serial: 2/23/18–3/30/18)	Brand
Mar.	*The Occident*	Heimweh (poem)	Faust
Apr. 27	*All-Story Weekly*	Silence (poem)	Brand
May 18	*All-Story Weekly*	A Rendezvous with Death (short novel)	Brand

June 8	*All-Story Weekly*	John Ovington Returns (short story)	Brand
July 13	*All-Story Weekly*	Devil Ritter (short novel)	Brand
July 20	*All-Story Weekly*	The Ballad of St. Christopher (poem)	Brand
Aug. 31	*All-Story Weekly*	Above the Law (short novel)	Brand
Sep.	*St. Nicholas*	My Heroes (poem)	Faust
Sep. 14	*All-Story Weekly*	Woodward's Devil (short story)	Brand
Oct. 19	*All-Story Weekly*	Bad-eye, His Life and Letters (short story)	Brand
Oct. 26	*All-Story Weekly*	No Partners (short novel)	Brand
Oct. 26	*Argosy*	The Double Crown (7-pt. serial: 10/26/18–11/30/18) (with John Schoolcraft as Peter Ward)	Frederick
Nov. 2	*Railroad Man's Magazine*	Harrigan! (5-pt. serial: 11/2/18–11/30/18)	Brand
Nov. 16	*All-Story Weekly*	The Great Stroke (short story)	Brand
Dec. 7	*All-Story Weekly*	The Untamed (6-pt. serial: 12/7/18–1/11/19)	Brand

1919

Feb. 1	*All-Story Weekly*	Victory (short story)	Brand
Feb. 15	*All-Story Weekly*	That Receding Brow (short story)	Brand
Mar. 1	*Argosy*	The Hammer (6-pt. serial: 3/1/19–4/5/19)	Frederick
Mar. 22	*All-Story Weekly*	Children of Night (5-pt. serial: 3/22/19–4/19/19)	Brand
May 3	*All-Story Weekly*	The Ghost (short story)	Brand
May 31	*Argosy*	The Higher Strain (short novel)	Frederick
June 14	*All-Story Weekly*	The Laughter of Slim Malone (short story)	Brand
June 28	*All-Story Weekly*	The Fear of Morgan the Fearless (short story)	Brand
Aug.	*Munsey's Magazine*	Hole-in-the-Wall Barrett (short story)	Brand
Aug. 9	*Argosy*	Luck (6-pt. serial: 8/9/19–9/13/19)	Frederick

Aug. 30	*All-Story Weekly*	"It Was Like This—" (short story)	Brand
Sep. 27	*All-Story Weekly*	The House That Steve Built (short story)	Brand
Oct. 11	*All-Story Weekly*	The Sacking of El Dorado (short novel)	Brand
Nov. 1	*Argosy*	Brain and Brawn (short story)	Frederick
Nov. 1	*All-Story Weekly*	Trailin' (6-pt. serial: 11/1/19–12/8/19)	Brand

1920

Jan. 3	*All-Story Weekly*	The Lost Garden (short story)	Brand
Jan. 31	*Argosy*	Crossroads (6-pt. serial: 1/31/20–3/6/20)	Frederick
Mar. 13	*All-Story Weekly*	Out of the Dark (short story)	Brand
Apr. 10	*All-Story Weekly*	Clung (6-pt. serial: 4/10/20–5/15/20)	Brand
May 29	*All-Story Weekly*	The Frigate Bird (5-pt. serial: 5/29/20–6/26/20)	Bolt
July 3	*Argosy*	Pride of Tyson (6-pt. serial: 7/3/20–8/7/20)	Frederick
July 10	*All-Story Weekly*	A Sagebrush Cinderella (short story)	Brand
July 24	*Argosy/All-Story*	The Ghost (short story)	Brand
Aug. 21	*Argosy/All-Story*	The Whisperer (short story)	Brand
Sep. 18	*Argosy/All-Story*	The Night Horseman (7-pt. serial: 9/18/20–10/30/20)	Brand
Nov. 25	*Western Story*	Jerry Peyton's Notched Inheritance (5-pt. serial: 11/25/20–12/25/20)	Baxter
Nov. 27	*Argosy/All-Story*	The Consuming Fire (short story)	Brand
Dec. 25	*Western Story*	The Man Who Forgot Christmas (short novel)	Frederick

1921

| Jan. 8 | *Argosy/All-Story* | Tiger (6-pt. serial: 1/8/21–2/12/21) | Brand |
| Jan. 15 | *Western Story* | The Cure of Silver Cañon (short novel) | Frederick |

Jan. 29	*Western Story*	Iron Dust (8-pt. serial: 1/29/21–3/19/21)	Baxter
Mar. 12	*Western Story*	His Back against the Wall (short novel)	Frederick
Apr. 9	*Argosy/All-Story*	White Heather Weather (7-pt. serial: 4/9/21–5/21/21)	Frederick
Apr. 16	*Western Story*	Donnegan (6-pt. serial: 4/16/21–5/21/21)	Baxter
May 21	*Western Story*	Jerico's "Garrison Finish" (short novel)	Frederick
June 18	*Western Story*	When the Wandering Whip Went West (short novel)	Frederick
July 9	*Western Story*	Bullets with Sense (short novel)	Brand
July 30	*Western Story*	When Iron Turns to Gold (short novel)	Baxter
Aug. 13	*Western Story*	Bull Hunter Feels His Oats (short novel)	Brand
Aug. 13	*Argosy/All-Story*	The Guide to Happiness (6-pt. serial: 8/13/21–9/17/21)	Brand
Sep. 3	*Western Story*	Madcap of the Mountains (7-pt. serial: 9/3/21–10/15/21)	Baxter
Sep. 10	*Western Story*	Outlaws All (short novel)	Brand
Sep. 24	*Western Story*	The Wolf Strain (short novel)	Brand
Oct. 1	*Argosy/All-Story*	The Seventh Man (6-pt. serial: 10/1/21–11/5/21)	Brand
Oct. 22	*Western Story*	Bull Hunter's Romance (short novel)	Brand
Oct. 29	*Western Story*	Ronicky Doone, Champion of Lost Causes (7-pt. serial: 10/29/21–12/10/21)	Manning
Nov. 12	*Western Story*	The Gauntlet (short novel)	Baxter
Nov. 19	*Western Story*	Riding into Peril (short novel)	Frederick
Dec. 3	*Western Story*	Sheriff Larrabee's Prisoner (short novel)	Dexter
Dec. 10	*Western Story*	The Man Who Followed (short novel)	Baxter

Dec. 10	*Argosy/All-Story*	Black Jack (6-pt. serial: 12/10/21–1/14/22)	Brand
Dec. 24	*Western Story*	The Gift (short novel)	Brand
1922			
Jan. 7	*Western Story*	Ronicky Doone and the Cosslett Treasure (8-pt. serial: 1/7/22–2/25/22)	Manning
Jan. 14	*Western Story*	The Fugitive's Mission (short novel)	Baxter
Feb. 4	*Western Story*	The One-Way Trail (short novel)	Baxter
Feb. 25	*Western Story*	The Emerald Trail (short novel)	Frederick
Feb. 25	*Argosy/All-Story*	Gun Gentlemen (5-pt. serial: 2/25/22–3/25/22)	Brand
Apr. 1	*Western Story*	Jim Curry's Compromise (short novel)	Brand
Apr. 8	*Western Story*	Three Who Paid (8-pt. serial: 4/8/22–5/27/22)	Baxter
Apr. 15	*Argosy/All-Story*	The Garden of Eden (6-pt. serial: 4/15/22–5/20/22)	Brand
Apr. 22	*Western Story*	Jim Curry's Test (short novel)	Brand
May 6	*Western Story*	King Charlie and His Long Riders (short novel)	Frederick
May 20	*Western Story*	Jim Curry's Sacrifice (short novel)	Brand
May 27	*Western Story*	King Charlie—One Year Later (short novel)	Frederick
June	*Ace High*	The Unhallowed House (short novel)	Frederick
June 3	*Argosy/All-Story*	His Third Master (6-pt. serial: 6/3/22–7/8/22)	Brand
June 17	*Country Gentleman*	Alcatraz (5-pt. serial: 6/17/22–7/15/22)	Brand
June 17	*Western Story*	The Shadow of Silver Tip (6-pt. serial: 6/17/22–7/22/22)	Baxter
June 24	*Western Story*	King Charlie's Hosts (short novel)	Frederick
July 8	*Western Story*	Slumber Mountain (short novel)	Frederick

July 15	*Western Story*	Ronicky Doone's Reward (6-pt. serial: 7/15/22–8/19/22)	Manning
July 22	*Detective Story*	The Painted Alibi (short novel)	Baxter
July 29	*Detective Story*	Walking Death (short novel)	Silver
Aug. 5	*Western Story*	The Bill for Banditry (short novel)	Frederick
Aug. 25	*Short Stories*	The Cross Brand (short novel)	Brand
Aug. 26	*Western Story*	Mountain Madness (short novel)	Baxter
Aug. 26	*Western Story*	Old Carver Ranch (7-pt. serial: 8/26/22–10/7/22)	Frederick
Sep. 9	*Detective Story*	The Night Rider (short novel)	Silver
Sep. 16	*Western Story*	Over the Northern Border (short novel)	Baxter
Sep. 30	*Western Story*	The Black Muldoon (short novel)	Dawson
Oct. 7	*Detective Story*	Rubies of Guilt (short novel)	Silver
Oct. 14	*Western Story*	Joe White's Brand (short novel)	Baxter
Oct. 21	*Western Story*	Without a Penny in the World (short novel)	Frederick
Nov. 4	*Detective Story*	The Hopeless Case (short novel)	Silver
Nov. 11	*Western Story*	Wild Freedom (6-pt. serial: 11/11/22–12/16/22)	Baxter
Nov. 25	*Short Stories*	Jargan (short novel)	Brand
Dec. 2	*Argosy/All-Story*	Kain (5-pt. serial: 12/2/22–12/30/22)	Brand
Dec. 9	*Detective Story*	Sealed for Fifty Years (short novel)	Silver
Dec. 9	*Western Story*	The Cabin in the Pines (short novel)	Frederick
Dec. 23	*Detective Story*	A Christmas Encounter (short novel)	Silver
Dec. 23	*Western Story*	The Power of Prayer (short novel)	Frederick

Dec. 30	*Detective Story*	Stolen Clothes (short novel)	Silver
Dec. 30	*Western Story*	Phil, the Fiddler (short novel)	Baxter

1923

Jan. 6	*Western Story*	Winking Lights (short novel)	Frederick
Jan. 27	*Western Story*	Under His Shirt (short novel)	Brand
Mar. 10	*Western Story*	Hired Guns (7-pt. serial: 3/10/23–4/21/23)	Brand
Mar. 17	*Western Story*	Two Sixes (short novel)	Baxter
Mar. 17	*Detective Story*	Black Shadows of Sawtrell House (6-pt. serial: 3/17/23–4/21/23)	Silver
Apr. 7	*Western Story*	''Sunset'' Wins (short novel)	Baxter
Apr. 21	*Argosy/All-Story*	The Darkness at Windon Manor (4-pt. serial: 4/21/23–5/12/23)	Brand
Apr. 28	*Western Story*	Gold King Turns His Back (short novel)	Frederick
Apr. 28	*Western Story*	The Bandit of the Black Hills (6-pt. serial: 4/28/23–6/2/23)	Baxter
May 26	*Western Story*	The Abandoned Outlaw (short novel)	Frederick
June 9	*Western Story*	His Name His Fortune (short novel)	Brand
June 30	*Western Story*	Little Sammy Green, ''Lucky Gent'' (short novel)	Brand
June 30	*Argosy/All-Story*	Dan Barry's Daughter (6-pt. serial: 6/30/23–8/4/23)	Brand
July 14	*Western Story*	Galloping Danger (6-pt. serial: 7/14/23–8/18/23)	Brand
July 28	*Western Story*	Black Sheep (short novel)	Baxter
Aug. 25	*Western Story*	''Safety'' McTee (short story)	Brand
Sep. 1	*Western Story*	Rodeo Ranch (short novel)	Brand
Sep. 1	*Western Story*	Seven Trails to Romance (6-pt. serial: 9/1/23–10/6/23)	Baxter
Sep. 15	*Western Story*	Wooden Guns (6-pt. serial: 9/15/23–10/20/23)	Brand

Oct. 13	*Western Story*	Slow Bill (short novel)	Frederick
Oct. 20	*Western Story*	Soft Metal (short novel)	Baxter
Nov. 3	*Argosy/All-Story*	The Stranger at the Gate (6-pt. serial: 11/3/23–12/8/23)	Brand
Nov. 24	*Western Story*	"Timber Line" (short novel)	Brand
Dec. 1	*Western Story*	The Whisperer of the Wilderness (6-pt. serial: 12/1/23-1/5/24)	Baxter
Dec. 8	*Western Story*	Uncle Chris Turns North (short novel)	Brand
Dec. 22	*Western Story*	The Boy Who Found Christmas (short novel)	Frederick

1924

Jan. 5	*Western Story*	Master and Man (short novel)	Brand
Jan. 19	*Western Story*	The Rock of Kiever (short novel)	Brand
Jan. 26	*Argosy/All-Story*	The Blackmailer (short novel)	Brand
Jan. 26	*Western Story*	Train's Trust (6-pt. serial: 1/26/24–3/1/24)	Baxter
Feb. 23	*Collier's*	Bulldog (short story)	Brand
Mar. 1	*Western Story*	Cuttle's Hired Man (short novel)	Brand
Mar. 8	*Western Story*	Four without Fear (6-pt. serial: 3/8/24–4/12/24)	Frederick
Mar. 22	*Argosy/All-Story*	The Man in the Dark (short story)	Brand
Mar. 22	*Western Story*	Lazy Tom Hooks Up with Skinny (short novel)	Brand
Apr. 10	*Short Stories*	One Hour Past Moonrise (2-pt. serial: 4/10/24–4/25/24)	Brand
Apr. 12	*Western Story*	The Welding Quirt (short novel)	Brand
Apr. 19	*Western Story*	Saddle and Sentiment (6-pt. serial: 4/19/24–5/24/24)	Brand
May 10	*Western Story*	Bared Fangs (short novel)	Baxter
May 31	*Western Story*	Argentine (6-pt. serial: 5/31/24–7/5/24)	Baxter

June 7	*Western Story*	The Gambler (6-pt. serial: 6/7/24–7/12/24)	Brand
June 21	*Western Story*	The Girl They Left Behind Them (short novel)	Frederick
July 5	*Western Story*	A Wolf among Dogs (short novel)	Frederick
July 12	*Western Story*	The Red Rider (short novel)	Silver
July 19	*Western Story*	The Boy in the Wilderness (short novel)	Baxter
July 26	*Western Story*	The Brute (short novel)	Baxter
Aug. 2	*Western Story*	The Love of Danger (6-pt. serial: 8/2/24–9/6/24)	Brand
Aug. 9	*Western Story*	The Race (short novel)	Baxter
Sep. 6	*Western Story*	Hired by Dad (short novel)	Baxter
Sep. 13	*Argosy/All-Story*	The Conquering Heart (short story)	Brand
Sep. 13	*Western Story*	Blackie and Red (short novel)	Brand
Sep. 13	*Western Story*	Larramee's Ranch (6-pt. serial: 9/13/24–10/18/24)	Baxter
Sep. 27	*Argosy/All-Story*	Clovelly (6-pt. serial: 9/27/24–11/1/24)	Brand
Oct. 4	*Western Story*	When ''Red'' Was White (short novel)	Brand
Oct. 4	*Western Story*	In the Hills of Monterey (6-pt. serial: 10/4/24– 11/8/24)	Frederick
Oct. 11	*Detective Fiction*	Champion of Lost Causes (7-pt. serial: 10/11/24– 11/22/24)	Brand
Nov. 15	*Western Story*	Chick's Fall (short novel)	Brand
Nov. 22	*Western Story*	Billy Angel, Trouble Lover (short novel)	Baxter
Dec. 13	*Western Story*	The Third Bullet (short novel)	Brand
Dec. 13	*Western Story*	Mountain Made (6-pt. serial: 12/13/24–1/17/25)	Baxter
Dec. 20	*Western Story*	Fortune's Christmas (short novel)	Brand
Dec. 27	*Country Gentleman*	Dark Rosaleen (5-pt. serial: 12/27/24–1/24/25)	Brand

1925

Jan. 3	*Western Story*	The Black Rider (short novel)	Brand
Jan. 24	*Western Story*	Beyond the Outposts (6-pt. serial: 1/24/25–2/28/25)	Morland
Feb. 21	*Detective Story*	The Crime by the River (3-pt. serial: 2/21/25–3/7/25)	Brand
Mar. 7	*Western Story*	Blackie's Last Stand (short novel)	Brand
Mar. 7	*Argosy/All-Story*	Señor Jingle Bells (5-pt. serial: 3/7/25–4/4/25)	Brand
Mar. 21	*Western Story*	The Black Signal (short novel)	Brand
Apr. 4	*Western Story*	Lew and Slim (short novel)	Brand
Apr. 11	*Western Story*	In the River Bottom's Grip (short novel)	Brand
Apr. 18	*Western Story*	In Dread of the Law (short novel)	Baxter
May 2	*Western Story*	Going Straight (short novel)	Baxter
May 16	*Western Story*	The Battle for Mike (short novel)	Baxter
May 23	*Western Story*	The Survivor (6-pt. serial: 5/23/25–6/27/25)	Brand
May 30	*Western Story*	The Outlaw Redeemer (short novel)	Baxter
June 27	*Western Story*	His Fight for a Pardon (short novel)	Baxter
July 4	*Western Story*	The Squaw Boy (6-pt. serial: 7/4/25–8/8/25)	Morland
Aug. 15	*Western Story*	On the Trail of Four (4-pt. serial: 8/15/25–9/5/25)	Brand
Sep. 12	*Western Story*	Fire Brain (6-pt. serial: 9/12/25–10/17/25)	Baxter
Oct. 3	*Western Story*	Sammy Gregg's Mustang Herd (short novel)	Brand
Oct. 17	*Western Story*	Gregg's Coach Line (short novel)	Brand
Oct. 24	*Western Story*	The Runaways (6-pt. serial: 10/24/25–11/28/25)	Baxter
Oct. 31	*Western Story*	Sammy Gregg and the Posse (short novel)	Brand

Nov. 7	*Western Story*	Not the Fastest Horse (short novel)	Frederick
Nov. 14	*Western Story*	The Range Finder (short novel)	Morland
Nov. 28	*Western Story*	Brother of the Beasts (short novel)	Brand
Dec. 12	*Western Story*	The White Cheyenne (6-pt. serial: 12/12/25–1/16/26)	Morland
Dec. 26	*Western Story*	No Man's Friend (short novel)	Brand

1926

Jan. 9	*Western Story*	The Tyrant (6-pt. serial: 1/9/26–2/13/26)	Challis
Jan. 16	*Western Story*	Sandy Sweyn Comes Out of the Wilds (short novel)	Brand
Jan. 30	*Western Story*	The Good Bad-man (short novel)	Baxter
Feb. 20	*Western Story*	Bluejay (6-pt. serial: 2/20/26–3/27/26)	Brand
Feb. 27	*Western Story*	The Man He Couldn't Get (short novel)	Baxter
Mar. 6	*Western Story*	The White Wolf (6-pt. serial: 3/6/26–4/10/26)	Frederick
Mar. 20	*Western Story*	The Vamp's Bandit (short novel)	Baxter
Apr. 17	*Western Story*	A Son of Danger (6-pt. serial: 4/17/26–5/22/26)	Brand
May 29	*Western Story*	Trail of the Stone-That-Shines (6-pt. serial: 5/29/26–7/3/26)	Morland
June	*Country Gentleman*	The Thunderer (4-pt. serial: 6/26–9/26)	Brand
June 12	*Western Story*	Acres of Unrest (6-pt. serial: 6/12/26–7/17/26)	Brand
July 17	*Western Story*	Bad Man's Gulch (short novel)	Baxter
July 24	*Western Story*	The Fugitive (short novel)	Brand
July 24	*Western Story*	Western Tommy (5-pt. serial: 7/24/26–8/21/26)	Frederick
Aug. 21	*Western Story*	The Valley of Jewels (short novel)	Brand

Aug. 28	*Western Story*	Trouble Trail (6-pt. serial: 8/28/26–10/2/26)	Baxter
Sep. 25	*Western Story*	The Border Bandit (short novel)	Brand
Oct. 2	*Western Story*	The Border Bandit's Indian Brother (short novel)	Brand
Oct. 9	*Western Story*	The Border Bandit's Prize (short novel)	Brand
Oct. 10	*Short Stories*	Jokers Extra Wild (short novel)	Brand
Oct. 30	*Western Story*	The Iron Trail (6-pt. serial: 10/30/26–12/4/26)	Brand
Nov. 6	*Western Story*	The Bells of San Filipo (6-pt. serial: 11/6/26–12/11/26)	Baxter
Dec.	*Far West Illustrated*	Comanche (5-pt. serial: 12/26–4/27)	Brand
Dec. 18	*Western Story*	Werewolf (short novel)	Brand
1927			
Jan. 15	*Western Story*	The Canyon Coward (short novel)	Brand
Feb. 12	*Western Story*	Smiling Charlie (6-pt. serial: 2/12/27–3/19/27)	Brand
Feb. 19	*Western Story*	Flaming Fortune (short novel)	Baxter
Mar. 12	*Western Story*	Lightning Lumberjacks (short novel)	Frederick
Mar. 26	*Western Story*	The Western Double (6-pt. serial: 3/26/27–4/30/27)	Baxter
Apr.	*Far West Illustrated*	Thunder Moon (5-pt. serial: 4/27–8/27)	Baxter
June	*Far West Illustrated*	Peter Blue, One-Gun Man (short novel)	Brand
June 4	*Western Story*	The Desert Pilot (short novel)	Brand
June 11	*Western Story*	The City in the Sky (6-pt. serial: 6/11/27–7/16/27)	Brand
July 2	*Western Story*	The Terrible Tenderfoot (short novel)	Baxter
July 16	*Western Story*	The Gentle Desperado (short novel)	Baxter
July 30	*Western Story*	Tiger, Tiger! (short novel)	Baxter

Aug.	*Far West Illustrated*	Sawdust and Six-Guns (6-pt. serial: 8/27–1/28)	Brand
Aug. 13	*Western Story*	The Silver Stork (6-pt. serial: 8/13/27–9/17/27)	Brand
Aug. 27	*Western Story*	Red Wind and Thunder Moon (short novel)	Baxter
Sep. 17	*Western Story*	Thunder Moon—Pale Face (short novel)	Baxter
Sep. 24	*Western Story*	Thunder Moon—Squawman (5-pt. serial: 9/24/27–10/22/27)	Baxter
Oct. 22	*Western Story*	A Lucky Dog (short story)	Frederick
Oct. 22	*Western Story*	Pleasant Jim (6-pt. serial: 10/22/27–11/26/27)	Brand
Nov. 19	*Western Story*	Forgotten Treasure (short novel)	Baxter

1928

Jan. 14	*Western Story*	Weakling of the Wild (6-pt. serial: 1/14/28–2/18/28)	Brand
Feb. 25	*Western Story*	Tragedy Trail (6-pt. serial: 2/25/28–3/31/28)	Baxter
Mar. 17	*Western Story*	The Path to Plunder (6-pt. serial: 3/17/28–4/21/28)	Brand
Apr.	*Far West Illustrated*	Outlaw Valley (5-pt. serial: 4/28–8/28)	Brand
Apr. 7	*Western Story*	The Magic Gun (short novel)	Frederick
Apr. 28	*Western Story*	The Gun Tamer (6-pt. serial: 4/28/28–6/2/28)	Baxter
May 12	*Western Story*	Three on the Trail (6-pt. serial: 5/12/28–6/16/28)	Brand
May 19	*Western Story*	Coward of the Clan (short novel)	Morland
June 2	*Western Story*	The Man from the Sky (short novel)	Morland
June 16	*Western Story*	Prairie Pawn (short novel)	Morland
June 23	*Western Story*	The Brass Man (6-pt. serial: 6/23/28–7/28/28)	Baxter
June 30	*Western Story*	Fugitives' Fire (short novel)	Morland
July 14	*Western Story*	Gunman's Goal (short novel)	Brand

Aug. 4	*Western Story*	Pillar Mountain (6-pt. serial: 8/4/28–9/8/28)	Frederick
Aug. 18	*Western Story*	The Bright Face of Danger (short novel)	Brand
Sep. 15	*Western Story*	Riders for Fortune (6-pt. serial: 9/15/28–10/20/28)	Baxter
Sep. 29	*Western Story*	Through Steel and Stone (short novel)	Brand
Oct. 13	*Western Story*	The House of Gold (short novel)	Brand
Oct. 27	*Western Story*	Silver Trail (6-pt. serial: 10/27/28–12/1/28)	Brand
Nov. 3	*Western Story*	Thunder Moon Goes White (short novel)	Baxter
Dec. 1	*Western Story*	The Lion's Share (short novel)	Baxter
Dec. 15	*Western Story*	Singing Guns (6-pt. serial: 12/15/28–1/19/29)	Baxter
Dec. 29	*Western Story*	The Flaming Rider (short novel)	Morland

1929

Jan. 12	*Western Story*	The Stranger (5-pt. serial: 1/12/29–2/9/29)	Brand
Jan. 27	*The American Weekly*	Mistral (9-pt. serial: 1/27/29–3/24/29) (newspaper supplement)	Brand
Feb. 16	*Western Story*	Hunted Hunters (short novel)	Baxter
Feb. 16	*Western Story*	The Winged Horse (6-pt. serial: 2/16/29–3/23/29)	Frederick
Apr. 13	*Western Story*	The Trail to Manhood (6-pt. serial: 4/13/29–5/18/29)	Brand
May	*Munsey's Magazine*	Blood and Iron (4-pt. serial: 5/29–8/29)	Brand
May 25	*Western Story*	Strength of the Hills (6-pt. serial: 5/25/29–6/29/29)	Baxter
June 29	*Western Story*	The Return of Geraldi (short novel)	Brand
July 6	*Western Story*	Rustlers' Rock (6-pt. serial: 7/6/29–8/10/29)	Manning
July 13	*Western Story*	Chinook (6-pt. serial: 7/13/29–8/10/29)	Frederick

Aug. 17	*Western Story*	While Bullets Sang (short novel)	Brand
Aug. 24	*Western Story*	Happy Valley (6-pt. serial: 8/24/29–9/28/29)	Baxter
Aug. 31	*Western Story*	Geraldi in the Haunted Hills (short novel)	Brand
Sep. 7	*Western Story*	The Danger Lover (short novel)	Manning
Nov. 2	*Western Story*	The Duster (short novel)	Brand
Nov. 9	*Western Story*	Two Bronchos (6-pt. serial: 11/9/29–12/14/29)	Baxter
Nov. 16	*Western Story*	Twisted Bars (short novel)	Brand
Nov. 30	*Western Story*	The Duster's Return (short novel)	Brand
Dec. 21	*Western Story*	The Horizon of Danger (6-pt. serial: 12/21/29–1/25/30)	Morland

1930

Feb. 1	*Western Story*	Twelve Peers (6-pt. serial: 2/1/30–3/8/30)	Brand
Feb. 22	*Western Story*	Cayenne Charlie (short novel)	Baxter
Mar. 15	*Western Story*	Tiger's Den (6-pt. serial: 3/15/30–4/19/30)	Frederick
Apr. 5	*Western Story*	Two Masters (short novel)	Brand
Apr. 12	*Western Story*	The Golden Coyote (short story)	Manning
Apr. 26	*Western Story*	White Hunger (short story)	Manning
Apr. 26	*Western Story*	Happy Jack (6-pt. serial: 4/26/30–5/31/30)	Baxter
May 3	*Western Story*	Sixteen in Nome (short novel)	Brand
May 10	*Western Story*	Battle's End (short novel)	Brand
May 17	*Western Story*	''Mother'' (short story)	Manning
May 24	*Western Story*	Shiver-Nose (short story)	Manning
May 31	*Western Story*	Yellow Dog (short story)	Manning
June 7	*Western Story*	Back to His Own (short story)	Manning
June 7	*Western Story*	The Stingaree (6-pt. serial: 6/7/30–7/12/30)	Brand

July 13	*The American Weekly*	The Golden Cat (14-pt. serial: 7/13/30–10/12/30)	Brand
July 19	*Western Story*	Daring Duval (6-pt. serial: 7/19/30–8/23/30)	Baxter
Aug.	*Railroad Man's Magazine*	The Mask of Ching Wo (6-pt. serial: 8/30–1/31)	Brand
Sep. 6	*Western Story*	Trouble's Messenger (6-pt. serial: 9/6/30–10/11/30)	Baxter
Oct. 18	*Western Story*	Rippon Rides Double (6-pt. serial: 10/18/30–11/22/30)	Brand
Dec. 6	*Western Story*	On Fortune's Back (6-pt. serial: 12/6/30–1/10/31)	Baxter

1931

Jan. 10	*Western Story*	Chip and the Cactus Man (short novel)	Brand
Jan. 24	*Western Story*	Chip Champions a Lady (short novel)	Brand
Jan. 31	*Western Story*	Chip Traps a Sheriff (short novel)	Brand
Mar. 14	*Western Story*	Twenty Notches (6-pt. serial: 3/14/31–4/18/31)	Brand
Apr. 25	*Liberty Magazine*	The Golden Day (short story)	Brand
Apr. 25	*Western Story*	Duck Hawk's Master (6-pt. serial: 4/25/31–5/30/31)	Baxter
May 30	*Western Story*	Valley Vultures (6-pt. serial: 5/30/31–7/4/31)	Brand
June 27	*Western Story*	Treasure Well (short novel)	Baxter
July 11	*Western Story*	Outlaw's Conscience (short novel)	Baxter
July 11	*Western Story*	The Rancher Returns (6-pt. serial: 7/11/31–8/15/31)	Frederick
July 25	*Western Story*	Clean Courage (short novel)	Baxter
Aug.	*Country Home*	The Rose of India (short story)	Brand
Aug. 22	*Western Story*	Golden Lightning (6-pt. serial: 8/22/31–9/26/31)	Brand
Sep. 12	*Western Story*	Gun Pearl Trail (6-pt. serial: 9/12/31–10/17/31)	Baxter
Oct. 17	*Western Story*	Spot Lester (short novel)	Brand

Oct. 24	*Western Story*	Tamer of the Wild (6-pt. serial: 10/24/31–11/28/31)	Morland
Oct. 31	*Western Story*	Nine Lives (short novel)	Brand
Nov. 14	*Western Story*	Torture Canyon (short novel)	Brand
Nov. 21	*Western Story*	Tramp Magic (6-pt. serial: 11/21/31–12/26/31)	Brand
Dec. 5	*Western Story*	Hawks and Eagles (short novel)	Baxter
Dec. 19	*Western Story*	Black Snake and Gun (short novel)	Baxter

1932

Jan. 2	*Western Story*	Black-Snake Joe (short novel)	Baxter
Jan. 2	*Western Story*	Dogs of the Captain (6-pt. serial: 1/2/32–2/6/32)	Brand
Jan. 9	*Western Story*	The Lightning Runner (6-pt. serial: 1/9/32–2/13/32)	Frederick
Jan. 23	*Western Story*	The Three Crosses (short novel)	Baxter
Jan. 30	*Western Story*	White-water Sam (short novel)	Morland
Feb. 13	*Western Story*	Speedy—Deputy (short novel)	Brand
Feb. 13	*Western Story*	White Wolf (6-pt. serial: 2/13/32–3/19/32)	Baxter
Feb. 20	*Western Story*	Outlaw Crew (short novel)	Brand
Feb. 20	*Western Story*	Rancher's Legacy (6-pt. serial: 2/20/32–3/26/32)	Morland
Feb. 27	*Western Story*	Seven-Day Lawman (short novel)	Brand
Mar. 5	*Western Story*	The Best Bandit (short novel)	Manning
Mar. 12	*Western Story*	Speedy's Mare (short novel)	Brand
Mar. 26	*Western Story*	Carcajou's Trail (short novel)	Brand
Mar. 26	*Western Story*	The Golden Spurs (6-pt. serial: 3/26/32–4/30/32)	Manning
Apr. 2	*Western Story*	Speedy's Crystal Game (short novel)	Brand
Apr. 2	*Western Story*	Lucky Larribee (6-pt. serial: 4/2/32–5/7/32)	Baxter

Apr. 9	*Western Story*	Mountain Raiders (short novel)	Morland
Apr. 16	*Western Story*	Red Rock's Secret (short novel)	Brand
Apr. 23	*Western Story*	Rawhide Bound (short novel)	Morland
May 14	*Western Story*	Speedy's Bargain (short novel)	Brand
May 21	*Western Story*	Greaser Trail (short novel)	Morland
May 28	*Western Story*	Range Jester (short novel)	Brand
June 4	*Western Story*	Paradise Al (short novel)	Manning
June 11	*Western Story*	The Geraldi Trail (4-pt. serial: 6/11/32–7/2/32)	Brand
July 9	*Western Story*	The Nighthawk Trail (short novel)	Brand
July 16	*Western Story*	Paradise Al's Confession (short novel)	Manning
July 23	*Western Story*	Mighty Lobo (4-pt. serial: 7/23/32–8/13/32)	Baxter
Aug. 20	*Western Story*	Outlaws from Afar (short novel)	Brand
Aug. 27	*Western Story*	Torturous Trek (4-pt. serial: 8/27/32–9/17/32)	Brand
Sep. 24	*Western Story*	The Law Dodger at Windy Creek (short novel)	Brand
Oct. 1	*Western Story*	All for One (4-pt. serial: 10/1/32–10/22/32)	Baxter
Oct. 25	*Sport Story*	Thunderbolt (3-pt. serial: 10/25/32–11/25/32)	Brand
Oct. 29	*Western Story*	Smoking Guns (short novel)	Brand
Nov. 5	*Western Story*	The Invisible Outlaw (4-pt. serial: 11/5/32–11/26/32)	Brand
Dec. 3	*Western Story*	The Two-Handed Man (short novel)	Baxter
Dec. 10	*Western Story*	Cat Hill Fugitive (4-pt. serial: 12/10/32–12/31/32)	Brand
Dec. 10	*Argosy*	The Longhorn Feud (6-pt. serial: 12/10/32–1/14/33)	Brand

1933

| Jan. 7 | *Western Story* | Señor Billy (short novel) | Baxter |

Jan. 14	*Western Story*	Montana Rides! (4-pt. serial: 1/14/33–2/4/33)	Evan
Jan. 28	*Western Story*	Speedy's Desert Dance (short novel)	Brand
Jan. 28	*Detective Fiction Weekly*	Steel Cut Steel (6-pt. serial: 1/28/33–3/4/33)	Brand
Feb. 4	*Western Story*	The Red Bandanna (short novel)	Baxter
Feb. 25	*Detective Story*	Printed Bait (short story)	Frederick
Feb. 26	*The American Weekly*	Luck and a Horse (5-pt. serial: 2/26/33–3/26/33)	Brand
Mar.	*Dime Western*	Death Rides Behind (short novel)	Brand
Mar. 4	*Western Story*	The Wolf and the Man (8-pt. serial: 3/4/33–4/22/33)	Baxter
Mar. 11	*Western Story*	The Stolen Stallion (book length)	Brand
Mar. 18	*Argosy*	The Masterman (6-pt. serial: 3/18/33–4/22/33)	Brand
Mar. 25	*Western Story*	Silvertip (book length)	Brand
Apr.	*Illustrated Love Magazine*	Mercy Anne (short story)	Brand
Apr. 15	*Western Story*	The Man from Mustang (book length)	Brand
Apr. 22	*Western Story*	Gunman's Gold (8-pt. serial: 4/22/33–6/10/33)	Frederick
Apr. 29	*Western Story*	Brothers of the West (book length)	Brand
May	*West Magazine*	The Quest (short novel)	Brand
May 20	*Western Story*	Silver's Strike (book length)	Brand
June 10	*Western Story*	Horseshoe Flat's Speedy Stranger (book length)	Brand
June 10	*Western Story*	Kingbird's Pursuit (8-pt. serial: 6/10/33–7/29/33)	Baxter
July	*Dime Western*	Black Thunder (short novel)	Brand
July	*West Magazine*	The Trail of the Eagle (short novel)	Brand
July 1	*Western Story*	The False Rider (book length)	Brand
July 22	*Western Story*	Riding Straight in Danger (book length)	Brand
Aug.	*Dime Western*	Guardian Guns (short novel)	Brand

Aug. 5	*Western Story*	The Iron Collar (book length)	Brand
Aug. 26	*Western Story*	The Fighting Four (book length)	Brand
Sep. 9	*Western Story*	Jingo (book length)	Brand
Sep. 9	*Argosy*	The White Indian (6-pt. serial: 9/9/33–10/14/33)	Brand
Sep. 9	*Western Story*	The Happy Rider (8-pt. serial: 9/9/33–10/28/33)	Baxter
Sep. 23	*Western Story*	Silver's Search (book length)	Brand
Oct.	*Harper's Magazine*	Only the Young Fear Death (poem)	Faust
Oct. 28	*Western Story*	Valley Thieves (5-pt. serial: 10/28/33–11/25/33)	Brand
Nov.	*Adventure*	Paston's Glory (short story)	Brand
Nov. 11	*Western Story*	Reata (short novel)	Baxter
Nov. 25	*Western Story*	Reata's Danger Trail (short novel)	Baxter
Dec. 9	*Western Story*	Reata's Desert Ride (short novel)	Baxter
Dec. 16	*Western Story*	Blue Water Bad Men (4-pt. serial: 12/16/33–1/6/34)	Brand
Dec. 16	*Argosy*	The Red Pacer (6-pt. serial: 12/16/33–1/20/34)	Baxter
Dec. 16	*Detective Fiction Weekly*	The Dark Peril (6-pt. serial: 12/16/33–1/20/34)	Brand
Dec. 23	*Western Story*	Reata and the Hidden Gold (short novel)	Baxter

1934

Jan.	*Harper's Magazine*	The Wedding Guest (short story)	Faust
Jan. 6	*Western Story*	Stolen Gold (short novel)	Baxter
Jan. 20	*Western Story*	Reata and the Overland Kid (short novel)	Baxter
Feb.	*Harper's Magazine*	A Special Occasion (short story)	Faust
Feb. 3	*Western Story*	The Tough Tenderfoot (6-pt. serial: 2/3/34–3/10/34)	Brand
Feb. 10	*Argosy*	The Naked Blade (6-pt. serial: 2/10/34–3/17/34)	Challis
Mar. 17	*Western Story*	Reata's Peril Trek (short novel)	Baxter

Mar. 17	*Argosy*	Brother of the Cheyennes (6-pt. serial: 3/17/34–4/21/34)	Brand
Mar. 17	*Detective Fiction Weekly*	X, the Murderer (6-pt. serial: 3/17/34–4/21/34)	Brand
Mar. 24	*Collier's*	Beyond the Finish (short story)	Brand
Mar. 24	*Western Story*	Gun Gift (6-pt. serial: 3/24/34–4/28/34)	Brand
Apr.	*Star Western*	Gunman's Bluff (short novel)	Brand
Apr. 28	*Argosy*	Montana Rides Again (6-pt. serial: 4/28/34–6/2/34)	Evans
May	*Star Western*	Lawman's Heart (short novel)	Brand
June	*Star Western*	Man beyond the Law (short novel)	Brand
June 2	*Western Story*	Valley of Vanishing Men (4-pt. serial: 6/2/34–6/23/34)	Brand
July	*The American Magazine*	Challenger (short story)	Brand
July	*Star Western*	Gallows Gamble (short novel)	Brand
July 7	*Detective Fiction Weekly*	Cross over Nine (6-pt. serial: 7/7/34–8/11/34)	Brand
Aug. 25	*Short Stories*	The Flood (short story)	Brand
Sep.	*Mavericks*	One Man Posse (short story)	Brand
Sep.	*Star Western*	Gunless Gunman (short novel)	Brand
Oct.	*Mavericks*	Sleeper Pays a Debt (short story)	Brand
Oct.	*Star Western*	Outcast Breed (short story)	Brand
Oct. 1	*Dime Detective*	Wet Money (short story)	Brand
Oct. 20	*Argosy*	Scourge of the Rio Grande (6-pt. serial: 10/20/34–11/24/34)	Brand
Nov.	*Mavericks*	Satan's Gun Rider (short story)	Brand
Nov.	*Star Western*	Gunman's Rendezvous (short novel)	Brand
Nov. 1	*Dime Detective*	Nine Parts Devil (short story)	Brand

Nov. 10	*Western Story*	Man of the West (6-pt. serial: 11/10/34–12/15/34)	Brand
Nov. 15	*Dime Detective*	The Unnumbered Door (short story)	Brand
Nov. 24	*Argosy*	The Firebrand (2-pt. serial: 11/24/34–12/1/34)	Challis
Dec.	*The American Magazine*	The Sun Stood Still (short story)	Brand
Dec.	*Mavericks*	Sleeper Turns Horse-Thief (short story)	Brand
Dec. 8	*Western Story*	Bad News for Bad Men (short story)	Owen
Dec. 15	*Liberty Magazine*	Name Your Price (7-pt. serial: 12/15/34–1/26/35)	Brand
Dec. 29	*Western Story*	The Red Well (short story)	Owen

1935

Jan.	*McCall's Magazine*	The Captain (short story)	Brand
Jan. 5	*Detective Fiction Weekly*	The Strange Villa (short story)	Brand
Jan. 12	*Detective Fiction Weekly*	The Little Father of Death (short story)	Brand
Jan. 26	*Detective Fiction Weekly*	The Scarred Back (short story)	Brand
Jan. 26	*Western Story*	The Fighting Coward (short story)	Owen
Feb.	*The American Magazine*	Charlie (short story)	Brand
Feb. 2	*Argosy*	The Great Betrayal (3-pt. serial: 2/2/35–2/16/35)	Challis
Feb. 9	*Argosy*	Rifle Pass (short story)	Brand
Feb. 9	*Detective Fiction Weekly*	The Man in the Shroud (short story)	Brand
Feb. 16	*Western Story*	Sun and Sand (short story)	Owen
Mar. 2	*Argosy*	Crazy Rhythm (short story)	Brand
Apr.	*McCall's Magazine*	Island of Safety (short story)	Brand
Apr.	*Star Western*	Gun-fighters in Hell (short story)	Brand
Apr. 6	*Argosy*	The Storm	Challis
Apr. 13	*Detective Fiction Weekly*	Treason against a King (short novel)	Brand
Apr. 27	*Detective Fiction Weekly*	The Gilded Box (short story)	Brand

May	*Elk's Magazine*	Paradise (short story)	Brand
May 11	*Detective Fiction Weekly*	Wings over Moscow (short story)	Brand
May 25	*Detective Fiction Weekly*	The Downfall (short story)	Brand
June 8	*Argosy*	The Cat and the Perfume (short story)	Challis
July	*Esquire*	Hummingbirds and Honeysuckle (short story)	Brand
July 13	*Argosy*	Claws of the Tigress (short novel)	Challis
July 20	*Argosy*	The Blackbirds Sing (6-pt. serial: 7/20/35–8/24/35)	Lawton
Aug. 3	*Argosy*	The Bait and the Trap (short story)	Challis
Aug. 10	*Argosy*	The Sacred Valley (6-pt. serial: 8/10/35–9/14/35)	Brand
Aug. 24	*Argosy*	The Pearls of Bonfadini (short story)	Challis
Sep. 7	*Argosy*	The Dew of Heaven (6-pt. serial: 9/7/35–10/12/35)	Challis
Sep. 21	*Detective Fiction Weekly*	''—Murder Me!'' (7-pt. serial: 9/21/35–11/2/35)	Brand
Oct. 1	*Adventure*	Beggar My Tailor (short story)	Brand
Nov. 30	*Collier's*	Thoroughbred (short story)	Brand
Dec. 7	*Detective Fiction Weekly*	The Bamboo Whistle (8-pt. serial: 12/7/35–1/25/36)	Brand
Dec. 14	*Argosy*	Perique (6-pt. serial: 12/14/35–1/18/36)	Lawton

1936

Jan. 25	*Argosy*	The Streak (6-pt. serial: 1/25/36–2/29/36)	Brand
Feb. 8	*Collier's*	The Small World (short story)	Brand
Mar.	*Cosmopolitan*	Internes Can't Take Money (short story)	Brand
Mar. 28	*Argosy*	The Song of the Whip (6-pt. serial: 3/28/36–5/2/36)	Evans
May 9	*Argosy*	Big Game (6-pt. serial: 5/9/36–6/13/36)	Brand
June	*The American Magazine*	Masquerade (short story)	Brand

June 7	*This Week*	Wine in the Desert (short story)	Brand
June 13	*Collier's*	Fixed (short story)	Brand
June 20	*Argosy*	The Golden Knight (7-pt. serial: 6/20/36–8/1/36)	Challis
June 27	*Collier's*	The Singular Horseman (short story)	Brand
June 27	*The Saturday Evening Post*	The Kinsale (short story)	Faust
July	*McCall's Magazine*	The Hound of the Hunter (short story)	Brand
July 18	*Collier's*	The Last Stretch (short story)	Brand
July 25	*Detective Fiction Weekly*	The Granduca (6-pt. serial: 7/25/36–8/29/36)	Brand
Aug. 8	*The Saturday Evening Post*	The Black O'Rourke (short story)	Faust
Oct. 17	*Detective Fiction Weekly*	Seven Faces (6-pt. serial: 10/17/36–11/21/36)	Brand
Nov.	*Cosmopolitan*	Five Minutes to Twelve (short story)	Brand
Nov. 15	*MacLean's Magazine* (Canadian)	A Seabold Fights (7-pt. serial: 11/15/36–2/15/37)	Brand

1937

Jan.	*Black Mask*	Bulldog (short story)	Brand
Jan. 2	*Argosy*	Viva! Viva! (short story)	Brand
Feb. 27	*Argosy*	The American (7-pt. serial: 2/27/37–4/10/37)	Challis
Mar. 6	*The Saturday Evening Post*	Johnny Come Lately (short story)	Faust
Mar. 20	*Argosy*	Pretty Boy (2-pt. serial: 3/20/37–3/27/37)	Brand
Apr. 3	*Collier's*	Dust Storm (short story)	Brand
Apr. 10	*Collier's*	Six Golden Angels (10-pt. serial: 4/10/37–6/12/37)	Brand
Apr. 24	*Argosy*	War for Sale (4-pt. serial: 4/24/37–5/15/37)	Brand
May 22	*Detective Fiction Weekly*	The Face and the Doctor (2-pt. serial: 5/22/37–5/29/37)	Brand

May 29	*Argosy*	The Smoking Land (6-pt. serial: 5/29/37–7/3/37)	Challis
June	*The American Magazine*	Devil Fly Away! (short story)	Brand
June 6	*This Week*	The Voice from the Record (4-pt. serial: 6/6/37–6/27/37)	Brand
June 12	*Argosy*	Bottle in the Sea (short story)	Brand
June 19	*Argosy*	Just Irish (short story)	Brand
June 27	*The American Weekly*	The Platinum Watch (3-pt. serial: 6/27/37–7/11/37)	Brand
July	*American Cavalcade*	To Meet in the Sun (short story)	Brand
July	*Cosmopolitan*	"Nifty" (short story)	Brand
July 24	*Detective Fiction Weekly*	The Death of Love (short story)	Brand
Aug.	*American Cavalcade*	The Nameless Member (short story)	Brand
Aug.	*Adventure*	The Saint (short story)	Brand
Aug.	*Complete Western Book Magazine*	Outlaw Buster (short novel)	Brand
Aug.	*Elk's Magazine*	Virginia Creeper (short story)	Brand
Sep.	*American Cavalcade*	Unhappy Landings (short story)	Brand
Sep. 4	*Liberty Magazine*	Bright Danger (10-pt. serial: 9/4/37–11/6/37)	Brand
Oct.	*American Cavalcade*	Brothers in the Sky (short story)	Brand
Nov.	*All-American Fiction*	The Champion (short story)	Brand
Nov.	*The American Magazine*	Three in the Dark (short story)	Faust
Nov.	*Double Detective*	Something Honest (short story)	Brand
Nov.	*The American Magazine*	Dust across the Range (4-pt. serial: 11/37–2/38)	Brand
Nov. 28	*This Week*	A Friend in the Night (short story)	Brand
Dec.	*All-American Fiction*	Lake Tyndal (short story)	Brand

Dec.	*The American Magazine*	They Stand So Tall (short story)	Baxter
Dec.	*Cosmopolitan*	Pringle's Luck (short story)	Brand
Dec. 4	*Collier's*	The Hill of Gasquet (short story)	Brand

1938

Jan.	*All-American Fiction*	Blind Bluff (short story)	Brand
Jan.	*The American Magazine*	Partners (short story)	Faust
Jan. 1	*MacLean's Magazine*	The Seventh Day (7-pt. serial: 1/1/38–4/1/38)	Brand
Jan. 9	*This Week*	A Silence in Tappan Valley (short story)	Brand
Jan. 29	*Western Story*	Eagles over Crooked Creek (short story)	Brand
Jan. 30	*This Week*	Forty-cent Fare (short story)	Brand
Feb.	*All-American Fiction*	Whistle Thrice (short story)	Brand
Feb.	*Cosmopolitan*	The Old Bean (short story)	Brand
Feb. 13	*This Week*	Turn of the Road (short story)	Brand
Mar.	*Black Mask*	The Silent Witness (short story)	Brand
Mar./Apr.	*All-American Fiction*	Nine Flights to Waterloo (short story)	Brand
Apr.	*Cosmopolitan*	Whiskey Sour (short story)	Brand
Apr. 24	*This Week*	Flower of Hell (3-pt. serial: 4/24/38–5/8/38)	Brand
Apr. 30	*Argosy*	The Bells of San Carlos (short story)	Brand
May	*The American Magazine*	What Price Story! (short story)	Brand
May/June	*All-American Fiction*	Speak No Evil (short story)	Brand
May 7	*Argosy*	The Living Ghost (6-pt. serial: 5/7/38–6/11/38)	Brand
June 15	*MacLean's Magazine*	Devil Dog (short story)	Brand
June 18	*Argosy*	Señor Coyote (2-pt. serial: 6/18/38–6/25/38)	Brand
July/Aug.	*All-American Fiction*	Fifteen Hundred Million (short story)	Brand
Aug.	*Blue Book*	The Flaming Finish (short story)	Brand

Sep.	*Blue Book*	Last Flight (short story)	Brand
Sep. 10	*Liberty Magazine*	Late Summer Song (short story)	Brand
Oct.	*Blue Book*	The Return of the Man Who was Killed (short story)	Brand
Nov.	*Cosmopolitan*	Death and Jimmy Warner (short story)	Brand
Dec. 17	*Argosy*	Young Doctor Kildare (3-pt. serial: 12/17/38–12/31/38)	Brand
1939			
Feb.	*Blue Book*	True Steel (short story)	Brand
Mar.	*Blue Book*	Half a Partner (short story)	Brand
Mar. 25	*Argosy*	Calling Doctor Kildare (3-pt. serial: 3/25/39–4/8/39)	Brand
Sep.	*Cosmopolitan*	The Secret of Doctor Kildare (short novel)	Brand
Sep.	*Good Housekeeping*	Miniature (short story)	Brand
Oct.	*Good Housekeeping*	Level Landings (short story)	Brand
1940			
Apr.	*Photoplay Magazine*	Doctor Kildare's Girl (short novel)	Brand
June 1	*Argosy*	Doctor Kildare Goes Home (4-pt. serial: 6/1/40–6/22/40)	Brand
Aug.	*Cosmopolitan*	My People (short story)	Brand
Sep.	*Elk's Magazine*	A Watch and the Wilderness (short story)	Brand
Nov. 29	*25th Reunion Class of 1915* (pamphlet)	We Are Going Home (essay)	Faust
Dec. 21	*Argosy*	Doctor Kildare's Crisis (4-pt. serial: 12/21/40–1/11/41)	Brand
1941			
Jan. 12	*The American Weekly*	Dead Man's Passport (8-pt. serial: 1/12/41–3/2/41)	Brand
Apr.	*Blue Book*	Luck of the Spindrift (4-pt. serial: 4/41–7/41)	Brand
May	*Cosmopolitan*	The People vs. Doctor Kildare (short novel)	Brand
July 5	*Argosy*	East Wind (short story)	Brand

| Aug. 31 | *This Week* | Cure for a Liar (short story) | Brand |
| Oct. 4 | *Argosy* | Seven Mile House (4-pt. serial: 10/4/41–11/29/41) | Brand |

1942

Jan.	*Harper's Magazine*	Distance (poem)	Faust
Mar.	*Cosmopolitan*	Doctor Kildare's Hardest Case (short story)	Brand
Sep.	*Esquire*	Taming of Red Thunder (short story)	Brand

1943

| July | *Esquire* | The Freeing of Yovan (short story) | Brand |
| Sep. | *Argosy* | Survival (short story) | Brand |

1944

Jan. 23	*The Brooklyn Eagle* (newspaper)	"Mister Christmas" (6-pt. serial: 1/23/44–2/28/44)	Brand
June 10	*The Saturday Evening Post*	After April (8-pt. serial: 6/10/44–7/29/44)	Faust
Aug.	*Argosy*	By Their Works (short story)	Brand

1945

| Jan. 27 | *Liberty Magazine* | First-Class Gentleman (short story) | Faust |

1948

Nov.	*Cosmopolitan*	Honor Bright (short story)	Brand
Nov. 21	*This Week*	The King (short story)	Brand
Dec.	*Fabulous Faust Fanzine*	Adventures by Land and Sea Autobiographical sketch	Faust
		The West Wind (poem)	Uriel

1951

| Feb. 11 | *This Week* | The Thief (short story: revision of "Our Daily Bread") | Brand |

1969

| Aug. | *The Faust Collector* | The Plow and the Horse (short story) | Faust |

1970

| Feb. | *The Faust Collector* | Follow the Herd (short story) | Faust |
| Nov. | *The Faust Collector* | The Garden (short story) | Faust |

1971

| Feb. | *The Faust Collector* | Dr. Kildare's Dilemma (2-pt. serial: 1st part) | Brand |
| Feb. | *The Faust Collector* | Summer Night at a Tavern (poem) | Faust |

1973

Jan.	*The Faust Collector*	Fellowship (poem)	Faust
		There Is No God (poem)	Faust
		Dr. Kildare's Dilemma (2-pt. serial: 2nd part {unfinished})	Brand

1990

| Fall | *Singing Guns* | The Second Chance (short story) | Faust |

1992

| Summer | *Singing Guns* | Upon Mycale, Among Priene's Ruins (poem) | Faust |
| | | If Love Can Follow (poem) | Faust |

_____ *ALPHABETICAL LIST OF PUBLISHED BOOKS* _____

All first editions are listed alphabetically, with title, byline, and year of publication. All alternate titles, both hardcover and softcover, are listed directly after the publication date, in parentheses thus: (= alternate title[s]) in alphabetical order.

Alternate American and British titles are listed in their proper alphabetical order in parentheses, without byline or publication date, but with the title of the first edition, thus: (alternate title = first edition title).

Alternate British titles are marked with {U. K.} or {U. K. only} if there is no U.S. edition.

ALCATRAZ, Brand, 1923 (= ALCATRAZ, THE WILD STALLION; DEVIL HORSE)

(ALCATRAZ, THE WILD STALLION = ALCATRAZ)

AMBUSH AT TORTURE CANYON, Brand, 1971

THE BAIT AND THE TRAP, Challis, 1951

THE BAMBOO WHISTLE, Frost, 1937

THE BANDIT OF THE BLACK HILLS, Brand, 1949

BANDIT'S HONOR, Manning, 1927 (= SIX-GUN COUNTRY)

BATTLE'S END/THE THREE CROSSES, Brand, 1990

THE BELLS OF SAN FILIPO, Brand, 1977

BEYOND THE OUTPOST, Morland, 1925

BIG GAME, Brand, 1973

THE BIG TRAIL, Brand, 1956

BLACKIE AND RED, Manning, 1926

BLACK JACK, Brand, 1970

THE BLACK SIGNAL, Manning, 1925

BLOOD ON THE TRAIL, Brand, 1957

THE BLUE JAY, Brand, 1927 (= RUSTLERS' RANGE)

THE BORDER BANDIT, Evans, 1947

BORDER GUNS, Brand, 1952

THE BORDER KID, Brand, 1941

THE BRONZE COLLAR, Frederick, 1925

BROTHER OF THE CHEYENNES, Baxter, 1935 (= FRONTIER FEUD; RUSTY {U. K.})

BROTHERS ON THE TRAIL, Brand, 1934

THE BRUTE, Manning, 1926

BULL HUNTER, Manning, 1924

BULL HUNTER'S ROMANCE, Manning, 1924

CALLING DR. KILDARE, Brand, 1940

CALL OF THE BLOOD, Baxter, 1934 (= RED HAWK AND WHITE HORSE {U. K.}; WAR PARTY)

CHEYENNE GOLD, Brand, 1972

CHILDREN OF NIGHT, Brand, 1928

CHIP CHAMPIONS A LADY/FORGOTTEN TREASURE, Brand, 1990

(CLEANED OUT {U. K.} = THE DUDE)

CLUNG, Brand, 1969 (= GHOST RIDER)

COWARD OF THE CLAN, Brand, 1991

(CROOKED HORN {U. K.} = THE OUTLAW)

THE CROSS BRAND {U. K. only}, Brand, 1993

CROSS OVER NINE, Butler, 1935

DAN BARRY'S DAUGHTER, Brand, 1924

DANGER TRAIL, Brand, 1940

DEAD MAN'S TREASURE, Brand, 1974

DEAD OR ALIVE, Brand, 1938 (= LANKY {U. K.})

THE DESERT PILOT {U. K. only}, Brand, 1993

(DESERT SHOWDOWN = TROUBLE TRAIL)

DESTRY RIDES AGAIN, Brand, 1930

(DEVIL HORSE = ALCATRAZ)

DIONYSUS IN HADES {U. K. only}, Faust, 1931

DR. KILDARE TAKES CHARGE, Brand, 1941

DR. KILDARE'S CRISIS, Brand, 1942

DR. KILDARE'S SEARCH, Brand, 1943

DR. KILDARE'S TRIAL, Brand, 1942

DONNEGAN, Baxter, 1923 (= GUNMAN'S RECKONING)

DRIFTER'S VENGEANCE, Brand, 1973

THE DUDE, Brand, 1940 (= CLEANED OUT {U. K.})

DUST ACROSS THE RANGE {U. K. only}, Brand, 1993

(A FAIRLY SLICK GUY {U. K.} = FIGHTIN' FOOL)

THE FALSE RIDER, Brand, 1947

(THE FASTEST DRAW = SEÑOR JINGLE BELLS)

FATE'S HONEYMOON {U. K. only}, Brand, 1926

FIGHTIN' FOOL, Brand, 1939 (= A FAIRLY SLICK GUY {U. K.}; SHOWDOWN
    {U. K.})

THE FIGHTING FOUR, Brand, 1944

FIRE BRAIN, Brand, 1926

THE FIREBRAND, Challis, 1950

FLAMING IRONS, Brand, 1948

FREE RANGE LANNING, Baxter, 1921 (= WAY OF THE LAWLESS)

(FRONTIER FEUD = BROTHER OF THE CHEYENNES)

FUGITIVES' FIRE, Brand, 1991

THE GALLOPING BRONCOS, Brand, 1950

GALLOPING DANGER, Brand, 1979

THE GAMBLER, Brand, 1954

THE GARDEN OF EDEN, Brand, 1963

THE GENTLE DESPERADO, Brand, 1985

THE GENTLE GUNMAN, Brand, 1964

(GHOST RIDER = CLUNG)

THE GOLDEN KNIGHT, Challis, 1937

GOLDEN LIGHTNING, Brand, 1964

THE GRANDUCA, Brand, 1973

(THE GUIDE TO HAPPINESS {U. K.} = THE TRAP AT COMANCHE BEND)

(GUNFIGHTER'S RETURN = JIM CURRY'S TEST)

GUN GENTLEMEN {U. K.}, Brand, 1924

GUNMAN'S GOLD, Brand, 1939

GUNMAN'S LEGACY, Evans, 1949 (= SIXGUN LEGACY {U. K.})

(GUNMAN'S RECKONING = DONNEGAN)

(GUNMEN'S FEUD = JERRY PEYTON'S NOTCHED INHERITANCE)

THE GUNS OF DORKING HOLLOW, Brand, 1965

THE GUN TAMER, Brand, 1929

THE HAIR-TRIGGER KID, Brand, 1951

HAPPY JACK, Brand, 1936 (= OUTLAW RIDER)

THE HAPPY VALLEY, Brand, 1931

HARRIGAN, Brand, 1971

HIRED GUNS, Brand, 1948

HIS THIRD MASTER {U. K. only}, Brand, 1925

(HORSEBACK HELLION = RED DEVIL OF THE RANGE)

HUNTED RIDERS, Brand, 1935

THE INVISIBLE OUTLAW, Brand, 1954

THE IRON TRAIL, Brand, 1938 (= RIDING THE IRON TRAIL {U. K.})

THE JACKSON TRAIL, Brand, 1932 (= THE OUTLAW TRAIL)

JERRY PEYTON'S NOTCHED INHERITANCE, Manning, 1925 (= GUNMEN'S FEUD)

JIM CURRY'S TEST, Manning, 1925 (= GUNFIGHTER'S RETURN)

THE KILLERS, Baxter, 1931 (= THREE ON THE TRAIL)

THE KING BIRD RIDES, Brand, 1936

KING CHARLIE {U. K.}, Baxter, 1925 (= KING CHARLIE'S RIDERS)

(KING CHARLIE'S RIDERS = KING CHARLIE)

KING OF THE RANGE, Austin, 1935

(LANKY {U. K.} = DEAD OR ALIVE)

LARRAMEE'S RANCH, Brand, 1966

THE LAST SHOWDOWN, Brand, 1975

LAWLESS LAND, Brand, 1983

(LAW OF THE GUN = THE SEVEN OF DIAMONDS)

(LONE HAND = SMUGGLERS' TRAIL)

THE LONG CHANCE, Brand, 1941 (= THE SAFETY KILLER {U. K.})

THE LONG CHASE, Brand, 1960

THE LONGHORN FEUD, Brand, 1933

THE LONG, LONG TRAIL, Baxter, 1923

LOST WOLF, Morland, 1928

(LUCK {U. K.} = RIDERS OF THE SILENCES)

LUCK OF THE SPINDRIFT, Brand, 1972

LUCKY LARRIBEE, Brand, 1957

(THE MAKING OF A GUNMAN = WESTERN TOMMY)

THE MAN FROM MUSTANG, Brand, 1942

(THE MAN FROM SAVAGE CREEK = RED DEVIL OF THE RANGE)

THE MAN FROM THE WILDERNESS, Brand, 1980

MARBLEFACE, Brand, 1939 (= POKER-FACE {U. K.})

MAX BRAND: COLLECTED STORIES, Brand, 1993

MAX BRAND: FIVE COMPLETE NOVELS (contents: DESTRY RIDES AGAIN; SIX-GUN COUNTRY; TROUBLE TRAIL; FLAMING IRONS; THE MAN FROM MUSTANG)

MAX BRAND'S BEST POEMS, Brand, 1992

MAX BRAND'S BEST STORIES, Brand, 1967

MAX BRAND'S BEST WESTERN STORIES, Brand, 1981

MAX BRAND'S BEST WESTERN STORIES Volume II, Brand, 1985

MAX BRAND'S BEST WESTERN STORIES Volume III, Brand, 1987

MAX BRAND'S FICTION RODEO (contents: SMILING CHARLIE; DESTRY RIDES AGAIN)

MIGHTY LOBO, Brand, 1962

MISTRAL, Brand, 1929

MONSIEUR, Challis, 1926

MONTANA RIDES!, Evans, 1933

MONTANA RIDES AGAIN, Evans, 1934

THE MOUNTAIN FUGITIVE, Manning, 1927

MOUNTAIN GUNS, Brand, 1985

MOUNTAIN RIDERS, Brand, 1946

THE MUSTANG HERDER, Manning, 1927

MYSTERY RANCH, Brand, 1930 (= MYSTERY VALLEY {U. K.})

(MYSTERY VALLEY {U. K.} = MYSTERY RANCH)

THE NAKED BLADE, Challis, 1938

THE NIGHT FLOWER, Butler, 1936

THE NIGHTHAWK TRAIL, Brand, 1987

THE NIGHT HORSEMAN, Brand, 1920

THE NOTEBOOKS AND POEMS OF "MAX BRAND," Faust, 1957

ON THE TRAIL OF FOUR, Manning, 1927

ONE MAN POSSE, Brand, 1987

THE OUTLAW, Brand, 1933 (= CROOKED HORN {U. K.})

OUTLAW BREED, Brand, 1955

OUTLAW CREW/THE BEST BANDIT, Brand, 1991

THE OUTLAW OF BUFFALO FLAT, Brand, 1974

(OUTLAW RIDER = HAPPY JACK)

OUTLAW'S CODE, Evans, 1954

(OUTLAW'S GOLD = THE TENDERFOOT)

THE OUTLAW TAMER, Manning, 1927 (= OUTLAW TAMER)

(OUTLAW TAMER = THE OUTLAW TAMER)

(THE OUTLAW TRAIL = THE JACKSON TRAIL)

OUTLAW VALLEY, Evans, 1953

THE PHANTOM SPY, Brand, 1973

PILLAR MOUNTAIN, Brand, 1928

PLEASANT JIM, Brand, 1928 (= SIX-GUN AMBUSH)

(POKER-FACE {U. K.} = MARBLEFACE)

PRIDE OF TYSON {U. K. only}, Brand, 1927

THE RANCHER'S REVENGE, Brand, 1934

RANGE JESTER/BLACK THUNDER, Brand, 1991

THE RANGELAND AVENGER, Baxter, 1924

RAWHIDE JUSTICE, Brand, 1975

THE RED BANDANNA/CARCAJOU'S TRAIL, Brand, 1991

RED DEVIL OF THE RANGE, Baxter, 1934 (= HORSEBACK HELLION; THE MAN FROM SAVAGE CREEK)

(RED HAWK AND WHITE HORSE {U. K.} = CALL OF THE BLOOD)

THE RESCUE OF BROKEN ARROW, Evans, 1948 (= REVENGE OF BROKEN ARROW)

THE RETURN OF THE RANCHER, Austin, 1933

(REVENGE OF BROKEN ARROW {U. K.} = THE RESCUE OF BROKEN ARROW)

THE REWARD, Brand, 1977 (= RONICKY DOONE'S REWARD)

RIDER OF THE HIGH HILLS, Brand, 1977

RIDERS OF THE PLAINS, Brand, 1940

RIDERS OF THE SILENCES, Frederick, 1920 (= LUCK {U. K.})

RIDE THE WILD TRAIL, Brand, 1966

(RIDING THE IRON TRAIL {U. K.} = THE IRON TRAIL)

RIPPON RIDES DOUBLE, Brand, 1968

ROGUE MUSTANG, Brand, 1984

RONICKY DOONE, Manning, 1926

(RONICKY DOONE'S REWARD = THE REWARD)

RONICKY DOONE'S TREASURE, Manning, 1926

RUSTLERS OF BEACON CREEK, Brand, 1935

(RUSTLERS' RANGE = THE BLUE JAY)

(RUSTY {U. K.} = BROTHER OF THE CHEYENNES)

(THE SAFETY KILLER {U. K.} = THE LONG CHANCE)

SAWDUST AND SIXGUNS, Evans, 1950 (= TENDERFOOT)

SECRET AGENT NUMBER ONE, Frost, 1936

THE SECRET OF DR. KILDARE, Brand, 1940

SEÑOR JINGLE BELLS, Manning, 1928 (= THE FASTEST DRAW)

THE SEVEN OF DIAMONDS, Brand, 1935 (= LAW OF THE GUN)

THE SEVENTH MAN, Brand, 1921

SEVEN TRAILS, Brand, 1949

THE SHADOW OF SILVER TIP, Baxter, 1925

THE SHERIFF RIDES, Austin, 1934 (= TRIGGERMAN)

SHOTGUN LAW, Brand, 1976

(SHOWDOWN = STRANGE COURAGE)

(SHOWDOWN {U. K.} = FIGHTIN' FOOL)

SILVERTIP, Brand, 1942

SILVERTIP'S CHASE, Brand, 1944

SILVERTIP'S ROUNDUP, Brand, 1943

SILVERTIP'S SEARCH, Brand, 1945

SILVERTIP'S STRIKE, Brand, 1942

SILVERTIP'S TRAP, Brand, 1943

SINGING GUNS, Brand, 1938

SINGLE JACK, Brand, 1950

SIX GOLDEN ANGELS, Brand, 1937

(SIX-GUN AMBUSH = PLEASANT JIM)

(SIX-GUN COUNTRY = BANDIT'S HONOR)

(SIXGUN LEGACY {U. K.} = GUNMAN'S LEGACY)

SLOW JOE, Brand, 1933

SMILING CHARLIE, Brand, 1931

SMILING DESPERADO, Brand, 1953

(SMOKING GUN TRAIL {U. K.} = SMUGGLERS' TRAIL)

THE SMOKING LAND, Brand, 1980

SMUGGLERS' TRAIL, Evans, 1950 (= LONE HAND; SMOKING GUN TRAIL
    {U. K.})

THE SONG OF THE WHIP, Evans, 1936

SOUTH OF RIO GRANDE, Brand, 1936

SPEEDY, Brand, 1955

THE SPLENDID RASCAL, Challis, 1926

SPY MEETS SPY, Frost, 1937

(STEVE TRAIN'S ORDEAL = TRAIN'S TRUST)

THE STINGAREE, Brand, 1968

THE STOLEN STALLION, Brand, 1945

STORM ON THE RANGE, Brand, 1978

STRANGE COURAGE, Evans, 1952 (= SHOWDOWN)

THE STRANGER, Brand, 1963

THE STRANGER AT THE GATE {U. K. only}, Brand, 1926

THE STREAK, Brand, 1937

(STRIKING EAGLE {U. K.} = VENGEANCE TRAIL)

THE SWORD LOVER, Frederick, 1927

TAMER OF THE WILD, Brand, 1962

(TENDERFOOT = SAWDUST AND SIXGUNS)

THE TENDERFOOT, Brand, 1953 (= OUTLAW'S GOLD)

(THREE ON THE TRAIL = THE KILLERS)

THE THUNDERER, M. B., 1933

THUNDER MOON, Brand, 1969

THUNDER MOON'S CHALLENGE, Brand, 1982

THUNDER MOON STRIKES, Brand, 1982

TIGER {U. K. only}, Brand, 1923

TIGER MAN, Baxter, 1929

TIMBAL GULCH TRAIL, Brand, 1934

TORTURE TRAIL, Brand, 1965

TRAGEDY TRAIL, Brand, 1951

TRAILIN', Brand, 1920

(THE TRAIL OF THE PANTHER {U. K.} = THE UNTAMED)

TRAIL PARTNERS, Brand, 1956

THE TRAIL TO SAN TRISTE, Baxter, 1927

TRAIN'S TRUST, Baxter, 1926 (= STEVE TRAIN'S ORDEAL)

THE TRAP AT COMANCHE BEND, Manning, 1928 (= THE GUIDE TO HAPPI-
NESS {U. K.})

(TRIGGERMAN = THE SHERIFF RIDES)

TROUBLE IN TIMBERLINE, Brand, 1984

TROUBLE KID, Brand, 1970

TROUBLE TRAIL, Brand, 1937 (= DESERT SHOWDOWN)

TWENTY NOTCHES, Brand, 1932

THE UNTAMED, Brand, 1919 (= THE TRAIL OF THE PANTHER {U. K.})

VALLEY OF JEWELS {U. K. only}, Brand, 1993

VALLEY OF VANISHING MEN, Brand, 1947

VALLEY THIEVES, Brand, 1946

VALLEY VULTURES, Brand, 1932

VENGEANCE TRAIL, Brand, 1941 (= STRIKING EAGLE {U. K.})

THE VILLAGE STREET, Faust, 1922

(WAR PARTY = CALL OF THE BLOOD)

(WAY OF THE LAWLESS = FREE RANGE LANNING)

WESTERN ROUNDUP (contents: PILLAR MOUNTAIN; PLEASANT JIM)

WESTERN TOMMY, Manning, 1927 (= THE MAKING OF A GUNMAN)

THE WHISPERING OUTLAW, Baxter, 1926

THE WHITE CHEYENNE, Brand, 1960

THE WHITE WOLF, Brand, 1926

WILD FREEDOM, Brand, 1981

WINE ON THE DESERT, Brand, 1940

WOODEN GUNS, Baxter, 1925

YOUNG DR. KILDARE, Brand, 1941

——— *CHRONOLOGICAL LIST OF PUBLISHED BOOKS* ———

All listings are first English language in the United States except where noted by {U. K.}. In these cases the first or only publication was in the United Kingdom. All entries include the publication year, the title of the book, the publisher, the byline under which Faust published the book, and alternate titles where there has been a title change or alternate editions where there has been a byline change or a more recent U.S. edition (for books originally first published in the United Kingdom). When a serial or compilation has been substantially abridged, this is noted, as is the case with a story rewritten by someone other than Faust.

Original magazine serial publications on which a book is wholly or partially based appear in brackets [ ]. Included are: the original title (in some short story collections if the story title was changed for book reprint it is noted as a reprint title followed by the original magazine title), the publication in which it appeared, the format (i.e., short story, serial, poem, etc.), the dates of the publication, and the byline under which the magazine work originally appeared.

Yr.	*Title*	*Publisher*	*Byline*
1919	THE UNTAMED	Putnam	Brand

[magazine serial version: ''The Untamed'' by Max Brand (in six parts) in *All-Story Weekly* (12/7/18–1/11/19)]

[alternate title: THE TRAIL OF THE PANTHER {U. K.} (Corgi, 1967) by Max Brand]

| *1920* | TRAILIN' | Putnam | Brand |

[magazine serial version: ''Trailin' '' by Max Brand (in six parts) in *All-Story Weekly* (11/1/19–12/6/19)]

| *1920* | RIDERS OF THE SILENCES {**abridged**} | H. K. Fly | Frederick |

[magazine serial version: ''Luck'' by John Frederick (in six parts) in *Argosy* (8/9/19–9/13/19)]

Yr.	Title	Publisher	Byline

[alternate title and edition: LUCK (London: Hodder and Stoughton, 1926) {**abridged**} by Max Brand]
[alternate title and edition: RIDERS OF THE SILENCES (Dodd, Mead, 1986) {**abridged**} by Max Brand]
{Note: the text of the 1986 version was abridged and substantially rewritten by another without credit.}

1920 THE NIGHT HORSEMAN Putnam Brand
[magazine serial version: "The Night Horseman" by Max Brand (in seven parts) in *Argosy All-Story Weekly* (9/18/20–10/30/20)]

1921 FREE RANGE LANNING {**abridged**} Chelsea House Baxter
[magazine serial version: "Iron Dust" by George Owen Baxter (in eight parts) in *Western Story Magazine* (1/29/21–3/12/21)]
[alternate title and edition: WAY OF THE LAWLESS (Dodd, Mead, 1978) {**abridged**} by Max Brand]

1921 THE SEVENTH MAN Putnam Brand
[magazine serial version: "The Seventh Man" by Max Brand (in six parts) in *Argosy All-Story Weekly* (10/1/21–11/5/21)]

1922 THE VILLAGE STREET AND OTHER Putnam Faust
POEMS
[contents: "The Village Street," "Sonnet," "The Torches," "To a Lady," "On a Grecian Funeral Monument," "Youth," "Hope," "The Skylark," "Brooklyn Bridge in a Sea Fog," "A Song," "Sunday," "The Little Men," "Balin," "Balin's Song to His Sword," "Buccaneer," "The Stars," "Fairyland," "The Parting" (reprint), "The Last Adventure" (reprint title for "The Long Road"), "The Secret" (reprint), "Legend of St. Christopher" (reprint title for "The Ballad of St. Christopher")]

1923 DONNEGAN {**abridged**} Chelsea House Baxter
[magazine serial version: "Donnegan" by George Owen Baxter (in six parts) in *Western Story Magazine* (4/16/21–5/21/21)]
[alternate title and edition: GUNMAN'S RECKONING (Dodd, Mead, 1976) {**abridged**} by Max Brand]

1923 ALCATRAZ Putnam Brand
[magazine serial version: "Alcatraz" by Max Brand (in five parts) in *Country Gentleman* (6/17/22–7/15/22)]
[alternate titles: ALCATRAZ, THE WILD STALLION (Dodd, Mead, 1959) by Max Brand and DEVIL HORSE (Warner, 1974) by Max Brand]

1923 THE LONG, LONG TRAIL Chelsea House Baxter
[magazine serial version: "Madcap of the Mountains" by George Owen Baxter (in seven parts) in *Western Story Magazine* (9/3/21–10/15/21)]
[alternate edition: THE LONG, LONG TRAIL (Dodd, Mead, 1974) by Max Brand]

1923 TIGER {U. K.} Hodder and Brand
Stoughton
[magazine serial version: "Tiger" by Max Brand (in six parts) in *Argosy All-Story Weekly* (1/8/21–2/12/21)]

Yr.	Title	Publisher	Byline

1923   CHILDREN OF NIGHT {U. K.}   Hodder and   Brand
                                                      Stoughton
[magazine serial version: "Children of Night" by Max Brand (in five parts) in
All-Story Weekly (3/22/19–4/19/19)]
[alternate edition: CHILDREN OF NIGHT (L. Harper Allen, 1928) by Max
Brand]

1924   DAN BARRY'S DAUGHTER   Putnam   Brand
[magazine serial version: "Dan Barry's Daughter" by Max Brand (in six parts)
in *Argosy All-Story Weekly* (6/30/23–8/4/23)]

1924   THE GUIDE TO HAPPINESS {U. K.}   Hodder and   Brand
                                                      Stoughton
[magazine serial version: "The Guide to Happiness" by Max Brand (in six parts)
in *Argosy All-Story Weekly* (8/13/21–9/17/21)]
[alternate title and edition: THE TRAP AT COMANCHE BEND (Chelsea House,
1928) {**abridged**} by David Manning]
[alternate title and edition: THE TRAP AT COMANCHE BEND (Thorndike,
1993) {**abridged**} by Max Brand]

1924   GUN GENTLEMEN {U. K.}   Hodder and   Brand
                                                      Stoughton
[magazine serial version: "Gun Gentlemen" by Max Brand (in five parts) in
Argosy All-Story Weekly (2/25/22–3/25/22)]
[alternate edition: GUN GENTLEMEN (Chelsea House, 1928) by David Man-
ning]
[alternate edition: GUN GENTLEMEN (G. K. Hall, 1993) by Max Brand]

1924   CLUNG {U. K.}   Hodder and   Brand
                                                      Stoughton
[magazine serial version: "Clung" by Max Brand (in six parts) in *All-Story
Weekly* (4/10/20–5/15/20)]
[alternate edition: CLUNG (Dodd, Mead, 1969) by Max Brand]
[alternate title: GHOST RIDER (Pocket Books, 1971) by Max Brand]

1924   THE RANGE-LAND AVENGER   Chelsea House   Baxter
[magazine serial version: "Three Who Paid" by George Owen Baxter (in eight
parts) in *Western Story Magazine* (4/8/22–5/27/22)]
[alternate edition: THE RANGELAND AVENGER (Dodd, Mead, 1985) by Max
Brand]

1924   BULL HUNTER   Chelsea House   Manning
[compilation of "Bullets with Sense" by Max Brand in *Western Story Magazine*
(7/9/21) and "Bull Hunter Feels His Oats" by Max Brand in *Western Story
Magazine* (8/13/21)]
[alternate edition: BULL HUNTER (Dodd, Mead, 1981) by Max Brand]

1924   BULL HUNTER'S ROMANCE {**abridged**}   Chelsea House   Manning
[compilation of "Outlaws All" by Max Brand in *Western Story Magazine*

(9/10/21), ''The Wolf Strain'' by Max Brand in *Western Story Magazine* (9/24/21), ''Bull Hunter's Romance'' by Max Brand in *Western Story Magazine* (10/22/21)]

1925   THE BRONZE COLLAR   Putnam   Frederick
[magazine serial version: ''In the Hills of Monterey'' by John Frederick (in six parts) in *Western Story Magazine* (10/4/24–11/8/24)]

1925   KING CHARLIE   Hodder and   Baxter
                                              Stoughton
[compilation of ''King Charlie and His Long Riders'' by John Frederick in *Western Story Magazine* (5/6/22), ''King Charlie—One Year Later'' by John Frederick in *Western Story Magazine* (5/27/22), ''King Charlie's Hosts'' by John Frederick in *Western Story Magazine* (6/24/22), ''The Bill for Banditry'' by John Frederick in *Western Story Magazine* (8/5/22)]
[alternate title and edition: KING CHARLIE'S RIDERS (Chelsea House, 1925) {**abridged**} by David Manning]
[alternate title and edition: KING CHARLIE'S RIDERS (G. K. Hall, 1993) {**abridged**} by Max Brand]
{Note: American editions contain abridgments of only the first three novelettes, entirely omitting ''The Bill for Banditry.''}

1925   HIS THIRD MASTER {U. K.}   Hodder and   Brand
                                              Stoughton
[magazine serial version: ''His Third Master'' by Max Brand (in six parts) in *Argosy All-Story Weekly* (6/3/22–7/27/22)]

1925   JERRY PEYTON'S NOTCHED   Chelsea House   Manning
         INHERITANCE
[magazine serial version: ''Jerry Peyton's Notched Inheritance'' by George Owen Baxter (in five parts) in *Western Story Magazine* (11/25/20–12/25/20)]
[alternate title and edition: GUNMEN'S FEUD (Dodd, Mead, 1982) by Max Brand]
{Note: For the first installment *Western Story Magazine* was still being issued every Thursday. In December 1920, the day of publication switched to every Saturday.}

1925   JIM CURRY'S TEST {**abridged**}   Chelsea House   Manning
[compilation of: ''Jim Curry's Compromise'' by Max Brand in *Western Story Magazine* (4/1/22), ''Jim Curry's Test'' by Max Brand in *Western Story Magazine* (4/22/22), ''Jim Curry's Sacrifice'' by Max Brand in *Western Story Magazine* (5/20/22)]
[alternate title and edition: GUNFIGHTER'S RETURN (Dodd, Mead, 1979) {**abridged**} by Max Brand]

1925   THE SHADOW OF SILVER TIP   Chelsea House   Baxter
[magazine serial version: ''The Shadow of Silver Tip'' by George Owen Baxter (in six parts) in *Western Story Magazine* (6/17/22–7/22/22)]
[alternate edition: THE SHADOW OF SILVER TIP (Leisure Books, 1994) by Max Brand]

Yr.	Title	Publisher	Byline

1925 BEYOND THE OUTPOST   Putnam   Morland
[magazine serial version: ''Beyond the Outposts'' by Peter Henry Morland (in
six parts) in *Western Story Magazine* (1/24/25–2/28/25)]

1925 THE BLACK SIGNAL {**abridged**}   Chelsea House   Manning
[compilation of: ''The Black Signal'' by Max Brand in *Western Story Magazine*
(3/21/25), ''Lew and Slim'' by Max Brand in *Western Story Magazine* (4/4/25),
''In the River Bottom's Grip'' by Max Brand in *Western Story Magazine*
(4/11/25)]
[alternate edition: THE BLACK SIGNAL (Dodd, Mead, 1986) {**abridged**} by
Max Brand]

1925 WOODEN GUNS   Chelsea House   Baxter
[magazine serial version: ''Wooden Guns'' by Max Brand (in six parts) in *Western Story Magazine* (9/15/23–10/20/23)]
[alternate edition: WOODEN GUNS (Chivers North America, 1993) by Max
Brand]

1926 BLACKIE AND RED {**abridged**}   Chelsea House   Manning
[compilation of: ''Blackie and Red'' by Max Brand in *Western Story Magazine*
(9/13/24), ''When 'Red' Was White'' by Max Brand in *Western Story Magazine*
(10/4/24), ''Blackie's Last Stand''by Max Brand in *Western Story Magazine*
(3/7/25)]
[alternate editions: BLACKIE AND RED (Chivers North America, 1994)
{**abridged**} by Max Brand]

1926 FIRE BRAIN   Putnam   Brand
[magazine serial version: ''Fire Brain'' by George Owen Baxter (in six parts) in
Western Story Magazine (9/12/25–10/17/25)]

1926 HARRIGAN! {U. K.}   Hodder and   Brand
                                               Stoughton
[magazine serial version: ''Harrigan!'' by Max Brand (in five parts) in *Railroad
Man's Magazine* (11/2/18–11/30/18)]
[alternate edition: HARRIGAN (Dodd, Mead, 1971) {**abridged**} by Max Brand]

1926 THE SPLENDID RASCAL   Bobbs-Merrill   Challis

1926 THE BRUTE {**abridged**}   Chelsea House   Manning
[compilation of: ''The Boy in the Wilderness'' by George Owen Baxter in *Western Story Magazine* (7/19/24), ''The Brute'' by George Owen Baxter in *Western
Story Magazine* (7/26/24), ''The Race'' by George Owen Baxter in *Western Story
Magazine* (8/9/24)]

1926 BLACK JACK {U. K.}   Hodder and   Brand
                                               Stoughton
[magazine serial version: ''Black Jack'' by Max Brand (in six parts) in *Argosy
All-Story Weekly* (12/10/21–1/14/22)]
[alternate edition: BLACK JACK (Dodd, Mead, 1970) {**abridged**} by Max
Brand]

Yr.	Title	Publisher	Byline

1926 THE STRANGER AT THE GATE {U. K.}   Hodder and   Brand
Stoughton

[magazine serial version: ''The Stranger at the Gate'' by Max Brand (in six parts) in *Argosy All-Story Weekly* (11/3/23–12/8/23)]

1926 TRAIN'S TRUST   Chelsea House   Baxter

[magazine serial version: ''Train's Trust'' by George Owen Baxter (in six parts) in *Western Story Magazine* (1/26/24–3/1/24)]

[alternate title and edition: STEVE TRAIN'S ORDEAL (Dodd, Mead, 1967) by Max Brand]

1926 RONICKY DOONE {**abridged**}   Chelsea House   Manning

[magazine serial version: ''Ronicky Doone, Champion of Lost Causes'' by David Manning (in seven parts) in *Western Story Magazine* (10/29/21–12/10/21)]

[alternate edition: RONICKY DOONE (G. K. Hall, 1993) {**abridged**} by Max Brand]

1926 THE WHITE WOLF   Putnam   Brand

[magazine serial version: ''The White Wolf'' by John Frederick (in six parts) in *Western Story Magazine* (3/6/26–4/10/26)]

1926 MONSIEUR {**abridged**}   Bobbs-Merrill   Challis

[magazine serial version: ''The Tyrant'' by George Challis (in six parts) in *Western Story Magazine* (1/9/26–2/13/26)]

1926 RONICKY DOONE'S TREASURE   Chelsea House   Manning
{**abridged**}

[magazine serial version: ''Ronicky Doone and the Cosslett Treasure'' by David Manning (in eight parts) in *Western Story Magazine* (1/7/22–2/25/22)]

[alternate edition: RONICKY DOONE'S TREASURE (G. K. Hall, 1994) {**abridged**} by Max Brand]

1926 THE WHISPERING OUTLAW   Chelsea House   Baxter

[magazine serial version: ''The Whisperer of the Wilderness'' by George Owen Baxter (in six parts) in *Western Story Magazine* (12/1/23–1/5/24)]

[alternate edition: THE WHISPERING OUTLAW (Leisure Books, 1994) by Max Brand]

1926 FATE'S HONEYMOON {U. K.}   Hodder and   Brand
Stoughton

[magazine serial version: ''Fate's Honeymoon'' by Max Brand (in five parts) in *All-Story Weekly* (7/14/17–8/11/17)]

1927 ON THE TRAIL OF FOUR {**abridged**}   Chelsea House   Manning

[magazine serial version: ''On the Trail of Four'' by Max Brand (in four parts) in *Western Story Magazine* (8/15/25–9/5/25)]

[alternate edition: ON THE TRAIL OF FOUR (Dodd, Mead, 1967) {**abridged**} by Max Brand]

1927 THE GARDEN OF EDEN {U. K.}   Hodder and   Brand
Stoughton

[magazine serial version: ''The Garden of Eden'' by Max Brand (in six parts) in *Argosy All-Story Weekly* (4/15/22–5/20/22)]

[alternate edition: THE GARDEN OF EDEN (Dodd, Mead, 1963) by Max Brand]

Yr.	*Title*	*Publisher*	*Byline*
1927	PRIDE OF TYSON {U. K.}	Hodder and Stoughton	Brand

[magazine serial version: ''Pride of Tyson'' by John Frederick (in six parts) in *Argosy* (7/3/20–8/7/20)]

| *1927* | THE MOUNTAIN FUGITIVE {**abridged**} | Chelsea House | Manning |

[compilation of: ''In Dread of the Law'' by George Owen Baxter in *Western Story Magazine* (4/18/25), ''Going Straight'' by George Owen Baxter in *Western Story Magazine* (5/2/25), ''The Battle for Mike'' by George Owen Baxter in *Western Story Magazine* (5/16/25)]

[alternate edition: THE MOUNTAIN FUGITIVE (Leisure Books, 1994) {**abridged**} by Max Brand]

| *1927* | THE BLUE JAY | Dodd, Mead | Brand |

[magazine serial version: ''Bluejay'' by Max Brand (in six parts) in *Western Story Magazine* (2/20/26–3/27/26)]

[alternate title: RUSTLER'S RANGE (Hillman Western Novel of the Month, no. 9, no date except © 1926 but this edition appeared in 1942) by Max Brand]

| *1927* | THE TRAIL TO SAN TRISTE | Chelsea House | Baxter |

[magazine serial version: ''Four without Fear'' by John Frederick (in six parts) in *Western Story Magazine* (3/8/24–4/12/24)]

[alternate edition: THE TRAIL TO SAN TRISTE (Dodd, Mead, 1983) by Max Brand]

| *1927* | THE SWORD LOVER | Watterson | Frederick |

[magazine serial version: ''The Sword Lover'' by Max Brand (in seven parts) in *Argosy* (11/10/17–12/22/18)]

| *1927* | WESTERN TOMMY | Chelsea House | Manning |

[magazine serial version: ''Western Tommy'' by John Frederick (in five parts) in *Western Story Magazine* (7/24/26–8/21/26)]

[alternate title and edition: THE MAKING OF A GUNMAN (Dodd, Mead, 1983) by Max Brand]

[alternate edition: WESTERN TOMMY (G. K. Hall, 1993) by Max Brand]

| *1927* | BANDIT'S HONOR | Chelsea House | Manning |

[compilation of: ''The Outlaw Redeemer'' by George Owen Baxter in *Western Story Magazine* (5/30/25) and ''His Fight for a Pardon'' by George Owen Baxter in *Western Story Magazine* (6/27/25)]

[alternate title and edition: SIX-GUN COUNTRY (Dodd, Mead, 1980) by Max Brand]

| *1927* | THE OUTLAW TAMER {**abridged**} | Chelsea House | Manning |

[compilation of: ''Brother of the Beasts'' by Max Brand in *Western Story Magazine* (11/28/25), ''No Man's Friend'' by Max Brand in *Western Story Magazine* (12/26/25), ''Sandy Sweyn Comes Out of the Wilds'' by Max Brand in *Western Story Magazine* (1/16/26)]

[alternate title and edition: OUTLAW TAMER (Dodd, Mead, 1988) {**abridged**} by Max Brand]

Yr.	Title	Publisher	Byline

1927 THE MUSTANG HERDER {**abridged**}   Chelsea House   Manning
[compilation of: "Sammy Gregg's Mustang Herd" by Max Brand in *Western Story Magazine* (10/3/25), "Gregg's Coach Line" by Max Brand in *Western Story Magazine* (10/17/25), "Sammy Gregg and the Posse" by Max Brand in *Western Story Magazine* (10/31/25)]
[alternate edition: THE MUSTANG HERDER (Thorndike Press, 1994) {**abridged**} by Max Brand]

1928 PLEASANT JIM   Dodd, Mead   Brand
[magazine serial version: "Pleasant Jim" by Max Brand (in six parts) in *Western Story Magazine* (10/22/27–11/26/27)]
[alternate title: SIX-GUN AMBUSH (Popular Library, 1955) by Max Brand]

1928 SEÑOR JINGLE BELLS   Chelsea House   Manning
[magazine serial version: "Señor Jingle Bells" by Max Brand (in five parts) in *Argosy All-Story Weekly* (3/7/25–4/4/25)]
[alternate title and edition: THE FASTEST DRAW (Dodd, Mead, 1987) by Max Brand]

1928 LOST WOLF   Macy-Masius   Morland
[magazine serial version: "The Squaw Boy" by Peter Henry Morland (in six parts) in *Western Story Magazine* (7/4/25–8/8/25)]
[alternate edition: LOST WOLF (A. L. Burt, 1928) by Peter Morland]
[alternate edition: LOST WOLF (Dodd, Mead, 1986) {**abridged**} by Max Brand]

1928 PILLAR MOUNTAIN   Dodd, Mead   Brand
[magazine serial version: "Pillar Mountain" by John Frederick (in six parts) in *Western Story Magazine* (8/4/28–9/8/28)]

1929 THE GUN TAMER   Dodd, Mead   Brand
[magazine serial version: "The Gun Tamer" by George Owen Baxter (in six parts) in *Western Story Magazine* (4/28/28–6/2/28)]

1929 TIGER MAN   Macaulay   Baxter
[alternate edition: TIGER MAN (G. K. Hall, 1994) by Max Brand]

1929 MISTRAL   Dodd, Mead   Brand
[magazine serial version: "Mistral" by Max Brand (in nine parts) in *The American Weekly* (1/27/29–3/24/29)]
{Note: Race track story set in the East but marketed as a Western story by Warner Books.}

1930 MYSTERY RANCH   Dodd, Mead   Brand
[magazine serial version: "The Path to Plunder" by Max Brand (in six parts) in *Western Story Magazine* (3/17/28–4/21/28)]
[alternate title: MYSTERY VALLEY {U. K.} (Hodder and Stoughton, 1930) by Max Brand]

1930 DESTRY RIDES AGAIN   Dodd, Mead   Brand
[magazine serial version: "Twelve Peers" by Max Brand (in six parts) in *Western Story Magazine* (2/1/30–3/8/30)]

Yr.	Title	Publisher	Byline

1931 DIONYSUS IN HADES {U. K.}   Blackwell   Faust
(epic poem)

1931 SMILING CHARLIE   Dodd, Mead   Brand
[magazine serial version: ''Smiling Charlie'' by Max Brand (in six parts) in *Western Story Magazine* (2/12/27–3/19/27)]

1931 THE KILLERS   Macaulay   Baxter
[magazine serial version: ''Three on the Trail'' by Max Brand (in six parts) in *Western Story Magazine* (5/12/28–6/16/28)]
[alternate title and edition: THREE ON THE TRAIL (Dodd, Mead, 1984) {**abridged**} by Max Brand]

1931 THE HAPPY VALLEY   Dodd, Mead   Brand
[magazine serial version: ''The Happy Valley'' by George Owen Baxter (in six parts) in *Western Story Magazine* (8/24/29–9/28/29)]

1932 VALLEY VULTURES   Dodd, Mead   Brand
[magazine serial version: ''Valley Vultures'' by Max Brand (in six parts) in *Western Story Magazine* (5/30/31–7/4/31)]

1932 TWENTY NOTCHES   Dodd, Mead   Brand
[magazine serial version: ''Twenty Notches'' by Max Brand (in six parts) in *Western Story Magazine* (3/14/31–4/18/31)]

1932 THE JACKSON TRAIL   Dodd, Mead   Brand
[magazine serial version: ''The Geraldi Trail'' by Max Brand (in four parts) in *Western Story Magazine* (6/11/32–7/2/32)]
[alternate title: THE OUTLAW TRAIL (Hillman Western Novel of the Month 13, n.d., © 1932 but this edition appeared in 1942) by Max Brand]
{Note: Because Geraldi was a character who appears in THE KILLERS (Macaulay, 1931) by George Owen Baxter in order to retain Max Brand's exclusive identity Dodd, Mead renamed the character ''Jesse Jackson'' for their book edition.}

1933 SLOW JOE   Dodd, Mead   Brand
[magazine serial version: ''The Golden Spurs'' by David Manning (in six parts) in *Western Story Magazine* (3/26/32–4/30/32)]

1933 MONTANA RIDES!   Harper   Evans
[condensed magazine serial version: ''Montana Rides'' by Evin Evan (in four parts) in *Western Story Magazine* (1/14/33–2/4/33)]
[alternate edition: MONTANA RIDES! (Signet, 1950) by Max Brand]

1933 THE LONGHORN FEUD   Dodd, Mead   Brand
[magazine serial version: ''The Longhorn Feud'' by Max Brand (in six parts) in *Argosy* (12/10/32–1/14/33)]

1933 THE RETURN OF THE RANCHER   Dodd, Mead   Austin
[magazine serial version: ''The Rancher Returns'' by John Frederick (in six parts) in *Western Story Magazine* (7/11/31–8/15/31)]
[alternate edition: THE RETURN OF THE RANCHER (Warner, 1972) by Max Brand]

Yr.	Title	Publisher	Byline

1933 THE OUTLAW   Dodd, Mead   Brand
[magazine serial version: "On Fortune's Back" by George Owen Baxter (in six parts) in *Western Story Magazine* (12/6/30–1/10/31)]
[alternate title: CROOKED HORN (London: Hodder and Stoughton, 1934) by Max Brand]

1933 THE THUNDERER   Derrydale Press   M. B.
[magazine serial version: "The Thunderer" by Max Brand (in four parts) in *Country Gentleman* (6/26–9/26)]
[alternate edition: THE THUNDERER {U. K.} (Hale, 1994) by Max Brand]
{Note: Race track story set in the East but marketed as a Western story by Hale.}

1934 TIMBAL GULCH TRAIL   Dodd, Mead   Brand
[magazine serial version: "Blood and Iron" by Max Brand (in four parts) in *Munsey's Magazine* (5/29–8/29)]

1934 CALL OF THE BLOOD   Macaulay   Baxter
[magazine serial version: "The White Indian" by Max Brand (in six parts) in *Argosy* (9/9/33–10/14/33)]
[alternate title: RED HAWK AND WHITE HORSE (London: Hodder and Stoughton, 1934) by George Owen Baxter]
[alternate title and edition: WAR PARTY (Dodd, Mead, 1973) {**abridged**} by Max Brand]

1934 THE SHERIFF RIDES   Dodd, Mead   Austin
[magazine serial version: "Silver Trail" by Max Brand (in six parts) in *Western Story Magazine* (10/27/28–12/1/28)]
[alternate title: TRIGGERMAN (Dell, 1952) by Frank Austin]
[alternate edition: THE SHERIFF RIDES (Warner, 1973) by Max Brand]

1934 THE RANCHER'S REVENGE   Dodd, Mead   Brand
[magazine serial version: "Gun Gift" by Max Brand (in six parts) in *Western Story Magazine* (3/24/34–4/28/34)]

1934 MONTANA RIDES AGAIN   Harper   Evans
[magazine serial version: "Montana Rides Again" by Evan Evans (in six parts) in *Argosy* (4/28/34–6/2/34)]
[alternate edition: MONTANA RIDES AGAIN (Paperback Library, 1966) by Max Brand]

1934 RED DEVIL OF THE RANGE   Macaulay   Baxter
[magazine serial version: "The Red Pacer" by Max Brand (in six parts) in *Argosy* (12/16/33–1/20/34)]
[alternate title: HORSEBACK HELLION (Signet, 1950) {**abridged**} by George Owen Baxter]
[alternate title and edition: THE MAN FROM SAVAGE CREEK (Dodd, Mead, 1977) {**abridged**} by Max Brand]

1934 BROTHERS ON THE TRAIL   Dodd, Mead   Brand
[condensed magazine version: "Brothers of the West" by Max Brand in *Western Story Magazine* (4/29/33)]

Yr.	*Title*	*Publisher*	*Byline*

1935 THE SEVEN OF DIAMONDS   Dodd, Mead   Brand
[magazine serial version: "Rustler's Rock" by David Manning (in six parts) in *Western Story Magazine* (7/6/29–8/10/29)]
[alternate title: LAW OF THE GUN (Monarch, 1959) by Max Brand]

1935 KING OF THE RANGE   Dodd, Mead   Austin
[magazine serial version: "Strength of the Hills" by George Owen Baxter (in six parts) in *Western Story Magazine* (5/25/29–6/29/29)]
[alternate edition: KING OF THE RANGE (Grosset & Dunlap, 1942) by Max Brand]

1935 HUNTED RIDERS   Dodd, Mead   Brand
[magazine serial version: "Weakling of the Wild" by Max Brand (in six parts) in *Western Story Magazine* (1/14/28–2/18/28)]

1935 BROTHER OF THE CHEYENNES   Macaulay   Baxter
[magazine serial version: "Brother of the Cheyennes" by Max Brand (in six parts) in *Argosy* (3/17/34–4/21/34)]
[alternate title: RUSTY (London: Hodder and Stoughton, 1937) by George Owen Baxter]
[alternate titles and editions: BROTHER OF THE CHEYENNES (Signet, 1949) {**abridged**} by Max Brand and FRONTIER FEUD (Dodd, Mead, 1973) {**abridged**} by Max Brand]

1935 RUSTLERS OF BEACON CREEK   Dodd, Mead   Brand
[magazine serial version: "The Winged Horse" by John Frederick (in six parts) in *Western Story Magazine* (2/16/29–3/23/29)]

1935 CROSS OVER NINE   Macaulay   Butler
[magazine serial version: "Cross over Nine" by Max Brand (in six parts) in *Detective Fiction Weekly* (7/7/34–8/11/34)]

1936 HAPPY JACK   Dodd, Mead   Brand
[magazine serial version: "Happy Jack" by George Owen Baxter (in six parts) in *Western Story Magazine* (4/26/30–5/31/30)]
[alternate title: OUTLAW RIDER (Monarch, 1960) by Max Brand]

1936 SECRET AGENT NUMBER ONE   Macrae Smith   Frost
[compilation of "The Strange Villa" by Max Brand in *Detective Fiction Weekly* (1/5/35), "The Little Father of Death" by Max Brand in *Detective Fiction Weekly* (1/12/35), "The Scarred Back" by Max Brand in *Detective Fiction Weekly* (1/26/35), "The Man in the Shroud" by Max Brand in *Detective Fiction Weekly* (2/9/35)]

1936 THE SONG OF THE WHIP   Harper   Evans
[magazine serial version: "The Song of the Whip" by Evan Evans (in six parts) in *Argosy* (3/28/36–5/2/36)]
[alternate edition: THE SONG OF THE WHIP (Paperback Library, 1967) by Max Brand]

1936 THE KING BIRD RIDES   Dodd, Mead   Brand
[magazine serial version: "Kingbird's Pursuit" by George Owen Baxter (in eight parts) in *Western Story Magazine* (6/10/33–7/29/33)]

Yr.	Title	Publisher	Byline

1936 THE NIGHT FLOWER   Macaulay   Butler
[magazine serial version: "The Dark Peril" by Max Brand (in six parts) in *Detective Fiction Weekly* (12/16/33–1/20/34)]
[alternate edition: THE NIGHT FLOWER (International Polygonics, 1987) by Max Brand]

1936 SOUTH OF RIO GRANDE   Dodd, Mead   Brand
[magazine serial version: "Tiger's Den" by John Frederick (in six parts) in *Western Story Magazine* (3/15/30–4/19/30)]

1937 TROUBLE TRAIL   Dodd, Mead   Brand
[magazine serial version: "Trouble Trail" by George Owen Baxter (in six parts) in *Western Story Magazine* (8/28/26–10/2/26)]
[alternate title: DESERT SHOWDOWN (Popular Library, 1955) by Max Brand]

1937 SPY MEETS SPY   Macrae Smith   Frost
[compilation of "Treason against a King" by Max Brand in *Detective Fiction Weekly* (4/13/35), "The Gilded Box" by Max Brand in *Detective Fiction Weekly* (4/27/35), "Wings over Moscow" by Max Brand in *Detective Fiction Weekly* (5/11/35), "The Downfall" by Max Brand in *Detective Fiction Weekly,* (5/25/35)]

1937 THE STREAK   Dodd, Mead   Brand
[magazine serial version: "The Streak" by Max Brand (in six parts) in *Argosy* (1/25/36–2/29/36)]

1937 THE GOLDEN KNIGHT   Greystone Press   Challis
[magazine serial version: "The Golden Knight" by George Challis (in seven parts) in *Argosy* (6/20/36–8/1/36)]

1937 THE BAMBOO WHISTLE   Macrae Smith   Frost
[magazine serial version: "The Bamboo Whistle" by Max Brand (in eight parts) in *Detective Fiction Weekly* (12/7/35–1/25/36)]

1937 SIX GOLDEN ANGELS   Dodd, Mead   Brand
[magazine serial version: "Six Golden Angels" by Max Brand (in ten parts) in *Collier's* (4/10/37–6/12/37)]

1938 THE IRON TRAIL   Dodd, Mead   Brand
[magazine serial version: "The Iron Trail" by Max Brand (in six parts) in *Western Story Magazine* (10/30/26–12/4/26)]
[alternate title: RIDING THE IRON TRAIL (London: Hodder and Stoughton, 1938) by Max Brand]

1938 THE NAKED BLADE   Greystone Press   Challis
[magazine serial version: "The Naked Blade" by George Challis (in six parts) in *Argosy* (2/10/34–3/17/34)]
[alternate edition: THE NAKED BLADE (Lancer, 1967) by Frederick Faust]

1938 SINGING GUNS   Dodd, Mead   Brand
[magazine serial version: "Singing Guns" by George Owen Baxter (in six parts) in *Western Story Magazine* (12/15/28–1/19/29)]

Yr.	*Title*	*Publisher*	*Byline*

1938 DEAD OR ALIVE Dodd, Mead Brand
[magazine serial version: "Cat Hill Fugitive" by Max Brand (in four parts) in *Western Story Magazine* (12/10/32–12/31/32)]
[alternate title: LANKY FOR LUCK (London: Hodder and Stoughton, 1939) by Max Brand]

1939 MARBLEFACE Dodd, Mead Brand
[magazine serial version: "The Tough Tenderfoot" by Max Brand (in six parts) in *Western Story Magazine* (2/3/34–3/10/34)]
[alternate title: POKER FACE (London: Hodder and Stoughton, 1939) by Max Brand]

1939 FIGHTIN' FOOL Dodd, Mead Brand
[condensed magazine version: "Jingo" by Max Brand in *Western Story Magazine* (9/9/33)]
[alternate title: A FAIRLY SLICK GUY (London: Hodder and Stoughton, 1940) by Max Brand]

1939 GUNMAN'S GOLD Dodd, Mead Brand
[magazine serial version: "Gunman's Gold" by John Frederick (in eight parts) in *Western Story Magazine* (4/22/33–6/10/33)]

1940 THE DUDE Dodd, Mead Brand
[magazine serial version: "Man of the West" by Max Brand (in six parts) in *Western Story Magazine* (11/10/34–12/15/34)]
[alternate title: CLEANED OUT (London: Hodder and Stoughton, 1940) by Max Brand]

1940 THE SECRET OF DR. KILDARE Dodd, Mead Brand
[condensed magazine version: "The Secret of Dr. Kildare" by Max Brand in *Cosmopolitan* (9/39)]

1940 DANGER TRAIL Dodd, Mead Brand
[magazine serial version: "The Happy Rider" by George Owen Baxter (in eight parts) in *Western Story Magazine* (9/9/33–10/28/33)]

1940 CALLING DR. KILDARE Dodd, Mead Brand
[magazine serial version: "Calling Dr. Kildare" by Max Brand (in three parts) in *Argosy* (3/25/39–4/8/39)]

1940 WINE ON THE DESERT AND OTHER Dodd, Mead Brand
STORIES
[contents: "Our Daily Bread" (first publication), "Oh, Wonderful!" (first publication), "The Wedding Guest" (reprint), "A Special Occasion" (reprint), "Charlie" (reprint), "Hummingbirds and Honeysuckle" (reprint), "The Small World" (reprint), "Internes Can't Take Money" (reprint), "Wine on the Desert" (reprint title for "Wine in the Desert"), "Fixed" (reprint), "The Kinsale" (reprint), "Lew Corbin, Gentleman" (reprint title for "The Last Stretch"), "The Luck of Pringle" (reprint title for "Pringle's Luck"), "Men Get Old" (reprint title for "What Price Story!"), "A Watch and the Wilderness" (reprint)]

Yr.	Title	Publisher	Byline

1940 RIDERS OF THE PLAINS   Dodd, Mead   Brand
[magazine serial version: "Acres of Unrest" by Max Brand (in six parts) in *Western Story Magazine* (6/12/26–4/17/26)]

1941 THE BORDER KID   Dodd, Mead   Brand
[magazine serial version: "Riders for Fortune" by George Owen Baxter (in six parts) in *Western Story Magazine* (9/15/28–10/20/28)]

1941 YOUNG DR. KILDARE   Dodd, Mead   Brand
[magazine serial version: "Young Dr. Kildare" by Max Brand (in three parts) in *Argosy* (12/17/38–12/31/38)]

1941 THE LONG CHANCE   Dodd, Mead   Brand
[magazine serial version: "The Western Double" by George Owen Baxter (in six parts) in *Western Story Magazine* (3/26/27–4/30/27)]
[alternate title: THE SAFETY KILLER (London: Hodder and Stoughton, 1942) by Max Brand]

1941 DR. KILDARE GOES HOME   Dodd, Mead   Brand
[magazine serial version: "Dr. Kildare Goes Home" by Max Brand (in four parts) in *Argosy* (6/1/40–6/22/40)]

1941 VENGEANCE TRAIL   Dodd, Mead   Brand
[magazine serial version: "Gun Pearl Trail" by George Owen Baxter (in six parts) in *Western Story Magazine* (9/12/31–10/17/31)]
[alternate title: STRIKING EAGLE (London: Hodder and Stoughton, 1942) by Max Brand]

1941 SILVERTIP   Dodd, Mead   Brand
[condensed magazine version: "Silvertip" by Max Brand in *Western Story Magazine* (3/25/33)]

1942 DR. KILDARE'S CRISIS   Dodd, Mead   Brand
[magazine serial version: "Dr. Kildare's Crisis" by Max Brand (in four parts) in *Argosy* (12/21/40–1/11/41)]

1942 THE MAN FROM MUSTANG   Dodd, Mead   Brand
[condensed magazine version: "The Man from Mustang" by Max Brand in *Western Story Magazine* (4/15/33)]

1942 DR. KILDARE'S TRIAL   Dodd, Mead   Brand
[condensed magazine version: "The People vs. Dr. Kildare" by Max Brand in *Cosmopolitan* (5/41)]

1942 SILVERTIP'S STRIKE   Dodd, Mead   Brand
[condensed magazine version: "Silver's Strike" by Max Brand in *Western Story Magazine* (5/20/33)]

1943 DR. KILDARE'S SEARCH   Dodd, Mead   Brand
[compilation of "Dr. Kildare's Girl" by Max Brand in *Photoplay* (4/40) and "Dr. Kildare's Hardest Case" by Max Brand in *Cosmopolitan* (3/42)]

1943 SILVERTIP'S ROUNDUP   Dodd, Mead   Brand
[condensed magazine version: "Horseshoe Flat's Speedy Stranger" by Max Brand in *Western Story Magazine* (6/10/33)]

Yr.	Title	Publisher	Byline

1943 SILVERTIP'S TRAP   Dodd, Mead   Brand
[condensed magazine version: "Riding Straight in Danger" by Max Brand in *Western Story Magazine* (7/22/33)]

1944 THE FIGHTING FOUR   Dodd, Mead   Brand
[condensed magazine version: "The Fighting Four" by Max Brand in *Western Story Magazine* (8/26/33)]

1944 SILVERTIP'S CHASE   Dodd, Mead   Brand
[condensed magazine version: "The Iron Collar" by Max Brand in *Western Story Magazine* (8/5/33)]

1945 SILVERTIP'S SEARCH   Dodd, Mead   Brand
[condensed magazine version: "Silver's Search" by Max Brand in *Western Story Magazine* (9/23/33)]

1945 THE STOLEN STALLION   Dodd, Mead   Brand
[condensed magazine version: "The Stolen Stallion" by Max Brand in *Western Story Magazine* (3/11/33)]

1946 VALLEY THIEVES   Dodd, Mead   Brand
[magazine serial version: "Valley Thieves" by Max Brand (in five parts) in *Western Story Magazine* (10/28/33–11/25/33)]

1946 MOUNTAIN RIDERS   Dodd, Mead   Brand
[magazine serial version: "Blue Water Bad Men" by Max Brand (in four parts) in *Western Story Magazine* (12/16/33–1/6/34)]

1947 THE BORDER BANDIT   Harper   Evans
[compilation of "The Border Bandit" by Max Brand in *Western Story Magazine* (9/25/26), "The Border Bandit's Indian Brother" by Max Brand in *Western Story Magazine* (10/2/26), "The Border Bandit's Prize" by Max Brand in *Western Story Magazine* (10/9/26)]
[alternate edition: THE BORDER BANDIT (Paperback Library, 1967) by Max Brand]

1947 VALLEY OF VANISHING MEN   Dodd, Mead   Brand
[magazine serial version: "Valley of Vanishing Men" by Max Brand (in four parts) in *Western Story Magazine* (6/2/34–6/23/34)]

1947 THE FALSE RIDER   Dodd, Mead   Brand
[condensed magazine version: "The False Rider" by Max Brand in *Western Story Magazine* (7/1/33)]

1948 THE RESCUE OF BROKEN ARROW   Harper   Evans
[magazine serial version: "The Horizon of Danger" by Peter Henry Morland (in six parts) in *Western Story Magazine* (12/21/29–1/25/30)]
[alternate title: THE REVENGE OF BROKEN ARROW (London: Jenkins, 1951) by Evan Evans]
[alternate edition: THE RESCUE OF BROKEN ARROW (Paperback Library, 1967) by Max Brand]

Yr.	Title	Publisher	Byline

1948 FLAMING IRONS {**abridged**} Dodd, Mead Brand
[magazine serial version: "The City in the Sky" by Max Brand (in six parts) in *Western Story Magazine* (6/11/27–7/16/27)]

1948 HIRED GUNS {**abridged**} Dodd, Mead Brand
[magazine serial version: "Hired Guns" by Max Brand (in seven parts) in *Western Story Magazine* (3/10/23–4/21/23)]

1949 GUNMAN'S LEGACY Harper Evans
[condensed magazine serial version: "Rancher's Legacy" by Peter Henry Morland (in six parts) in *Western Story Magazine* (2/20/32–3/26/32)]
[alternate title: SIXGUN LEGACY (London: Jenkins, 1950) by Evan Evans]
[alternate edition: SIXGUN LEGACY (Paperback Library, 1967) by Max Brand]

1949 THE BANDIT OF THE BLACK HILLS Dodd, Mead Brand
[magazine serial version: "The Bandit of the Black Hills" by George Owen Baxter (in six parts) in *Western Story Magazine* (4/28/23–6/2/23)]

1949 SEVEN TRAILS Dodd, Mead Brand
[magazine serial version: "Seven Trails to Romance" by George Owen Baxter (in six parts) in *Western Story Magazine* (9/1/23–10/6/23)]

1950 SMUGGLERS' TRAIL Harper Evans
[magazine serial version: "Scourge of the Rio Grande" by Max Brand (in six parts) in *Argosy* (10/20/34–11/24/34)]
[alternate titles: SMOKING GUN TRAIL (London: Jenkins, 1951) by Evan Evans and LONE HAND (Bantam, 1951) by Evan Evans]
[alternate edition: SMUGGLERS' TRAIL (Paperback Library, 1967) by Max Brand]

1950 SINGLE JACK Dodd, Mead Brand
[magazine serial version: "Comanche" by Max Brand (in five parts) in *Far West Illustrated* (12/26–4/27)]

1950 THE FIREBRAND Harper Challis
[compilation: "The Firebrand" by George Challis (in two parts) in *Argosy* (11/24/34–12/1/34), "The Great Betrayal" by George Challis (in three parts) in *Argosy* (2/2/35–2/16/35), "The Storm" by George Challis (in three parts) in *Argosy* (4/6/35–4/20/35)]

1950 SAWDUST AND SIXGUNS Harper Evans
[magazine serial version: "Sawdust and Sixguns" by Max Brand (a six-part serial) in *Far West Illustrated* (8/27–1/28)]
[alternate title and edition: TENDERFOOT (Paperback Library, 1967) by Max Brand]

1950 THE GALLOPING BRONCOS Dodd, Mead Brand
[magazine serial version: "Two Bronchos" by George Owen Baxter (in six parts) in *Western Story Magazine* (11/9/29–12/14/29)]

1951 THE BAIT AND THE TRAP Harper Challis
[compilation of "Claws of the Tigress" by George Challis in *Argosy* (7/13/35),

Yr.	*Title*	*Publisher*	*Byline*

"The Bait and the Trap" by George Challis in *Argosy* (8/3/35), "The Pearls of Bonfadini" by George Challis in *Argosy* (8/24/35)]

1951 THE HAIR-TRIGGER KID   Dodd, Mead   Brand
[magazine serial version: "Duck Hawk's Master" by George Owen Baxter (in six parts) in *Western Story Magazine* (4/25/31–5/30/31)]

1951 TRAGEDY TRAIL   Dodd, Mead   Brand
[magazine serial version: "Tragedy Trail" by George Owen Baxter (in six parts) in *Western Story Magazine* (2/25/28–3/31/28)]

1952 BORDER GUNS   Dodd, Mead   Brand
[magazine serial version: "The Brass Man" by George Owen Baxter (in six parts) in *Western Story Magazine* (6/23/28–7/28/28)]

1952 STRANGE COURAGE   Harper   Evans
[magazine serial version: "Daring Duval" by George Owen Baxter (in six parts) in *Western Story Magazine* (7/19/30–8/23/30)]
[alternate title and edition: SHOWDOWN (Paperback Library, 1967) by Max Brand]

1953 OUTLAW VALLEY {**abridged**}   Harper   Evans
[magazine serial version: "Outlaw Valley" by Max Brand (in five parts) in *Far West Illustrated* (4/28–8/28)]
[alternate edition: OUTLAW VALLEY (Paperback Library, 1967) {**abridged**} by Max Brand]

1953 SMILING DESPERADO   Dodd, Mead   Brand
[magazine serial version: "The Love of Danger" by Max Brand (in six parts) in *Western Story Magazine* (8/2/24–9/6/24)]

1953 THE TENDERFOOT   Dodd, Mead   Brand
[magazine serial version: "Saddle and Sentiment" by Max Brand (in six parts) in *Western Story Magazine* (4/19/24–5/24/24)]
[alternate title: OUTLAW'S GOLD (Warner Books, 1976) by Max Brand]

1954 OUTLAW'S CODE {**abridged**}   Harper   Evans
[magazine serial version: "The Lightning Runner" by John Frederick (in six parts) in *Western Story Magazine* (1/9/32–2/13/32)]
[alternate title and edition: OUTLAW CODE (Paperback Library, 1968) {**abridged**} by Max Brand]

1954 THE GAMBLER   Dodd, Mead   Brand
[magazine serial version: "The Gambler" by Max Brand (in six parts) in *Western Story Magazine* (6/7/24–7/12/24)]

1954 THE INVISIBLE OUTLAW   Dodd, Mead   Brand
[magazine serial version: "The Invisible Outlaw" by Max Brand (in four parts) in *Western Story Magazine* (11/5/32–11/26/32)]

1955 SPEEDY   Dodd, Mead   Brand
[magazine serial version: "Tramp Magic" by Max Brand (in six parts) in *Western Story Magazine* (11/21/31–12/26/31)]

Yr.	Title	Publisher	Byline

1955 OUTLAW BREED   Dodd, Mead   Brand
[magazine serial version: "A Son of Danger" by Max Brand (in six parts) in *Western Story Magazine* (4/17/26–5/22/26)]

1956 THE BIG TRAIL   Dodd, Mead   Brand
[magazine serial version: "The Trail to Manhood" by Max Brand (in six parts) in *Western Story Magazine* (4/13/29–5/18/29)]

1956 TRAIL PARTNERS   Dodd, Mead   Brand
[magazine serial version: "All for One" by George Owen Baxter (in four parts) in *Western Story Magazine* (10/1/32–10/22/32)]

1957 LUCKY LARRIBEE   Dodd, Mead   Brand
[magazine serial version: "Lucky Larribee" by George Owen Baxter (in six parts) in *Western Story Magazine* (4/2/32–5/7/32)]

1957 THE NOTEBOOKS AND POEMS OF Dodd, Mead   Faust
   "MAX BRAND"   John F. Schoolcraft,
               editor
[contents: (poems) "Briareus," "Ceyx and Halcyone," "Dorothy Parker," "Gethsemane," "I Wakened," "I'll Have No Gods," "The Island of Ios," "La Belle France," "My Sweat," "Old Friends," "Rain," "So Poor," "Time Gives Burdens," "To My Soul," "Tom and Jerry," "What Love Is There," "Song to Mars" (reprint), "The Last Adventure" (reprint title for "The Long Road"), "The Secret" (reprint), "Only the Young Fear Death" (reprint), "Distance" (reprint)]

1957 BLOOD ON THE TRAIL   Dodd, Mead   Brand
[magazine serial version: "The Wolf and the Man" by George Owen Baxter (in eight parts) in *Western Story Magazine* (3/4/33–4/22/33)]

1960 THE WHITE CHEYENNE   Dodd, Mead   Brand
[magazine serial version: "The White Cheyenne" by Peter Henry Morland (in six parts) in *Western Story Magazine* (12/12/25–1/20/26)]

1960 THE LONG CHASE   Dodd, Mead   Brand
[magazine serial version: "Old Carver Ranch" by John Frederick (in seven parts) in *Western Story Magazine* (8/26/22–10/7/22)]

1962 TAMER OF THE WILD   Dodd, Mead   Brand
[magazine serial version: "Tamer of the Wild" by Peter Henry Morland (in six parts) in *Western Story Magazine* (10/24/31–11/28/31)]

1962 MIGHTY LOBO   Dodd, Mead   Brand
[magazine serial version: "Mighty Lobo" by George Owen Baxter (in four parts) in *Western Story Magazine* (7/23/32–8/13/32)]

1963 THE STRANGER   Dodd, Mead   Brand
[magazine serial version: "The Stranger" by Max Brand (in five parts) in *Western Story Magazine* (1/12/29–2/9/29)]

1964 GOLDEN LIGHTNING {**abridged**} Dodd, Mead   Brand
[magazine serial version: "Golden Lightning" by Max Brand (in six parts) in *Western Story Magazine* (8/22/31–9/26/31)]

Yr.	*Title*	*Publisher*	*Byline*

1964 THE GENTLE GUNMAN {**abridged**}   Dodd, Mead   Brand
[magazine serial version: ''Argentine'' by George Owen Baxter (in six parts) in
Western Story Magazine (5/31/24–7/5/24)]

1965 TORTURE TRAIL   Dodd, Mead   Brand
[magazine serial version: ''Torturous Trek'' by Max Brand (in four parts) in
Western Story Magazine (8/27/32–9/17/32)]

1965 THE GUNS OF DORKING HOLLOW   Dodd, Mead   Brand
[magazine serial version: ''The Silver Stork'' by Max Brand (in six parts) in
Western Story Magazine (8/13/27–10/17/27)]

1966 RIDE THE WILD TRAIL {**abridged**}   Dodd, Mead   Brand
[magazine serial version: ''Dogs of the Captain'' by Max Brand (in six parts) in
Western Story Magazine (1/2/32–2/6/32)]

1966 LARRAMEE'S RANCH   Dodd, Mead   Brand
[magazine serial version: ''Larramee's Ranch'' by George Owen Baxter (in six
parts) in *Western Story Magazine* (9/13/24–10/18/24)]

1967 MAX BRAND'S BEST STORIES   Dodd, Mead   Brand
                                                   Robert Easton,
                                                   editor
[contents: ''The King'' (reprint), ''Honor Bright'' (reprint), ''Wine on the Des-
ert'' (reprint title for ''Wine in the Desert''), ''Our Daily Bread'' (reprint), ''The
Wolf Pack and the Kill'' (excerpt from ''Harrigan!''), ''Internes Can't Take
Money'' (reprint), ''The Claws of the Tigress'' (reprint), ''The Silent Witness''
(reprint), ''The Kinsale'' (reprint), ''A Life for a Life'' (excerpt from CALLING
DR. KILDARE), ''The Luck of Pringle'' (reprint title for ''Pringle's Luck''), ''A
Special Occasion'' (reprint), ''The Sun Stood Still'' (reprint)]

1968 RIPPON RIDES DOUBLE {**abridged**}   Dodd, Mead   Brand
[magazine serial version: ''Rippon Rides Double'' by Max Brand (in six parts)
in *Western Story Magazine* (10/18/30–11/22/30)]

1968 THE STINGAREE {**abridged**}   Dodd, Mead   Brand
[magazine serial version: ''The Stingaree'' by Max Brand (in six parts) in *Western
Story Magazine* (6/7/30–7/12/30)]

1969 THUNDER MOON {**abridged**}   Dodd, Mead   Brand
[magazine serial version: ''Thunder Moon'' by George Owen Baxter (in five
parts) in *Far West Illustrated* (4/27–8/27)]

1970 TROUBLE KID   Dodd, Mead   Brand
[compilation of ''Chip and the Cactus Man'' by Max Brand in *Western Story
Magazine* (1/10/31) and ''Chip Traps a Sheriff'' by Max Brand in *Western Story
Magazine* (1/31/31)]

1971 AMBUSH AT TORTURE CANYON   Dodd, Mead   Brand
          {**abridged**}
[compilation of ''Spot Lester'' by Max Brand in *Western Story Magazine*
(10/17/31), ''Nine Lives'' by Max Brand in *Western Story Magazine* (10/31/31),
and ''Torture Canyon'' by Max Brand in *Western Story Magazine* (11/14/31)]

Yr.	*Title*	*Publisher*	*Byline*

1972 THE LUCK OF THE SPINDRIFT Dodd, Mead Brand
[magazine serial version: "The Luck of the Spindrift" by Max Brand (in four parts) in *Blue Book* (4/41–7/41)]

1972 CHEYENNE GOLD {**abridged**} Dodd, Mead Brand
[magazine serial version: "The Sacred Valley" by Max Brand (in six parts) in *Argosy* (8/10/35–9/14/35)]

1973 DRIFTER'S VENGEANCE {**abridged**} Dodd, Mead Brand
[compilation of "Speedy—Deputy" by Max Brand in *Western Story Magazine* (2/13/32), "Seven-Day Lawman" by Max Brand in *Western Story Magazine* (2/27/32), and "Speedy's Mare" by Max Brand in *Western Story Magazine* (3/12/32)]

1973 BIG GAME Warner Paperback Brand
  Library
[magazine serial version: "Big Game" by Max Brand (in six parts) in *Argosy* (5/9/36–6/13/36)]

1973 THE GRANDUCA {**abridged**} Warner Paperback Brand
  Library
[magazine serial version: "The Granduca" by Max Brand (in six parts) in *Detective Fiction Weekly* (7/25/36–8/29/36)]

1973 THE PHANTOM SPY {**abridged**} Dodd, Mead Brand
[magazine serial version: "War for Sale" by Max Brand (in four parts) in *Argosy* (4/24/37–5/15/37)]

1974 DEAD MAN'S TREASURE {**abridged**} Dodd, Mead Brand
[magazine serial version: "Perique" by Dennis Lawton (in six parts) in *Argosy* (12/14/35–1/18/36)]

1974 THE OUTLAW OF BUFFALO FLAT Dodd, Mead Brand
{**abridged**}
[magazine serial version: "The Mask of Ching Wo" by Max Brand (in six parts) in *Railroad Man's Magazine* (8/30–2/31)]

1975 THE LAST SHOWDOWN {**abridged**} Dodd, Mead Brand
[compilation of "The Duster" by Max Brand in *Western Story Magazine* (11/2/29), "Twisted Bars" by Max Brand in *Western Story Magazine* (11/16/29), and "Duster's Return" by Max Brand in *Western Story Magazine* (11/30/29)]

1975 RAWHIDE JUSTICE {**abridged**} Dodd, Mead Brand
[compilation of "Reata" by George Owen Baxter in *Western Story Magazine* (11/11/33), "Reata's Danger Trail" by George Owen Baxter in *Western Story Magazine* (11/25/33), and "Reata's Desert Ride" by George Owen Baxter in *Western Story Magazine* (12/9/33)]

1976 SHOTGUN LAW {**abridged**} Dodd, Mead Brand
[compilation of "Hawks and Eagles" by George Owen Baxter in *Western Story Magazine* (12/5/31), "Black Snake and Gun" by George Owen Baxter in *Western Story Magazine* (12/19/31), and "Black Snake Joe" by George Owen Baxter in *Western Story Magazine* (1/2/32)]

Yr.	*Title*	*Publisher*	*Byline*

1977 THE BELLS OF SAN FILIPO {**abridged**}   Pocket Books   Brand
[magazine serial version: "The Bells of San Filipo" by George Owen Baxter (in six parts) in *Western Story Magazine* (11/6/26–12/11/26)]

1977 RIDER OF THE HIGH HILLS {**abridged**}   Dodd, Mead   Brand
[compilation of "Reata and the Hidden Gold" by George Owen Baxter in *Western Story Magazine* (12/23/33), "Stolen Gold" by George Owen Baxter in *Western Story Magazine* (1/6/34), and "Reata and the Overland Kid" by George Owen Baxter in *Western Story Magazine* (1/20/34)]

1977 THE REWARD {**abridged**}   Pocket Books   Brand
[magazine serial version: "Ronicky Doone's Reward" by David Manning (in six parts) in *Western Story Magazine* (7/15/22–8/19/22)]
[alternate title: RONICKY DOONE'S REWARD {**abridged**} (G. K. Hall, 1995) by Max Brand]

1978 STORM ON THE RANGE {**abridged**}   Dodd, Mead   Brand
[compilation of "Treasure Well" by George Owen Baxter in *Western Story Magazine* (6/27/31), "Outlaw's Conscience" by George Owen Baxter in *Western Story Magazine* (7/11/31), and "Clean Courage" by George Owen Baxter in *Western Story Magazine* (7/25/31)]

1979 GALLOPING DANGER {**abridged**}   Dodd, Mead   Brand
[magazine serial version: "Galloping Danger" by Max Brand (in six parts) in *Western Story Magazine* (7/14/23–8/18/23)]

1980 THE MAN FROM THE WILDERNESS   Dodd, Mead   Brand
{**abridged**}
[magazine serial version: "Mountain Made" by George Owen Baxter (in six parts) in *Western Story Magazine* (12/13/24–1/17/25)]

1980 THE SMOKING LAND   Capra Press   Brand
[magazine serial version: "The Smoking Land" by George Challis (in six parts) in *Argosy* (5/29/37–7/3/37)]

1981 MAX BRAND'S BEST WESTERN   Dodd, Mead   Brand
STORIES {**abridged and rewritten**}   William F. Nolan,
    editor
[contents: "Wine on the Desert" (reprint title for "Wine in the Desert"), "Virginia Creeper" (reprint), "Macdonald's Dream" (title for the rewritten " 'Sunset' Wins"), "Partners" (reprint), "Dust across the Range" (title retained for rewritten serial), "The Bells of San Carlos" (reprint)]

1981 WILD FREEDOM {**abridged**}   Dodd, Mead   Brand
[magazine serial version: "Wild Freedom" by George Owen Baxter (in six parts) in *Western Story Magazine* (11/11/22–12/16/22)]

1982 THUNDER MOON'S CHALLENGE   Dodd, Mead   Brand
{**abridged**}
[compilation of "Red Wind and Thunder Moon" by George Owen Baxter in *Western Story Magazine* (8/27/27), "Thunder Moon—Pale Face" by George Owen Baxter in *Western Story Magazine* (9/17/27), and the beginning of "Thun-

Yr.	*Title*	*Publisher*	*Byline*

der Moon—Squawman'' by George Owen Baxter (in five parts) in *Western Story Magazine* (9/24/27–10/22/27)]

1982 THUNDER MOON STRIKES {**abridged**}   Dodd, Mead   Brand
[compilation of the conclusion of ''Thunder Moon—Squawman'' (see above) and ''Thunder Moon Goes White'' by George Owen Baxter in *Western Story Magazine* (11/3/28)]

1983 LAWLESS LAND {**abridged**}   Dodd, Mead   Brand
[compilation of ''Speedy's Crystal Game'' by Max Brand in *Western Story Magazine* (4/2/32), ''Red Rock's Secret'' by Max Brand in *Western Story Magazine* (4/16/32), and ''Speedy's Bargain'' by Max Brand in *Western Story Magazine* (5/14/32)]

1984 ROGUE MUSTANG   Dodd, Mead   Brand
[compilation of ''Paradise Al'' by David Manning in *Western Story Magazine* (6/4/32) and ''Paradise Al's Confession'' by David Manning in *Western Story Magazine* (7/16/32)]

1984 TROUBLE IN TIMBERLINE   Dodd, Mead   Brand
[compilation of ''The Quest'' by Max Brand in *West* (5/33), ''The Trail of the Eagle'' by Max Brand in *West* (7/33), and ''Outlaw Buster'' by Max Brand in *Complete Western Book Magazine* (8/37)]

1985 MAX BRAND'S BEST WESTERN   Dodd, Mead   Brand
STORIES: Volume II {**abridged and**   William F. Nolan,
rewritten}   editor
[contents: ''The Fear of Morgan the Fearless'' (reprint), ''Dark Rosaleen'' (title retained for rewritten serial), ''Cayenne Charlie'' (title retained for rewritten short novel), ''The Golden Day'' (reprint), ''Outcast'' (title for rewritten ''Outcast Breed'')]

1985 MOUNTAIN GUNS {**abridged**}   Dodd, Mead   Brand
[magazine serial version: ''Trouble's Messenger'' by George Owen Baxter (in six parts) in *Western Story Magazine* (9/6/30–10/11/30)]

1985 THE GENTLE DESPERADO {**abridged**} Dodd, Mead   Brand
[compilation of ''The Terrible Tenderfoot'' by George Owen Baxter in *Western Story Magazine* (7/2/27), ''The Gentle Desperado'' by George Owen Baxter in *Western Story Magazine* (7/16/27), ''Tiger, Tiger!'' by George Owen Baxter in *Western Story Magazine* (7/30/27)]

1987 ONE MAN POSSE {**abridged**}   Dodd, Mead   Brand
[compilation of ''One Man Posse'' by Max Brand in *Mavericks* (9/34), ''Sleeper Pays a Debt'' by Max Brand in *Mavericks* (10/34), ''Satan's Gun Rider'' by Max Brand in *Mavericks* (11/34), ''Sleeper Turns Horse-thief'' by Max Brand in *Mavericks* (12/34), and ''Sun and Sand'' by Hugh Owen in *Western Story Magazine* (2/16/35)]

1987 MAX BRAND'S BEST WESTERN   Dodd, Mead   Brand
STORIES: Volume III {**abridged and**   William F. Nolan,
rewritten}   editor
[contents: ''Reata's Peril Trek'' (title retained for rewritten short novel), ''Crazy

Rhythm'' (reprint), ''Dust Storm'' (reprint), ''A Lucky Dog'' (reprint), ''The Third Bullet'' (title retained for rewritten short novel), ''Half a Partner'' (reprint), ''The Sun Stood Still'' (reprint)]

1987   THE NIGHTHAWK TRAIL {**abridged**}   Dodd, Mead   Brand
[compilation of ''Nighthawk Trail'' by Max Brand in *Western Story Magazine* (7/9/32), ''Outlaws from Afar'' by Max Brand in *Western Story Magazine* (8/20/32), ''Speedy's Desert Dance'' by Max Brand in *Western Story Magazine* (1/28/33)]

1989   THE NEW FRONTIER   Doubleday   Brand
                                           Joe R. Lansdale,
                                           editor
{Note: First publication of ''A First Blooding,'' a section of Faust's unpublished novel, WYCHERLY}

1990   BATTLE'S END/THE THREE CROSSES   Tor   Brand
[contents: ''Battle's End'' (reprint) and ''The Three Crosses'' (reprint)]

1990   CHIP CHAMPIONS A LADY/   Tor   Brand
     FORGOTTEN TREASURE
[contents: ''Chip Champions a Lady'' (reprint) and ''Forgotten Treasure'' (reprint)]

1991   COWARD OF THE CLAN   Putnam   Brand
[compilation of ''Coward of the Clan'' by Peter Henry Morland in *Western Story Magazine* (5/19/28) and ''The Man from the Sky'' by Peter Henry Morland in *Western Story Magazine* (6/2/28)]

1991   FUGITIVES' FIRE   Putnam   Brand
[compilation of ''Prairie Pawn'' by Peter Henry Morland in *Western Story Magazine* (6/16/28) and ''Fugitives' Fire'' by Peter Henry Morland in *Western Story Magazine* (6/30/28)]

1991   THE RED BANDANNA/CARCAJOU'S   Tor   Brand
     TRAIL
[contents: ''The Red Bandanna'' (reprint) and ''Carcajou's Trail'' (reprint)]

1991   OUTLAW CREW/THE BEST BANDIT   Tor   Brand
[contents: ''Outlaw Crew'' (reprint) and ''The Best Bandit'' (reprint)]

1991   RANGE JESTER/BLACK THUNDER   Tor   Brand
[contents: ''Range Jester'' (reprint) and ''Black Thunder'' (reprint)]

1992   MAX BRAND'S BEST POEMS   Fithian   Brand
                                        Robert Easton and
                                        Jane Easton, editors

[contents: ''To Chaucer,'' ''Sometimes,'' ''Leonard,'' ''To Love,'' ''My Country,'' ''Athens,'' ''Sappho,'' ''At Mission Hill,'' ''Wordsworth'' (reprint), ''Judgment'' (reprint), ''Foscari'' (reprint), ''Ulysses and Circe'' (reprint), ''Strange Things Are Found'' (reprint), ''College Sonnets'' (reprint), ''To Arthur Ryder'' (reprint), ''The Sonnet'' (reprint), ''Fools All'' (play excerpt, ''Fools All, a Com-

edy in One Act''), "The Long Road" (reprint title for "The Last Adventure"),
"The Ride to Camelot" (reprint excerpt), "Bed Time" (reprint), "Cleopatra and
Creon" (reprint excerpt from "One of Cleopatra's Nights"), "Defense of Guen-
evere" (reprint), "The Village Street" (reprint), "On a Grecian Funeral Monu-
ment" (reprint), "To a Lady" (reprint), "A Song" (reprint), "Dionysus in
Hades" (reprint excerpt), "Only the Young Fear Death" (reprint), "Olympe"
(reprinted from the short story, "The Wedding Guest"), "In the Valley of Hatsu-
Se" (reprint excerpt from the short novel, "Treason against a King"), "The
Secret" (reprint), "Lavia" (reprint excerpt from the serial, "The Blackbirds
Sing"), "Blondel and Richard" and "Elspeth" (reprint excerpts from the serial,
"The Golden Knight"), "March Wind" (reprint excerpt from the serial, "The
Song of the Whip"), "Tom and Jerry" (reprint), "I'll Have No Gods" (reprint),
"My Sweat" (reprint), "So Poor" (reprint), "Old Friends" (reprint), "The Island
of Ios" (reprint), "Gethsemane" (reprint excerpts), "What Love Is There" (re-
print), "Briareus" (reprint excerpt), "Afterword from the Poet" (reprint notebook
excerpt)]

1993 VALLEY OF JEWELS {U. K.}   Hale   Brand
[magazine version: "The Valley of Jewels" by Max Brand in *Western Story
Magazine* (8/21/26)]

1993 THE CROSS BRAND {U. K.}   Hale   Brand
[magazine version: "The Cross Brand" by Max Brand in *Short Stories*
(8/25/22)]

1994 DUST ACROSS THE RANGE {U. K.}   Hale   Brand
[magazine serial version: "Dust across the Range" by Max Brand (in four parts)
in *The American Magazine* (11/37–2/38)]
{Note: This was the first book publication of the unabridged serial as Faust wrote
it.}

1994 THE DESERT PILOT {U. K.}   Hale   Brand
[magazine version: "The Desert Pilot" by Max Brand in *Western Story Magazine*
(6/4/27)]

1994 THE COLLECTED STORIES OF MAX   University of   Brand
        BRAND   Nebraska Press
                                          Robert and Jane
                                          Easton, editors
[contents: "John Ovington Returns" (reprint), "Above the Law" (reprint), "The
Wedding Guest" (reprint), "A Special Occasion" (reprint), "Outcast Breed"
(reprint), "The Sun Stood Still" (reprint), "Secret Agent Number One" (reprint
title for "The Strange Villa"), "The Claws of the Tigress" (reprint excerpt),
"Internes Can't Take Money" (reprint), "Fixed" (reprint), "Wine on the Desert"
(reprint title for "Wine in the Desert"), "Virginia Creeper" (reprint), "Pringle's
Luck" (reprint), "The Silent Witness" (reprint), "Miniature" (reprint), "Our
Daily Bread" (reprint), "Honor Bright" (reprint), "The King" (reprint)]

1994 THE SACKING OF EL DORADO   Chivers North   Brand
                                          America
[contents: "Bad-Eye: His Life and Letters" (reprint), "The Ghost Rides To-

Yr.	*Title*	*Publisher*	*Byline*

night!'' (reprint title for ''The Ghost''), ''The Consuming Fire'' (reprint), ''A Sagebrush Cinderella'' (reprint), ''The Fear of Morgan the Fearless'' (reprint), ''The Sacking of El Dorado'' (reprint)]

1995 THE RETURN OF FREE RANGE LANNING   G. K. Hall   Brand
[contents: ''The Black Muldoon'' (reprint), ''Gunman's Bluff'' (reprint), ''The Return of Free Range Lanning'' (reprint title for the restored ''Iron and Dust'')]

1995 SIXTEEN IN NOME   Five Star Westerns   Brand
[compilation of ''Sixteen in Nome'' by Max Brand in *Western Story Magazine* (5/3/30) and ''Battle's End'' by Max Brand in *Western Story Magazine* (5/10/30)]

1995 MURDER ME!   St. Martin's Press   Brand
[magazine serial version: '''—Murder Me!'' by Max Brand (in seven parts) in *Detective Fiction Weekly* (9/21/35–11/2/35)]

1996 THE GHOST WAGON AND OTHER   University of   Brand
GREAT WESTERN ADVENTURES   Nebraska Press
                                 Jon Tuska, editor
[contents: ''The Ghost Wagon'' (reprint title for the restored ''The Cure of Silver Cañon''), ''Rodeo Ranch'' (restored reprint), ''Slip Liddell'' (reprint title for the restored ''Señor Coyote''), ''A Matter of Honor'' (reprint title for the restored ''Jerico's 'Garrison Finish' '')]

1996 THE BLACK RIDER AND OTHER   University of   Brand
STORIES   Nebraska Press
                                 Jon Tuska, editor
[contents: ''The Black Rider'' (reprint), ''The Dream of Macdonald'' (reprint title for the restored '' 'Sunset' Wins''), ''Partners'' (reprint), ''The Power of Prayer'' (restored reprint)]

A FAUST FILMOGRAPHY

This compilation has been revised and enlarged with the help of William F. Nolan. Sources include the three volumes of the CATALOG OF COPYRIGHT ENTRIES, CUMULATIVE SERIES: MOTION PICTURES, for 1912–39, 1940–49, and 1950–59, respectively, published by the United States Copyright Office, Library of Congress; the annual volumes 1937 to 1968 of the INTER-NATIONAL MOTION PICTURE ALMANAC, published by Quigley Publications, New York; THE LIBRARY OF CONGRESS CATALOGS: THE NATIONAL UNION CATALOG, 1953–1957, MOTION PICTURES AND FILM STRIPS; THE AMERICAN FILM INSTITUTE CATALOGUE: FEATURE FILMS 1911–1920, FEATURE FILMS 1920–1930, FEATURE FILMS 1931–1940; THE FILM DAILY YEARBOOK 1954; and THE LIBRARY OF CON-GRESS AUTHOR CATALOG, 1948–1952: FILMS, as well as studio records, Library of Academy of Motion Picture Arts and Sciences archives, Brandt & Brandt agency records, and Faust memorabilia and correspondence. Listings include motion pictures derived in any way from Faust's writings. Though the filmography may seem extensive, it does not include at least twenty Faust stories, novels, and titles of works to which motion picture rights were sold but from which no films appear to have been made. The story, magazine, serial, or novel from which each film derives is listed under its title, or its connection with Faust's work is explained in a note. When there was no title change, there is no specific attribution. The filmography is organized chronologically by year of release and includes the title of the film, the distributing company, and the principal cast members.

──────────────────── *SILENT FILMS* ────────────────────

	Film Title	Distributing Company	Principal Cast Members
1917	THE ADOPTED SON	Metro Pictures	Francis X. Bushman Beverly Bayne
1918	LAWLESS LOVE (''Above the Law'')	Fox	Jewel Carmen Henry Woodward
1918	KISS OR KILL (''Mr. Cinderella'')	Universal	Herbert Rawlinson Priscilla Dean
1920	BULLET PROOF (''Luck'')	Universal	Harry Carey Kathleen O'Connor
1920	THE UNTAMED	Fox	Tom Mix Pauline Starke
1920	A THOUSAND TO ONE (FATE'S HONEYMOON)	Associated Pictures	Hobart Bosworth Ethel Grey Terry
1921	TIGER TRUE (TIGER)	Universal	Frank Mayo Fritzi Brunette
1921	CHILDREN OF THE NIGHT (CHILDREN OF NIGHT)	Fox	William Russell Ruth Renick
1921	WHO AM I?	Select Pictures	Claire Anderson Niles Welch
1921	SHAME (CLUNG)	Fox	John Gilbert Anna May Wong
1921	THE NIGHT HORSEMEN (THE NIGHT HORSEMAN)	Fox	Tom Mix May Hopkins
1921	TRAILIN'	Fox	Tom Mix Eva Novak
1922	IRON TO GOLD (''When Iron Turns to Gold'')	Fox	Dustin Farnum Marguerite Marsh
1922	HIS BACK AGAINST THE WALL	Goldwyn Pictures	Raymond Hatton Virginia Valli
1922	THE FIGHTING STREAK (FREE RANGE LANNING)	Fox	Tom Mix Patsy Ruth Miller
1922	JUST TONY (ALCATRAZ)	Fox	Tony (horse) Tom Mix
1922	CROSS ROADS (CROSSROADS)	Merit Film Corp.	Franklyn Farnum Genevieve Burt

{Note: In some states such as New York this film was exhibited under the title THE LARIAT THROWER.}

1923	THREE WHO PAID (THE RANGE-LAND AVENGER)	Fox	Dustin Farnum Bessie Love

	Film Title	Distributing Company	Principal Cast Members
1923	MILE-A-MINUTE ROMEO (GUN GENTLEMEN)	Fox	Tom Mix Betty Jewel
1923	THE GUNFIGHTER (HIRED GUNS)	Fox	William Farnum Doris May
1924	THE VAGABOND TRAIL (DONNEGAN)	Fox	Charles "Buck" Jones Marian Nixon
1924	AGAINST ALL ODDS ("Cuttle's Hired Man")	Fox	Charles "Buck" Jones Dolores Rousse
1925	CHAMPION OF LOST CAUSES	Fox	Edmund Lowe Barbara Bedford
1925	THE BEST MAN (SEÑOR JINGLE BELLS)	Fox	Tom Mix Clara Bow
1926	THE FLYING HORSEMAN ("Dark Rosaleen")	Fox	Buck Jones Gladys McConnell

{Note: Charles Jones, who had been using the praenomen "Buck" for his Western films, legally changed his name at this time to Buck Jones.}

1928	THE CAVALIER ("The Black Rider")	Tiffany-Stahl Productions	Richard Talmadge Barbara Bedford

{Note: While not a sound film, this release did have a music and effects track that contained the song, "My Cavalier," with words by R. Meredith Wilson and music by Hugo Riesenfeld.}

SOUND FILMS

	Film Title	Distributing Company	Principal Cast Members
1931	FAIR WARNING (THE UNTAMED)	Fox	George O'Brien Louise Huntington
1931	A HOLY TERROR (TRAILIN')	Fox	George O'Brien Sally Eilers
1932	WHISTLIN' DAN (THE UNTAMED)	Tiffany	Ken Maynard Joyzelle Joyner

{Note: While this film was based on an "original" screenplay by Stuart Anthony, it had earlier served as the basis for BORDER LAW (Columbia, 1931) starring Buck Jones. Maynard, who invariably played characters with the praenomen Ken, in this case adopted the screen name of "Whistlin' Dan," a covert reference surely to the Faust character, Whistlin' Dan Barry.}

1932	DESTRY RIDES AGAIN	Universal	Tom Mix Claudia Dell

Film Title	Distributing Company	Principal Cast Members
1937 INTERNES CAN'T TAKE MONEY	Paramount	Barbara Stanwyck Joel McCrea
1938 YOUNG DR. KILDARE	M-G-M	Lew Ayres Lionel Barrymore

{Note: This and the following six films were produced from original screen stories written by Faust.}

1939 CALLING DR. KILDARE	M-G-M	Lew Ayres Lionel Barrymore
1939 THE SECRET OF DR. KILDARE	M-G-M	Lew Ayres Lionel Barrymore
1939 DESTRY RIDES AGAIN	Universal	Marlene Dietrich James Stewart
1940 DR. KILDARE'S STRANGE CASE	M-G-M	Lew Ayres Lionel Barrymore
1940 DR. KILDARE GOES HOME	M-G-M	Lew Ayres Lionel Barrymore
1940 DR. KILDARE'S CRISIS	M-G-M	Lew Ayres Lionel Barrymore
1941 THE PEOPLE VS. DR. KILDARE	M-G-M	Lew Ayres Lionel Barrymore
1941 DR. KILDARE'S WEDDING DAY	M-G-M	Lew Ayres Laraine Day

{Note: This and subsequent films in this series were based on characters Faust had created in his Kildare stories, the rights to which he had sold to M-G-M. Lew Ayres, and the Kildare character he played, were dropped from the series after the next entry, but Lionel Barrymore continued on in the role of Dr. Gillespie, which he had been playing in all the M-G-M entries. These films are followed by an asterisk (*).}

1941 DR. KILDARE'S VICTORY*	M-G-M	Lew Ayres Laraine Day
1942 POWDER TOWN	RKO-Radio Pictures	Victor McLaglen June Havoc

{Note: Faust worked on this film without screen credit.}

1942 CALLING DR. GILLESPIE*	M-G-M	Lionel Barrymore Donna Reed
1942 DR. GILLESPIE'S NEW ASSISTANT*	M-G-M	Lionel Barrymore Van Johnson
1942 THE VALLEY OF VANISHING MEN	Columbia	Bill Elliott Carmen Morales

{Note: A serial of fifteen episodes, each released separately: Chapter One: "Trouble in Canyon City"; Chapter Two: "The Mystery of the Ghost Town";

Film Title	Distributing Company	Principal Cast Members

Chapter Three: "Danger Walks by Night"; Chapter Four: "Hillside Horror"; Chapter Five: "Guns in the Night"; Chapter Six: "The Bottomless Well"; Chapter Seven: "The Man in the Golden Mask"; Chapter Eight: "When the Devil Drives"; Chapter Nine: "The Traitor's Shroud"; Chapter Ten: "Death Strikes at Seven"; Chapter Eleven: "Satan in the Saddle"; Chapter Twelve: "The Mine of Missing Men"; Chapter Thirteen: "Danger on Dome Rock"; Chapter Fourteen: "The Door That Has No Key"; Chapter Fifteen: "Empire's End." This serial was produced for Columbia Pictures by Larry Darmour Productions. According to a Brandt & Brandt memo dated May 7, 1942, Faust, who was then working for Columbia Pictures, was paid $250 for use of this title, which at that time, had appeared only as a four-part serial in *Western Story Magazine* (6/2/34–6/23/34).}

1943	DR. GILLESPIE'S CRIMINAL CASE*	M-G-M	Lionel Barrymore Van Johnson
1943	THE DESPERADOES	Columbia	Randolph Scott Glenn Ford

{Note: This film was based on an original Faust screen story.}

| 1943 | THE DEERSLAYER | Republic | Bruce Kellogg Jean Parker |

{Note: Faust worked on this film without screen credit.}

| 1944 | IN OUR TIME | Warner Bros. | Ida Lupino Paul Henreid |

{Note: Faust worked on this film without screen credit.}

| 1944 | COVER GIRL | Columbia | Rita Hayworth Gene Kelly |

{Note: Faust worked on this film without screen credit.}

| 1944 | UNCERTAIN GLORY | Warner Bros. | Errol Flynn Paul Lukas |

{Note: Based on a screenplay by Faust and Laszlo Vadnay.}

| 1944 | THREE MEN IN WHITE* | M-G-M | Lionel Barrymore Van Johnson |
| 1944 | THE CONSPIRATORS | Warner Bros. | Hedy Lamarr Paul Henreid |

{Note: Faust worked on this film without screen credit.}

1944	BETWEEN TWO WOMEN*	M-G-M	Van Johnson Lionel Barrymore
1946	RAINBOW OVER TEXAS ("Señor Coyote")	Republic	Roy Rogers Dale Evans
1947	DARK DELUSION*	M-G-M	Lionel Barrymore James Craig
1948	THE ADVENTURES OF DON JUAN	Warner Bros.	Errol Flynn Viveca Lindfors

{Note: Faust worked on a screen story by this title but received no credit.}

Film Title	Distributing Company	Principal Cast Members
1950 MONTANA	Warner Bros.	Errol Flynn Alexis Smith

{Note: Although Ernest Haycox was credited for the original screen story on which this film was based (and his 40,000 word "novel" still exists), Faust also had worked on a Western screenplay in 1943 intended as a vehicle for Errol Flynn while under contract at Warner Bros. The title of his screenplay is MONTANA with a plot opening in New Orleans and moving to Butte, Montana, but without the cattleman-vs.-sheepman theme of the Haycox story which was filmed. The situation may have been similar to the instance where writer Tom W. Blackburn was assigned by Warner Bros. to write a screenplay titled COLT .45 when almost thirty other screenplays with that title had been started by other writers. In Haycox's case, as in Blackburn's, it was his screenplay the studio ultimately filmed.}

Film Title	Distributing Company	Principal Cast Members
1950 SINGING GUNS	Republic	Vaughn Monroe Ella Raines
1950 BRANDED (MONTANA RIDES!)	Paramount	Alan Ladd Mona Freeman
1951 FRENCHIE	Universal	Joel McCrea Shelley Winters

{Note: The plot of this film was an obvious imitation of the 1939 screen version of DESTRY RIDES AGAIN.}

Film Title	Distributing Company	Principal Cast Members
1951 MY OUTLAW BROTHER (SOUTH OF RIO GRANDE)	Eagle-Lion	Mickey Rooney Wanda Hendrix
1955 DESTRY (DESTRY RIDES AGAIN)	Universal	Audie Murphy Mari Blanchard
1957 THE HIRED GUN	Rorvic/M-G-M	Rory Calhoun Anne Francis

{Note: The Faust estate was paid $250 for a quit claim to the title HIRED GUNS in order to clear the rights for this film based on a story by Buckley Angell.}

ABOUT FREDERICK FAUST

William F. Nolan

This bibliography is a greatly expanded, revised, and updated version of the original "Works about Faust" listing I prepared for my book, MAX BRAND: WESTERN GIANT (Bowling Green University Popular Press, 1985). Although checklists of works by Faust had been printed as early as 1948, no extensive bibliography of works about this author existed prior to my first listing. That I would be the one to compile such a list is not surprising, since I have been collecting works by and about Faust for over fifty years. As this bibliography attests, I have written more about Faust than any other critic (some fifty-five book, magazine, and newspaper pieces, beginning in the 1940s); my Faust collection stands as the world's most complete, filling five floor-to-ceiling bookcases in my den. Beneath my high school yearbook photo is the prophetic caption: "To carry on for Max Brand."

A great deal of material about Faust has appeared in the ten years since my initial listing. As Frederick Faust's literary reputation has grown, a steady progression of profiles, essays, and reviews has been printed relating to his life and his fiction. All but the most minor of these are included in this bibliography, fully annotated. Each of the four sections is arranged chronologically; page numbers are missing only on those items clipped from original sources. For fans, collectors, scholars, and librarians, I trust that this bibliography will provide a worthwhile research tool.

I. BOOKS ON FAUST

THE MAX BRAND COMPANION [MBC] is the fifth book to deal directly and wholly with Faust—following two compilations of essays and articles about him, a biography, and a critical study. In total, they offer a comprehensive portrait of one of history's most prolific storytellers.

MAX BRAND: THE MAN AND HIS WORK, edited by Darrell C. Richardson. (Fantasy
Publishing Company, 1952) Hardcover, 198 pages.

Published eight years after Faust's death, this compilation is a direct offshoot of Richardson's amateur magazine, *The Fabulous Faust Fanzine.* The contributions are mixed as to quality, and there are factual errors. The cover portrait of Faust was drawn by Haskell Richardson, brother of the editor. Four photos are included: a cover shot of the December 7, 1918, issue of *All-Story Weekly,* featuring Dan Barry in "The Untamed"; a picture of Faust's study in Italy where he composed his verse; a picture of Faust as part of the staff on the university publication, *The Occident,* taken in 1915, and a frontispiece portrait. The chapter prefaces are by Richardson.

Contents (eight chapters, bibliography)

"Introduction" by Richardson, dated August 1, 1951. (pp. 11–14)

"The Life and Works of Max Brand" by Richardson. (pp. 15–51)
The first extensive attempt at a Faust biography in book format.

"Bohemian Days with Max Brand" by John L. Schoolcraft. (pp. 53–58)
Reprinted from *The Fabulous Faust Fanzine* (see Section III). A personal memoir by one of Faust's close friends, dealing with their university days and their early struggles in New York as beginning professional writers. Warm and affecting. {Editors' Note: Reprinted in MBC.}

"Twenty-Five Million Words" by Edward H. Dodd, Jr. (pp. 59–65)
Reprinted from *Publishers Weekly* (see Section III). The first full article ever printed on Faust is herewith collected in book format. Of historic importance. (There is also a "Postscript" to this piece by John Blair.) {Editors' Note: Reprinted in MBC.}

"A Farewell to Max Brand" by Steve Fisher. (pp. 67–72)
Reprinted from *Writer's Digest* (see Section III). A moving, highly-emotional memoir by one of Faust's studio pals at Warner Bros. {Editors' Note: Reprinted in MBC.}

"Max Brand and the Western Story" by S. Allen McElfresh and Richardson. (pp. 74–92)
Reprinted, in part, from *The Fabulous Faust Fanzine* (see Section III). A revised and expanded overview of the pulp Western and Faust's place in the genre.

"Interesting Facts about Faust's Prolific Production" by William F. Nolan. (pp. 93–103)
A compilation of various facts I had gathered (through 1951) relating to Faust and his works.

"Fantasy in the Writing of Max Brand" by Richardson. (pp. 105–122)
Reprinted, in part, from *The Fabulous Faust Fanzine* (see Section III). A revised and expanded discussion of the fantasy books and stories in the Faust canon. Covers eight books and seven shorter works with detailed plot discussion. States: "Faust basically wrote fairy tales—but grown-up fairy tales."

"The Death of a War Correspondent" by Jack Delaney. (pp. 124–126)
Reprinted from *Harper's,* where it was originally titled "Frederick Faust Again" (see Section III). A battlefield account of Faust's death in Italy.

"Bibliography of the Works of Frederick Faust" by Richardson (with Russell Gale, Cecil

Hinote, Stanley Haynes, Darrel LeFever, S. Allen McElfresh, William F. Nolan, Philip Richman, and Carl Brandt). (pp. 129–198)

Revised, expanded, and updated (into 1952) from the original listing in *The Fabulous Faust Fanzine*. Consists of: Pseudonyms of Frederick Faust; Descriptive Listing of the [then 150] Published Books of Frederick Faust; Anthologies and Special Faust Associational Items; Listing by Title of Faust's Published Books; Faust Titles Published as Pocket Novels; Original Magazine and Newspaper Works; Reprinted Magazine Material; Articles about Frederick Faust and His Works; Addenda to the Bibliography.

Although this listing has been corrected, extended, and updated in publications, it retains value since it is the only Faust bibliography to detail his work under separate magazine headings, and under separate pen names, within each magazine.

MAX BRAND: THE BIG "WESTERNER," by Robert Easton (University of Oklahoma Press, 1970). Hardcover (also issued in trade paperback): 330 pages.

A full biography by Faust's son-in-law, husband to Faust's daughter, Jane Faust Easton. A superb job of family research and personal history, it is particularly notable for collecting Faust's letters concerning his participation as a war correspondent in World War II, offering the only detailed record of Faust's service and death in the 1944 Italian Campaign. Many other Faust letters are quoted, along with poems and brief samples of his fiction, although there is no attempt at a critical analysis of Faust's work. While he is basically quite sympathetic to his subject, Easton (a professional writer with many books to his credit) does not hesitate to reveal Faust's flaws, and he never allows the man himself to be obscured behind a mountain of productivity. Contains eight photos of Faust (from 1915 into 1943), plus pictures of his family, friends, and editors, along with early magazine covers from *All-Story Weekly* featuring his work, and stills from several of his films. A total of 33 photo pages, including a frontispiece portrait.

A portion of the text was reprinted in TWENTIETH-CENTURY LITERARY CRITICISM (see Section II). It is important to note that Easton's biography was the springboard for all subsequent academic work on Faust. Prior to 1970 Faust was not considered a worthy subject of study by the nation's academic community. Easton's book penetrated this literary wall.

Contents (prologue/epilogue, 26 chapters, bibliography)

"A Boy and a Valley"

"The University of California"

"Wanderings"

"Canada"

"New York"

"A Young Writer"

"In Uniform at Last"

"Western Novels"

"A Touch of Death"

"The Uphill Road"

"England"

"Florence"

"Ireland and Italy"

"U.S.A., 1929"

"Destry Rides Again"

"Editors and an Agent"

"Ordeal by Writing"

"Fictional Summits"

"A Faustian Olympiad"

"Two Women"

"Dionysus in Hollywood"

"Deepening Conflicts"

"Farewell to New York"

"Outward Bound"

"Combat Correspondent"

"The Stuff of Dreams"

"A Faust Bibliography" (magazine and newspaper works, plus a title listing of 170 Faust books, into 1970)

"Film, Radio and Television Appendix"

"A Faust Filmography" (expanded and updated from my listing in *The Fabulous Faust Fanzine*—see Section III)

"Books about Faust"

MAX BRAND: WESTERN GIANT: THE LIFE AND TIMES OF FREDERICK SCHIL-
LER FAUST, edited by William F. Nolan (Bowling Green State University Popular Press, 1986). Hardcover (also issued in trade paperback): 175 pages.

A compilation of essays, articles, reviews, and memoirs, with a comprehensive checklist, this book attempts to place Faust in a wide personal and professional perspective.
With editor's entry prefaces. No photos.

Contents (twelve sections and a bibliography)

"Introduction: The Fabulous Faust" by William F. Nolan. (pp. 1–4)
Offers a Faust profile and overview of the book's contents.

"A Sketch of My Life" by Frederick Faust. (pp. 5–9)
Reprinted from *The Fabulous Faust Fanzine* (see Section III). Taken from a letter
Faust wrote to his daughter Jane in 1939 (when he was forty-seven), this is the only
extended piece of autobiography from this publicity-shy author. Deeply emotional
and revealing. {Editors' Note: Reprinted in MBC in its entirety.}

"Memories of My Father" by Jane Faust Easton. (pp. 10–17)

Excerpted from her privately published book, MEMORIES OF THE '20s AND '30s (see Section II). Of major biographical importance, written with grace and wisdom. The only direct memoir offered by an intimate family member.

"The University Years" by Harvey Roney. (pp. 18–22)

Reprinted from *The Faust Collector* (see Section III). Memoir from a close friend at the University of California. Illuminating and informative view of Faust's life on campus. {Editors' Note: Reprinted in MBC.}

"Faust's Military Interlude" by Gilbert J. McLennan. (pp. 23–25)

Edited from an earlier version in *The Fabulous Faust Fanzine* (see Section III). Brief but important memoir by a man who served with Faust in the 97th Canadian Battalion in 1916 (known as "The American Foreign Legion"). {Editors' Note: Reprinted in MBC.}

"Bohemian Days on Grub Street" by John Schoolcraft. (pp. 26–30)

Reprinted, in part, from *The Fabulous Faust Fanzine* (see Section III), but augmented with material from Schoolcraft's unpublished manuscript, "The Fabulous Faust: His Life and Letters." A vital, revealing portrait of the early writing days in New York by a lifelong friend. {Editors' Note: Reprinted in MBC.}

"Destry and Dionysus" by Martha Bacon. (pp. 31–36)

Reprinted from *The Atlantic* (see Section III). A marvelous memoir/essay by the daughter of Faust's teacher and close friend, Leonard Bacon. Deals with their life in Italy prior to World War II. A major piece. {Editors' Note: Reprinted in MBC.}

"The Death of a War Correspondent" by Jack Delaney. (pp. 37–39)

Reprinted from *Harper's* (see Section III), where it was printed as "Frederick Faust Again." A firsthand battlefield report.

"A Farewell to Max Brand" by Steve Fisher. (pp. 40–44)

Reprinted from *Writer's Digest* (see Section III). A key item in relation to Faust's work in Hollywood. Recalled by a studio friend who shared these years with Faust. {Editors' Note: Reprinted in MBC.}

" 'Heinie' Faust: A Collective Portrait" (pp. 45–54)

Assembled from a variety of Faust's friends, family, critics, his agent, editors— in all, twenty individuals. Reveals many aspects of Faust as man and writer. Biographically vital.

"A Selection of Reviews and Critical Commentary on Faust Books" (pp. 55–62)

Excerpted sections covering review commentary on twenty-one Faust books, from the 1920s into 1984. A representative critical look at Faust's work over six and a half decades.

"Max Brand and the American Western Story" by Samuel A. Peeples. (pp. 63–71)

A detailed overview of the genre and Faust's place in it, with a perceptive analysis of his writing style. A key essay, written with vigor and backed by intensive scholarship. Reprinted in TWENTIETH-CENTURY LITERARY CRITICISM (see Section II).

"A Bibliographical Checklist of Works by and about Frederick Faust" by William F. Nolan. (pp. 72–174)

The most extensive listing, by far, of work by and about Faust, consisting of:

"Works by Faust"

Books: A Byline Listing (covering 213 Faust books, through 1985, arranged by pen name in chronological order, with full magazine origins)

Books: A Title Listing (covering 260 titles, originals and variants)

Fiction (covering some 600 works from 1910 and arranged chronologically, year by year)

Plays and Sketches (covering his works from high school and the University of California, 1911–1916)

Verse (the first listing anywhere of Faust's poetry, covering eighty-plus college poems and extending into his collected book verse. In all, some 112 poems are listed.)

Non-Fiction (items from 1912 into 1973, including notes, letters, essays, etc.)

Films (covers 24 silent films and 35 sound films either adapted from his books and stories or written directly by Faust for the screen)

Radio, Television, and Stage Adaptations (covering all known items from 1932 into 1972). Data not complete.

Books about Faust

Books Containing Material on Faust

Magazine and Newspaper Items

Papers on Faust

(These sections formed the basis for this bibliography)

MAX BRAND, by William A. Bloodworth, Jr. (Twayne Publishers, 1993). Hardcover: 189 pages.

The first full-length critical study on Faust by the president of Augusta College, Georgia. Bloodworth began writing about Faust in 1981 (see ''Max Brand's West'' in Section III) and spent six years on an aborted biography, turning to this volume (part of the United States Authors Series) in 1990. It took three years to complete. The book covers some eighty-three Faust books, stories, poems, plays, and other work and is divided into genre sections. Biographical data are mixed with critical analysis throughout as Faust's life is tied to his work. Avoiding the dry, pedantic tone and content associated with most academic studies, Bloodworth delivers a clear, reasoned view of Faust without excessive praise or condemnation. He considers him in the light of popular culture as a major American storyteller. Certainly this study is essential and pivotal in understanding Faust as man and writer. With a frontispiece photo of Faust, taken in 1941 in California.

Contents (preface and career chronology, fifteen chapters, with notes, bibliography)

''Max Brand and Frederick Faust''

''California''

''Becoming Max Brand''

''The Untamed''

''Your Forte Is the West''

''Western Story Magazine''

''Life and Poetry on a Grand Scale''

''Singing Guns and Destry Rides Again''

''Pulp Problems''

"Indian Stories"

"Last Westerns"

"Detectives and Spies"

"Historical Adventures"

"Hollywood"

"Dr. Kildare"

"Selected Bibliography" (lists eighty-one books as "Primary Works" and eighteen entries in "Secondary Works" relating to major book and magazine items about Faust

Full chapter notes.

———— *II. BOOKS CONTAINING MATERIAL ON FAUST* ————

This listing covers more than sixty books relating to Faust. All primary reference volumes that list Faust as an entry have been included. However, if the
entry is extremely brief and/or adds nothing to known data, the volume has been
excluded. I have also been selective with regard to anthologies containing Faust
works. If a full-page biography is printed, the book is usually included, but
anthologies with brief notes on Faust are *not* listed. Novels in which Faust is
treated as a fictional character are included.

WANDERER'S CIRCLE, by Cornelia Stratton Parker (Houghton Mifflin, 1934). On
   Faust: pp. 302–304.
This travel book includes a warm account of the author's visit to Faust's villa in Italy.

SEMI-CENTENNIAL: SOME OF THE LIFE AND PART OF THE OPINIONS, by
   Leonard Bacon (Harper, 1939). On Faust: pp. 212–213.
In a chapter titled "Florence," the author draws a brief portrait of his friendship with
Faust in Italy.

TWENTIETH CENTURY AUTHORS, edited by Stanley J. Kunitz and Howard Haycraft
   (H. W. Wilson, 1942). On Faust: p. 181, with photo of Faust.
The first reference work to attempt a detailed career entry, as "Brand, Max." Based
heavily on the 1938 Edward H. Dodd, Jr. piece in *Publishers Weekly.* (See "Twenty-
Five Million Words" in Section III.)

"E" COMPANY, by Frank O'Rourke (Simon & Schuster, 1945). On Faust as "Max
   Hickman": pp. 130–132, 135–136, 139, 144, 154–157.
This novel is dedicated "To Max Brand," and the author, who had met Faust before
entering the war, here employs him as a fictional magazine correspondent named "Max
Hickman" who dies in battle. The parallel is clear—since Faust was with E Company
in Italy on the day of his death in 1944.

GREAT TALES OF THE AMERICAN WEST, edited by Harry E. Maule (The Modern
   Library [Random House], 1945). On Faust: p. xvi.
One of the first influential reprintings of Faust's classic short story, "Wine on the
Desert." (It has appeared in many subsequent anthologies and is Faust's most familiar
shorter work.) In his introductory overview of the genre, Maule sees Faust as a bridge

between the earlier immature Westerns and "the best of Western stories as we know them today . . . in which attention to character study and literary finish replaced the old emphasis on action."

THE BLUE DEVILS IN ITALY, by John P. Delaney (Infantry Journal Press, 1947). On Faust: pp. 60, 75, 283.

Account of the Italian Campaign in World War II in which Faust died as a war correspondent. Brief references to Faust by "Jack" Delaney.

THE FICTION FACTORY: FROM PULP ROW TO QUALITY STREET, by Quentin Reynolds (Random House, 1955). On Faust: pp. 180–192.

An account of Faust's years with *Western Story Magazine* (*WSM*) is provided in this comprehensive history of Street & Smith. Reynolds is not entirely accurate, but his portrait of Faust is lively and detailed, highlighting Faust's relationship with Frank Blackwell, editor of *WSM*. The author reproduces the contents page of *WSM* for April 2, 1932, showing Faust at work under three pen names in this issue. A portrait photo is also included.

THE NOTEBOOKS AND POEMS OF "MAX BRAND," by Frederick Faust, edited by John Schoolcraft (Dodd, Mead, 1957). On Faust: pp. 7–8. "Introduction" by R. E. (Robert Easton).

Beyond the verse, a fascinating one-hundred page "Notebooks" section contains quotations from Faust's notebooks and letters, forming a loosely knit autobiography. (This volume represents a heavily edited version of Schoolcraft's unpublished manuscript, "The Fabulous Faust: His Life and Letters.")

POETRY FROM HIDDEN SPRINGS, edited by Paul Jordan-Smith (Doubleday, 1962). On Faust: p. 65.

A one-page biographical sketch, "Frederick Faust," with a reproduction of his poem, "The Secret."

REMEMBER? REMEMBER?, by Charles Beaumont (Macmillan, 1963). On Faust: pp. 141–143.

A profile of Faust is included in the author's chapter, "The Bloody Pulps."

HORROR TIMES TEN, edited by Alden H. Norton (Berkeley, 1967). On Faust: p. 82.
A rare reprinting of Faust's horror novelette, "That Receding Brow," with a one-page biography of Faust. Relates his work to this fantasy genre.

MAX BRAND'S BEST STORIES, edited by Robert Easton (Dodd, Mead, 1967). On Faust: pp. ix–xv, 1, 7, 33, 45, 55, 63, 91, 149, 159, 185, 197, 215, 237.

Introduction (by the editor) titled "Max Brand and Frederick Faust" plus brief prefatory notes to each story. A frontispiece photo is included.

THE PULP JUNGLE, by Frank Gruber (Sherbourne Press, 1967). On Faust: pp. 112–124, 183.

In this unevenly written memoir of his pulp years, the author includes a chapter on Faust (based on their friendship at Warner Bros. in the early 1940s). Gruber is inaccurate on several counts, and his memory is not to be trusted. Of limited value.

ZANE GREY, by Frank Gruber (Walter J. Black, 1969). On Faust: pp. 108–109, 215.
Of interest here is not the author's error-studded two-page profile of Faust, but the fact that Zane Grey read Faust and "at one time had a number of Max Brand's books on a shelf."

THE UNEMBARRASSED MUSE: THE POPULAR ARTS IN AMERICA, by Russel
B. Nye (Dial Press, 1970). On Faust: p. 298.
In this massive overview, embracing all aspects of popular culture, the author allows
many textural errors to mar his extensive history. In discussing the Western, he is critical
of Faust as a formula writer, dubbing his work "rubberstamped adventure fiction."

THE SIX-GUN MYSTIQUE, by John G. Cawelti (Bowling Green University Popular
Press, 1971). On Faust: p. 98.
Under the heading "Max Brand (Frederick Faust)," the author selects Faust as the lead-
ing representative of his "Pulps and Paperbacks" Western school and lists twenty-two
Brand titles. (There is no biography or critical discussion.)

CHEAP THRILLS: AN INFORMAL HISTORY OF THE PULP MAGAZINES, by Ron
Goulart (Arlington House, 1972). On Faust: pp. 137–141.
In this study the author profiles Faust in his chapter "Cowboys" and quotes briefly from
several Faust Westerns.

DICTIONARY OF AMERICAN BIOGRAPHY, SUPPLEMENT THREE: 1941–1945,
edited by Edward T. James (Scribner's, 1973). On Faust: pp. 264–265.
In the entry, "Faust, Frederick Schiller," Hamlin Hill offers a two-page profile, ending
with commentary on Faust's verse. Hill claims that it demonstrates "an enormous knowledge of classical and medieval legend and myth, a romantic poetic style and a tightly
controlled and formal sense of prosody."

FAULKNER: A BIOGRAPHY, by Joseph Blotner (Random House, 1974). On Faust:
pp. 1123–1124.
In his comprehensive two-volume study of the prize-winning author Blotner recounts a
1940s screen collaboration between Faust and Faulkner at Warner's on THE DE
GAULLE STORY (never produced).

ENCYCLOPEDIA OF MYSTERY AND DETECTION, by Chris Steinbrunner and Otto
Penzler (McGraw-Hill, 1976). On Faust: p. 146.
A brief entry headed "Faust, Frederick (1892–1944)" covers seven of his mystery-related
novels.

A COMPANION TO CALIFORNIA, by James D. Hart (Oxford University Press, 1978).
On Faust: p. 135.
In his brief entry, "Faust, Frederick [Schiller]," Hart dubs him as "a professional writer
of adventure stories." There is no critical assessment.

THE UNTAMED, by Max Brand (Gregg Press, 1978). On Faust: pp. v–xii.
In this special edition of Faust's first published book, Jack Nachbar provides a critical
Introduction. Important not for content but because it marks the first academic interest
in Faust since Easton's 1970 biography.

WHO'S WHO IN HORROR AND FANTASY FICTION, by Mike Ashley (Taplinger,
1978) (originally published in England). On Faust: pp. 77–78.
The author states that Faust's "contribution to the weird field is limited but important"
and cites three magazine stories, the three "Dan Barry" novels, THE GARDEN OF
EDEN, and THE SMOKING LAND.

DESTRY RIDES AGAIN, by Max Brand (Gregg Press, 1979). On Faust: pp. v–xi.
Another special Faust edition, with a critical Introduction by Richard W. Etulain. With
eight pages of photos from the 1939 film version of this novel.

MEMORIES OF THE '20s AND '30s, by Jane Faust Easton (Santa Barbara, California,
         privately published, 1979). 157 pages. With 30 photos, five of Faust.
Photos include shots of the Faust villa in Italy, his wife, children, and servants. Faust's
eldest daughter has subtitled this memoir "Growing Up in Florence, New York and Los
Angeles." The period covered is from 1922 into September 1940 (when the author
married Robert Easton). Charming and warmly detailed, with many references to her
father. Some of the Faust-related sections were reprinted in MAX BRAND: WESTERN
GIANT as "Memories of My Father" (see Section I).

THE SMOKING LAND, by Max Brand (Capra Press, 1980). On Faust: pp. 7–8.
In this paperback first-book printing of Faust's only science-fiction adventure novel Robert Easton provides the Introduction. Text reproduced from the pulp pages of *Argosy*,
with the original illustrations that accompanied this serial in 1937.

TWENTIETH-CENTURY CRIME AND MYSTERY WRITERS, edited by John Reilly
         (St. Martin's Press, 1980). On Faust: pp. 172–179.
A brief biographical entry, as "Brand, Max," and a lengthy checklist of Faust's novels,
which is riddled with errors. Also lists some of his screen works. Of partial value is a
two-page critical sketch on Faust by Elmer Pry, relating his work to the mystery genre.

MAX BRAND'S BEST WESTERN STORIES, edited by William F. Nolan (Dodd,
         Mead, 1981). On Faust: pp. 1–21, 23, 34–35, 54–55, 100, 106–107, 210.
The editor's introduction, "Western Giant," offers a full profile of Faust, and there are
detailed prefatory notes to each entry.

THE AMERICAN WEST IN FICTION, edited by Jon Tuska (New American Library,
         1982). On Faust: pp. 218–219.
The editor provides a short profile of Faust as "Max Brand" in part III of this anthology,
"The West of the Storytellers." Reprints "Wine on the Desert."

FIFTY WESTERN WRITERS: A BIO-BIBLIOGRAPHICAL SOURCEBOOK, edited
         by Fred Erisman and Richard W. Etulain (Greenwood Press, 1982). On Faust:
         pp. 32–41.
The entry, "Max Brand (Frederick Faust)," is a worthwhile examination of Faust's
contribution to the genre by William Bloodworth. A brief bibliography of works by and
about Faust is included.

TWENTIETH-CENTURY WESTERN WRITERS, edited by James Vinson (Gale Re-
         search Co., 1982). On Faust: pp. 103–117.
A brief biographical entry, as "Brand, Max," and a lengthy, often incorrect checklist of
Faust's books, uncollected stories, verse, etc. The only real value here is William Blood-
worth's solid critical appraisal of Faust's Western fiction.

ENCYCLOPEDIA OF FRONTIER AND WESTERN FICTION, by Jon Tuska and Vicki
         Piekarski (McGraw-Hill, 1983). On Faust: pp. 90–96.
A basic biographical treatment as "Faust, Frederick," with a title listing of his books
and a listing of Western films based on his works.

THE PULP WESTERN, by John A. Dinan (Borgo Press, 1983). On Faust: pp. 13, 15–
         16, 49, 51–52, 71, 73–78, 107, 116.
This history of Western fiction in the mass-market pulp magazines of America contains
many references to Faust. Dubbed King of the Western pulp genre, he is cited as "the

principal moving force in the first and second Western pulp periods." A biographical profile of Faust (pp. 76–78) quotes from his fiction.

YESTERDAY'S FACES: A STUDY OF SERIES CHARACTERS IN THE EARLY PULP MAGAZINES, by Robert Sampson (Bowling Green University Popular Press, 1983). On Faust: pp. 210–225.
Subtitled "Volume 1, The Glory Figures," this profile of the action pulps features a lengthy study of Westerns and includes, in the chapter "Fifty Miles South, Near the Pecos," a detailed critical look at Brand's "Dan Barry" series, beginning with THE UNTAMED. This section of the book was reprinted in TWENTIETH-CENTURY LITERARY CRITICISM.

THE BRITISH SPY NOVEL: STYLES IN TREACHERY, by John Atkins (John Calder, 1984). On Faust: pp. 66–67.
In a chapter titled "The Chancelleries of Europe" the author comments at some length on Brand's novel THE PHANTOM SPY.

A. MERRITT: REFLECTIONS IN THE MOON POOL, edited by Sam Moskowitz (Oswald Train, 1985). On Faust: pp. 57–60.
Chapter 7 details a proposed collaboration between Merritt (editor of *American Weekly* and a well-known fantasist) and "Brand" on a novel, THE FOX WOMAN. Eventually Faust pulled out of the project due to a conflict of writing styles.

MAX BRAND'S BEST WESTERN STORIES, VOLUME II, edited by William F. Nolan (Dodd, Mead, 1985). On Faust: pp. 1–3, 41, 55, 113, 162.
Includes an Introduction and prefatory notes by the editor.

A LITERARY HISTORY OF THE AMERICAN WEST (Texas Christian University Press, 1986). On Faust: pp. 125–126.
In a section entitled "Lawmen and Outlaws," an overview of the American Western, Kent Steckmesser states that "the popularity of the mythical lawman was proved by the widespread acceptance of Max Brand . . . who sees his characters as demigods." Brief, provocative commentary.

MAX BRAND'S BEST WESTERN STORIES, VOLUME III, edited by William F. Nolan (Dodd, Mead, 1987). On Faust: pp. xi-xii, 1–2, 70, 87, 104–105, 145–146, 206, 221.
Includes an Introduction and prefatory notes by the editor.

THE NIGHT FLOWER, by Max Brand (IPL, 1987) (the first paperback reprinting of this novel, originally published in hardcover as by "Walter C. Butler"). On Faust: pp. 1–5.
In the Introduction (by William F. Nolan) Faust's mystery fiction is related to his other work, and the background of this novel is explored in a comparison to Dashiell Hammett's THE GLASS KEY.

POPULAR WORLD FICTION, edited by Walton Beacham and Suzanne Niemeyer (Beacham Publishing, 1987). On Faust: pp. 176–196.
In a long review/essay, "Max Brand/Frederick Faust, 1892–1944," Bradley University's Edgar L. Chapman provides a most provocative and illuminating look at Faust. He concentrates in particular on SINGING GUNS, DESTRY RIDES AGAIN, and the three Montana Kid novels, relating them to various popular markets, including motion picture adaptations. Thoughtful, well-developed commentary.

SELLING THE WILD WEST: POPULAR WESTERN FICTION, 1860 TO 1960, by
    Christine Bold (Indiana University Press, 1987). On Faust: pp. 76–77, 91–104.
In section 3, "Escaping from the Pulps," the author cites Faust, Zane Grey, and Ernest
Haycox as "the most famous, successful, and prolific authors of popular Western fiction"
in the period before World War I and extending beyond World War II. She devotes long
essays to each. In her "Max Brand" she postulates that, although Faust attempted to
distance himself, as a classical poet, from the formula works of Max Brand, he did not
wholly succeed: "It seems clear that his popular Westerns—which move from acknowledging classical prototypes to introducing their own superhuman figures—have the same
combination of mythological content and patterned form as his poetry."
    Her arguments in placing Faust firmly in the mold of a formula writer suffer from a
narrow perspective attained by a cursory reading of the Faust canon. (Only seventeen
Faust Westerns are actually cited in the essay.)

WESTERN AND HARD-BOILED DETECTIVE FICTION IN AMERICA, by Cynthia
    S. Hamilton (University of Iowa Press, 1987). On Faust: pp. 42–45, 50–52, 54,
    57, 94–119, 127.
In her lengthy essay, "Frederick Faust," British critic Hamilton comes to hasty conclusions based on a reading of only a bare dozen Faust Westerns; she attacks much of his
fiction as bitter, superficial, and self-mocking. Of interest as a slanted view of Faust,
with some probing insights along the way, Hamilton ultimately fails because the totality
of Faust's work cannot be fairly judged on so small a portion of his output. Her essay
is reprinted in TWENTIETH-CENTURY LITERARY CRITICISM.

LIFE AND WORK, by Robert Olney Easton with David Russell (University of Califor-
    nia, Santa Barbara, 1988). On Faust: pp. 141–145, 149, 162–166, 259–265.
Part of the university's Library Oral History Program, this is actually a book-length
interview with Easton, conducted by Russell. Easton, who married Faust's eldest daughter, speaks of Faust as a "literary mentor," placing him in a family context.

THE NEW FRONTIER: THE BEST OF TODAY'S WESTERN FICTION, edited by
    Joe R. Lansdale (Doubleday, 1989). On Faust: pp. 1, 13–14.
Prints a section of WYCHERLEY, Faust's unfinished Civil War novel, as "A First
Blooding," with an Afterword by William F. Nolan relating this segment to the existing
200–page manuscript. This novel was Faust's most serious attempt at quality prose fiction.

PLAYING DOCTOR: TELEVISION, STORYTELLING, AND MEDICAL POWER, by
    Joseph Turow (Oxford University Press, 1989). On Faust: pp. 3, 9, 10, 14, 19,
    23–24, 26, 52, 56–57, 61, 78, 241.
Beginning with "Kildare in the Context of His Time" in Chapter 1, Turow names Faust
as a prime influence in shaping medical drama for a mass-market audience. He treats the
Kildare series in detail, crediting Faust with creating the doctor-as-hero image in novels,
films, and motion pictures.

RIO RENEGADES, by "Terence Duncan" (William F. Nolan). (Zebra Books, 1989).
Dedicated to Faust, with a villain named "Barry Silver" (partially based on Faust) and
a colonel named "Maxwell Schiller Brandt," the novel utilizes all of Faust's pseudonyms
as various character names ("Sheriff Peter Henry Baxter," etc.). A Max Brand pastiche.

THE WESTERN PULP HERO, by Nick Carr (Starmont House, 1989). On Faust: pp.
    82–83.

Under the heading "Silvertip," the author describes Jim Silver, ranking him among the major pulp Western series characters. (No biographical material on Faust is included.)

THE AMERICAN WEST: FROM FICTION INTO FILM, by Jim Hitt (McFarland, 1990). On Faust: pp. 189–193, 315–316.

A profile of Faust in relation to his books-into-films and a checklist of twenty-four motion pictures produced from Faust works. The author claims that "by the 1930s, his books were outselling even Zane Grey."

LOVE AND WAR: PEARL HARBOR THROUGH V-J DAY, by Robert and Jane Easton (University of Oklahoma Press, 1991). On Faust: throughout the book, some 60 pages.

In this series of wartime letters, exchanged between the Eastons and intercut with personal narrative and updated commentary, Faust is constantly mentioned and discussed. His battlefield death provides an emotional high point, poignantly expressed. There are two photos of Faust in the book: one with his wife, Dorothy, and one with his daughter, Judy (at the horse races in Santa Anita, California).

HIDDEN IN PLAIN SIGHT: AN EXAMINATION OF THE AMERICAN ARTS, by Martin Williams (Oxford University Press, 1992). On Faust: pp. 75–78.

In the section "And a Few Words on Max Brand" the author admits that his reading of Faust consists of "five short stories and four novels." Williams found two of the novels "unreadable" but rated TORTURE TRAIL "more impressive, in some respects, than ROBINSON CRUSOE." He calls Faust "an American Balzac."

MAX BRAND'S BEST POEMS, edited by Robert and Jane Easton (Fithian Press, 1992). On Faust: pp. 7–16, 92–101.

Martin Greenberg delivers a brief Foreword, followed by the editors' introduction, "Max Brand and Frederick Faust," summing up the impact of Faust's verse: "Read as part of his life, his poetry completes the image of a Protean figure who strode through his era in many guises, like those mythic heroes and heroines he created in verse and in prose." William F. Nolan contributes an afterword, "The Poet and the Proseman," quoting Leonard Bacon's comment that "Faust was, to me, poetry incarnate."

DANGER IS MY BUSINESS: AN ILLUSTRATED HISTORY OF THE FABULOUS PULP MAGAZINES, by Lee Server (Chronicle Books, 1993). On Faust: pp. 26, 29, 137.

The author places Faust (with Edgar Rice Burroughs) at "the summit" among pulp writers, calling him "the titan of popular literature . . . responsible [with Burroughs] for setting the standards for excitement and color in popular fiction in this century." With a photo of Faust and a color reproduction of a 1929 "Max Brand" cover of *Western Story Magazine.*

KING COWBOY: TOM MIX AND THE MOVIES, by Robert S. Birchard (Riverwood Press, 1993). On Faust: pp. 159, 234, 248–249.

There are no biographical or critical data on Faust himself in this study, but eight films starring Mix and based on Faust's books and stories are discussed, with reviews quoted on each. One of the chapters is titled "Destry Rides Again" and details the star's debut in sound films via this Faust novel. Birchard claims that "Max Brand . . . provided the source material for several of Tom's best films." He also reveals that Mix planned a sequel to DESTRY RIDES AGAIN as DESTRY OF DEATH VALLEY. Stills from seven Faust/Mix films are included, with a poster from DESTRY RIDES AGAIN. The author claims that the title for THE UNTAMED was devised for Mix and caused Faust to change the book title from THE WILD GEESE. This is incorrect, as THE WILD GEESE was Faust's first title for THE NIGHT HORSEMAN. Indeed, the original 1920 Putnam edition has Faust's first title as the running head on every interior page. Only on the printed title page is it called THE NIGHT HORSEMAN.

TWENTIETH-CENTURY LITERARY CRITICISM, VOLUME 49, edited by Laurie Di Mauro (Gale Research, 1993). On Faust: pp. 34–61.

Under the heading "Frederick Faust, 1892–1944," there is a 30,000–word section of reprinted criticism from Robert Easton, Edgar L. Chapman, William A. Bloodworth, Jr., Robert Sampson, Samuel A. Peeples, and Cynthia S. Hamilton (see Sections I–III).

Shorter quotations from other critics are included, and Faust himself is quoted about his Westerns: "I've . . . used only one plot—the good man becomes bad and the bad man becomes good." The editor provides an Introduction to this material, listing fifty-two Faust books as "Principal Works." The extensive critical coverage in this key library reference volume, however belated, is an impressive demonstration of Faust's acceptance by the mainstream literary establishment. His fiction is treated as worthy of serious critical attention. A Faust portrait photo is included.

THE BLACK MASK MURDERS, by William F. Nolan (St. Martin's Press, 1994). On Faust: pp. 25–27.

This historical mystery novel, set in 1930s Hollywood, presents Faust as himself in a fictional encounter with Dashiell Hammett as they discuss an aborted Tom Mix Western.

THE COLLECTED STORIES OF MAX BRAND, edited by Robert and Jane Easton (University of Nebraska Press, 1994). On Faust: pp. ix–xx, 1–2, 17–18, 71–72, 88–89, 103–104, 147–148, 160–161, 209, 217–218, 236–237, 252–253, 261, 277–278, 290, 296–297, 309–310, 317, 335–336, 343.

In this Centennial Edition of Faust's best stories, William Bloodworth provides the Introduction and the editors introduce each selection with a perceptive and revealing biographical/critical preface. Taken together these carefully wrought prefaces are of genuine value in uniting the author's life with his fiction. A key Faust volume, offering further proof of literary distinction.

TRAILIN', by Max Brand (University of Nebraska Press, 1994). Issued in hardback and trade paperback editions. On Faust: pp. vii-xii.

In a biographical and critical Introduction to Faust's second published novel, Western history scholar Richard W. Etulain comments on "the hero's Oedipal search for his father [as] his trailin' becomes The Quest of all young men on such journeys." This theme reappears in many of Faust's subsequent Westerns.

THE UNTAMED, by Max Brand (University of Nebraska Press, 1994). Issued in hardback and trade paperback editions. On Faust: pp. v–x.

William A. Bloodworth, Jr., provides the critical Introduction to Faust's first published novel, pointing out that Max Brand's Western image in THE UNTAMED was shaped out of bitterness and hardship and that his early years of bruising ranch work as an orphan in California's San Joaquin Valley "scarred him internally and gave him no reason to sentimentalize the West."

WILD WEST SHOW!, edited by Thomas W. Knowles and Joe R. Lansdale (Wings Books [Random House], 1994). On Faust: pp. 84–87.

A profile of Faust with portrait photo titled "Frederick *Who*? Oh, You Mean Max Brand" by William F. Nolan is illustrated with a photo of Tom Mix as ''Destry'' and a paperback cover shot of DESTRY RIDES AGAIN, ''Max Brand's most famous Western novel.''

THE WESTERN STORY: A CHRONOLOGICAL TREASURY, edited by Jon Tuska
(University of Nebraska Press, 1995). On Faust: pp. xxiv, 89–91.
In reprinting Faust's ''Werewolf'' in this landmark anthology Tuska covers Faust in a biographical-critical essay, placing him in historical context within the framework of the American Western Story. Tuska's Introduction is monumental. An indispensable volume.

{Note: The Golden West Literary Agency has been providing textually important prefaces to Faust stories collected in such Brand books as THE SACKING OF EL DORADO: STORIES OF WESTERN ADVENTURE (Chivers North America, 1994) and THE RETURN OF FREE RANGE LANNING: A WESTERN TRIO (G. K. Hall, 1995), as has Jon Tuska in such anthologies as his SHADOW OF THE LARIAT (Carroll & Graf, 1995) and THE BIG BOOK OF WESTERN ACTION STORIES (Barricade, 1995). I have been told the agency will continue to provide such prefatory notes on the many Brand collections and anthologies it will prepare for book publication in forthcoming years.}

III. MAGAZINE AND NEWSPAPER ITEMS ON FAUST

This listing includes all known articles, tributes, profiles, and essays dealing with Faust. It is selective with regard to obituaries and reviews of books about Faust. Items about Faust as a student at the University of California, Berkeley, are excluded with the exception of the ''Little Bobbie'' item from 1915. Since David Fox is providing a complete listing elsewhere in this book of the contents of the three Faust-related magazines (*Fabulous Faust Fanzine, Faust Collector,* and *Singing Guns*), I have limited my commentary to key items from these publications. Page numbers are missing on clipped entries.

''A Little More of Little Bobbie,'' by Anon., *The Daily Californian* (4/27/15).
The campus editors comment on Faust's being revealed as the mysterious ''Littie Bobbie'' whose series of humorous, biting letters criticized the university.

''Fate's Honeymoon,'' by ''The Editor'' [Robert H. Davis], *All-Story Weekly* (7/14/17),
p. 177.
This editorial commentary accompanied the printing of Faust's first book-length serial (as Max Brand) in this Munsey magazine, proclaimed by Davis as ''an epochal event in American literature.'' Faust was twenty-five and just beginning his fiction career. In the next twenty-six years he would go on to complete 250 more book-length works.

''The Round-Up,'' by Anon. {Editors' Note: Frank E. Blackwell, reprinted in MBC},
Western Story Magazine (9/2/22), pp. 132–133.
The editor provides readers with a faked profile of ''George Owen Baxter,'' mixing biographical fact with fiction.

''The Mastery of Max Brand,'' by Anon., *Argosy All-Story Weekly* (6/30/23), pp. 481–483.

Editorial commentary on the Dan Barry series, with detailed plots of his magazine serials "The Untamed," "The Night Horseman," and "The Seventh Man." Written as a lead-in to the first serial installment of "Dan Barry's Daughter." Brand is described as "a master craftsman of the written word."

"The Round-Up," by Anon. {Editors' Note: Frank E. Blackwell, reprinted in MBC}, *Western Story Magazine* (9/15/23), pp. 132–133.
The editor profiles "Max Brand" for *WSM* readers, again mixing fact and fiction. A folksy Western lingo is employed, as the editor declares: "Gosh all hemlock, hope you all haven't got tired with our talkin' so much about one of our children."

"The Round-Up," by Anon. {Editors' Note: Frank E. Blackwell, reprinted in MBC}, *Western Story Magazine* (2/9/24), pp. 133–135.
An editorial account, written in the usual heavy Western lingo, of a New York visit by "Max Brand" during which a bull terrier is purchased (Faust bred bull terriers in Westchester). The dog turns out to be "stone deaf . . . but he's got a fine nose for scentin'." Brand keeps the animal.

"George Owen Baxter," by D. C. Hubbard, *Western Story Magazine* (4/28/28).
"Max Brand, Famous Western Author," by D. C. Hubbard, *Western Story Magazine* (6/2/28).
"David Manning," by D. C. Hubbard, *Western Story Magazine* (6/16/28).
The three profiles were written as promotion pieces in *WSM* and mixed biographical fact with fiction. A separate life was invented for these three Faust pen names in the magazine. {Editors' Note: Reprinted in MBC.}

"Writers of California," by Carey McWilliams, *Bookman* (12/30).
Contains a brief mention of Faust.

"The Men Who Make the Argosy: Max Brand," by Anon., *Argosy* (12/10/32), p. 141.
Part of a series of magazine profiles, this one detailing a visit "Brand" had in Texas with a pair of "old trappers" who supposedly gave him ideas for his Western tales. Accompanied by a photo of a young Faust (probably from his university days in Berkeley). He was forty when this piece appeared, and his real name was not revealed.

"Twenty-Five Million Words," by Edward H. Dodd, Jr., *Publishers Weekly* (3/26/38), pp. 1358–1360.
The first major profile on Faust and the first to reveal his true identity with regard to "Max Brand." Mainly discusses his "astonishing record" in which he is said to have been capable of 90,000 words in seven days. With a photo of seven foreign-language Brand Western novels and a U.S. edition of THE IRON TRAIL. Reprinted in MAX BRAND: THE MAN AND HIS WORK (see Section I). {Editors' Note: Reprinted in MBC.}

"Kildare Creator Is Killed in Italy," by Milton Bracker, *New York Times* (5/17/44).
Obituary. With a photo of Faust. He was quoted: " 'I want to see exactly how American troops act in battle,' he told the troops waiting with him for the start of the big push Thursday night. 'I'm going in with you, and I am going to write exactly what I see. If you do well, I'll tell it and, if you do badly, I'll tell that, too.' "

"Film Writer, 'Dr. Kildare' Author, Killed in Italy," by Anon., *Los Angeles Times* (5/17/44).

Obituary.

"Legendary 'King of the Pulps' Dies on Battlefield," by Anon., *San Francisco Chronicle* (5/17/44).

A detailed biography in which Faust is described as "tall, gangling, possessed of an almost Byronic spirit of rebellion." Obituary. With a photo captioned "Fabulous Faust."

"Max Brand, 51, Author, Killed at Front in Italy," by Anon., *New York Herald-Tribune* (5/17/44).

Another lengthy obituary in which the writer incorrectly claims that "Mr. Faust saw little of the West and met his first real cowboy long after his first Western story was published." With a photo.

"Max Brand Died Entering Battle with Infantry," by Russell Hill, *New York Herald-Tribune* (5/18/44).

A by-lined follow-up story in which Hill states: "I was with Faust on a troopship coming across from the U.S. and had many discussions with him about military strategy and military history." He writes of Faust's bad heart, claiming: "Internes used to queue up to listen to his irregular heartbeats through a stethoscope."

"By the Way," by Bill Henry, *Los Angeles Times* (5/21/44).

Henry devotes his column to an obituary of Faust.

"Frederick Faust's Work," by Frederick C. Mills, *New York Herald-Tribune* (5/22/44).

A memoir-tribute by a friend, mainly discussing Faust's verse. One of his poems is printed.

"Frederick Faust," by Leonard Bacon, *Saturday Review of Literature* (5/27/44), pp. 28–29.

Faust's friend and former teacher provides a heartfelt memoir, stressing the immense power that verse exerted in Faust's life. "Faust, to me, was poetry incarnate. He lived, moved, and had his being in, for, and because of it."

"Aesop and Faust," by Anon., *Newsweek* (5/29/44).

The obituary here dubs Faust "a literary Paul Bunyan."

"Frederick Faust, *et al.*," by Anon., *Time* (5/29/44).

This obituary is notable for a quotation ascribed to Faust: "No one is more than forty to fifty percent efficient, but when a man is backed into a corner by a man who intends to kill him, he can be as high as ninety percent efficient." With a photo.

"Mr. Frederick Faust," by J. A. S. (John Spranger), *London Times* (5/31/44).

A British friend who once toured the Greek islands with Faust fondly recalls their times together.

"Frederick Faust," by Anon., *Harper's* (7/44).

An obituary from the magazine Faust was representing at the time of his death.

"A Farewell to Max Brand," by Steve Fisher, *Writer's Digest* (8/44), pp. 31–33.

Fisher was a close studio friend at Warner Bros.; his essay-tribute to Faust is emotionally charged and deeply felt. "He had in him power and depth and beauty he'd never even tapped." Revealing and informative. Reprinted in MAX BRAND: THE MAN AND HIS WORK and in MAX BRAND: WESTERN GIANT (see Section I). {Editors' Note: Reprinted in MBC.}

"Frederick Faust Again," by Anon., *Harper's* (8/44).

Contains a detailed battlefield report of Faust's death by Sergeant Jack Delaney. Affecting and sincere. This was one of many tributes received by the magazine. Reprinted as ''The Death of a War Correspondent'' in both MAX BRAND: THE MAN AND HIS WORK and MAX BRAND: WESTERN GIANT (see Section I).

''The Fabulous Faust: In Memoriam,'' by Leonard Bacon, *University of California Alumni Magazine* (9/44), pp. 29, 38–39.

Bacon, winner of the Pulitzer Prize for verse in 1941, again pays tribute to his deceased friend in a full essay that recalls their early teacher-pupil relationship at the University of California, describing Faust as a man ''who powerfully affected every life he touched. . . . The points of an Irish hunter, a stroke in tennis, the virtue of a wine, the full meaning of an epigram, he could be exciting about any one of them.'' To him, Faust was indeed ''a great man.'' With a photo of Faust.

''Death of a Writer,'' by Fred Painton, *Writers Guild Magazine* (1944).

Unlocated. Painton was apparently overseas in May 1944 as a fellow war correspondent.

''Dear Mr. Fisher,'' by Frank O'Rourke, *Writer's Digest* (letters) (3/45).

A response to Steve Fisher's tribute by a young man who had been inspired to write by meeting Faust. O'Rourke describes the meeting and the first book (''E'' COMPANY) resulting from it (see Section II).

''The Fantasy of Frederick Faust,'' by Darrell C. Richardson, *The Philadelphia Science Fantasy Society News* (11–12/45).

An examination of Faust's outright fantasy. The plots of two short stories, two novelettes, and his serial, ''The Smoking Land,'' are discussed in detail.

''Strength!,'' by Chester D. Cuthbert, *The Fabulous Faust Fanzine* no. 1 (6/48), pp. ix–xii.

A reader's essay on Faust's writing style. Cuthbert sees Faust as ''under some powerful compulsion to discover the secret of strength.'' {Editors' Note: Reprinted in MBC.}

''Tribute to a Modest Man,'' by Phil Richman, *The Fabulous Faust Fanzine*, no. 1 (6/48), pp. xiii–xiv.

A profile with important quotations from several Faust letters to Richman, one of the first Faust collectors.

''Sidelights on Faust's Output,'' by W. F. Nolan, *The Fabulous Faust Fanzine*, no. 1 (6/48), pp. xix–xxi.

A gathering of facts about Faust's writing career, including comparison of the early pre-M-G-M Kildare with the series of novels and films.

''Once Upon a Time,'' by S. Allen McElfresh, *The Fabulous Faust Fanzine*, no. 1 (6/48), pp. xxxix–xl, xlii.

McElfresh, a Faust collector, makes the point that Faust was always a fantasist: ''Basically, [he] was a writer of fairy tales and fantasy, and his tales belong in no other category. It makes no difference that, formally, his themes deal with adventures in the West, cloak and dagger escapades in medieval Europe, piracy on the Spanish Main, or murders in New York. They are fantasies and fairy tales whatever their theme or locale.'' Persuasive and thought-provoking commentary.

''Concerning Faust Films,'' by William F. Nolan, *The Fabulous Faust Fanzine*, no. 2 (12/48), pp. 12–13.

The first printed listing of the films produced from Faust source material or worked on by him, based on extensive studio research. Some thirty-two films are listed, with overall commentary.

"More Sidelights on Faust," by William F. Nolan, *The Fabulous Faust Fanzine*, no. 2 (12/48), pp. 26–28.

Among the assembled information is the fact that Faust had told Phil Richman "that he had helped [John] Schoolcraft write THE BIRD OF PASSAGE," which is why the book was dedicated to him. Also Faust intended using the pen name "Henry Uriel" on a story for which a new pen name, "Max Brand," was substituted.

"The New Faust Mystery," by Chester Cuthbert, *The Fabulous Faust Fanzine*, no. 2 (12/48), p. 41.

Deals with the idea that Faust linked himself with the Faust legend and explored it constantly in his fiction: "Faust was deeply concerned with good and evil . . . whether real strength would serve one or the other, or was actually beyond both. Faust wrestled with the problem all his life: was he compelled to do so by his preoccupation with the Faust legend?" Arresting commentary.

"Heinie," by Carl Brandt, *The Fabulous Faust Fanzine*, no. 2 (12/48), pp. 46–47.

A memoir by Faust's longtime agent and friend who states that Faust "desired desperately to live gustily, with color in every action and background. But his unsafe heart condemned him to inaction, except the vicarious living he got from the tales he wrote." A fascinating portrait from an inside source. Partially reprinted in MAX BRAND: WESTERN GIANT (see Section I). {Editors' Note: Reprinted in MBC.}

"Faust and the Western Tale," by S. A. McElfresh, *The Fabulous Faust Fanzine*, no. 2 (12/48), pp. 51–52, 55.

An essay placing Faust within the Western genre. Reprinted, revised, with Darrell Richardson, as "Max Brand and the Western Story" in MAX BRAND: THE MAN AND HIS WORK (see Section I).

"Letters," *The Fabulous Faust Fanzine*, no. 2 (12/48).

Important letters printed in this issue include those from Carl Brandt, Steve Fisher, Jane Faust Easton, Frank O'Rourke, Phil Richman, John Schoolcraft, and R. Pinckney McLean (who, as a very close friend of Faust, reveals the background to Faust's work on his book of nonfiction, FIGHTER SQUADRON AT GUADALCANAL).

"Immortality," by Anon., *New York Herald-Tribune* (8/21/49).

Comment on the reissue of Faust's first novel, THE UNTAMED. From his 1949 perspective, the writer cannot imagine reaction to Faust half a century in the future: "Just how would a reader in 2000 A. D. regard a Brand 'Western?' . . . Historical? Sociological?" (Two years later, writing in the 12/51 issue of *The Fabulous Faust Fanzine*, collector S. Allen McElfresh stated: "The idea of Faust being published fifty years from today is absurd. He lacks the popularity and appeal. Maybe a Faust book or two will be published . . . ten to fifteen years from today [1966], but even that is doubtful.")

"The Life and Works of Max Brand," by Darrell C. Richardson, *Cincinnati Post* (8/23/49).

A profile of Faust.

"Bob's Bookshelf: Max Brand, King of the Pulp Writers," by Bob Campbell, *Los Angeles News* (1949).

A brief column profile by the president of the American Booksellers' Association.

"A Sketch of My Life," by Frederick Faust, *The Fabulous Faust Fanzine*, no. 3 (1/50), pp. 9–11.

The first printing of a long autobiographical letter Faust wrote to Jane Faust in the fall of 1939. An essential item. Reprinted in MAX BRAND: WESTERN GIANT (see Section I). {Editors' Note: Reprinted in MBC in its entirety.}

"Bohemian Days with Faust," by J. L. Schoolcraft, *The Fabulous Faust Fanzine*, no. 3 (1/50), pp. 17–19.

An important, vital memoir from one of Faust's dearest friends, detailing their early life in New York as a pair of penniless young writers (when a three-course dinner could be had for a quarter). Reprinted in MAX BRAND: THE MAN AND HIS WORK and, revised, in MAX BRAND: WESTERN GIANT (see Section I). {Editors' Note: Reprinted in MBC.}

"Faust's Military Interlude," by Gilbert J. McLennan, *The Fabulous Faust Fanzine*, no. 3 (1/50), pp. 24–26.

Faust in Canada recalled by a fellow soldier who served with him in "The American Foreign Legion." Reprinted and revised in MAX BRAND: WESTERN GIANT (see Section I). {Editors' Note: Reprinted in MBC.}

"More Faustiana," by William F. Nolan, *The Fabulous Faust Fanzine*, no. 3 (1/50), pp. 31–34.

Another gathering of facts based on extensive research, including the report of a visit to Munsey editor, Al Gibney (of *Argosy*), in New York. Gibney describes putting pressure on Faust for more Dan Barry books, even after Faust had killed off this character in THE SEVENTH MAN: "We begged Heinie to recreate Barry in the role of an illegitimate son. He positively wouldn't hear of it and flatly declared that Dan had always been true to Kate Cumberland. We did manage to wheedle a fourth novel, DAN BARRY'S DAUGHTER, out of him—but never the illegitimate son!"

"Faust and the Nietzschean Concept," by Frank J. Hartl, *The Fabulous Faust Fanzine*, no. 3 (1/50), pp. 35–38.

A major essay, written with verve and punch, placing Faust's great fictional villains in the tradition of Friedrich Wilhelm Nietzsche, "the greatest apostle of strength." He quotes Nietzsche: "In the battle of life, what we need is not goodness but strength, not humility but pride, not altruism but resolute intelligence." Thus Hartl ties Faust to the Nietzschean law: "Strength is the ultimate virtue." However, he makes it very clear that Faust was by no means a Nietzschean disciple and likely despised much of the German's philosophy but that he did espouse the idea of strength as a separate way of life, beyond good and evil.

"Letters," *The Fabulous Faust Fanzine*, no. 3 (1/50).

Of importance, letters from Carl Brandt, Ray Bradbury, Frank O'Rourke, and Dr. George W. Fish (Faust's lifelong pal, "Dixie," who was the model for Dr. Kildare).

"Max Brand's Western Style," by Samuel A. Peeples, *The Fabulous Faust Fanzine*, no. 4 (12/51), pp. 11–12.

An examination of Faust as a writer in the Western genre, with some shrewd observations and conclusions. Later, for MAX BRAND: WESTERN GIANT, the author revised and greatly expanded this piece as "Max Brand and the American Western Story."

"Richard—Mon Roi," by Vida Jameson, *The Fabulous Faust Fanzine*, no. 4 (12/51), pp. 30–32.

An essay-review of THE GOLDEN KNIGHT with perceptive plot analysis. Jameson praises the book as a combination of fantasy and fact, as "history-cum-legend."

"Letters," *The Fabulous Faust Fanzine*, no. 4 (12/51).
Important letters from: Steve Fisher, Gilbert J. McLennan, John Blair, William F. Nolan, and John L. Schoolcraft (who reports, in six letters from 1/50 to 9/51, that he completed a volume on Faust, "a personal history based primarily on his letters"). This book surfaced six years later, in a truncated form, as THE NOTEBOOKS AND POEMS OF "MAX BRAND" (see Section II).

"Greatest Pulpist," by Anon., *Time* (8/25/52).
A negative review of MAX BRAND: THE MAN AND HIS WORK in which it is claimed that "there was no real essence to Faust's writing—unless it was the gooey residue of boiled pulp." His fiction is also dubbed "fascinating babble" and summed up as "a phenomenal flow of unreality." With a photo of Faust.

"Max Brand: The Man and His Work," by William F. Nolan, *Rhodomagnetic Digest*
(1/53), pp. 53–55.
Review.

"Destry and Dionysus," by Martha Bacon, *The Atlantic* (7/55), pp. 72–74.
A pivotal piece, relating Faust to modern literature and verse. A memoir by Leonard Bacon's daughter, superbly written. Reprinted in MAX BRAND: WESTERN GIANT (see Section I). {Editors' Note: Reprinted in MBC.}

"Sir," by James J. Geller, *The Atlantic* (9/55), pp. 34–35.
A letter from the man who was responsible for Faust's being hired as a screenwriter at Warner Bros. Geller was a story editor at the studio and reported that Faust regarded himself "as a deep failure even though he commanded the highest prices in the . . . field."

"Max Brand: The Most Unforgettable Person I Have Ever Known," by Frank Gruber,
The Roundup (1/57), pp. 5–10.
Gruber, who knew Faust only during the final year of his life, recalls his studio friend in a memoir marred by errors. Sincere but carelessly written in Gruber's awkward pulp style.

"Destry Rides, Again and Again," by Herbert Mitgang, *New York Times* (4/19/59),
Section 2, pp. 1, 3.
Article on the opening of "Broadway's first Western musical," the stage adaptation of DESTRY RIDES AGAIN. Producer David Merrick is quoted: "The Max Brand book had all the basic elements for a musical. . . . I was not attracted by the movie versions at all."

"The Word Merchants," by Bill Heuman, *Writer's Digest* (3/64), pp. 33–38.
In this article on prolific writers, from Horatio Alger to Edgar Wallace, Faust is profiled in a section titled "He Wore Two Hats." Several errors mar the overheated text.

"Call-ing Doctor Kil-dare," by Sidney De Boer, *P&S Quarterly* (3/66), p. 20. Published
by the Alumni Association of the Columbia University College of Physicians and
Surgeons.
About Dr. George W. "Dixie" Fish, model for Kildare.

"Trade Winds," by Anon., *Saturday Review* (5/21/66).
A column devoted to a discussion of Dr. Fish as the basis for Dr. Kildare. The subject

is quoted: "Faust used to sit in the accident room at Roosevelt Hospital . . . taking notes of all he saw."

"The Creator of Dr. Kildare and Destry," by Robert Cromie, *Chicago Tribune, Books Today* (6/4/67).
A review of the Easton-edited collection, MAX BRAND'S BEST STORIES, that serves as a full profile of Faust, with photo. Easton is quoted: "Faust put dreams in print. He composed prose ballads. His importance as a popular mythmaker . . . is fundamental."

"King of the Pulps," by Stewart Kimble, *The Pulp Era* 69 (1–2/68).
Unlocated. Printed in a small-press publication.

"Heinie and the Chickens," by Frank Gruber, *The Faust Collector*, no. 1 (2/69), pp. 7–8.
A brief memoir regarding Faust in his Warner's period when Gruber had to deliver some chickens to his home in Brentwood, California. A minor piece.

"A Writer-to-Writer Tribute," by William F. Nolan, *The Faust Collector*, no. 1 (2/69), p. 11.
A brief tribute.

"Max Brand and the Mystery Story," by Bill Clark, *The Armchair Detective* (7/69).
Brief piece relating Faust to the mystery genre.

"Faust and *Western Story Magazine*," by Bill Clark, *The Faust Collector*, no. 3 (8/69), p. 9.
An important statistical examination of Faust's major pulp market. Clark reveals: "Faust appeared 834 times in 622 issues . . . he had 307 stories in the magazine . . . one third were serials, twelve averaged 50,000 words, and 175 others were over 20,000 words."

"The Faust Papers," by William F. Nolan, *The Faust Collector*, no. 4 (11/69), pp. 4–6.
Based on a visit to the Faust collection at the Bancroft Library in Berkeley, at the University of California. Many notes and letters are quoted. Forms a guide to this extensive collection.

"The Gaudy Pulps—and Their Fabled King," by William F. Nolan, *Los Angeles Times, Calendar* (11/23/69).
Syndicated, worldwide.

"Taxi, Speedy, and Silvertip," by Bill Clark, *The Faust Collector*, no. 5 (2/70), p. 5.
A piece showing how Faust attempted to inject the character of "Taxi" into other series beyond the Silvertip novels.

"The Man Who Was Max Brand," by William F. Nolan, *The Roundup* (3/70), pp. 1–2, 12.
A profile, with emphasis on his Western output.

"Herculean Writer," by John Blades, *Chicago Tribune* (3/12/70).
A review of Robert Easton's biography, MAX BRAND: THE BIG "WESTERNER." Here Faust is dubbed "the Charles Atlas of American literature."

"Max Brand: The Big 'Westerner,' " by Thorpe Menn, *Kansas City Star* (3/15/70).
A lengthy essay-review of the Easton biography in which the author sums up Faust as "a cultured American who failed in his ambition to be a classical poet but . . . accomplished more as an American mythologist." With a drawing of Faust.

"Life of Max Brand, a Fascinating Story," by Walker A. Tompkins, *Santa Barbara News-Press* (3/15/70), p. F-16.
Tompkins points out, in this review of the Easton biography, that Faust lived in Santa Barbara for a time and that his widow, Dorothy Faust, lived in the city for several years following World War II. With a photo of Robert Easton.

"Personal History," by William Decker, *Saturday Review* (3/28/70).
"Never was a man's name more appropriate to his personal demons," states Decker in this review of the Easton book. Sees Faust as having lived "a tormented life."

"Prolific He Was, and Unknown Too—Except as 'Max Brand,' " by Robert Ostermann, *National Observer* (4/6/70).
The author is stunned by Faust's production as he reviews the Easton biography, declaring "that he did write more stories, read by more people, than any other writer of record."

"Max Brand: Hiding behind Myriad Names," by E. R. Hagemann, *Courier-Journal* (4/26/70).
Hagemann was chairman of the English department at the University of Louisville. In his review of Easton's biography he calls this "an important book about an important man."

"The One-Man Fiction Factory," by Ferol Egan, *American West* (5/70).
Egan claims that it was Western fiction that saved Faust, "a minor poet on the brink of starvation." His review of Easton's book points out that the key fact about Faust was that "he believed in the American Dream."

"Max Brand," by David Dempsey, *New York Times Book Review* (5/3/70), p. 8.
This full-page feature review of Easton's book reflected major critical coverage. The author notes that Faust "was on a treadmill of his own creation and there was no way to stop it." With a photo of Faust with two of his children, plus photos of pulp magazine covers featuring his fiction.

"Big Westerner Was Prolific Tale-Teller," by Chester D. Cuthbert, *The Winnipeg Tribune* (Canada) (6/13/70), p. 18.
Cuthbert, who had contributed to *The Fabulous Faust Fanzine*, again writes of Faust's "search for the secret of strength" in this Canadian review of Easton's biography.

"Max Brand: The Big 'Westerner,' " by Richard W. Etulain, *Western American Literature* (7/70).
Western scholar Etulain in his review is not satisfied with the scope of Easton's book: "It centers on Faust the man . . . but it attempts little evaluation of Faust the writer."

"Seven Years with Heinie Faust," by Harvey Roney, *The Faust Collector*, no. 7 (8/70), pp. 1–4.
A memoir by a school chum of life at Berkeley. Biographically important. Reprinted as "The University Years" in MAX BRAND: WESTERN GIANT (see Section I). {Editor's Note: Reprinted in MBC.}

"Max Brand: The Big Westerner," by John G. Cawelti, *Journal of Popular Culture* (Fall/70), pp. 566–569.
Popular culture authority Cawelti in his essay-review echoes Etulain in his frustration over the scope of Easton's biography, stating that "we still need a solid analytical study of Faust's work in its context as a major example of the popular culture of the 1920s

and 1930s.'' Such carping on the part of Etulain and Cawelti overlooks the fact that Easton was writing a personalized biography, not a critical study. It was left to William Bloodworth to produce the first full-length critical treatment of Max Brand (see Section I).

"The Remarkable Max Brand," by Dale L. Walker, *The West* (11/70), pp. 18–19, 42–45.

Although this lengthy profile of Faust is written with authority and careful attention to fact, it presents nothing new. With a Faust photo and a shot of several of his paperback and hardcover Westerns.

"Fiction Machine," by Anon., *London Times* (12/4/70).

This British review of Easton's biography compares Faust with several other prolific, fast-production authors, concluding that Faust "has a strong claim to have been the fastest and one of the most voluminous writers of all time."

"Max Brand: The Big 'Westerner,' " by Theodore Peterson, *Journalism Quarterly* (Spring/71), pp. 147–148.

Peterson draws a parallel between Faust and F. Scott Fitzgerald and states that Faust was "a man far more complex than the heroes of his popular stories."

"Jack London and Max Brand," by Chester D. Cuthbert, *Styx* (Canada) 2 (1973), pp. 23–25.

The parallel here is between Faust and Jack London, and there is solid reason to believe that Faust was influenced by London's work, echoed in his Klondike adventures.

"The Doctor with the Best Bedside Manner," by Jane Ardmore, *Photoplay* (3/74), pp. 26–27, 64–66, 68.

Biographies of the stars who portrayed Dr. Kildare in films and TV, from Lew Ayres to Richard Chamberlain.

"Max Brand: The King of the Pulps," by "Frank Anmar" (William F. Nolan), *Topper* (3/76), pp. 69–71.

A full profile, with a photo of Faust and five of his pulp magazine covers.

"The Phenomenon of Max Brand," by William F. Nolan, *The Roundup* (7/76), pp. 6–8, 11.

Information and statistics on Faust's Western fiction, with a Faust photo and a photo of William F. Nolan.

"A Max Brand Check-List," by William F. Nolan, *The Roundup* (8/76), pp. 9–11.

A bibliographical companion piece to the above, listing Faust's Western novels and films.

"George W. Fish, 81, 'Dr. Kildare's' Model," by Anon., *New York Times* (2/2/77).

Obituary. With data on his friendship with Faust.

"Max Brand: Pulp King," by William F. Nolan, *Xenophile* (5–6/77), pp. 2–12.

Includes appendix, "Max Brand's Pulp Characters," by Nolan. The cover illustration on this issue, featuring a lengthy profile, portrays Faust surrounded by his most famous characters. Inside, photos of nine pulp magazines are shown, with fiction under his various pen names.

"The Image of the Indian in Max Brand's Pulp Western Novels," by Edgar L. Chapman, *Heritage of Kansas* (Spring/78), pp. 16–39.

The first full-scale critical essay on Faust's work, dealing with his "Indian novels," in which Chapman credits Faust with an advanced sensitivity to the Indian, portraying

Native Americans with sympathy and understanding. In doing so, "Brand was clearly ahead of his time." Extremely well done, demonstrating careful scholarship and a full knowledge of the Faust canon. Reprinted in TWENTIETH-CENTURY LITERARY CRITICISM (see Section II). {Editors' Note: Revised and expanded in MBC.}

"The Soul of Frederick Faust," by Robert Easton, *Westways* (6/78), pp. 30–33, 72–73, 76–77.
One of the finest essay-profiles ever written on Faust: tender, lyrical, emotionally moving. With color photos of his pulp and slick magazine covers and with shots of Faust, his wife, and their villa in Italy.

"Max Brand: The Great Storyteller Who Became Reluctant 'King of the Pulps'," by William F. Nolan, *Los Angeles Times Book Review* (5/6/79), pp. 2–3.
Another feature profile on Faust, "the human plot machine."

"Frederick Faust Collector," by Dale L. Walker, *The Roundup* (6/79), pp. 8–11.
About the Faust collection of Charles Stever, with photos of Stever, Faust, and Walker.

"The Rise of the Western," by Gary Topping, *Journal of the West*, no. 19 (1/80), p. 33.
An overview of the Western as a literary genre, with several authors discussed, including Faust.

"Max Brand's Westerns Ride On," by Edwin McDowell, *New York Times* (9/14/81).
A review-essay on MAX BRAND'S BEST WESTERN STORIES with photos of Faust and two stills from film and stage versions of DESTRY RIDES AGAIN.

"Max Brand's West," by William A. Bloodworth, Jr., *Western American Literature* (Fall/81), pp. 177–191.
Another major critical essay on Faust dealing with eighteen of his Western novels, in which Professor Bloodworth examines Faust's fictional landscape. Reprinted in TWENTIETH-CENTURY LITERARY CRITICISM (see Section II).

"Max Brand: Lorenzo of the Pulps," by Dale L. Walker, *The Retired Officer* (2/83), pp. 22–26.
Walker recycles his Faust material for another magazine profile. With photos.

"Growing Up in Berkeley, 1900–1917," by Dorothy Rieber Joralemon, *American West* (7–8/83), pp. 42–48.
With many photos from the period. Written by a University of California classmate who comments: "In our puritanical community, [Faust's] reputation was in collapse: too much drunkenness and other assorted vices not in the Victorian tradition." Faust is only briefly mentioned, but the piece is important for its historical background.

"Destry Rides Again . . . and Again . . . and Again," by David L. Fox, *Favorite Westerns* (Summer/84), pp. 31–33.
A media history of Faust's most famous Western. With a portrait of Tom Mix and stills from two other film versions of the novel.

"Unforgettable Frederick Faust," by Robert Easton, *Reader's Digest* (12/85), pp. 197–198, 201–203.
A mass-market profile with a painting of Faust hunched over his typewriter. According to Easton: "The man who most affected my life was Frederick Faust."

"Max Brand Part of Writer Robert Easton's Life," by Cheri Matthews, *The Modesto Bee* (2/25/86), p. 4.

A profile piece, with photos of Faust and Easton, announcing a lecture by Easton on "Max Brand of Modesto."

"Max Brand: Western Giant," by William Bloodworth, *Western American Literature* (5/87), p. 73.

A review of the book he calls "a true labor of love."

"Western Colossus," by David L. Fox, *The Westerner* (Spring–Summer/87), pp. 42–43. A brief profile with a Faust photo and stills from his films. Says Fox: "Frederick Faust had the rare ability to set our imaginations free."

"Shakespeare of the Western Range," by George A. Baker, *The Far-Westerner* (10/88), pp. 5–29.

The entire issue of this digest-sized magazine is devoted to Faust, with several of his letters quoted, photos of his high school in Modesto, and three photos of Faust, two from his student days. Faust poems are also reprinted. Contains important information about his early years.

"Writers Who Made the Pulps: George Challis," by C. E. Cazedessus, Jr., *The Fantasy Collector* (4/89), pp. 2–3.

A brief rundown of Faust's Challis titles, with nine *Argosy* covers featuring Challis reproduced.

"The Paperback Books of Frederick Faust," by William F. Nolan, *Singing Guns*, no. 1 (Spring/89), pp. 3–18.

Lists 177 first paperback editions into 1989, under six pen names. With photos.

"First Encounter," by Leo A. Hetzler, *Singing Guns*, no. 2 (Summer/89), pp. 6–9.

From a letter Professor Hetzler sent to Robert Easton. Makes classic comparisons to Shakespeare and others.

"Faust's Mystery Fiction: A Checklist," by William F. Nolan, *Singing Guns*, no. 2 (Summer/89), pp. 10–23.

Lists thirteen published books, eleven serials (unpublished in book format), and some fifty novelettes and short stories. With photos.

"Silvertip: Part 1—The Stolen Stallion," by David L. Fox, *Singing Guns*, no. 2 (Summer/89), pp. 24–28.

The beginning of an ongoing series in which Fox dissects and discusses the Silvertip novels. He continues this series in *Singing Guns*, nos. 3–9. With photos.

"The Making of a Medical Man: Max Brand's Young Doctor Kildare," by Susan L. Zodin, *Singing Guns*, no. 2 (Summer/89), pp. 32–36.

The beginning of a four-part series in which Zodin dissects and discusses the Kildare novels. She continues this series in *Singing Guns*, nos. 3–5. With photos. {Editors' Note: Reprinted in MBC.}

"Max Brand's California Roots," by William Bloodworth, *Singing Guns*, no. 3 (Summer/90), pp. 4–11.

An illuminating research piece on Faust's early boyhood in Modesto, California, based on interviews and newly discovered source material.

"Shakespeare's Presence in Faust's Westerns," by Leo A. Hetzler, *Singing Guns*, no. 3 (Summer/90), pp. 15–21.

The title says it all. Faust revered the work of Shakespeare, and Hetzler brings them together. Of solid worth. {Editors' Note: Reprinted in MBC.}

"Statistics on Faust's Western Output," by William F. Nolan, *Singing Guns*, no. 3 (Summer/90), pp. 23–26.
A year-by-year breakdown on Faust's 1917–1939 Western fiction, a total of 388 pieces, including his "Far North" tales.

"A Sexual Perspective in the Works of Max Brand," by Jack Ricardo, *Singing Guns*, no. 3 (Summer/90), pp. 28–30.
The author attempts to fit Faust's male characters into a homosexual frame, questioning Faust's basic "sexual perspective." {Editors' Note: Reprinted in MBC.}

"The Real Max Brand: Some Thoughts on One Western Life," by William Bloodworth, *Singing Guns*, no. 4 (Fall/90), pp. 4–13.
The printed text of a paper delivered in 1984 (see Section IV). Bloodworth claims that Faust "came closer in his Westerns to writing about himself than he did in any other kind of popular fiction."

"Comments on 'A Sexual Perspective'," by Leo Hetzler, William F. Nolan, and Ed Gorman, *Singing Guns*, no. 4 (Fall/90), pp. 43–48.
Each of the three strongly disputes the idea that Faust was a repressed homosexual or that he was bisexual. In a postscript the editor, Dave Fox, agrees with them. To see such elements in his work is to misread the canon. {Editors' Note: Reprinted in MBC.}

"The Paperback Books of Frederick Faust—'Max Brand'," by William F. Nolan, *Paperback Parade* (3/91), pp. 22–29.
A revised and updated version, with book photos, of the earlier listing in *Singing Guns*. (This issue also reprints Nolan's *Xenophile* profile, "Max Brand: Pulp King.")

"Some Thoughts on Realism in Faust's Westerns," by Leo A. Hetzler, *Singing Guns*, no. 5 (Spring/91), pp. 14–30.
Another superb critical contribution, Hetzler earns his place among the major Faust critics with this lengthy and perceptive essay. Must reading for anyone seriously interested in the work of Frederick Faust. {Editors' Note: Reprinted in MBC.}

"From Whistling Dan to Dr. Kildare: Series Characters among the Published Books of Frederick Faust," by William F. Nolan, *Singing Guns*, no. 5 (Spring/91), pp. 42–60.
The first such listing adds up to sixty-two books and twenty-one characters, each of whom is described, with origins noted, dated in order of creation. With photos.

"Max Brand, the True King," by William F. Nolan, *The Western Review* (12/91), p. 8.
A defense of Faust as the true King of the Pulps.

"The Multiple Worlds of Frederick Faust," by William F. Nolan, *Singing Guns*, no. 6 (Fall-Winter/91), pp. 4–8.
A first listing of Faust's non-Western works, arranged under: The Italian Renaissance, Knighthood, Dog Stories, The Spanish Inquisition, Mythic Gods, High Society, Rural Farm Life, Love Stories, Espionage, Boxing, Piracy on the Spanish Main, The Medical Profession, Football, The Civil War, Ironworkers, World War I, World War II, Steeplechase Racing, The Irish, The French Revolution, Latin American Revolutions, The Art World, Aviation, Shipwrecks, The South Seas, Early California, Canada, Fantasy and Science Fiction, The Argentine, Historicals, Men and Horses, Crime and Mystery, The Yukon, Alaska. And they say that Max Brand wrote only Westerns! {Editors' Note: Reprinted in MBC.}

"The More Things Change . . . Frederick Faust's View of Higher Education," by William Bloodworth, *Singing Guns*, no. 6 (Fall-Winter/91), pp. 9–12.

Bloodworth describes Faust as "the most brilliant and prolific student writer of both poetry and prose, on a campus blessed with many good writers."

"Italian Westerns and Faust," by Leo A. Hetzler, *Singing Guns*, no. 6 (Fall-Winter/91), pp. 18–22.

Many parallels are drawn between the heroes of Italian films of the Old West and Faust's own characters. With photos of Clint Eastwood and others.

"Faust and Films: The Silent Years," by Carl Hutt, *Singing Guns*, no. 6 (Fall-Winter/91), pp. 27–33.

A discussion of the silent films based on Faust material, with photos of stills and posters.

"From Karl May to Frederick Faust: Some Observations from Germany," by Elisabeth Wäke, *Singing Guns*, no. 6 (Fall-Winter/91), pp. 45–53.

A German reader compares the work of Faust to the European Westerns of writer Karl May. With photos.

"Your Forte Is the West," by William Bloodworth. *Singing Guns*, no. 7 (Summer/92), pp. 4–15.

A section from Bloodworth's working manuscript of MAX BRAND (see Section I). Deals with the early writer-editor exchanges between Faust and Bob Davis, who sends him the cover art for THE UNTAMED, declaring: "This is going to be the turning point in your . . . life"—as indeed it was. {Editors' Note: Reprinted in MBC.}

"The 'Lost' Novels of Frederick Faust," by William F. Nolan, *Singing Guns*, no. 7 (Summer/92), pp. 21–26.

A listing, with commentary, of Faust's thirty-four full-length works never published in book format. Three shorter novellas (under 50,000 words) are also listed. With photos.

"My Encounter with Faust's Novels," by Edgar L. Chapman, *Singing Guns*, no. 7 (Summer/92), pp. 42–46.

Chapman, associate professor of English at Illinois' Bradley University, discusses his gradual addiction to reading Max Brand. Summing up, he says: "Reading Faust . . . when he's at the top of his form can be a very liberating experience."

"The Western Novels of Max Brand," by Ben Bridges [pseudonym for David Whitehead], *Book and Magazine Collector* (8/93), pp. 40–49.

This British publication, published for collectors, here treats Faust with a full profile and a "Max Brand UK Bibliography" of Faust books printed in England. (The listing contains many errors and omissions.) With a photo of Faust and with photos of some Faust books published in the United Kingdom.

"Max Brand," by N. Lester, *Book and Magazine Collector* (11/93), pp. 92–93.

A letter from a Faust reader in England, correcting several errors in the Bridges piece. Norman Lester has collected Faust "since 1920" (seventy-three years) which surely must stand as an all-time record.

"Thoughts on Max Brand's 'The Garden of Eden'," by Leo A. Hetzler, *Singing Guns*, no. 8 (Summer/95), pp. 6–12.

A detailed examination of this offbeat Faust tale that, as Hetzler points out, "stands outside the corpus of Faust's Westerns" (relating to the story's religious-philosophical content). {Editors' Note: Reprinted in MBC.}

"Faustian Statistics," by William F. Nolan, *Singing Guns*, no. 8 (Summer/95), pp. 13–24.

More facts on Faust's output, comparing him with John Creasey and Georges Simenon in terms of overall production, and including statistics on Faust's 900–plus works: 188 book-length serials, 25 complete book-length novels, 194 short stories, 274 novelettes, 13 sketches and plays, and 225 poems.

"Frederick Faust, Soldier," by Herbert Wadopian, *Singing Guns*, no. 8 (Summer/95), pp. 15–19.

A personal battlefield account of Faust's four days (in May, 1944) with Lieutenant Wadopian's platoon on the Italian front. Written as a letter in July, 1945. {Editors' Note: Reprinted in MBC.}

"A Hero's Death: New Facts on the Last Hours of Frederick Faust," by William F. Nolan, *Singing Guns*, no. 8 (Summer/95), pp. 20–21.

A newly discovered front-lines report, showing that Faust, on the night of his death, while wounded, faced enemy fire to obtain ammunition for a trapped gunner. {Editors' Note: Reprinted in MBC.}

" 'Pringle's Luck': Why Faust Went to War," by Elisabeth Wänke, *Singing Guns*, no. 8 (Summer/95), pp. 22–33.

In a lengthy and insightful essay, using Brand's World War I short story as her basis, Wänke explores Faust's driving compulsion to demonstrate his courage under full battle conditions.

"Faust's Use of History and Authentic Geography for His Western Fiction," by Edgar L. Chapman, *Singing Guns*, no. 8 (Summer/95), pp. 42–57.

Chapman demonstrates that Faust's so-called never-never land of the West was often historically accurate and that the author also utilized Western history in several of his novels, particularly in relation to the legend of Billy the Kid and the shoot-out at the O.K. Corral. And, again, he makes the point that Faust's Indian novels were all based on tribal fact.

"Argosy—and the Amazing Max Brand," by William F. Nolan, *Argosy* ([1]/96).

A full profile of Faust and his years with the *Argosy* publications, with many covers of *Argosy* reproduced, featuring his work under various pen names.

IV. PAPERS ON FAUST

"The Formula Fallacy: The Westerns of Max Brand," by Ernest L. Bulow. Paper presented at the Popular Culture Association's national meeting in 1973.

"The Figure of a Gentleman: The Silvertip Novels of Max Brand," by Jack Nachbar. Paper presented at the Popular Culture Convention, Chicago, 1976.

"The Mentor Figure in Max Brand's Westerns" [title not verified], by Robert Metz. Paper presented at the Popular Culture Convention, Chicago, 1976.

"The Outlaw as Heroic Outsider in Max Brand's Westerns: From Dan Barry to the Montana Kid," by Edgar L. Chapman. Paper presented at the Popular Culture Convention, Chicago, 1976.

"The History of a Hero: A Study of Max Brand's DESTRY RIDES AGAIN," by David L. Fox. Thesis written for Western Carolina University, 1984.

"The Real Max Brand: Some Thoughts on One Western Life," by William A. Bloodworth, Jr. Paper presented at the Western Literature Association meeting, 1984.

"The Dangerous Equipment of Fiction," by William A. Bloodworth, Jr. Paper presented at the Western Centennial Symposium, American Heritage Center, Wyoming, 1992.

"Max Brand's Place in the Four Phases of the Popular Western," by Edgar L. Chapman. Paper presented at the Western Centennial Symposium, American Heritage Center, Wyoming, 1992.

FAN PUBLICATIONS

David L. Fox

''Fan'' interest in Faust began in the pages of the very pulps where his fiction was appearing, particularly in the letters sections of *Argosy* and *Western Story Magazine,* throughout the 1920s and 1930s. There, before the mystique of Faust's personal life arose, praises would be heaped, far more frequently than criticism, upon Faust stories or serials in previous issues, often pleading for more of the same but also occasionally chiding the editor for the author's departure from expected patterns. Often these appraisals did little more than rank the stories in order of preference; sometimes they complimented Faust under two or three pseudonyms in the same letter, or they vaguely compared him to the magazine's other regular authors, and to himself. Though perhaps not the product of highbrow literary acumen, essential distinctions and judgments were nevertheless being made. Faust's style was being discovered; the biography was beginning to take shape; the quasi-cult following was being established. To some extent the fanzines were an extension of this incipient scholarship.

By the time of Faust's death in 1944 his popularity was commonly acknowledged, the public appetite having been well served by him in the pulps, in books, in films, and in the paperback market that was beginning to emerge. And there it might have remained, or stalled, had it not been for the cadre of loyal fans, especially those whose initiation began with the pulps, who became collectors of the ephemera and preservers of the arcane. To be sure, reprints of Faust's works continued, and the circulation of the three fan magazines was insufficient to have had much direct influence on marketing decisions. Further, if the 'Nineties' resurgence of Faust titles in print continues to flourish, it will be due to the merit of the works themselves, to the inherent storytelling mastery that made them successful in the first place. Yet the concurrent academic interest in Faust seems to be descended from the same recognition of talent that infused the motives of those who shared in the excitement and collegiality of the fanzines. It is perhaps not entirely presumptuous to think that the existence of the fan publications has been (and still is) a significant part in securing for Faust the critical elevation he so certainly deserves.

In the tables that follow each section, entries are listed under sometimes arbitrary headings, more or less in the order of appearance in the magazine. Annotations are intended as a guide for identifying the Faust topics or titles involved, but they do not necessarily summarize all of the authors' worthwhile findings. Where possible, reference to more accessible reprint versions of the articles is given. Other sources for Faust's work are not provided except for those works considered to be obscure. For instance, full citations are not given for most of Faust's contributions to *The Occident* and *The Pelican,* student publications at the University of California at Berkeley. The bibliography in this book will provide complete details for Faust's early verse and prose as well as the professional works.

———— *I. THE FABULOUS FAUST FANZINE, 1948–1951* ————

Four years after Faust's death, the first of the amateur publications devoted exclusively to Max Brand was inaugurated. Darrell C. Richardson, an avid collector of many pulp genres, had already compiled and distributed an index of Faust titles, and, along with a revision of that effort, he brought out the first issue of *The Fabulous Faust Fanzine,* in June 1948. (All issues originated at Darrell C. Richardson's Covington, Kentucky, address.) Richardson had begun collecting Faust's writings in 1943, acquiring a broad familiarity of the pulp field in general and becoming an authority on Faust in particular. His landmark publication set high standards for the ones that followed.

The 8½ × 11-inch format of *The Fabulous Faust Fanzine* (*FFF*) was enhanced with line drawings by Richardson's brother, Haskell, and a cover by William F. Nolan, which represented the Western emphasis of Faust's work, as well as a likeness of Faust in a decidedly stoic demeanor. With modifications to reflect the issue number and date, this cover pictorial was used for all four of the hefty "zines." Each, published irregularly, reprinted some amount of poetry or short fiction by Faust, with original and reprint essays and other material. Some issues featured actual, pasted-in dust jackets of Faust novels in current release. The first issue ran to eighty pages, the others slightly fewer, amounting in its four issues to a tremendous amount of information.

Richardson's work, and the material it brought together, was of inestimable value to the casual collector as well as the serious researcher. Much of the information in the magazine was reedited for MAX BRAND: THE MAN AND HIS WORK, providing a more durable and accessible form for the biography of Faust (by Richardson himself), tributes and literary appraisals, statistical data, and a bibliography that tracked the pseudonymous fiction from pulps to hard covers. Some of this material has since been superseded or, rather, perhaps merely updated by more extensive research, but for its time Richardson's work was a compilation of the most accurate information available and is still useful. Furthermore, it remains fascinating for the enthusiasm of its contributors and the period it reflects. Many of the articles (reprints themselves in some cases) have found republication elsewhere, but it is a transporting experience to hold in one's hands the original and truly fabulous *FFF*. One need only be aware of the labyrinthine scope of the material, until then uncataloged, to appreciate the efforts of Richardson and his contributors, including especially William F. Nolan, S. Allen McElfresh, Philip Richman, among others.

Contents of *The Fabulous Faust Fanzine,* Vol. 1, No. 1 (June 1948)

Reprint Fiction by Faust

"Partners"

"Cure for a Liar"

"Convalescence" (Part 1 of 3) (Faust's first published story in *All-Story Weekly*)

Reprint Poetry by Faust

"Distance"

"The Village Street"

"Dionysus in Hades" (first stanza only)

"On a Grecian Funeral Monument"

"Balin's Song to His Sword." [Richardson also prepared a full-length version of "Balin," which had comprised a major portion of Faust's *The Village Street.* With illustrations by William F. Nolan, the edition was limited to a hundred copies and sold to Richardson's readership as a separate twenty-four page booklet in the same general format as the magazine. Subtitled "From Malory's Narrative of the Dolorous Stroke," the poem is pleasant enough to read—its drama is well handled and some descriptive passages are quite good—but it is perhaps, with its tercels and poniards and falchions, too much of a "jongleur tale" for this century. Richardson called it a "novel in verse," and Faust could undoubtedly have turned it into a successful historical novel, had he so chosen.]

"Only the Young Fear Death"

"To a Lady"

"Sonnet"

"Hope"

"Sunday"

Articles

"The Poetic Soul," by Leonard Bacon from *The Saturday Review of Literature* (5/27/44). Bacon stresses Faust's quest for poetry as a "sacred art" and depicts Faust himself as "poetry incarnate." Faust's failure to achieve greatness in verse was due to what Bacon terms "some perfectionist demon." It is here that Bacon provides the apt and often quoted summation that, though out of joint with the twentieth century, Faust's "Dionysus in Hades" is "nobly planned, nobly felt, nobly written."

"Strength!!!" by Chester Cuthbert. A survey of Faust's preoccupation with the uses and effects of power, his "obsession with the idea that strength is beyond good and evil." Admitting to a shortage of biographical certainty, Cuthbert nonetheless attempts to equate Faust's literary "compulsion to discover the secret of strength" with the writer's personal search for answers. He concludes that Faust's "romantic viewpoint weakened his work," yet Faust remains "one of the most original writers of modern times."

"A Tribute to a Modest Man," by Philip Richman. A look at some details of Faust's prolific production rate, set against some typically self-effacing letters from "a very obscure hard-working and ordinary fellow," as Faust depicted himself.

"Sidelights on Faust's Output," by William F. Nolan. Includes notes on Faust's work in Hollywood, statistics, Faust's writing habits, pseudonyms, Dr. Kildare predecessors and sequels, title changes, etc. This and similar articles in subsequent issues formed Chapter 6 of Richardson's MAX BRAND: THE MAN AND HIS WORK.

"Rare Faust Volumes," by Darrell C. Richardson. Discusses hard-to-find editions, even then, of Faust's works.

"Max Brand Lives On," by John Blair. The assistant production manager of Dodd, Mead discusses sales of Faust titles.

"Frederick Faust." A brief biographical sketch originally appearing in *Harper's*.

"The Death of a War Correspondent," by Jack Delaney. Originally in *Harper's* (8/44) and included in MAX BRAND: THE MAN AND HIS WORK.

"The Fantasy of Frederick Faust," by Darrell C. Richardson. Originally published in *The Philadelphia Science Fantasy Society News* (11–12/45) and expanded for Chapter 7 of Richardson's MAX BRAND: THE MAN AND HIS WORK. This early version discusses "John Ovington Returns," "Devil Ritter," "That Receding Brow," "The Lost Garden," and the George Challis science-fiction serial, "The Smoking Land." The later, enlarged article included references to fantasy elements in many other works, including the Western tales.

"Faust the Writer," by Brandt and Brandt. A brief biographical sketch from Faust's literary agents.

"Why I Like Faust Stories," by Darrell Le Fever. Mentions several favorite Faust heroes and characterizes Faust's mold as producing variations on the "lazy good-for-nothing fellows of misguided bent."

"Faust the Dreamer," by William F. Nolan. Uses an "author's note" from Faust's 1923 serial, "The Darkness at Windon Manor," as a window on the author's private side, his soul, spirit, impulses—or, as Nolan concludes, that inner self which made Faust "an extreme idealist, a man of deep emotions and wildly romantic dreams."

"Once Upon a Time," by S. Allen McElfresh. Points out parallels between Faust's fiction and fairy tales. McElfresh discusses several Faust heroes (or "super-men" and "demi-gods"), distinguishing between what he terms Faust's "informal fantasy," which subtly permeates most of the works, and the "formal" attempts, such as "The Smoking Land." For storytelling style, McElfresh suggests that Faust is similar to Robert Louis Stevenson.

"Portrait of a Great American," by William F. Nolan. Cites a bare-bones obituary to establish the general success with which Faust had kept his public persona at a minimum and goes from there to fill in the details known primarily to the coterie of fans who searched for years to piece together Faust's life and career.

"Keep Climbing," by Carl Brandt. Echoes of Faust's guiding principles in a brief statement originally published in *This Week* magazine (4/25/48).

Biographies

Obituaries from *Time* (5/29/44) and *The Saturday Evening Post* (undated, but probably from the issue announcing the posthumously published Faust serial, "After April," beginning 6/10/44), and publicity accounts from *Western Story Magazine* (6/2/28) by D. C. Hubbard, *Argosy, Esquire,* and *Blue Book* magazines, all undated.

An Index of the Works of Frederick S. Faust

A chronological listing of (1) Faust's magazine appearances, classified by periodical title, giving type of work and, for serials, an installment count; also indicates series characters and sequels; (2) reprinted magazine works; (3) first-edition book versions, categorized under pseudonym; (4) projected titles of paper and hardcover titles. An updated version was included in Richardson's MAX BRAND: THE MAN AND HIS WORK.

Miscellaneous

Short items such as notes about future Faust books and movies, personal accounts of collectors and fans, and "Editorial Ramblings."

Contents of *The Fabulous Faust Fanzine*, Vol. 1, No. 2 (December 1948)

Reprint Fiction by Faust

"The Small World"

"Convalescence" (Part 2 of 3, continued from the first issue)

"Forty-Cent Fare"

Reprint Poetry by Faust

"The West Wind"

"Dragon Teeth"

"The Secret"

"The Skylark"

"The Last Adventure"

"The Song of the Falcon"

Articles

"A Farewell to Max Brand," by Steve Fisher. A tribute by the writer who had known Faust in their Warner Bros. days. His recollections cover many instances of the warmth, energy, and shyness of Faust's personality, with emphasis on Faust's generosity, literacy, and productivity. Originally written for *Writer's Digest,* the article appends a paragraph from a variant version from *Argosy* and is included in Richardson's MAX BRAND: THE MAN AND HIS WORK. {Editors' Note: Reprinted in MBC.}

"Concerning Faust Films," by William F. Nolan. One of the first rank of Faust experts, Nolan uncovered in this early piece of research some significant Faust connections. Discusses films based on Faust's magazine fiction between 1917 and 1947, including projects left uncompleted or assigned to other writers.

"Twenty-Five Million Words," by Edward H. Dodd, Jr. Reprinted from *Publishers Weekly* (3/26/38), the article begins the ongoing task of accounting for Faust's total output. Dodd discusses many industry details, from Faust's earnings (four cents per word, the top rate at the time) to his peak hourly output (fourteen pages). {Editors' Note: Reprinted in MBC.}

"More Sidelights on Faust," by William F. Nolan. Anecdotes about written notes found with Faust when he died in Italy, his fascination with horses, details on some of the pseudonyms, his Yorktown series, Nolan's collection of Faust materials, and comments about a few of Faust's characters.

"Adventures by Land and Sea," by Evan Evans. A brief "biography" created in 1933 by Faust to give *Harper's* readers a glimpse of one of the magazine's writers.

"The Last Days," by Herbert Wadopian. A short sketch by Faust's platoon leader in Italy. Wadopian later gave a more detailed account of Faust's last days (see *Singing Guns Magazine* below).

"The New Faust Mystery," by Chester D. Cuthbert. Another effort by a collector who attempted to acquire everything Faust wrote.

"Killed in Action," *New York News* (5/17/44). Obituary.

"The Tale of a Hobby," by Philip Richman. An account of Richman's seven-year correspondence with Faust, a luncheon meeting with him in 1935 that led to his involvement in promoting the publication of some eighty Faust books, and other incidents relevant to his unique collection of Faust pulp material.

"My Faust Collection," by Darrell C. Richardson. The title is indicative, along with occasional comments evaluating the Faust titles reported on. {Editors' Note: Reprinted in MBC.}

"Heinie," by Carl Brandt. Reports of Faust's generosity, particularly in support of young writers or old friends, which Brandt (as Faust's literary agent) attributes to the examples Faust learned from his absorption of ''The Golden Age of Italy.'' {Editors' Note: Reprinted in MBC.}

''The Most Prolific Writer,'' by Coleman Nipper. Faust's output compared to that of other noted writers.

''Faust and the Western Tale,'' by S. Allen McElfresh. A preliminary survey, later to appear as Chapter 5 of MAX BRAND: THE MAN AND HIS WORK, where it was retitled ''Max Brand and the Western Story,'' by McElfresh in collaboration with Richardson, and supported by novelist Sam Peeples.

''Another Faust Fantasy,'' by Darrell C. Richardson. A discussion of '' 'Sunset' Wins,'' an ''off-the-trail yarn'' which the author adds to the list of fantastic tales (begun in the previous issue).

Miscellaneous

Editorial, book reviews, letters from readers, index addenda, book jackets and other pictorial matter. The reviews include brief clippings from many sources, primarily *The New York Times Book Review*. The letters include some anecdotes of meetings with Faust. ''Tips on Faust Tales'' offers brief synopses and critical commentaries on numerous works, many available only in the original pulps.

Contents of *The Fabulous Faust Fanzine*, Vol. 1, No. 3 (January 1950)

Reprinted Faust Fiction and Other Prose Pieces

''Woodward's Devil''

Introduction to ''Humming Birds and Honeysuckle'' (previously unpublished in this complete version)

''Convalescence'' (Part 3, conclusion)

''The House of Rulaki'' {Editors' Note: Reprinted in MBC.}

''Five Minutes to Twelve''

''A Sketch of My Life.'' From a letter to Faust's daughter Jane in 1939. A poignant and illuminating description of the hardships and yearnings Faust experienced. {Editors' Note: Reprinted in MBC in its entirety.}

''Brother John'' (one-act play)

''Campus Moralists''

Reprinted Faust Poetry

''Song to Mars''

''Youth''

''The Night''

''A Sea Call''

''The Parting''

''Brooklyn Bridge in a Sea Fog''

''Dawn''

Articles and Features

"More Faustiana," by William F. Nolan. As in preceding issues, these notes range far and wide, including facts about abridgments that occurred when serials were transmitted to book form, comments from friends and associates of Faust, the radio production of "Singing Guns," notes on motion picture versions of some Faust works, Faust's last Westerns, and much more.

"Faust and the Nietzschean Concept," by Frank J. Hartl. Drawing on a reading of a great many Faust works—Westerns, the Renaissance tales, sports stories, the Kildare series, the detective fiction, and more—Hartl finds Faust's heroes to be all of a kind: "the Nietzschean mold," the superman. His thesis is supported by the fact that Faust "wholly agreed with Nietzsche that excellence could be developed only by a constant struggle against mediocrity" (see Robert Easton's MAX BRAND: THE BIG "WESTERNER," p. 41). On the other hand, Steve Fisher vigorously denounced the whole idea in a letter in Vol. 2, No. 1.

"Some Comments of Faust," by Charles W. Wolfe. A pulp collector's appraisal of the Kildare stories.

"Personal Glimpses," by Bill Clark. Remarks on Faust's generous nature, comparisons to other popular writers of the period, and an enumeration of the "five plots" Faust used repeatedly.

"Immortality," by John K. Hutchens. A brief forecast of Faust's lasting appeal.

"Bohemian Days with Faust," by John L. Schoolcraft. Contains a clarification of Schoolcraft's role in the collaborations he and Faust engaged in, as well as anecdotes revealing the origin of the "Max Brand" pseudonym and other steps in the formative years of Faust's career. A version of this sketch later appeared as Chapter 2 of MAX BRAND: THE MAN AND HIS WORK. In cooperation with the Faust family, Schoolcraft also completed an "official" biography (unpublished) and edited THE NOTEBOOKS AND POEMS OF "MAX BRAND." {Editors' Note: Reprinted in MBC.}

"Max Brand Book Sales," by John Blair. Updates Edward Dodd's figures (see Vol. 1, No. 1, above).

"Faust's Military Interlude," by Gilbert J. McLennan. Reminiscences by a member of the 97th Canadian Battalion, which Faust joined in 1916. The sketch provides a composite look at the soldier-of-fortune attitudes of "the American Foreign Legion," which attracted Faust. Included in Nolan's MAX BRAND: WESTERN GIANT. {Editors' Note: Reprinted in MBC.}

Miscellaneous

Editorials, "Tips on Faust Tales" (brief synopses and commentary, some by readers and some reprinted from professional reviews, similar to the same department in the previous issue). Index, addenda, letters, and pictorial matter.

Contents of *The Fabulous Faust Fanzine,* Vol. 2, No. 1 (December 1951)

Articles and Features

"Max Brand's Western Style," by Samuel L. Peeples. The Western novelist (who also wrote as "Brad Ward") credits Faust with influencing the direction of the Western story by creating a new pattern, "a never-never land, a West That Never Was."

"The Fast Production Writer," by L. Ron Hubbard. Originally appeared as a letter in *Argosy.* Hubbard briskly defends the steady output of the prolific writer against the occasional achievement of the slower "artist," putting Faust in the company of O. Henry, Dickens, and Scott.

"He Couldn't Say No," by Cleve Cartmill. Assumes Faust's productivity was due to commitments to editors that he would not break. A writer himself, Cartmill questions whether Faust had time for "fun." He makes a serious point regarding the similarities between some Faust stories and some O. Henry stories.

"Richard Mon Roi," by Vida Jameson. A synopsis-review of Faust's THE GOLDEN KNIGHT.

"Pseudo-Faust Works," by Darrell C. Richardson. Settles some questions about works erroneously attributed to Faust, including some "Peter Dawson" stories, as well as writers bearing actual names of some Faust pseudonyms.

Reprinted Fiction and Other Prose by Frederick Faust

"A Note and a Letter." Quotations from a note discovered by Faust's daughter Jane, with the editorial suggestion that it might have formed the basis for "that one *great* book Faust always intended to write someday." The letter, written to Faust's wife Dorothy, 4/8/44, just a few weeks before his death, reveals his wish to be assigned to a company of Negro troops, among whom he had talked and taken notes toward "a great story." Faust also suggested that, though apart, they might be joined spiritually by reading DON QUIXOTE simultaneously. He spoke of reaching maturity, noting that Quixote was fifty-six when he began the fulfillment of his dream. Faust was fifty-two at the time.

"Editorial from *The Pelican*"

"The Eternal Triangle" [originally "The Silent Witness" in *Black Mask Detective Stories,* 1938]

"Sartor Resartus"

"On the Origin of Damn"

Reprinted Poetry by Frederick Faust

"Wordsworth"

"Stradivarius"

"Sonnet"

"The Little Men"

"Legend of St. Christopher"

"Fairyland"

"The Torches"

"Buccaneer"

"The Stars"

"A Song"

"A Ringer"

Miscellaneous

Editorial, book reviews (excerpts from *New York Times* and *New York Herald-Tribune*), "Tips on Faust Tales," letters from readers (including some significant remarks by Peeples, Schoolcraft, Fisher, McElfresh, and Nolan), pictorial matter, and an announcement that this issue would be the last.

—————— II. THE FAUST COLLECTOR, 1969–1973 ——————

The Faust Collector was begun with the encouragement of pulp writer Frank Gruber who had worked with Faust in Hollywood (see Gruber's THE PULP JUNGLE). William J. Clark, a longtime collector and authority on Faust, published the first issue in February 1969 and continued quarterly through nine issues with a final tenth issue in 1973. All issues were produced at Clark's California address. The first issue (which carried a memoir by Gruber) appeared in a digest-size format professionally printed by the Pulp Era Press, with the remainder in 8½ × 11-inch typewritten format. The first cover carried an ink drawing by G. M. Farley, and the remainder used a similar pose rendered by George Barr contained in an oval lariat that went on to form part of the title. This artwork lent an extremely effective air of excitement to the publication. Clark, a statistician and computer expert, compiled his own Faust index and was indefatigable in searching out titles, word counts, and other details of Faust's work. (For a profile on Clark, see *Singing Guns,* Vol. 1, No. 6.)

Like *The Fabulous Faust Fanzine,* the *Collector* consisted of Faust reprints and original contributions, along with tidbits of information about Faust's life, work habits, pseudonyms, announcements of forthcoming new books, and so on. Its limited length (twelve pages in first issue, ten thereafter) prevented lengthy examinations of critical concerns, but the frequency and regularity of its issues made up for this brevity. In addition, the information was always quite helpful and provocative.

Contents of *The Faust Collector,* Vol. 1, No. 1 (February 1969)

Articles

"How Many Words," by William J. Clark. Discusses the problems of tallying Faust's total output, due to unsold manuscripts, uncertainty over pseudonyms, and undiscovered works in obscure magazines, editorial abridgments, etc. Clark's estimate is 25 million words.

"Did He or Didn't He?," by William J. Clark. Uses an entry from Faust's notebooks to examine the extent of Faust's participation in the writing of THE GREY CHAR-TERIS by Robert Simpson.

"Heinie and the Chickens," by Frank Gruber. A humorous recounting of a problem encountered by Gruber when Faust threw a party during his days at Warner Bros.

Max Brand's Western Magazine, by the editor. Lists the thirty-three issues of the 1949–1954 publication and the titles (variants and originals) of the Faust stories reprinted in them.

"A Writer-to-Writer Tribute—Across the Years," by William F. Nolan. A personal tribute by a writer whose imagination was captured at age fourteen by a Faust novel. Nolan also gives credit to Richardson's previous fan publication for giving him his "real start as a writer." (Untitled in this issue, but given this title in "Editorial Ramblings" in second issue.)

"Max Brand, The Big 'Westerner,' " review of the book by Robert Easton, reprinted from the University of Oklahoma catalog, spring and summer 1969.

Reprinted Fiction by Faust

"The King is Dead," a short story written when Faust was a junior at Modesto High School and published in the 1911 yearbook. The story is followed by editorial remarks regarding the provenance of this story.

Miscellaneous

Numerous short pieces and fillers touching on Faust's life and works.

Contents of *The Faust Collector,* Vol. 1, No. 2 (May 1969)

Reprinted Faust Fiction and Poetry

All Faust material in this issue is from the Modesto High School publication, *The Sycamore,* from Faust's senior year.

"The Fate of Llewellyn Cadmon" (short story)

"The Magic Drought" (poem)

"The Three Arts" (poem)

"The Paragon" (poem)

Miscellaneous

"Editorial Ramblings," by William J. Clark. Announcements of forthcoming Faust books, working titles, and word counts of some works, and other short pieces.

"Debunking the Legends," by William J. Clark. Deals with the myth that Faust never rewrote once a manuscript was finished.

"The Montana Kid," by George Barr. An excellent drawing of the Faust character.

Contents of *The Faust Collector,* Vol. 1, No. 3 (August 1969)

Original Faust Fiction

"The Plow and the Horse" (short story)

Reprinted Faust Poetry

"The Baseball Bat"

"Ode to a Beer Opener"

"Calls to Glory" (This and the two preceding poems are from *The Pelican,* the humor magazine of the University of California during Faust's student days.)

"What Will You Do," from *The Occident.* (This poem also appeared in THE VILLAGE STREET in a slightly altered version. There is a first-stanza comparison of the two versions. See annotation under "Faust in *The Occident*" below.)

Miscellaneous

"A Farewell to Max Brand," by Steve Fisher. (Reprinted from *Writer's Digest,* 8/44.) {Editors' Note: Reprinted in MBC.}

"Faust and *Western Story Magazine,*" by William J. Clark. An overview of the magazine from 1901, when it was known as *Buffalo Bill Stories,* through the days when Faust contributed, by Clark's count, 306 stories.

"Faust in *The Occident,*" by William J. Clark. A chronological listing of Faust's poems, essays, plays, short stories, and critical reviews from 1912 through 1918, the vast majority of which are poetry.

Miscellaneous

"Editorial Ramblings," by William J. Clark. Announcements of forthcoming Faust titles and other brief notes.

Contents of *The Faust Collector,* Vol. 1, No. 4 (November 1969)

Reprinted Faust Fiction

"Mercy Anne"

Reprinted Faust Poetry

"Guenevere"

"Hastings"

"The Bards"

Articles

"The Faust Papers: A Visit to the Faust Collection at the University of California in Berkeley," by William F. Nolan. A significant description of the enormous quantity of unpublished material Faust left behind and which was assigned to Bancroft Library after the death of Dorothy Faust: handwritten notebooks, poems, descriptions, letters to and from Faust, and countless other fragments of written matter. Of special interest, considering the disdain in which Faust is generally thought to have regarded his Western tales and the lack of historical accuracy in them, is a huge card file of ''Western Facts.'' Nolan gives more than a simple inventory, using his examination of the papers to construct a vivid sketch of Faust the father-friend-dreamer.

Miscellaneous

''Editorial Ramblings,'' by William J. Clark. Announcements of forthcoming Faust books and other short pieces.

''The Scarcest Title,'' by William J. Clark. Describes his rare copy of THE VILLAGE STREET AND OTHER POEMS by Frederick Faust and lists the full contents of the volume.

''Frederick Faust Published in Sweden [and Hungary] through 1968,'' by Göta Gillberg. Gives titles and dates of translations of nineteen Faust works.

Contents of *The Faust Collector,* Vol. 2, No. 1 [Whole No. 5] (February 1970)

Original Faust Fiction

''Follow the Herd''

Reprint Faust Prose and Poetry

''The Common Law''

''The Bards''

Articles

''Taxi, Speedy, and Silvertip,'' by William J. Clark. Deals with character names, and some changes by Frank Blackwell, Faust's editor at *Western Story Magazine.* Also lists the sequence of the Silvertip series, along with the working titles of each installment.

Miscellaneous

''In Memory of Frank Gruber,'' by William J. Clark. A tribute to a colleague of Faust and the man who had encouraged Clark to publish the magazine.

''Two Reviews,'' by William J. Clark. Brief descriptions of Robert Easton's MAX BRAND: THE BIG ''WESTERNER'' and Steve Fisher's THE HELL-BLACK NIGHT.

''Editorial Ramblings,'' by William J. Clark. Lists titles of some unpublished short stories by Faust.

''Recommended Reading,'' by William J. Clark. Lists the addresses of other fan-oriented publications.

Contents of *The Faust Collector,* Vol. 2, No. 2 [Whole Number 6] (May 1970)

Articles

"Destry and Dionysus," by Martha Bacon. Reprinted from *Atlantic Monthly* (7/55). {Editors' Note: Reprinted in MBC.}

Reprinted Faust Poetry

"Judgment"

Miscellaneous

"Meet the Collector," by William J. Clark. A profile of a Faust collector in New Zealand.

"Editorial Ramblings," by William J. Clark. Brief comments, including the announcement that the last two pages of this issue and subsequent issues will be devoted to an alphabetical list of Faust works for the benefit of subscribers who wish to use it as a checklist for their collections.

"The Big Westerner," by William J. Clark. Lists some publications that carried reviews of Easton's biography of Faust and quotes from a letter that describes a meeting with boxer Gene Tunney and Faust.

Contents of *The Faust Collector,* Vol. 2, No. 3 [Whole No. 7] (August 1970)

Articles

"Seven Years with Heinie Faust," by Harvey Roney. A detailed memoir by a Berkeley classmate and lifelong friend, covering Faust's rebellious academic years and the unsettled few years thereafter. {Editors' Note: A version of this sketch, somewhat abridged and titled "The University Years," appears in MBC.}

Miscellaneous

"Meet the Collector," by William J. Clark. An introduction by Clark and a description by the collector of another hobby, unrelated to Faust.

"Editorial Ramblings," by William J. Clark. Brief notes, little pertaining to Faust, except for a paragraph detailing the interest in Faust from such locations as Ceylon and Canada.

Contents of *The Faust Collector,* Vol. 2, No. 4 [Whole No. 8] (November 1970)

Original Fiction by Faust

"The Garden"

Reprint Poetry by Faust

"Bjornsen"

"Strange Things Are Found"

Miscellaneous

"Editorial Ramblings," by William J. Clark. Brief notes, including a refutation of some errors in "The Remarkable Max Brand," by Dale L. Walker in *The West* (11/70).

Contents of *The Faust Collector,* Vol. 3, No. 1 [Whole No. 9] (February 1971)

Original Faust Fiction

"Dr. Kildare's Dilemma" (two chapters of an unfinished Kildare story, to be concluded in the next issue) {Editors' Note: Reprinted in MBC.}

Original Faust Poetry

"Summer Night at a Tavern"

Miscellaneous

"Editorial Ramblings," by William J. Clark. Brief notes on recent and forthcoming Faust books. Also includes some remarks about unpublished works and gives a few examples from Faust's "Plot Notebook."

III. SINGING GUNS: A JOURNAL OF COMMENT AND ANALYSIS (1989–1995; CURRENT)

The title of this amateur magazine comes from Faust's 1928 serial, one of his best works and one of the most frequently reprinted. It was chosen, as stated in the initial issue, because it represented "both the poetic qualities of Faust's flowing, image-making style, and the tense urgency that pervades the exciting action sequences." As editor, I also recalled the affects of my youthful exposure to another Faust favorite, RANCHER'S REVENGE. Some recent research, at that time, into yet another superior Faust novel, DESTRY RIDES AGAIN, had led to correspondence with William F. Nolan who, as in the case of the two prior fan publications, provided experience, expertise, and encouragement to the emergence of this one. Material by Nolan has appeared in every issue.

The aim of *Singing Guns* was stated in its subtitle, but the viewpoint of the collector was not absent. All issues have been illustrated with reproductions of pulp illustrations, first-edition dust jackets, paperback covers, even comic book versions of Dr. Kildare and Silvertip. Authoritative checklists and bibliographic information appeared regularly. But the primary goal has been to treat Faust as a writer deserving serious critical consideration. Several of the contributors have been scholars of major importance in Faust research, as the contents listing will show. Most issues have also contained original or reprinted Faust prose and poetry. All issues originated at the editor's address at 922 Tilley Creek Rd., Cullowhee, NC 28723.

Always in digest format *Singing Guns* was begun as a quarterly but for part of its life has had an irregular schedule. Over the same time it has expanded from thirty-six pages to sixty-eight and is still extant. Although its publication schedule is variable, inquiries and manuscripts can be sent to the editor.

Contents of *Singing Guns,* Vol. 1, No. 1 (Spring 1989)

Articles and Reviews

"The Paperback Books of Frederick Faust: A Checklist of First Softcover Editions 1928–1989," by William F. Nolan. Gives dates and book numbers for 177 Faust titles in paper editions. Also includes a list of Faust books in hardcover editions only. Although much new material has come out since then, this authoritative list is invaluable to collectors and researchers. A revised and expanded version appeared in *Paperback Parade* (3/91).

"Mostly Murder: Reviews of Faust's Mystery Fiction," by David Fox and Sherry B. Fox. Brief review of CROSS OVER NINE, THE NIGHT FLOWER, and SIX GOLDEN ANGELS.

"Eagles over Crooked Creek [review]." An analysis of this "Hugh Owen" short story.

"Sun and Sand [review]." Analysis of another "Hugh Owen" story. This story is recommended for its parallels to Faust's classic "Wine on the Desert," which it precedes by one year.

Miscellaneous

"Essentials." Reviews Nolan's MAX BRAND: WESTERN GIANT.

"A Western Reading List." Cites a twenty-five-title list, compiled by the Western Writers of America (WWA), of the Best Western Novels Ever Written, which includes Faust's DESTRY RIDES AGAIN.

"On the Back Cover." A reproduction of a British paperback edition of SINGING GUNS with a brief discussion of the history of this work, including remarks on the 1950 film version.

Contents of *Singing Guns,* Vol. 1, No. 2 (Summer 1989)

Articles and Reviews

"First Encounter," by Leo Hetzler. Begins as a memoir but includes some observations on themes and symbolism in Faust Westerns. A discerning reader, Hetzler suggests that Faust adapted elements of other genres to the Western: the Gothic tale, mysteries, the Holmesian detective, and the Private Eye.

"Faust's Mystery Fiction: A Checklist," by William F. Nolan. The introduction to this bibliography provides a much-needed reminder that Faust had impressive accomplishments in the mystery-suspense field, with twenty-five full-length mystery novels and numerous shorter works. Cites data on magazine and book formats, as well as versions adapted by radio, television, and films.

"Silvertip, Part I: THE STOLEN STALLION," by David Fox. Begins an examination of Faust's longest continuing Western character, the hero of thirteen tales.

"Powell's Army #8: Rio Renegades," by "Terence Duncan." A review of this Faust pastiche (by William F. Nolan writing under a house pseudonym) in which all of Faust's pseudonyms are assigned to characters (Colonel Maxwell Schiller Brand is one example), as well as other Max Brand motifs.

"The Making of a Medical Man: Max Brand's Young Dr. Kildare," by Susan Zodin. A discussion of the relationship between the original Faust story and the motion picture treatment. {Editors' Note: Reprinted in MBC.}

"Tributes," by William F. Nolan. Includes a quotation concerning Faust by Western writer Frank O'Rourke, who had dedicated to "Max Brand" his first book, "E" COMPANY, in which Faust is embodied in the character of war correspondent Max Hickman.

Miscellaneous

"A Collector's Letter." A facsimile of a 1939 letter signed by "Max Brand."

"The Quotable Faust." Selected passages from several Faust works.

"Bookshelf." Readers' additions to the WWA list in issue no. 1.

"Essentials." Addresses of pulp dealers. Also a brief filler in which contemporary Western writer Cameron Judd is compared to "Max Brand."

"Transformations." Reproduces *Argosy*'s 1934 illustration for the "George Challis" serial, "The Naked Blade," and the same title in a 1937 edition, the only paperback to be published under Faust's name.

Back cover. Reproduces a Faust inscription and signatures of "Max Brand" *and* Frederick Faust.

Contents of *Singing Guns,* Vol. 1, No. 3 (Summer 1990)

Articles and Reviews

"Max Brand's California Roots," by William Bloodworth. An excellent account of the adolescent years of "a writer who was in flight from himself." Drawn largely from Schoolcraft's earlier interviews as well as Bloodworth's 1985 personal contacts with Dr. John Cooper, a close friend of Faust's during the Modesto years.

"Shakespeare's Presence in Faust's Westerns," by Leo Hetzler. In a close and intelligent reading of several Faust titles, Hetzler shows how scenes in the novels parallel the plays, from villains in "Othello" to the balcony scene in "Romeo and Juliet." Hetzler also compares Faust himself to the Bard's Prospero, "creating and peopling a world 'such as dreams are made on.' " {Editors' Note: Reprinted in MBC.}

"A Sexual Perspective in the Works of Max Brand," by Jack Ricardo. Discusses what the author sees as a homosexual element in Faust's masculine characters. He also attempts, vainly and with dubious foundation, to extend this idea to Faust himself. Ricardo's views were unanimously repudiated by others in the next issue. {Editors' Note: Reprinted in MBC.}

"The Making of a Medical Man, Part II: Max Brand's Dr. Kildare," by Susan Zodin.

Continues the examination with analysis of CALLING DR. KILDARE and DR. KILDARE'S SEARCH. {Editors' Note: Reprinted in MBC.}

"The Silvertip Series, Part II: SILVERTIP," by David Fox. Examines the novel, with emphasis on the hero's adherence to a vow.

Reprinted Faust Nonfiction

"We Are Coming Home." An essay prepared by Faust for the Berkeley class reunion held in San Francisco in 1940. This was the only printed piece of nonfiction to appear during his professional career. In 1915 Faust had been a feisty student; here, in tender and melancholy maturity, he paints a picture of the wartime moods that, unique to the Class of '15, still bind them to their sense of Alma Mater.

Miscellaneous

"Frederick S. Faust: A Brief Chronology." Highlights certain achievements in Faust's life.

"Three Poems on Faust's World," by Lee Prosser. Evocative verse inspired by "a poet at heart" from a successful poet and editor.

"The Quotable Faust." Aphorisms and philosophical passages gleaned from several Faust works.

"Essentials." Notes on current books containing work by and about Faust.

Back Cover. Features a reproduction of an all-Faust issue of *Famous Spy Stories* (1940).

Contents of *Singing Guns*, Vol. 1, No. 4 (Fall 1990)

Articles and Reviews

"The Real Max Brand: Some Thoughts on One Western Life," by William Bloodworth. A paper presented at the 1984 meeting of the Western Literature Association in Reno. A good summation of Faust's development as a writer and a person. Includes portions of letters from Faust to his literary agent, Carl Brandt, in which Faust comments on some works in progress. Bloodworth also argues for the critic's right to investigate biography in assessing a writer's work.

"A Meeting of Two Writers," by Rocco Musemeche. A sketch of Faust's meeting with fellow pulpist Theodore Roscoe, whose forte was the realm of terror and weird adventure. The two occasionally shared cover billing in *Argosy* during the thirties.

"Fabulous Faust Facts," by William F. Nolan. Includes brief remarks on Faust's productivity, entering the slick magazine market, and other details.

"Admirable Plagiarism," by James L. Henry. Points out some common traits in the fiction of Faust and Jack London, citing in particular THE UNTAMED and THE CALL OF THE WILD.

"Dr. Kildare's Private Life," by Susan Zodin. Discusses THE SECRET OF DR. KILDARE and other titles in the series. {Editors' Note: Reprinted in MBC.}

"The Silvertip Series, Part III: THE MAN FROM MUSTANG," by David Fox. Focuses on the hero's mythic, otherworldly aura and the incremental introduction of the archvillain, Barry Christian.

Reprint Prose by Faust

"Oscar Wilde: A Survey of Some of his Prose Writings." From *The Occident* (10/12), the essay reveals a remarkable degree of literary perception and critical acuity in the young Faust. Faust dissects several of Wilde's controversial works, including "Salome," some fairy tales, and DORIAN GRAY. One might discern in Faust's evaluation of Wilde some of his own literary predilections.

Original Prose by Faust

"The Second Chance," with "A Preface to a Lost Classic," by William F. Nolan. One of the Yorktown series, a framework devised by Faust as a challenge to his creativity: the sinking of the passenger ship would be told from a different viewpoint each time. One of several previously unpublished stories, the manuscript of this one bore Faust's name rather than a pseudonym, suggesting that he himself was pleased with the results. {Editors' Note: Reprinted in MBC.}

Miscellaneous

"Some Questions and Conundrums," by "Prof. V." In a whimsical tone, these probing questions offer some intriguing, sometimes offbeat, avenues for further research and study.

"Death of a Mountain Man," by Harold Lee Prosser. Rendered in both Spanish and translation, this verse, says Prosser, is "a parable" in which Faust is conceived as a seer, understanding and describing the nature of death.

"The Quotable Faust." From the novels, brief excerpts presenting Faust's views on poetry, courage, and the loss of the frontier.

Letters from Readers. Refutations of Ricardo's article in the previous issue. Lengthy rebuttals by Hetzler and Nolan, with a shorter excerpt by Ed Gorman. {Editors' Note: Reprinted in MBC.}

"Miscellany." A brief commentary, with illustration, of the novelized version of UNCERTAIN GLORY, by Herb Meadow, based on Faust's screenplay (in collaboration with Laszlo Vadnay) for Warner Bros. in 1944.

Cover. Contains a reproduction of the 1947 Penguin edition of MONTANA RIDES AGAIN, in which Faust (as Evan Evans) is hailed as innovator who has "restored to the frontier novel its pristine legendary quality."

Contents of *Singing Guns*, Vol. 1, No. 5 (Spring 1991)

Articles and Reviews

"Eddie Bennett, Faust Collector Deluxe," by Rocco Joame Musemeche. A profile of a highly respected pulp collector and dealer. Focuses on the Faust items most in demand.

"The Silvertip Series, Part IV: SILVERTIP'S STRIKE," by David Fox. Discusses the introspective side of the hero, as well as Faust's precise sense of detail.

"Some Thoughts on Realism in Faust's Westerns," by Leo A. Hetzler. Challenges the assumption that, because he incorporated classic myths into them, Faust uses his characters to "openly question the veracity of the old tales" of chivalry and other artificial images of the Old West. Hetzler makes a strong case for Faust's deliberate use of a Dickensian "higher" realism. {Editors' Note: Reprinted in MBC.}

"From Whistling Dan to Dr. Kildare: Series Characters among the Published Books of Frederick Faust," by William F. Nolan. An important guide, tabulating nineteen Faust creations and providing publication data for magazine, hard cover, and paperback formats of each.

"Some Problems of Chronology in the Kildare Saga," by Susan Zodin. A clarification of the confusion arising from M-G-M's continuation of the Kildare films after Faust stopped writing the series. {Editors' Note: Reprinted in MBC.}

Reprinted Faust Fiction

"The House of Rulaki." {Editors' Note: Reprinted in MBC.}

Miscellaneous

"News and Views." Short items including Faust's lucky number, a review of Robert Easton's LIFE AND WORK, which includes anecdotes about Faust, and HOODWINK, a crime novel by Bill Pronzini, which has as one character "the new Max Brand."

"Faust and *Western Story Magazine*." Reproduces two examples (of some twenty instances) of issues carrying three Faust works under different pseudonyms.

"The Faust Trail," by William F. Nolan. Identifies some twenty different Faust titles using the word *trail*.

"Mr. Baxter and Mr. Brand." Reproduces two 1929 letters to *Western Story Magazine* from readers unaware that their two favorite writers were the same man.

"The Quotable Faust." Aphorisms and other brief excerpts from Faust's fiction.

"Miscellany." Announces two audiocassette versions of Faust's works.

Contents of *Singing Guns*, Vol. 1, No. 6 (Fall 1991/Winter 1992)

Articles and Reviews

"The Multiple Worlds of Frederick Faust," by William F. Nolan. A representative listing of titles by category, showing the wide range of subject matter covered by Faust's fiction. {Editors' Note: Reprinted in MBC.}

"The More Things Change . . . : Frederick Faust's View of Higher Education," by William Bloodworth. Discusses Faust's criticism of education at Berkeley. Includes excerpts of some Faust works from *The Pelican*.

"Italian Westerns and Faust," by Leo A. Hetzler. A look at Faustian themes in the cinema of Sergio Leone.

"The Fun of Collecting Faust," by Samuel A. Peeples. Expresses a preference for Faust's historical novels, by a collector, novelist, and screenwriter who credits Faust's THE

BORDER BANDIT as the inspiration for his own first published novel. {Editors' Note: Reprinted in MBC.}

"Faust and Films: The Silent Years," by Carl Hutt. Discusses film adaptations of Faust works, beginning in 1917.

"Love and War: Pearl Harbor through V-J Day by Robert and Jane Easton. A Review," by William F. Nolan. The book is built around the World War II letters and later reflections of Faust's daughter and son-in-law, and Nolan excerpts a few of the letters dealing with Faust.

"From Karl May to Frederick Faust: Some Observations from Germany," by Elizabeth Wänke. May, the German author of dozens of novels set in an American West he had never seen, is discussed in contrast to Faust. Wänke also comments on numerous Faust characters and describes her route of discovery from early reading of May, eventually leading her to Faust's THE UNTAMED.

"William J. Clark: Trailblazer in Faustiana," by Rocco Joame Musemeche. A profile of the editor of *The Faust Collector*.

"The Silvertip Series: SILVERTIP'S ROUNDUP, THE FALSE RIDER, and SILVER-TIP'S TRAP," by David L. Fox. Discusses the three novels as a trilogy within the series, sharing plot lines, characters, and themes.

Reprinted Faust Prose

"Jude the Obscure" from the 9/13 issue of *The Occident*. Faust delineates the "conditional failure" of Hardy's novel, a shortcoming of the Greek dramatist's concept of nobility and justice, of heroes "struggling magnificently with the inevitable." This viewpoint reveals something of Faust's own sense of values in his work.

"Cast of Characters, from THE ADVENTURES OF DON JUAN: A Screen Treatment (with an introduction by William F. Nolan)." Completed in 1944, shortly before he shipped off to Italy as a war correspondent, Faust's colorful characterizations for the Warner Bros. film can be considered his last work of fiction. Faust also prepared a lengthy story outline for the film, although the final script was reworked by other writers.

Miscellaneous

"A Rare Faust Signature." An inscription in a copy of THE VILLAGE STREET, dated May 29, 1922 (29 was Faust's "lucky number").

"A Letter from William F. Nolan." Addenda to his list of series characters in the previous issue.

"The Quotable Faust." Brief excerpts from several Faust works.

Back cover. Announces the publication of a biography of pulp artist, J. Allen St. John, by Darrell C. Richardson, editor of *The Fabulous Faust Fanzine*.

Contents of *Singing Guns,* Vol. 1, No. 7 (Summer 1992)

Articles and Reviews

" 'Your Forte Is the West,' " by William Bloodworth. An in-depth story of Faust's association with Bob Davis, editor at the Munsey Company, who encouraged Faust to concentrate on Westerns. Focuses on ''The Untamed'' (which Faust dedicated to Davis) and its sequels. A version of this article appears as Chapter 5 in Bloodworth's MAX BRAND. {Editors' Note: Reprinted in MBC.}

''A Personal Indebtedness,'' by D. B. Newton. The Western novelist describes his ''moment of discovery'' of Faust, in 1928, and credits Faust as the inspiration for his own writing career. {Editors' Note: See Newton's essay in MBC.}

''The 'Lost' Novels of Frederick Faust: Full-Length Works Unpublished in Book Format,'' by William F. Nolan. Provides magazine information, including word counts, of the dozens of serials and book-equivalent-connected novelettes that have never achieved book format.

''My Encounter with Faust's Novels,'' by Edgar L. Chapman. A reminiscence centered on the author's early introduction to Faust's DEAD OR ALIVE and his later return to Faust's novels with a critically mature view after becoming a professor of literature.

''The Best Western Writer of 'Em All,'' by Samuel A. Peeples. Some critical remarks on Faust, Zane Grey, and others.

''Fifty Years with the King of the Pulps: A Bibliography of William F. Nolan's Writings about Frederick Schiller Faust,'' by Tim Sinniger. A detailed listing of the dozens of published essays, introductions, and other pieces by the man who vowed in 1945 ''to carry on for Max Brand.''

''More Series Characters by Frederick Faust,'' by Patrick Parenteau edited, with additions, by William F. Nolan. Provides a register of the serials and short fiction involving continuing characters that have not been published in book form and clarifies some ambiguities regarding nonseries characters with similar names. A follow-up to Nolan's article in *Singing Guns*, no. 5.

''The Silvertip Series, Part VI: SILVERTIP'S CHASE,'' by David L. Fox. Discusses the installment in which the hero acquires his wolf companion, Frosty, and the ''iron collar'' of Silvertip's code of honor.

''The Stuff of Dreams,'' by Robert Easton. Dramatically recounts Faust's final days. Reprinted from Easton's MAX BRAND: THE BIG ''WESTERNER.''

Original Poetry by Faust

''Two Poems.'' From Faust's previously unpublished works, undated. Consists of ''Upon Mycale, among Priene's Ruins'' and ''If Love Can Follow.''

Miscellaneous

''The Quotable Faust.'' Comments from letters and notebooks in the Faust papers at the Bancroft Library, University of California at Berkeley. Collected by William F. Nolan.

''Max Brand's Best Poems. A Review,'' by Leo A. Hetzler. Discusses and excerpts poetry from the anthology by Robert and Jane Easton.

Letters. Contains readers' evaluations of Faust, including some comments of critical value.

"A *London Times* Tribute to Mr. Frederick Faust," by J. A. S. (probably John Spranger). A brief memoir by a traveling companion during Faust's tour of Greek islands in the early 1930s. Also includes a Reuters dispatch regarding Faust's death.

Contents of *Singing Guns*, No. 8 (Summer 1995)

Articles and Reviews

"William Bloodworth's *Max Brand*: A Review," by William F. Nolan. An appraisal of Bloodworth's lucid and penetrating critical study from Twayne in 1993.

"Thoughts on Max Brand's THE GARDEN OF EDEN," by Leo A. Hetzler. An in-depth look at the biblical imagery and "Æschylean vision" in the 1922 serial, which "stands outside the corpus of Faust's Westerns." {Editors' Note: Reprinted in MBC.}

"Faustian Statistics," by William F. Nolan. An updated look at the total Faust output, some 28 million words, with comparisons to Creasey and Simenon.

"Frederick Faust, Soldier," by Herbert Wadopian. An account of Faust's last hours by the lieutenant of the platoon to which Faust was assigned. {Editors' Note: Reprinted in MBC.}

"A Hero's Death: New Facts on the Last Hours of Frederick Faust," by William F. Nolan. An account of Faust's participation in the battle action "on a shell-pocked Italian hillside in May of 1944," based on newly discovered information by a soldier who was there. {Editors' Note: Reprinted in MBC.}

"Pringle's Luck: Why Faust Went to War," by Elisabeth Wänke. Intensive observations on Faust's 1937 story, and ALL QUIET ON THE WESTERN FRONT, as well as Faust's personal desire to "get over there" with the rest of the soldiers.

"Faust's Use of History and Authentic Geography for His Western Fiction," by Edgar L. Chapman. An in-depth exploration of possible sources for Faust's depictions of Indian and Mexican cultures and the use of Wyatt Earp and Billy the Kid as analogues for numerous Faust characters. Includes a bibliography and other notations.

"The Silvertip Series, Part 7: THE FIGHTING FOUR and SILVERTIP'S SEARCH," by David L. Fox. More evidence of Faust's concerns with good versus evil and with the role of the creative artist versus man of action.

"The Collected Stories of Max Brand. A Review," by David L. Fox. Deals with the 1994 anthology edited by Robert and Jane Easton and in some detail with "The Wedding Guest" (1934). The collection is an important showcase for Faust's range and development as a serious writer and increasingly conscious artist.

Original Poetry by Faust

"Six Poems." Drawn from "Dead Man's Passport," Faust's 1941 serial, at a period when Faust was attracted to Chinese poetry and imitated it in this novel, set in Shanghai. {Editors' Note: Reprinted in MBC.}

Miscellaneous

"Frederick Faust, the Blue Devil." A reprint of a portion of an item by Albert Hemingway, from a newsletter of the 88th Infantry Division, which Faust accompanied into Italy in 1944.

"Faust's Reading List." A paragraph from a letter to Munsey editor Bob Davis in which Faust expresses his interest in reading *Argosy* fiction.

"Grand Openings: Irresistible First Paragraphs in the Fiction of Frederick Faust," by J. G. Brownley. A discussion of the narrative techniques in "A Silence in Tappan Valley," a short story from 1938.

"Now Picture This . . . ," a selection of effective similes from numerous Faust works.

"Some Flaws in Western Fiction Bibliography," by E. Hamilton Jackson. Points out errors in credits to Faust in WESTERN SERIES AND SEQUELS: A REFERENCE GUIDE (Garland, 1986).

THE MULTIPLE WORLDS OF FREDERICK FAUST

William F. Nolan

It has long been my intention to separate the works of Faust into subjects beyond his Westerns. It is well and good to talk about his amazing range of subject matter but something else again to pin down the exact areas of his fiction. No one has ever compiled such a listing, and this present one does not pretend to be complete as to titles within a given genre.

In other words, I am providing just a few titles under each heading to give the reader some idea of which stories fit where. For dates of publication and magazine origin, I refer the reader to the Faust Bibliography above which lists all of Faust's fiction. The titles I have chosen to include under each heading are representative but not complete. With this listing, however, the full range of subject matter covered by Faust is revealed for the first time. Here, then (in no particular order), the multiple worlds of a master storyteller.

THE ITALIAN RENAISSANCE
THE FIREBRAND
THE BAIT AND THE TRAP
"The Cat and the Perfume"

KNIGHTHOOD
"Balin"
THE GOLDEN KNIGHT

DOG STORIES
"Bulldog"
"The Conquering Heart"

LOVE STORIES
"Out of the Dark"
"The Gambler and the Stake"

"Turn of the Road"
"Late Summer Song"
"Rose of India"

THE SPANISH INQUISITION
THE SPLENDID RASCAL

MYTHIC GODS
DIONYSUS IN HADES

HIGH SOCIETY
"Kain"
"Who Am I?"
HIS THIRD MASTER
"The Ghost"
"A Special Occasion"
"The Wedding Guest"

PIRACY ON THE SPANISH MAIN
THE NAKED BLADE
"The Dew of Heaven"
"Clovelly"

THE MEDICAL PROFESSION
YOUNG DR. KILDARE
CALLING DR. KILDARE
THE SECRET OF DR. KILDARE
DR. KILDARE TAKES CHARGE
DR. KILDARE'S CRISIS
DR. KILDARE'S TRIAL
DR. KILDARE'S SECRET
"Whiskey Sour"
"Internes Can't Take Money"
"My People"
"Dr. Kildare's Dilemma"

FOOTBALL
"Thunderbolt"

THE CIVIL WAR
"A Watch and the Wilderness"
"A First Blooding"

THE IRISH
"The Black O'Rourke"
"Just Irish"
"The Kinsale"
"Devil Fly Away"

THE FRENCH REVOLUTION
"The American"

LATIN AMERICAN REVOLUTIONS
"Viva! Viva!"
"Return of the Man Who Was Killed"

"A Seabold Fights"
"East Wind"

THE ART WORLD
"The Hammer"

AVIATION
"Paston's Glory"
"To Meet in the Sun"
"The Nameless Member"
"The Flaming Finish"
"The Last Flight"
"True Steel"

THE ARGENTINE
THE GALLOPING BRONCOS
THE GENTLE GUNMAN

MEN AND HORSES
"Beggar My Tailor"
"Challenger"
"The Last Stretch"
"Beyond the Finish"
"The Singular Horseman"
"Miniature"
"Name Your Price"
"Thoroughbred"

RURAL FARM LIFE
"The Golden Day"
"The Sun Stood Still"
"The Champion"
"Virginia Creeper"
"The Taming of Red Thunder"

ESPIONAGE
SECRET AGENT NUMBER ONE
SPY MEETS SPY
THE BAMBOO WHISTLE
"War for Sale"
"The Sole Survivor"
"Blind Buff"

BOXING
"Pretty Boy"
"They Stand So Tall"
"Fixed"
"Brain and Brawn"

IRONWORKERS
"Johnny Come Lately"
"Nifty"

WORLD WAR I
"The Luck of Pringle"
"Charlie"
"The Hill of Gasquet"

WORLD WAR II
"After April"
"The Freeing of Yovan"

STEEPLECHASE RACING
THE THUNDERER
MISTRAL

SHIPWRECKS
"The Captain"
"Island of Safety"
"Bottle in the Sea"
"The Second Chance"

THE SOUTH SEAS
"Harrigan!"
DEAD MAN'S TREASURE
THE LUCK OF THE SPINDRIFT
"The Blackbirds Sing"

EARLY CALIFORNIA
"In the Hills of Monteray"

CANADA
THE STINGAREE
"The Tyrant"
"Lightning Lumberjacks"

FANTASY AND SCIENCE FICTION
THE SMOKING LAND
"Devil Ritter"
"That Receding Brow"
"The Lost Garden"
"John Ovington Returns"

HISTORICALS
"The Double Crown"
"White Heather Weather"
"One Glass of Wine"

THE YUKON
MIGHTY LOBO
THE WHITE WOLF
"Chinook"
"The Masterman"
"Devil Dog"
"Carcajou Trail"

ALASKA
TORTURE TRAIL

SIXTEEN IN NOME
"Two Masters"

Let it be duly noted that I have included, in this listing, several books and stories which were printed as Westerns but were actually stories of the Yukon, of Argentina, of horse racing, the Civil War, Early California, and farm life.

I am tempted to break down farther some of Faust's Westerns into "American Indian Tales," "Rio Grande Border Tales," etc., but I will resist this on the basis that these plainly belong with his overall Western titles.

For now, we are finally able to answer that often-asked question: "Sure, I know he wrote a lot of Westerns . . . but what *else* did he write?"

THE FUN OF COLLECTING FAUST

Samuel A. Peeples

As an avid reader of the pulps, particularly *Argosy,* from the time I was about ten, I preferred the science fiction and fantasy, such as Edgar Rice Burroughs and A. Merritt, and Ray Cummings, and apart from my first love, Zane Grey, I didn't care too much for Westerns until I started reading Charles Alden Seltzer's serials in my favorite weekly magazine. In 1932 *Argosy* announced the return of Max Brand to its pages, and, having already tried Walt Coburn on his "return" and finding him not to my liking, I started "The Longhorn Feud" with some doubts which were promptly realized, as I detested the story and thought it was worse than Walt Coburn's. So Max Brand remained on my NG [no good] list for a couple of years.

Then *Argosy* started a serial by "George Challis"—rather openly known to "be" Max Brand under another name—"The Naked Blade," which I devoured avidly; the storyline was lifted almost verbatim from an older favorite of mine, TO HAVE AND TO HOLD by Mary Austin, but, if anything, it buckled and swashed even better . . . ! I promptly decided I'd try more of Max Brand (et al.) and found dozens of titles in the San Francisco Public Library stacks. I was lost: Zane Grey had found a third Western writer with whom to share my affection.

My first Faust collection vanished during the war, but in 1946 I made the acquaintance of Paul S. Latimer who then lived in Oakland, and we've been friends ever since . . . forty-five years! We shared a fondness for *Argosy* and its writers, especially Burroughs and Faust, and Paul's collecting habits re-inspired my own, and we had many wonderful book-hunting jaunts around the San Francisco Bay Area, locating old "hidden" bookstores as far away as Sacramento . . . and even taking an annual trip to the shops in Southern California. At that time Faust titles were available for an average of fifty cents apiece . . . original editions and reprints alike! Even with a limited amount of money to spend (about

$10 for a whole day of book-looking and buying) my collection grew. I have all (except one title swiped by another collector-fan) of Faust's books in hardcover first editions. That one I have in a G&D [Grosset & Dunlap] copy on my shelf to remind myself of the cupidity of collectors!

I don't know which I enjoyed most, Paul Latimer's company on these special jaunts or the books I added to my ever-growing collection. Paul was—and is—a great companion and a marvelous friend. (Even though I used to envy some of his acquisitions!)

Now, nearly half a century later, I still read and enjoy Faust and can see on my shelves titles that I remember finding on a book jaunt with Paul. Latimer always wrote in pencil in every book he bought where he found it, the date, and other details—which after a few years makes them invaluable as souvenirs of long-gone days. I wish I'd done the same, but I always had an objection to writing in books, preferring them as I found them. I always leave the prices I paid in them, and it's a shock to open a treasured item and be reminded that I picked it up in some Goodwill outlet for a nickel!

While my long-suffering wife (we just celebrated our Golden wedding anniversary this year) still insists I've always been a pack rat by nature, she's encouraged my book collecting. I have complete first-edition sets of Zane Grey, Edgar Rice Burroughs, A. Merritt, Sax Rohmer—and most of the rest of my youthful favorites, including Rafael Sabatini. Yes, I do have favorites, but my list (I've never actually compiled one) would include at least one title from each of my favorite authors. Now, as an older man, I still re-read them and find that my taste has changed—but not all that much. Sax Rohmer has diminished in rank for me, while Faust and Zane Grey have risen along with Edgar Rice Burroughs.

My best-loved Faust titles are not his Westerns, with one or two exceptions, but rather his historical novels, followed by his mysteries—the latter are, I think, among his most original and exciting work. Those I don't have in magazine form (only a few) are represented by photocopies. Strangely enough, the first Faust work I ever truly enjoyed remains one of my top favorites—"The Naked Blade."

I haven't had much time of late to pore over my books, but in thinking of this brief article I found myself pulling down Faust titles—and bringing up a flood of wonderful, warm memories of places and people who are now long gone. Tom Greene, a great friend, who passed away thirty years ago, gave me several Faust titles he'd found, including a pristine first in dust jacket of THE WHITE WOLF, and holding it and looking at it today brought Tom back in memory vividly. I remember his pleasure in handing me this treasure, so long ago; it made my eyes moist. As we get older, memories are perhaps our greatest pleasure. So my collection of books remains important in my life—and the source of continued pleasure in many forms, not the least of which is re-reading them, and realizing just what consummate writers men like Frederick Faust were.

In the crumbling pages of old pulp magazines are yarns that should be required reading in every American school. But in this age of television and hard rock and boom boxes, young people who read for lasting pleasure are becoming fewer and fewer. But things—life itself—seem to go in cycles, so, one of these days, you'll see a kid like I was—on a bus, a park bench, a sofa at home, on the lawn under a tree—with his nose buried in a wonderful story, and, if there's any justice in the world, one written by Max Brand—or Faust by any other name.

MY FAUST COLLECTION

Darrell C. Richardson

One of the most prized items in my Faust collection is a mint copy of THE THUNDERER by M. B. This limited-edition volume is bound in red leather with considerable gold leaf trim, which includes a horseshoe design on the front and, with the excellent Paul Brown drawings, it is a fine job of binding crafts-manship.

Other books that I especially prize are my copy of DIONYSUS IN HADES, which has been personally inscribed by Faust, and THE TEN-FOOT CHAIN, one of his earliest writings to appear between hard covers. I have all Faust titles except one in first editions but especially valued is my set of the early Putnam first editions: THE UNTAMED, THE NIGHT HORSEMAN, THE SEVENTH MAN, DAN BARRY'S DAUGHTER, TRAILIN', ALCATRAZ, FIRE BRAIN, and THE WHITE WOLF—all by Max Brand. Also prized are THE BRONZE COLLAR by John Frederick and BEYOND THE OUTPOST by Peter Henry Morland. All of these are among the earliest published books of Faust. I also value a first edition of THE BLUE JAY, which was the first Faust book pub-lished by Dodd, Mead & Company. Before I leave the books—I admire my mint copy of WINE ON THE DESERT with jacket, not only because it was a gift of John Blair of Dodd, Mead, but because I consider this book of short stories the finest of Faust's prose writing to be placed between book covers. My collection of Faust's published books is complete, lacking only THE VILLAGE STREET.

One of the major sections of my collection is the many bound volumes of excerpted magazine tales. The magazine tales are bound in brown book cloth in a uniform set and are labeled "Works of Frederick Faust." Stories are bound and classified as to type, pseudonym used, and by magazine. For example, all the tales from *Blue Book* are bound in one volume, while tales from *Detective*

Fiction Weekly are bound together in a set of five volumes. From *Western Story Magazine* I have many bound volumes of excerpted stories. My general plan has been to bind about three complete serials, or ten complete short novels, to a volume. I group tales chronologically when possible and usually separate the tales according to the pseudonym used. For example, I have thirty Max Brand short novels bound ten to a volume. The same is true for George Owen Baxter and John Frederick. I have some few volumes of short novels, mostly by Peter Henry Morland and David Manning, that contain also a short novel or so by Brand, Baxter, or Frederick in order to fill out the volume. "Montana Rides!" by Evan Evans and "The Tyrant" by George Challis are bound in a single volume, as those were the only two uses of these pseudonyms in *Western Story Magazine.*

One particular volume of tales from *Western Story Magazine* is my special pride and joy! It contains "Sheriff Larrabee's Prisoner" by Martin Dexter, "The Black Muldoon" by Peter Dawson, "The Red Rider" by Nicholas Silver, all the short novels by Hugh Owen, "In Nature's Cruelest Trap" by John School-craft, and all six of the "Golden Coyote" tales by David Manning.

The seven "Reata" novels of Baxter are bound in a single volume, and the thirteen "Silvertip" novels and serials make up three volumes. A feature of Volume I of "Silvertip" is the original drawing by Rodeiveld of Silvertip which has been used as a trade mark (in a circle) on the various jackets illustrating the Silvertip books. "Peter Blue, One-Gun Man," Max Brand's only complete novel from *Far West Illustrated,* is bound as the lead tale in a volume with the three "Chip" novels. Some of the complete *Western Story* serials that I have bound include: "The Stingaree," "Rippon Rides Double," "The Invisible Outlaw," "Trouble's Messenger," "Duck Hawk's Master," "The Wolf and the Man," "Mighty Lobo," "Galloping Danger," "Seven Trails to Romance," "Chinook," "The Bells of San Filipo," "Two Broncos," and "Saddle and Sentiment."

I also have filed in manila envelopes at least one or more serial parts from every Faust serial in *Western Story Magazine* which has not yet been printed in book form. In some cases I lack only one serial part to complete a tale. As I completed serials, and other stories, I bound them into sets.

From *Argosy* I have excerpted and bound only the stories that were published since 1932. Before this date I have a huge set of *Argosy* going back to early 1900, and the Faust tales during this period have not been removed but are in the complete magazine within my pulp magazine collection. (The same applies for the *All-Story* tales and stories in magazines such as *All-American Fiction* and others where I collect the magazines as well as the Faust tales.) Such later *Argosy* novels are "The Longhorn Feud," "The Masterman," "Scourge of the Rio Grande," "The Streak," "Big Game," "The Living Ghost," and others are bound three serials to a volume. The three "White Indian" stories form a volume, the two South Sea novels of Dennis Lawton another, and George Owen Baxter's "The Red Pacer" and Evan Evans's "Montana Rides Again" and

"The Song of the Whip" make up a third volume. The four *Argosy* "Dr. Kildare" stories make another volume; "The Naked Blade," "Dew of Heaven" and "The Smoking Land" comprise another; and the complete "Firebrand" series finishes up the Challis set. In a large omnibus volume is bound "War for Sale" and various shorts such as "Pretty Boy," "Señor Coyote," "Rifle Pass," "Crazy Rhythm," "Viva! Viva!" "Bottle in the Sea," "Just Irish," "Bells of San Carlos," and "Finish Pylon" by Peter Dawson (pseudonym for Jonathan Hurff Glidden *not* Frederick Faust).

Other items in my Faust collection which I prize highly are original paintings and drawings of the illustrations for Faust book jackets and magazine stories. For example, I have framed above my Faust book collection the large painting in color by Rodeiveld which was done for the jacket illustration for THE FALSE RIDER. Also framed is the original illustration from FLAMING IRONS. Others are filed and eventually more will be framed.

Not bound are hundreds of tales from the "slicks" and odd sized publications such as *Collier's, Harper's, McCall's, The Saturday Evening Post, MacLean's, Good Housekeeping, Cosmopolitan, The American Magazine, Liberty, Country Gentleman, Photoplay, This Week, American Weekly, Elks,* and *Esquire.*

Various other bound volumes include stories from such publications as *Adventure, Short Stories, Dime Detective, Greater Western, Golden West, Black Mask, Double Detective, Sport Story, Star Western, Mavericks, Munsey, Triple Western,* and *Railroad Man's Magazine.*

In many cases I have Faust stories excerpted and bound, but I also have them in the complete original magazines. In my collection of over 20,000 pulp magazines are more than 100 titles which are complete. These include all science fiction and fantasy magazines and hundreds of titles in the realm of adventure, Western, mystery, hero titles like The Shadow, Doc Savage, etc.

For forty years I have had a complete file of *Argosy* and *Argosy All-Story* from 1900 through the 1940s when it ceased being a pulp. Recently I found the only missing issue of *All-Story* from 1910 for my collection and now have this grand magazine complete, every issue 1905–1920. I major on the main-line pulps like *Adventure, Blue Book, Popular, Top-Notch, Short Stories, New Story, All-Around* and other all-fiction types which ran for decades. Even from these long runs of titles I have located duplicates through the years and have excerpted selected Faust stories and bound them in my brown cloth volumes.

Some of the works of Faust are considered truly rare collector's items. THE VILLAGE STREET AND OTHER POEMS was published by Putnam's in 1922. This slim volume of ninety-eight pages bound in green paper on boards was dedicated to Thomas Downey. It was the first and one of the few books to be published under his own name. I had searched for this book for nearly fifty years without locating it. During these several decades I have been in contact with many hundreds of Faust fans, collectors, and dealers and still need only this title to have all Faust books in first editions.

Some people consider DIONYSUS IN HADES published by Basil Blackwell in 1931, and printed in England at the Shakespeare Head Press, St. Aldates, Oxford, to be his rarest book. This edition was limited to 500 copies and dedicated to Walter Morris Hart. It was bound in ¼ buckram and paper with uncut edges. Though a very scarce book, several copies have passed through my hands. My own copy has been personally inscribed by Faust, as follows:

December 19, 1931

To Dorothy and Simeon from Heine, to help you to be moderns.

Frederick Faust

THE THUNDERER by M. B. (the only use of this pen name) was a Derrydale Press Book in 1933 in a limited edition of 900 copies. It has great illustrations by the famous painter of horses, Paul Brown. This story originally appeared in *Country Gentleman*. "The Thunderer" is a great jumping horse and this tale ranks as a minor classic in the field of horse stories. All Derrydale Press books are valuable and this is a prized collector's item.

THE TEN-FOOT CHAIN, OR CAN LOVE SURVIVE THE SHACKLES, published by The Reynolds Publishing Company, New York, in 1920 contains one of the first Faust stories to see book publication. This was a symposium of four tales written about the same theme. The tales resulted from a dinner meeting of four authors and an editor. Dr. Means, one of the authors, tossed the question: "What mental and emotional reaction would a man and woman undergo, linked together by a ten-foot chain, for three days and nights?" This query precipitated such an uproar that Bob Davis, editor of the Munsey Magazines, asked each writer to record his version of the tale.

The four tales about "The Ten-Foot Chain" are as follows: "An Indian Jataka" by Achmed Abdullah, "Out of the Dark" by Max Brand, "Plumb Nauseated" by E. K. Means, and "Princess of Percheron" by Perley P. Sheehan.

"The Ten-Foot Chain" is seldom seen and most Faust collections lack this title in its initial appearance in *All-Story Weekly*; the cover was devoted to this symposium and the pictures of all four authors were published on the cover. This was one of the first published pictures of Faust who was very seldom photographed. His true identity remained unknown not only to the literary world but also to the general public for years to come. My copy of the book, the only copy I've ever seen, still retains its dust jacket.

The collecting of foreign editions of Faust books is indulged in by some collectors. I have many of these from several different countries. Many of these are unusual collector's items. While traveling in Europe several years ago, I found some Zane Grey, Edgar Rice Burroughs, and Max Brand titles in a book shop in the northern Flemish-speaking part of Belgium. Among these were copies of TIGER in Flemish published in Antwerpen, and a copy, with jacket, of WAR FOR SALE (Oorlog te Koop) published in Rotterdam. The jacket copied the magazine cover from its appearance in *Argosy*.

There are many other unusual and scarce Faust collector's items, such as movie material, the early Hillman softcover titles, British editions like "penny dreadfuls" with color covers, printed under pseudonyms like George Owen Baxter, etc., and countless other items too numerous to mention.

Though many Faust stories in books, newspapers, and magazines may not be referred to as collector's items, a long list of his works seems to be scarce and difficult to locate. Many of the books published under pseudonyms such as Peter Henry Morland, Walter C. Butler, Frederick Frost, John Frederick, and Frank Austin are not easy to find. Some titles under the pseudonyms George Owen Baxter and David Manning fall under the rare category. A few of the titles under the famous pen name Max Brand are scarce books. Perhaps the rarest of these is WINE ON THE DESERT, published by Dodd, Mead in 1940. CHILDREN OF NIGHT published by L. Harper Allen, New York, in 1928 is a seldom-seen book. It was published as a regular hardback and also issued in a paper edition bound on boards with an illustrated cover in color. It was very much *abridged* from its original magazine appearance.

A number of Faust yarns in magazines are scarce in part because they appeared in obscure and short-lived publications which seem to have disappeared from the scene. *American Cavalcade* was a digest-size magazine which published four Faust stories in 1937. After many years of searching I still lack all but one of these issues. *The American Weekly* and *This Week* were supplements to newspapers. Though they had huge circulation, few issues survived because they were thrown out with newspapers in the trash can. Some of Faust's best stories were in these two periodicals, and they were a high-paying market for writers. Very few back-issue dealers in magazines handled these, and they are difficult to find. Some other publications that seem hard to find are *Country Gentleman, Elks Magazine, Country Home, Illustrated Love Magazine, Ace-High, Black Mask,* and *Mavericks.* In my own experience I have found the old pulp magazines easier to locate than more recent "slick" magazines like *The American Magazine, Cosmopolitan, Collier's, Esquire, Good Housekeeping, Liberty, McCall's,* and *The Saturday Evening Post.* The pursuit of rare Faust items is an interesting and rewarding quest.

The cover of *Argosy All-Story Weekly* for January 8, 1921, with the first installment of "Tiger" by Max Brand and later that year when "The Guide to Happiness" began in the issue for August 13, 1921.

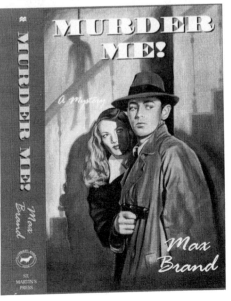

Detective fiction by Frederick Faust. ''Walking Death'' under the byline Nicholas Silver showcased in Street & Smith's *Detective Story Magazine* for July 29, 1922; the two-part serial, ''The Face and the Doctor,'' beginning in *Detective Fiction Weekly* for May 22, 1937; and MURDER ME! successfully published as a hardcover book by St. Martin's Press in 1995.

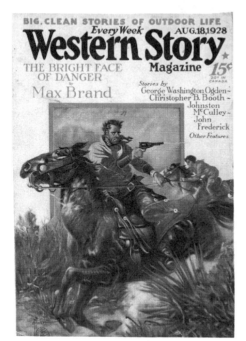

"The Bright Face of Danger" by Max Brand began in Street & Smith's *Western Story Magazine* for August 18, 1928. John Frederick, another Faust pseudonym, was showcased on the same cover. The issue for March 5, 1932, showcased three Faust pseudonyms and no one else. This was a frequent occurrence.

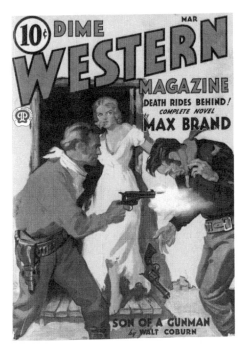

The first Western short novel by Max Brand appeared in *Dime Western* in the issue for March 1933. The Max Brand name on a competing Western fiction magazine irritated Street & Smith. In 1935 Street & Smith created *Western Winners,* offering reprint fiction from earlier issues of *Western Story Magazine*, principally stories by Max Brand who by that time no longer appeared in *WSM* under the Max Brand byline.

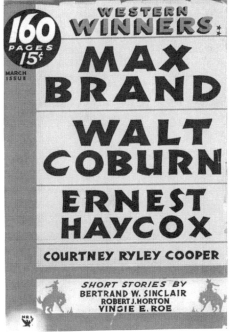

During the mid-1930s Faust's fiction began appearing in such slick magazines as *Liberty* and *Collier's*.

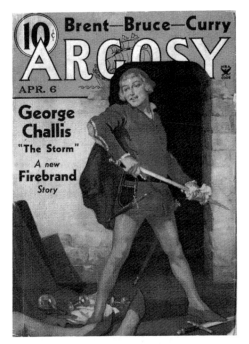

All-Story Weekly and *Argosy* had always been ready markets for Faust's historical fiction. His finest historical novels, under the byline George Challis, began appearing in *Argosy* in the 1930s. His final Western short novel also began in *Argosy* in the issue for June 18, 1938, as a two-part serial. This short novel has now been restored as "Slip Liddell" and appears for the first time as Faust wrote it in THE GHOST WAGON AND OTHER GREAT WESTERN ADVENTURES published by the University of Nebraska Press in 1996.

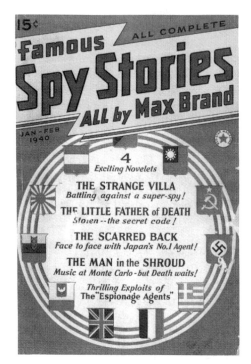

The first issue of the Munsey Company's new *Famous Spy Stories* for January–February 1940 was devoted entirely to stories by Max Brand. He dominated later issues as well. In December 1949 Popular Publications launched *Max Brand's Western Magazine*, a monthly that lasted until Popular ceased publishing pulp magazines in September 1954.

The Bull Hunter stories appeared in Street & Smith's *Western Story Magazine* under the Max Brand byline and the serial "Western Tommy" under the John Frederick pseudonym. These bylines were changed for the book editions when they appeared from Chelsea House, Street & Smith's book publishing division.

The first edition from G. P. Putnam's Sons of THE WHITE WOLF by Max Brand in 1926 featured a dust jacket with powerful archetypal imagery. Dodd, Mead's cover for PILLAR MOUNTAIN, employed a similar motif done with great simplicity.

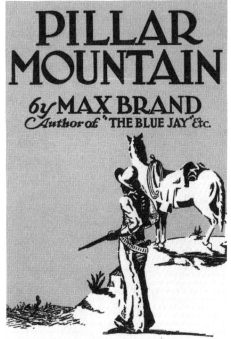

In the 1930s for Faust's horse racing and spy fiction, the jacket covers reflected the prevailing mood of art deco.

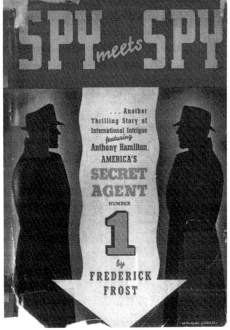

In the late 1930s and the 1940s book jacket art often reflected images projected by Hollywood films. Faust's THE IRON TRAIL from Dodd, Mead and THE BAIT AND THE TRAP from Harper & Bros. were no exceptions.

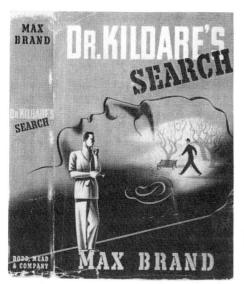

The Dodd, Mead jackets for the Dr. Kildare novels tended to reflect a psychological surrealism influenced by Salvador Dalí, while the reprint editions tended to use images of Lionel Barrymore and Lew Ayres from the popular M-G-M film series.

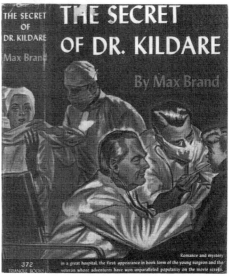

Max Brand remains a top-selling author. His COLLECTED STORIES from the University of Nebraska Press helped to further Frederick Faust as a major American literary artist. SIXTEEN IN NOME is one of four new hardcover Westerns appearing annually in Five Star Westerns, published by Thorndike Press in hardcover editions and by Brilliance Corporation simultaneously in full-length audio editions.

BELLES LETTRES AND LITERARY CRITICISM

THE HOUSE OF RULAKI

Frederick Faust

First published in The Occident *in 1913 when Faust was a student at Berkeley,*
"The House of Rulaki" was subsequently reprinted in The Fabulous Faust
Fanzine.

He met Rulaki on such a day as exists only in the South Seas and in books. It
was at that period in the evening, when the west is yet pink enough to make
one conscious that day has been but does not obtrude the fact upon the attention
with flaring strokes of color. The languor in the air, in the wind, was rich as
perfume, and the mind went out in a thousand strong feelings while the body
was content to lie passively. But not the body of ''Hercules'' Martin. The vigor
of the Occident was still tense in his muscles; the Orient was as yet only strong
because of its newness. The littered studio, the thousand dreary details of his
Parisian life, had indeed been washed from his memory, and, while his will lay
dormant, his instincts grew younger by several thousand years. Yet he still had
what to the Eastern mind is a species of insanity, an over-plus of energy which
must be expended in exercise.

Therefore on that night he followed his custom of swimming in the surf,
plunging out through the breakers, and then floating on his back in the long,
lazy swells that rise and fall as gently, as evenly, as the breasts of a sleeping
woman. Confident in his strength and the swimmer's skill, he had paid no attention to the stories of the whirlpools which sweep close in upon the coast of
Tutuila, develop in one fearful moment, and draw down many a strong swimmer.
But on this night, surely of all nights a fated one for Martin, while he lay

drowsily content in the warmth of the water and half conscious of the astonishing nearness of the stars and moon, he felt a sharp current whirl him around. The suddenness of the thing left him dazed. He could only fight blindly for his life. It was a long, nightmare fight, and, when the whirlpool relaxed its grip, he was far out from land, his arms numb with weariness and only moving through the force of instinct, and his lungs choked with water. It was clearly impossible to reach shore, and Martin shouted for help. He confessed this afterward with shame, and indeed for such a man as Martin it was a matter of shame.

It takes a loud voice to reach past the sound of the breakers, but the fear of death was as air in his big lungs, and he was heard. After a time, he swears it was hours, during which his progress had become a thing almost as terrible as death itself, he heard a reassuring voice which he answered. Rulaki says that she was guided by his voice, that and something else. Next the moon flashed on a white arm and forehead, and, as the swimmer approached him, she bade him swing in behind, place his left hand on her right shoulder, and throw his head far back. In this way they made slow progress to the line of the breakers, by which time Martin was so far recovered that he could make his own way to the shore. There they collapsed together, he too tired to express gratitude, or she to expect it.

They rose to their elbows, facing each other at the same moment. Martin always thought that this was a miracle, in a small way. But Rulaki thought that it was something else. I remember when I first saw Rulaki so that I am not surprised that Martin first sat up, then stood bolt upright, and stared dumbly. To Rulaki, as he stood there, his wet body alive in the moonlight and that mighty chest still heaving, he was a god. Then she spoke in that wonderful voice of hers. I could never find the word for it, but Parker says that it was *warm*. Still Martin only stared and said nothing. He felt a hunger within him, a hunger that was not for food, and which for the first time in his atheistical life made him wonder if after all he had the thing popularly known as a "soul."

Rulaki arose. "You are very tired," she said, "and you will be cold. My palace is there," she continued, extending her arm toward the house she had inherited from her trader father, "and, if you will come, you may rest until you are able to go home. I will give you brandy, real brandy." She added this with a smile.

The house of Rulaki is set on a high rise of ground. All around it roll the besieging waves of forest, splashing it here and there with a spray of green vines. Martin caught his breath, and his eyes brightened when he saw it. Rulaki nodded and smiled appreciatively.

"I feel the same way about it after all this time," she said.

The door was opened to them by a Negro boy clad in a loose jacket and green knee-pants bordered with white. Below his knees his legs were bare, and on his feet were sandals. He grinned welcome to Rulaki and bowed deferentially to Martin. Rulaki handed Martin a gaily-colored dressing gown of some rich stuff which caressed the skin.

"Be seated," she said, after Martin had thrown the robe about him with a sudden consciousness of his scanty garb. "I will come again at once. Terry," she said to the boy, "bring brandy . . . and here"—finding a silver cigarette case—"are cigarettes."

Martin sank into something which was between a divan and a Morris chair and vastly comfortable. Then he selected a cigarette and lighted it at a suspended lamp which burned the faintest of perfumes. Presently the Negro entered, bearing a bamboo tray on which rose a bottle of Grande Chartreuse and two thin stemmed glasses. These he placed on a small table on Martin's right hand. Martin filled the glasses. When he looked up, the Negro was still waiting.

"That is all," said Martin, and the boy disappeared.

Left to himself, Martin looked about the room. It had impressed him when he first entered as being peculiarly comfortable and complete, neither oppressing the eyes with elaborate decoration nor wearying the mind with a bare monotony. When he set himself now to analyze its charm, he was astonished to find no pictures on the walls, whether of animate or inanimate objects. Soft scroll work only ran here and there, grotesque at the first examination, beautiful at the second. The furniture was all appropriate, but not of any one pattern. In fact, it presented an astonishing variety of material, color, and form. Finally Martin noticed that the room was smaller than he had at first thought. The prevailing light and cheerful tones lent it an exaggerated sense of spaciousness. His observations were interrupted by the entry of Rulaki, laughing as she came. I have seen Rulaki in a hundred costumes and thought of each: "No one but she should wear that." So it was now with Martin. It was a simple thing she wore, a flowing effect of Japanese pattern, yet to Martin it appeared, he knew not why, to possess something of the majesty, something of the mystery, of priestly robes.

"They tell me I should go on the stage, I change dresses so quickly," said Rulaki.

"It has been a short time," said Martin clumsily.

"Oh," she cried, "you have not touched the cordial. See! It's the true Chartreuse." She raised a glass between his eyes and the lamp, which shone through the delicately green liquid until it became a sparkling, living thing, before she handed it to him. "I will pledge you an old toast," she said, taking the other glass. "The Waves of Tutuila and the gifts of the gods they bring us."

"The waves of Tutuila," said Martin seriously, "I shall ever trust to their guidance."

The strong cordial swept the blood up into his face. He leaned forward to look at her, although she was so close he might have touched her with his hand. For the first time he saw the vein which frequently ran a vine of timid blue along her throat. He reached again for the Chartreuse. "Let us find another toast," he said.

Within a week all of his luggage was brought to the house of Rulaki. They had almost quarreled about it, for he naturally wished that she should come to him rather than he to her. In the end she conquered for, when he teased, she was inflexible, and, when he commanded, she wept. So he came to live in the house of Rulaki, the house which Rulaki loved almost as if it had been a part of her. For a time people said many things, but at last the talking died away and stopped, and everything was taken as a matter of course. After all, Rulaki was only a half-breed.

It was at about this time that Parker visited them. After supper they lounged on the porch which opened out over the ocean.

"You're hitting up the nicotine rather lively, aren't you?" said Parker, when Martin lighted his fourth cigarette since black coffee.

Martin looked up quickly. "Does it show?" he asked. "I *have* been going at it rather heavy."

"Oh," cried Rulaki, "why shouldn't he smoke? He likes it."

"Of course," said Parker, noting the unusual sallowness of "Hercules" Martin's skin. "But it's rather hard on a fellow here." He struck himself on the chest.

"Doing much swimming lately, Henry?"

"No," he answered, dropping his chin upon one hand and staring out into the night, "no, I haven't been swimming much. I'll have to start again. It's so lazy here in Tutuila . . . so infernally lazy." He threw the cigarette out the window.

"Swimming is too much hard work," said Rulaki, "except now and then at night."

She leaned back among the cushions of her hammock, delirious curves from ankle to throat. Her lips opened once, as if she were about to speak; then her eyes closed, and she breathed a long breath of content. There was a minute's silence while Martin gazed moodily at her. Far off on the ocean Parker saw the light of an outgoing ship dwindle, twinkle, and go out.

"I forgot that I have brought you a *Courier des Arts,*" he said, recalling himself suddenly and producing the paper from his hip-pocket. "Thought you might be glad to know how your painters' world is going on." He watched Martin's face, hoping for a change, and the change came.

"Thanks," Martin said eagerly, reaching for the paper and commencing to run through its pages. "You'll excuse me for a moment, won't you? What's this? Antoni! Not Francisco Antoni? Yes, by the Lord, Francisco Antoni! A year ago he was just a promising cub, and now he's famous!"

"Have you been painting much lately?" asked Parker.

"No," answered Martin, "no . . . in fact, I haven't done anything since I've been in Tutuila."

He glanced at Rulaki, but she was fast asleep, and her lips were slightly parted, smiling.

"I'll leave you to your journal," said Parker, rising.

Martin made no answer. He was gazing at Rulaki. At the door Parker glanced back again. The journal was crumpled in Martin's hand, and he was leaning forward to look at her, although she was so close that he could have touched her with his hand. Parker tip-toed out.

It is a strange resolve that will endure over night in Tutuila, but Martin's purpose held. Themes for his picture were by the hundred in his mind and only waiting for his brush. All that lacked was a model. Naturally Rulaki occurred to him, and, still more naturally his choice was made on the instant. When he broached the subject to her the next day, she was very obstinate. They had walked up the hillside for a little distance and were lying together under an exceptionally tall and heavily foliaged palm.

When he explained his purpose to her, she was very obstinate for a long time. "If you should make me on the canvas, line for line and every color just as I look, would it be me when you were done? See," she went on, "there was a silly officer boy. . . ."

"What!" said Martin.

"He was only a big boy and very, very silly. I think he was more in love with my hair than with me . . . he used to say. . . ."

"It's beautiful hair," said Martin, letting one hand luxuriate in the dark, silky mass. "Haven't I ever told you how beautiful it is?"

"Do you think it is?"

"Of course."

"Tell me again."

"It's foolish for me to go on describing, for I can never say it right. Did you ever go out and look at the sky at night when the stars are very few and the sky is so close that you can almost touch it? It seems deep, deep black, yet you can feel the blueness in it."

Rulaki thought for a moment, chin on hand and eyes studious. "Yes," she whispered breathlessly, lifting her eyes.

"Well, that is like your hair. Mind, I don't say that it is just the same, for your hair has something different, finer, more beautiful . . . why! . . . it's a part of you."

"There!" cried Rulaki triumphantly, "that is just what I wanted to say but couldn't. If you painted every line and color just like me, still it wouldn't be me, and it would stay there to lie about me forever. The officer boy I started to tell you about. . . ."

"Damn the officer boy. If he. . . ."

"Sh-h," laughed Rulaki, closing his mouth with her hand. "He had a great big camera, and he teased me until I let him take pictures of me, lots and lots of them. But when he showed them to me, my . . . how disappointed I was. I could recognize my face, but it was not the *real* I. Won't you understand?"

"The officer boy was a fool," began Martin angrily. "Besides, no camera can do what a trained hand can do. It's what is called art, Rulaki, to show the inside of things as much as the outside. That's what I'm going to try to do for you."

"I don't like it," said Rulaki sulkily.

"But think," said Martin, "just think that, if I *can* paint you as you are, you may live forever."

"Live forever! Live forever!" cried Rulaki savagely. "Why should I care to have a picture of me live forever when I'll be dead and . . . and . . . nasty."

A wave of warmer air rolled around them, and Martin settled himself more comfortably.

Rulaki crept closer to him and slipped one arm under his head. "Why do you want to work and paint pictures?" she murmured in his ear.

"Because . . . ," he began.

"Sh!" cried Rulaki. "Listen."

From above came the caw of a bird, faint from the distance and yet wonderfully clear. Martin looked up through the branches and out into the great quiet of the sky.

"It is better to be like this, after all," he said. "I will place you against all the pictures that were ever painted. I will give them all up for you."

"No, no," laughed Rulaki, "for yourself."

It was a habit of Rulaki's to laugh at critical moments. She laughed even when the crash came about two months later. Martin was never a financier, and his entire fortune, which was considerable, had become tangled in some shaky railroad stock. Now he went to the wall with every cent.

"What matter?" cried Rulaki gaily. "I have enough for two . . . yes, more than enough, and we might as well spend it all."

Martin lighted a cigarette and inhaled several full puffs before he replied. "I have fallen pretty far," he said slowly, with his eyes on the floor. "But I don't think that I can live at the expense of a woman. At least not yet," he added bitterly.

They were silent for a time, and I think that Rulaki trembled.

"What will you do?" Rulaki asked at last.

"I will go away," said Martin, "go away to Paris. Perhaps, when I'm there, the dead part of me will come to life, and all that I've lost will come back to me. If I can, I'll make enough money in a year to come back to you and stay."

"But what have you lost that you must go so far away to get it back?" she asked. "Do you mean the money?"

"You won't understand me," said Martin, "but I'll try to tell you. I want to get hungry again, the kind of hunger that gets down in a man's bones and tortures him. It's the hunger for power over the souls of men." He extended his hands with their long fingers, already less indicative of power than they had been a few months before. "If you could have known what those hands have done when the hunger was on me . . . but the hunger is gone. I've eaten and I've drunk . . . I've lived and I've loved. You don't understand me . . . you can't . . . but the hunger's gone. Oh, God! shall I ever get it back?"

"I don't understand," cried Rulaki, white and bewildered. "You are going away, far away across the oceans, to be hungry?"

"I shall come back," he said, "with money."

"Men come to Tutuila," she returned quietly, "and of these some go away, and those who go away never come again. Take me with you."

"To starve, perhaps?"

"But I have much money."

"In Europe the man cares for the woman. No, I shall go alone . . . I must work . . . and I must be alone. You shall wait here for me. Will you wait?"

A chorus of laughter reached them from a group of sailors who were climbing up into the hills from the beach.

"Yes," said Rulaki, "I will surely wait for you."

Thereafter she was very quiet, and neither wept nor pleaded. I think she felt that some Nemesis had come upon her, for her happiness had been too great. So she met it proudly but unresistingly, as one should meet the inevitable. She did not even ask to go with him again, for something made her understand.

The hill on which Rulaki's house stands is in full view of the harbor and not a long journey from it, so that Martin could stay with her until the last moment. She would have gone down to the boat with him. This he would not allow.

"If I should see you standing there on the shore while I sailed out into the night, it would be too much, as though I were sailing forever out and away from your life," he said.

In the final moment after Martin had kissed her for the last time and they stood together at the door, she clung to him for a few seconds and stared hungrily into his face, as if she were drawing something from it to keep forever. Then she smiled and waved him down the hill. Part way down he turned to look again. It was night, and the same moon which had shown her to him for the first time among the waves was now ghostly pale upon her face. She was still waving. It is in that way that I like to think of her, smiling and waving, to make *him* think that she was hopeful and confident.

When he had placed his suitcase in his stateroom, he went out upon the stern of the ship to look again upon the house of Rulaki. There was no need of any moon to help his sight. The entire house was in flames.

I was walking down the street with Parker the other day, when Martin, no longer "Hercules" Martin, passed us. For some moments afterward we were silent.

"Martin," said Parker, as though we had just been talking on the subject, "might have been a great painter . . . and, after all, Rulaki was only a half-breed."

CONVALESCENCE

Frederick Faust

In reviewing THE GHOST WAGON AND OTHER GREAT WESTERN AD-VENTURES (University of Nebraska Press, 1996) by Max Brand in the Am-arillo, Texas, Sunday News-Globe, *Doris R. Meredith observed that in Max Brand's fiction "one is immediately struck by the timelessness of the language. There is no slang to date the story and distract the reader." Faust's study of classical models served him well in terms of his style, but it was not quite so pristine at the beginning. "Convalescence," marking Faust's first appearance in a national-circulation magazine, appeared under his own name in* All-Story Weekly.

"I'm glad you gave him this private room, Miss Allen," said the doctor. "I should have mentioned it myself if I had thought. He must be kept quiet . . . absolutely."

They leaned over the still figure on the bed, his head swathed in bandages to the bridge of his nose, no sign of life about him save that one hand gripped the coverlet on which it lay.

"Absolute quiet," repeated the doctor.

"Yes, doctor," said the head nurse.

"The bullet just missed the brain. Very unusual case, but with perfect care he may live through. Must have perfect care, though. Put a good nurse on this case. Let's see. What about that girl with the red hair . . . I mean the one who had red hair when she began training?"

The head nurse controlled a smile. "Margaret Flanders," she said, "yes, I think she is the one for this case."

"Put her on during the nights."

She stepped into the corridor outside the room and spoke to an orderly. In a few moments Margaret Flanders entered. The hair which had once been red was now soft brown and waved demurely under the white cap, and the steady purposefulness of her eyes belied the rather unusual pallor of her face. She received the directions of the doctor with the usual hospital formula of "yes, Doctor," and failed to show any excitement as he waxed emphatic with particulars toward the end.

Left alone with the patient, she first drew the window shade so that a shadow fell across his face, then she stood by the bed and regarded him fixedly for several minutes. Something on his wrist startled her attention. She leaned over and drew back his sleeve, revealing a narrow white scar which curved for several inches up his arm.

Margaret Flanders closed her eyes and stood for a time with a thoughtful frown. She raised the curtain again so that the full light of the sun fell on the unconscious man's face and leaned over him, as though she were trying to look up under the bandages. But they concealed his identity as fully as a mask.

Half an hour later she was speaking with the clerk of the storage room. "I want to see the property of that man who was brought in last night, shot through the head, Jim," she said to the clerk. "What's his name?"

"Don't know," he answered. "They filed the stuff here under the name of John Doe. Nothing on him to identify him except a blackjack." He smiled wisely into her expressionless face. "Guess he's a hard one, all right," he went on, as he laid a little cloth bag on the door counter. "Here's the stuff they took from his pockets. Will he live?"

She fumbled the contents of the bag one by one, a roll of bills, a pocket knife, a watch, a wallet, the blackjack (innocent seeming enough in its snug leather cover), and a large bunch of keys. She held the keys for a moment in the hollow of her hand. They were of many sizes, some of them Yale keys, some plain keys, and nearly all filed curiously about the edges.

As the clerk turned a little away, she dropped the bunch of keys into the pocket of her apron. When he looked up again, she was busy tying up the mouth of the bag. "There's nothing here to identify him," she said as she gave back the bag. "Yes, I think he will live." She paused a moment and stared vaguely into a far corner of the room. "I am quite sure he will live." As she walked back toward her patient's room, she was smiling strangely, and her head was bent forward.

It was a bitter watch by day and night for the next two weeks to save the wounded man, but at the end of that time Margaret Flanders, a little thinner and paler than before and with a trace of purple shadows under her eyes, received orders to remove the bandages about the upper part of her patient's face. She went about the task with even more delicacy and hesitation than the condition of her patient demanded. She had undone the first roll when his hand went up and caught her fingers firmly.

"Now tell me straight," he said. "When this bandage comes off my eyes, will I see you as pretty as I've been imagining you all these nights? Are you like your voice and like the touch of your hands?''

''My hands and my voice are both part of me,'' she answered with a low, brooding laugh, ''but I haven't the least idea whether or not you'll find me pretty.''

He drew a deep breath. ''Don't think I'm faking any funny stuff,'' he said.

''Not a bit,'' she answered, ''all sick men have queer imaginations.''

His hand remained steadfastly prisoning hers. ''You may think me a bit queer,'' he replied, ''but I'm not. I'm handing you the cold dope. When I lay here all this time, I've had a mighty big chance to think things over. At first I wasn't very keen whether I lived or not, but, while I lay here, I got to listening to the sound of your dresses swishing about and to your voice . . . which is some voice, take it from me . . . and then the easy way you have with your hands . . . which, I may also remark, are some hands. . . . Well, say, lady, I've got a picture of you cached away in my brain that's a cross between a rising moon and a saint on a stained-glass window pane. Now, put me right. What am I going to see when I look at you?''

She laughed softly again. ''I can't describe myself,'' she said. ''I haven't a mirror here, and my memory is very short.''

''All I want to know,'' he persisted, ''is whether I'll have to forget your face and remember that you've got a beautiful soul, and then close my eyes again, and think back to the short stories I've read so I can say nice things to you.''

''Well,'' she replied, ''I hope you won't think about my soul.''

With deft hands she removed the last roll of bandage, and he lay looking up to her. His eyes grew suddenly wide, and a faint blush on his cheeks answered the sudden color of her face.

''It is seven o'clock,'' she stated. ''The day nurse will be here any moment, and I must go.''

He caught at her dress. ''Don't go,'' he pleaded. ''I'm remembering things so fast now that my head is dizzy.''

She extricated her dress from his hands and walked to the door, smiling back at him.

''You'll come back?'' he called.

''Yes, tonight,'' she answered.

''If you don't come back, honest, I'll tear off the rest of these bandages while the day nurse is not looking.''

The door closed upon her half-mocking laughter.

That day was a hard one for the day nurse. Her patient rolled and tossed uneasily, and suddenly he would lie still, and she would be conscious of the unfaltering stare of eyes that had given defiance too often to danger, a glance that made her turn almost unawares, as if to seek for some protection. As the evening drew on, he grew feverish as if with excitement.

''Tell me what's the matter?'' she pleaded. ''Does your head pain you very much?''

A brief smile relaxed the stern lines of his face. "My head's all right," he answered. "It's something inside my head that bothers me. Say, what time is it?"

"Fifteen minutes to seven."

"That's when the night nurse comes on, isn't it?"

"Margaret Flanders? Yes. She's a lovely girl, don't you think?"

"Sure," he said, "Margaret . . . what did you call her?"

"Margaret Flanders."

"Oh," he said, his whole figure relaxing somewhat under the bedclothes, and a frown came on his forehead. "Do you ever call her Madge for short?" he continued, the frown disappearing.

"Don't you think she's much too dignified for a nickname?"

"Hmm," he growled, "I suppose so. Sure she is. Say, tell me on the level, is she late ever?"

"No, nurses aren't often late in this hospital."

"Does she live far away?"

"What a lot of questions," laughed the nurse. "I'm sure I don't know."

"She might be late," he mused heavily. "I sure hope she's on time. Say, what time is it now?"

"Thirteen minutes to seven."

"Thirteen more minutes. Say, did she always look the way she does now?"

He closed his eyes with grim determination and tried to while away the time by counting sheep jumping over a stile. At last the door opened; he heard a murmur of voices; and then he knew the day nurse had gone and that the night nurse had come. He welcomed her with a sudden smile and open eyes.

"Gee," he said, stretching out his hand, "it's great to see you again. This has been a rotten long day. Rotten long. You've no idea."

She made no answer, and he continued to study her with dumb satisfaction as she moved about the room.

"Come over here a moment, won't you?" he pleaded at last. "Say," he continued, when she stood by the bed, "do you know that, if you had red hair instead of that soft brown, and if you were a little different around the eyes . . . I don't know how, I'd feel like calling you Red Madge?"

She smiled on him inscrutably. "And if you were not in a hospital," she replied in a level voice, "and if you wore a cap a bit to one side of your head and pulled down over your eyes, I'd feel like calling you Jimmy Erickson."

His face grew paler and his eyes suddenly wide with astonishment. "Red Madge," he whispered, then he dropped one hand back to cover his eyes. "It *can't* be you! Your hair was red, bright red, and your eyes were different. Say, Madge, *is* it you, honest?"

"Sure it's me, silly."

"But in a hospital?" He raised himself suddenly on one elbow. "What's the game? Aw, go on, you can trust me. You know I'm a silent guy."

"There isn't any game."

He leaned back on the pillows and smiled on her complacently. "Anyway, it's mighty fine to see you again, Madge. Put her here."

They shook hands silently. They were both smiling now, but each in a different manner.

"So you're not here on a game?" he mocked.

"No."

"Say, Madge, you always were a peach on the silent stuff, but I should think you'd loosen up to me. I never did a pal dirt, did I? Maybe there's some way I can help. Is there?"

"You're on the wrong track, Jimmy," she smiled. "There's nothing but red lights ahead on that line. Switch over and get a new start."

He grinned at her contentedly. "You're a wonder, all right," he acknowledged. "I'm sure enjoying your little act, and, believe me, I'm some critic of this sort of a show. But cut the silky stuff, Madge. If you keep on kidding me, I'll laugh myself sick again. All right, if you won't loosen up, I'll leave you alone.

"But tell me this, Madge, where have you been all this time? The old gang is all busted up, the best old gang that ever made life hell for the New York bulls. It was you that held us together, old girl. The count swore you'd double-crossed us when you disappeared two years ago when we was in the midst of our biggest game. You remember the John Gleason stunt we were pulling when you went out of sight? Say, loosen up a couple of notches and give me the straight of it. Why did you cut and run? Or did someone make you run?"

"I want to know first how you came to be laid up here," she answered.

"Then you'll tell me why you ditched us?"

"Sure I will."

"It was that rotten Bull McDonald. You never had no use for him, and I guess you had the dope. You could always sort of smell out a phony crook, Madge. Well, this guy McDonald . . . God, I get crazy when I think of it." His eyes left her face and his lips narrowed to a thin, straight line. "This guy McDonald," he continued after a pause, "got Jess Wildcome for his lady, and he was sure strong for her."

"That pale-eyed thing?" remarked Margaret scornfully.

"Sure," grinned Jimmy, "he never had no taste. He never had no eye for the right thing. He knows about as much about girls as I do about Shakespeare." He paused to gloat over his metaphor. "I got a hunch that's about as close to nothing as there is," he continued. "But that's not all. Not by a lot. No, the sweetest part of it was that that fat-headed bum thought *I* wanted Jess. Why, if he'd get a pair of glasses, he wouldn't want her himself." He laid a hand upon Margaret's, and his eyes went soft. "Besides, you know where I'd hang out if I got a chance."

She drew her hand away, and her eyes were vague.

Jimmy sighed. "Anyway," he went on, "once this mutt got the bulge of the idea that I was pining away for Jess, he went the limit. I happened to have a glass of beer with her in McCarthy's one night and in come Bull McDonald and pipes us off before we got past the foam. He went up to Jess and grabbed her by the shoulder like he owned her. Maybe he did.

"Anyway he got pretty rough. He wouldn't look me in the eye, but he says: 'What the devil are you doing in here with Jimmy? Doing me dirt on the side, eh?' It made me pretty sore to hear a full-grown guy talk to a Jane like that, even if she does look like an advertisement for the Salvation Army. I says very soft to Bull, and speaking like a gentleman: 'Cut out the rough, Bull, and stow the Bluebeard stunt. She ain't got no key to no secret chamber.'

"At that, Bull turns on me and begins to cuss me. I guess he was a sailor or something once, or maybe he used to drive mules . . . anyway the way he swore sounded like Billy Sunday on a drunk. It got under my skin more than it should have, maybe. Anyway, I planted him on the chin while he was still going full blast.

"That busted the music box, all right. He went down in a heap. Jess screamed, of course. She never had no sense. But I got her by the arm and kidded the bouncer along with a five-spot, and we managed to get out of the place.

"The next day I heard that Bull McDonald was on my trail with a gun. Happy Pierson tipped me off. But I didn't pay any attention to him. Happy has a way of handing out the bull, you know. Well, that's all there is to it. I was coming out of the alley when it happened. The yellow dog didn't give me a chance. Stepped up behind me and says down low: 'I got you, Jimmy, damn you, and you'll never have to be got a second time!' I whirled around, and the gun went off at the same time. I woke up here.

"Did I tip off the police? Say, am I a rotter? Not me. The police are all right, but once in a while they happen to get track of things. They might get Bull before I do, that's all. And when *I* get Bull. . . ." He closed his eyes and smiled.

"Bull is a cur," said Margaret. She clenched her hands fiercely. "Sometimes I wish I were a man. God, how I wish it."

"You're all right as you are," stated Jimmy critically. "I wouldn't have you changed. Not any way. No. But say, let me in on the Gleason stunt, will you, and how you disappeared?"

"It's a long story, Jimmy."

"I hope it takes all night," he grinned. "Won't it be rich to tell the straight stuff to the boys when I get out of this?"

She strummed the slim fingers of one hand meditatively against her chin, and a faint smile of reminiscence touched her lips. "It seems as if I have to dream back into another life just to remember it," she began. "You recall we were trying to get from this John Gleason the paper containing the assay of a mine in California?"

"Sure," said Jimmy. "Didn't the count and I trail him all the way across the continent? The game of it was that he knew that our gang was on his track, and he knew both the count and me. I'll bet he didn't close his eyes half an hour at a time all the while we were tracking him. He sure looked dead for sleep when he hit the Grand Central in this little old town.''

"You boys did a good job, all right," she said. "You'll know just how good it was when I get through with my story. But the point was that he reached New York, and I rented a swell apartment opposite his hotel."

"Sure," said Jimmy, "you were to keep watch on him, and a bad job you made of it, too, Madge. I guess it was the first bad job of your life."

"The best job I ever did," she said with a strange smile. "The very best, Jimmy, and yet I was trying my hardest at the rottenest game I ever tried. Oh, it seems a long, long time ago, Jimmy."

"Go on," said Jimmy. "Cut out the sighs and tell me the dope. This is getting pretty deep for me."

She regarded him half with wonder and half with amusement, as a child looks upon a playmate after years of separation. "I did keep watch on him," she said at last. "I saw him register at the hotel across the street from my apartment, just as we expected he would. Then I waited for him to come out. I knew that he daren't stay inside with that assay in his pocket. He wouldn't be able to meet his financier until the next day. In the meantime he would want to be with people. I knew he would not dare to sit in a room for fear he would go to sleep and, once asleep, he never knew when we would get at him. So I waited just inside the door of the apartment house and pretty soon, sure enough, out he came and stood on the steps of the hotel.

"He looked mighty big, standing over there. It looked a larger job than I could tackle. But even then I didn't dream just how big a job it would be. I had made up my mind to a game. I had a box of knockout pills, and I determined to get him into my apartment and give him one." She stopped, shivering slightly, and closed her eyes. "I ran down the steps of the apartment house just as he started down his steps on the opposite side of the street," she continued, "and walked a bit down the street and then started to cross to his side."

"By Jove," exclaimed Jimmy, "this is as good as a horse race, to hear you tell it. Go on."

"The street was covered with hard snow," she said, avoiding Jimmy's intent eyes, "and that gave me an idea. I reached the sidewalk a few paces ahead of him, and, as I stepped up from the gutter to the pavement, I pretended to twist my ankle, gave a little cry, and sort of collapsed on the snow." Remembering, she threw back her head and laughed low in her throat, an ominous little chuckle. "Oh, Jimmy," she cried, "Sarah Bernhardt never had anything on the way I did that tumble! I lay with one hand on my ankle, and one arm supporting me, and my head thrown back, and my eyes closed. It was a great pose.

"Then I knew he was leaning over me, and I shivered. It was a real shiver, too, because all at once I remembered all the stories we had heard about that silent John Gleason." She smiled reminiscently. "But I didn't find him so very silent," she said. "Anyway, when I opened my eyes a little, his face was close to me. I never saw such a worried face on a man. I guess he hadn't slept for weeks from the way he looked. His eyes you could hardly see, the shadows were so deep around them. All around his mouth ran deep furrows. You boys must certainly have dodged him like his own shadow. But he wasn't done yet. I knew that by the square jaw and the straight set of his lips. I knew I'd have my hands full with him.''

'' 'You have sprained your ankle?' he said.

'' 'Yes,' I said in a sort of breathy voice that went off into a half moan. 'And it hurts awfully!' I stopped a minute and closed my eyes and breathed hard. I could feel his eyes studying me. Then I said: 'Will you please telephone for a taxi or something to take me home?'

''He began to rub his chin as if he were thinking hard. Then he said: 'And leave you sitting on the snow with a sprained ankle? Do you live on this block?'

''Of course, I had a hard time keeping from a grin. It was so easy I was almost ashamed. Gee, I was a fool! 'Yes,' I said, 'I live in that apartment house across the street.'

'' 'I could carry you back,' he said.

'' 'No,' I began, pretending to be pretty weak and incoherent with pain, 'I ... I . . . . ' I broke off as though I couldn't stand it any more, and dropped my face into my bent arm, and burst into weeping. I had found out that most men can't stand to hear a girl cry, especially when you sort of choke up between sobs. I didn't need to cry then, but I wanted to make sure of him. I wanted to do an artistic job that the gang would praise me for. Jimmy, while I lay there crying, I was really thinking of how the story would sound when I told it to you boys.''

''It sounds great, Madge,'' said Jimmy. ''Gee whiz, lady mine, didn't I always say you were the queen of the lot?''

She drew a deep breath through stiff lips. ''Oh, Jimmy,'' she cried, ''I'm ashamed, ashamed to think back to it! What a strange creature I must have been. Anyway I heard him say: 'Come on, I'll have you home in a jiffy,' and then his arms went round me as gently as a mother picks up a baby, and away I went up into the air. He was an awful tall man, Jimmy. And strong? My, he was a regular giant.''

Jimmy scowled grimly. ''I ain't any infant's food baby myself,'' he declared. ''I'd like to meet up with this Gleason chap. Go on. He picked you up in his arms. I got that all right. Huh!''

''He carried me back across the street,'' she continued, smiling faintly, ''and I dropped my head against his shoulders and let out a sob once in a while to make him think I was using all my self-control to keep down a cry of agony. When we stood inside the entrance of the apartment house, I whispered very weakly: 'You may leave me here. I think I may be able to get upstairs.' Then I waited a minute, nearly shaking for fear he'd take me at my word. But not he. He was a dead game chap, all right.

'' 'Where is your floor?' he asked.

'' 'Second,' I said. 'Apartment has the whole floor.'

"And he commenced to climb the stairs with me. Half way up the stairs I thought I'd better faint. The great point was to get him inside my room. After that, things would take care of themselves, but I was deadly afraid he would leave me at the door. So I fainted. Nothing less would have convinced him how far gone I was. I went weak and soft as a rag in his hands. He stopped in the middle of the flight and raised my head to his shoulder so that it wouldn't fall back. Then I felt two hard, cold lips touch mine.''

"Hell!'' cried Jimmy, starting up in his bed. "You felt *what?* Madge, do you mean to say . . . aw, say, this makes me all sick inside.''

He leaned back wearily on the bed and closed his eyes. She continued as if she had not heard him.

"At the door I pretended to get conscious and started taking quick, short breaths. He lowered me to the floor. I opened the door and dragged myself inside. I stood without looking at him.

" 'Thank you,' I told him. 'I . . . I . . . ,' and then I stopped and stood with my eyes closed, groping against the wall for support. The next minute he had me in his arms and took me over to a couch that stood at one side of the room. I opened my eyes. 'I am so sorry,' I said, smiling up to him, 'that I fainted. Thank you so much for helping me home. I can manage now.'

" 'Look here,' he said, 'I know something about sprained ankles. Let me bandage yours.'

"Before I could stop him, he had started to untie my shoelace. It gave me a thrill then, and I went cold. Of course, when he took the shoe off, he would find no swelling. I wondered how I could bluff it through. Then he said: 'Maybe I can bandage it up before the swelling starts.' That gave me a hope again. So I pretended that the pain overcame me again and sank back into the pillows. He was wonderfully gentle while he took the shoe off.''

"I'd like to get my hands on the big stiff,'' growled Jimmy, apropos of nothing.

" 'Now,' he said gravely, 'if you'll tell me where I can get hot water and bandages, I'll leave you to take off the stocking.'

" 'But . . . ,' I began, as if I were going to protest.

" 'Tut, tut!' he said and waved his hand, as if he were brushing away all my arguments into thin air, 'don't be silly about it.'

" 'There's a basin in the bathroom over there,' I said after a little pause, as if I were thinking it over. 'And I think you'll find a roll of bandages in the little toilet cupboard in the same room.'

"By the time I got my stocking off, he came through the door again with a towel thrown over his shoulder and carrying the package of bandages and the basin of steaming water. My, he looked as official as a waiter. I sat on the edge of the couch and held my leg tight with both hands above the ankle, as if I were trying to keep the pain from spreading. He knelt down and took the heel of my foot into the hollow of his hand.

" 'The trouble is,' he said critically, 'that your foot is much too small to walk upon' and here he scowled up to me 'and the heels of your shoes are too high.'

" 'I shall have them lowered,' I said meekly, and put my foot into the water with a little indrawn breath, as if the pain were going. He kept frowning away at my foot which got all pink in the hot water, and then he drew one finger very lightly over the arch of my foot. I turned away and blushed. Oh Jimmy, something snapped inside me then, and I wanted to cry.

"Afterward he dried my foot with a towel. When he came to the toes, he looked up and I had to bite my lips to keep from a smile, it was so tickly. He laughed at me then, and I didn't know what to do."

"Huh," snapped Jimmy, "I'd have punched him on the chin."

" 'It's funny,' said John Gleason. 'Why, your foot isn't as big as my hand. I suppose that's why I can't notice any swelling so far. We must have caught it just in time.'

" 'And how can you be so gentle with such . . . with such . . . ,' I began.

" 'With such big hands?' he finished for me, as he commenced to pass the bandage around my foot and over my ankle. 'Only from long practice in the football training quarters.'

" 'You played football,' I asked him, and I noticed the thick set of his shoulders.

"He pointed to a scar on one side of his forehead. 'That's a touching little reminder,' he said, 'where one of the boys stepped on my face. And it was during a practice scrimmage at that.'

" 'Oh,' I cried, 'what a disgusting game!'

"Indeed, I did hate the game when I saw his poor scarred face. Then just the shadow of a smile touched his mouth. I guess he isn't the kind that smiles often.

" 'Yes,' he said, 'I guess it's only a game for India rubber men like me with hard hands and hard hearts.'

"It made me feel pretty bad to hear him call himself that when there I was being treated by him as if he were my big brother, and me all the time trying some way to do him dirt. When a woman's bad, she's awful, awful bad, Jimmy."

Jimmy was staring moodily into one corner of the room. He made no answer.

"Then he got up and stood towering over me," she went on. " 'Is there anything here with which I can make you a hot drink?' he said.

" 'Oh,' I said, 'don't trouble. I have kept you too long.'

"He smiled at me. 'Not a bit,' he said, and with that started for the kitchen.

"What a clattering he made among the pans. Once he came to the door to ask where I kept the sugar. He had thrown his coat off and stood with an apron tied about his waist. In one hand he carried a saucepan and the rolled-up shirt revealed the corded strength of his arms. Such whip-cord muscles. Then he went back to the kitchen, and pretty soon I heard him singing in a roar of a bass voice:

> Oh, I am a friar of orders gray,
> And down the valley I take my way;
> My long bead roll I merrily chant,
> Wherever I wander no money I want,
> And why I'm so plump the reason I'll tell,
> Who leads a good life is sure to live well.

"When he returned again, he carried a tray all carefully arranged with toast on a plate, a steaming pot of chocolate, a little jar of jam, two butter knives, two pats of butter, and a bowl of lump sugar. He set the card table in front of me, the tray upon it, and then drew up a chair on the opposite end of the table. It made me feel sick to do it, but I had gone too far to draw back now. I reached inside the purse and got hold of the knockout pills.

" 'This is truly domestic,' said silent John Gleason, 'a scene like this may only be found in the homes of married couples after some ten years of living together. Your hair, for instance, is a bit toweled where it rubbed against my shoulder, and I am in my shirt sleeves . . . do you mind? Yes, this is the great test of married life, for after ten years of domesticity we sit thus, and the proof of the happy life is that I do not miss my morning paper, and you are too much interested in your sprained ankle to remember that your hair is in disarray.'

"I smiled a little back to him. I had put in the knockout pills while he was talking. He was looking away at the moment. I guess my hand shook as I passed him the chocolate. He looked down at it and stirred the sugar around slowly. Suddenly he leaned over to me.

" 'Has any one man got a chance against a gang?' he said.

"I went cold inside. I guess my eyes went wide. 'No,' I stammered, 'I guess not. Why?'

" 'Because I have a gang against me,' he said, 'and I am trying to fight them single-handed. I tell you, it is too much of a job for one man to tackle.' Here he set down the cup. 'Will you be a pal to me and help me out?' he said.

"I tried to think, but I felt his eyes burning on me out of the hollow of his face. 'God knows I'll try to do every right thing by you.'

" 'Put it there,' he said, 'you're the real thing, little partner.'

"Well, I shook hands with him, then he went on to say just what was happening to him, how he had started from San Francisco with the assay of a rich new mine and how a gang of crooks had got wind of it, and they were going to try to get the assay from him, and how he hadn't dared to sleep for a week, almost.

"He leaned closer at that and put a hand on mine. His hand was awfully large and cold. 'I've got to sleep,' he said. 'I won't be able to see my financier who would back our mine until tomorrow. I can't last another day. God, no! They will get me before tomorrow.'

"He dropped his face into his hands and groaned aloud. Oh Jimmy, it's a fearful thing to see a big, strong . . . honest man like that groan and give up.

"Suddenly he raised his head and his face was brighter. 'Have you got an extra bed here?' he asked.

"Then I saw what was coming. I was desperate, but I couldn't dodge those questioning eyes of his. 'Yes,' I said.

" 'And may I use it? Be a real pal to me. You've got to hang with me against that gang. They will never dream that I am here. If I leave here, I am lost.'

"Jimmy, I couldn't say no, could I, to a man like that? Then I thought to myself that it would be easy to get the paper from him while he slept.

" 'There's a bed in that room there,' I said. 'Of course you can use it any time.'

"He got up without a word. Now that he felt safe, every line of his face dragged down. He was letting his will go. He walked toward the door I had pointed out, then hesitated, and came back toward me. A wallet was in his hand. When he spoke, his voice came dragging out as if he already was half asleep.

" 'In this wallet is the assay they're after,' he said. 'Keep it for me till morning. Somehow I feel safer with it in your hands.'

"Then he went off to bed. I heard the springs groan as he flung himself on the bed. After a minute I heard his heavy breathing and slipped in to see him. He lay with his arms thrown out crosswise and his head collapsed to one side just as he had fallen. His whole body seemed to be drinking in sleep and rest. I drew the cover over him, went out, and closed the door so that his breathing wouldn't sound in the next room."

"And do you mean to tell me," cried Jimmy, "that he was in that room when I went to see you that day? And that you had the wallet? And that all that stall about your broken ankle which kept you from tracking Gleason was a joke and that you pulled the wool over my eyes?"

"That's it, Jimmy. Will you ever forgive me for it?"

He struck his hand across his eyes. "But why did you disappear afterwards?" A sudden light of horrified understanding broke across his face. "Madge, for God's sake!" he cried. "You didn't go away with Gleason the next day?"

She grew a little pale under his stare. "Wait," she said. "My story is just beginning. I went to bed that night after looking at Gleason again. He had remained in the same position all day. I woke up the next morning to a rapping on my door, then Gleason's voice. 'Hey, there, wake up!'

" 'I am awake.'

" 'Then dress and come out here,' he called. 'I have something important to tell you.'

"I dressed as fast as I could and went out to him. He was a different man, standing in the corner of the room with his hands clasped behind him and most of the lines and hollows gone from his face.

" 'You don't seem to be limping this morning,' he said.

"I remembered then, and went red and pale, I guess.

" 'Never mind,' he said, 'where's the wallet?'

"I gave it to him without a word. He looked to see that the assay was there.

All my world was whirling around in my head. I felt helpless as a baby before him.

" 'Now,' he said, 'I'm going to give you a straight talk, Red Madge.'

"I shrank away from him when I heard that name, and I guess my eyes were as big as moons.

" 'Oh,' he said, 'don't faint away. I knew you the first moment I clapped my eyes on you. You should have known I would. Yours isn't a common face, my dear, and your hair isn't a common color.'

"Here he grinned a little, and I hated him with all my heart."

"Good for you," said Jimmy. "Now you're talking."

" 'Did you think you took me in with that circus fall?' went on John Gleason. 'My dear girl, it was very badly done. You should learn more finesse. It was very bad indeed. If you are going to be a crook, be a clever crook. The one thing the world can't forgive a thief is stupidity. And did your pals call while I was asleep? And did you double-cross them because you hadn't the heart to give away the poor, simple-minded, heavy-handed blockhead who lay fast asleep in the next room? Why, this is as good as Shakespeare brought up to date.'

"I simply dropped into a chair, and buried my face in my hands, and cried. I hadn't any more courage. But pretty soon I felt his hand on my shoulder, and he was saying little comfortable things which didn't mean anything but made me stop crying. And then he wiped my face with his big handkerchief, and patted my head, and said I would be all right in the end.

"Oh, Jimmy, how he talked to me then. He told me all about the life I was in. He told me where it would all end, and he told me what every woman's happiness really consists of, and how I was bound to miss it all. Then he talked about his home, and how he had been a boy, and about his mother, and the good, clean people he had always lived among.

" 'You haven't had the chance, Madge,' he said, 'not half of a chance. Everything went wrong with you from the first. All that you have saved is a clean body, but what a topsy-turvy, twisted mind you have, Madge! My dear, they have spoiled everything about you, these dirty curs who have exploited your cleverness. They have spoiled everything about you except the possibility of a return to the dear, quiet ways of good womanhood.

" 'Now listen to me. You are going to put everything you have in a heap, your money and your trinkets and your clothes, and you are going to burn it all up, all except enough to wear. And when you burn those clothes, you will burn your past. Here is two hundred dollars of clean money. Take it and make a clean start. Start all new. Get simple clothes. Go to work at honest work. Be a trained nurse. Learn to *give,* instead of always trying to *get* something for nothing. The more you give out of an empty heart the fuller that heart will grow with happiness.'

"He said a little more, and then he got up and shook hands with me, and I promised him, man to man, to try to do as he told me to do. Then he walked out of the room and out of my life.

"That's all, Jimmy, except that I have tried hard these two years to do as he told me, and I am very happy, and very sad, too. And I hope you won't hate me for double-crossing you that time."

He drew a deep breath and closed his eyes. "You're so far away from me, Madge," he said. "There is a whole world between us. You belong to such men as John Gleason now, and my hands fall away from you, Madge, because they are . . . slimy."

Jimmy fell strangely silent during the rest of his convalescence. His eyes followed Madge dumbly about the room, but he rarely spoke. The wonder and the aloofness had never gone from his gaze, and sometimes it hurt her like a spoken reproof, but she went on her way. His recovery was rapid now, and she watched his increasing strength with a vague dread of the day when he should walk out of her life and disappear among the shadows of New York.

But it chanced that on the evening of his release from the hospital it was her night off, and she was curiously happy and anxious at the same time when he asked her to go out with him. It was a crisp February night, glitteringly clear, and, as Jimmy took the fresh sweep of the outdoors for the first time in many weeks, his shoulders snapped back and his chin went high.

"Let's walk," he said, "just walk and walk till we get tired, and after that . . . well, after that, I suppose it's good bye. What a long good bye it will be, Madge, eh?"

She looked at him closely but made no answer, and they walked on without direction. They came to the Fifty-ninth Street bridge and turned onto it instinctively. At the central arch they stopped. For half an hour neither of them had spoken.

Before them stirred the ominously lighted shadows of the East River, and on either side the lights of Brooklyn and New York blinked through the night. Jimmy took off his hat.

"Madge," he said, "in a few hours most of those lights will go out and you will be in bed and fast asleep, but I go back to the other life, to the shadows that run always under the lights. Ain't it queer how there are two worlds inside this funny old life of ours? There's your life with the steady happiness that keeps on and never changes, and there's my life where the lure and the draw is the big drunk of the gambling chance. There's the calm old age at the end of your life, but at the end of a life of a guy like me there's just a . . . morning after. What a funny old world.

"By rights," he went on, "we should be standing on opposite sides of this bridge, there's such a river in between us." He groaned faintly and turned to her and tilted her head so that her steady eyes looked up to him. "And still I love the gambling chance," he muttered. "Madge, dear, there's only one fine thing in my life, and that's loving you, and honest to God, I've kept my life clean of other women since I met you. Madge, is it a gambling chance? Will just plain love ever make a guy like me worthy of a girl like you?"

She drew his arm closer about her and smiled gravely up at him. "Sometimes

I don't care the least bit about worthiness," she said, "but I like you a terrible lot, Jimmy . . . oh, such an awful lot you'd never guess!"

"Madge," he whispered, "you're not kidding me along? You wouldn't double-cross me now? Madge."

A moment later he stepped back from her with a sunken head.

"Aw, what's the use?" said Jimmy. "I've made a rotten mess of things, Madge, and why should I mess up two lives instead of one? And how could we get married? God, what a fool I am. The bunch of fancy keys I've been collecting all my life was lost at the hospital. It'll be a long time before I can break back into the old game without them."

She handed him the bunch of keys. "I got them from the clerk," she said. "I thought maybe you wouldn't want them back, so I didn't say anything. Jimmy, do you need them terribly bad? Jimmy dear, can't we do without them? They won't unlock any door where we both can enter now. Won't you make my way your way? We can go to some other place where the old gang can't draw you back, and we can start all over and pull together hard, and make a home."

"Madge," he said, "what is it they say when a man is getting well after being terrible sick?"

"Convalescence," she said.

"Well," he said after a silence, "I reckon I've been sick most of my life, but I'm all well now, Madge, all well."

A light jingling, a glittering of falling light, and a splash came up to them from the river far below.

"If the New York bulls knew what had just happened, Madge," said Jimmy Erickson, "I think they'd all have a drink to celebrate."

THE SECOND CHANCE

Frederick Faust

In the 1930s Faust wrote seven stories about the sinking of a passenger liner he called the Yorktown, *and each story was told from the perspective of a different passenger. Three of these* Yorktown *stories appeared in* McCall's *in 1935 and one in* Argosy *in 1937. "The Second Chance" remained unpublished at the time of Faust's death along with two others. It was finally published in* The Faust Collector. *Eventually all seven stories will be gathered together in book form.*

Louise Campbell wakened in the night with a racing heart and smallness of breath, as though the darkness were stealing her life. The panic had jerked her upright in bed before her hand found the electric switch. Even with the light on, she still felt the horror near and seemed to see a withdrawing vapor of darkness. Two bells sounded so far and faint on the ship that they were hardly more real than thought. It was one o'clock. Only an hour and a half before the heavy drug had closed her eyes. Now she could only sleep with a dangerous quantity of the narcotic. The one mercy for which she could thank God was that in late June He sent the dawn early.

She lay back on the pillows. The doctors told her that complete relaxation was almost the equivalent of sleep, but she could not relax until she had found a subject for pleasant thought, and of late she had searched too often among her memories, as one might flutter the pages of a thick book, without finding the happy places. That fumbling through the past became a frenzy. She tried to look forward, but the daydreams also, which had been the most soothing prelude to sleep, those sky-blue fancies which often had made her laugh softly in her bed, would come to her no more. She was walled within the continually shrinking space of the present moment.

On deck breathing would be easier, but the thought of making the effort to rise and dress made her heart shudder with weakness. Yet, she realized, to lie awake in the cabin would be a nightmare more horrible because it was conscious. Experience helped her as a whip helps a slave. She got up at once and went to the clothes closet.

On the left were lounging gowns and dressing robes and exquisite colorful embroideries. In fact, that had been her chosen style of dress for all occasions of the day or night until her illness of three years before. She had been able to dress like a girl then because Time had scarcely handled her for thirty-seven years, leaving to her always the same blue and golden beauty. But, between the days when she entered and left the hospital, his fingers had bruised her face—horribly beneath the eyes and striking all of the sweet childishness from her mouth. Until then, she had spent her days like an immortal—and now she must dress in black to escape observation. Over the gowns she ran her desolate hands to make a choice among the shadows. Her body was still fresh, lovely, and young, but she dared not show so much as the grace of her arms through any film of gauze or lace, the contrast so darkened the guilty ugliness of her face.

It was only when she was done that she ventured to put on the bright things in her wardrobe. In that way, she sometimes could forget the picture that waited when she lifted her glance to a mirror. She could avoid the glass except when she was doing her hair or putting on the dull make-up with which she tried to obscure her features a little, but, whenever she had to confront that new image, strange thoughts would fly in her mind. It was as though a witch had cursed her; or again, because of the courage that was her virtue, she let conscience say that her new face was that of the evil she had done. It was the immediate cause of the change that she revolted against most, for surely all modern good sense tells women that they need not have children unless they wish to. The operation itself had been simple enough; it was the unlucky complications afterward that gave her a month of agony which was written in her face. When she went into the hospital, she looked not more than her late twenties; when she came out, she seemed twenty years older.

So she dressed herself in black. When she drew on her slippers, she smiled a little because she remembered the day on the beach when Anton Wolf, the strong man, had held both her feet in the grasp of one hand and had lifted her above his head so that she stood at a balance with her outstretched arms while the crowd took breath before it could shout. The Sunday supplements had rejoiced the world with that picture, but, ah, what a pity that the camera had not been able to show the millions the blue and gold of her beauty and the sunny gilding of her body! Why had not color photography been perfected? Science, like a stupid wastrel, had let her slip through the fingers of time, and all that the world had of her was the gibbering shadow of Louise Lombard which had walked across some miles of Hollywood negatives, a poor, poor ghost.

She put on a beret to cover the shine of her hair and a cloak whose stiffened collar could be drawn like a mask over her face. Before she left the room, habit made her glance over it. She could escape from it now, but she would have to return. The time had gone when every step she took might be toward an adventure. The men were lost to her; she was anchored in herself. And then her eye lighted on the full vial of veronal. Why had she never thought of it before? That, of course, was the easy way out—so far out that there would never be any return. She picked up the vial and went up at once to the promenade deck.

There was a moon above a softly blowing mist, and the sea flowed quietly away beneath with a tarnished sheen. She gripped the rail with both hands and looked up. If there had been one star, or the thinnest edge of the moon's brilliance, she would have felt that she could live; but a denser fog rolled in, and she breathed the cold of it. She had tried before, many times in the last three years since the day when Eddie Steinworth had told her that she no longer was worth a damn in the movies. Not that the movies mattered so much; men had been her profession, her career, her triumph, but now, when men looked at her, they narrowed their eyes and disgust curled their lips. Once she had lain down with a gas tube between her teeth, but the first sweet, horrible taste of the stuff ended that attempt. She had tried a revolver, steadying her wrist with the grasp of her left hand, forcing the gun up until the chilly lips of it touched her temple. She had leaned for an hour at a fortieth story widow, but her arms had stiffened and would not let her slip away into freedom. But veronal would make everything so easy.

She went into the smoking room, empty at this hour except for a poker game of five at one of the larger corner tables and two other smaller groups. She sat at a side table with her back toward the rest, the collar of her coat well raised as Bliss, the fat-faced smoking-room steward, approached. The flow of his body into a great, outstanding belly filled her with an unnamable disgust. He put down a small plate of sandwiches, a silver dish whose compartments contained salted almonds, green olives, little roasted peanuts.

"Take that stuff away!" she commanded.

"Certainly, madame," said Bliss, picking up the dishes. He did not need to exercise any self-control; the fat swinishness of his good nature was never perturbed.

"Bring me a French vermouth," she ordered.

"With lemon peel?"

"Yes," she answered.

Of all her men, what one would she wish to have filling the chair opposite? Those she had married and divorced were most easily brought to mind. They were all alive; any one of them might actually be on this ship and that was strange, considering how dead they were in her mind. Even Barney Shay, who had married her on her eighteenth birthday, was only sixtyish now. She thought of him almost with kindness because, unlike the others, he had not learned to hate her after she drained him of money and cast him off. Cecil Warren, her youngest and last, was a dozen years younger than she. He would look more like a son than a husband now. He had been her most disgraceful mistake, just a bit of bad thinking and carelessness. It was ironically proper that he should have been the ruin of her beauty. He had lived beside her like a mortal near a goddess, but, after the operation, he had looked at her once and disappeared. The others had been bounders, playboys, or headlong egotists, but Cecil Warren was simply contemptible. Yet it was he who would have been the father of the child! If she had gone through with the thing, perhaps that curse of sudden age would not have come over her face; perhaps, when the child lay in her arms, a normal instinct would have enriched her with happiness. But she always had detested children, and, when she thought of the nameless, faceless, unborn thing, she felt only a sickness of body and mind.

The fat hand of Bliss, dimpling at the wrist, slid the vermouth onto the table before her. She paid with a dollar bill and swayed her head a little to dismiss him, yet she found in herself a slight gratitude to the gross steward because he reminded her that men, for whom she had existed, are all insatiable pigs. She had a right to despise them and their greed far more than she regretted any evil she had done. She poured the veronal, to the last drop, into the glass and, holding up the pale gold of the liquor, watched the highlight that trembled in the heart of it; then she raised the daintily curving brim to her lips and lifted her eyes to the future.

The glass was cold. The chill from it struck through her entire body as though, at that moment, she had stepped from warmth and light into outer darkness. The poisoned vermouth moistened her lips, but they would not part to receive it. Bliss would find her sleeping too heavily to be roused; she would be carried to the ship's hospital where that iron-faced Doctor Nash would look at her and quickly understand. She would soon be gone, and the ship would travel on with all its lights shining, its passengers deep in the slumber of the well fed, its lookout peering anxiously through the mist. But they could not see even as far as the first step of the journey which she was to make alone.

She lowered the glass. Except for the last three years she had never been alone. Wherever she went, men appeared as mysteriously as migrating birds, and it was unnatural that she should drop beyond ken unattended. She was ready to leave a life which she detested, but she could not go out alone.

Other failures made it easier for her to give up this attempt. She rose with a sudden shrug of her shoulders and went quickly out onto the promenade. The mist was less, or the moon seemed stronger on the starboard side where the long row of steamer chairs had been folded and roped in standing groups except for one blanketed figure which still reclined in a solitary chair. It was only recently that loneliness in others had attracted Louise Lombard, and she recognized the novelty of the attraction as she veered a little toward the sleeper. It was a woman. Not the moonlight but a very dim glow from a window fell on her face, and Louise Lombard sheered away suddenly.

It was Katherine Wayland who was hurrying to Europe to join her husband before her child was born. She looked paler than ever and yet ethereally pretty, also; the full coming of womanhood made the face of the girl lovely, but even the doubled folds of the blankets could not hide the swollen distortion of her body.

Louise Lombard spat out a breath and then ran her hands down over the slender smoothness of her body. There are two kinds of women, she thought, and there have always been two kinds; and God must have intended it so. Just as some men hoard their money, adding bit by bit to build up security, there are others, her men, who threw it to the wind of a good time. Also, everyone has a right to her own opinion.

She made the round of the deck slowly because her thoughts stopped her now and then. When she came to the port door of the smoking room, she looked in not with any purpose of entering but because she had a curious desire to see the shining of that glass of golden vermouth which had death hidden so carefully under the bitter of the wormwood. She was in time to see Bliss pick up the abandoned drink and carry it toward the bar; he was still in profile when he poured the vermouth down his throat.

She started to cry out that it was poison; the doctor would prevent danger with a stomach pump. But then she realized how much that confession would mean. She had boarded the ship under an assumed name with some difficulty, but under the pressure of such a circumstance her identity was sure to come out, and how the newspaper bloodhounds would fasten on that story: LOUISE LOMBARD ATTEMPTS SUICIDE AT SEA. FORMER SCREEN BEAUTY . . .

After the first impulse to give the warning was checked, she thought of another thing that was important. She could not tell how the veronal killed and whether, before the end, there were nausea, a swelling or distortion of the face, frantic struggles against death. But Bliss would show her the entire truth, and, if it were not too revolting, she could follow his involuntary example. She felt no pity. Bliss was only one of the swine, and it did not matter when his ghost went stumbling, blubbering, arms a-grope through the outer darkness. And if she went on, quickly, how could she be supposed to know what had happened? She went on quickly.

An ecstasy possessed her, a bodily sensation of delight. The stupid pleasure of most women is merely to bring life into the world, she felt, but Louise Lombard was handling death, literally tasting it with an exquisite connoisseurship. She hardly knew where she walked, except that she had seen the pale, suffering face of Katherine Wayland somewhere.

An appetite for more delicious knowledge drove her. Then she was again at the open door of the smoking room. She looked into the bar and saw Bliss, sagging like a loosely-filled sack, perched on one of the tall stools, yawning; because it was after two o'clock, the fool would be thinking. But ah! The depth of knowledge which only she, of all the world, could impart to him. It was right that the swine should die first and trample the way out before the more elected spirits of men and women followed.

Here the *Yorktown* swayed a little to the starboard and kept on listing a trifle as though a very long, gentle wave were passing under the keel.

It was best for her, under any circumstances, not to be found staring through the doorway at the sinking body of Bliss. So she went forward and leaned at the rail. The *Yorktown* began to shudder, and an odd drumming sound passed through the ship. Something slid out of the fog near the prow at the same time; it was long and very low and dark. Vaguely she saw it nuzzle the bow just where it curved out to the full width of the hull. Then it slid on down the side with a decreasing speed.

Something showered up from it, and here the moon parted the mist to show her that that whirlwind in still air was composed of gulls and sooty terns which rose and fell like the swirling head of a fountain. They seemed to have risen, parasites, from the back of a sea-monster. But now she saw that it was a ship with sharp bows, a deck almost awash out of which sprouted the stumps of three masts. The fallen spar pointed like a cannon at the great wall of the *Yorktown*. No bow-waves curled from the cutwater of the derelict, no wake left a widening pattern behind her; she came with the sea, softly. Already the birds began to drop back to her, settling on the sway of cordage, balancing their long, curved wings; then a deeper fog swallowed her astern.

Louise Lombard became aware that the throbbing shudder no longer troubled the *Yorktown*; the hum and quiver of the engines had ceased. A false sense of motion still seemed to carry them forward, but Louise knew that they were lying still, as though the touch of the derelict had poisoned the life of the great ship. She thought of Bliss, the fat steward, yawning on his stool in the bar, then she went up to the boat deck and up to the game deck above it to sit on a bench and watch the interweaving designs of the fog beneath the moon.

Her thoughts would not progress; something happening to the ship held her in the present moment. She heard feet thumping over the decks at a run; bells rang as dimly as voices heard through the deadening wall of ether. Then the whistle blew six short blasts, followed by a long hoot.

All the *Yorktown* wakened at once. Officers, sailors, appeared on the boat deck; a murmur of feet and voices poured upwards. They were rising about her like a swarm. She leaned over the rail and called to a sailor who was coiling down a rope on the deck just beneath: "What's it all about, Jack?" He looked up at her so suddenly that his mouth pulled open; then he bent his head and went on silently with his work. Down on the promenade were many people gathering. She heard now and then a sharp outcry, the rest murmurs.

A tall, bending figure in uniform paused beside her: "Go down to the boat deck!" he commanded. "Get down there at once!"

The officer went on, and Louise Lombard sat where she was, dreaming that perhaps she was not to die alone, after all. The bench, she noticed, had altered a little beneath her as though the ship were being lifted from the stern by a wave that never ebbed, and it was this which made her see that the *Yorktown* was slightly down by the head. An instant later a scurry came up all the four companionways from the promenade, a scurrying, the whisper of dresses like the wind, and a rapid little murmur suppressed, not unlike the noise of a stream along a hillside. These were all women or children tugged along by the hand. The officers met them with pointing arms and sharp commands, shepherding them in small groups in front of the double rows of the boats. The women seemed trying to make it all a whispering secret, but the big-throated men were giving the mystery away.

A voice called, quiet with awe: "Billy! Billy! Where are you?" Then, in a sudden screech: "Billy! Who's seen my boy? He's in shorts. He's only ten. Billy! Billy! Oh, my God, where's my son!"

The eyes of Louise Lombard half closed; she drew in a long breath through her teeth with a sound like straining water. She told herself at once that she did not care. Her unborn son had killed her beauty, and, even if he had lived, what return would he have made to her for that?

A boat filled on the port side. One of the officers was handing in the passengers and reassuring them: "Now this is going to be all right. Just keep your heads. Sit tight. We've got to have these drills. Sit fast and hold on a little. No more danger than in an elevator."

The boat filled; the davits bent outwards. Two sailors began to hand the ropes of the tackle, and the lifeboat dropped gently from view. Louise Lombard, surveying the vastness of the *Yorktown,* found it hard to believe that even the vast throat of the ocean could swallow such a morsel, but she knew that the ship was being abandoned in the middle of the sea. Boats swung out on the starboard and to port. They were lowered away.

"Shall I help you to a place in a boat?" asked a voice above her. Louise Lombard looked up at Michael Carmichael, who was lifting his gray cap to her. She had seen him here and there, moving with a quiet step and sometimes with a faint smile. A whisper among the passengers had told her his name. He was someone important. Now that she saw him so close she realized that he had been walking up and down in her thoughts since her first glimpse of him. The treacherous moon, at this moment, divided the mist and looked straight down upon her face, but no shadow of surprise or disgust appeared in Michael Carmichael. He held out his hand, smiling still. "Won't you let me take you to a boat?" he repeated.

The quiet of his eyes told her that he was seeing everything, and yet to him certainly she was appearing as no less than a woman. Thin images out of the past rushed through the eyes of Louise Lombard faster than even landscapes whirled away across the windows of a train. She knew that she was confronting at least a reality worth more than all the shadows which had filled her brain, like a sick man who tastes wine for the first time, and on his final day.

"I'll stay here . . . a while," she said, and turned her back on him. She faced a blankness of moving fog with silly little creatures astir in it. All the lives on the *Yorktown* were so petty compared with the one man she might carry down.

That deep voice continued beside her: "You know we all can have the same idea when we're tired . . . but sleep and a touch of friendship make a difference, don't you think? Please let me take you to the boats."

Because there was no sham of priestly unction for the very sake of this utter reality, grief wrung the soul of the woman. In her soul there was little taste of the distinction between grief and any other pain. That was why she whirled about and cried: "Ah, damn the boats! I'll stay here!"

Even then he waited for a moment until she turned her back the second time. At last he was gone, leaving her in such a blankness that she saw and heard nothing except the chirping voices and the dwarfed forms that were in her past. She wished she had asked him why he bothered about her. She yearned desperately to learn what effect her bruised and starving face had had upon him. She knew the answer would come from a profound knowledge of life which she herself could neither touch nor see.

Something like a padded fist struck the *Yorktown* and shook it slightly with a following sound like the rush of wind or of water. The long deck heeled to the starboard and sent her staggering across to the lower rail. There had been a list of twenty or thirty degrees before the ship steadied again. It seemed to be sweeping sideways on an unending wave.

She saw the clumsy women tumbled in heaps on the deck beneath. Some of them screamed. Some of them clung together as though the water were even now closing over them. She wanted them all! She grudged every boatload that sank from the davits toward the second chance of life. Yet how good would that chance be if the storm, which the falling barometer had promised the evening before, should arrive? Not to go alone into the outer night but in a flock swifter than sea birds? Let all the future days be shut away—all the days for all of them.

The noise from the men that stirred her, as though her own throat uttered it, had ended. Now the women on the boat deck were being herded to the starboard side alone. A few random exclamations told her why: the cant of the vessel made it impossible to launch all the remaining boats on the port side. The gate to safety was narrowing—not half of those who remained could escape through it.

The *Yorktown* was uttering two blasts on the fog horn every two minutes. It was after one of these that a tumult spread all around the hidden promenade deck, a yelling of despair as though the sea were reaching now for those unseen men. Up the four companionways came a pressure that staggered the men on guard. They beat that pressure away. It came again. She could hear the blows struck that knocked the mob leaders down.

It was good this way, thought Louise Lombard. Down there on the promenade they knew by this time that half the boats were useless and that the remainder could contain only a portion of their number. They were tasting death not in one great swallow but distilling the cold poison gradually against the palate. It was better, it was perfect this way, for at the best what one of them had rubbed elbows with death daily for three long years? This was merely a little last-minute ripening of their souls before they passed along with her upon the great journey.

A moment of comparative quiet followed, as more boats put off and dropped over the starboard rail. Six of the twelve, well loaded, already had gone down toward safety, when the *Yorktown,* poised for its long downward rush, lifted and trembled like a spear in a hand grasp, and the heart of Louise Lombard trembled also, raised with joy to find in herself no fear.

From the unseen crowd on the promenade deck she heard voices strangled in mid-cry by fear, the trampling of feet like thunder on the horizon, then harsh shouting from the sailors who guarded the companionways. A last rush for the boat deck was starting.

She wanted the stampede to break down the barriers and flood the upper deck because she would be standing here above them, watching the yelling panic which would make all further launching of the boats impossible. So the *Yorktown* would sweep downwards, and the clusters of struggling humanity, like knots of fighting cats, would be swallowed by the same wide throat that drank down the liner. But the crews which manned the companionways seemed perfectly competent to discharge their duty, particularly those who were commanded at the aft-port companionway by the chief surgeon, Doctor Nash. Fresh from the operating room in long white garments, he looked like one who played the ghost in the play, or like an even more symbolic figure. She knew him less by his dim features in the moonshine and more by the extreme rigidity of his military carriage.

Three times a tumbling wave of figures struggled up to the feet of the doctor and fell away again. The fourth effort was more sustained. Men rose as high as the waist above the deck in spite of the poised automatic of the chief surgeon. He leveled the gun; erratic sparks sprang from the muzzle of it. A noise like the chatter of a riveter rattled for an instant in her ears, and the wave of passengers receded. Perhaps one of them had reached Nash with a stabbing knife or a bullet, for he himself faltered backwards, throwing an arm up across his face.

"Now!" screamed Louise Lombard. "Now! Now's your chance!"

It seemed as though those men on the stairway might have heard her. They lunged upwards in uncontrollable numbers that swept the guard aside. An active fellow in a sweater and cap knocked the chief surgeon headlong, picked up his fallen gun, and ran on.

At the three other companionways, as though one break in the dam had ruined the whole strong wall of discipline, the passengers flooded upwards and a new voice, great and wild, rang from the *Yorktown* into the sky. To Louise Lombard they were the mob, the supernumeraries, the color and sound effects of her last and greatest stage. All courage, all steadfast manliness, now would be dissolved in the mob frenzy, she hoped. But no, there were still officers who stood against the rush till they were overwhelmed like small islands by a flood. When she saw this, she looked upwards with a cringing, sudden expectancy; but there was only a luminous entanglement of the fog beneath the moon. She glanced hungrily down again.

A filled boat was leaving the davits when the rush commenced. Perhaps the terror of it made the life crew clumsy, for, while the stern-rope paid out slowly, the bow tackle went on the run and spilled the living cargo. Their screaming shrilled in the top of her brain, diminished, and went out suddenly like fire blown down the wind. The sea had them, and the boat, headed down, dropped, dangling, from view. Then the panic-driven stormed the lifeboats which remained.

To the rearward of that madness other men came more slowly, all those steadier souls who wished for life, but only if there were some dignity in the keeping of it. But the mob had beaten the women down or thrust them backwards, a lighter flotsam, to the rear of the press. That fellow in the sweater who had felled the doctor and taken his gun was now in a boat amidships, active as a fighting ape. With a club in one hand, the automatic in the other, he cleared the benches quickly of the human tumble which had overheaped them. Continually the crowd surged at him and fell back again, dreading him more than it feared the sea. With a voice that shouted hoarse and far through the tumult, like the cry of a seabird against a storm, he picked his crew now. The chosen tumbled aboard to help their master keep back the unelect. He was a man; the rest were nothing.

From that center of glorious action Louise glanced over the fringes of the crowd just beneath her and marked a woman with pale, blown hair who struggled again and again to make forward through some momentary gap in the throng. As the path closed in heavy tumult, she would shrink away once more, desperately shielding her body with her arms. Thrown back from the last effort against the cabin wall, she stared where the despairing are bound to look, upwards. And Louise recognized Katherine Wayland.

A numbness spread through the brain of Louise. She pressed her hands against her body where pain seemed to be. Bitterness was in her mouth. The world receded as once before it had wavered and been lost behind the impenetrable wall of ether, and an overwhelming sense of loss poured through her soul. In that sickness of the mind she turned her head and saw against the lifting port rail of the game deck, like two figures in the sky, tall Michael Carmichael with a woman close to him.

What right have the Katherine Waylands to wear the child-look, the passive despair? And what right had a girl beside Carmichael to smile upwards at him as though she found in him space and future enough to enclose her soul forever? She was that French maid with the pale, pure face which the moon was outlining now in soft fire. But what was she to stand in the midst of such a revelation as Louise Lombard had dreamed of but never seen. Or had she even dreamed of it, in fact? Death could not harm that girl beside Carmichael because, for her, existence was complete. It seemed to Louise that her heart was being crushed between two walls of cruel understanding that had come to her how much too late!

That voice which rang like the distant croaking of a gull came to her again and for a wild moment it seemed to her that it was a bodiless cry rising from her own spirit.

"One more place! One woman for luck!"

It was the man in the sweater, blood-drenched now but still the perfect master of his boat and its crew.

Louise Lombard raced down the nearest steps to the boat deck, to the side of Katherine Wayland. "A place for you . . . if you'll come . . . if you'll fight for it!" she screamed. Katherine Wayland turned her head from that distorted face, but Louise caught hold on her, shrilling: "Stand up, damn you! Stand up and fight for the two of you. There's one place waiting!"

And through a momentary gap she dragged the girl. The gap closed around her, but still she found a way. Her free hand was armed with talons to claw a passage through. The davits were bending, the boat was swaying out, but still it was not clear of the deck when the two women reached it. Louise Lombard looked up at the man in the sweater, a snarling face that dripped with blood.

"Here!" she cried. "This one! This is your luck!" And she thrust Katherine Wayland forward. Many hands, reaching over the gunwale, gripped the loose, falling body and dragged it on board. The boat sank from the davits at once and passed from view.

Louise Lombard watched it disappear, and it seemed to her that something of herself was being launched to find a second chance. The crowd swept her back and forth on waves and counterwaves. The screaming had grown more frightful, but, still with a strange joy, she watched the smooth running of the ropes through the pulleys as the boat descended.

The moon, throwing aside the clouds like bow waves from the prow of a silver ship, drove suddenly near, and Louise Lombard felt the brightness enclose her. The *Yorktown,* lifting her stern still higher, was running downhill toward her grave.

DR. KILDARE'S DILEMMA: A FRAGMENT

Max Brand

With the exception of the first two, all of the subsequent Dr. Kildare stories were written expressly for motion pictures, and Faust even sold screen rights to the characters to M-G-M. However, after each movie was made, he could then sell the story to his book publisher. M-G-M by this same contract reserved the right to make movies of Kildare stories that were not written by Faust, and this they did in DR. KILDARE'S WEDDING DAY. In it, Nurse Mary Lamont is killed. Therefore in the next story Faust himself wrote about Kildare for the studio, "Dr. Kildare's Hardest Case," there is mention of the fact that Jimmy has lost his girl. Faust's personal choice, however, was that Mary Lamont should not die. If he acceded to the studio's storyline in the short novel he wrote for M-G-M, he had his publisher reverse it for the book edition, and the ending was changed so that Jimmy and Mary are still engaged. When William J. Clark was given this unfinished Kildare story to publish in The Faust Collector, *he had to decide which road to take. "Is Mary dead or isn't she?" he asked. His choice was to go along with the studio. Below, since Faust's text has now been restored as he wrote it, Mary Lamont is alive. It is worth adding that this story could not have been filmed, even had Faust been able to complete it, since Lew Ayres, who played Dr. James Kildare in the M-G-M films, was a conscientious objector and refused to serve in the U.S. armed forces. This action on his part led to Ayres's contract being terminated by M-G-M and Kildare's being dropped as a character from the series, which henceforth had Lionel Barrymore as Dr. Gillespie carrying on with a new assistant. Faust, of course, had a much different scenario in mind for his character than it was possible, under the circumstances, for the studio to have brought to the screen.*

I

Pearl Harbor and her forty-sixth birthday came upon Mrs. Florence Harned Wilton at almost the same moment and surprised her into giving up the world, or at least a great portion of it. She closed the Florida house, sold the Wyoming ranch, put the Sixty-third street house on the market, and moved into the Waldorf Hotel, for she realized that the time had come for her to leave the greener pastures and pass into her period of Works and Days. She could not help retaining some of her old habits, such as that lift of the head which discouraged the double chin and gave her an altogether unnecessary air of hauteur. She returned to many things which she had lost or forgotten, and among others she remembered that she had a daughter. It was not that she ever had been moved by any but the most loving thoughts about her child, but, since Sylvia grew up preferring the Harned horses to the Wilton yachts, naturally she had seen less and less of the girl. Now that she renewed their acquaintance, she discovered Sylvia in such a state of mind that she at once called a conference with the girl's father and the family physician, Dr. Randall Eliot.

They met in the Harned double-decker apartment on Fifth Avenue, where Florence really felt more at home than in any other place in the world because she had spent so much time buying the furniture and the rugs which were to match the eighteenth-century English pictures of Benjamin Harned. In later years she left such matters to interior decorators, but, when she had married Ben Harned, she approached the establishment of a home with diligence and the best intentions.

Today, instead of settling down in the library or in the huge living room, she chose to take Ben and the doctor to the small conservatory which overlooked the park because the aquarium was there, and it soothed her to watch the goldfish drift among the water plants like translucent birds through a strange forest. The movement of those tenuous fins, involved and softly curving like mists in the wind, seemed to her the symbol of perfect social grace. She enjoyed all this the more for contrast because her own approach was, as a rule, abrupt to the point of brusqueness. She detested unmannerly creatures who stamped, who banged on the table with their fists, or who lifted their voices like loudspeakers, but she rarely came to the end of a day without doing all three.

As she settled the two men in the little room, she took a good breath and a pleasant look at the fish which shimmered half seen in the water, arranging themselves in lovely Chinese patterns. Then she let forth a blast.

"How long is it since you last looked at your child?" she asked of Benjamin Harned.

"At Sylvia?"

"Have you any others?" snapped Florence Harned Wilton.

He turned a little pink. He could bowl over whole boards of directors with a word, but Florence always angered and frightened him. A sauce, as it were, of sweet and sour, no matter what subject was served.

"Of course not. I see Sylvia nearly every day," he said.

"But do you *look* at her?" asked Mrs. Wilton savagely.

He glanced toward the doctor for support, but old Dr. Eliot was smiling down at his interlaced fingers and was no use whatever.

The mother continued presently: "The point is that the child has gone to the devil."

"What?" cried the father.

"Well, she's on the way, at least," said Mrs. Wilton. "She's lost her grip. Her mind's shattered."

"You're not trying to tell me that Sylvia's mind . . . ?" he said.

"Well, go on . . . finish your sentence," she demanded.

"I mean to say . . . ," he stammered.

"Say it, then. Hysterical. The girl's hysterical," said Florence. "Do you know what she's done?

"Please tell me, my dear," said the father, wiping his face, for he was in a sweat of real anxiety.

"Do you know that she's sold her whole string of show horses?"

"Well, but wouldn't you call that a war measure?"

"War, my foot! What does a baby like Sylvia know about war?"

"But the jumpers . . . you know, everybody's doing it."

"Sylvia isn't everybody, I thank God. She's one of the most selfish little egotists that ever drew breath perhaps, but she's always had her own point of view and kept to it in spite of you and me and the devil, as you very well know, or ought to know. But where do I find her now? Gone to the devil and dragged down into the slums of the city."

"No," gasped Benjamin Harned.

"Don't sit there saying 'no' like a baby blowing bubbles," she shouted. "It doesn't change the fact that she's acting like a common working girl, trudging among the outpatients of a charity clinic. I saw her striding about in clothes at least six months out of fashion and her hair, her lovely hair . . . a completely neglected mess. Hysterical! I tell you, that's a mild word for Sylvia. Something pathological has happened to her. Doctor Eliot, stop sitting there . . . say something . . . you're supposed to keep an eye on this idiot family. Do *you* know anything about this?"

"I do," said the doctor.

"Then why don't you speak up?" she demanded.

"Because I'm asked now for the first time," he answered softly.

"Then quick. What is it?"

"Sylvia has fallen in love," said Dr. Eliot.

"Love? Oh, heavens, is that all? Are you serious?" asked the mother. She sat back in her chair and gave half her attention to the goldfish, mysteriously interweaving, gold and green, through the water.

"Well, that's all right, then, isn't it?" asked Harned. "Love . . . I mean . . . what?"

"I'd say that Sylvia is in rather a bad state, though," admitted Dr. Eliot.

"Ah, would you? In what way?" asked Florence. "If the fellow's married already, there can be a divorce for him, can't there?"

"He's not married," said Dr. Eliot.

"Don't tell me that he's a monk, or something horrible?" she asked.

"The point seems to be," said the doctor, "that Sylvia's been attracted to an extremely old-fashioned young man. You remember reading fairy stories and legends about odd creatures, men and women, who fall in love only once?"

"I remember. I've read such things. And heartbreak, what?" said Harned, recalling more and more of this recondite subject. "They died of heartbreak and all that. Tremendously mid-Victorian."

"My God, Ben, you give me a deep pain sometimes," said Florence.

"Do I?" he asked. "I'm sorry, dear. I didn't mean to be offensive, really. But let's get back to the man. *Why* doesn't Sylvia marry him and have it over and done with?"

"The young fellow in question," said the doctor, "is already engaged to marry someone else."

"Not want to marry Sylvia?" said the mother. "Doctor, don't tell me that he's a psychological freak of some sort?"

"No," said Dr. Eliot. "This fellow appears to be genuinely in love, and that's enough for him."

"Ah? Really?" asked Harned.

"Who is she?" snapped Florence.

"Just a . . . well, just an ordinary hospital nurse, you know."

"You mean a mere nobody?" asked Mrs. Wilton. "I could conceive a young man completely dazzled by someone . . . but a common little nurse? Well, is he a little bit retarded or something?"

"I believe not," said the doctor. "He's not old enough to be well known in his profession, but in his hospital he's considered a genius. You've heard of Doctor Leonard Gillespie?"

"Oh, yes," said Florence. "He's a great name. A mindreader, or something, isn't he?"

"Well, somewhat the same thing . . . a diagnostician," said Dr. Eliot. "And this Doctor Kildare is his assistant. After forty-odd years of work, after hunting half that time to find a brain into which he could pour what he himself knows, just two or three years ago Gillespie ran onto this Kildare and found in him what he wanted. Mind you, it meant for him an opportunity . . . in my profession, it would be called a divine opportunity . . . to learn, but it also meant slaving terribly, night and day, drudging and dredging up facts and yet keeping the instinct clear and clean and fresh so as to look deeper than the eye generally does."

"But I don't understand . . . ?" said Harned.

"Ben, for the sweet mercy of heaven, be still," commanded Florence. "Go on, dear Doctor Eliot, please."

"There's just a whisper abroad," said the doctor, "that this Kildare is a contrary youngster who occasionally wants to work out things his own way and causes a devil of a mess . . . but, as I've said, he's not well known. He's just a young rumor and legend, a bit of gossip, you might say. I learned about him when I began to look into the work Sylvia is doing for the clinic at Blair Hospital.''

"So, now . . . let's have a conclusion," said Florence. "This lad with the extra-size brain is in love with a common nurse. So . . . ?"

"Shall I be brutally frank?" asked the doctor.

"You always are, in the end," said Florence, "so why not now?"

"Well, then, I conclude that, at present, this young Doctor Kildare loves his girl and his work more than he loves anything else. This seems to include Sylvia."

"He knows, of course," suggested Ben, "that Sylvia could buy and build his hospital? Then there's nothing for it but to send the nurse away on a trip and see that she's amused."

"Benjamin, my darling, will you please be quite still for a little moment?" said Florence. "The point is, Doctor, that this Kildare pays no attention to Sylvia, but she still keeps on worshipping at the shrine . . . scrubbing the floor of it, as it were?"

"That, I should say, is just about the case," admitted the doctor.

"Just one moment. There she is now, isn't she . . . ? Oh, Sylvia? Come here a moment, my dear," called the mother.

A young woman came into the doorway and began pulling off her gloves. She wore a tailored suit and a small tweed hat. Her shoes, yellow to go with the suit, were scuffed and dirty.

"Hello, Mum," she said. "How do you do, Doctor? Hi, Pops. You people want me for something?"

"Sit down, sweet. You look tired," said her mother.

"No. I won't sit down," said Sylvia quietly but disposing of the subject with absolute finality.

"The subject we were discussing was young Doctor . . . ," began her father.

"Benjamin!" said his former wife.

He was still.

Sylvia looked about at them. She smiled a little. "You were talking about young Doctor Kildare. Is that it?" she asked.

"Why, we were interested in this new work of yours, darling, of course," said Florence. "And he seems to be a part of it."

Sylvia laughed softly, leaning her head back against the wall. "You've been taking me all apart, haven't you?" she said. "Poor little rich girl and such a good, good boy, and slum clearance, and rest in the country for the ailing poor, such a problem, isn't it all?"

She kept her voice perfectly sweet and low, as the poet recommends, but something alarmed her mother.

"Just relax and be yourself, Sylvia," she said. "It's all right, dear. There are whole regions of happiness in this world that you haven't touched yet. You're just a little overwrought now, my sweet."

"You're too kind, all of you," said Sylvia, without smiling at all.

A maid hurried into the room.

"Telephone for you, Miss Sylvia. The hospital calling."

Sylvia went to answer.

"Did you notice her, Doctor?" whispered the mother. "Did you see her eyes? She frightened me. She's in the most dreadful condition. Why, she's apt to do *any*thing."

The voice of Sylvia came to them clearly, saying: "Yes, yes. No. . . . I do not. . . . 'Not' is the word I used. . . . I'm so sorry I didn't make myself clear. I don't intend to return to the hospital. . . . I'm so glad you understand now. . . . No, I shall not change my mind tomorrow. No, you need not trouble Doctor Kildare. I don't wish to speak to him. . . . Quite final. I'm so sorry. Good bye."

"Ah, that's good, now, isn't it?" said Harned. "She's broken everything off, you see."

"Oh, Ben, you exquisite, witless idiot," said Florence through her teeth.

II

Sylvia came back into the doorway for a moment. "Do you need me here for a review, or may I go take a bath?" she asked.

"Do get your bath," said her mother. "And shall I come and rub the back of your neck? You know that tired place, sweet?"

"Please don't bother," said Sylvia. "Good bye, Doctor. Good bye, Mum. So long, Pops."

She went away, her footfall lost to silence instantly in the thickness of the great living room rug.

"Now, my dear," said Harned, "you've got to admit that she was perfectly let down and easy. She's simply through with a mistake. She's my daughter. That's all."

"Oh God, Benjamin," said Florence, "if she were only your daughter, what a simple problem she would make. Ben, my dear old thing, can't you rally a moment from that fatty degeneration of the brain and see *anything*?"

"Now, please don't get yourself into a state, dear Missus Wilton," said Dr. Eliot.

"I'm not in any state," she answered, "except that I can see that that girl is ready for murder. Relaxed? She's as relaxed as a butcher knife. I only hope it's not her own throat she tries to cut. Doctor Eliot, you *know* I'm right."

"You are indeed," he said.

"And it's a dangerous moment for her?"

"*Most* dangerous, I should say," remarked the doctor.

"But dear heavens . . . God above us," muttered Harned. "*Are* you serious, actually?"

"Be still. My dear old Benjamin, please, please, please be still before you make me start screaming. I want to be calm, and you drive me insane, insane, *INSANE!* It's your idiocy that the poor child has inherited. I'm sure she never got that terrible temperament from me. Doctor, tell me what to do. Shall I go into her room?''

''I don't think you could get in there,'' said Dr. Eliot. ''We must try to have a sedative . . . perhaps brought to her in a drink.''

''She doesn't drink anything . . . hardly water, even,'' said her mother.

''No?'' asked the doctor.

''On account of her damned figure,'' said the mother. ''I don't see how women can be such perfect fools.''

Harned abandoned all pretense of knowing. ''Will somebody please tell me what this is all about?'' he asked. ''The poor girl seemed quite all right to me. A little more polite than usual, I might say.''

''Did you see her eyes?'' demanded his former wife. ''Did you see the stare in her eyes? Listen. Listen.''

They all heard, far away, the tapping of a hand on a door. Then the voice of the maid said: ''Doctor Kildare is here to see you, Miss Sylvia. No, not on the telephone, but in person. . . . Yes, Miss Sylvia. . . . Yes, I shall.''

''Has she told him that she'll see him?'' whispered Florence Wilton.

''I'll tell him that in any case he mustn't leave,'' suggested Harned, starting for the door.

''Benjamin,'' she gasped.

He paused. ''Well?'' he asked. ''And why not? He seems important to us all just now, doesn't he?''

A heavier knock sounded, apparently at the same door.

''It isn't the maid,'' said the voice of a man. ''This is Jimmy Kildare. I want to see you.''

There was a pause. Mrs. Wilton held Harned by both lapels of his coat.

''If you move . . . if you speak . . . if you breathe . . . ,'' she warned.

He did not move or speak or breathe. The knocks came at the door again, much more heavily than before.

''Very well,'' they heard the raised voice of Kildare saying, ''but you won't walk out before you've settled a few of the details. That would be a ratty thing to do. . . . Never mind. I'll wait here at your door.''

''How does he dare?'' asked Florence Wilton, making the words on her lips without breath. ''The clumsy, tactless idiot.''

''In her own house, too, the fool,'' said Harned. ''It's time for me to take a hand out there and. . . .''

''You dare to move, you precious . . . ,'' said his former wife in the same voiceless way.

He did not dare to move. The pause just beyond the living room continued for another vital moment. Dr. Eliot stood up from his chair with the polite smile rubbed entirely from his face. The mother closed her eyes. Harned, gradually partaking of the mutual alarm, watched with fascinated eyes the pulse in the big purple vein that appeared at the side of her throat. He told himself that, after all, she *was* like other women, she *did* feel the emotions of a mother. This was very wonderful, but in his own heart grew a hollow sense of panic.

There was an indeterminate sound in the distance.

"She's opened the door," whispered the white lips of Florence Wilton.

To their straining ears the voice of Sylvia came quite clearly. "I'm afraid it seemed a bit sudden and melodramatic," she said. "But I was tired."

Far more clearly they made out the brusque voice of the young doctor, saying: "I don't think you were very tired."

"Ah, you don't?" from Sylvia.

"We don't need to talk about what's really the matter," said Kildare. "The others don't understand. They'll take your word that it's only a matter of being tired. And that will save your face."

"Save my face?" answered Sylvia, her voice strangely indrawn.

"Never mind about that," said Kildare. "I've brought a few items for you to check. Then we bow you out of the picture."

Out in the conservatory they all heard, or seemed to hear, a faint rustling of papers.

"We don't need to stand here," said Sylvia. "We can sit down in the library."

"Neither of us needs to waste any time," said Kildare. "This is a sort of exercise in algebra . . . we cancel a factor out . . . that sort of thing."

"You have a very odd manner," said the girl.

"I have a damned good reason for having a very odd manner," he told her.

"This ruins everything," groaned Harned, but his words were stifled by his own hand upon his mouth.

"What reason, if you please?" asked the girl.

"Don't be small. Be your full size, please," said Kildare.

Wrangling with her, actually . . . the fool . . . the fool! said the silent agony of the mother.

"In what way?" asked Sylvia, with a growing tension in her answer. "I hope that I've done as much for the hospital as the hospital has done for me."

"This is the way you talk, is it?" asked Kildare with a brutal heaviness. "I thought the whole problem of that out department was settled . . . now it's thrown back on our hands."

"You'll miss the money I've been giving, but I can see to it that. . . ."

"Money? . . . rot," said Kildare. "But the drive and the enthusiasm and the *apparent* kindness that made them love you. . . ."

"They didn't love me. . . ."

"They poured out everything like water for you. But I understand why you walked out."

"You do?"

"We thought you were one of us," said Kildare. "For my part I thought you were grown up. I didn't know you were a baby who still had to be fed with praise."

"I don't have to be."

"And patted on the back and admired," said Kildare, rushing on.

"Jimmy!" cried the voice of Sylvia, broken suddenly. "Don't."

"I didn't mean to go so far," said Kildare. "But you filled the whole situation like a storybook angel this morning . . . and now you're gone."

"I'm not gone, if you really need me," said the shuddering voice of the girl. "Only, let me be alone a minute . . . I mean I don't want to be alone . . . Jimmy, I mean I'm so frightfully miserable."

"Are you, Sylvia?" he asked, very gentle. "What is it?"

"It's a ghastly headache. I think it's migraine. It drives me entirely crazy."

"I'll tell you what," said Kildare. "You go to bed and rest, will you?"

"Shall I?" asked the girl.

"Oh, dear heavens," whispered the mother, "she loves him. How she loves him."

"That's right. You try to get some sleep," said Kildare.

"You order it?" she asked.

"As your doctor."

"As my doctor?" she laughed a little. "Yes, Doctor," she said.

"And then tomorrow or this afternoon I'll ring you."

"This afternoon . . . please?" she said.

"This afternoon, of course," said Kildare. "I'm mighty glad this wasn't a real break."

"You don't despise me too much for nerves and things?"

"I know what headaches can do. Now get in there and dive into bed. Quick. . . . Are you there . . . ? Never mind undressing. Lie flat on your back. Your eyes closed? Good girl. And good bye."

"Don't let him go," murmured Florence Wilton, unable to move. "Bring him out here, Benjamin. . . . I hope I'm not going to faint. Doctor? He's a fool, and the girl's throwing herself right at his feet. Headache, indeed!"

Harned returned with a strongly built young man beside him, a blunt, fighting jaw, and a look about the eyes of dissipation, or of overwork.

"This is Sylvia's mother, Missus Wilton," said Harned, "and here's Doctor Eliot, who's taken care of us all. When you called, as a matter of fact, we were all talking about Sylvia. She hasn't seemed very well, and we thought you'd add your advice. Won't you sit down with us?"

"Thank you," said Kildare. "Are you Randall Eliot? Yes, I've read your two books. The second one was a little hard for me, but I managed it. It seems a very beautiful piece of work, sir."

"I don't suppose Gillespie had time for it?" asked Eliot a little wistfully.

"I read the last chapters aloud to him . . . his eyes aren't perfect any more, you know," said Kildare. "But I'm afraid he doesn't agree with you as I do. He still thinks J. R. Hammond's work is the best word on the subject."

"Ah . . . exactly . . . kind of you," said Eliot, disappointed in spite of this young man's admiration. "Now suppose we come to the subject of Miss Harned. What do you think?"

"Your opinion comes many, many years before mine, sir," said Kildare with such an honest modesty that Mrs. Wilton looked again at him, blinking her eyes a little.

"They've had *my* opinion," said Eliot. "Now let's have yours."

"Of course, for your regular fee," said Harned.

"Benjamin," said the silencing lips of his former wife.

"My dear Missus Harned," said Kildare, "your daughter has spent money by the tens of thousands on our hospital. We couldn't pay her back . . . not with blood. But it seems to me that she's suffering from a severe emotional strain. I hoped that we'd been helping her by keeping her interested and working at the hospital. And just now I was . . . er . . . bullying her a little and pretending to be angry because she was leaving us. So she's back again . . . but I'm afraid that I'm making a blundering diagnosis here, sir."

"Not at all, but just coming to the point in a few words?" said Eliot.

"What I suggest has an old-fashioned savor to it," said Kildare. "It sounds like a grandfather's tale. But, actually, I think Sylvia is very, very deeply in love."

A great accumulated breath issued from the lips of Mrs. Wilton.

Harned said, staring at Kildare: "Doctor Eliot seems to agree with you."

"Ah, does he? I'm glad to be on your side of the fence, sir," said Kildare. "If you agree, then I suppose we can almost conclude that the diagnosis is right."

"And then the next step?" asked Harned dryly.

"The next step is to find out the name of the man, I suppose," said Kildare. He felt all their eyes upon him and grew a little conscious of his clothes, which were in fact as graceless and shapeless as old bags.

"Perhaps," said Mrs. Wilton, "we might throw some light on that subject?"

Dr. Eliot broke in in a sharp voice: "I don't think so . . . not as yet. But we'll do our best when we can."

III

Dr. Eliot discovered that he was going Kildare's way and drove him back to the hospital. It was an early spring day but winter had come back to ice the streets of Manhattan and blow a loud horn around its corners. Dr. Eliot drove with his chin dropped into the scarf that swathed his throat.

"Since you'll be seeing her almost every day at the hospital," said the veteran, "you'll have a good chance to make observations. It ought not to be too hard to discover the man in the case. What do you think?"

"Perhaps a man in service," said Kildare. "Somebody overseas, it might be."

"What would you advise when we find him? A frank talk to let him know what's happening?" asked Eliot.

"If I may advise, no," answered Kildare. "You don't mind me improvising ideas like this?"

"My dear young man," said Eliot, his voice a little dry, "go right ahead. I find it stimulating."

"Well," said Kildare, "we want to try for the permanent happiness of Sylvia, don't we? Might it not be rather bad to break the news to the man in the case? Merely to tell him that this girl has lost her head over him? Put it in the usual talk. She's 'dizzy' about him. Or she's 'off her feed.' It's hard to talk seriously about such a thing. The man might be flattered, because she's rather a pretty girl, don't you think?"

Dr. Eliot looked at him and almost ran into a big Army truck. "Yes. I do think so," he said. "I think she's rather beautiful. Quite, in fact."

"Really?" said Kildare, wearily looking askance at Eliot. "So the man in the case would be flattered at first. But wouldn't he find the girl cheapened? Isn't the old adage true? Do you mind adages, Doctor Eliot?"

"No, sir, go right ahead," Eliot answered with extraordinary snap and precision.

"Well, isn't there the saying," said Kildare, "that the man must pursue and the woman flee? I mean to say, without a contest there is no victory, no glory, all that sort of thing."

"Ha," said Dr. Eliot.

"At the same time," said Kildare, "one must take it for granted that there is an obstacle . . . perhaps a preference for some other woman, perhaps preoccupation in his work. Something of this sort has created the gap between Sylvia and the man. Because it's such a decided gap she begins to feel entirely thwarted. She has the air of a person who is giving up. And that's very bad, wouldn't you say?"

"I certainly would damned well say that it's very bad," replied Dr. Eliot.

"I hope you won't think I'm cheapening Sylvia," said Kildare, "but sex and all that sort of thing . . . I beg your pardon."

"Quite all right. I agree. Go on, damn it!"

"Well, sir, it hits me pretty close to home, actually."

"Does it?" exclaimed the doctor, his car swerving violently.

"It does," said Kildare. "I like to see people fight. And *she's* fighting. She throws herself into our charity cases. With her whole heart. And *what* a heart! She wants to fill her mind so completely that she won't have a chance to think of the other thing. Oh, yes, she's fighting like a trooper. It's sort of terrific in a sense."

"I agree," said Dr. Eliot harshly.

"I mean to say, such a good-looking girl and a huge fortune that doesn't exactly make her any the less attractive . . . for a girl like that to be stymied, you know?"

"Why, it sounds crazy. Perhaps it *is* crazy!" exclaimed Dr. Eliot, and brought his car to a stop in front of the hospital. He said: "You wouldn't advise telling the man of the case?"

"I seriously wouldn't," agreed Kildare.

"Even if he were drawn into a marriage . . . you think it would make for a bad future?"

"If you don't mind me having all these opinions," said Kildare, "she knows that there's a distance between them now. If she thinks that anything except nature . . . except real love, I mean . . . has brought them together, she'll be suspicious of everything so long as they live together."

"I think you're right," murmured Dr. Eliot, and moved his car headlong into the traffic like a racer proud of a new machine.

Kildare, looking after the speeding car, felt that he had annoyed the doctor in some way. He could not remember what he had done that was wrong except that he had expressed a good many opinions, and old men find it hard to listen to the young for any length of time. He was sorry, for he liked Dr. Eliot and respected his work very much. He felt, as he turned into the hospital, that he had lost a good opinion for which he would have given a good deal.

Before he even checked in at Gillespie's office or reported at the clinic the good effect of his call on Miss Harned, Kildare took the express elevator to the roof and went out on the sun deck, for he remembered that he had not seen Tucker since early the day before. The sun was getting through the broken sky from time to time, and no doubt they would have Tucker under the glassed-in portion of the roof, because Gillespie had given orders that they should put him where he could see the sky as much as possible, almost in spite of the weather. He was now, in fact, alone at the top of the great building, his eyes moving with the sweep of the clouds.

Tucker Brown was eleven and death was so close to him that the delicate blue shadow lay before it on his face. Disease had been consuming the marrow of his bones with an agony for so long that Tucker had almost forgotten what peace meant. Therefore he lived with pain quietly, like an angel in the calm of heaven. He had been given up so long that the hospital was aware of him through its whole nervous system, and the beauty of his daily life and thought made the great institution feel more pain, it seemed, than was given to Tucker himself. When he saw Kildare, he smiled. There was a faint sheen of moisture on his face, and Kildare wiped it away. It was the secret they shared that this slight perspiration meant extra pain—what real excess of agony Kildare could dream but never know. Gradually the mind of the boy returned from the world of thought to his favorite doctor.

"Suppose you began all over at the very heart, Doc," he said. "Who would you be?"

"You mean, Sullivan, Jeffries, Willie Heston, or Bill Tilden, or who?" asked Kildare.

"Yeah. The whole lot."

Kildare sat by him, thinking. "I don't know. It's hard to choose, isn't it?" Tucker Brown smiled.

"Who would *you* be?" asked Kildare.

"Gee, I'd be Babe Ruth," answered Tucker. "He was so smart, they say he even seemed fast on the bases."

"He did," agreed Kildare.

"*You* didn't see him, Doc, ever?"

"Once. I saw him once."

"You *did!* Tell me."

Consumed with delight to have his nearest hero tell of the greatest of them all, the eyes of Tucker shone. The blunt fingertips of Kildare found the pulse of Tucker fading, pausing, hurrying, and always seeming about to stop with weariness. His touch studied these signs of death while he was saying: "I never saw anybody stand up to the ball the way the Babe did."

"He turned around so's he had to look at the pitcher over his right shoulder, didn't he?"

"That's right."

"And when he took a good whang at the ball . . . tell me."

"When he took a good swing at the ball, if he missed, sometimes he was spinning so hard that he had to jam the bat into the ground to keep from falling."

"But when he cracked it?"

"When he hit it," said Kildare, "you only asked where . . . you didn't have to ask how far it was going. The ball came off the bat with a ring, as though it was iron. I can hear that sound still, right in the top of my head."

"Go on," whispered Tucker.

"They were likely to go anywhere," said Kildare, "but, the day I watched, he hit a couple over the right field fence."

"Only a couple?" asked Tucker.

"Yes. He was having a bad day at bat."

"I bet. How many runs did he knock in?"

"Only four, outside of what he scored."

The laughter of Tucker almost closed his eyes. "My goodness, you just think of that," he said. "My jiminy, my jiminy, you just think! How far did the ball go?"

"Both of them were aimed at the same plot in the sky, right over the second story of the right-field bleachers. They went there on a straight line."

"The second story? *Over* the *second* story?"

"That's as far as I could see them," said Kildare. "They were still traveling as far as I could see."

"Oh, my," breathed Tucker. "Who were they playing?"

"Cleveland. And Cleveland was in first place that day. But the Babe broke their hearts."

"Poor old Cleveland. Poor old Indians," said Tucker. "They never did much good after that?"

"Not much good," answered Kildare. "The Babe just about wrecked them. They couldn't stand the strain. Every time he came to bat the infield went back twenty yards, the right fielder ran right back till he was standing against the fence at the foul line . . . first baseman played short right. Everything was all twisted out of shape . . . and then he'd knock those balls where they *couldn't* be fielded, except with an airplane."

"Except with an airplane," echoed Tucker, laughing with a faintly musical sound. "I'll bet *you* would've been a good player, Doc. I'll bet you would've been a dandy."

"No, I wasn't much good."

"Oh, I just bet you would've made a second baseman, where they've got to think so fast. And run one way and throw the other. I can just see you! But seeing the Babe, that was about the best day you ever had, wasn't it?"

"That *was* a great day," agreed Kildare. "You think of anything you want?"

"No . . . hardly," said Tucker Brown.

"You want something. What is it, Tucker?"

"Suppose I could just snap my fingers and . . . there it would be."

"Well, suppose," said Kildare.

"Miss Harned would be sitting over there, reading to me."

"Maybe we can get her."

"Oh, no, she's got to go dashing around doing things for a lot of people."

"You like her, Tucker?"

The boy considered a pleasant problem for a time. "You know something?" he asked.

"Go ahead," Kildare replied.

"If she's not smiling one way, she's smiling another. It's always coming or going. I lie here and pretty near forget what she's reading about. She looks up, and I'm laughing. She don't know why. But she laughs right back. She don't mind being laughed at."

"Doesn't she?" asked Kildare.

"Nope. Not so long as it's all in the family."

"I'll send her up here," said Kildare.

"No, no! But you might say that you and I were talking about her. That might put her in mind of coming. And then. . . ."

His voice went out, gradually, like a light entering a mist. The blue around his mouth turned green-white and the perspiration shone on his face again. Kildare chose not to be seeing these symptoms of a new and profound agony. He merely hummed a song as he filled the needle with the sedative.

Afterward he went down to the offices which he shared with Gillespie. It was a dull day, with not more than a dozen people in the waiting room, half of them looking as though they had come from the far corners of the earth for even the war which throttled commerce with bombs and blasting could not keep a certain number of adventurers from sifting through for the sake of their lives. Doctors in Persia, in Argentina, in South Africa, in all the far places, had thrown up their hands and left their patients to turn toward a last hope, like dying believers toward Mecca. Their goal was their own health, but, by the time they reached Gillespie, they had made such efforts that they were purified in a strange way as though by devotion to a high cause. The glance of Kildare still was running over their faces when Dr. John Fielding came out of Gillespie's office. He was the doctor's doctor, carrying on the inevitably lost fight against the cancer which consumed the great man.

"How is he?" asked Kildare.

"He's tired . . . very tired," Fielding replied.

"I must take over more," said Kildare, pinched with sudden pain.

"No, it's not that kind of tired," said Doctor Fielding. He remained for a moment, his medical bag swinging slowly back and forth, like a pendulum marking out strangely important seconds of time. But he could not find the right words. He merely repeated: "It's not that kind of tired." Then he went on. "They're talking about you in there right now," he said over his shoulder as he went out.

IV

In the office, in fact, were two Blair Hospital residents of the year before, Charlie May and Daniel Repton. A squat fellow with the face and complexion of a toad was with them. May and Repton hailed Kildare cheerfully, but he hardly had eyes for them. He was recognizing the toad, first with his eyes and then with his whole mind and spirit, for that was William O. Hollis.

He was being introduced to Dr. Hollis. The yellow-green eyes of Hollis showed no recognition. The whites were the same color. It was impossible to look at them without disgust. Hollis held a thick cigar in the center of his mouth. He puffed it, the smoke dribbling out from both sides and rolling up into the inflamed eyes. To Kildare this monster was beautiful for he knew what acid had eaten away the whole outer rind of this man's body, and for what purpose it was being handled in the Hollis laboratory when it exploded. He accepted the disfigured hand of Hollis with reverence.

Instead of acknowledging the introduction, the grotesque said: "We're starting a base hospital to get to the front. A base hospital that will be a field hospital and only the best we can get go with us. We could make you second in command, Major Kildare. I'd be the top. But we knew we had to talk to Gillespie before we talked to you. The Army will have to waive all the rules and take us intact, by the way."

"All right, then. Get out . . . get out," commanded Gillespie, lying back in his wheelchair with his eyes closed. "Get out and let me talk to him."

They left the office, saying other things that Kildare did not hear, for he was stunned. But, since Gillespie remained with his eyes closed for the moment, he remembered what Fielding had said and began to study the old man's face intently for signs of that weariness, that extra fatigue about which the cancer specialist had spoken so significantly.

It was, of course, nonsense that the old man should be still alive. The creeping fire of the disease long ago should have consumed him coldly, except that something of the spirit seemed to be interposed continually, so that the plague consumed this rather than the flesh. But now, as Kildare looked at the white storm of the hair and the savagely battered face, he thought for an instant that he understood what Fielding had meant. The spirit itself was failing, perhaps, and would leave the body unreinforced, to burn away as swiftly as smoking tinder, touched by wind. As he looked down into that aged face, the depth and greatness of the disaster sickened him as though he were on a height, tempted to throw himself away. His instinct would have set the clock of his teacher's existence in tune with that of Tucker Brown, hurrying away the last few moments of its remaining time.

"Open the window," commanded Gillespie, and the strength of his voice scattered half the fears of Kildare at once.

He opened the window. "Yes, sir?" he said.

"You hear?" asked Gillespie.

Now that he listened to the outer world, Kildare heard distinctly a military band which was striking up not far away.

"Thinking about a uniform, aren't you?" asked Gillespie.

"Not seriously," answered Kildare.

"Why not?"

Kildare was silent.

"Why not think about a uniform? You think day and night about the war, don't you? So why not a uniform?"

"There's always a war wherever you are, sir. I'm glad enough to be fighting it with you."

"Ha!" exclaimed Gillespie. "That's a sort of pretty speech. Pretty enough to make to a girl. D'you think I'm a damned woman, Kildare?"

Again Kildare was silent.

"The fact is," said Gillespie, "that the war changes everything. It has to. Why should it pass into the lives of a hundred and thirty million Americans without affecting you and me? Can you give me a reason?"

"We're already doing something," answered Kildare. "Anything that serves the whole people, as you serve them. . . ."

"Not another damned word of that," broke in Gillespie. "Dangerous to talk like that about serving the whole people with our work? Why not serve them directly, with our own hands and heads, where the service would be worthwhile, in touch with the enemy?"

Kildare waited.

"You're burning to go," said Gillespie.

"No, sir."

"Your heart is tearing gradually in two. Admit it."

"No, sir."

"You lie."

"I do not."

"You confoundedly and damnably lie, Jimmy."

Kildare took a breath.

"Why, a civilian is hardly more than half a man during a war," said Gillespie. "Take women. Will they look at a man out of uniform? They will not. Why not? Because they have instincts, and their instincts are right about such fundamentals. Women have no good ideas at all about education . . . but they have the best ideas in the world about service. The women want us all to get into uniforms and march for the front."

"I'm not going to the front," said Kildare.

"Oh, you're not?"

"No, sir. I'm staying in Blair Hospital."

"With the old crank, Leonard Gillespie?"

"Yes, sir."

Gillespie sighed. "Well, then," he said, "I suppose that I'll have to tell you the truth. I wanted not to. You have feelings. I wanted not to hurt them. Kildare, I order you to go to the front in the Hollis unit."

"I refuse to go, sir," said Kildare.

"Damnation, don't talk back to me!"

Kildare leaned at the back of the chair. "Very well, sir . . . I'll be silent."

"I see I've got to give you the whole truth," groaned Gillespie. "It's this . . . I thought that I had the ideal pupil, the fellow who had the brain, the ability to observe, the talent for remembering, the human touch, the patience to learn what I have to give. I thought you had all of these qualities, and you *have* them. I wasn't wrong, but there's one angle from which you're a total failure. A man cannot keep on amassing information and storing it and holding it ready like a granary ready for the world in time of famine . . . a man cannot do this unless he is willing to introduce a certain air of the impersonal into his attitude. You understand?"

"Yes, sir."

"Now, take that boy . . . the one with the rotten bones . . . I forget his name."

"Tucker Brown, sir."

"Well, take Tucker. He means too much to you. He's incurable. Therefore, you should shelve him. There should be a place in your brain to which you relegate the lost causes. You hear me?"

"I do."

"But you don't put the lost causes on shelves. You plunge in and try to bring them out. Pleasant to think about. Damned Christian, and all that. Democratic, too. But you can't have this in a great doctor. That's your damning fault. The result is that, after thinking this over, I've decided that it's better for you to carry on with what I've already given you. It's a good deal. You won't forget it. You'll be a good doctor. You'll be a distinguished doctor. But you'll never be a great man of science. There's the brutally cold edge, the sharp steel edge of the truth, which I wished to avoid telling you.''

"There's still something else," said Kildare after another moment for breathing. "Even if I can't do anything in myself, I can be of service to you."

"You can. But I can get somebody else. Somebody just about as good."

"No," said Kildare.

"Somebody to all intents and purposes just as good."

"No," said Kildare.

"Damn it, Jimmy, you can, of course, be useful to me, but I have to make a choice. Out there on the firing line or near it, you may save hundreds of lives, prevent thousands of distortions of body and soul. I have to choose between having you here with me, and letting you go for our country. . . . Do you know that I love you, Jimmy?''

"We are pretty close to one another, I hope," said Kildare.

"We are, I thank God. And the reason I thank Him, is that in giving you up I'm making a real sacrifice for the other fellow . . . the man in the street . . . the land of the free and the home of the brave. You know, I believe in all those stale phrases. They're as fresh as a song to me. So, Jimmy. I'm giving you up for our country. Don't argue. Just pack your things and get out.''

"No, sir," said Kildare.

"By God, you mean that you won't go when I send you?"

"I must think a bit about it," said Kildare.

"Why should you have to think? Why can't you make up your mind at once, like a man?''

Kildare laid his hand on the shoulder of the old man. "You like to make yourself out a brutal tyrant, don't you?'' he asked.

"Why, damn it," said Gillespie, "I'm simply talking facts."

"Tucker isn't so well," said Kildare.

"Don't change the subject on me, young man! Who are you talking about, anyway?''

"You know perfectly well who I'm talking about."

"I do not. I don't spend my life on lost causes. I have no idea what you mean. I try to keep a general point of view. I would not waste hours that might be useful to thousands on the case of a little boy who. . . ." He saw that he had revealed his knowledge. He sighed and let his head fall against the back of the chair. "I'm a terrible liar, Jimmy," he said.

"You are, sir," said Kildare.

IN MEDIAS RES

EAGLES OVER CROOKED CREEK

Max Brand

"Eagles over Crooked Creek" was the last story Frederick Faust published in Western Story Magazine *for which he had once customarily written a million and a half words a year. It came after a two-year hiatus from the magazine and differs remarkably in tone from the fiction that had preceded it.*

Two eagles were fighting at the head of the cañon, and the wind blew them and their screaming out over Crooked Creek, so that everyone looked up from the streets and some of the younger lads even took random shots at the pair. But the people were glad, really, to hear the screeching of the eagles, because it meant that winter definitely had left the mountains, and the spring was there to stay. Men thought of taking off flannel underwear; women thought of cleaning house. Young Chuck, coming up the trail into Crooked Creek for the first time in two years, proud of his seventeen years and his new horse, divided his mind between the eagles and the town itself. It seemed to have shrunk; the weight of the winter had pressed the buildings down and narrowed the streets. He was half way into town before he saw anyone he knew, and that was old Ben Whalen, his uncle's partner. Ben stalked down the middle of the street, leading that ancient horse, Pepper, which still showed his name in the arch of his scrawny neck and the flattening of his ears, but Time was the permanent famine that roached his back and tucked up his belly. Old Ben Whalen was among men what Pepper was among horses, loose-kneed, gaunt, with the hanging flesh of his face tucked up at the corners of his eyes and his mouth.

"Hey, Ben!" called Chuck, and galloped his piebald up to the old man.

Pepper began to prance without going any faster. Ben Whalen sluiced himself around and squinted over his shoulder. "Don't go knockin' your dust over me, young feller," he said.

"Hey, Ben, don't you know me?"

"Why, you kind of appear like little Chuck," said Ben. "What you taken and done? Growed up?"

"I kind of been growing," admitted Chuck. "Where's Uncle Cal?"

"Yeah, you've taken and growed up on us," said Ben, as they reached the foot of the cañon where the road turned up among the rocks.

"Where's Uncle Cal?" repeated Chuck.

"No use you riding up this trail," answered Ben. "Cal always was a loon, and he's gone and spent the winter over by the Sugar Loaf. He got a dream that the Sugar Loaf was all veined up with gold, and he's gunna get at that gold as soon as things thaw out, so's to be ahead of the rush." Ben spat, then he laughed and smoothed his chin with his whole hand, a careful gesture which he inherited from the days when he wore a full beard. He repeated, as he turned up the cañon road: "There ain't any use you coming. You won't find Cal up there no more."

"I'll come anyway," said Chuck.

Ben stopped short, and Pepper bumped his nose on the shoulder of his master. "What for would you be such a damn' young fool?" asked Ben. "Cal ain't up there, and I ain't one for much company."

"I'd like to see the old shack anyways," said Chuck and laughed.

Ben Whalen mounted Pepper and slumped into the saddle. There was a jingling of tin cans from the pack which sat over the hips of the old horse.

"How's Pepper's sight?" asked Chuck. "Can he see pretty good now?"

"He can't see nothing no more," answered Ben. "Why else would I've been leading him through the street? But he knows the three miles of the cañon trail like it was wrote out on the palm of his hand."

"How old is Pepper?" asked Chuck.

"Don't be chatterin,' " said Ben. "They don't raise up boys with no manners these days. They all keep squawkin' like them eagles up yonder."

So Chuck was quiet, unoffended because he knew Ben from of old. For that matter Uncle Cal was as silent as any sourdough, but for Chuck this trip was a return to something more than people. It was a voyage back into his childhood, where even mountains and rocks possess a living spirit that changes. And all the way up the cañon he watched with admiration how the old horse, Pepper, followed the sharp windings of the path that followed the twists and the leapings of the creek. There was never a misstep all the way. Only when they came to the head of the steep way, Pepper tried to veer off to the left instead of going straight on toward the shanty. Ben Whalen cursed the old gelding, and kicked him, and reined him the right way, but to the last step Pepper continued to sag to the left.

"Growed out of his good sense, the old fool," commented Ben, and began to unstrap the pack.

Chuck carried it into the shack in his strong young arms. It was the same flimsy structure, built of wide, warped boards with cracks through which the sunshine striped the floor with fuzzy yellow lines of light. The winter had blown through those crevices enough snow dust to paint the stove all over with a new coating of red rust, but there was little else in the single room that could take harm. More perishable stuff, of course, would be lodged in the small cellar through the winter.

"You tell me where, and I'll put things away," said Chuck.

"You take yourself off and leave me be," said Ben, leaning on his rifle and staring gloomily around him.

So Chuck went outside. Pepper was no longer standing in front of the shanty. He had gone off to the side, and there he hung his head and switched his ragged old tail at the flies which swarm thickest and bite deepest in the early spring. The grass stood up quite high in the place where Pepper was standing, and yet it was not for the grass that the gelding had gone there. He did not crop a blade of it, but hung his head as though he were tethered to a hitching rack.

Chuck sat down on the door sill. The little house was just the same, except that like everything else it had shrunk. The cañon, too, was narrower, and the walls no longer lifted so high, and the water roared neither so musically nor on so deep a note. It seemed to Chuck that, as one grows older, the world sifts away through the fingers, so what could remain inside the gaunt hands of old men like Ben or Uncle Cal? He turned and looked toward the great Sugar Loaf, frosted with blue and white toward the summit. Then he looked back down the cañon. It was not only smaller, but it was changed, for surely in the old days he had been able to look past more than two bends of the walls. There had been a rift, an outlet, and the eye was not stopped by the two joining sides of rock.

Chuck stood up and drifted to the side. The piebald, noisily ripping at the grass and jangling its bit, nevertheless followed him, and this warmed his heart. Now, as he passed to the right, Chuck saw that the cañon in fact opened a little. It was exciting. It was as though a door were swinging wide in his mind. He found the exact point from which, he could have sworn, he used to look down the narrows of the ravine. He could see past the second bend and caught a glimpse beyond the third, a narrow slot of blue sky that let the eye shoot onwards. That, as he remembered it, was exactly what he used to see from the threshold of the old shack.

He turned, bewildered, and saw that the shanty stood, in fact, well over to the right. But Pepper was exactly in line with him and that glimpse through the third bend of the ravine. There was something ghostly about it that brought a chill into his blood in spite of the strong mountain sunshine. He went up to Pepper, and the old horse jerked up his head and flattened his ears. He walked in front of Pepper. The ears and the pinched nostrils showed anger, but the filmy eyes showed nothing but the endless twilight within the mind. Stepping back, Chuck's foot sank into a hole. He looked down and saw, where the grass was beaten down, that the lips of the little depression made an exact square, like a posthole filled up. But no posts had ever stood near the old shack, none at all except the two of the hitching rack! An idea stranger than life or death made

Chuck shuffle back and forth through the grass until he found, eight feet away, another square hole exactly like the first.

He took off his sombrero and rubbed the sweat from his face. The wind came off the mountains and blew his head cold, but the blood in his body was already well iced. For here, where he stood, the hitching rack of the shanty once had been!

He moved back through that taller grass, still scuffing with his heels, and again he found a depression. It was not a narrow hole mouth, this time, but a long line. Still scuffing, he traced a depression inches deep which turned at four corners and outlined a space ten feet long.

"By the jumping thunder," said Chuck, "this is where the shack used to stand. Those were the postholes. This is the old cellar that's been filled in. . . ."

"What you doin' over there?" shouted Ben Whalen. "What's the matter with you, over there?" He stood in front of the shanty with his rifle at the ready. "Come here!" called Ben. "Come on over here! What you doin' there?"

Chuck looked with yearning toward the piebald horse which still followed at his heels, but he was not even tempted to jump for the saddle, because he could remember Ben Whalen's talent for putting bullet holes through tin cans flung as high as one pleased. If the grass had been a little taller, Chuck would have dropped into it and tried to disappear like a mole. Instead, he had to walk stiff legged because his knees were rigid with terror toward the old man on the threshold of the cabin.

"What you doin' over there, anyway?" asked Ben Whalen.

"I dropped a coupla dimes outa my pocket," said Chuck. "I dropped 'em out when I pulled out my sack of Bull Durham. They went flip off into the grass, and I started kicking around in it to find 'em."

"Why for would you kick around in the grass if you wanted to find something?" asked Ben. "There ain't any sense in doing that. . . . I got an idea that you're a liar, Chuck, like your pa and your Uncle Cal and your grandpa all was liars before you!" He grew very angry. "You hear what I'm saying?" shouted Ben.

"Hey . . . don't swing that gun around," said Chuck. He threw up his hands in a gesture that was purely instinctive. Then desperate fear tempted him, and he caught at the end of the rifle barrel.

"Will you? Will you?" screeched Ben Whalen. He jerked back on the gun. The front sight ripped half way across the palm of Chuck before his grip held fast. He flung his other arm around Ben and hugged him close. It was like embracing a skeleton, and all the strength went out of Ben in a moment. His hands left his rifle. As Chuck jumped back from him, holding the rifle, old Ben simply leaned against the side of the door with a hand pressed to his side, panting. His mouth was open, sagging the lines of his face longer and longer.

"What's the matter with you, Chuck? You gone crazy or something?" asked Ben.

"I'm crazy enough to go and dig up that whole place!" shouted Chuck. "I'm crazy enough to dig clean to the bottom of the old cellar yonder, till I find out what you were coverin' up! I'm just crazy enough for that.''

''What cellar?'' asked old Ben.

''There! Right yonder where the house used to stand.''

''What you mean, Chuck? Who'd take and move a house? Who'd have such a loony idea as that?''

''You took and done it yourself,'' said Chuck. ''Post by post and plank by plank, you took and done it your own self. I'm gunna find why, if I have to dig right to the bottom of the cellar.''

''Don't you do it, son,'' said Ben. ''That ain't a cellar no more. That's a grave!''

A voice that Chuck never had heard before came out of his own throat: ''Uncle Cal! It's Uncle Cal!'' he was crying

''Yeah. That's where he lies,'' said Ben. ''Maybe you'll be wanting to take me back to town, Chuck?''

He mounted the blind horse, and, while Chuck rode behind with the rifle at a balance across the pommel of his saddle, Pepper went down the slope with his absurd prancing.

''It was Pepper that showed you the way, wasn't it?'' asked Ben.

''Yeah. Pepper showed me.''

''Dog gone his old heart,'' said Ben. ''I guess he's gunna outlive me, after all.''

''Ben, will you tell me how it happened?'' pleaded Chuck, looking with pity on that bent and narrow back.

''I dunno,'' said Ben. ''I guess I've got kind of old and cranky.''

He looked up where the two eagles, after giving up their battle for a time, had joined combat again in the middle of the sky. They seemed higher now, but their screaming came plainly to the ears of Chuck. Old Ben kept staring upwards while the blind horse carried him with careful feet down the trail.

POEMS

Frederick Faust

Dear Friend

The rain is falling.
Like the brush of a great painter
It makes the hills harmonious with the sky.
It has thickened the air of the valley
And tarnished the face of the river.
So that now the great waters flow unseen;
Their course is only through the mind.
The garden, too, is dying in this false twilight.
Only the pomegranate tree flames with bright beauty
As though the sun had returned to it alone.
Suddenly I am happy;
For I think of you, my friend, through the darkness of many years.

Written in the Mind

The flame which lived in the lantern
Has shown me the face of the writing.
It has conducted me among great names
Like a happy traveler among the mountains.

All poems are grouped by source. In some cases only one poem may be represented, but if the source appears at the end of several poems, then all of the poems prior to that source belong to that source.

It has awakened golden voices.
But now the lantern is dead;
The voices are silent.
Only what was written in the mind
Remains living in the room beside me.
I am left alone in the darkness
And find myself repeating a name.

My Soul

Why are you despondent, my soul?
I am weary of these continual reproaches
For most of my life is spent in your service.
If I have fed myself with roast suckling pigs,
With tender bamboo shoots, pastries, and samsu,
Nevertheless you never were forgotten.
Where was it, far away, that I showed you the evening
Rushing upon the city like a tide of gold?
Do you forget that hour in the desert
When we listened to the water from the pump
Falling into the great tank
With a brazen reverberation and a silver ringing sound?
You have walked through the solemn hollows of the mountains;
You have heard the birds singing at night;
You have watched the flight of the doves
Dropping down through the twilight;
We have listened together to the poets.
What more will you have of me?
If the horse cannot jump the wall
Is it not foolish to feed him the spur?
You should have chosen some mighty poet or hero,
It is not in the least my fault
That you chose to inhabit this commonplace house.

On the Death of My Young Son

My thought was that in the darkness
He came to me with the stars, saying:
Oh, my father, weep no more for me.
The high gods, the spirits of the sky,
Have taken me away to their gardens.
They dared not let me live
For I had learned their secret from the wind,
Their secret for which they tremble
Lest men should hear it and no longer pray,
No longer feed the undying ones with sacrifice.

But you, oh my father, remember
And keep this truth warm in your heart:
More than the mountains at dawn,
More than the rivers of peace,
More than sleep and dreams,
More than silence and stars,
More than these is death beautiful.

My Last Day

When my last day has come,
Let me be seated by the southern window.
My closed eyes shall not see, in the sunshine,
The peonies in the garden
Or the willows or the river beyond them,
But the blue hills far away shall join me with my past.
Then in my mind be sure that I shall not behold
The dragon hall of audience
Or the thousand tapers and the thousand lords
Attending the dawn and His Majesty.
Neither shall I remember the far frontier,
The arrows, the kettle drums, the shouting,
The cold wind and the aching wounds.
No, for I shall seem to float again on the lake
Where as a boy I have drifted
With clouds above me and clouds far beneath,
Voyaging through a silent heaven
With you, my lady.
The three score years are dust that vanished.
How shall I, then, feel bitter regret
That you were taken from me
By the long road that journeys toward the north?
Wherefore should I weep like a child
Because we could not grow old together?
It is remembering you
That keeps my heart young forever.

These Mountains

Not even weary labor can pass these mountains,
They are as lofty as time.
They hold the sun far away.
The light of the moon is lost in the wild valleys.
The pine trees bend before a storm
Even when the wind is still.
In my heart now my home is remembered

Where summer made itself the year
But even winter made itself welcome,
Where hate could not live an hour
And to love was as easy as drawing breath.

—*from* DEAD MAN'S PASSPORT

Be the walls triple brass and the gates of steel,
   Be the guards appointed and armed,
   Yet at your feet before dawn I kneel,
   For the life of the lover is charmed.

   Here in the silence and the dark hour,
      The petals are coldly furled,
   But open again, my dear, my flower,
      My blossom of all the world.

   Oh, that my voice were the golden sun,
      For with a gentle art
   I'd touch the petals one by one
      And open wide your heart.

—*from* SEÑOR JINGLE BELLS

   Is it the wind that has ruffled your hair?
      Is it the night wind
   That has blown the stars into your eyes?
Or is it love that has made you mysterious?

   All ye who crawl on your bellies;
   All ye of the sixty-three kinds,
   Listen to the voice of a friend.
   Let there be peace between us.
Peace to you and to yours I swear;
   Swear peace to me and to mine.
   Out of your holes come forth,
   Come forth all ye out of the grass
   To look in my face and to swear.
   I shall not harm you or yours;
   You shall not harm me or mine
In the name of God, in the name of His prophet.

—*from* ''War for Sale''

And this shall be my knell, be my knell;
And this shall be my knell—my knell.
   And this shall be my knell:
   Sam, I hope you go to hell,

Sam, I hope you sizzle well—
Damn your eyes!

—from TRAILIN'

If Troy town burned down for Helen's lips,
Bright with kisses and wine;
If Hero's love was worth a death,
Then what shall pay for thine?
The game is drawn, the dice are set,
But who shall cast for Nicolette?

But I have seen her dance at night
Under a cloud-tossed moon,
And ever as she danced she sang
A strange and humming tune.
Oh, fearless hearts cannot forget
The beauty that is Nicolette!

She rather hears than tales of love
A charger's galloping;
She loveth deeds and fierce repute—
Fame is her wedding-ring!
Oh, death himself hath never met
A mistress such as Nicolette!

—from THE SWORD LOVER

May thy sleep be as deep
As the depths of my love for thee;
May thy dream ever seem
Sweet remembrance of constancy.

—from THE GUIDE TO HAPPINESS

I have come in from the sea,
The salt of it has cracked my lips,
The salt of it burns in my eyes;
My belly is sick with the taste of the sea,
But now I tread the shoaling water,
The soft sand is under my feet,
The green of the forest blesses my eyes,
And the wind laughs in my heart and over my head.

I have been very far away from you.
The high green mountains of twilight lay between us.
The terrible dark ocean of night lay between us.
I journeyed on through the storm, hopeless,

And suddenly I reached the white beach of the dawn,
I saw my home and the bright morning of your face.

—*from* DEAD MAN'S TREASURE

On the white mantle lay the Indian red
Of rubies, emeralds like the eyes of green
Scattered the floor, and from her shining head
Cast down, the coronet of pearls was seen
Through shadow by its own imperious light;
But Iseult like a star dissolved in night
Was lost from high Tintagel in. . . .

Be not haughty; be not cold,
Daphne from Apollo fled
With her beauty's wealth untold;
Daphne is with Helen dead.
It is true the wounded tree
Fills with bloom where fruit shall be,
Be not cruel, for tomorrow
Finds you old and ends my sorrow.
And that I knew and then I sang:
The silver apples from your girdle hang.

We are but cups to hold the wine
Of love, the fragrant, the divine.
Be not distant in your pride.
Though in velvet youth you dress,
Time the thief is at your side;
Praise only love for loveliness.
Never let the wind blow bare
The golden pollen from your hair;
But let the treasure be carried home,
The honey lodged within the comb.
That I felt and therefore sang:
"The silver apples from your girdle hang."

The boatman on the side of death,
The soft stream of forgetfulness,
Elspeth, would stay his oar, Elspeth
And looking on your loveliness
Would fail to row you to the dead
But like a dreaming child would slowly bend his head.

That space of shadow or of light
Where stars shine and the winds take breath
Was never crossed by mortal wight,
Elspeth, but you may rise Elspeth,

To music more than that of strings;
Ah, what a sound of singing, and a noise of wings.

Take you a heaven nearer earth,
For there my lonely song shall rise
To join you on the fields of mirth
And the blue meadows of the skies;
My lonely songs shall find you there
Until you breathe my sorrow like a sweeter air.

Pull out the lance-head; broach my side
Like an old cask of Bordeaux' pride,
For many men of my death shall drink.
By God, the silver goblets clink
And ringed around by hungry eyes
Another free companion dies.
Like a fool from home my soul goes forth,
So here's the testament of my-worth.
My broken spear with the pennon on her
I give Pierre for his broken honor;
My poniard is Alfredo's part,
To be a cat's tooth in his heart;
My sword to Stephen and a prayer
That it break in battle and leave him bare;
My horse and spurs to John Thyvelle
To lighten him on the way to hell.
And here's my purse that with strong hands
I filled and emptied of house and lands,
The saint I prayed to, the God I served,
The liege from whom I never swerved.
Give it to Joan that she may be
One night alone with my memory.

Westerly, blow westerly!
No other wind can blow to me
The larksong or the smell of rain
Or carry me to my love again
No other wind can blow to me
But westerly, blow westerly.

—*from* THE GOLDEN KNIGHT

What shall I do with this weariness of light?
The day is like the eye of a prying fool
And the thought of a lover is burdened by it.
Only the star and the moon have wisdom.
Of all the birds there is only a single one,
Of all the birds one who knows that night is the time for song.

And I of all men understand how to wait for darkness.
Oh, my beloved, are you, also, patient?

—*from* THE BAIT AND THE TRAP

The breast of a bird, how soft;
Breast of a cloud, softer and softer;
But softest is the breast of night.

Long night, soft night, long, long night;
And two breathing together;
In the breast of night two breathing.

Now the morning stands on the hill;
Now the morning lies on the water.
It is still. It is waiting. It is still.

The thought of her comes to me like the fall
Of dew that gilds the morning, like the fall
Of rain in the hot, dusty throat of August;
Like wings between the morning and the night
She comes to me; but only in my thought.

Let not my ladder be her golden hair
For climbing to her heart, but let it be
Her sweet, clear laughter, like a winding stair.

Darkness walls in the soul; man is not seen
Save in the lightning flashes of his deeds.

—*from* THE LUCK OF THE SPINDRIFT

Love is not happiness.
A horse under hell;
A sword under hand;
And red wine for the belly;
But love is not happiness.

Love is not happiness.
Seeing is longing;
Winning is doubting;
Leaving is sorrow;
But love is not happiness.

Gather the starlight
And weave me a mantle.
Dip it in evening blue.
Weave me a mantle;
And fringe it with moonshine

And weave me a mantle
To walk with my love.

—*from* MONTANA
RIDES AGAIN

THE QUOTABLE FAUST

compiled by David L. Fox and William F. Nolan

One may take chances with a revolver, which is a careless and sometimes a foolish weapon; but there is a sort of philosophical calm about a rifle which discourages questions and sudden starts, and brave attempts.

—from PLEASANT JIM

He accepted the thing at last; he had endured enough to trust time as a healer and the pain which made his heart small today would be less tomorrow and still less the next day until at last it was lost in the mute throng of sorrows which are the soul of this sad life of ours.

—from TRAGEDY TRAIL

And in that sun-flooded, cheap little room, with its bare, unpainted floor, and its bare, unpainted walls, and the gaping cracks of the board ceiling, he had a great thought that sobered him and made him look up. So our great moments come, in spite of dinginess, two or three in a life of which they compose the lasting wealth. Why should there be more? And if there is only one light, it is enough to show the ship across the dark sea.

—from MYSTERY RANCH

We admire great men for great deeds, but we do not love them for the same reasons. Heroes are apt to be a bit cruel, and conquerors are callused across the knuckles and the heart. But when, now and then, we meet gentleness with valor, and modesty with might, and above all, perhaps, when we find honesty in the place of sheer ambition, we are unnerved, and kindliness flows in upon all the secret places of the soul and a sort of worship issues from us.

—from SAWDUST AND SIXGUNS

There is nothing which so tickles the vanity of a man as to be wrapped in a mist which the understanding of others cannot penetrate.

—from THE SPLENDID RASCAL

Of all our acquaintances the face in the mirror is the only trustworthy adviser. He has that disquieting habit of saying what he thinks and thinking what he says, a very Diogenes whose lantern lights up the comfortably shadowed corners of our conscience. He repays without the slightest exaggeration our smiles and our laughter, our frowns and our tears. He will not flatter. He cannot cajole. We reckon our minutes by the ticking of a clock, but the face in the mirror gives us the large and pitiless measure of the years.

—from FATE'S HONEYMOON

This world in which we have been placed . . . this wonderful and beautiful world in which we have been placed has been given into the hands of people of two kinds. The one are producers; the others are non-producers. . . . Their [the producers'] responsibility is great; their work is important, . . . but it cannot be all-important. Against them cannot be balanced the class of detestable idlers, thieves, vagabonds, or all the rottenness of a society which has no concern except to amuse itself. But as a counterpoise to the producers, in all countries which can be called great, there always has been and ever must be a class necessarily small which is ready to prize honor more than cash, and to follow bright glory like a star.

—from MISTRAL

A politician, it may be taken, is one who controls without seeming to have the upper hand. A politician works from the inside; by means of a smile he does more than by means of a blow.

—from OUTLAW VALLEY

Those who dwell in cities cannot know the sky. They are only aware, now and again, of a pleasant blueness against which the bricks of some distant wall make a line of red; or they see, as they look up from an open carriage, a whirl of stars flowing through the heavens in a narrow street fenced in by the shadowy walls of the great buildings on either side. This is all that city dwellers can know of the sky.

—from SADDLE AND SENTIMENT

Youth gives sprightly grace, but its very litheness leaves many an angle of brain and body. Youth is unfinished. It wears, with its irregularities, brain and body.

—from "Kain"

Friendship is not sold by the yard; neither is it traded for merchandise; but it is rather like gold, and sometimes the hardest rocks give the richest strike.

—from THE SHERIFF RIDES

The annals of the mountain desert have never been written and can never be written. They are merely a vast mass of fact and tradition and imagining which floats from tongue to tongue from the Rockies to the Sierra Nevadas. A man may be a fact all his life and die only a local celebrity. Then again, he may strike sparks from that imagination which runs riot by camp fires and at the bars of the crossroads saloons.

In that case he becomes immortal. It is not that lies are told about him or impossible feats ascribed to him, but every detail about him is seized upon and passed on with a most scrupulous and loving care.

—from ''Luck''

We have no frontier, now. Fast-driven passenger expresses snake across the country from end to end, blotting out time and distance. Or if a man's thoughts must be sent and not his person, he flashes them instantly and cheaply across the wires. And ten thousand newspapers pour forth floods and floods of news so that nothing can happen in one corner of the country that is not known in every other part of it, so long as it is beautiful, strange, terrible, or in the least degree important. From East to West, from North to South, we read the same papers and books, hear the same music, and live according to the same standards. Our food is the same, our clothes are the same, and our thoughts are the same. And every moment of existence welds this gigantic empire into a closer-knit, stronger unit, furnishes it with a stronger and more universal ideal, links every particle of it into an entity called the United States which in physical power is to the Roman Empire what the Roman Empire was, let us say, to a single sprawling province like Africa. So we have no frontier.

And because we have no frontier, we are forced to digest the poison which is generated in the social body, and take it back into the blood, so that who can say to what ignominious end our muscular greatness will come?

—from SAWDUST AND SIXGUNS

A brave man is not content with one defeat. He rises from the floor of the ring after the first knockdown and struggles again. Fierce pride rises in his heart. Pride strengthens his limbs. Pride wipes the mist from before his eyes. Pride reserves his muscles for another struggle. So many a defeat is turned into a victory.

—from MIGHTY LOBO

Poetry is a bit extravagant. The blessing is that it has wings. The curse is that the wings are apt to carry us out of sight. We fly too near the sun, and the clear sense melts out of us, and we come down with a thump in an absurd huddle and leave the air full of feathers.

—from THE GOLDEN KNIGHT

Now, there is sometimes needed only a word to unlock the most startling truths in the mind. Green was never seen in the sky until a poet looked at the West some thousands of years after civilization and saw that color there. But all the rest, expecting blue above them, found only blue.

—from TIGER MAN

Hunger is the great bender of dignity.

—from THE LUCK OF THE SPINDRIFT

Where is it among the poets . . . that they speak of the danger and the loveliness and the wildness and the song of the sea, and find it like the delightful peril and the beauty and the strangeness of the voice of woman?

—from THE LUCK OF THE SPINDRIFT

He wore no monocle, and yet he had a sort of eyeglassed air of superiority. Even his few intimates in the East found that manner unpleasant; to a Westerner it was simply maddening.

—from WOODEN GUNS

How often one hears the remark concerning a patiently working horse: "If only it knew its strength!" The same thing is rarely said about a man, for the picture which fills the eye is of the great bulk of twelve or fifteen hundred weight of bone and muscle turned in revolt, smashing the wagon it pulls and the harness which attempts to control it, killing the driver with the blow of a hoof, or destroying the rider with a crunch of teeth stronger than a tiger's. If a man is wakened to lawlessness his power is yet more terrible. He banishes with a gesture of the mind the load of duty at which he has been tugging. He annihilates the law by merely denying it. He trebles his strength by freedom which is absolute. He adds to the strength of a man the strength of a wild beast by casting himself loose from society.

—from "Master and Man"

I feel as if I've seen your face many times. But that's true of all the beauties. They open the heart and give one something important to think about. They connect one with great thoughts. Great crimes, great follies, great tragedies, great mercies, nothing small should come from a woman with a face like yours.

—from BORDER GUNS

Courage is the possession, the special treasure, of no nation. Americans are as brave as the next nation. But they did a good deal of running at Bull Run.

—from SONG OF THE WHIP

There is no cleanser of the mind like a morning bath. The same cold, whipping spray which calls up the pink blood, glowing through the marble of the skin, drives the ache of sleep from the brain, and washes away at once all the recorded thoughts of yesterday.

—from TRAILIN'

As for the Bible, he had felt it to be a great and dreary book fit for old women and Sunday, but, when the conversation-hunger drove him, he opened it perforce—and was suddenly lost in talks of old wars, wild vengeances, strange prophecies, inspired men.

—from WILD FREEDOM

Great horses fill the mind of a man more than any other thing in the world. A dog may be brave and devoted; or a child may be true; or a friend may be faithful; but the very essence and business of a horse is that he lay down his life for his master.

—from TWENTY NOTCHES

Following are comments from letters and notebooks in the Faust Papers at the Bancroft Library, University of California at Berkeley, collected by William F. Nolan in 1969.

If you wish to select one among the seven cities of my youth, seek among Malory, wine, the Aegean, Athens, Chaucer, the ballads—and then look out through the Golden Gate.

A horse can understand more of one's speech than most men.

All that can save fiction is enormous verve, a real sweep, plus richness of character, blood that can be seen shining through.

After the age of ten, all studies except math were a joke to me.

I am the most famous campus drunk.

I feel the suspense . . . the sheer movement of a yarn.

Of this I am certain—that I have sold my soul.

God cannot exist alone. He must have god-like men.

Why is my verse so difficult, so dead, so dull to other people?

I have finished the plots for two musicals [in Hollywood]. I never go to musicals.

The preparations of food must become an art, and the eating of it must be a ceremony.

Sex is like wine. A little of it seasons life, but it must not be taken too seriously.

I cannot write prose if I *think* . . . I don't believe that Shakespeare stopped to think out reasons for doing things. I believe he simply worked by instinct, the sure workman's instinct.

Have recently sent thirty-eight poems to our leading magazines and received thirty-eight poems back from our leading magazines.

So it will be when we are dead that perhaps our lives will stand for something.

A typewriter is almost like a human being to me.

I am beginning to believe that I shall never be able to write anything but pulp paper stuff.

Maturity is that age at which men no longer hope for perfect happiness.

The fool laughs at illusions; the wise man spends his life in contemplation of them.

Winter is the most human season, because, being most barren, it is most full of hope.

People who don't believe in the beauty of life are really the defeated ones.

TWENTY-FIVE MILLION WORDS

Edward H. Dodd, Jr.

This article about Frederick Faust first appeared in The Publisher's Weekly, *March 26, 1938. Dodd at the time was Faust's publisher at Dodd, Mead & Company, which successfully published the Max Brand books from 1927 until 1988.*

They pay him the top rate—four cents a word—for all his stuff, and there are very few men who get that. Certainly his stories sell better in book form than those of any other regular pulp man. But his most potent claim to this top position is his productivity. Here we have figures—shattering, staggering figures which no one else can touch.

The real name of this man is Frederick Faust. He has published under thirteen pen names and is writing currently under five. His first great success was THE UNTAMED which in 1918 swept him among the top ranking Western authors in a few weeks. And if you will read the review of THE IRON TRAIL in the Sunday *Times* for January 23, 1938, you will realize he is still very much there. His best known pseudonym is Max Brand and the Western story has been his widest medium. I have seen an issue of a *Western Story Magazine* with four serials in it—all of them by Faust under different names.

Max Brand has been working for about twenty years and during that time he has published some twenty-five million words. Now that is a lot of words to have set in type. I don't know how far they would run if set on one line, but I know that Margaret Mitchell would have to write nearly three GONE WITH THE WINDs a year for twenty years to catch up with him. I have the exact figures of his present-day rivals taken from the files of the Congressional Library, and they show that he has written as much in twenty years as Edgar Wallace, J. S. Fletcher, and E. Phillips Oppenheim, all thrown in together, have written in a total of a hundred and five years! At about this point dime novels will flash into the old-timer's mind. But, although the number of these books is not unimpressive, the total wordage is bush league stuff. Frederick Van Renssalaer Dey under the pseudonym of Varick Vanardy started off the Nick Carter dime novels under the Street & Smith imprint. When Dey died in the early 'Twenties, the series was continued by Frederic Ormond, John Russell Coryell, and Frederick William Davis. These authors added forty-six titles, bringing the total up to sixty-two. At 30,000 words apiece this competition fizzles out with less than two million total. If you will credit Max Brand with this coming year's output, which is all ready and scheduled but not yet published, you can throw Nick Carter into the scales with Wallace, Oppenheim, and Fletcher and still not balance Max Brand. To find a possible competitor we have to hark way back to the days when Walter Scott was turning out the Waverly novels. But in support of his records we have only legends—no figures.

To the ordinary writer this sort of literary mass production is nothing short of terrifying. Mechanically it means stenographers in relays, hour after hour with no let up, and an incredible amount of black coffee. Creatively it means giving birth to ideas at a rate that would make even a mother plant aphis blush with envy. And don't forget that this is the most inventive sort of writing—no scenic descriptions or lists of atmospheric detail here, but plots, plots, plots, crowding upon each other, action rattling into action, everything different. Of course this kind of writing cannot be done twelve hours a day, year in and year out, but it has to be pretty constant to *average,* as Max Brand does, a book in three weeks. As for records we have no data for comparisons, but here are some marks to shoot at:

1 hour	14 pages
1 day	107 pages
3 days	50,000 words
7 days	90,000 words
1 year	700,000 words

Now what do all these words mean and what is done with them? In dollars and cents they mean a substantial living to the author—one that is likely in a good year to reach six figures. In printed matter in the United States alone these words mean eighty-five books, fifty-five short stories, 201 novelettes, and 196 serials. The subjects of the 453 magazine tales are many and various as follows, by far the greatest number being Westerns:

Westerns	328
Alaska	13

Chinese	3
Mystery	21
Secret Service	10
Historical	21
Miscellaneous	57

Faust uses numerous pseudonyms not only because he writes so much, but also to build up separate reputations in these different fields. His Westerns vary somewhat in type—Mexican border, horse, outlaw, rancher stories whose heroes are brainy weaklings and others which extol the exploits of supermen. The best are the straight outlaw type. Those in which a horse is the hero are the least successful.

It would take an Einstein to calculate the number of times all these words are read. The books sell around 20,000 copies. The circulations of the better pulp magazines in which Max Brand (in various guises) appears run about a quarter of a million. Serials running in five and six issues would, of course, equal five or six [novels] and novelettes two or three short stories. If your head is not reeling by now, you will multiply the whole mass by three or four on the assumption that each magazine is read by that many different people.

Let's first multiply 25 million words by 250 thousand magazines, then add eighty-five books at an average of 75,000 words multiplied by 20,000 circulation, and triple that for the number of readers. The answer is 22,950,000,000,000 words. Which shows what happens when Einstein isn't on the job and is probably more people than ever have lived or will live, indicating that a few generations of mid-Western grasshoppers must needs be devoted Western fans.

All that is pretty impressive. But remember that these figures are strictly American. If you were to wander through Europe, however, and ask booksellers in Budapest, Vienna, Prague, Warsaw, Berlin, Amsterdam, etc., who, in their opinion, was the best-selling American author, I warrant the answer would almost inevitably be Max Brand. For some curious reason which an enterprising psychologist ought to uncover, Europe, and unexpectedly middle Europe, has an apparently unquenchable thirst for Western stories. Mysteries and romances, which easily outsell Westerns in this country, must need constantly to eat the dust of the six-shooting lads on the galloping mustangs. For what must be an equally curious reason, very few Western fans are to be found in Italy and France.

Excluding pirated publications such as appear frequently in Japan, Holland, and the Balkans, Max Brand is published in ten foreign countries. By far the largest consumer is England where they start a book off at 7/6 [7 shillings, 6 pence], shoot it after a year or two into a 3/6 [3 shillings, 6 pence] edition, then to 2 shillings, and finally wind up with a sixpenny paperbound article. Germany is next in quantity, but Hungary, Czechoslovakia, and Poland rarely miss a title. In Spanish his books look like magazines, 6½ × 9½ inches.

Add to this twenty-five moving pictures, one of which, THE UNTAMED, has been remade three times, once as a silent, twice as a talking picture. This is an average of better than one a year, and I think you will have a hard time finding any author who can tie that percentage. Some of these pictures are the old-fashioned, non-talking kind of Wild West shows that find their way all over the world and which will very likely still be touring around China and Uganda another twenty years hence. Top all this off with two volumes of poems, and you will know why Mr. Frederick Faust, alias Max Brand, alias this and that, has managed to keep busy during the last twenty years.

What manner of man do you conjure up with all these figures whirling around in your head? Do you see a tall fellow, six feet two with broad shoulders and a massive head? Do you hear a resonant, cultured voice, and sense the predilection of a gourmet for rare wines and fine victuals? Do you visualize him living in a villa in the Italian hills with a surpassingly beautiful wife, with two children of college age? Do you think of him as a dreamy talker of boundless imagination who could hold you spellbound by the hour as he discoursed on anything from Omar Khayyam to China Clippers? If you do, you're good. For that is just the sort of man Max Brand is!

STRENGTH!: SOME IMPRESSIONS OF MAX BRAND

Chester D. Cuthbert

This article appeared originally in The Fabulous Faust Fanzine. *It has been revised for this book by the author.*

Argosy All-Story Weekly magazine presented serially the first Max Brand story that I read, and years passed before I learned that the writer's real name was Frederick Faust. The story was probably "Tiger," though I recall that "Clovelly" and "Señor Jingle Bells" were also printed about that time. I have twice re-read the last-named story in book form and consider it one of the most unusual stories ever to have been granted print in a pulp-fiction magazine.

It is an axiom of the pulp-fiction field that right must always triumph over wrong, that only the good man can win the girl. But "Señor Jingle Bells," philanderer, bravo, bank robber, and kidnapper, who by evil machination brings within his power a fine young woman, accomplishes all his purposes by force of strength. Of all Faust's works with which I am acquainted, this is the most striking example of his obsession with the idea that strength is beyond good and evil.

The problem of what constitutes strength appears to have obsessed him all his life. Regardless of the mood which swayed his belief at the various times when his stories were written, Faust's theme was always strength. No writer has developed the theme in such detail and at such length. Faust made it his joyous task to portray the most glorious feats of strength and action that he could imagine. And the gratitude I felt, other hero-worshippers can imagine better than I can describe.

The impact of the three stories I have named was so powerful that I read his "Whistlin' Dan Barry" trilogy and DAN BARRY'S DAUGHTER as soon as I knew that they were available in book form. Dan Barry is one of the great characters of all Western fiction, and his nostalgic longing for the freedom of the wild strikes the universal chord of the primitive in all who read of him. Kate Cumberland's struggle to tame that outlaw wildness, which is carried on into the story of their daughter, is no mean portrayal of woman's civilizing influence throughout the ages.

THE WHITE WOLF, TRAILIN', and ALCATRAZ were the next books I read, the first and third of these emphasizing Faust's love of dogs and horses, respectively, which plays so large a part in his writings. Of some titles obtained from England, THE GARDEN OF EDEN and HARRIGAN! were unusual stories, and THE GUIDE TO HAPPINESS amused me more than any other book of Faust's. THE GARDEN OF EDEN, like "The Ballad of St. Christopher," and, if my recollection is correct, "Kain," was written to show the humbling effect upon strength, of the realization that power has been based upon misconception or error. The first-named story is an instance, of which there are many in Faust's work, of simple goodness rather than mental or physical strength triumphing over guile and is in direct contrast to "Señor Jingle Bells." "The Ballad of St. Christopher" is a poem, crude and rough-hewn, but so challenging a vehicle of its author's philosophy at the time of its publication in 1918 that it should be "required" reading for all who are interested in Frederick Faust the man.

"The Longhorn Feud" commenced a long series of stories in *Argosy* after Max Brand had made no appearance in its pages for many years. "The Naked Blade" by George Challis I did not at first recognize as Faust's work, thinking it an attempt by a new writer to imitate Max Brand. Then I learned—I think from a writer's magazine—that "Max Brand," "George Challis," "Evan Evans," and "George Owen Baxter" were one and the same. I therefore bought MONSIEUR by George Challis, considering it a much better story than "The Naked Blade."

SINGING GUNS is an instance of a class of story which Faust wrote to identify strength with good. This has been the predominant note in his more mature work, and, while the stories sounding this note have not always been among his best, they have carried conviction. I read four of the Dr. Kildare stories, thinking them fine work and probably the best in craftsmanship of all Faust's fiction.

I do not know whether I have read a representative selection of his work, but approximately one-eighth of his published stories have come my way; many of them I've read twice, and some oftener. I have read them only because I enjoyed reading them; I have never subjected them to a critical appraisal because I wished, if possible, to retain without diminution the thrill of admiration they awakened in me. Whenever a Faust book happened along, I would begin reading it with eager anticipation and was seldom disappointed; but I was reading on many subjects sufficiently interesting to occupy my time, and I never became a collector of Faust's work. The few tales whose effect was not wholly pleasurable only point up the fact that there are few writers who have given me better entertainment value for the time I have spent reading their work.

But what kind of man was this master storyteller? I had no biographical data excepting four paragraphs which appeared in *Argosy* for December 17, 1932, and conveyed almost no facts. And the writers' magazine had stated merely that he was one of the world's most prolific writers, with an estimated annual income of $100,000 from his writings alone. Only two conclusions did I reach: he cared little for money, and he was under some powerful compulsion to discover the secret of strength.

Faust never declared himself. During his lifetime he forbade publication of biographical data which were likely to reveal his personality or, at least, refused to give out such information. Only his poetry and a few stories were published as "by Frederick Faust."

My opinion is that, at an early age, Faust found himself unable to face life squarely, mainly because he could not find a satisfactory philosophy. Supremely conscious of his titanic energy, he feared himself. Worshipping strength, he could not decide how to embody his potentialities in a career which would meet his ideal. That is why, when he turned to writing, so many of his stories have as theme, "What is Strength?" He always thought, perhaps subconsciously: "If I can only find out what true strength is, then I'll know how to live, and then I'll live!" But he never solved the problem, though I think he came mighty close occasionally, and so he never really lived. He sought refuge in romantic idealism. His heroes were projections of his dreams, and he spent his tremendous energy in putting them on paper because he was afraid of using that energy in his own life. Faust was an amazing character. If he hadn't been a great writer, he would have been a bandit, or general, or saint. He could never have been mediocre. It may have been a mercy to the world that he turned to writing. On the other hand, he might greatly have benefited the world in some other sphere of activity.

I may be wrong; Faust may have been another Jack London, but I doubt it. London, in his books, described life as he lived and saw it. Faust described life as he wished it could be. Faust was living a dream; his was not a normal life. Take some incidents that are known of him: going "over the top" with only a walking stick—in modern warfare, living in a villa in Italy—when he was writing mainly of other locales, supporting an army of unemployables—when he was himself so amazingly industrious, and took such joy in his industry—were these not acts committed because they were romantic, and only incidentally for other reasons? Faust was an idealistic dreamer, a noble soul. He could inspire his readers with his visionary conception of romantic action, but he could not help them in any practical way to cope with life itself.

This romantic viewpoint weakened his work. As an instance, let's take the start of the poem "Balin." Balin is riding along a pleasant road, a soldier of fortune, apparently, but aimless, purposeless. He is supposed to be a man of hardened maturity, yet a man of truly strong character, when mature, is rarely without purpose. Faust gives Balin no reason for existing other than to serve Nerys and avenge her brother. He even remarks, near the conclusion of the poem: "Nerys was dead, and through his fingers poured his life, loose sand." Balin rides on, once more aimless, purposeless. Only the romantic necessities of the situation have given him any life in Faust's imagination, and the reader can get no more than Faust can give.

At heart, Faust was such a sentimentalist that he had to make his heroes seem strong by every means he could devise. Even Señor Jingle Bells couldn't be the bold badman consistently. Faust had the romantic touch to perfection. He could make a few hours of high adventure seem more worthwhile than a lifetime of sober, industrious, useful work.

And now, how can I summarize Max Brand's effect upon me? In much of his work there is a tendency to melodrama and a consequent overdrawing of both character and incident. Occasionally he essayed realism, but his writing was mainly romantic: it deals with the materials of adventurous life, but in a manner so pervaded by the writer's personality as to convey a dream-like effect. Many of his plots are superficial and unreal, and the characters mere puppets acting as the master pulls the strings. Yet admiration for the master disarms all criticism, and I continue his story, fascinated under a spell from the first word to the last. Faust's ability to construct a story has been equaled by few pulp-fiction writers, and he practiced the psychology of sustained suspense so expertly that material extraneous to the story's action is seldom found. His descriptive passages are so blended with the development of character and action that the reader is swept on without pause.

If those who say that a writer can be original only to the extent that he expresses himself, then Max Brand must be considered one of the most original writers of modern times. Despite his being so prolific, Faust's style at its best is surprisingly even and thoughtful. His shrewd observations concerning life and human reaction to it are worth study. Like all highly individual writers, Faust is a dangerous model for imitators; his mannerisms of style, while suitable for him, would be jarring and disconcerting in the work of any other writer.

The news of his death in Italy in 1944 was a sad blow, softened only by the fact that he survives in a mountain of printed work which may be mined almost inexhaustibly by the average reader and whose size is known only to the expert student. I thank Frederick Faust for many of the most pleasurable hours of my life. Whenever I think of him, the word "strength" flashes into my mind. Certainly, if he failed to discover the secret of strength, he was ever eagerly in search of it, and he has left many clues for other seekers.

YOUR FORTE IS THE WEST

William A. Bloodworth, Jr.

The following essay was adapted from the manuscript of MAX BRAND, a book in the Twayne United States Authors Series. All quotations from correspondence between Frederick Faust and Robert H. (Bob) Davis are taken from Davis's papers in the New York Public Library.

"The Untamed," which began as an *All-Story Magazine* serial in December 1918 and was published as a book in March 1919, turned out to be a crucial work for Faust. He knew, even as he was writing it but especially after it was published, that the story was possibly the beginning of real success. Before it appeared, he had been providing a steady stream of fiction for Munsey magazines but had not been paid more than the standard rate for his work, and Max Brand, as a Munsey author, had not developed a particular following among readers. "The Untamed" changed all of this. And much of the credit was due to Faust's editor at the Munsey Company, Bob Davis, who not only spurred him to write the novel but who also encouraged him to stick to Westerns, including the powerful sequels to "The Untamed."

————————————— *I* —————————————

Faust wrote to Davis about the story which became "The Untamed" in February 1918, indicating that Davis had been involved in shaping ideas for the serial. Faust also worried about the title, which to that point had been simply "Whistling Dan." "I don't like Whistling Dan as a title, Chief," Faust wrote. Apparently, Davis and Faust had already discussed extensively the idea of the story. "This is the story of an atavism, a terrible fighter. I think when he learns of his almost weird power through his first fight the blood lust should go to his head like wine. He should be in a perpetual struggle to hold himself back from violence.'' Faust thought that a better title might be either ''The Lone Wolf'' ''because Dan will feel himself shut off from the rest of mankind by his peculiar nature,'' or ''Wine of Power.'' But Faust admitted that neither title was exactly right.

He wanted something right because the story had a particular interest for him, especially in the strange character of his protagonist. What Dan Barry does is less important than what Dan Barry is, and, even when Faust had only started the story, he sensed that he was tapping into powerful, perhaps even mythic sources, for his character.

By April Faust had finished the story. ''Here's 'The Untamed,' '' he told Davis in a note accompanying the manuscript. ''If you find it O.K., will you shoot the needle into your finance department and have them send out a check?'' Faust also noted that he had not taken Davis's opinion on the final episode of the novel. Davis apparently suggested that a minor character needed more development, but Faust explained that to do so would have ''blurred the main characters.'' He was probably right, but the note suggests how involved Bob Davis had been in his editorial role.

The story was a long time moving from completion in manuscript to its magazine and book appearances. Part of the problem had to do with the times. The war was on. In June 1918, Faust himself had finally managed to enlist in the Army, hoping as always to be sent to Europe but ending up at an Army Engineers' camp in Virginia for the duration of the conflict. In addition to the war the nation was battling the flu, which Faust himself contracted and survived. The Munsey staff around Bob Davis was hard hit, however. Also the war made it hard for the Munsey Company to buy sufficient quantities of paper. Finally, though, on October 13, 1918, Davis sent Faust a copy of the cover for the magazine issue in which the first episode of ''The Untamed'' would appear:

I send you herewith a cover of ''The Untamed.'' It's some good-looking job, Kid. This is going to be the turning point in your literary life. Don't smear yourself all up and down the map in the meantime. It's always darkest before dawn; and the damnedest, finest dawn ever heard of is ready to bust in the East. I could put this in very exquisite English, as you know, but I won't do it because you don't like poetry from me.

But Faust did like the advice and support and, in fact, dedicated the book version of ''The Untamed'' to Davis. George Putnam published the book six months later in a handsome edition of 374 pages that sold for $1.50 and quickly went into a second printing. The story was soon snapped up by Hollywood. Putnam himself had told Faust that Douglas Fairbanks might buy it and play the title role himself. As it was, Faust had to settle for a 1920 Fox production starring Tom Mix. But it was still, in Davis's terminology, a pretty fine dawn. In April 1919, when the book was selling well, Faust told Davis: ''By the way, 'The Untamed' is not *my* book; it's *our* book.''

Davis was also helpful with the two novels that served as sequels to THE UNTAMED. These were published as THE NIGHT HORSEMAN and THE SEVENTH MAN, carrying the story of Dan Barry forward to his death. Not only did Davis advise Faust on his manuscripts, but he insisted that he soak up some of the flavor of the real West by taking a trip to El Paso, Texas, where he even visited a working ranch. Yet any interest in the reality of the West, on Davis's part, was tempered by his knowledge that Faust worked better out of imagination than out of observed fact. At one point during his trip Faust indicated in a letter to Davis that he was interested in writing about a particular trial. Davis's advice was to "fight shy of it." "It is easier to dream fiction than to fake facts." The advice was not lost on Faust. He did not quite understand what it was about his first Western book that made such an impression on readers. He told Davis: "I still fail to see why 'The Untamed' has gone over, and it makes me feel that we can knock them dead with the sequel. For that reason I'm anxious to get back to New York and hit the collar again. No question about it, I work a hell of a pile better with than away from you." He also wondered whether the public was sick of the "proper man" as a hero; it was all he knew that might explain the appeal of THE UNTAMED. He was, of course, right.

In the next eighteen months he proceeded to turn out not one but two sequels to the story that had "gone over" so well. They, too, did well. Also he wrote several other Westerns for Munsey, generally avoiding the "proper man" as hero. He had discovered, with Bob Davis's assistance, a real forte. In later years he would not always write good Westerns, and he would certainly not restrict himself to that genre. Also he would claim, as necessary, that he cared not a whit for Westerns. But the truth was otherwise.

In August 1920, Faust saw his creation on the silver screen at the Capitol movie house in New York. The next day he wrote to Bob Davis about the film.

Dear Chief:

I got Miss Temple's telegram about THE UNTAMED showing at the Capitol. That sounded pretty good. I went up and took a look. Jesus, what a blow-out!

I'll tell you what, they inserted a dexterous knife and cut out everything that approached good stuff in the story. They had a tin whistle going behind the stage every time Dan appeared, and it was so damned ludicrous that the audience began to laugh. They used few of the important scenes, and the ones they did use they wrested from their real meaning. They made it a joke picture, and to cap the climax they threw in the happy ending which of course spoiled the whole yarn. The whole point of Dan's character and his coming to life were obscured. The incidents rattled off so swiftly that it was almost impossible to follow the meaning of the picture. The narrative was twisted, changed, cut at will. And when Kate is in the cabin in the mountains, they frame it so that her virtue is threatened.

In a word, it's a cheesy piece of work. I went all set for a pretty good show, even though the original story is nothing to get wild about. I saw, without exaggeration, the worst picture I ever laid eyes on. Between you and me, I think Tom Mix is okay, but his directors are a joke.

And in conclusion, can't we have something to say about the way our stories are done? Can't we get in touch with the birds who write the scenarios? Can't we write the scenarios ourselves? I'd rather put more time in and get less out than see such fearful botches. You'll say more violent things than that if you should ever be unlucky enough to have to see that abortion on the screen. When am I going to see you?

Thine,
Max

It is obvious that Faust cared about the story he had created and thought it had points worth preserving. Whether his reaction to the screen version of THE UNTAMED influenced his attitude toward his later work is hard to tell. Much of what he said later on, as well as much of what he turned out on his typewriter, suggests that he wrote mainly to get the stories out into magazines and money into his bank accounts. But, guided by Bob Davis, THE UNTAMED and its sequels were more than merely lucrative.

II

In THE NIGHT HORSEMAN and THE SEVENTH MAN, the sequels to THE UNTAMED that Bob Davis had urged Faust to write, the off-center quality of themes and characters continued. Taken together, the three novels constitute a strange but powerful bit of popular American literature.

Faust had trouble with the sequels. He had finished "The Untamed" in April 1918, and by May was mentioning to Davis the idea of a sequel entitled "The Wild Geese." In fact, on May 15 he sent Davis several pages of a scenario for the beginning of the sequel. But it lacked direction, and Davis had not been very encouraging about it. Faust had at least two reasons for staying on the trail of Dan Barry, however. First, he needed to capitalize on the success of THE UNTAMED while it was still in the public eye; he admitted to his wife, Dorothy, that their hopes for the future were pinned to the sequel. Second, even though he claimed not to know why THE UNTAMED went over so well, he certainly was aware that he had somehow uncovered themes that satisfied large numbers of readers.

On November 3, 1918, however, he told Davis that his efforts on the idea of "The Wild Geese" were an absolute bust. But by June 1920, the story was done, and Faust was trying to find a better title than "The Wild Geese" while starting on the third Dan Barry novel. "The Night Horseman," the title settled on, finally began appearing in *Argosy All-Story Weekly* (the title reflecting a merger of two Munsey magazines) in mid-September 1920, twenty-two months after "The Untamed" had begun its run in the magazine. More than a year later, in October 1921, the third Dan Barry novel, "The Seventh Man," began appearing in the magazine. Like "The Untamed," each sequel was published as a hardcover book by Putnam several months after the last weekly episode appeared in the magazine.

The three Dan Barry novels thus were written over three and a half years of Faust's career, a period which also saw the appearance of fourteen other serials as well as many novelettes and short stories. Moreover, in 1923, two years after the publication of "The Seventh Man," Faust returned to the setting and characters (*sans* Dan Barry himself) in DAN BARRY'S DAUGHTER. While he was certainly not obsessed with his creation and first great success, he devoted a remarkable amount of attention to it. Somewhat for this reason, but more pointedly for his extended treatment of a Western hero outside the realm of a "proper man," THE NIGHT HORSEMAN and THE SEVENTH MAN are important features of the Max Brand legacy.

In the second novel Faust returned to the Kate Cumberland–Dan Barry relationship in an extraordinarily complicated plot involving the temporary "taming" of the hero. The novel opens with Kate's father, Joe Cumberland, near death and apparently needing the presence of Dan Barry to sustain his life. To lure Barry back both for Joe Cumberland's sake and to save him from his own wildness, his friend, Buck Daniels, strikes Barry on the face. The ploy works, and Barry comes raging back to the Cumberland ranch. He is often described as a wolf or a werewolf by those who fear his arrival. Kate, however, is able for a while to create in Barry some sense of human compassion. In a chapter entitled "Victory," Barry puts his hand in hers and decides that he will not kill Buck Daniels. But, when he faces Daniels and refuses to fight him, he seems lonesome, even saying: "I feel sort of lost and lonesome . . . like I'd thrown somethin' away that I valued most."

In the end Dan Barry is returned to wildness. After two men refuse to fight him, thus frustrating his atavistic desires, Barry returns to the Cumberland ranch during a terrific nighttime storm and demands that Kate leave the ranch and come with him. In a scene more symbolic of rape than of love the woman is once more drawn to Barry by his mysterious personal power. At the very close of the novel she and Barry ride off into the night on Barry's powerful black horse with an even darker name: Satan. When they leave, Kate's father dies, and an observer wonders whether what has happened (especially the winning, so to speak, of Kate by Barry) is "God's work or devil's work."

The answer is by no means clear, nor does it become a great deal clearer in the final novel about Dan Barry. In THE SEVENTH MAN Faust again created a plot which turns upon furious action, motivated by a lust for revenge. It begins with Dan Barry married to Kate Cumberland. Several years have elapsed since the tumultuous final scene of the previous novel. Barry and his wife appear to have settled down to a life of peaceful domesticity and the raising of a child in a mountain cabin. Early in the story Kate feels that Dan is safe from the uncontrollable rage that she had seen before in him: "There was no danger," she thinks, "of him ever slipping back into that terrible other self"; she would "never again have to dream of that whistling in the wind."

Her expectations are shattered, however, when a sheriff's posse shoots a borrowed horse out from under Barry as he attempts to help a friend evade the lawmen. At the death of the horse Barry is overcome by the internal wildness that his years of marriage with Kate had suppressed. He first shoots a member of the posse, thinking it right—in his untamed mood—to avenge a horse's life with a human life. Then, finding that he has been betrayed by the very friend whom he had earlier tried to help, he promises to take a total of seven lives to even the score.

The plot of THE SEVENTH MAN is largely the story of Barry's rage and revenge. He kills six men with ease, the sixth being the sheriff. The seventh man is the friend, Vic Gregg, who had betrayed him in the opening episodes. Getting to the seventh man is the primary task of the novel's plot. But Faust introduces a secondary—yet more interesting—conflict in the story. This is the conflict between Dan and Kate Barry, husband and wife, two lovers fated now by Dan's rage to lose each other. As he hunts his seven victims, Barry lives in a cave alone with Satan and Black Bart, his horse and dog. At one point Kate sends their daughter, Joan, with a message. Joan, aged four or five, shares her father's personality, especially his strange ability to communicate with wild animals. When she comes to Barry at his cave, she stays, taking a coyote pup as a pet and forcing her mother, now on the other side of a moral chasm from her husband, to fight for her return.

Ultimately this strange Western turns not on some resolution between Dan and those whom he pursues. Rather, it shifts with a deadly finality to the complicated conflict between Barry and his wife. By the conclusion of the story Kate has managed to recapture her daughter from Barry's mountain cave. She and Joan then move to the home of her now-deceased father. Barry finally arrives at the Cumberland ranch, looking for Joan and whistling his strange music. Kate, whose love for Barry has never ceased despite his murderous rage against the killers of the horse, realizes now that her husband will remain forever untamed. Therefore in a moment of terrible, mixed emotion—a combination of love and fear—she takes a small pistol which Barry had taught her to use, aims it at his heart, and shoots him. It is obvious that she is the only person capable of killing him.

The meaning of this event in the story is complicated. Above all, it points to the departure of Faust's Western narratives from stories similar in setting and characters. Under the example of Owen Wister and Zane Grey, the Western had become by 1921 the carrier of a national mythology. The Western hero was society's salvation, the answer to corruption and lawlessness. The violent potential of the hero was a deadly but often hesitant means of fighting fire with fire. THE VIRGINIAN (Macmillan, 1903) had been archetypal in this regard. Its title character appears first in the novel as a young man with the attributes of a tiger. But as the story develops, so does the Virginian's innate qualities of civility. In the end he sheds blood reluctantly, even killing a former friend, because it is something he must do in order to maintain social order. This kind of logic, with its implied apologia for violence, its participation in what Richard Slotkin refers to as ''regeneration through violence'' in his book of that title, merges with a romantic plot that pulls together the Western ways of the hero with the Eastern background of the heroine.

Thus the classic Western ends on a note of hope in which the coming together of hero and heroine is truly generative and progressive. This is the typical ending also of Zane Grey's Westerns. Such stories restate the ''frontier thesis'' first announced by Frederick Jackson Turner in 1893—that the primitive simplicity of life on the frontier has been the key determinant of American character and virtue. Faust obviously felt little compunction about not investing in the frontier thesis. Although he is frequently mentioned in the same breath with writers like Zane Grey, his Westerns are of another order. They do not, as a rule, provide a mythic affirmation of the frontier experience. They use presumed elements of that experience for the sake of action and conflict, but they seldom extol the value of Western history or assert the virtues of the frontier past over the present.

The killing of Dan Barry by his wife at the end of the Dan Barry trilogy denies the power of love as a stabilizing force in society and—by extension— suggests that the Western hero and all he represents is, after all, a matter of violence and death without regeneration. The contrast to Grey's novels in this regard is striking. In RIDERS OF THE PURPLE SAGE (Harper, 1912) the gunman, Lassiter, is ultimately united with and symbolically transformed by his relationship with the heroine. In NEVADA (Harper, 1928) a character burning with restlessness finds stability and purpose when he falls in love with a sixteen-year-old beauty. In Max Brand, however, Kate Barry sends a bullet through the wild heart of her untamed spouse.

FREDERICK FAUST'S WESTERN FICTION: AN OVERVIEW

Jon Tuska

O, it is excellent
To have a giant's strength, but it is tyrannous
to use it like a giant.

—Shakespeare

It was a young voice as thin and clean as rays of starlight and there was
an upward springing in it, as life should be at the beginning.

—Frederick Faust

We have lingered in the chambers of the sea / By sea-girls wreathed with
seaweed red and brown / Till human voices wake us, and we drown.

—T. S. Eliot

I

The immediate occasion that caused Frederick Faust to write Western stories
was the extraordinary success and popularity of Zane Grey. Grey's "Desert
Gold" was serialized in Street & Smith's *The Popular Magazine* in 1913, after
which he began selling first serial rights to his Western novels to Robert Hobart
Davis at the Munsey publications. Bob Davis serialized "The Light of Western
Stars" in *Munsey's Magazine* in 1913. "The Lone Star Rangers" appeared as
a five-part serial in *All-Story-Cavalier Weekly* in 1914. "The Last of the Duanes" was cut from nearly 90,000 words to a short novel of less than fifty pages
and appeared in a single issue of *The Argosy*. Davis claimed his reason for this
condensation was that the serial, as Grey had written it, involved the deaths of
no less than eighteen characters and was, therefore, much too violent. "The
Desert Crucible," which became THE RAINBOW TRAIL (Harper, 1915), was
serialized in *The Argosy* and was followed by "The Border Legion." Grey then
entered the slick magazine market with "Wildfire," serialized in *The Country
Gentleman* in 1916, and never returned to pulp magazines except in reprints.

Bob Davis needed someone to replace Zane Grey. He chose Frederick Faust, a California writer then living in New York. Born in Seattle, Washington, at a very early age Faust moved with his parents to the San Joaquin Valley in California. His parents were poor and, apparently to compensate for a life in which there was sometimes not enough to eat, he turned to medieval romantic literature and his own vivid imagination for solace. It was the extraordinary amount of physical labor Faust did as a youth which strained and enlarged his heart. Later many of his protagonists would be confronted early on in his narratives with similarly brutal manual labor. When orphaned, he went to live with a distant relative, Thomas Downey, a high school principal.

Faust was sixteen when Downey introduced him to a Classical education. Greek and Latin literature and mythology fired Faust's mind and remained a lifelong frame of reference. As late in his career as "Gunman's Bluff" it was not unusual for Faust to include in a description of an impending gunfight a Classical reference: "Martindale converged on Rafferty's saloon. Not all of Martindale, for the women and children remained at home, of course, and they formed the whispering chorus against which the tragedy was enacted." Faust's images and even his characters would shimmer and intimate those once bright forms born in the vivid light of the lands bordering on what Herodotus would call ἡ δε ἡ Θαλασσα (the sea) and Julius Caesar *mare nostrum* (our sea). Years hence, when Faust found himself in one enchanted land of the Mediterranean, he commented: "Wherever there is Greece there is magic. And when mountains or islands appear blue, there is usually a silver or golden slope shining through the mist. One rarely finds a landscape that is all dark." Faust would find the dark landscapes, though, as did Odysseus, and he would project them outward into the mountain desert of the great American West, but always there was the brilliant light in the pantheon of the firmament. Homer, Vergil, Dante, Shakespeare, Æschylus, yes—not so much Sophocles, and never Euripedes (who dared look into the abyss and saw that the universe at base was irrational and therefore incomprehensible to reason)—these were the purveyors of the worlds and the moods which preoccupied Faust, and they left their eternal imprint on what he wrote.

It must be stressed, however, that moods and spiritual landscapes are not the same thing as references to Classical mythology. Robert Easton in MAX BRAND: THE BIG "WESTERNER" (University of Oklahoma Press, 1970) felt that "Faust introduced old world myth into the new world West. This— with his poetic approach—is his unique contribution to the Western story." In the six-part serial, "The Untamed," Faust compares his protagonist, Dan Barry, who is whistling when seen for the first time, to the woodland god, Pan. Jack Nachbar in his Introduction to the Gregg Press' hardcover reprint edition of THE UNTAMED in 1978 called the reader's attention to this and numerous other Classical references to be found in the text of what became Faust's first Western novel. The references are there, as they are throughout many of Faust's Western stories, but all such references are largely gratuitous and never organic.

These references in THE UNTAMED do not provide any additional dimension to Dan Barry's character. After he is compared to Pan, no further literary use is made of this similarity in terms of what happens in the story. Moreover, Faust's comparison of the final confrontation in THE UNTAMED between Dan Barry and Jim Silent with the epic battle between Achilles and Hector in Homer's "Iliad" is even spurious since Dan's motive is shown as more instinctual than heroic.

One of the convictions of Classical Antiquity that struck the strongest chord in Faust was the belief that to die in battle was the best, most heroic kind of death, a romantic notion perhaps best articulated by Horace when he wrote: *"Dulce et decorum est pro patria mori."* Horace used the Latin word *decorum* here as a cognate for the Homeric sense of καιρός (due measure)—it is both sweet and *fitting* to die for one's fatherland. The notion of fitting in this context means that the act performed is consonant with the highest aspirations of the natural order that governs all things in the universe. Faust's desire to be in battle was what prompted him to try getting into the Great War by emigrating to Canada. This, and all of his subsequent efforts, however, were of no avail and in 1917, in New York, unable to get shipped overseas even in the ambulance corps, Faust turned to what from then on would be his principal aim in life: to become a major poet. In a letter of protest to *The New York Times,* working at manual labor and voicing his outrage, Faust objected to the social injustice of his lot and, fortuitously, was given assistance by Mark Twain's sister. It was she who first brought Frederick Faust and Bob Davis together. Faust's acumen and immense talent impressed Davis at once.

There is an anecdote told of their first encounter to which I am inclined to lend credence. Presumably Davis, as a way of testing Faust's ability as a writer, gave him the nucleus of a story idea, sent him down the hall to a room where there was a typewriter to see what he could do with it, only for Faust to return later that day with a story that was immediately publishable. That story was titled "Convalescence." After that Faust became a regular contributor to *All-Story Weekly* which was one of the Munsey magazines Davis edited. By the time Faust sold his third story to Davis, he had adopted Max Brand as his byline. There was a sound reason for a pseudonym beyond any desire for anonymity. The United States was at war with Germany, and anything German was considered anathema by many. What name could be more recognizable as German in origin than Faust?

In 1918 Faust wrote his first Western fiction for *All-Story Weekly,* although a five-part mining serial from the previous year that Davis retitled "Fate's Honeymoon" in *All-Story Weekly* begins in the contemporary West. Faust's first Western story in terms of the American West as a sustained setting is the short novel, "Above the Law," followed by the short story, "Bad-Eye, His Life and Letters." Davis is known to have given Faust some Zane Grey serials to read in preparation for writing Western stories. William F. Nolan in his Introduction to THE BEST WESTERN STORIES OF MAX BRAND quoted Faust as saying:

"Davis handed me copies of Zane Grey's LONE STAR RANGER and RIDERS OF THE PURPLE SAGE. Told me to read 'em and see what I could do along those lines." On the face of it these were curious novels for Davis to have given Faust. THE LONE STAR RANGER (Harper, 1915) is a hybrid combining Davis's condensed version of "The Last of the Duanes" as Part One with a section of the serial "The Lone Star Rangers" as Part Two. It is probably Grey's weakest book in that decade primarily because the condensed version of "The Last of Duanes" doesn't really fit with the other serial.

Based on the internal evidence of Faust's own early Western fiction, I believe he also unquestionably read Zane Grey's THE HERITAGE OF THE DESERT (Harper, 1910) and THE BORDER LEGION (Harper, 1916). "Above the Law" shares many similar plot ingredients with THE BORDER LEGION, and Faust's THE UNTAMED has a variation of these same plot ingredients as does the six-part serial, "Luck," in *The Argosy*. Jack Nachbar in his Introduction to the Gregg Press' edition of THE UNTAMED noted that "several of the characters are motivated by virtues straight out of the traditions of King Arthur and his Knights of the Round Table. The members of Silent's outlaw gang . . . feel a bond of honor toward the gang similar to those of Arthur's knights for one another. A further indication of the gang's knightly basis is their demand that Kate Cumberland be treated with respect, a demand out of character for desperado killers but quite in character for men true to a code of chivalry." There is no question that this view of honor among thieves and a code of chivalry for desperadoes was a fixed idea with Faust, and one that persisted. In "Luck," when Jim Boone and his gang are first seen, Faust replays the same theme with even greater accentuation.

Each of them should have ridden alone in order to be properly appreciated. To see them together was like watching a flock of eagles every one of which should have been a solitary lord of the air. But after scanning that lordly train which followed, the more terrible seemed the rider of the great black horse. Yet the king was sad, and the reason for his sadness was the riderless horse which galloped so freely beside him.

The rider on the great black horse, "the king," is Jim Boone. He is sad because in the course of robbing a train his only son, Handsome Hal, was killed. When Pierre le Rouge comes to replace Hal with this gang, he also shares their sense of a bond of honor, a bond that can survive everything except Bob McGurk's fiendish and systematic revenge for the way the gang rallies around Pierre le Rouge when McGurk demands Pierre be expelled from the mountain desert.

It is safe to state, I believe, that Faust was the first to emphasize the loyalty of gang members to the degree that he did. Contemporary Western writers like B. M. Bower in her saga about Chip Bennett and the Happy Family at the Flying U and Clarence E. Mulford in his saga about Hopalong Cassidy and the Bar-20 crew reserved this kind of loyalty for these extended families consisting of their heroes and their rangeland friends. Loyalty, for Faust, was one of the greatest virtues, and should a man lose that, he has lost everything.

In Zane Grey's THE BORDER LEGION Jim Cleve and Joan Randle have an altercation after which Cleve goes off in anger to join Jack Kells's gang. Joan follows Cleve and becomes for much of the story Kells's personal prisoner. There is a similarity here with Kate Cumberland's attempt to seek out Jim Silent's gang in the hope that her presence among them will be sufficient to dissuade Dan Barry from killing them all. The major difference between the two narratives is that, while Kate is made a prisoner of the Silent gang, no relationship develops between her and Jim Silent as it does between Joan and Jack Kells. Instead, Kate's captivity is the occasion for Lee Haines, Silent's right hand, and Buck Daniels, a gang member, to conspire together to effect Kate's escape. Haines, in this sense, is a reversal of the thug, Gulden, Kells's apish right hand who lusts after Joan and wants to chain her naked in a cave. Haines, not Silent, is the one who falls in love with Kate.

I suspect that Mescal—Grey's heroine in THE HERITAGE OF THE DESERT who rides a mare called Black Bolly with Wolf, her faithful wolf-dog, always at their side—was the inspiration for what Faust in THE UNTAMED transformed into the striking images of Dan Barry, his stallion, Satan, and his wolf-dog, Black Bart. Indeed, Faust was obviously so taken with this triumvirate of human, horse, and dog that he resorted to it again in the Bull Hunter stories of 1921, in the Lost Wolf stories, and, later in the 1930s, in the Silvertip series. Satan stands fifteen hands high compared to Parade in the Silvertip series who stands seventeen hands high. It isn't until DAN BARRY'S DAUGHTER that we learn that Black Bart weighs one hundred and thirty pounds. Frosty in the Silvertip series weighs one hundred and fifty pounds. One error that Faust consistently made in the Dan Barry saga—and one he did not repeat in the Silvertip series—is that Black Bart is always shown as being in the lead when Dan is riding hard and fast on Satan, the wolf-dog serving as guide to the trio. It must have been pointed out to Faust that, no matter how capable Black Bart might be, he could not possibly run faster than a stallion!

Grey's major influence on Faust, however, has little to do with the kinds of Western stories each wrote. It consists rather in the fact that both Grey and Faust, in their finest Western fiction, eschewed realism in preference for psychodramas in the realm of the dream and the archetypes of the collective unconscious, even though they went about it in very different ways. Grey tied his dreams to a vivid depiction of the wilderness and the vast terrain of the West as he personally experienced it. This was combined with his obsessional eroticism tempered, and even disguised, for his readers by means of a powerful and sustaining context of romance. Faust plunged instead into the no less vast cavity of the human soul—the expanse that is without measure, as Heraclitus said—and for him the experience must have been much as he would later describe it in 1926 for Oliver Tay in what became THE BORDER BANDIT.

He was seeing himself for the very first time; and, just as his eye could wander through the unfathomed leagues of the stars which were strewn across the universe at night, so he could turn his glance inward and probe the vastness of new-found self. All new!

Dan Barry, Satan, and Black Bart in THE UNTAMED are not really a triumvirate Western hero, traditional or otherwise, but instead an archetypal projection of the shadow: "They seemed like one being rather than three. The wolf was the eyes, the horse the strong body to flee or pursue, and the man was the brain which directed, and the power which struck." It is Jim Silent, Dan Barry's antagonist, who in his first fight with Dan brings to him "this first taste of his own powers—this first taste . . . of blood!" Dan is more feral than human and that is how he is depicted when, as an "ominous crouched animal with the yellow eyes, the nameless thing which had been Whistling Dan before, sprang up and forward with a leap like that of a panther."

Robert Easton suggested in his biography of Faust that much of the plot of THE UNTAMED is actually an imaginative distortion of Faust's very personal conflicts at the time he wrote it. He and Dorothy Schillig had only recently married (hence, Bob Davis's humorously coining the title "Fate's Honeymoon" in subtle reference to the event), and Faust was apparently torn between his desire to live only to write poetry and his growing responsibilities toward his family. Easton wrote: "Barry is trying to come to grips with himself. He is torn between adventurous freedom (war, action) and love (Dorothy, baby), between civilized society (the here, the now) and unresolved possibilities that lie out yonder where the wild geese call (the possibilities of poetry)." If this is an accurate assessment of the spiritual climate in which this novel was conceived— and I take it to be so—then the ending to this story was unresolved in the author's mind and a sequel had to be written. Faust actually continued Dan Barry's saga through two more books, THE NIGHT HORSEMAN and THE SEVENTH MAN, before Dan is dead, killed by the heroine, Kate Cumberland, a desperate act prompted by Kate's determination to protect their daughter from him. It is Joan Barry's story, narrated after her father and her mother are both dead, that concludes the saga in DAN BARRY'S DAUGHTER. The only resolution at which Faust could arrive to Dan Barry's schizoid dilemma was for Dan Barry to die—and at the hands of the woman who both desperately loves him and who is terrified of him.

For the rest of his life Faust never could resolve this dilemma in himself. Maybe it was only resolved for him on the battlefield in Italy where he died. It is the same dilemma that Jack London varied in CALL OF THE WILD (Macmillan, 1903) where Buck is seen to choose the wilderness and reversed in WHITE FANG (Macmillan, 1906) where White Fang chooses domestic life with his master. With Jack London, I suspect, this dilemma was more a premise than the source of constant emotional anguish and turmoil it was for Faust. I have already made reference to THE BORDER BANDIT. The conflict within the third and final part of this novel is the wild and free life lived by the Mexican bandits and by Yellow Wolf, the Comanche brave who befriends Oliver Tay, and its alternative. Oliver begins this narrative in three parts searching for wholeness but deserts this goal at the conclusion through his love for a woman. The struggle at the center of Faust's THE WHITE WOLF or the Dan Barry stories is now focused far more precisely, but the resolution is bathed in irony. Yellow Wolf's inner voice is the last one heard as he reflects: "To each man his own strength. To each man his own weakness. But, alas, what weakness was so great as the love of a woman? For it seemed to him that already he saw the mighty shoulders of Oliver Tay bowed to the plow."

In THE SEVENTH MAN Dan Barry is shown pursuing a tamed and civilized life with Kate and their young daughter, Joan. Vic Gregg has been making improvements on his mining properties so he will have enough money to marry Betty Neal. One night in town Vic and Betty have an argument because of her intention to attend a dance with Blondy Hansen. Vic and Blondy shoot it out in a saloon. Vic becomes a fugitive and is wounded by a bullet fired by the pursuing sheriff. Dan saves him, taking him to the mountain cabin where he, Kate, and Joan are living. The family strikes Vic as a happy one, although Dan can be very intimidating with little Joan. When Dan, pretending to be Vic, tries to mislead the sheriff's posse, the horse he is riding is hit. Dan retaliates by killing a member of the posse. Dan is determined to finish off the rest of the posse as well as Vic who, he thinks, has betrayed him. Dan Barry's attacks followed by the pursuit of him make for one of the most exciting chases in all of Western fiction.

The conclusion of THE SEVENTH MAN, where Kate feels compelled to kill Dan to protect Joan from him and his murderous impulses, is scarcely the happy ending to be found in Zane Grey's stories or in the majority of Western fiction being written at the time. Nor is this a lone example of a Western story by Faust ending in tragedy. In the fourth and final short novel, "The Bill for Banditry" in *Western Story Magazine,* comprising KING CHARLIE, Billy English, the protagonist, who has sacrificed years of his life to raise, nurture, and educate Louise Alison Dora Young finds all of his hopes for happiness and fulfillment ultimately destroyed because he believed the lie told to him by the tramp, King Charlie, that Charlie is his father. Jim Curry in the third and final short novel, "Jim Curry's Sacrifice" in *Western Story Magazine,* comprising JIM CURRY'S TEST abandons all hope of love and happiness when he returns to being the bandit known as "The Red Devil" in order to permit an old man to retain an illusion about his worthless son. To stay within a classical context, it is very much a matter of how the opposing themes of what Henrik Ibsen regarded as a "life-sustaining illusion" and what Homer meant by "fitting" are resolved in a Faust Western story that determines whether the story is a tragedy or a comedy. Just as Jim Curry sacrifices his life to preserve a "life-sustaining illusion," so Happy Jack in "The Gift" in *Western Story Magazine* saves his life by preserving an old man's "life-sustaining illusion" that his lost son is returned to him.

It is perhaps most revealing of Faust to recall here "Slip Liddell" which first appeared under the title "Señor Coyote" in two installments in *Argosy*. It is the last Western short novel Frederick Faust was to write, and *Argosy* was a fitting place for it to have been published since his earliest Western fiction had been sold to *All-Story Weekly* and *The Argosy* owned by The Frank A. Munsey Company. With the issue dated 7/24/20 these two magazines were merged to form *Argosy/All-Story Weekly*. Finally with the issue dated 10/5/29, any reference to *All-Story Weekly* was dropped. As the bleakness of the Great Depression seemed like it would never end, irate readers of *Western Story Magazine* in the early 1930s began to complain about "fairy tale" stories by Faust under various pseudonyms. While it is true that Faust did often seem to write fairy tales, few could know the exhaustive research notes he had compiled on every aspect of Western life from animal husbandry to mining, from transportation to the culture and history of many Indian nations. Perhaps no one except his wife, Dorothy, knew how acutely Faust had suffered during his early years as a farm and ranch laborer. She forbade the children ever to mention those years in his presence. But it was from this well of early sorrow, and from the sustained misery of his later life, that Faust created so many of the subtexts in his Western stories, as in his fiction generally. *"In animi doloribus solitudines captare,"* Cicero once wrote, "in anguished souls solitudes are captured." In Faust's stories it is often only a glance, a gesture, a brief and fleeting glimpse that reveals the depth of personal suffering residing behind the surface of even the brightest fairy tale.

Near the end of "Slip Liddell" Slip and Skeeter are talking.

"Slip, it's kind of funny. This morning I was thinking that we had years and years and years laid out ahead when we'd be seeing each other now and then, and you'd be laid up in the back of my mind like a bit of summer weather, and all that. And now here it is the end, already. It makes me feel queer. It makes me feel kind of sick in the stomach. . . . And good bye!"

She was out the window in a flash, but in the open air she turned again.

"Should I come back? Would you kiss me good bye?" she asked.

"You don't have to come back for that," he said. And he picked up her hand and leaned over and kissed it with a long, light pressure of his lips.

Afterward she lifted the hand to her cheek. She began to laugh, but the laughter staggered and went out suddenly.

"Slip!" she whispered. "I'm not going to live long after you."

"Stop talking rot!" he commanded.

"I never could be another man's," said Skeeter.

"Wait, Skeeter . . . ," he called, leaning across the window sill.

But she already was gone into the night.

"There was so much unexpressed feeling that could not be entirely portrayed," Loren Grey, Zane Grey's younger son and a noted psychologist, once recalled about his father, "that, in later years, he would weep when re-reading one of his own books." If Faust seldom read any of his fiction once it was published and kept most of it locked away in a cabinet, forbidding his children to read it, to avoid contact with so much deeply concealed emotion may have been part of the reason, just as it may explain why he tended to disparage what he wrote. In "The One-Way Trail" by George Owen Baxter in *Western Story Magazine,* for almost a decade Alison Chalmers has been Sheriff John Clark's ward. One night to his shock he hears an incredible sound.

It must be Alison, and yet—Alison laughing? It was impossible! To be sure, in the old days when her father was alive, she had been a merry little child. But, now that he thought upon it, it was years and years since he had heard her laugh. It was a sufficiently horrible thought, this one that a young girl had not laughed for so long a time that he could not remember, but the sheriff did not dwell on the horror.

The emotional power in the subtexts of Faust's psycho-dramas can be at times so absolutely devastating that surely he would, like Sheriff John Clark, want to distance himself from them.

It is perhaps also worthy of note that Bob Davis's reason in 1914 for rejecting Zane Grey's "Last of the Duanes"—that there was too much violence in it— was apparently no longer a valid premise for him in 1917 since Dan Barry in the three volumes of his saga is far more violent than Buck Duane is in Grey's serial. At this late date, with LAST OF THE DUANES (Five Star Westerns, 1996) finally published as its author intended, it would appear that Davis's second thoughts were perhaps more apt. In telling evidence of the classic stature the Dan Barry saga has gained it is only necessary to reflect that seventy-five years after THE UNTAMED first appeared both it and its companion volumes were reprinted by the University of Nebraska Press with great success. At about the same time the entire saga was also issued in full-length audio by Books on Tape, as well as in large print, and first editions of the Dan Barry books appeared in translation, first in the Czech Republic and then in the Slovak Republic. Obviously, whatever its origins in Faust's tormented psyche, the spiritual and psychological appeal of the Dan Barry saga has been able to touch the human soul generation after generation, and as such it may now be regarded as a meaningful contribution to world literature.

II

In assembling the fiction to appear in THE SACKING OF EL DORADO, I went back and read all of the Western short stories that Faust wrote immediately after publication of "Above the Law" and during the period which saw the first appearance of his earliest Western novels, THE UNTAMED, TRAILIN', and THE NIGHT HORSEMAN. In these early stories Faust was feeling his way, developing and rehearsing his psychological themes, trying again and again to find the best way possible to express them in a dramatic narrative.

"Bad-Eye, His Life and Letters" and "The Ghost" in *All-Story Weekly* both rely on a subtle interplay between illusion and reality. James Jerrold Melrose, known among the local inhabitants of Truckee as Bad-Eye, is killed during a barroom brawl. When a young woman shows up whose last name is Melrose, Masters, who owns the bar and hotel where Bad Eye died, and Mac, the bartender who dispatched the wastrel, believe she is the widow. An elaborate comedy of errors ensues until she reveals herself to be a very distant cousin whose sole purpose in coming to Truckee was to find out why her friend, who had married Bad-Eye and had been supporting him for years in his drunken frivolities, has stopped hearing from him. In the next story an armed thief known as The Ghost has a hide-out that allows him to vanish, seemingly into the air. A gunman is engaged by the mining community on which he has been preying to run down the outlaw. The Ghost turns out to be the town drunk, a man known locally as "Geraldine." He succeeds in making it appear that the gunman, rather than being the bounty hunter the community thought he was, is himself actually The Ghost. Geraldine manages to escape with all the loot from his depredations. Interestingly, the same sequestered hide-out and a very similar outlaw are later to be found in "Clung," a six-part serial that ran in *All-Story Weekly* in 1920.

In "Gunman's Bluff" there is a silent observer: "The Chinaman grinned and bobbed his head at her. Chinamen never understood anything except how to be kind. And that's the lesson the world needs most." However, it would not be until Les Savage, Jr., wrote the original version of HANGTOWN (Ballantine, 1956) and introduced among his Chinese characters a Chinaman who has had his tongue cut out by a Missouri Pike that the Sophoclean ideal would at last be achieved in Western fiction: a silent character whose very presence speaks far more eloquently and imperishably than either the protagonist or the chorus. Yet, if Faust's imaginative treatment of the Chinese on the frontier did not venture in this direction, "Clung" was his earliest effort to tell a story about a Caucasian raised by a member of another race, in this case by Li Clung, so that intellectually, culturally, and spiritually—in short, all but biologically—Clung *is* Chinese. He is looked down upon as a "Chink" and dismissed by many of the local Caucasians. It is also perhaps notable that, while CLUNG appeared in book form in the British market a few years after the magazine serial, it wasn't published in the United States in book form until Dodd, Mead & Company brought it out in 1969. When Pocket Books issued its mass merchandise paperback reprint edition in 1971, fearing perhaps that a "Chinese" protagonist would discourage readers, the title was inappropriately changed to THE GHOST RIDER! Yet, it is in CLUNG that I suspect one witnesses the first manifestation of the impulse of later Faust serials featuring Caucasians raised among various Indian nations who ultimately find themselves as bewildered by their mixed heritage as Clung does.

The praxis of "The Fear of Morgan the Fearless" in *All-Story Weekly* hinges on how fragile is human psychology when Morgan, a fearless outlaw, is confronted by the superior confidence of the man who is hired to hunt him down and capture him. The strain of the confrontation is painful as Morgan's bravura is so reduced by intimidation that finally, without any resistance, he allows his guns to be taken from him by the man he had intended himself to shame or to kill. Of all of Faust's early themes the psychological principle of breaking the spirit of a man, or an animal, would be one that he varied most often. It is anticipated in "The Laughter of Slim Malone" in *All-Story Weekly* and is to be found, albeit again in a subtle variation, in "Jerico's 'Garrison Finish' " in *Western Story Magazine,* in "The Power of Prayer" in *Western Story Magazine,* and in " 'Sunset' Wins" in *Western Story Magazine.* It is by means of psychological reduction that Dr. Clinton Aylard shames Harrison Colby in WOODEN GUNS only to have the same strategy work just as effectively against him, as once it worked for him, when Big Jim Conover comes for a showdown with the doctor. Aylard's reputation as a gunfighter, in fact, first came about because, upon seeing the widely feared Big Jim Conover, he could detect as a medical man that Conover's right side, including his gun hand, is paralyzed. Faust employed another variation of this affliction theme, even to the protagonist's suffering from a partial paralysis of his right hand, as late as "Gunman's Bluff" in *Star Western.* "The Sacking of El Dorado" in *All-Story Weekly* is still another variation, combining the power of psychological reduction with the interplay between illusion and reality when Blinky Meyers comes to dominate El Dorado through deception and artifice before his reduction by the policeman whom he shot and left for dead in New York.

"A Sagebrush Cinderella" in *All-Story Weekly* is an evocation of fairy tales and the legendry of knight errantry. Jacqueline During, from whose point of view much of the story is told, is a totally charming, fascinating character. She is introduced at once.

She lay prone upon the floor, kicking her heels together, frowningly intent upon her book. Outside, the sky was crimson with the sunset. Inside the room, every corner was filled with the gay phantoms of the age of chivalry. Jac would not raise her head, for if she kept her eyes upon the printed page it seemed to her that the armored knights were trooping about her room. A board creaked. That was from the running of some striped page with pointed toes. The wind made a soft rustling. That was the stir of the nodding plumes of the warriors. The pageantry of forgotten kings flowed brightly about her.

Jac in this fetching short novel is in her way the unfinished prototype for Jacqueline Boone, one of the two heroines in "Luck" and the tragic heroine we see for the last time in the sequel to that serial, "Crossroads" in *The Argosy*—as well as Jacqueline Stoddard, the heroine of WOODEN GUNS.

"Luck," in my opinion, is quite possibly the most significant and poignant novel Faust wrote up to this time, notwithstanding the Dan Barry saga. While he seems not to have been an especially religious man, Faust certainly was not above exploiting the imagery and symbols of the Old Testament and the New Testament if they served the theme he had in mind. In "Luck" the dominant symbol is the silver crucifix given to Pierre le Rouge by Father Victor, the Jesuit who has raised and seen to Pierre's education.

> The stern priest dropped his head. He said at last: "I have nothing saving [*sic*] one great and terrible treasure which I see was predestined to you. It is the cross of Father Meilan. You have worn it before. You shall wear it hereafter as your own." He took from his own neck a silver cross suspended by a slender silver chain, and the boy, with startled eyes, dropped to his knees and received the gift.
>
> "It has brought good to all who possessed it but, for every good thing that it works for you, it will work evil on some other. Great is its blessing and great is its burden."

Unfortunately the authentic text of this magnificent story has never appeared in book form as Faust wrote it, neither in the 1920 first edition as RIDERS OF THE SILENCES by John Frederick nor the later edition in 1988 extensively revised by William F. Nolan without credit as RIDERS OF THE SILENCES by Max Brand. From the 1920 book version some of the mystical significance attached to the crucifix that Pierre le Rouge wears was excised in the editorial process and even more is absent from the 1988 version. Yet, without this element, the meaning of the story is totally altered, and what occurs in "Crossroads" is really incomprehensible, for it is Jack, as she is known, who is left in possession of the magical cross at the conclusion of "Luck." By restoring this element, "Luck" becomes as the author intended the first installment in the life of one of his finest and most memorable tragic heroines and is actually the beginning of Jacqueline Boone's story. "Crossroads" is its conclusion. Jack, like Clung and Thunder Moon and many another Faust protagonist, finds only anguish in her mixed nurture. Raised as a boy, Jack wants to be thought of as a man, except by the man with whom she is in love, Pierre le Rouge, while Pierre is in love with Mary Brown and can be no more than a friend to Jack. Dane Coolidge in HIDDEN WATER (A. C. McClurg, 1910) was the first to use the theme of the two heroines—introduced by Sir Walter Scott in WAVERLY—in a Western story. But this theme in Coolidge's story is not developed so grippingly and memorably as it is in "Luck." Beyond this, "Luck" has two powerful scenes of psychological reduction, first when Pierre le Rouge reduces the pitiless avenger, Bob McGurk, and again when Jack confronts McGurk and takes his horse. Indeed many of the characters in "Luck" find their worst fears become reality and, very often, in the confrontation of those fears they undergo a psychological reduction. Jack, alone, is made stronger by her confrontation for, in losing Pierre, she is able to find herself.

"The Consuming Fire" in *Argosy/All-Story* is another variation on the theme of illusion and reality. Ed Raleigh, when he reaches his majority, leaves home to prospect as his father had before him, even though his father has forbidden him to do it. When he reaches Sierra Padre, where his father met his mother, Ed encounters old Martin who wants to go down into the valley to kill Pete Raleigh for eloping with his girl years before. Pete Raleigh shows up, seeking his son, and old Martin, who has been determined for years to settle the score, doesn't recognize him as the man he claims to want to kill.

Even at the very beginning there was already something of the archetypal about Faust's Western fiction, and frequently his earliest short stories as well as his serials have about them qualities commonly associated with legendry, myths, parables, drawing a degree of their vividness from the same primal sources as folk tales. To understand what Faust is about, in fact, it is necessary to keep this perspective in mind. The only politicians a reader encounters in any Faust Western story are state governors, and these men are embodiments of Plato's ideal of the philosopher-king with, sometimes, a bit of the flair of Shakespeare's Prospero thrown in for good measure, especially in his curtain speech at the conclusion of ''The Tempest'' when the conjurer asks of his audience:

> As you from crimes would pardon'd be,
> by your indulgence, set me free!

Vic Gregg is granted a pardon by the governor at the conclusion of THE SEVENTH MAN. He is the first of what became a long line of Faust protagonists who, by this means, are granted a second chance in life. Lee Porfilo in THE MOUNTAIN FUGITIVE like Pierre le Rouge trained as a youth in the art of boxing by a priest has the promise of a pardon from the governor at the end. Jack Richards at the conclusion of THE WHISPERING OUTLAW is given the choice by the governor of death or a year at hard labor. SINGING GUNS derived from a serial published in 1928 has perhaps the most memorable instance of a benign and forgiving governor. When Sheriff Owen Caradac explains to the governor's secretary why he has nurtured the terrible desperado, Annan Rhiannon, the reader is told:

Politicians are lovers of human nature, and they love humanity because they understand. . . . Tears came for an instant into the eyes of the governor's secretary, for he was a Westerner, and west of the Rockies hearts are as soft as hands are hard.

Isobella Dee, one of the two heroines in SINGING GUNS, is able at last to persuade the governor to pardon Rhiannon. As Sheriff Caradac sums it up:

''If you'll stand your trial, the governor has promised his pardon to you if you're convicted. D'you hear? It ain't legal. God bless our governor, he's too damn' big to be legal.''

Faust's last important Western story from this early period about which I wish to say a word is TRAILIN'. It is one of Faust's few narratives prior to his coming to Street & Smith that is a pure pursuit story, relying almost solely on delayed revelation. It combines both mystery and suspenseful parallel plotting with a childish and sullen protagonist who can scarcely be viewed as a hero. In the East Anthony Woodbury learns that his father's real name is not John Woodbury but John Bard. When his surrogate father is murdered, Anthony goes West to learn his true identity. In searching a deserted house, Anthony walks cautiously on the rotted floors as he thinks of that "fabled boat of Charon which will float a thousand bodiless spirits over the Styx but which sinks to the waterline with the weight of a single human being." Sally Fortune is rather an offbeat heroine, possessed of a bit of Jacqueline Boone's pretense of masculinity.

With deft, flying fingers she rolled a cigarette, lighted it, and sat down cross-legged. Through the first outward puff of smoke went these words: "The only thing that's a woman about me is skirts. That's straight."

Anthony's real father is a rancher named William Drew. He towers over others "as the Grecian heroes loomed above the rank and file at the siege of Troy. He was like a relic of some earlier period when bigger men were needed for a greater physical labor."

Size would become increasingly a factor in the physical make-up of Faust's characters, particularly his protagonists, but in part this is also to be viewed as an embodiment of the belief Faust had that "there is a giant asleep in every man. When that giant wakes, miracles can happen." That, too, increasingly was to happen in Faust's Western fiction—the encounter with the miraculous. Indeed, much of the tone of twentieth-century American fiction outside of the Western story has been that of realism, naturalism, and materialism. The human soul, accordingly, shrank until it was often little more than an atrophied collection of quiet resentments and bitter, petty neuroses. Faust could instead—as he did in THE GARDEN OF EDEN—provide a Western story in which not a single shot is fired and in which the protagonist, David Eden, confesses to Ruth Manning as they leave his sequestered valley: " 'How wonderful are the ways of God!' " Leading his horse, Glani, with Ruth astride, David remarks: " 'Through a thief he [God] has taught me wisdom; through a horse he has taught me faith; and you, oh, my love, are the key with which he has unlocked my heart!' " The Biblical overtones that run throughout Faust's Western fiction are as striking and unique as his imagery from Classical literature. Indeed, Zane Grey's avowed pantheism is wan beside the vivid evocation of the presence of God in Faust's fiction, whether as the Great Spirit of the Plains Indians or the Christian Deity.

Walt Coburn in his fiction during his Golden Age, from 1926 through 1934, frequently evoked *El Señor Dios* but never with quite the same conviction as Faust did in his stories. Apostate though he may have been, when Faust was writing a story that required an act of faith, he was capable of demonstrating it with the utmost conviction. As late as the short novel, "Lawman's Heart," in *Star Western,* when Dr. Channing dies, "a bullet, mercifully straight, struck the consciousness from him, and loosed the life from the body, and sent the unharmed spirit winging on its way." Later still is "The Bells of San Carlos," appearing in *Argosy* in 1938. It is not such a great step from the miraculous to the mystical, and it is a step Faust took more than once in his Western stories. It is indeed an easy one for a poet to take, and Faust regarded himself his lifelong as above all a poet. "*Laudato sie, Misignore, cum tucte le tue creature, spetialmente messor lo frate sole, lo quale iorno et allumini noi per loi,*" sang Saint Francis of Assisi. "Praised be Thou, my Lord, through all Thy creatures, but especially honoréd Brother Sun, who makes the day and who through the day illumines us." Faust and his family spoke Italian and his granddaughter, Adriana, Judy's only child, lives today in Florence, the city Faust so loved. Brother Pascual, the friar in the serial Faust titled "The Valley of the Dead" and Don Moore at *Argosy* retitled "Montana Rides Again," and Fray Luis in this story are two of the most formidable members of the clergy to be found in all of Faust's Western fiction. Their presence in a story offered Faust the opportunity to embrace, as only a poet might, that seeming paradox of life where, if what is cherished becomes lost and is surrendered without regret, only then can it ever really be found.

At the close of "Crossroads," Dolores has the silver crucifix that Jack had once received from Pierre le Rouge. Oñate, a tyrannical sheriff, is terrified, thinking of the psychological reduction he will experience through a confrontation with Dix Van Dyck.

At that instant the face of Dolores grew positively demonic, but, when he opened his eyes again, her face was again gentle.

"But suppose I save you from him?"

"Dolores!" He clutched her by either arm. "I will robe you in silks . . . gold on your wrists and diamonds on your fingers . . . jewels in your hair. You shall walk on the petals of roses and sleep in satins and down. Dolores, Dolores, Dolores! Save me! He is the devil . . . no man. He walks on me in my sleep. I die every night. No walls and no guards can save me!"

"I will," said the girl.

"Ah, God!" breathed the sheriff. "You mock me again!"

"With this cross," said the girl, "I will save you, my Oñate."

"The cross?" he whispered in breathless hope, like a child hearing the tale of a nurse—a tale of horror and unreal marvels.

Yet, if it is clearly by means of an act of grace that the Deity influences the lives of humans and animals in some of Faust's Western stories, there is another pervasive force in the psychic world of his fiction, flickering always in the dark heavens, the no less inexorable law of destiny, of fate, of *rota Fortunae*. It is as if, even more than Dante, Faust sought to embrace the medieval unity and yet to remain withal a pagan devoted no less to the magic and wonder of Classical Antiquity. For Faust, in his Western fiction, these diametrically opposed and philosophically contradictory forces may be regarded as co-present. Did he really believe in them? The only answer at which I can arrive is that he believed in them as much as Shakespeare did—as dramatic motifs, as sources for a numinous, resonant imagery capable of conjuring the deepest emotional responses from his audience. If he himself could not make the leap of faith across the abyss, many of his characters are able to do it.

III

More than half of the six hundred stories and serials of varying lengths that Frederick Faust wrote in his lifetime are Western stories. From nearly the beginning the special magic of a Faust Western story comes about through its setting in that land of the mountain desert, a place for him as timeless as the plains of Troy in the hexameters of his beloved Homer and as vivid as the worlds Shakespeare's imagery projected from the bare stages of the Globe. However, I do not believe he would have written nearly so many Western stories and serials were it not for a most providential confluence between his genius and the editorial needs of Street & Smith Publications, in particular the ready and nearly insatiable market in the offing at *Western Story Magazine.*

The real Buffalo Bill Cody had died in Denver, Colorado, on January 10, 1917, and, with his passing, interest in his ongoing adventures had waned. In 1919, just before leaving on a trip to France, Ormond G. Smith, president of Street & Smith, told Henry Ralston to sell the *New Buffalo Bill Weekly* for whatever he could get. When Ralston found no takers, he came up with another idea which he presented to George Smith, vice-president of Street & Smith. Why not revamp the magazine into one devoted to general Western fiction and call it *Western Story Magazine?* George Smith liked the idea and gave Ralston a free hand to do just that. On July 12, 1919, the first issue of *Western Story Magazine,* dated September 5, 1919, and priced at 10¢, went on sale on newsstands.

Beneath the title was a notice that ran for the next eight weeks: "Formerly *New Buffalo Bill Weekly,*" and also a reminder that its contents were "Big Clean Stories of Western Life." Already in the first issue there was established an editor's page titled "The Roundup" and, among other things, readers were promised that "the best writers of Western adventure stories will entertain you." In large part, throughout its thirty-year history, this proved to be a truthful statement. Henry Ralston, who had begun with the company in 1898 and would not retire until 1950, still had his name on the declaration of ownership when the magazine was published for the last time with the issue dated 8–9/49. Ralston had designed *Western Story Magazine* as a bi-weekly, but by November 1920 circulation had reached 300,000 copies per issue, and George Smith decided that the time had come for the magazine to become a weekly.

Faust's first appearance in *Western Story Magazine* was with the five-part serial titled "Jerry Peyton's Notched Inheritance" in 1920. For *Western Story Magazine* he created a new pseudonym—George Owen Baxter—and in succeeding years would add to this string numerous other *noms des plumes.* In fact, Faust became so prolific a contributor to this magazine over the next decade that he might have a serial by David Manning, a serial by George Owen Baxter, and a novelette by Max Brand all running in the same issue, and this remained the case as late as the issue dated 4/2/32. "How did I get hold of Faust?" recalled Frank E. Blackwell, the editor of *Western Story Magazine*. "Bob Davis was over-bought. Munsey found it out, told Bob he'd have to shut off buying for as long as six months, and use up some of the stuff in the safe. Faust, always in need of money, no matter how much he made, came to me with a story. I bought it. He was mine, and mine only from there on." Thanks largely to the popularity of Faust's tremendously prodigious contributions, circulation of *Western Story Magazine* increased to 2 million by 1922. The cover price was also increased to 15¢. On an average issue Street & Smith showed a profit of as much as $100,000. Blackwell could afford to pay Faust's rate of a nickel a word.

For the first twenty-five years of the magazine's publishing history "The Roundup" in *Western Story Magazine* was the place where letters from readers were quoted, surveys as to the kind of stories readers wanted in the magazine were conducted, and previews of stories or a new serial beginning in the next issue could be found. Blackwell, who edited the magazine for all the years that Faust was a contributor, wrote this anonymous column and would occasionally showcase various authors in it or even quote from letters received from authors whose names were familiar to regular readers. For what was called the Christmas number dated 12/25/20, there was a short novel titled "The Man Who Forgot Christmas" by Faust under his John Frederick byline and the final installment of "Jerry Peyton's Notched Inheritance" by George Owen Baxter. "How begin the new year right?" Blackwell asked in "The Roundup." "Could there be a better way than by reading *Western Story Magazine*? *No.* And we hope you will agree with us."

Faust's contributions to *Western Story Magazine* first began reaching extraordinary proportions with the new year. "The Cure of Silver Cañon" by John Frederick appeared in the issue dated 1/15/21 and "Iron Dust," an eight-part serial by George Owen Baxter, began in the issue dated 1/29/21. Blackwell made a casual reference to this particular Faust persona in "The Roundup" for the issue dated 1/14/22 when he commented that "George Owen Baxter was in this morning and he agrees with this C. O. Dodge fellow from Oroville, California. . . ." In "The Roundup" for the issue dated 3/10/23 Blackwell related another conversation he had had with Baxter in his response to a query from a reader: "We have taken that up with Baxter several times. He is a perverse sort of cuss, that Baxter fellow is. In some ways we like it in him. He has strong opinions. 'How about it, George?' we asked him. 'In that "Iron Dust" story, do they get married? Does the man go after the pony or the girl?' Well, we asked him so hard that he wrote a sequel to it. . . ." The protagonist in "Iron Dust" is Free Range Lanning. He was the first Faust character to become so popular with readers of *Western Story Magazine* that Faust was prevailed upon to write a sequel. Over the years there would be many other characters concerning whom readers would make a similar demand.

In "The Roundup" for the issue dated 2/25/22 Blackwell requested: "Stand up, Max Brand, and answer Wallace W. Harris of Covington, Virginia. What? Max not present! Hark! It seems to us we hear the clicking of a typewriter. We'll bet he's out yonder in the mesquite with a lantern and his black piano, hammering away at another good yarn. Go down and put it up to him, Wallace."

Blackwell must have been amused by this byplay with Faust's multiple author personalities since he was wont, upon occasion, to quote a letter from one reader conveying his dissatisfaction with a David Manning story while praising one by George Owen Baxter. When "Wooden Guns" was beginning in the issue dated 9/15/23, Blackwell provided a detailed portrait of its author in "The Roundup": "Take Max Brand. My, but he's a fine upstandin' boy. If you want to see a typical product of the West, just cast your glance on Max. . . . One thing, though, Max isn't good at, and that's talkin'. No, sirs and ladies, when it comes to conversation, Max is sure weak. He's got all gifts the gods can hand out, save one, the gift of gab. If you're alone with him, and he likes you, you may get a little more than yes and no answers, by puttin' questions; but in a crowd, say, he might just as well be a hitchin' post, for all the noise he makes. . . . It's Max's eyes that get you most. Pale blue eyes they are, and with a look in 'em that comes when the person as owns 'em has spent much time alone in the open places. Max looks at you—yes, he's a straight looker, but with a look that seems to go through, past you, and way, way out yonder."

In a very real sense during the years 1921 through 1933 Frederick Faust *was Western Story Magazine.* It was his stories and serials and, to a lesser extent but certainly worthy of mention, stories by Robert J. Horton and Robert Ormond Case, that won legions of readers for *Western Story Magazine* and that so singularly accounted for its extraordinary popularity. Yet, more than any other author of Western stories at the time, Faust's narratives concentrate on the psychology, indeed on the souls, of his characters. They are archetypal psychodramas in which what events mean to the protagonists and how they affect their souls are what the stories are really about, and, while Faust had a natural sense of fast pacing, there is little violence in his Western fiction after 1920. In "Outlaws All," a short novel by Max Brand first appearing in *Western Story Magazine,* gunfighter and outlaw Pete Reeve returns to his shack. He finds that Bull Hunter, a good-natured giant of a man who is his partner, has managed during Pete's absence to capture and tame a wolf known as The Ghost.

"He don't like me, hey?" grumbled Pete Reeve, gradually adjusting himself to the strange state of affairs which he had found in his shack. "Well, no more do I like him. But . . . what's it mean, Bull? What you done to him?"

"Treated him like a dog," said Bull quietly, "and that's just turned him from a wolf into a dog. Look at that. No wolf, no real, full-blooded wolf, could ever be tamed. They're wild all the way through. But this Ghost is half dog, Pete. The wolf shows on the outside; he's all dog on the inside."

"Half dog? Half snake!" said Pete Reeve, partly in disgust and partly with relief. He sat down on a box and examined the snarling giant more closely. "My, but he's got a devil's disposition, Bull. And that's The Ghost? But you're right, Bull. I know wolves back and forth and sidewise and there never was a real one that ever run quite as big or as heavy in the shoulders as that. And there never was one near as broad across the eyes. Nor with a coat near as silky as that. Besides, he's clean-skinned. Not the wolf rankness about him."

Bull nodded and looked admiringly at his companion. "You sure see things, Pete," he said. "I never noticed none of those things."

"I see the outside," said Pete shortly, "but I got an idea you see a lot more on the inside than I'll ever be able to see."

In THE RETURN OF THE RANCHER, Gaspar Sental has been persuaded— for a sum of money—to lead his old friend, Jim Seton, into a trap where Seton is to be killed from ambush. At the last moment Sental tries to convince Seton to turn his back on protecting Henry and Molly Ash from their own folly, to return with him to old Mexico. Seton looks into Sental's eyes and Gaspar Sental looks straight into Seton's. Was he after all, Sental wonders to himself, a traitor?

"Listen to me!" said Sental. "You are coming away with me. This is no country for you. There is no joy in you. It is a dry land. The people in it are dry. But come away with me to my own country. Do you hear me, my dear friend, my old friend?"

"I must stay here."

"Can nothing move you? You see what money I show. I have more, also."

Seton hesitated a moment. Then he laughed.

"Do you know something, Gaspar?"

"Tell me, *amigo!*"

"I mean, do you know how you act about this money?"

"No, but tell me that."

"You act as if it were blood money . . . you're so anxious to spend it quickly, with a friend."

"Blood money," cried Gaspar Sental.

Then he laughed.

But between the words and the laugh, Seton had looked into his soul, and he saw there that which turned his heart sick.

"At least," said Sental, "ride up the road with me a little, and we'll talk it over."

Then Seton knew, for certain. He looked steadily into the face of his old companion. Each had meant life or death to the other.

"Yes," he said. "Let us go!"

Seton outwits the trap and sends the ambusher packing. Sental is devastated by what he has done. Seton ignores Sental's complicity. He remembers only when he saved Sental's life.

"It was not your wounds that ached, when you paused there at the bridge," said the Mexican. "It was your heart to see what a cur I had become."

"I did not, Gaspar. Talk no more of it."

"I *must* talk more. There was once a blow you gave me when we were playing foolishly with one another. . . ."

Seton went to him and took the reins of Sental's horse in his grip.

"Listen to me!"

"Yes?" said Sental.

His face was working, the mouth twitching at the corners, the forehead corrugated with deepest agony.

"You spoke of the night when I dragged you down the trail, Gaspar. Now let me tell you . . . I remember nothing between us since that night."

"Do you mean it?"

"Here is my hand, Gaspar."

"I am not worthy to touch it. You should have shot me down!"

"And lost you? I am not such a fool! Besides, you're not likely to die of old age . . . now that El Blanco is trailing you as he was trailing me. Take my hand, Gaspar!"

It is scenes and moments such as these that distinguish the Western stories written by Frederick Faust. There is action, motion, constant momentum, but the author's concern is not really focused on these but rather on what is most important and most intimate and most meaningful in our lives, what alone ultimately matters. Love, friendship, loyalty, courage are affirmed, yet beyond even these is the prospect of redemption. It comes about through human interaction in stories that are never really plot-driven but depend on human character almost entirely for their motive and progression—the spiritual capacity for sublimity as well as despair, the potential for decency that exists in every human being, and the possibility even in the outcast, the criminal, the socially and politically disenfranchised to attain through one gratuitous act true nobility of soul.

Robert Ormond Case related in an article titled "The Difference Is Real People" in *The Roundup* in October 1958, the name given to the house organ of the Western Writers of America, that in 1932 Blackwell was informed "that competition was hurting *WSM,* income had dwindled to a mere million a year and he must therefore retrench, and at once. How? By eliminating the five-cent writers from his payroll. Regretfully Blackwell did so. This did no particular or immediate damage to a demon producer like Faust—he merely extended his working day and sold his output across the board—but what it did to me shouldn't happen to a dog. Abruptly, from a nonchalant $1,500 plus income per month, surrounded by children who had grown accustomed to wearing shoes and eating regularly—we were a three-car family living in a five bedroom three-bath house with only the grand piano paid for—my income during the next 10 months was exactly nothing."

In the issue dated 3/26/32 Blackwell in "The Roundup" announced: "Banner issue next week, folks. The first installment of a great serial by George Owen Baxter. Baxter calls his latest (and many of you will think it his best) 'Lucky Larribee.' Dashing title that! and the story does not belie its name. Then there is a complete novel by Max Brand. Brand's handle for the story is 'Speedy's Crystal Game,' and it's as fast as its name. Comes along toward the end of the magazine the second installment of 'The Golden Spurs' by David Manning. And then, folks, with next week's issue begins a serial by a new man, Evin Evan: 'Montana Rides.' Some of the critics on this here editorial ranch have declared this yarn to be something extra. We await your verdict. She sure does move, that's one thing certain.'' Again Frederick Faust was the author of all of these stories.

As late as March, 1933, Faust was still commanding his 5¢ a word. An eight-part serial by George Owen Baxter titled "The Wolf and the Man" began in the issue dated 3/4/33. The issue dated 3/11/33 had—in addition to an installment from this serial for which Faust was paid $500—a book-length novel by Max Brand titled "The Stolen Stallion" for which payment was $2,000. For the issue dated 3/25/33 in addition to the serial installment there was another book-length novel by Max Brand titled "Silvertip" and again, for that issue, he was paid a total of $2,500. That month Faust was still able to earn $6,000 from just *Western Story Magazine!*

The crisis that hit *Western Story Magazine* during the early 1930s was due only in part to the Great Depression. There was also a lot more competition, from Clayton Publications such as *Ace-High Magazine* and *Ranch Romances,* from Fiction House's *Lariat Story Magazine* and *Action Stories* and *Frontier Stories* (this last purchased by Fiction House from Doubleday, Doran in 1929), from Doubleday, Doran's *West* and *Short Stories,* and beginning in late 1932 from *Dime Western* published by Popular Publications. While Faust was still in Italy, Blackwell held several conversations with his agent, Carl Brandt, and complained that maybe part of the problem was that Faust was now writing "too well," that plot was vanishing in the wealth of characterization. Brandt assured Blackwell that he would advise Faust to concentrate more on plot and action. He had resisted Blackwell's first efforts to reduce Faust's word rate, and he was not above selling to the competition so that in March 1933, "Death Rides Behind" by Max Brand appeared in *Dime Western* and also a six-part serial, "The Masterman" by Max Brand, began in *Argosy.* Blackwell resented this practice. His feeling was that *Western Story Magazine* had made a heavy commitment to Faust for over a decade and, now that the magazine had come upon hard times caused by a depressed economy and strong competition in the magazine market, Faust should be willing to make the same commitment reciprocally by continuing the number and quality of his submissions for somewhat less payment until the present crisis had passed. The problem in this for Faust was that no matter how much he earned he was perpetually in debt and financial accommodation was simply beyond his ability.

In truth, what was happening at *Western Story Magazine* in the early 1930s had less to do with the way Faust wrote his stories than with the way in which the Western story was being packaged by competing pulp magazines. The most successful pulp magazines launched by Street & Smith in the late 1920s were

Complete Stories and the revamped *Wild West Weekly.* These magazines offered readers all stories complete in a single issue. Serials often prompted subscriptions so a reader wouldn't miss an installment. As the economic collapse stretched out into years, choices had to be made, such as purchasing a single issue without a commitment to purchase more. The very name of Popular Publications' *Dime Western* signified the new emphasis on a lower price. Only when the first issue of Popular Publications' *Star Western* appeared, dated October 1933, at a cost of 15¢ did one know that the worst of the depressed magazine market had passed. However, *Star Western* offered readers 160 pages as opposed to *Western Story Magazine*'s 130 pages for the same money. Blackwell's response was to cut back to one serial in four installments with more short novels in each issue. As long as the magazine still had Faust, this proved an effective strategy.

Beyond these economic and marketing factors, Popular Publications in their Western pulp magazines introduced a new dimension in the Western story. The Western protagonists in their magazines were increasingly shown as men surrounded by armed camps of opposing factions and are seemingly threatened from all sides. This was not the kind of narrative structure Faust had ever employed in his serials. The obvious financial appeal of a serial to an author was that it could be assigned back to him and published as a hardcover book. Short novels of 30,000 words or less did not accommodate this secondary market or the cheap hardcover reprints which followed first book publication. Notwithstanding, Carl Brandt encouraged Faust to write short novels instead of serials and to stress series characters—hence Reata, Speedy, and so many more, above all Jim Silver, were created during this period, amplifying the penchant Faust had always had for continuing characters.

There is every indication that from the beginning Faust worked and reworked his stories and polished them. Although he did keep his book editions locked away, he finally made an exception of their being off limits to his daughter, Judy, whom Faust upon occasion, when she was older, did encourage to read his novels. It was probably due to his own refusal to read his published work, however, that he was unaware of how there had always been some editorial intervention in his Western fiction. The first time he chose to include a number of Mexican characters in a serial—in "Crossroads: A Sequel to Luck"—it is evident that the pejorative term "greaser" was substituted by the editor for the word "Mexican" in Faust's narrative voice. This may be somewhat understandable, if not exactly pardonable, since the U.S. Army had been recently involved in numerous border clashes with Pancho Villa's revolutionaries and anti-Mexican sentiment was running high. There would seem to be less excuse a decade later for Blackwell's altering Faust's title of "The Death Trail" to "The Greaser Trail" in *Western Story Magazine.*

As Faust's rate was indeed cut by Street & Smith in late 1933 to 4¢ a word and his agent sold more of his Western fiction to competing magazines, the degree of editorial intervention also increased to a much greater extent than had ever been true with Faust stories sold to Street & Smith. Rogers Terrill, editor of *Dime Western* and *Star Western,* had had his training at *Action Stories* and only occasionally had written a story for Street & Smith (where he once had his name on a cover with Max Brand *and* George Owen Baxter). Terrill bought Faust's "The Strange Ride of Perry Woodstock" and retitled it "Death Rides Behind" for Max Brand's first appearance in *Dime Western.* It is interesting to contrast how Terrill was able, by editorial intercession, to turn Faust's poetic imagery and sterling prose into ½¢ a word pulp writing. Here is how Faust opened the story:

An owl, skimming close to the ground, hooted at the very door of the bunkhouse. That door was wide, because the day had been hot and the night was hot, also, and windless. Therefore, Perry Woodstock jumped from his bunk, grabbed his hat in one hand and his boots in the other, and still seemed to hear the voice of the bird in the room, a melancholy and sonorous echo.

   The owl hooted again, not in a dream but in fact, farther down the hollow, and Woodstock realized that he had not been wakened by the voice of the cook calling to the 'punchers to "come and get it," neither was it a cold autumn morning at an open camp, neither was there frost in his hair nor icy dew upon his forehead, and his body was not creaking at all the joints. . . .

And here is how Terrill altered that opening scene:

The door of the bunkhouse was wide, because the day had been hot and the night was hot, also, and windless. Perry Woodstock jumped from his bunk, grabbed his hat in one hand and his boots in the other. Something had awakened him. Some sound had come to that door. He stood tense for a moment.

   His nerves were on edge, his heart pounding with the effect of some strange alarm. . . .

Faust was invariably a master of understatement and eschewed the obvious. His knowledge of human character was too subtle. This, too, was repaired by Terrill, as illustrated by the way Faust ended this story:

"Rosemary!" he broke out at her. "I've got to say something to you."
   "Don't," she said. "because words are silly things between us, now!"

And the way Rogers Terrill recast that ending:

"Rosemary!" he broke out at her. "I've got to say something to you!"
   "Don't," she said, "because words are silly things between us, now. When two people are in love they have no need for them. . . ."
   And together, riding stirrup to stirrup, they left the mountain top where love and death had waged grim battle for the pair of them.

When Street & Smith had first threatened to cut Faust's word rate in 1932 to 4¢ a word, Don Moore at *Argosy* jumped into the fray and guaranteed Faust 5¢ a word for 200,000 words a year. Agents frequently pre-sold pulp magazines fixed wordage by established writers on an annual basis. Yet by early 1934 Faust was getting 2¢ a word virtually everywhere in pulp magazines. Both he and Carl Brandt agreed that the only way to cope with the depressed economy was for Faust to move into slick magazines which paid much better. Faust, studying the market, readily realized that restrictions in the slicks were more rigid and confining than they had ever been in the pulps. Writing for *Western Story Magazine,* he had had to concern himself with such general notions as a pursuit plot, which Blackwell preferred, or delayed revelation. Writing for the slicks, he realized that the editors sought to dominate a contributor's mind. Attitudes and ideas were everything. Beyond entertainment, which both pulp and slick fiction alike provided, slick fiction had to deliver an ideological message to readers which agreed with the editorial policies of the magazine and these were dictated by the advertisers and their agencies. Perhaps it is for this reason that so much of the slick fiction of the 1930s and 1940s has become hopelessly dated while pulp fiction from that same period still pulsates with imagination and iconoclasm. Ideology is time-bound. Faust wrote for the pulps for most of his career and possibly this is why his stories have continued to live and to be loved.

The year 1934 really marked an almost total break between Faust and *Western Story Magazine.* His Western stories were appearing regularly in *Star Western* and *Mavericks,* both Popular Publications, as well as *Argosy.* Blackwell was so wounded by Faust's seeming desertion from the magazine that had supported him for so many years that he wouldn't feature the name Max Brand even when he bought a Faust story, and the two short stories Blackwell bought by Faust in 1935 were run under the pseudonym Hugh Owen. In 1936 and 1937 Faust did not appear in *Western Story Magazine* at all. In fact, he would appear in the magazine only one more time.

I do not know if Faust and Blackwell personally communicated after 1934. Blackwell did send a note of condolence to Faust's widow following Faust's death as a combat correspondent in Italy in 1944. For better or worse the management at Street & Smith blamed Blackwell for the decline of *Western Story Magazine* and reduced its cover price to 10¢. By 1938 Blackwell was ousted and was briefly replaced by Ronald Oliphant. Francis L. Stebbins took over briefly in early 1939 until John Burr, who was hired from Dell Publications to edit *Wild West Weekly,* assumed the editorship of *Western Story Magazine.* Burr remained editor for its last decade during which time it went from a weekly to a bi-weekly and then, in 1944, to a monthly and changed its name to just *Western Story* with the issue dated 6/8/40.

In a way *Western Story Magazine* never really recovered from Faust's departure. Faust had made it something that was treasured by its many readers. Under John Burr's editorship, the same writers who were regular contributors to *Dime Western, Star Western, 10 Story Western, Ace-High Western Stories, Big-Book Western, New Western, Action Stories, All Western, Ranch Romances,* and numerous other Western fiction magazines were the same ones to be found in *Western Story.* Only in the five serials featured in *Western Story* in the years 1941 through 1943 written by Peter Dawson (pseudonym for Jonathan Hurff Glidden) did some of the magic return to its pages, and it was for this reason, no doubt, that these serials were divided into seven installments rather than into the usual five or six which again became commonplace during the mid-1930s.

In view of the fact that more than two-thirds of Faust's Western fiction appeared in Street & Smith magazines, averaging about a million and a half words a year, a few general observations about it would not be out of order. Something W. Somerset Maugham said about one of the world's great painters in DON FERNANDO (Doubleday, Doran, 1935) might well be applied to Faust's Western fiction as well. "When you see many of a painter's pictures together, you may find in them often a certain monotony. An artist can only give you himself and he is unfortunately always very like himself. The startling thing about El Greco is that, such was his vitality, he can under the most unlikely conditions give you an impression of variety." No less remarkable is the expansiveness of Faust's imagination when it comes to the Western story as a form of literary art and the fecundity with which he would vary his themes, examining problems and dilemmas of the human condition from numerous disparate viewpoints. No matter how much Frank Blackwell or Carl Brandt might tell Faust that he was writing stories that were too character-driven, he could never really change the way he wrote. In order to write, he was fond of saying, "I must be able to dream."

As early as 1921, writing as George Owen Baxter, Faust had commented about Free Range Lanning in "Iron Dust" that Lanning "had at least picked up that dangerous equipment of fiction which enables a man to dodge reality and live in his dreams." Brave words! Yet, beyond this, and maybe precisely because of the truth in them, much that happens in a Western story by Frederick Faust depends upon the interplay between disparate dreams and reality. Barney Quince in "Forgotten Treasure" in *Western Story Magazine* is plagued by memories for which he cannot account: "He slept at last but a wild and broken sleep in which he dreamed that he dreamed, and the dream became reality, and reality became the dream, so that he sat up in the morning, pale, faint, with a heart that fluttered weakly in his breast, as though he had been climbing mountains all night long." It is thanks to this interplay that so much that Faust wrote impresses us with its vitality and variety.

Faust's last important series of interrelated novels which he wrote for *Western Story Magazine* appeared in the years 1933 and 1934 and brought back a new variation on the triumvirate of the early Dan Barry stories. Jim Silver, better known as Silvertip, in the first of these stories, "The Stolen Stallion," pursues the stallion, Parade, to the point of mutual exhaustion. His quest is finally fulfilled, and Silver even wins a race riding Parade. " 'I've spent a life, so far, trying to find one thing I really wanted,' " Silver comments at the end. " 'I've got it now, and I'm going to use it. I don't know for what.' " Frosty, the hundred-and-fifty-pound wolf, completes this new trio in "The Iron Collar" in *Western Story Magazine*. Silvertip persists in his vague mission through the adventures recorded in these thirteen novels, in many of them battling his arch-enemy, Barry Christian, and in "The False Rider" in *Western Story Magazine* even confronts a *Doppelgänger*. Still, there is nothing in "The Stolen Stallion" or its immediate sequel, "Silvertip," which would give an indication that these novels were intended to launch a new series character and, based on internal evidence, the order in which the series of novels was conceived and in which they appeared in *Western Story Magazine* gives no real indication of any in-herent chronology. Perhaps for this reason, when Dodd, Mead began publishing the Silvertip stories in a uniform edition of hardcover books in the 1940s, no internal chronology was followed, either. Ever since, Silvertip titles have spo-radically appeared in reprint without acknowledgment that it was a series until Dodd, Mead finally began a new program of systematic reprints in the 1980s, curtailed about half way through when they went out of business. David L. Fox, writing about the Silvertips in *Singing Guns* (Fall 91/Winter 92), was no doubt correct that "it is apparent that, consciously or not, Faust had something in mind when he wrote these tales. Whether it was a plan that didn't quite become coherent or whether it was merely a mood that resulted, desultorily, in specific imagery is not clear. The fragments are there, however, and while they may not quite coalesce, they do lend an enticing atmosphere to these novels."

Ultimately, perhaps, the Silvertips are linked psycho-dramas in which Faust reprised again and again the battle with the shadow in Silver's struggles with Barry Christian and others and projected by this means the irresolutions and contradictions in his own psychic life. He was unable to resolve the contradic-tions in his psyche and so was doomed to wander amid the shades of his own inner underworld. Yet, if the final battle was lost and if the price he finally paid was staggeringly high, the consequences of projecting his struggles enriched and enlivened the world of his imaginative creations and the moods of that dark turmoil haunt the tenebrous trails along which Silvertip must pass as ceaselessly as if abandoned in the circles conjured by Dante's pivotal canticles in the "Pur-gatorio." It is also evident, I suspect, to the sensitive reader that Silvertip be-came a creative straight-jacket for Faust. He remains more obscure in thirteen book-length adventures than any other Faust protagonist even in a short novel. Faust was at last trying to write action instead of character, and, if he commented bitterly on what he wrote for pulp magazines, perhaps the anguish he experi-enced in having to write these stories for Blackwell remained foremost in his memory rather than the halcyon days of the 1920s when his imagination was allowed to roam at such liberty in the mountain desert.

"Eagles over Crooked Creek" in *Western Story Magazine* was the last story Faust published in the magazine for which he had written more of his Western fiction than for any other periodical. It is a short, short story, a fine farewell filled with symbolism and sadness. Young Chuck learns that old Ben has murdered his long-time partner, Uncle Cal. As they descend from the mountain, the screaming eagles are again fighting in the sky as old Ben's blind horse, sure in his footing, travels knowingly down a path made familiar by countless similar passages through the many years. Perhaps in this blind horse, Pepper, is the symbol of the god of Faust's unconscious who, as Polyphemus, was destined now forever to walk in darkness, following the same path. Once he abandoned the Western story, although he continued to write well and produced some of his finest fiction, in a true sense never again would Frederick Faust dream so vividly. Perhaps human voices had awakened him, but greater realism tarnished forever what had once been the most pristine magic.

IV

In 1921 Faust made the painful and, for him, tragic discovery that he had a chronic and incurable heart condition from which he might die at any moment. Different parts of his heart would beat at different rates and, sometimes, would seem not to beat at all. This may have been due in part to physical strain as a youth, partly from overwork in the present, but an even greater factor may have been emotional in origin in Faust's erratic, contradictory, and tormented life. After consulting a number of cardiac specialists, Faust became no less depressed over the lack of progress in his literary work than he was about his physical condition and sought consultation with H. G. Baynes in the United Kingdom, a Jungian analyst, and finally conversed with C. G. Jung when Jung passed through London. Jung did not take Faust as a patient, but he did advise Faust that his best hope was to live a simple life. Faust did not undertake, as Hermann Hesse had following his sessions with Jung, the ordeal of confronting the sources of his inner torment and achieving wholeness within his own soul. Jung's advice Faust seemingly rejected because he went to Italy where he rented a large villa, lived extravagantly, and was perpetually in debt. If Faust believed that to be able to write the prose fiction he wrote he had to dream, part of that dreaming may have been the life style he pursued in his Florentine villa. What Faust would not accept as a dream was his intention to write great poetry, even though on one occasion he had to publish his poetry himself.

Faust came to love the grand gesture—pretending that time, money, and courtesy were endless, while privately he was besieged and overburdened by his many debts. The bills did compel him to do one thing: to write at an amazing rate for various pulp magazines. It is to the time he spent amid Jungian ideas, however, that is perhaps owed the kinds of dreams he dreamed in many of his finest stories beginning in 1926 and the nature of the psycho-dramas enacted within them. Faust had by 1930 in his personal library all five of the books by C. G. Jung that had been translated into English. His exploitation of Jungian imagery was used most intensely in the early 1930s, and it is little wonder that it was during this period that he produced some of his finest work.

It is not my intention to suggest that all, or even most, of Faust's Western stories be submitted to a literary analysis in terms of Jung's theories of Analytical Psychology, nor would I wish a Jungian analysis of a few of Faust's Indian characters to be applied in general to all of his Indian characters. However, a knowledge of the Jungian psychological system of thought can illumine an additional dimension in a number of Faust's Western stories and to this extent may be useful in bringing about a deeper understanding of the psychological conflicts in his narratives.

Faust wrote to Leonard Bacon from London on October 5, 1925:

I have seen Jung. He told me, in short, that the only way to be honest in writing was to search my own mind, because no outsider could put his finger on what was bunk in me and what was real. . . . I think Jung is right and a writer has to be his own doctor. But oh, how I should like to lean on someone! . . . I have said good bye to Baynes, who sails for Africa tomorrow. He is a fine fellow and he has put me right about a lot of things, but I am afraid that psychoanalysis will never turn the trick for me. Baynes as a man seemed to me absolutely the right stuff but as a scientist not at all. And I got the same impression out of Jung. Have you ever read any of his writings in the vein of a prophetic book from the Bible? I gathered an impression that there is a great deal of mist and mystery in Switzerland.

In an essay revised for the last time in 1954 titled *"Über die Archetypen des kollectiven Unbewussten"* ["The Archetypes of the Collective Unconscious"], Jung observed:

It is generally believed that anyone who descends into the unconscious gets into a suffocating atmosphere of egocentric subjectivity and in this blind alley is exposed to the attack of all the ferocious beasts which the caverns of the psychic underworld are presumed to harbor. . . . Whoever goes to himself risks a confrontation with himself. . . . This confrontation is the first test of courage on the inner way, a test sufficient to frighten most people away, for the encounter with ourselves belongs to the more unpleasant things that can be avoided so long as we can project all that is negative into the environment.

"Werewolf" by Max Brand in *Western Story Magazine* involves just such an inward journey for Christopher Royal who is convinced he is a coward and flees a confrontation with Harry Main who is a gunfighter. There comes a time in this story—when Christopher encounters the aged Indian, the old wise man— that the terrain shimmers with the multiple affinities of meaning conjured by the unconscious, which Vergil once sought to capture within an image both awesome and sinister: *numina magna deum.* For Christopher, in fleeing, finds that he is become a wanderer, a searcher, and it is in the deep fastnesses of the wilderness through the medium of the ancient Indian that he is confronted with the terrors of his own soul and the meaning of his life. He has found love, as deep and abiding as it is ever given to human beings to know, but it is lost to him until his own spiritual odyssey shall have completed its course, until he has had his spirit vision, confronted the terrifying shadow within, with only the mournful howl of an ancient werewolf to accompany him on this lonely, and terrible, and anguished journey to the center of his soul. Having experienced the terrors of his own unconscious, Christopher is no longer afraid of a mere mortal; but ''to the end of his life, while all the rest of his hair was black, there was a decided sprinkling of gray about the temples, and one deep crease drawn down the very center of his forehead. The werewolf had put its mark upon him.''

Faust knew the journey to the center of his soul would be a terrible struggle and was fearful of it. He wrote to Leonard Bacon in a letter dated November 16, 1927, from the Villa negli Ulivi almost a year after ''Werewolf'' appeared:

I haven't gone to Jung. I intended to and would have been in Zurich on October first. But in the meantime while schooling a green hunter over a wall in Ireland, this summer, I broke my leg and ankle and used up Jung's time in bed. We have other complications now which make me plan to stay close at home for a time and work like hell to make money. The most important thing is that Dorothy will have a baby in February. We both are tremendously happy about it, but between providing for a baby, paying doctor bills, furnishing a new house, building a wing onto it, etc., you can see that I can't afford even such a necessary luxury as Jung.

When I am far away from [them], I always feel like thumbing my nose at Jung, Baynes, & Co., but I have committed myself far enough to go ahead with the thing. In the meantime I have vague plans of trips through Africa, Asia, etc. No doubt I want to drift because I hate to stand still long enough to face myself; perhaps Jung can anchor me, but while I want to be helped, I can only be helped after a fight which will be so really awful that Jung probably would tell me to go to hell. Which is probably where I belong.

In ''Lucky Larribee'' in *Western Story Magazine,* Faust had all the elements in hand to realize the dream of achieving wholeness even if he himself might not be able to attain it. The protagonist is introduced in this way: ''Larribee was plain no good. Larribee was low.'' He is sent by his father to live with his cousin's family where he proves lazy, shiftless, and spends most of his time in town drinking and playing cards (even upon occasion cheating). What changes all this is the appearance of Sky Blue, the magnificent stallion that has never been ridden. Dan Gurry is the owner and he hopes that one of the cowboys in the district will be able to break Sky Blue so he can race him. Larribee has a run-in with Josiah Ransome III, son of Major Ransome, a rich and very influential man in the district, and he bests him. Ransome becomes bitter about his humiliation. One cowboy after another is thrown off by Sky Blue until it is Larribee's turn and he is able to ride him easily. Larribee, attracted to Arabelle Ransome, bets her the ring she is wearing that he will ride Sky Blue. The ring which she surrenders reluctantly has a special meaning and her freely giving it will mean a total commitment. There is something magical and marvelous about the entire episode and Arabelle is not so much a character as a projection of the anima [even her very name comes from the Latin in which *ara* is altar as in *ara maxima Herculae* and means literally "beautiful altar"]. However, Larribee cannot worship at this shrine before he has achieved wholeness.

In a race against Colonel Pratt's thoroughbred mare, Sky Blue and Larribee become as a centaur. Larribee leans forward in the saddle and "out his lips came a thin, small, sharp straining cry. Sky Blue lifted his head and pricked his ears. He thought he had heard that sound before, the scream of a hawk, half lost in a windy sky, or was it the far-distant neigh of a neighboring stallion from another hilltop? But, with pricked ears and head lifted for a moment, he listened to the cry of joy which had rushed from the throat of the man, and in that instant they were welded together, made of one flesh, of one brain, of one mighty spirit!" When they catch up to the colonel and his mare, "the colonel looked around at them as though the earth had been split and the steeds of Poseidon had risen out of the gap." While living in Italy, Faust hired a tutor to help him learn ancient Greek so he might read Homer in the original. It was an act which brought a new dimension to his fiction and new resonance to his style.

Ransome places a burr beneath Sky Blue's saddle and the horse bucks off Larribee at his highest moment of fulfillment and recognition, the stallion fleeing then so swiftly he cannot be caught again. With this begins the pursuit part of the story and, in terms of the psycho-drama which goes on beneath the dream-like surface, it brings about the transformation of Larribee through his ordeal until he becomes known first to the Indians and then to everyone alike as "the" Larribee. Dan Gurry, Colonel Pratt, and Larribee begin the pursuit. An encounter with Cheyenne Indians, also after the stallion, puts Larribee in the position of giving back to Shouting Thunder his life—for Larribee has the power to kill him and does not. Shouting Thunder makes Larribee a blood brother, Larribee's first step in reconciling with the shadow, the inferior part of his nature which, as Jung once noted, is frequently projected into the dusky form of the American Indian in dreams by Americans. " ' . . . He gave me life, and spared my soul,' " Shouting Thunder thinks. " 'Therefore I shall spare his soul. We shall stand up together among the Sky People. If there is one horse between us, I shall run on foot and he shall sit in the saddle!' " So it becomes a quaternity, a mandala, in the pursuit of Sky Blue with the shadow also in pursuit, the mysterious white leader of the Crows. Shouting Thunder in this psycho-drama assumes the role of the old wise man, the one who will act as Larribee's guide into the realm of the archetypes of the collective unconscious.

On the surface this pursuit story has Sky Blue as its objective, a stallion that refuses now to have its will broken, that once trusted a human being and was injured, and will never surrender again. One by one the quaternity drops off, Gurry dying to make room for the new member of the quadrant constellation, the Crow leader, the white man who is also an Indian and who was responsible for Sky Blue's injury in the first place. Josiah Ransome is Larribee's shadow, a man who went to live among the Crows after Sky Blue's flight. When they first confront each other, Larribee is uncertain of Ransome's identity, mistaking him for Shouting Thunder. The conflict in this novel is resolved psychologically, not physically as is so often found in more conventional Western fiction. Only when Larribee willingly sets Sky Blue free, after having captured him, does the horse follow Larribee of his own accord. In Larribee's soul the drama has been to find the self and Sky Blue is the means by which this search is fulfilled: "His inward richness of mind would be the knowledge that the horse was free and happy. . . ."

Larribee cannot achieve wholeness until he has overcome his estrangement to the shadow, until he has reconciled with it, at which point the fever which has driven them all, the fever to possess, to capture Sky Blue abandons him and he is free at last, whole at last, in quite the way Jung had suggested to Faust he could free himself of the demons which possessed him. Shouting Thunder as the old wise man is the source of wisdom who leads Larribee to the self, to wholeness: "He was really far beyond the realm of reason. He was in that dreamy realm of the mystic to which Shouting Thunder had introduced him. Remembering the words of the Indian, he told himself that whatever fate ruled this world, it had determined beforehand what man, if any, should ride Sky Blue." In the event, it is not even Larribee who rides Sky Blue, but the projection of the anima, the feminine side of his soul. Once Larribee achieves wholeness, accepts the shadow as part of himself, the conflicts are resolved and Ransome and he agree that with all the dangers ahead and around them they are fortunate to have each other for company even if they do not speak to each other. Arabelle makes her decision. Sky Blue has touched the earth. He has left his wrong steps behind him, it is observed, as so too has Larribee. In the way Hermann Hesse learned from Arthur Schopenhauer, so Faust learned from the Greeks and Larribee learns from experience that fate rules life, not us. It is, as Jung had once observed, not—I think, therefore, I am—but rather, the thought occurs within me. How did I make this misstep, Schopenhauer asked, and then did I really make it? How else explain the alterations in Sky Blue's color, as when Larribee is shocked to discover that "it seemed to him that the horse of his imagining had grown larger and that it was black." Or when Major Ransome and Larribee's father are together watching at dusk and the major asks what color is the horse that is being led by the man? " 'Dark,' said Larribee. 'Black, I should say, but this light is bad.' The major leaped from his chair. 'Black, did you say?' he exclaimed. 'A big, powerful looking black horse?' 'No, not big. Compared to the horse the girl is riding, it's no more than a pony.' 'Compared to the horse that the girl is riding?' echoed the major, baffled, and straining his eyes vainly. 'But Arabelle's little mare would never—what sort of horse is she riding, then?' 'A high-headed demon,' said Larribee, 'that dances along like a racer on parade, a light-colored horse, a luminous horse. He has the head of a stallion.' " The words shimmer with subtle meanings. In fact, every story Faust ever wrote seems to have to a degree both surface action and a subtext, a story within the story that functions on the deepest level.

Tertullian in DE CARNE CHRISTUS wrote: "*Certum est quia impossible est.*'' Or as Josiah Ransome puts it: '' 'But Larribee—damn him!—is the only man who's given up Sky Blue and, therefore, he'll be the only man who'll get him.' '' Larribee was lost, but now as *the* Larribee he is found. Sky Blue was lost, so he is found. It is a realm, as Shouting Thunder knows, beyond reason. When Faust chose to call his protagonist ''Lucky'' he meant the words as Hesiod had—ταων ευδαίμων τε καὶ ὄλβιοζ—or lucky [fortunate, well-starred, eudaimonious] is Larribee with respect to them (the days of his life).

Although the elements of Jungian psychology are in rather a pure state in ''Werewolf,'' by the time Faust came to write LUCKY LARRIBEE Jungian theory was by then integrated eclectically into the imagery of Classical Antiquity and its literary concerns as well as with the tenets and beliefs of early Christianity. In these terms it is interesting to contrast LUCKY LARRIBEE with a Faust Western story that embodies many of the same themes but written before his exposure to Jungian ideas, ''Galloping Danger,'' a six-part serial in *Western Story Magazine.* The book edition was first published as GALLOPING DANGER more than fifty years later and in a somewhat abridged version. Eventually the text will be restored in book form as well as Faust's original title, THE QUEST OF LEE GARRISON.

This novel is a masterpiece in which no event and no character is extraneous, in which every thread of the story and every theme is developed with precision, and in the magazine version it never loses its poetry. The opening scene involves flashbacks to the dreadful home life from which Lee Garrison fled as a teenager until the focus comes back to the present in a lonely line shack and Lee's encounter with a dying Indian who has lost his life in a thousand-mile pursuit across the mountain desert of a magnificent gray stallion known as Moonshine. Lee determines to capture the horse himself, trailing him on foot over hundreds of miles until, both nearly dropping from exhaustion, the two have a confrontation. This sequence is no less thrilling than similar pursuits of horses in LUCKY LARRIBEE or THE STOLEN STALLION. As happens with Sky Blue in LUCKY LARRIBEE, rather than be ridden by a man Moonshine takes flight over a waterfall. A hoof is injured, and Lee first rescues the stallion from the maelstrom of the river and then gently nurses the animal until the hoof is healed.

In the course of his pursuit of Moonshine, Lee had discovered a rich outcropping of gold and bargained its whereabouts to an old prospector named Guttorm for a pipeful of tobacco. Now, atop Moonshine with whom Lee has developed a deep bond, Lee rides into the camp of Buddy Slocum, a former jockey on his way to the gold fields at Crooked Creek. When the two men play cards, Slocum loses and accuses Lee of being a cheat. Later in an abandoned cabin encountered on the trail, Lee finds a woman's glove and becomes convinced that the woman whose hand will fit this glove is his only true love, a notion Lee owes to his favored Malory whose book he reads over and over. When Lee rides into Crooked Creek, he pens Moonshine in a corral behind the boarding house where he takes a room. This marks ''the beginning of slavery for Moonshine.'' Indeed, from this point on the reader's sympathy is with Moonshine who has been taught to trust a man and who will, as a result, experience one disastrous humiliation after another.

Lee cannot help but reflect, as he explores this gold camp, that "truly there was a burden in civilization." He is also transformed by the gold camp so that Faust can observe about him that "one self had died, and a new self gripped the whiskey glass. . . ." Guttorm has taken sole credit for the strike and hates the sight of Lee who is an embarrassment to him. The old prospector has brought his dying young son to Crooked Creek and has total faith that a quack doctor named McLeod will be able to keep him alive. Eventually the boy dies, and McLeod proposes a partnership with Lee who, by this time, has earned for himself a somewhat unsavory reputation. Trying to get rid of the money he won from Slocum, Lee gambles with it, only to learn that he has the Midas touch and wins ten times what he sought to lose.

Alice, a dance-hall girl Lee sees for the first time sitting in an open window, is the one he believes to be the lady of the glove. Alice rides bareback on Moonshine as Lee walks by their side. The comparison between the glove and Cinderella's slipper is even made overtly by Faust after it is found not to fit Alice's hand. In a variation on the theme of the two heroines, Sally McGuire is now introduced, a rich man's daughter in love with Handsome Harry Chandler who has lost all of his money but still owns a race horse named Laughter. Harry challenges Lee to a race, the winner to take the other's horse. Lee agrees. Sally tries to convince Lee to lose the race so Harry may retain his pride and the two can then marry. Lee does want to throw the race for Sally, but Moonshine won't let him. Moonshine won't have his spirit broken, not even by Slocum, riding Laughter, who quirts the stallion across the nose during the race. When Moonshine wins, Harry surrenders Laughter and leaves town.

Lee overhears Sally's father saying to her: " 'A man that needs a woman's saving isn't worth being saved.' " It is a statement that directly contradicts a common theme in Zane Grey's Western romances. The glove is found to fit Sally's hand. To secure his happiness with Sally, Lee rides out of town to where Harry Chandler is camped. Harry, seeing Lee and Moonshine approach, fires a shot at them and hits Moonshine. His second shot kills the stallion. Harry flees while Lee sits on the ground, cradling Moonshine's head in his lap. When Sally and her father arrive, Sally declares her love for Harry Chandler. In the final very brief scene that concludes this story Sally confesses to her father that the glove in which Lee has put so much stock was never hers at all. Unlike Larribee, Lee Garrison's quest is in pursuit of an illusion. He wins the unquestioning love of Moonshine, and, in his indifference to the stallion and his pursuit of an illusion, Lee brings about Moonshine's destruction. Rather than ending on a note of hope, much less the achievement of wholeness, the ending to THE QUEST OF LEE GARRISON is one of sustained irony. Garrison has managed to destroy all that was noble and best in his life.

———————————————————————— *V* ————————————————————————

Each morning Faust devoted to poetry. His afternoons were reserved for his fiction. He had deadlines set, and he did his best to meet them, the afternoons often extending into the hours of darkness. He was a one-man fiction factory, and he did it by himself, sitting before a battered typewriter he called "my oldest friend," pounding out every word with two fingers. Dorothy proof-read all that he wrote for many years, and it is to her that is owed the small number of technical errors which were allowed to remain in his stories and serials. In TWENTY NOTCHES, the protagonist, a tramp referred to as the Sleeper, at one point is made a prisoner and escapes with the help of a pistol smuggled to him. He fires two shots and, although he has no ammunition, he afterward reloads the spent chambers. Yet, while in Louis L'Amour's Western fiction this kind of thing is commonplace, in Faust it is conspicuous when it occurs because it occurs so rarely. TWENTY NOTCHES is one of Faust's "fairy tale" Westerns but that is not to imply that it is without its referents to Homer's world. The Sleeper has in his possession for a time what is believed to be a magical gun and "as the strange flower of the moly, white blossom and black root, had saved Odysseus, so the thought of the gun and its equal magic saved the tramp." At another moment in the story, "the Sleeper stood up and almost laughed in the darkness. So Perseus, with winged heels and the magic sword, might have stood beside the Gorgon."

When he wrote poetry in the mornings, Faust would feel a good day one in which he might write three lines. In the afternoons, his sleeves rolled up, he banged out thirty pages of a story with none of the passion for revision he showered on his poetry, although he did revise his fiction. Faust used to like to read aloud to his family and friends after dinner, and he had committed thousands of lines from Shakespeare to memory. He would also read aloud from Milton and Chaucer. Carl Brandt, who became Faust's agent in 1925, was over the years a devoted friend as well. Faust might follow Shakespeare or Milton with his own poetry. Brandt felt that "Faust had a beautiful speaking voice and read poetry musically, with passion and conviction. I would sit and listen to him read. Drugged by the spell of his voice, at three in the morning, I'd be convinced that his verse was great. But in the next day's cold white light, reading the same lines, it became clear how personal a thing his poetry was, and how little of it was really publishable."

For all of his obsession with the ostentation of wealth and with its ready acquisition one of his more common themes, Faust himself seems never to have been the least interested in accumulating money, only in spending it. It was in its way as much a mania with him as the race track would prove for T. T. Flynn or building houses and lavishing gifts on relatives and secretaries would be for Zane Grey. Also, as was the case with Zane Grey, as dependent as Faust was on Dorothy and as much in love with her as he claimed to be, he seemed after 1930 incapable of fidelity and became involved from time to time with other women. Possibly Faust could only keep dreaming the eternal dream of the anima by plunging amid all those fair forms he sought out in his waking life. Unlike St. Augustine, however, who in his CONFESSIONES admitted that eventually he came to realize the power and majesty behind all those fair forms, the *primum mobile* responsible for their creation, for Faust they brought him nothing but torment and filled much of Dorothy's life with anguish. No god from the unconscious or beyond shouted his name and burst his deafness, as one had for Augustine. Yet, a theme as persistent in Faust's Western fiction as the narrative structure of a pursuit story and delayed revelation is the possibility for spiritual redemption. Often the most profoundly moving scenes in Faust's narratives are the instances where a character manages to achieve personal salvation by a confrontation with the shadow within as happens to Annan Rhiannon in SINGING GUNS, to Jack Ripley in SMUGGLERS' TRAIL, and to Gaspar Sental in THE RETURN OF THE RANCHER—to give only three examples among many.

A close friend of Faust's once suggested that in his poetry Faust should cease writing about mythical gods and titans to which Faust replied: "It isn't really a preference for those themes, but a lack of all other themes that determines my choice. Since modernity is impossible, what remains?" It is perhaps this same posture which explains Faust's preference for a Western story set in no particular time frame and in no particular place but rather in the vast domain of the imagination where marvelous things can and do happen and, more importantly, a world in which a reader can accept them as happening. Notwithstanding this proclivity for the timelessness of the unconscious combined with a distaste for modernity, Faust sometimes seems guilty of introducing all manner of anachronisms into a Western story. In "Riders for Fortune" serialized in *Western Story Magazine* and published later as THE BORDER KID, one character makes reference to someone turning on a big ceiling light, and another sees a man dodging "very like a football player running through a crowded field." Yet, in truth, in a timeless world no such thing as an anachronism is conceivable. Moreover, it was a convention in much of the fiction in *Western Story Magazine* in the 1920s that the events depicted were supposed more or less to have occurred somewhere in the West in the very recent past no matter what the actual chronological year.

Because Faust himself had for so long been an underdog—so much so, even, that a follower of Alfred Adler's Individual Psychology might make a solid case of explaining Faust's extravagance and his terrific, driving energy as an almost frenzied compensation for perceived inferiority—his fiction invariably transforms the underdog, elevates him, becomes for the underdog an apotheosis and a perpetuation. Similarly, some of Faust's finest creations are his Mexican and Indian characters, many of whom embody the highest virtues in Faust's moral lexicon. There is the notorious bandit leader, Mateo Rubriz, in the three novels about the Montana Kid. There are the four Mexicans who help Oliver Tay in THE BORDER BANDIT nearly attain his quest for wholeness. Most often

Cheyenne Indians occupy the role of the old wise man as when Broken Knife befriends Johnnie Tanner in VENGEANCE TRAIL. Johnnie is much in need of such a spiritual guide in the West because upon his arrival there from New York, the reader is told, Johnnie "swept his eye around the vast and circling skyline of the prairie, and it seemed to him that here, where the heavens were wider, the hearts of men were greater also. Their passions were more important. Hatred was more than human; it was devilish. And in friendship there was something divine." Indeed, friendship with Indian characters is divine in such serials as the Rusty Sabin saga which came to comprise three books: CALL OF THE BLOOD, BROTHER OF THE CHEYENNES, and the conclusion of the trilogy first serialized as "The Sacred Valley" in *Argosy* and later published as CHEYENNE GOLD; in the Thunder Moon stories; and, above all, there is the remarkable "The Horizon of Danger" serialized in *Western Story Magazine* and later published as THE RESCUE OF BROKEN ARROW.

Street & Smith's book publishing arm, Chelsea House, began issuing Faust's serials from *Western Story Magazine* in the 1920s as novels by George Owen Baxter and David Manning. The name Max Brand, which had been used on all the early Putnam books, now was reserved for the books published by Dodd, Mead & Company which took over the Max Brand book publishing program from G. P. Putnam's Sons with publication of THE BLUE JAY. Yet some of Faust's finest Western fiction appeared under the name Evan Evans, novels which were polished with unusual care. It was under pressures from his agent that Faust found himself coming more and more to the United States, usually leaving his family behind in Italy. For periods of time he was literally a captive of Carl Brandt, working many long hours in Brandt's office, revising a story or writing a new one to specification. It was in 1932 that the president of Harper's, Cass Canfield, told Faust that Zane Grey's sales had dropped off to 30,000 copies a year. Dodd, Mead had been enjoying great success with the Max Brand books. Harper's wanted its own line of Westerns from Faust, and so the Evan Evans series began.

Hollywood beckoned. Faust had been selling stories to motion picture companies for years, and his first major success was when Fox Film Corporation bought THE UNTAMED as the basis—however unlikely—of a vehicle for Tom Mix. Even Faust's parodying of the closing books of "Odyssey" in DESTRY RIDES AGAIN was adapted as a vehicle for Tom Mix's comeback in talking pictures. Universal, which made the film, paid Faust $1,500 for the screen rights. The appeal of Hollywood now for Faust was that he would be paid $1,000 a week, or more, to work on screenplays. Faust brought his family to Hollywood and, seemingly, turned his back on Europe which appeared relentlessly bent on another war. While at M-G-M, he breathed new life into his Dr. Kildare character—Paramount Pictures had earlier made a film based on Faust's first Kildare story—and an entire series was launched starring Lew Ayres as Kildare and Lionel Barrymore as Dr. Gillespie.

Switching from studio to studio, never very happy, and often drinking heavily despite the tenuousness of his heart condition, Faust talked more and more about great writers who had started writing their most noteworthy fiction in middle age, because he was middle-aged and he feared with his motion picture commitments, his slick magazine writing and, despite his steady outpouring of stories and novels, he would never achieve his goal. Those who worked with him in Hollywood were amazed at his fecundity, his ability to plot stories. Faust himself had some simple advice on the process: read a story half way through and then imagine how it will end. Then put on a new beginning and you have a different story, one all your own. However, for all of his incessant talk about plot and plotting, Faust's Western fiction is uniformly character-driven. His plots emerge from the characters as they are confronted with conflicts and frustrations. If the sub-texts often reveal depths of anguish in his characters, a word might also be said about Faust's humor. It is so often present, and one instance among thousands that particularly stands out in my memory is found in TIMBAL GULCH TRAIL where the humor is sustained by the constant contrast between irony and naiveté. Beyond this, so many of his characters are truly unforgettable, from the most familiar such as Dan Barry and Harry Destry to the marvelous creations of José Ridal in BLACKIE AND RED, or Gaspar Sental in THE RETURN OF THE RANCHER, or the two old-timers, Jim and Harry, in TIMBAL GULCH TRAIL. Yet, whatever flashes of a soul in anguish or the leavening evocation of humor he might provide, Faust in his Western stories cherished above all the virtue of hope. It is the vital force that inspires so much of what he wrote. If courage is the emotional dynamic that infuses his Western fiction with its energy, it is hope that irradiates its soul. At times, indeed, it even introduces, rather than concludes, the story—as in the first sentence of THE SEVEN OF DIAMONDS: "It was not the end of the desert; it was better than that; it was the point when despair ended and hope became a certainty."

Faust had missed the Great War. He refused to miss the Second World War. He pulled enough strings to become a war correspondent, and he sailed to the Italian front where he lived with the men in foxholes, in mud. They were green troops in some of the bloodiest conflict of the entire war, men who had grown up reading his stories with their superhuman heroes and their grand deeds. It was there he died, on the dark night of May 12, 1944, from a shrapnel wound.

VI

Faust has been condemned by those who admire realistic detail in Western fiction for ignoring historical accuracy and for often failing to provide even minimal descriptions of his frontier settings. Too often, it may appear, his plots are pursuit stories and his protagonists in quest of an illustrious father or victims of an Achilles' heel; but these are premises and conventions that are really of little consequence. He has been criticized for basing his images of Indians on the accounts of James Willard Schultz and George Bird Grinnell, who romantically championed the Cheyennes but took sides against their enemies, the Pawnees. Such a criticism overlooks the main thrust of Faust's Indian narratives: his Indian characters are not totally comprehensible as realistic Indians any more than any Faust character is to be taken as an attempt to draw accurately from life. His characters are psychic forces. In Faust's fiction as Robert Sampson concluded in the first volume of YESTERDAY'S FACES (Bowling Green University Popular Press, 1983), "every action is motivated. Every character makes decisions and each must endure the consequences of his decisions. Each character is gnawed by the conflict between his wishes and the necessities of his experience. The story advances from the first interactions of the first characters. It continues, a fugue for full orchestra, ever more complex, modified by decisions of increasing desperation, to a climax whose savagery may involve no bloodshed at all. But there will be psychological tension screaming in harmonics almost beyond the ear's capacity."

There will come a time, probably well into the next century, when a reevaluation will become necessary of those who contributed most to the eternal relevance of the Western story, and in this reevaluation unquestionably Zane Grey and Frederick Faust will be elevated while popular icons of this century, such as Owen Wister, judged solely in terms of their actual artistic contributions to the wealth and treasure of world literature, may find their reputations diminished. In such a reevaluation Faust might well emerge in common with Jack London as a purveyor of visceral fiction of unique emotional power and profound impact that does not recede with time. Faust's Western fiction is timeless in its setting and in this respect shares the same domain as Homer. Faust was extraordinarily productive and, with more than 200 published Western novels and story collections to his credit and a hundred more still to appear in book form, it goes without saying that a false impression can be gained by reading an inferior effort.

However, for this reason a word of caution might also be in order. Beginning with some of the Chelsea House compilations and the Dodd, Mead editions starting at the time of FLAMING IRONS published in 1948—a typically inappropriate title for what was first called "The City in the Sky" when serialized in *Western Story Magazine*—Faust's Western fiction underwent abridgment to stress the action and often what was so fine in the original stories became compromised by the interpolations of hack work and editorial revisions by other hands. Many of the stories in the Nolan collections, in fact, are not really Faust's work. As of 1992, a thorough-going effort commenced to restore Faust's work to what he originally wrote, using authentic texts or the author's own typed manuscripts. The consequence of this situation, though, is that a critical literary study of Faust's contributions to the Western story is not really possible without access at least to the original magazine versions and a critical commentary based largely, or exclusively, on the book editions published after Faust's death addresses more often the inadequacies of Faust's editors rather than Faust's fiction as he wrote it.

Sometimes the cutting was not severe. "Western Tommy" runs 55,500 words over five installments in *Western Story Magazine* and as WESTERN TOMMY, published by Chelsea House in 1927, is 55,400 words. Many times, though, the abridgments have been to the significant detriment of the stories as Faust wrote them. "Ronicky Doone, Champion of Lost Causes" comes to 72,200 words over seven issues of *Western Story Magazine* but in the Chelsea House edition is a mere 56,400 words. "The Tyrant," one of Faust's most compelling psychodramas concerned with a man's relationship with fate, is 64,300 words over six issues of *Western Story Magazine* and only 59,000 words in the book edition, MONSIEUR. The deletion of those 6,000 words and the inept but deliberate deconstruction of Faust's hexametric prose rhythm turned a powerfully metaphysical and metaphorical drama into a mediocre period piece about quaint rural French-Canadians. "Black Jack" over six installments in *Argosy/All-Story* comprises 87,000 words, and BLACK JACK is barely over 60,000 words. Instead of allowing the story to come to its logical conclusion, all the poetry and profundity of the text were excised, and the text was brutally condensed by Dodd, Mead.

Yet, the worst example of editorial tampering is unquestionably the Thunder Moon stories. Faust wrote a five-part serial titled "Thunder Moon" that was published in *Far West Illustrated* then the short novel, "Red Wind and Thunder Moon," in *Western Story Magazine*. A second short novel, "Thunder Moon—Pale Face," in *Western Story Magazine* followed, a second five-part serial—"Thunder Moon—Squawman" in *Western Story Magazine,* and a final short novel, "Thunder Moon Goes White," in *Western Story Magazine.* THUNDER MOON in the 1969 Dodd, Mead edition is an abbreviated version of the serial, "Thunder Moon." THUNDER MOON'S CHALLENGE is, quixotically, a compilation of "Red Wind and Thunder Moon," "Thunder Moon—Pale Face," and the first half of the second serial, "Thunder Moon—Squawman." THUNDER MOON STRIKES is a compilation consisting of the second half of "Thunder Moon—Squawman" and the novelette "Thunder Moon Goes White." The Thunder Moon stories, however, have now been restored as Faust wrote them and are available in hardcover editions from the University of Nebraska Press. In order to do justice to this series, the final short novel has to stand alone, something perhaps considered uncommercial by Dodd, Mead, but the University of Nebraska Press was willing to publish the four books in this manner so as to preserve the integrity of Faust's narratives.

Dodd, Mead, along with Chelsea House and Bobbs-Merrill in the 1920s, was not the only publisher to make serious and detrimental editorial abridgments of Faust's work. "Outlaw Valley" in five installments in *Far West Illustrated* is 68,700 words, and the book edition, OUTLAW VALLEY, is only 64,900. On the other hand, in several notable cases (most of them occurring while Faust was still alive), his manuscripts would be sent to Street & Smith as well as to the subsequent book publisher. The book publisher might actually cut less of the text than the magazine publisher. "The Path to Plunder" in six installments in *Western Story Magazine* runs only 74,500 words whereas the book edition, MYSTERY RANCH, is longer by 400 words. The same is true for THE UN-

TAMED and TRAILIN'. Both in their book editions are some 400 words longer than in the serial versions.

A writer ought to be judged by his best work. In this case such an evaluation, of course, can only come once it is determined what is Faust's work as he wrote it and what is not. However, even once that has been done, such a list cannot hope to be comprehensive since Faust's most remarkable achievement is not that he wrote so much, but rather that so much of what he wrote is so fine! Perhaps the best place to begin with him is THE UNTAMED and the subsequent Dan Barry stories, SILVERTIP for that series, and MONTANA RIDES! for that series. CALL OF THE BLOOD is perhaps as fine a place as any to begin reading Faust's Indian stories. Beyond these, there are LUCKY LARRIBEE, THE BORDER BANDIT, THE RESCUE OF BROKEN ARROW, GUNMAN'S LEGACY, SAWDUST AND SIXGUNS, STRANGE COURAGE, and what is now titled THE QUEST OF LEE GARRISON. Notwithstanding, reading these novels in their abridged book editions can be only a fraction of the experience one will have when reading them in their original unexpurgated versions. In due course all of Faust's fiction will be restored to the way he wrote it.

If editorial hindrance and the exigencies of book publishing with regard to length are not enough, the serious critical treatment of Faust's Western fiction has been further complicated by the years of so many pseudonyms, not only in magazines but in book appearances as well; although within recent years Max Brand has become his only byline, and all that he wrote will eventually appear or reappear under this name. William F. Nolan perhaps said it best when he remarked that the finest of Faust's stories "form a rich legacy, bright threads from the vast tapestry of adventure he left us." His finest fiction can be enjoyed on the level of adventure or on the deeper level of psychic conflict. However, it is unjust to dismiss Faust's Western fiction, as Christine Bold did in SELLING THE WILD WEST (Indiana University Press, 1987), by quoting Faust's own disparaging comments about his Western stories. Faust in his heart knew that he had not resolved the psychic conflicts he projected into his fiction, and so he could not be expected to speak highly of it. He held out hope to the last that the resolutions he had failed to find in life and in his fiction could somehow, miraculously, be achieved on the higher plane of his poetry. But Faust is not the first writer, and will not be the last, who treasured least what others have come to treasure most. It may even be possible that a later generation, having read his many works as he wrote them, will find Faust to have been truly one of the most significant American literary artists of the twentieth century.

SOME THOUGHTS ON REALISM IN FAUST'S WESTERNS

Leo A. Hetzler

An earlier version of this essay appeared in Singing Guns.

Realism is a word that has many meanings. It may refer to the literary Realism that began in France in the 1840s. In its first phase it emphasized detailed description of physical, real-life surroundings. In its next phase it examined daily living and found it gray, monotonous, and empty, an uninteresting tapestry bereft of any bright threads. Again, realism may refer to the portrayal of characters that ring psychologically true to life. In this sense a folktale such as "The Ugly Duckling" may be more real than some Realist novel. Finally, there is the ordinary, common-sense meaning: life as we know it from our experience. Although I shall be making references to the first two meanings, my ordinary use of realism will be that of the third.

Any discussion of realism in Faust's Westerns must confront the fact that he transferred to the Old West the classic heroes and myths: warriors of the Trojan War, knights of Arthur's Round Table, and folk heroes of medieval and Norse romances. This he did quite consciously. In WESTERN TOMMY, for instance, Tommy Mayo arms himself with the same deliberate care and pride that a Greek hero would take. Thus his saddle is embossed with scenes that took two generations of craftsmen to complete: Faust spends two pages describing its series of scenes in this Western version of the shield of Achilles. Further, Tommy announces that he will live a hero's life. He will not hoard his moments but live them to the full: three to five years at the most, surrounded by friends, and then one of those friends will betray him—" 'When the finish comes, I won't have any regrets.' " Again, in THE BLACK SIGNAL the townspeople look upon Lew Melody "as a sort of Achilles, fated to a short but a glorious life."

And Dan Barry, with the tragic restlessness of the god, Pan, within him always yearns to follow where the wild geese fly.

Samuel A. Peeples in "Max Brand and the American Western Story" suggests that such transference by Faust "beguiles us not with what was but what might have been, if this were a different world. . . . Once committed to Faust's word wizardry, your interest is so absorbed that you find yourself dwelling in the dream world he has created without questioning its reality." I think that this charge of "unreality" is too strongly stated. It is true, of course, that the men and women featured in Greek, Roman, and medieval epics, dramas, and folktales have been "heightened" to a grandeur necessitated by the genres of epic and tragedy. But are they, then, to be looked upon wholly as non-human, wholly unrealistic? Think of Orestes, Achilles, Launcelot, Gawain: how invulnerable were they? How blameless? How untouched by ill chance, deception, and betrayal? One recalls that, of all the classic heroes, only Hector is stainless; of all the Arthurian knights, only Galahad is innocent. And both die young. Moreover, Chaucer, Shakespeare, Arnold, Browning, Tennyson, and Eliot—as Faust did— used such legendary figures to cast an intensely realistic eye on their own age, for these legends told of humanity's continuing struggle against personal weaknesses within and evil forces without. These ancient legends told of a striving, with many failures, to live rightly and justly. And they told of moments of hopelessness, when there was left only an unbowed spirit. It is in this sense that Faust followed the road of the classic "heroic."

However, Peeples does not appeal to this defense of Faust's resurrecting the old heroes and mythic actions. Rather, he finds an actual realism in Faust's transference of heroes-as-doers-of-mighty-deeds, because the real Old West was indeed "a saga filled with daring, heroic action, and bitter strife." It was, in truth, a time of grandiose gestures and colorful figures. I would offer, as my own example, the instance when in Virginia City the loss of a mine as rich as the Comstock Lode changed hands on a single cut of cards. Peeples notes that towering characters:

. . . stepped full-blown from history into the wildest of Western novels. . . . No fictional gunfighter, no matter how gunslick he may be described, can compare with the real article, John Wesley Hardin, of Texas, who could do tricks even cowboy actors can't match—not to mention killing forty men in single combat.

And yet Faust himself rejects such an argument. He was too much of a realist to depict his heroes on a grand scale as perfect figures. In the Old West he saw no demi-gods striding the earth. In fact, he doubted the truth of most of Western folklore. Hence, first of all, in his novels he had certain of his main characters openly question the veracity of the old tales. In THE STREAK Blondy doubts the truth of the traditional honor code of the gun duel. Buying bullets for his encounter with the vicious expert gunman, Calico Charlie, Blondy looks longingly at a case of shotguns—with one of those he would have some small chance of surviving. "But," he thinks, "the weapon of Western chivalry is the revolver," with a challenge delivered and a time and place named:

And then Blondy wondered if, after all, things had ever happened that way. Was it not all a matter of tradition, legend, and many foolish stories written into the books? When men fought with fists or guns, was there anything knightly about it, or wasn't it usually a matter of a brawl, a savage flurry of words, voices suddenly cursing, and then: "Take this, damn you!"

Faust goes even farther in THE GENTLE DESPERADO. A lying uncle has raised Robert Fernald on false tales of the Old West, in which supposedly he rode with Wild Bill Hickok, lived with Indians, and hunted with Buffalo Bill. Although Robert believes these stories, Faust from the outset makes it quite clear to the reader that the uncle is fabricating. Further, it is important to note that Faust does not present the uncle as a good-natured guardian, seeking merely to entertain the boy: rather, he has made himself into a hero so that Robert would never suspect that he has robbed his nephew of his $60,000 inheritance. Exaggerated legends from such a source, then, are not to be accepted by the reader with an amused tolerance.

It is somewhat surprising that Faust should so openly question the truthfulness of the popular images of the Old West. After all, his writing contract asked for nothing more than that he passively work within the margins of certain given patterns. Why did he daringly call in question the pillars holding up those patterns? Basically, I think, it was his sense of integrity as an artist-creator that led him first to question and then answer the accusations raised by certain Eastern critics of the Western.

Faust was not content merely to voice strong doubts about the legends of the Old West. He took a second step, one that is present in almost every one of his Westerns: to reveal in some detail exactly how heroic legends were born and how they grew. First, the reader is taken through the actual episode; for example, the protagonist is fearful, without much hope, but—in the end—lucky. Then the news reaches the town in this form: "the hero sought out the encounter and laughed at what was not even a challenge to him." Then successive reports exaggerate even farther. And the protagonist's protests are taken for a hero's modesty. But what a reader is most aware of—and this is a key point if one is to understand Faust's thinking—is that, in the actual episode, despite the man's fear and hopelessness, he was indeed a "hero" in a realistic meaning of that term.

As a specific example, let us return to that episode of Blondy's buying those bullets in THE STREAK. He had just returned from charging up a hill with an empty gun where reptilian Calico Charlie lay in supposed ambush. Now, as he waits for the store's door to be unlocked, he takes one last look at the store, for he knows that within an hour he will be dead:

. . . a gun gripped in the little claws of Calico Charlie, the muzzle of it jerking up in rapid vibrations as the shots were poured forth; and his own body torn and battered by those shots tearing through the flesh, thudding home like heavy fists, smashing the bones. That was the picture he kept seeing blown across the stars.

He fans his gun: "Had any of even the most famous old gunmasters been able to accomplish the thing [he was doing]? Or was it chiefly talk, rumor, legend again—always legend. Fairy stories. . . ." Blondy smiles to himself and Wilkes, the storekeeper, remarks:

"You laugh, eh? But I suppose you must have taken a good ten years to learn the trick of it. . . ."

Yes, that was the way legend grew. Blondy felt himself in the breath-taking presence of its birth at that moment. Wilkes would say, out of his own mind, that The Streak with his own life had told him so. . . .

And now, to complete the legend Blondy knew that he must not stand before Calico Charlie in the orthodox fashion, with his forefinger on the trigger, trying to plant a lucky shot . . . the chance of the condemned man who was given the pitiful little stylus with which to face the charge of the lion in the arena. But even that chance Blondy must cast away because the pitiless legend of The Streak demanded that he should fan the hammer of his revolver.

Then Blondy saunters into the saloon headquarters of the enemy, packed with henchmen who know of the price on his head. He stands loosely at the bar with his back turned to them all and says quietly: "Let me have one of those cold beers, Reilly, will you?" This is humble courage in a man who is fearful inwardly as he remembers that he has never had even a minute's practice with a gun. And it is worth repeating—a complete episode similar to this may be found in almost every Faust Western.

That Blondy in skill and bravery equals what the legends had boasted leads us to Faust's third step: a conviction that the Old West has never died out. Teddy Roosevelt discerned this in the 1890s while working with his ranch's cowboys. As an instance from Faust let us recall Robert Fernald, raised on the stories of his uncle in THE GENTLE DESPERADO. In despair, he finds that he can win only some of the boxing matches in the weight classes above him, can hit only off-the-center of a quarter thrown into the air, can hit a dime at thirty paces only once in four times, and can run only most of a day. Again, in THE BIG TRAIL Tom Fuller circa 1910 proves to be as daring, capable, and courageous as his father had been in the 1860s. Early in the story a blacksmith replies to the charge that the Old West is dead by remarking that people have been saying this for generations: fur traders said it when they first saw a wagon and oxen arrive, the oxen drivers when they first spotted a mule train, the muleteers when a stagecoach passed them:

And then comes the railroad and everybody says that the East is sure let all through the West, and there ain't any more West at all. . . .

They went a further step, when the automobiles came along. And they say that the automobiles are gunna fill this land. But I say they ain't.

He points out that there are too many deserts, mountains, and rivers to challenge and toughen and inspirit the dwellers:

It's the country where they's room to breathe, to think, room to step and hit nobody's corns but your own . . . nor the time ain't ever gunna come when a few wild men don't ride out from that there desert, and over them hills! And I tell you, too, that the time will never come when the West'll be safe for a fool!

This oration finds its proof in DUST ACROSS THE RANGE, a short novel set in the year 1937. Faust makes it specifically contemporary: Harry Mortimer is a university graduate in agriculture, working in the West to prevent soil erosion. Eight Civilian Conservation Corps youths assist him in fighting a dust bowl storm. But Faust just as specifically establishes a bridge from the Old West to the New, for Harry is as determined and resourceful as any ranch boss from the 1880s. Indeed, a central episode takes place in a saloon that in the days of the Old West had been the scene of numerous gunfights—three bullet holes, in fact, still pierce its swinging doors. A seventy-year-old bartender from that era offers an old toast: "Here's to the fight and to them that shoot straight, and damn the man that breaks the mirror." Faust's modern hero, Harry, unarmed hurls himself into seven cowboys whose pistols are already half drawn, although he is not able, despite the toast, to keep the mirror from a bullet. The girl, Louise Miller, as any heroine of the Old West works in the storm alongside of the men and risks her life to prevent bloodshed. Further, the CCC lads are true heirs of their cowboy precursors: they protect Harry, avenge him, and are ready to fight for him. Of course, this mirroring of the Old West works the other way, too: if the folk of the 1930s confront human evil and natural disaster with such strength, who is to deny some germ of truth existed in those tales of yesteryear?

Somewhat related to this is the anti-realism charge of anachronism made against Faust. For instance, in the midst of Old West fast action the reader stumbles upon a telephone or a truck. Of course, Faust did commit some anachronisms, despite his file on Western data. But the instinctive charge of anachronism, whenever a critic encounters anything considered modern, reveals, I think, the ignorance of later-day Easterners. However, the historical truth is that posses-on-horseback did ride on into the era of the telegraph, the automobile, and the telephone; such devices simply made the posse's net more effective, increasing the odds against Faust's harassed outlaws. Further, Easterners forget that in the early 1900s, mining towns were still being founded, power struggles still taking place, and banks still being robbed. Silverton, Colorado, would be such an example. Finally, it is in this area (around 1912) when Faust himself associated with working California cowboys and listened to their tales.

A more particular question for our topic is this: what degree of realism is there in these "knights" of Faust? Certainly they find themselves in more action and outer conflict than real life offers to the ordinary person: the genre of the Western demands this. Yet Faust goes deeper than physical action and creates central characters who are far more humanly real than a reader might expect. First of all, a surprising number of Faust's Westerns—perhaps one third—have as the central character a person who has no skill with guns or other weapons. Some are even physically handicapped. Why did Faust choose such protagonists, so lacking in promise and so taxing of his inventive powers? Faust had to entertain with adventure, of course, but I think that he also desired—pushing the Western to its limits—to present life as he had experienced it. And one essential element in that experience was voiced by Destry in his solemn moment of reconciliation. He now sees that most men are mostly good and, more significantly, are "capable, now and then and here and there of great deeds inspired by love and high aspirations." Indeed, the boy Willie, near death in his arms, is just such a human: to save Destry, he had thrown his life away in confronting an evil man whom even Destry feared.

In VALLEY THIEVES we encounter another character who performs "great deeds inspired by love and aspiration"—Bill Avon. He is a small rancher, a husband and father, his home only a shanty, average in intelligence, awkward, has little skill with guns. Although this novel is one of the "Jim Silver" series, Bill is the central character and the real hero. Even though he considers himself "just a dull, ordinary drone," he steps forward to prevent a corrupt sheriff from shooting an unarmed man. When Silver tells him he cannot accompany him into certain death, Bill insists and explains: "I'll never be able to face my son." Under torture, he lies to Barry Christian, knowing that within hours his lie will be discovered; later he shouts defiance in Barry's face. Offered a safe pass if he will desert Silver, he recalls for the reader:

I would like to say that I answered right up, that I shouted it, and that I cried out that I would rather die than see Jim Silver done in on account of the rest of us. But the fact is that for a second I thought about the shack on the ranch, and the smell of the coffee in the kitchen, and the sound of Charlotte singing quietly over her sewing, and the way the taste of coffee and tobacco mixes in the mouth.

I came to with a gasp and said, "No, no, Jim! We stand together."

Bill even returns to the enemy's stronghold. At the end, Barry Christian speaks derisively of him to Silver: "You choose some pretty clumsy weapons." Silver disagrees.

In another "Jim Silver" novel, VALLEY OF VANISHING MEN, the central character again is but an ordinary cowhand, Ben Trainor, who sets out to find his brother. He has no skill either as a gunman or as a fighter: he knows he is "no hero." Yet, filled with fear, he nevertheless acts bravely and honorably again and again.

In LARRAMEE'S RANCH Faust chose as his hero a gentle, frail, pale-faced youth who has a crippled leg, wears glasses, and though a Westerner has never fired a gun nor ridden a horse. His first act upon leaving home to face the world is to rescue a frightened rabbit. Yet, by posing as a menacing and dangerous man of dark mystery, he outbluffs gunmen and captures the infamous Night Killer. Challenged to ride a man-slayer horse, he first has to read a book on "horse breaking." In the end, Tom is surprised that he has succeeded despite his lack of cleverness and bravery. The reader knows better.

Yet what of such "super-heroes" as Destry or Jim Silver? Even here, Faust is careful to show that they have their share of human weaknesses. Destry is beaten to the draw by the man he fears, Bent, and only a lucky shot saves him. Moreover, Faust often stresses that even the top gunmen must depend on luck. The most detailed discussion of this is in ON THE TRAIL OF FOUR. In SILVERTIP'S SEARCH Silver is often unnerved with fear:

He knew that it was fear that had come into him like the cold, damp breath of a cellar.
. . . He kept seeing the dead man, Lawson, sit up on the trail, and then rise, and walk to him with dead eyes, and laughter . . . dark forms were crouching there in the shadows, ready to start out at him . . . shudders were working up and down the flesh of his back.
. . . He set his teeth against that weakness so hard that a fine perspiration broke out on him.

Again, Silver's friend, Taxi, seemingly without any human emotion but loyalty, nevertheless explodes into jealousy in VALLEY THIEVES over his displacement at Silver's side by another. Very realistically he gives way to anger in bitter, wounding words that cut Silver to the quick. As a final instance, Silver's usual insight fails him when, in STOLEN STALLION, he refuses to believe the fool, Charlie Moore, that Brandy is the sire of Parade.

An entirely different facet of realism is the controversial question whether fictional characters who have a personal commitment to traditional moral values and who struggle to live up to that code can be considered *realistic*. Recently I read a number of reviews of the TV production of "Lonesome Dove," and they all attacked it for its lack of realism—for depicting "a West that never was." By this they did not mean it was historically false but rather it was morally false: they found the evil and weak-willed characters to be realistic, but they could not believe in those characters who were honorable, who sacrificed their well-being and risked their lives for others, who kept their word, who stood fast against great odds, who never forgot their unjust deeds. One answer to cynical critics—and one that author, Larry McMurtry, could make—would be that the good characters (as well as the bad) were based upon his own predecessors— their diaries, letters, and tales—reinforced by research. As a parallel example one recalls that, when Charles Dickens was criticized at the turn of the century for romanticizing members of the lower classes by endowing them with "unrealistic" self-dignity or dry sarcasm or sublime insights, G. K. Chesterton could only reply that one could meet such poor in the streets of modern London every day.

It is true that Faust's protagonists, even con-men and outlaws, do have an unusually high code of honor: loyalty to friends, not taking advantage of the weak, not shooting to kill unless absolutely necessary. They struggle and they learn. How unrealistic are they? To be sure, the genre of the Western in the 1920s and 1930s expected such behavior to a certain degree. But might not Chesterton also reply: "Look among working men and you will meet such men"? One place we might look is Faust's own life, where a generous spirit found its culmination as he lay dying: he sent the medics away to two boys near him: "They're worse off than I."

Counter to the convention of happy endings then current, Faust sometimes concluded his tale tragically or in a bittersweet tone. Who can forget the final paragraphs of THE SEVENTH MAN, where Faust with restrained power depicts the death of Dan Barry, shot by the woman he loves—with Buck Daniels weeping aloud, Les Haines with his face in his hands, and a wedge of wild geese flying low across the moon? In "The Dream of Macdonald" Faust tells in stark, bald prose the series of injustices that destroyed Macdonald's reputation. This bare, heart-rendering recital reinforces the poignancy of his noble, tragic death. Such injustices are the dark shadows that continually threaten most of Faust's heroes. In THE DUDE the likable, witty ex-convict never reveals his deep love for Molly Loftus, because he is a social outcast. The heroic Juanita in THE BLACK SIGNAL never marries, because the man she loves weds another. Again, many heroes, such as Tommy Mayo in WESTERN TOMMY, ride off, breaking the girl's heart. The ending of THE GENTLE DESPERADO is bittersweet, with bitterness predominant. Fernald does marry, but he also yearns for his former adventurous life: "Still his eyes were fixed on the wild heights of life, and he despised the quiet ways in which he found himself." Finally, Faust more often than not did not leave his hero materially rich: his couples become merely small ranchers. Thus in RAWHIDE JUSTICE Faust resists the temptation to have the heroine, kidnapped as an infant by Gypsies, turn out to be an heiress.

Faust's realism in description of places, things, seasons, and times of the day or night need not be touched upon here, for he is a master of the highest rank in this. His inventiveness in fresh similes is without equal. Although his places are not geographically real, they always ring true. As an example of his descriptive powers, I shall quote only from a passage in RUSTLERS OF BEACON CREEK about a late fall roundup:

That autumn night was both wet and cold; the wind blew hard, with frost in its breath and anger in its roar; it was trying to bring on a sweeping victory of winter all at one blow. . . . They sat up from their damp blankets, shuddering, and clasped their sleepy bodies in their arms, wondering if they had the strength to rise, and wondering if rising were worthwhile; the next instant the wind had passed its fine sword blade through and through them and they abandoned all doubt. They began to drag on socks stiff with frost, and then the bitter pain of boots. . . . Morning appeared only on the clock, for it was dark as pitch. . . . Under such hardships, riding twelve to twenty hours a day, stiffened with cold and beaten with wind, men marching in an army for the salvation of their country would have collapsed and died like flies. But these 'punchers were working for pay and foolishness. . . .

Finally, detailed descriptions that marked the first phase of French Realism appear in Faust mostly in regard to food. For example, in RIPPON RIDES DOUBLE Rippon lovingly prepares the ingredients for his Mulligan stew, composing an array of little dishes "like a musician, adding theme to theme to make the harmony grow." A different instance of detail is found in OUTLAW BREED where Phil Slader's mind races on for two pages, thinking what $500 would buy. Faust was effective, too, in small details. The Alaskan bartender in MIGHTY LOBO reads through the Want Ads in a San Francisco paper five months old, marking certain ones with his thumbnail and all the while shaking his head or raising his eyebrows. Or young Jimmy in THE STREAK emphatically strokes his forehead where his hero, Blondy, had been wounded.

What one might call "sociological" realism is also present in Faust's Westerns. He was well aware of corruption in law enforcement, business, and politics. In the matter of injustice and the law, he depicts numerous brutal "bull" detectives, such as the two who beat Paradise Al savagely in ROGUE MUSTANG on a trumped-up charge of vagrancy (the two had actually found $428 on him), and they plan to continue the clubbing when they get him to jail. Perhaps the most detailed description of the tortures inflicted on state prisoners appears in THE LONG CHASE. Tom Keene spends three years in "Little Ease" for protecting a cripple from a brutal guard. Years later, when an inspector checks on reports of brutality, Tom, like the other prisoners, lies, fearful of Warden Tufter's reprisals. Again, in reference to political corruption, wealthy men, such as John Miller in DUST ACROSS THE RANGE, are shown to control elected officials. In DESTRY RIDES AGAIN one recalls the blunt letter from the President of T. and O. Company reminding legislator, Clyde Orrin, that they are already paying him $10,000 a year for favors; if he does not get them a "fat" tax cut, his political career will be at an end; if he is successful, he'll receive a $10,000 bonus, plus a governorship or a U.S. Senate seat.

In the matter of racial tolerance Faust realistically confronted current, widespread prejudice. He was indeed a man ahead of his time. In his Westerns it is his villains who make racial slurs against Indians, Mexicans, and Negroes—and it is his heroes who look upon these races as fellow human beings. Faust has young Destry prejudiced against Mexicans and Negroes early in the story, but only so that his later moment of enlightenment will be more striking and affecting. Then, too, his novels centering on Indian life are admirably empathetic and realistic in their portrayal of a wide range of Indian experience. In the Red

Hawk series his artful treatment of the god of the Cheyennes, Sweet Medicine, is movingly lyrical and reverent. As for Negroes, they appear frequently and are always dealt with as diverse persons—the best compliment a writer can pay. They range from the highly intelligent and noble slave, Luke, in THE LONG CHANCE to the loyal giant, Soapy, in RIDERS OF THE PLAINS. Similarly, Mexicans—men, women, and children—have varying personalities. One of my favorites is the con-man, Pedro Aquiller, master of many languages and varied American dialects in THE BIG TRAIL. In addition, William Nolan cites "Outcast Breed" for its typically Faustian theme of "the problem faced by a man of mixed blood fighting to survive prejudice and hostility."

Realism in characterization was discussed earlier from the viewpoint of legendary heroes. I would like to make a few observations about other aspects. First, there is a surprising variety of characterization to be found in Faust's Westerns, given the circumstances under which these hundreds of books were written, for Faust poured out his prose at an astonishing rate—in a relatively short period, more than 30 million words in fiction. One would have expected, then, repeated patterns with repeated types—villains, for instance. Certainly Faust was obligated only to produce fast action, and he had the disguise of numerous pen names. Yet he taxed his creative powers, despite the pressure of deadlines, to bring forth new, fresh characters and push his Western stories beyond traditional limits.

Recall, for instance, the character, Tonio, in VALLEY VULTURES. Charlie Dexter is trailing the mass murderer, Scorpio, who had begun his life of terror with the massacre of Charlie's family. He meets Tonio, whose face is horribly disfigured from a blow of a horse's hoof. Tonio tells Charlie that he, too, is on a vengeance trail against Scorpio, whose corrupting friendship has ruined his life. Scorpio had seduced Tonio's innocent fiancée and a short time later abandoned her. Again, he had urged Tonio to waste a year of his life chasing a wild stallion; while taming it, his handsome face was utterly destroyed; and after a bond of love was formed with the horse, Scorpio shot it. Yet, Tonio admits, Scorpio has winning ways: once, when Tonio tried to stab Scorpio but succeeded only in getting his own throat cut, it was Scorpio who nursed him back to health. Tonio ends by declaring that he can only succeed in killing Scorpio. Tonio's agonized narration takes some thirty pages. But then it is revealed that Tonio *is* Scorpio—he is a schizophrenic. As Tonio dies, he grips his throat and hoarsely cries: "Scorpio, Scorpio, you are choking me."

In the tragedy, JIM CURRY'S TEST, two characters undergo change but in opposite directions. Jim Curry gives up his career as the non-violent Red Devil bandit and, amid the affection of a rancher's family, matures into a new life; he and the rancher's daughter fall in love. But the rancher's son, Charlie Mark, assumes the role of the Red Devil and descends into evil and kills wantonly. In the tragic ending, to save Charlie from a posse, Jim once again assumes the role of the Red Devil. As a final, brief instance of main characters, MIGHTY LOBO has non-stop action, involving a gold mine, a missing brother, and vengeful

Indians. Yet, for the reader the focus of the novel is the psychological action within the five main characters: each is a puzzle, and hence the reader never can guess in what direction the plot will jump.

I shall not attempt here a discussion of the degree of realism in Faust's Western women, for it is so extensive a topic that it demands a full essay in itself. Here certain themes of realism would emerge: that women usually are more perceptive than men—for instance, the girl in the stagecoach in JIM CURRY'S TEST; that women have greater inner strength than men—Jim Silver avers: " 'Women stand pain better than men . . . ' " in VALLEY OF VANISHING MEN; that women can be the greater hero—"Outcast Breed," RUSTLERS OF BEACON CREEK, SLOW JOE, MIGHTY LOBO, two in THE RANGELAND AVENGER, "Black Jack," and many others.

Realism in the portrayal of evil and villainy is presented by Faust because of his gifts of invention and his mastery of words. Think of the opening scene of "Black Jack"—the laughing outlaw rides openly down the main street of Garrison City to see his newly born son; a rifle pokes out between curtains, and the outlaw's life is ended by a shot in the back. But this villainy is nothing compared to the heartlessness of so-called "good" society in condemning the son, simply because of "tainted blood." In this book there is no humor nor hope; indeed, until the penultimate page, it is expected that the son will die under the same exact circumstances as his father.

Dickens could convey, noted Chesterton, a "higher" realism—that is, places and persons are presented to the reader, not as having been imprinted on Dickens's mind, but rather as having Dickens's mind and mood imprinted *into* them—an "eerie" realism. This is often Faust's type of realism: for example, his evocative portrayal of the evil Cary clan and their abode, their savage women and brutal children in VALLEY THIEVES. Bill Avon is taken to Old Man Cary:

The smell of the cooking broth was stale through the room. Everything seemed to be soaked with the greasy odor, as though that same pot had been boiling there for years. Mutton was the smell, and if you know mutton, you know what I mean. . . . Old Man Cary . . . still had the great Cary frame which his descendants had inherited from him. . . . But there was no flesh on him. He was eaten away. Death had been at him for a long time and death was still at work. . . . His face had shrunk so that it seemed very small, unmatched to the size of his head, like a boy's face under a mature skull. And his eyes were bright, sharp, young, under the wrinkling folds of the lids.

Along with Dickens, Faust peopled his novels with minor characters who come to life on the page, such as the coffin maker in VALLEY VULTURES, or the boy, Slim, in THE BLACK SIGNAL, reclining against the forelegs of his little bronco, playing his harmonica: "If this ain't swell harmony, I'm a goat!" Or the simplicity of the stagecoach driver in FALSE RIDER: when the pitiless Barry Christian shoots the lead horse to stop the coach, the driver ignores the rifle and weeps openly over the horse: "There's a mare that never said 'No.' ... I've been drunk behind her, and she's made better time when I was drunk than when I was sober. ... There's a mare that was a lady, and I loved her." Dr. Blinky, the sneak thief in THE DUDE who is terror stricken as he accompanies the Dude on a robbery, in his dying moments provides perhaps the most realistic and finest death scene in Faust's fiction. Or Hank Cleeves, turned evil and now dying, remembered by Destry as a childhood friend: "Tall, wiry, pale, thoughtful, an ironic and caustic boy, walking apart from the rest, acclaimed as a genius by boys with lesser talents for the making of sleighs, and toys of all sorts." Or Cold Feet as he prays aloud before a masked lynch mob in THE RANGELAND AVENGER:

"Our Father in Heaven, forgive them as I forgive them. ... Let no knowledge of the crime they are committing come to these men. Fierce men, fighters, toilers, full of hate, full of despair, how can they be other than blind? Forgive them, as I forgive them without malice."

One minor character who takes on life every time he appears is Taxi, introduced first in SILVERTIP'S ROUNDUP as he arrives in the West to avenge a friend's death. Deceptively dapper and only twenty-two, Taxi already is an extremely capable New York City underworld figure. If one seeks to find realism in characterization at its most perfect, read these first eighteen pages—every thought, gesture, and all the dialogue are artfully rendered. Here is proof that Faust is a writer of first rank. In barren Horseshoe Flats, a town that had been optimistically laid out in broad streets and isolated buildings, Taxi is a city mouse caught in a desert under a hawk. He hates the place. Putting some wild flowers on his friend's grave, he turns away "because he did not want to see the flowers die on Joe's grave." He is embittered at discovering that the girl who had caused the murder, Sally, is so plain. I could continue to synopsize the action, but only an actual reading of the whole can convey what Faust has wrought. By the end of the book, Taxi knows he could live in no place but the West and could love no girl but Sally.

Finally, in this matter of characterization, mention must be made of Faust's realism in depicting animals. Note how often he enters into their minds and feelings. More than half of SILVERTIP'S CHASE, for instance, is seen through the eyes of the wolf, Frosty, and his mate, and in one episode a grizzly bear. Faust goes farther in STOLEN STALLION: he gives dialogue to the stallion, Brandy, to his mare, Mischief, and to their colt, Parade. This is a risky device if not done well. But Faust is not playing Aesop nor does he desire to ascend to the mythic heights of a Richard Adams in WATERSHIP DOWN. Rather, he wants to bring the reader to a greater realism in empathizing with his wild animals. And he succeeds well.

One last aspect of realism needs a brief comment: Faust's deep insights into life that continually surprise the reader. For example, in SINGLE JACK Apperley says of love in a male: "Only once in our lives, perhaps, we find her who possesses the key of mystery which unlocks the heart and lets the wind of an unknown country pass through all the chambers." In TRAIL PARTNERS no human is more innocent than Slope, and yet he avers: "I have done such things that they wake me up at night. . . . I'm afraid to face them, even out here in the open light of day! . . . I'm better than no one. I'm only worse than I should be." Again, in THE FALSE RIDER Silver reflects that a mob made up of good men is far worse than one consisting of badmen, "because the mere consciousness of honesty is apt to make the members of the crowd feel that every emotion in the heart is justifiable and should be followed with safety." And one recalls that insightful passage when the dying Willie's sigh causes Destry's breast to lift "as the breast of a mother stirs when the infant moves beside her, at night. He felt all of paternity, all of motherhood, also, since both qualities lie mysteriously buried in the heart of man." Such mysteries thronging "down on the sad soul of Destry," touching "them in their flight as a child might hold up its hands and touch moths flying in the night," lead him to the insight that all men are "peers" because all humans share in the same mystery of having been created partly "out of the soil" and partly "out of the heavens." Life and death appeared to him thus: "Life was a queer thing. It was a great and continued war to maintain it. But to lose it, how simple! Like dropping a golden coin into a dark sea!" Such are the realistic insights that enrich a reader of Faust's Westerns.

I would say that Faust saw life's reality as a vast panorama, with millions of different shades of varied colors—dark and bright, foolish and sublime, frenzied, and still, cynical and romantic. He held that most Westerners, as indeed most of humankind, sought to live according to certain traditional moral ideas. Thus in THE BIG TRAIL a wise doctor asserts that the honest man is the "only one who really exists and really lives." Further, in that same novel Faust demonstrated the deeper realities of what his experiences in life had disclosed to him: that amid fear, bravery can appear; that amid hopelessness, one more attempt will be made; that amid uncertainties in love, vows will be taken. Indeed, for Faust, in THE BIG TRAIL his romantic Kate Lane and his doubting Thomas Fuller are both right, for life encompasses them both. And like the heroic common man, Bill Avon, in VALLEY THIEVES, Faust recognized that, although we are sometimes lost in a blind darkness, yet in other moments we look about "as though I were a child, reading a book of wonders."

ONE MAN'S FAUST

Dwight Bennett Newton

This essay, written by an author of seventy Western novels and numerous short stories, was specially requested by the editors and appears here for the first time.

I

In the spring of 1928 a twelve-year-old Kansas City youngster, ambitious to be a writer, had reached a crossroads. After five years spent in the best of all training grounds, the Oz books—reading them over and over, studying the prose style of L. Frank Baum (an excellent craftsman, by the way), and learning something about characterization, dialogue, and viewpoint—I'd begun to think I was too old for fairy stories but had no idea where to turn for a replacement. Then, lo! On a rainy April day I came upon a copy of *Western Story Magazine* (''Big, Clean Stories of Outdoor Life'') that my brother had left lying around from the previous summer. I couldn't know that the future course of my life was about to be set for me.

Naturally I knew about Westerns from Saturday matinees at the silent movies with Tom Mix and Hoot Gibson, but I'd never read a pulp magazine. Unabashed by its cover art, I opened this one to the first story, ''The Gentle Desperado,'' by someone named George Owen Baxter (''author of 'The Terrible Tenderfoot,' etc.'') and took a glance at the opening sentence: ''Catalina, sitting half seen among the trees, beckoned Robert Fernald with a scattered gleam of lamps among the shadows.''

Hey! I thought. *This fellow's as good as L. Frank Baum!* I finished that story, and all the others. None seemed anywhere near as well written as Baxter's, except for the closing installment of a six-part serial, ''The City in the Sky,'' by Max Brand whose style I thought was astonishingly like Baxter's.

I went digging again in the closet and unearthed additional numbers from 1927. I read "The Terrible Tenderfoot" and the rest of "The City in the Sky" (and along with them a story by Robert Ormond Case who, in later years and despite the difference in our ages, was to become a cherished friend and colleague). Already it was clear beyond any doubt that this city-bred youngster, who had never been farther west of the Missouri state line than Topeka, possessed an enduring affinity for that whole exciting region that lay beyond. And why not? After all, I'd never been to the land of Oz, either.

Nearly seventy years later I've seen my share of the West and spent my adult life writing stories about it—all due to the magic of nineteen words stumbled upon, wholly by accident, at a moment when I was ready to appreciate them. Naturally I had to find out if *Western Story Magazine* was still being published after all that time—when you're twelve, a year seems about as long as a decade. Yes, it still was; and Max Brand was writing for it—or, George Owen Baxter, or whatever the man's real name might be. I was convinced they had to be the same person long before I discovered a copy of Baxter's serial, "The Gun Tamer," published as a book with Brand's name on it. By now I was taking my fifteen cents each week to the Crown Drug Store at St. John and Elmwood, where I would buy one of their two copies of the magazine and stick it inside my shirt so that no one (except the druggist, of course) would know my guilty secret. I'm afraid my poor mother was distraught, at first, until I sat down one day while she was sewing and read to her for a bit. I can still remember the way she looked at me, in astonishment, and exclaimed: "Why, they're real *stories,* aren't they!" After that she never made any more trouble for me, especially when it turned out that my uncle, a Methodist minister, liked reading Westerns himself for relaxation.

I'd hit pay dirt with the May 12 issue, featuring the first installment of Brand's "Three on the Trail." To my twelve-year-old ear the opening sentences read almost like a poem and could have been printed as one:

> The landlord leaned in the doorway.
> He had not paused to knock,
> But, softly turning the knob,
> Had let the draft
> Carry the door
> Wide.

An English teacher could have pointed out the alliterations in the first line; the assonances of "not," "paused," "knock," "softly," "knob"; and the lilting rhythm throughout, though, of course, English teachers never do this sort of thing except with authentic, certified *poetry* ("And *l*ive a*l*one in a bee-*l*oud g*l*ade"). Just the same, I knew all I needed to: whatever else he was, this Max Brand was a poet!

And, that *story!* James Geraldi, making his debut, proved himself the peer of

Douglas Fairbanks in the most romantic movie that I had ever yet seen: THE THIEF OF BAGDAD (1924). Flat broke, he paid his bill from the crooked hotel keeper's own wallet and then, while the law was being summoned, climbed out of a window to the roof where he leaped with ease to the house adjoining (pausing only for a bow to a cheering crowd, gathering in the street). Having entered this building through a skylight, he took cover behind the first door he came to—and, naturally, encountered a beautiful girl who would soon be asking him to undertake a life-or-death mission. What more than this could any twelve-year-old possibly ask of the person who had replaced L. Frank Baum as his favorite author? From the magic of Oz to the magic of Max Brand: it was an obvious transition!

I had sampled other pulps by now. I rather liked *Argosy All-Story Weekly* for its policy of running four serials in every issue, but for the time being I remained faithful to *Western Story Magazine* since it was the one that regularly featured Max Brand. I often wonder how many of us are still around who were among those lucky readers of Frederick Faust—getting his works hot off the press, the first time anywhere, along with the funky but rather charming illustrations of Frank Tinsley? They came at us fast, usually at the rate of a book-length serial each month and a novelette or two besides. In June 1928, for example, there was "The Brass Man" plus the "Paul Torridon" novelettes that eventually became COWARD OF THE CLAN. In August, it was "Pillar Mountain"; in September, "Riders for Fortune"; in October, "Silver Trail"; in December, "Singing Guns"; in January, 1929, "The Stranger"; in February, "The Winged Horse"; in April, "The Trail to Manhood"; and so on. I absorbed them all. (Most would be given other titles when they went into book form, but, of course, these are the names by which I will always remember them.)

As stories by Peter Henry Morland, John Frederick, and David Manning appeared, I was to grow more and more bewildered: these, too *had* to be pseudonyms—except that it was physically impossible for one person to turn out such vast quantities of carefully crafted prose! It would not be until 1935 that *Esquire* finally revealed the name of the man in the villa at Florence, writing poetry with a quill pen while batting out a million words and more of pulp fiction every year. It seemed that Frederick Faust's prose wasn't polished at all. It simply came that way off the top of his head!

As it happened, I had stopped reading him a couple of years before—in 1933, to be exact. It was Silvertip that turned me off. By then I was seventeen and a good deal more critical. In this new series, it seemed to me, Faust must have written himself out and now was doing a kind of travesty on everything that had come earlier. Jim Silver, with those little horns of gray at his temples and the whole familiar array of props—a superhorse, a sidekick, a pet wolf, and still another of Brand's supervillains of whom I'd already grown very tired (all of them identical clones of that more famous "Napoleon of Crime," Sherlock Holmes's nemesis, Doctor Moriarty): as far as I was concerned the whole setup belonged in *Wild West Weekly*.

What to me was even worse, most of the magic and the poetry seemed to have drained out of Faust's prose, leaving such turgid and melodramatic stuff as the following from SILVERTIP'S TRAP:

What a man was Barry Christian! No wonder that the cream of the criminal brains of the West was eager to follow him wherever he might lead.

Then the thought of Naylor turned back to Jim Silver, riding with the men of Elsinore on behalf of the law. No doubt, close to him rode that slender man with the pale, bright eyes—Taxi. Those two might be strong enough to wreck all the forces of the great Christian. It seemed to Naylor a battle of supermen—and he was a useless force in the encounter.

That is truly awful stuff, pure half-cent-a-word pulp at any price! I decided the time had come to call it a day on Max Brand, and in all of 1934 I bought just one copy of *Western Story Magazine* out of curiosity. Yes, he was still at it, with what I didn't realize at the time would be his very last serial for Frank Blackwell. At about the same period a diary entry tells me that I read one of his "Sleeper" novelettes in a magazine called *Mavericks,* and that I thought he had simply recycled a plot from his "Duster" series of a few years before. Brand was just about through. It was too bad, really.

I know now, of course, that Faust wasn't "written out" in 1933; he was merely exhausted. For that was the year when he published 1,830,000 words— no doubt a record no one else is ever likely to match. Nor for that matter was anyone likely to want to, unless driven by some hopeless economic bind, like the one from which Faust never seemed able to extricate himself. At one point, in that final year, he set himself to turn out four 50,000–word novels in sixteen days, desperately hoping that way to pay off some part of his colossal debt. I wish I could have known that! If SILVERTIP'S TRAP was one of those four-day novels, it would have explained everything.

In the years following I completely lost sight of Faust. My own failed attempts to write Westerns being temporarily on hold, I was now into philosophy and literature and Greek history and no longer wasting my time on magazines, and so I had no idea at all that he was starting to appear in *Harper's* and *Collier's* and *The Saturday Evening Post.* The movie, INTERNES CAN'T TAKE MONEY, caught me completely by surprise, along with its authentic Faustian dialogue: "The kid has eyes in the ends of his fingers!" Also by surprise, in February 1937, I found a serial entitled "The American" running in *Argosy,* and thought it the best thing of Faust I had ever read.

I might add that about this same time I'd finally turned out a salable story, although the magazine paid on publication and it wouldn't be until April 1938— ten frustrating years since the day I first discovered Westerns—that I at last saw myself in print. (As it happened, the year of my debut would also mark the *final* appearance of Max Brand in a Western pulp magazine.) I think it might be of interest, if maybe a little embarrassing, to quote briefly from "Brand of the

Hunted'' by D. B. Newton from *Western Novel and Short Stories Magazine* (7/38).

Chapter VII
The Sun Rises

It would be many days before the doctor could remove the bandages from Mahan's face, but it was such a relief to learn that he had not been blinded, after all, that he was content to wait.

For the present, it was quite enough to sit here in the coolness of the hospital ward, and hear the voices of Polly Haines and the lower tones of her father.

It was by far the coolest spot he had yet found in Mesquite; but then he was told that he was not in Mesquite at all: the sheriff had moved him, while he was still unconscious, to the hospital at Willow Springs.

As soon as he recuperated, no doubt, the trial would begin!

This passage is obviously written in what I should have to call a half-cent-a-word version of Faust's abbreviated, or "Dick and Jane" mode, right down to the closing exclamation point (except that, to be truly authentic, instead of "Mahan's face" I ought of course to have written "the face of Mahan"). I doubt that I was consciously doing an imitation; I'd absorbed so much of Max Brand that the words seemed to come out this way of their own accord. I should add that it never happened again: once into print, I began adapting my style, chameleon-like, to match the environment of whatever magazine I happened to be writing for. Writers, like all threatened species, learn the art of survival.

———————————————— *II* ————————————————

Some years ago the late Bernard DeVoto made a reference to what he called "interchangeable Westerns in basic pidgin." There was a certain amount of justice in that, I'm afraid. Many Westerns are no more likely than other types of category fiction to serve as paragons of literary excellence. Even Cherry Wilson—one of my favorite writers from the old *Western Story Magazine,* author of "The Throwback," "Empty Saddles," and other fine novels—could commit such a passage as this, from the opening installment of a serial: " 'Go!' cried the girl, advancing on him. 'Go, Pete Challoner!' And there was a blaze in her blue eyes then before which even his stubborn spirit quailed."

I could have assured DeVoto that in Frederick Faust at least there was one Western writer utterly incapable of any such barbaric string of words as "then before which even"—or for that matter, of a sentence like one by W. Somerset Maugham in THEN AND NOW, a novel of Renaissance Italy that I quote from memory: "He had taken him from the gutter, he had taught him to win friends and influence people, and this is how he rewarded him." Faust had absolute command of the language. As with everything else he wrote, his Westerns—

pounded out, we are told, like automatic writing, without pause and never to be looked at again once a page left his typewriter—are virtually beyond reproach. (In the twenty-odd books of his that I have lately been reading, I managed to spot just two dangling participles and one misuse of "imply" and "infer"!) One could well imagine, as I once did, that he must spend hours correcting and polishing; and, of course, he didn't.

He had two styles, one of which I referred to a moment ago as a sort of "Dick and Jane" mode consisting of brief paragraphs, each usually containing a single sentence. He used this only occasionally, when it suited his purpose. Here is an example, from the opening of THE GUN TAMER:

There was no harm in sending the colonel's daughter to the dance, as everyone in the household agreed.

She had been raised so delicately that nothing so rude and rough as a bandanna bedecked cowpuncher possibly could enter her inner horizon.

Besides, she was only seventeen, and, as the colonel said: "Only a child, much younger than her years. Of course, there's no place for men in her thoughts!"

So they got her ready for the dance.

The colonel had been begged to lend dignity to the affair by lending his presence, and, since the colonel had more dignity than he knew what to do with, he accepted the invitation almost in those terms.

His wife went, too.

The chapter goes on like this for a devastating portrait of the arrogant colonel and his cowed and diffident wife. (Faust continued using the technique off and on throughout the book, but this wasn't customary with him.)

The style he normally used was a different matter entirely. Once the creative juices started flowing, particularly with the excitement of beginning a new story, Faust's mind must have been so crowded with ideas and images that only the most flexible style could express them all, at the same time giving his writing a musical quality, lying somewhere between poetry and prose. He accomplished this with punctuation and with a careful balancing of his sentences, letting some of them run out into complex shapes full of dependent clauses that one has to read closely, word by word, in order to absorb it all. Here's the beginning of THE SEVEN OF DIAMONDS:

It was not the end of the desert; it was better than that; it was the point where despair ended and hope became a certainty. Through the dusty air the eye still held on a round distance to the mountains and the shadows of their gorges, but that distance was as nothing compared with the marches which lay behind his back! He halted his horse, which was trembling and feverish with desire to get at the water, and looked back to the dimly dissolving horizon, sketched not by pen or pencil, but by a brush dipped into misty colors, and running as flat as the palm of the hand. It looked like infinity.

This was most unusual pulp writing, even for the rather sedate pages of *Western Story Magazine*; later, in the 1930s when something a good deal like "Dick and Jane" became prevalent with the advent of a lot of new magazines, certain editors were tempted to cut Faust's prose to ribbons; but in my day no true fan would have dreamed of skipping a word of it, for fear of missing some gem of description, some telling bit of characterization. From THE SEVEN OF DIAMONDS again: "His black beard gave him a formidable appearance; . . . but at close hand, one saw a brown eye, as open and harmless as the eye of a calf." And every sentence would draw him deeper into that personal, private West that was Max Brand's unique creation.

Sometimes, it's true, when interest flagged or Faust was working under too much pressure, the prose might suffer from melodrama and plain bad writing, as in SILVERTIP'S TRAP. On occasion, too, when he wanted to complete the poetic cadence of a sentence without actually having anything more to say in it, he could even resort to empty verbiage:

He heard a groan from Lowell, at this point, and, stepping back to the fallen boy, he quietly and quickly prepared a gag which he fitted between the teeth *of the man of the law*. Then with Lowell's own irons, he fettered the hands and the feet *of the deputy*. (Italics added.)

Bad writing, again, and really very silly—trying to devise some sort of conclusion to these sentences, he has ended up restating, twice in a row, what the reader already knew perfectly well—that Lowell is a deputy sheriff. Faust could have corrected it easily enough with something on this order: "He heard a groan from Lowell and delayed a moment while he fashioned a gag from the boy's handkerchief, afterward shackling him hand and foot with his own irons." Well, no, it's not in Faust's style; but at least every word *says* something—and, incidentally, my version offers information that he simply chose to ignore: what the gag was made of. A moment's revision was all it would have cost him; but, of course, in 1929—at five cents a word—revision was something Faust could not be bothered with—and would not, for some time to come.

III

In a published interview a few years ago, after having acknowledged my indebtedness to Max Brand, I added for some reason: "I can't read him now." At the time, I suppose, I knew what I meant, but it was an uncharitable remark and still bothers me. Partly on that account I decided, not long ago, the day had come to do something I'd never got around to before: try reading again, for the first time, some of those stories that had impressed me so as a youngster and find out how they actually looked to me so long after.

I soon discovered that, if anything, Faust's writing looked even better now than I'd remembered: years spent sweating out salable prose of my own have

only increased my awe at his facility with words and his inexhaustible capacity
for invention. The level of literacy in our culture not being what it was seventy
years ago, I can imagine some readers today would have trouble relating to the
more leisurely pace and intricacy of his prose; for me, to read it at its best, with
its effortless flow and its weight of ideas and images and freshly minted language—and then imagine that typewriter chattering away without pause, at forty
or fifty words a minute—is to wonder how anyone could have managed this.

Another thing about Faust that I'm sure I wouldn't have appreciated fully at
the age of twelve is his skill with female characters, exactly right for the kind
of story he told, in Westerns or any other genre. Maizie Delmar, Polly Noonan,
Louise Asprey, Helen Forman, Leslie Carton, Kate Lawrence—the list goes on
and on, each woman different and memorable yet all of them definitely sisters
under the skin: baffling creatures, courageous and whole-hearted, but also unpredictable and clearly much smarter than the heroes who find themselves constantly at a loss knowing what to make of them. These women, at least in my
opinion, are Faust's prime creations, and he obviously enjoyed them, for the
scenes involving them are among the most entertaining and gracefully written
in whichever book they happen to appear.

As to those favorite stories I mentioned, there were a couple I especially
wanted to reread because they were the ones that established Max Brand as my
favorite author. ''Three on the Trail'' was, unfortunately, available only in one
of those unsatisfactory Dodd, Mead abridgments, and I found myself constantly
looking in vain for favorite bits of writing that weren't there; but even in that
shape it held up well enough—a highly enjoyable romp of a book, with many
happily unexpected turns of plot. On the other hand, ''The City in the Sky''
(with its dreadful book title, FLAMING IRONS) proved disappointing. It still
had great action and atmosphere, and a really dandy premise: the baffling quest
for a town that no one seemed ever to have heard of. But at the very end, when
the secret of the steel box was finally revealed, this time I could see—as I hadn't
before—that it left so many questions without logical answers that Faust's story
fell apart in my hands; I had to wonder if he himself had been aware of the
trouble. Even so, it could never take away the pleasure a twelve-year-old had
had in reading it.

Another thing I learned: to read a book straight through will reveal flaws that
can be missed when it's taken in installments over a six-week period. Faust,
I've more than once discovered, tended to be careless in maintaining a consis-
tency of tone. He could allow PILLAR MOUNTAIN to drift away from poetry
into farce (in Chapters 7 to 9) and then to badly handled melodrama as at the
end of Chapter 24. For an even worse example: after a genuinely interesting
first half a 1921 serial for *Argosy* called ''The Guide to Happiness'' (published
in book form under the inexplicable title THE TRAP AT COMANCHE BEND)
takes a plunge into rather unfunny slapstick and becomes stuck there, while
Nancy Scovil, one of his most promising heroines, is thoroughly trashed by its
silliness.

Or, he would go the other way: "The Path to Plunder" (book title: MYS-TERY RANCH) makes a great beginning with a couple of hilariously funny chapters and leads the reader to hope that for once Max Brand has decided to write a comedy. Alas, the comedy comes to an abrupt halt, and he finds himself instead in a rather turgid murder mystery; even the appearance of an engaging chap named O'Shea, in the second half, can't save it or make it the book it had started out to be.

Of course I concede that, as a professional, I'm likely to give more importance to things like this than someone reading for pleasure and not much concerned with technical matters. At twelve I doubt that I would have paid much attention to them either, when certain other things bothered me considerably more. For one, it seemed to me that the inhabitants of Max Brand's West spoke a very, very strange language, consisting in large part of a number of expressions they all used, over and over—"this here," "gunna," "old son," "you hear me talk?" and so on—along with an occasional phonetic misspelling. Why single out the word "nacheral," I wondered, when nobody ever hears it pronounced any other way?

What is more, in moments of drama these people comported themselves in the oddest ways: their eyes would turn yellow; they would break out in perspi-ration, groan aloud, and smite their brows, or shake a fist above their heads—even stagger with emotion and have to clutch at the furniture to steady them-selves. In short, they behaved very much as I used to see actors do in the old silent movies, especially in slapstick comedies where they threw pies at one another. But Max Brand described it all with a straight face, in a manner I could never comprehend; he certainly knew people in real life didn't act like this, so was it meant to be camp? Or did he expect his readers to be naive enough to take it straight? With Faust, much of the time I've had to admit I wasn't sure *what* he was up to.

Which brings me to the thing that used to puzzle me the most. This was a particular episode that for some reason kept recurring in his books, a scene involving a pet or some other small animal, a cat or a dog or perhaps a parrot—in one instance a squirrel that sneaked in from outdoors. The moment this crea-ture appeared, a reader of Faust knew it was going to eat a morsel of poisoned food, and its death would save the unsuspecting hero (or, at least once, the heroine). Just how often Faust may have used this piece of business I really don't know; but I ran across it quite a few times in these Westerns I've been reading, from the 1920s, and also in "Perique," a South Sea island story that *Argosy* ran in 1935. That time, the hero gave a bite to a parrot but for once the bird survived, and Perique was left to enjoy his meal.

What's going on here? Did Faust have some kind of obsession with this theme, or was it merely a convenient way to fill up a chapter or two? In any event he doesn't seem to have cared what the thousands of readers following his work in Street & Smith's *Western Story Magazine* might think about it. To me this repeating of one incident, varied only in the most minor details, suggested indifference, or perhaps even contempt for Frank Blackwell, his magazine, and anyone who read it. I didn't want to think that of my favorite author; still, it may not have been too far off the mark, to judge from one comment by Faust in 1921: "I have recently sold to Blackwell two novelettes and two serials so very terrible that even my hardened mind shuddered when I heard he had sent out the checks." But presumably he wasn't above cashing them.

IV

If my opinions on the subject of Westerns have undergone any changes since 1928, this is not merely due to encroaching age but also because of fifty-odd years spent plying my trade as a writer of popular fiction. I saw my job to be one of creating decent men and women who seemed real enough to be believable, likable enough for a reader to care about them, and vulnerable enough (and therefore definitely *not* superhuman) that a reader might be concerned about their fate. Basically a story would work only so far as everything that happened in it was plausible, possible, and convincing.

And at every moment, as I wrote, there was a voice at my ear that kept prompting me with anxious questions: *Are you sure the thing rings absolutely true? Would he actually have said that? Would she really do this?* It was a bad moment for me when I couldn't answer a positive yes. So, now, as if from habit, while I'm in the act of reading a Max Brand Western, that voice is still there, still in business, still nagging: *Do you honestly think a girl could fool anyone into believing she was two people by switching between different-colored wigs?* Or: *Do you accept the notion of a complete counterfeiting layout hidden behind a waterfall?* Or: *Would this kid grow to manhood living in a cave with a family of bears, without ever once considering trying to make his way out of the mountains and look for the house where he used to live?* Or—and this is a good one—: *Can you see a man, with both hands tied behind him, escape from his enemies by doing a back flip through an open window, then get onto his feet and go running to his ground-tied horse? And, when with a single kick of his boot he has flipped the reins up onto the animal's back, can you see him—hands still tied—making a powerful leap that puts him astride the saddle, where a single word to his horse sends them galloping away to freedom? Can you? Answer yes or no!*

There seems to be a problem here of reasonable limits. I don't have to be reminded that it is a combination of a slightly skewed vision and deliberately exaggerated dramatic effects, coupled with—and sometimes working against—fine poetic prose and extraordinary descriptive powers that give the "Max Brand West" its unique, almost hypnotic attraction. I know I'd have been lucky to possess a tenth of his talent and skill; moreover, I'm convinced he created something really fresh when he introduced Greek mythology, with stunning effect, into those first Dan Barry novels (even though he spoke of them himself as "silly stuff").

On the other hand, I also have to say that his too-literal attempt to rewrite the "Iliad" as a Western in HIRED GUNS did nothing much for Homer or for the Western story, and neither did Harry Brown's later attempt at the same trick in THE STARS IN THEIR COURSES—that's all it ever was, a trick. In my opinion the so-called mythic vein runs very thin in Faust's later books, aside from borrowing a gimmick from the Theseus legend for one of them. His heroes, usually big and heavily muscled and sometimes not all that bright, sound more like Hercules than Achilles; but, in fact, my impression is that it was really *himself* whom Faust liked to use as the chief physical model for the whole lot. The fact that he gave one of them his own defective heart, in MARBLEFACE, might be thought to clinch the argument.

The honest truth is that after all the years I've been reading him my ideas about Frederick Faust are fairly tentative. He has so many contradictions that I don't pretend to understand very much about him or the things he wrote. But I know there are others around who would be glad to enlighten me. "You ask the wrong questions," one Faust aficionado will say. "You mustn't carp about literal reality. Faust works out his themes on a deeper level, where his genius makes even the supposedly implausible seem true. You've got to change your mind set, or you'll never understand him." To which another will answer: "Baloney! The man wrote for money . . . *lots* of money, with his tongue firmly in his cheek. Just go with the magic, and, if something doesn't make sense, take it as camp . . . the way everybody does with Sherlock Holmes nowadays. You mention DESTRY RIDES AGAIN? A good example! Who can take seriously anything that happens in a town named Wham?"

At which point I'm glad to let them have it out to their own satisfaction.

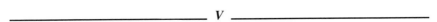

V

"One of these days," Faust promised his wife, "we will start better fiction rolling." And it did happen, when the Great Depression undermined at last the five-cent word rate he'd enjoyed at *Western Story Magazine,* and he had to retool for other markets. It's astounding how quick he was at adapting to something like a dozen new fields, and how fast his agent would be selling him to the top-paying slicks. There seemed to be nothing Faust couldn't do if he set his mind to it. But then, before he'd had time to establish a firm new base, he simply threw over fiction writing, which had never actually interested him much—"this horrible, dragging, walking prose"—for the richer lure and anonymity of Hollywood. Even there, he managed to create a brief vogue with his Dr. Kildare series, before he finally went to Italy, where everything came to an end.

It's useless to speculate what he might have done with the twenty or thirty years left him afterward had he survived the war. There was, of course, no afterward; almost by accident and by default the Frederick Faust who had wanted to be remembered for his verse would be eclipsed by an alter ego who had been made famous through two decades spent hacking one particular kind of fiction that Faust disdained.

And yet . . . ? Sometimes I can't help wondering if he didn't protest too much, because along toward the end of a day in September 1932, on which he appears to have written an entire 27,000–word Western novelette between breakfast and midnight, we find him jotting this, in what seems almost a mood of euphoria: "9.05 P.M. Only nineteen pages to do, now. Everything is walking along, and the end of the story is in sight, and it's a peach. A perfect pippin. . . . The world seems a good old place."

I know I've gone on the offensive myself, any number of times and warded off comments about my craft by joking that I wrote Westerns under pen names so that my mother wouldn't know what I did for a living, while actually I loved the books I wrote and took immense pride in putting the very best into them that I knew how. In my case, by contrast with Faust, the words would come slowly and sometimes with considerable effort; and yet it hasn't always been like that. Once in a great while, for an hour or so, there was magic! Suddenly, everything worked; the words seemed almost to appear on the page faster than I could hit the typewriter keys, while my conscious mind tagged along to find out which exactly correct word would be the next to come dropping from my fingers. Those were the unexpected high moments, when I somehow stumbled into peak efficiency and knew an exhilaration such as I was never to forget.

And, for all his disclaimers, I wonder if Frederick Faust might not have felt something like this at least part of the time, when he sat down to his daily twenty pages and watched his mind go into overdrive. Perhaps it was what he referred to when he wrote once of "the growing pile of manuscript at my right, and this childish happiness in me." I surely like to think so. Reading is much more pleasurable if you can feel the author got *some* amount of joy from his work.

Today I have stacks of Max Brand novels, a good many more than by any other one writer. Even now I can pick one up at random and instantly be caught in the magic of its language. I'm aware, of course, that at some point I may come upon something that makes me mad enough to toss the book aside, but sooner or later I'll probably be back to finish it because of some jewel of prose I may find in the next paragraph, or the possibility of meeting still another of those remarkable women.

Or, is it simply because reading Max Brand can make me feel I'm twelve years old again?

THE LIFE AND WORKS OF MAX BRAND

Darrell C. Richardson

*An earlier version of this essay was published in MAX BRAND: THE MAN
AND HIS WORK. The author subsequently revised it for this book.*

I thought it well to include a few personal glimpses and a few anecdotes about
Faust the man as well as Faust the writer. These will help to reveal the stature
of the man. He had many sides to his nature, but they all demonstrated his
amazing zest for life.

Faust's heart was a constant anxiety and handicap to him through the years.
He suffered great pain and terrible insomnia year after year. He played a good
game of tennis and golf against doctors' orders. According to them he should
have been dead twenty years before he was. One of his daughters wrote me: "I
believe that his gigantic will to live pulled him through many moments when
other men would have given up. The whole story is one of miracles all the
way."

In an article in *Time* (5/29/44) Faust is described as "a massive man with a
long, chiseled face; his appetites for work and living were enormous. He could
lock himself in a hotel room with two typewriters and a bottle of Irish whiskey,
emerge four days later with a neatly typed, complete magazine serial." Other
writers have long been interested in Faust's terrific ability to pound out the
wordage. The same article in *Time* relates Faust's explanation of his capacities:
"No one is more than forty to fifty percent efficient, but, when a man is backed
into a corner by a man who intends to kill him, he can be as high as ninety
percent efficient." Faust never explained just why he was backed up so desperately into his productive corner. But he loved rich living, and that took the
kind of money he made.

An editorial in *Cosmopolitan* (12/37) had this to say about Faust: "A prolific author is Max Brand. . . . He is a man of tremendous, burning energy and wild enthusiasm which he uses to write as much as a million and a half words a year. He is a Niagara Falls of stories harnessed to an electric typewriter. Max Brand is only one of the names he has used, because he writes so much that no publisher could print it all under the same byline.''

Calling Max Brand ''one of the world's most prolific writers,'' an editorial in 1935 in *Esquire* went on to say: ''His books are translated practically wherever books are read. His reputation has been largely made in romantic Western stories. During the last couple of years, however, he has practically deserted the so-called action story and has appeared in *Post, McCall's, This Week,* and *Harper's.* He still maintains a pretty high rate of production, being among the fortunate few whose fertility never seems to run thin.''

It was this unlimited source of ideas which he had that fascinated all the writers who knew him. His mind seemed saturated with more plots than he could ever use. In a letter to Philip Richman, dated February 19, 1934, Faust wrote: ''I am sure I wrote more during the early 'Twenties than the 1930–1933 period. There were early years when I rapped out the stuff pretty fast, particularly in the summer of 1920 when in one period of thirteen days I wrote a serial, two long novelettes, and 190,000 words. This sort of writing is improvisation rather than composing, of course. (You understand that what I write you is not for repetition, because it would seem like cheap boasting. Therefore, I have avoided publicity of every kind.) Altogether I've written between twenty-four and twenty-five million words during seventeen years, or the equivalent, at 70,000 words a book, of some three hundred and fifty novels. These are rather startling facts, but I want to call your attention to the undoubted truth, that one fairly good novel would outweigh all the mass of material which I have written. Your extreme interest in my yarns has led me to equip you with more facts about a very obscure hard-working and ordinary fellow.'' This letter, written some ten years before his death, does more than give us a firsthand picture of Faust's unbelievable productivity. It reveals the modesty and the transparent humility which seemed a natural part of him.

It would appear that the average person feels that a prolific writer cannot also be a *good* writer. Yet some of the world's best writers like Charles Dickens, O. Henry, and Sir Walter Scott had terrific production speed and could really roll out the wordage. Although Faust wrote more than any other person ever did, Carl Brandt said of Faust's production a few years back: ''He writes everything himself directly on the typewriter. He does not dictate nor has he any help beyond the fact that he likes to have someone to act as listener while he paces the floor and develops his story idea.''

Faust had the habit many writers have of jotting down ideas as they came to him. Writing me while vacationing at Villa Rosina in Florence, Italy, Jane Faust Easton (Faust's elder daughter) wrote: ''I am enclosing on a pink slip one of my father's notes. It was his habit to always carry around a notebook with him, and he was forever jotting down things that came to mind through the day. It would be impossible to estimate how many hundreds of these notebooks he filled in his lifetime." Here is Faust's note which was enclosed:

We are always reading the distinguishing qualities or talents of a man into all his actions. As a matter of fact, sometimes he expresses one faculty through another. When he is at his highest, there is a little God mixed in. When an artist steps into his working mood, he is retreating from himself into another self. He is re-seeking, and this process is a mystery. An artist will be a hearty and profane fellow in his leisure moments because in his working time he is doing something akin to praying.

Perhaps the idea in this little note would have been developed into a novel if Faust had lived. It might even have been that one *great* book Faust always intended to write someday. Who knows?

During a recent trip to San Francisco I visited most of the bookstores, which is my usual custom when I visit any city. In the Argonaut Book Shop the owner, Mr. R. D. Haines, told me that Faust was a customer of his for many years. He rarely visited the shop—but instead telephoned orders. On one occasion he called and requested copies of everything that could be located in a two-week period on clipper ships. At other times he would request stacks of books on other subjects. In this manner he acquired information on a great variety of subjects. With his retentive memory he absorbed knowledge for future reference.

Faust did not care for his children to read his stories. He did not even maintain a collection of his own books, let alone his hundreds of magazine serials and stories. His daughter Judith wrote me that he gave away to friends from time to time some of his very best books, such as THE BLUE JAY, THE WHITE WOLF, THE GOLDEN KNIGHT, and THE THUNDERER. According to Judith Faust, "all in all, he was a most provoking father to have, when it came to reading matter." She related: "Pop told me of one story he wrote when he was in the Army, I believe, with a severe bout of influenza. It was written when he had a high fever and was about a man in the same state. He was in desperate straits for money and the story sold. Have you any idea of the title?" I am sorry that I cannot identify the story.

According to Jane Faust Easton, her father never talked of his writing as the children grew up and forbade his children to read his books, which he kept well hidden behind doors in his study. "He referred to them as 'bread and butter' and poured his real soul and greatest belief in his verse."

Faust was half-Irish and something of an actor with plenty of blarney, according to his daughter Judith. "The Irish part of him was the part that gave him his immense tolerance and his need to make others happy. He never sat in judgment. He loved to spread his elbows at the board and listen 'to scoundrels and kings' alike, and for that reason he knew few men of his own caliber. His description in MONSIEUR of the people surrounding that man, though exaggerated, was not far from his own case."

There is another side of Faust's personality that cannot be ignored. All of his friends mention it. It was especially apparent to his wife and his children who loved him most. I am referring to the immense personal kindness of the man—his unselfish generosity to others. Carl Brandt related that people who had been kind to him in his early days could always count on him for help when needed. Several thousand dollars went to help an associate editor who had been kind to him, after the man became an invalid.

If Faust had never written for the pulps at all, he could still have made a good living out of his work which appeared in the "slick" magazines. In all, about seventy-five stories were published in slick magazines like *The Saturday Evening Post, Collier's, This Week, Esquire, The American Magazine, Cosmopolitan, McCall's,* and *Harper's.* Twelve stories appeared in *Cosmopolitan* alone, and three of these were book length. In 1937–38, Faust had stories appearing in *The American Magazine* under three different pen names over a three-month period. These included his serial, "Dust across the Range," which appeared under the Max Brand pseudonym; a short story by Frederick Faust; and another story under the George Owen Baxter pseudonym. Several of these tales from the slicks were collected into the only anthology Faust prepared of his short stories. If I should be asked to pick the one published book of Faust's which I consider of greatest literary merit, I would unhesitatingly choose this one: WINE ON THE DESERT AND OTHER STORIES. This book, published by Dodd, Mead in 1940, contains fifteen short stories. Most of the stories appeared originally in various slick magazines from 1934 to 1940, though two of the stories had no previous appearance and two others were revised for book publication.

W. Somerset Maugham once said: "Just as there is no obligation to read fiction, there is no obligation to like it. The only thing that really matters to you is what a work of art says to you." It is on this basis that I presume to choose several pieces of Faust's writing which I consider among his best work. I do not claim that these stories are the best in literary merit; I merely say that they appealed to me most. One of the stories in addition to the title story which stand out in the book is "A Watch and the Wilderness." This is a tender and tragic story of the Civil War. At the close of the narrative, which is filled with pathos, the dying Yank sharpshooter murmurs to his Confederate killer: "*carmina morte carent*" [songs are immune from death]. As the youth says these last words, the birds in the trees are still singing, and the Confederate is examining the beautiful watch, with the picture of the boy's sweetheart, which has been destroyed by the bullet that killed him.

Another piece that stands out in this collection is "Charlie." It is the tale of a desperate experience during World War I. It is the story of men facing death. But it is also the story of a horse—and how God used the major's horse, Charlie, to lead the remaining lost survivors of the Second Battalion across the dark and foggy no-man's-land to safety.

"A Special Occasion" and "The Wedding Guest" saw magazine appearance in *Harper's.* They are masterpieces of a literary man. Not only do they show the mark of a writing craftsman, not only do they demonstrate shrewdly drawn characters, but they are wonderful stories as well. I rather imagine that Faust himself was speaking through one of his characters in the following lines from "The Wedding Guest": "Once, when I was in Italy, I remember leaving the heat of Florence to go to the Lido, and sitting in the deep shadow of a hotel verandah, and never turning my head, for fear the world behind me would not be as happy as my heart, and simply watching the high wall of the sea with white sails climbing it and taking the blue stain of distance as they reached the top."

"Hummingbirds and Honeysuckle," another story in this collection, defies classification. Perfectly integrated, narrated with plausibility, the events are close to fantasy; yet they seem real. Smoothly and carefully constructed, the ending is something of a bombshell. With unsurpassed aplomb, Faust writes a story which is of a type naturally expected to have first appeared in *Esquire*.

"Oh, Wonderful!" and "Our Daily Bread" were written especially for book publication and had no previous printing. However, "Our Daily Bread" in slightly abridged form and with a different ending was published in *This Week* under the title "The Thief." The picture of the refined Mrs. Sidney M. Lester walking into Kahn and Seidelman's Grocery every day at about five-thirty and stealing a loaf of bread, and then walking with dignity out into the street, is unforgettable. And the courtesy and the benevolence of the Kahns and the Seidelmans warms the heart.

"Oh, Wonderful!" is not only an extremely well-written story but is truly unique. The leading character in the tale we never see at all—we only get an occasional description of him from characters in the story that do. He never once walks on the stage, yet he is the leading actor in the drama. How do the other characters in the story describe him? Each and every one describes him as—Oh, Wonderful!

"Men Get Old" first appeared in May 1938 in *The American Magazine* as "What Price Story!" The former title more aptly describes the central theme of the narrative. Well told, it is the human, poignant picture of George Burleigh, formerly a great news reporter, fighting a losing battle to keep from washing up. And when the crisis comes, and Burleigh loses his courage, Jan Simmons steps in and kills those dangerous mobsters, Lefty Ginnis and Turk Lavine. Though Burleigh dies, Simmons gives him credit for the heroic encounter and a four-column head makes a hero of the once great man who lost his nerve. Why did he funk out? Men get old....

One of Faust's little-known stories, "Mr. Christmas," is a realistic story of everyday people, including several crooks. As usual in Faust stories, one crook is not quite as bad as you would imagine him to be. Dufferin, a young aristocrat who has lost his nerve, develops into such a Santa Claus at the climax that he earns the nickname "Mr. Christmas." In so doing, he not only regains his lost nerve but wins the woman he had lost three years before. Though dubbed a novel and appearing in six installments of *The Brooklyn Eagle* back in 1944,

"Mr. Christmas" is barely long enough to be called a novelette. Short on quantity—but long on quality—it ranks in my book as one of Faust's better tales.

"Harrigan!" is by no means one of Faust's better stories. Yet, it is interesting, different, and not his usual type. "Harrigan!" first appeared in 1918 as a serial in *Railroad Man's Magazine* and was published as a book in England a few years later. Harrigan is a strong character. He is a huge, flame-haired Irishman, and the story concerns his struggles (mostly over Kate Malone) with Black McTee, an equally large and powerful Scotchman. The story begins on the Honolulu waterfront, and the setting for the other forty chapters, except the last, is the high seas. Shipwrecks, fights, mutiny, and the dreadful enmity with Black McTee mark the progress of Harrigan as he travels across the South Seas. Judith Faust in a letter to me wrote: "The description of the storm in 'Harrigan' was based on an actual storm my father and Dr. Fish experienced on a tramp steamer going to Honolulu."

Among the outstanding off-trail Westerns penned by Faust is SEÑOR JIN-GLE BELLS. Though a Max Brand *Argosy* serial, it was published as a book by David Manning. In his article, "Strength," Chester D. Cuthbert wrote: "It is an axiom of the pulp fiction field that right must always triumph over wrong; that only the good man can win the girl. But Señor Jingle Bells, philanderer, bravo, bank robber, and kidnapper, who by evil machination brings within his power a fine young woman, accomplishes all of his purposes by force of strength. Of all Faust's work with which I am acquainted, this is the most striking example of his obsession with the idea that strength is beyond good and evil."

Only once did Faust use the pseudonym Lee Bolt. Under this name he wrote "The Frigate Bird" back in 1920. The hero of the tale, John Axson, is described as "a young man of extraordinary strength of both body and mind, but exceedingly ugly." Among the legion of powerful men in hundreds of Faust stories, Axson is in a class by himself. He is a super thief—a frigate bird—because he robs only thieves. His prey is the top criminals of the underworld. Axson has to plunder, but he plunders for the sake of another—and this little mystery makes the story. The blurb on the cover of *All-Story* that featured "The Frigate Bird" further describes the story as "the foreclosure on a mortgaged soul."

Faust did not write so much about people who might exist, as he did of people the reader would like to believe could exist. According to Samuel A. Peeples: "This haunting sense of balladry, of legend-building, is outstanding in his George Challis novels, THE FIREBRAND and THE BAIT AND THE TRAP. In THE GOLDEN KNIGHT, his attempts at realism cheat the character of Richard the Lion-Heart of some of this heroic legendry." Nonetheless, THE GOLDEN KNIGHT was deservedly one of the more popular books Faust ever wrote.

The New York Herald-Tribune of October 10, 1937, said of THE GOLDEN KNIGHT: "Besides a knack for conveying medieval sights, sounds, and smells expressively and pungently, George Challis can produce knights who are [now personalized as] human beings. We are thinking especially of his portrait of Richard the Lion-Heart. A bit phenomenal as a warrior perhaps, but engagingly human as a man. Mr. Challis seasons his dish with the spice of wit and the sauce of romance. The result is very gratifying.'' *The New York Times* of October 13, 1937, said: ''If you like a rousing adventure story about one of the great historical personages whose glamour has defied time . . . you will find THE GOLDEN KNIGHT wholly delightful. It is a tale of stout and generous imaginings, full of breezy humor, packed with lusty characterization and without a dull moment.'' The *Saturday Review of Literature* on October 30, 1937, said: ''This is a thoroughly enjoyable historical novel notable for its humor as well as its derring-do. Frances Ludlow, in selecting this sprightly novel as editor's choice for October, says, 'It is very hard to describe the pleasurable excitement of discovery THE GOLDEN KNIGHT gave me. A lusty, exciting, humorous, beautiful tale.' ''

Faust must have had a special pride in the George Challis pen name because practically every story written under this pseudonym is top notch. Harper's revived this pseudonym. Mr. Evan Thomas of Harper's wrote me that they planned to issue THE FIREBRAND under the Evan Evans name. I immediately advised him to use the George Challis name since it was much better known than he may have thought. Thomas replied: ''I am interested that you advise me to use the Challis name instead of Evan Evans and would like to hear more about that. Because we were going to use the Evans name, we have been planning to hold this project off for another four years, but using the Challis name we could do it sooner.'' The George Challis name was eventually used for THE FIREBRAND. It sold about 100,000 copies and was chosen for the Adventure Book Club and the Doubleday Family Book Club.

There were seven ''Firebrand'' stories. It was not until after plans were nearly complete for the two books that Mr. Thomas learned there was one ''Firebrand'' tale he had not seen: ''The Cat and the Perfume.'' After sending him my bound volume of the complete ''Firebrand'' series from *Argosy,* Thomas wrote: ''We have already made a contract for two books to be made up out of the first three and last three. (1. 'The Firebrand,' 'The Great Betrayal,' and 'The Storm'; 2. 'Claws of the Tigress,' 'The Bait and the Trap,' and 'Pearls of Bonfadini.') We had no knowledge of 'The Cat and the Perfume.' A strange business because I was just certain that there must be some intervening story and was unable to find it.''

Sometime later he wrote: ''I have read 'The Cat and the Perfume' and it is very good. But I still think we'd better plan to stick to the material which we already have a contract for. We're going to have to do some cutting on the first three even at that, and some editing on the last three to provide a little more continuity.''

The George Challis name was used mostly for historical novels with the emphasis on sword play and medieval romance. Other books to appear under the pseudonym are THE NAKED BLADE, THE SPLENDID RASCAL, and

MONSIEUR. MONSIEUR appeared originally—of all places—in *Western Story Magazine* under the title "The Tyrant." THE SPLENDID RASCAL is one of the two Faust novels which did not first see print in a magazine. The *Boston Transcript* of June 23, 1926, said of this novel: "Never, never (and we make no reservation) did we take a cruise so continuously and luridly thrilling as this, filled with a hair-raising adventure which proves that the author's imagination is of that type which rules the world, certainly that of fiction." The *New York Evening Post* observed: "There is a pleasant flavor of Kingsley's 'Westward Ho!' and all who like vivid he-manry flashing the busy blade, moonlit moments touching the swift course of blooded action with tender romance, will enjoy the story."

THE NAKED BLADE is a tale of buccaneers and pirates and the old Spanish Main. The *New York Herald-Tribune* of June 5, 1938, observed: "THE NAKED BLADE is as vigorous as they come full of resounding phrases and the clash of arms."

Early in his career Faust had intended for John Frederick to be his "historical" pseudonym. Some of the very fine historicals to appear under this name were "The Double Crown," "The Hammer" and "White Heather Weather." The second long novel Faust ever wrote was a historical called "The Sword Lover," which appeared in 1917 in *Argosy* under the Max Brand name. However, it was printed in book form under the John Frederick pseudonym. THE BRONZE COLLAR by John Frederick was first printed in *Western Story Magazine* as "In the Hills of Monterey." It is a historical novel of old California. The *New York Times* of February 22, 1925, said of THE BRONZE COLLAR: "This story has all the elements of a brave and beguiling tale, brave and gallant enough to beguile a sleepless night or a dull journey."

Faust wrote an occasional historical under the Max Brand pseudonym. Several of these were novelettes in length. Perhaps the outstanding one of these was "One Glass of Wine!" in the October 6, 1917, issue of *All-Story*. The setting is medieval London, and the hero, Richard Henshaw, a penniless country lad bored with a dull life, goes to London. In a week he has become fabulously wealthy, sought after by society, and the lover of Dorothy Canfield, the most beautiful heiress in England! None but a Faust character could accomplish so much in so little time and still remain plausible.

I consider "Clovelly" about the best historical Faust ever wrote. It appeared in *Argosy* in 1924 under the Max Brand name. Two additional good George Challis *Argosy* serials that have never yet hit book form are "The Dew of Heaven" (an "Ivor Kildare" story and a sequel to THE NAKED BLADE) and "The American," a story of the French Revolution. I believe Harper's passed up a good thing in not publishing several of these fine historicals in book form, using the George Challis pseudonym.

Faust did some very good mystery and detective stories. Among his better whodunits are "Six Golden Angels," "Bright Danger," "Champion of Lost

Causes,'' "Seven Mile House," and the three Clovelly detective stories from *Dime Detective.*

As "Walter C. Butler" he wrote a couple of good adventure books: CROSS OVER NINE and THE NIGHT FLOWER, both published by Macaulay. *The New York Times* for August 16, 1936, said of THE NIGHT FLOWER: "Action gets strongly under way on the first page of this exceptionally solid crime novel with the holdup of an armored truck . . . the manifold intricacies of the plot are worked out with flawless skill. What is extremely rare in a story of this genre, one can never positively foresee just what will happen next, or correctly conjecture what the conclusion will finally bring forth. The reviewer confidently chooses this book (he keeps an eye closely on the field) as the best written, most artfully constructed, and thoroughly interesting crime-adventure novel published thus far within the year.''

His pseudonym "Nicholas Silver" was reserved almost entirely for whodunits. Most of these appeared as novels in *Detective Story Magazine.* The July 29, 1922, *Detective Story Magazine* contained a novel by Nicholas Silver, the first use of this pseudonym. In the editorial column, called "Headquarters Chat," Nicholas Silver was introduced as "a brand-new writer, new not only to these pages, but to all other magazines." The editorial goes on to say that most writers have one or two stories and then they are finished. The editor continued: "Let's hope that Silver is one of the rare exceptions. We have a real hunch that he will prove to be." It goes without saying that "Silver" was one of the exceptions!

Faust was also adept at handling the situations necessary for stories about espionage and international intrigue. His "War for Sale" was voted one of the best stories ever to appear in *Argosy.* When the Anthony Hamilton "spy" novels were printed in book form by Macrae-Smith, Faust merely changed his own last name slightly and the result was Frederick Frost—another pen name. These three books—SECRET AGENT, NUMBER ONE, SPY MEETS SPY, and THE BAMBOO WHISTLE—show Faust's powers as a fictioneer to good advantage. *The New York Times* of May 17, 1939, had this praise for SECRET AGENT NUMBER ONE: "With Monte Carlo for a setting, Mr. Frost has produced an international spy story that might have come from the pen of Oppenheim himself. . . . It stirs the pulse and gives the reader a happy hour or two of vicarious excitement and that, no doubt, is what the author set out to do." The same newspaper later described SPY MEETS SPY as "a slick and competent item of its kind. Mr. Frost has the knack all right." The December 5, 1937, issue of *The New York Times* reviewed THE BAMBOO WHISTLE: "This makes a swift yarn that will have any reader wondering from page to page what will happen next. This third novel by Frederick Frost is more ingenious and more exciting than either of the others." All of the Anthony Hamilton stories had their first appearance in *Detective Fiction Weekly* under the Max Brand pseudonym.

Other Faust pseudonyms were invented just for certain books or for special story types. For example, when back in 1933 Dodd, Mead wanted to publish several Faust titles a year, another pseudonym, Frank Austin, was concocted.

Three books appeared under this fictitious moniker. Dennis Lawton was used only twice for a couple of *Argosy* serials with a South Seas setting. Several very fine Indian stories were published under the Peter Henry Morland pseudonym. Two of these, BEYOND THE OUTPOST and LOST WOLF, appeared in book form. A number of very fine Indian stories also appeared under the George Owen Baxter byline. One of these Baxter Indian stories, CALL OF THE BLOOD, was described in *The New York Times* for March 11, 1934, as "well told, it is the human, poignant picture of a young man's struggle to emerge successfully from the conflicting duality of his personality and environment. (Rusty Sabin, the white hero of the book, was reared by the Indians.) A brisk moving tale this is, with originality and action told by a man who seems to possess knowledge of the workings of the Indian's mind, his life, and his customs." There were two other Rusty Sabin Indian stories, BROTHER OF THE CHEYENNES followed its predecessor into book form, but the third of the trilogy CHEYENNE GOLD, based on the serial "The Sacred Valley," was not printed as a book until 1972.

M.B., initials for Max Brand, was used as a *nom de plume* for THE THUNDERER, which originally saw print as a serial in *Country Gentleman.* It was published in 1933 by Derrydale Press in a deluxe edition at $7.50 per copy. The review in *The New York Times* from November 26, 1933, said: "Richly bound in red leather stamped with gold and copiously illustrated by an artist (Paul Brown) equally adept at drawing horses and human beings, THE THUNDERER is the sort of book one would naturally select for a sportsman friend. Michael Carmicheal was twenty-one when he left the farm to make his way into the world. . . . How this frail and scholarly youth who had spent his childhood reading Greek and Latin and old-world romances while his father and brothers toiled on the land, how this book-wise innocent fared in the battle for survival, provides material for a charming story of rural life. Sharing honors with Michael is a five-year-old plow horse which the boy bought from a farmer at the instigation of his friend, Rance Turner. Uncle Rance had once been a famous trainer of race horses, but now in his old age he subsisted on the meager taking of a blind vegetarian. A tragedy he felt even more keenly than the loss of his sight was the accidental death of The Thunderer, the greatest stallion he had ever trained. . . . With The Thunderer Rance would certainly have won the Steeplechase Classic, the Chester Cup, and with the Cup, a fortune. The five months of strict discipline which Michael underwent in the schooling of Duffer made a man of a timid boy. The account of the race is particularly well managed, a climactic episode so graphically described that the reader shares every thrilling moment." This book ranks as a minor classic in the field of horse stories.

The Dr. Kildare books are perhaps more widely known than anything Faust has written. They are excellently done. Charles W. Wolfe, writing in *The Fabulous Faust Fanzine,* commented: "In 1938 I picked up an *Argosy* and started reading a Dr. Kildare story. From then on I followed the cases of this famous hero avidly, and believe there was no series which ever impressed me so profoundly. I don't claim to have a medical education, but I did take enough courses in biological science to know that the Dr. Kildare stories are among the most scientifically accurate writings ever offered by a fiction author of any age. The knowledge and information stored in the brain of Frederick Faust must have been enormous. With his volume of output, he could not have had time for such extensive research, but apparently he was the one man in the world who did not need it, for he seemed to 'know' his subject in 'most any field he chose.''

PILLAR MOUNTAIN is a typical Max Brand Western. I would not dog-matically say it is his best Western, but it has all those ingredients that his readers like best. Here is what the *Saturday Review of Literature* for October 13, 1928, had to say about this novel: "Mr. Max Brand is one of the ablest manufacturers of Western fiction. This one is a good Western and something more. Mr. Brand has injected a good deal of humor into it . . . an infusion which few other writers in this field manage successfully . . . and he has also endowed it with an atmosphere suggestive of some myth from the childhood of the race, a folk tale of Hercules or Siegfried. Like Siegfried, his hero, Philip, was reared by an old man in the wilderness aloof from humankind; and when this hero of gigantic strength and childlike innocence comes down among men his deeds are touched with just the right degree of fantastic exaggeration. . . . The climactic fight between Philip and the man known only as the 'Colonel' brings in a motive dear to the first Greek and Teutonic storytellers, and is handled with a skill and a power worthy of the theme. Westerns, when they are well done, are good entertainment, but Mr. Brand is of sufficient caliber to go hunting bigger game.''

MONTANA RIDES! under the Evan Evans pseudonym, is skillfully done, and could well be called a classic of Western fiction. *The New York Herald-Tribune* of June 18, 1933, said: "Western heroes who ride hard and shoot straight clutter the fictional scene. Their exploits have become so familiar that readers are inclined to ride hard in the opposite direction and shoot straight for some other sort of novel. The ranch routine and the rescue rigmarole have been done so often that they are almost as automatic as the revolvers that puncture the narratives. All of which explains why our sombrero is off to Evan Evans who has shattered the formula neatly in MONTANA RIDES! and turned out a yarn with intelligence.'' The other two Montana Kid books, MONTANA RIDES AGAIN and THE SONG OF THE WHIP, are in the same class with their predecessor.

Early in 1950, we were startled to find the following information in "The Congressional Library Catalog Supplement'' (Vol. 12, 1948):

Faust, Frederick (1892, 1944). "The Gate''; scenic oratorio for sale, chorus, and or-chestra; actors and narrator. In two parts. Nineteen scenes. Libretto by Max Brand (pseud.), Mirza Hamad Sohrab, and Julie Chanler; Music by Max Brand (pseud.). New York Associated Music Publishers, Inc., 1944. 61 pages.

Shortly thereafter we discovered that Max Brand had adapted Oliver Wendell Holmes's well-known poem, "The Wonderful One-Hoss Shay,'' as an orchestral work and that it had been recorded by the Philadelphia Orchestra under Eugene Ormandy. This information excited us no end and made us wonder just how versatile this fellow Faust was anyway. I wrote the Associated Music Publishers in New York and obtained copies of "The Gate" and further information about "The Wonderful One-Hoss Shay." I had a feeling all the time that there was a big mistake somewhere and this author must be another Max Brand. This conjecture turned out to be correct, and "The Congressional Library Catalog" had simply made a mistake. The Associated Music Publishers put me in touch with Max Brand of Hollis, Long Island, New York, and he confirmed that he had never had any connection with the late Frederick Faust and that Max Brand was his real name.

There were other instances in which stories were, for a time at least, reputed to be Faust tales. In the June 1933 *Story* there was a short story called "Roadside Incident" by Evan Evans. To quote *Story*: "Evan Evans, a native of Wisconsin, is a young writer of twenty-eight, now doing research in early American Literature at Harvard." So, not only had we turned up a Max Brand who wasn't Faust, but we had also turned up an Evan Evans who was not Faust.

Somewhat the same thing happened with a story called "Finish Pylon" in the April 1943 *Argosy* by Peter Dawson. Knowing Peter Dawson to be a Faust pseudonym, this was considered another Faust yarn. However, the publisher tells us this story was by Jonathan Glidden who also used the same pseudonym, Peter Dawson. Under this *nom de plume* he has written some good Western novels.

One of the last stories Faust wrote was a long novel, "After April." According to the editors of *The Saturday Evening Post*: " 'After April' . . . is the strange and disturbing love story of a man and a woman who had experienced in their lives the worst which a war, already old and skilled in the flagellation of human hearts, can bestow. For persons who have looked upon death and those other things which are more unbearable, there can be no happy ending— nor any unhappy ending, either. For their sufferings are merely historical warp and woof in the tapestry of human experience." In this novel we catch a glimpse of Faust's literary maturity. It makes one wonder what Faust might have produced, had he averaged writing only one book a year rather than twenty.

It is interesting, though vain, to speculate concerning the work Faust would have done had he lived for many more years. Surely in his later maturity he would have reached new heights in literary expression. Under the heading "Hollywood Colossus," *Newsweek,* after reporting Faust's death, had this to say: "His six-foot frame concealed a medical oddity—a 'fibrillator' (quivering muscles) heart, usually fatal within a few years, but which had defied the strain Faust put upon it. Indeed, he liked to confound the doctors by playing vigorous golf and tennis. From the Italian battlefield where Faust died, Russell Hill, *New York Herald-Tribune* correspondent, dryly observed: 'It is possible he was hit by mortar fire, and it is possible that when he was wounded his fibrillator heart finally gave way.' "

It seems altogether fitting that Faust himself should have the last word on death:

Only the young fear death,
A god has crossed their path, and they are sure
Of happiness, if it would but endure.

Only the young fear death;
For when companions vanish on the way
And leave us one by one,
Is it not better done
Than to come lonely to the end of day?

Only the young fear death.
The aged speak not of it. At the door
They stand with cheerful faces to the last,
Like men who on the homeward way have passed
The steps of darkness many times before.

—from *Harper's Magazine* (10/33)

A SEXUAL PERSPECTIVE IN THE WORKS OF MAX BRAND

Jack Ricardo

This article first appeared in Singing Guns.

The name of the author on the front cover of the book struck my eye: Max Brand. It was such a masculine name; it was such a simple name. And, as I later learned, the name was also fictitious. But, at the same time, I didn't know Max Brand from "Mad Max." The book was obviously a Western novel because a drawing of a cowboy graced the paperback cover. I bought the book.

I had read other Western novelists. Zane Grey, of course, whom I enjoyed. His love of the country, his concern about conservation and the treatment of animals shone through on the pages of his books. And Louis L'Amour, most of whose stories I found little more than heterosexual love tales bound together in a Western setting. And, in my opinion, rather shallow.

But Brand soon became my favorite. Mainly because his Western stories revolved around tough men, his descriptive prose ultra-masculine. For the most part Brand's heroes were rugged men, strong men, mythic men. His stories told about men who learned to live with other men, or hated them. Men whose relationships were stronger with each other than with women.

Women, of course, were involved in the plot. But many times only as a diversion, a necessity of the heterosexual times when the books were originally published. But even in this context, Brand's description of women differed sharply from his description of men. Contrast the men with the women in THE KING BIRD RIDES. The King Bird meets up with the marshal who is chasing him:

He had taken care, in making that moonlight call, as though it had been upon a sweetheart. . . . He stood there, laughing in the moonlight, as fine a picture as ever had filled the eyes of Marshal Jim Hampton. . . . He laughed again, very gently, and there was almost a caress in his eyes as they dwelt on the face of the marshal.

And then the female is introduced through the King Bird's eyes. "It was a girl. That was clear in spite of her man's overalls, and the bandanna around her neck, and the battered old sombrero on her head."

Where do King Bird's sympathies lie? It's obvious, even though by the end of the story King does live happily ever after with the female. Again, the necessity of the times. But King's most profound relationships are with men, not with the woman.

Consider the meeting of two men in MOUNTAIN RIDERS:

Derry went down to the creek and filled the pot with water. As he came back, he was walking slowly, for it seemed to him that he had entered a new life—that everything he had done before that had been as nothing, and that he never before had found a real man—not even that hardy Yankee skipper, so handy with fists and tongue.

As he reached the fire, he suddenly extended his hand. Rainey took it with an almost hesitant gesture and, looking up, smiled into the face of Derry. And Rainey had the look, at that moment, of a very happy but rather guilty boy.

I began to buy every available paperback of Brand's that I could find at flea markets or thrift shops. And the more I read of Brand, the more I wondered about the man. Who was he? I did some research and found out. Max Brand was a married man with three children, and he died at a relatively early age. His real name was Frederick Faust.

Now comes the crux of the matter in my interest in Brand the man. I was first attracted to Brand by his name, then by his words. The masculine texture of the books, his wonderful heroes. I'm homosexual, and I wondered if Brand was. From what I've discovered so far, it seems he was not. But my research isn't complete. There are too many empty holes in his biography. Yes, Faust's bouts with alcohol are well known, and his affairs with other women besides his wife are chronicled. But there still remain questions.

In MAX BRAND: WESTERN GIANT (Bowling Green University Popular Press, 1985) Faust was called "the man of mystery." Author William F. Nolan quotes Faust's daughter about her father's continuous partying: "There were many long nights when he didn't return until dawn." She also goes on to say: "Casual strangers would drop by and remain in our guest room for days or weeks." Most, if not all, of these casual strangers were male.

In Nolan's book Martha Bacon, Faust's young neighbor in Florence, Italy, talks about Faust's life in California. "Faust drinks with Irish poets, polo players, and movie stars . . . he supports promising artists and once-promising drunks."

Carl Brandt, Faust's agent and friend, is also quoted in the same book: ". . .

there never was a time when he was not supporting at least one lame duck. . . . At one time, there were fifteen of them on his payroll.'' Mostly men.

In MAX BRAND: THE BIG ''WESTERNER'' (University of Oklahoma Press, 1970) author Robert Easton describes some of these guests and strangers. An ''. . . editor, drunken cab driver, impoverished poet . . . an itinerant pianist from a local night club, a merchant mariner home on leave met in a bar, might practically live at his house.'' While living in Florence, Easton goes on to say, ''Faust periodically indulged in wild parties with a group of male friends.'' While assisting in the training of Italian athletes before the 1936 Olympics, Easton quotes Faust as saying: ''I was staggered by the physical splendor of the Italian men.''

What do these observations mean? Nothing. Maybe. They could only be the reactions of a heterosexual man who preferred gallons of booze and the rugged company of other men. Or they could be an understated description of a man who drank because he couldn't cope with his sexual feelings toward other men, of a man who kept company with other men for less than altruistic reasons. Speculation? Of course.

Can it ever be proved that Frederick Faust, Max Brand, was a closet homosexual or bisexual? Probably not. Not yet. But, from where I sit, I think it's a possibility.

COMMENTS ON JACK RICARDO'S "SEXUAL PERSPECTIVE" ARTICLE: A SYMPOSIUM

This colloquy of responses appeared in the next issue of Singing Guns.

―――――――――――――― *I* ――――――――――――――

Leo A. Hetzler

The question Jack Ricardo raises, whether there is evidence in Faust's Westerns that he was homosexual or bisexual, is a valid critical inquiry. Our present generation is acutely aware of literary homosexual nuances, whether made consciously or unconsciously by either the author or his characters. In the past thirty-five years male friendships in fiction have been studied and queried, from Huckleberry Finn and Jim (suggested by Leslie Fiedler) to Batman and Robin. Further, Mr. Ricardo shows admirable critical restraint in his tentative conclusion: he suggests only a "perhaps."

However, from the evidence Mr. Ricardo offers and from my own reading of Faust's Westerns and other of his novels, I cannot agree even with this qualified "perhaps." First of all, the quotations and instances cited by Mr. Ricardo must be interpreted within their proper context. Objectivity is achieved only if one is faithful to the context. And, of course, one must not omit from a source anything that would alter its meaning.

Mr. Ricardo's first quotation is from THE KING BIRD RIDES:

He had taken care, in making that moonlight call, as though it had been upon a sweetheart. . . . He stood there, laughing in the moonlight, as fine a picture as ever had filled the eyes of Marshal Jim Hampton. . . . He laughed again, very gently, and there was almost a caress in his eyes as they dwelt on the face of the marshal.

But Mr. Ricardo omits the two preceding sentences that would explain the essential point of this passage. Faust is stressing that the King Bird, after having evaded a posse of thirty men and a relay of a hundred horses for seven days and nights over a rugged terrain, enters the enemy camp on the seventh night without a smudge or wrinkle in his clothes: "He was always one to pay the greatest attention to his clothes. He could come out of the wildest desert as out of a bandbox. Even his boots he had rubbed up . . . otherwise they would not have been gleaming, surely. He had taken care, in making this moonlight call. . . ."

Again, the first ellipsis in Mr. Ricardo's quotation actually covers some three pages. Here the reader would discover why the King Bird has come: to lead the marshal away to where a fair gun duel can take place. Hence, it is also made evident that the word "caress" in the final sentence is the kind of "caress" that a lion makes with its paw upon the head of a lamb about to be torn to pieces. The King Bird has calmly come to kill the marshal.

The girl in overalls and sombrero mentioned by Mr. Ricardo is stringing barbed wire, and this explains her garb. But, thinks the King Bird, "no man or boy ever had elbows turned in just this fashion, with such neatness and delicacy." Although Helena (a "Helen of Troy" connotation) Blair's wit is as barbed as the wire she is stringing, the reader discerns that she loves the King Bird. Later, her essential womanliness is stressed when she is abducted to nurse a wounded, kidnapped boy. However, Helena is not the girl to whom the King Bird is presently engaged: that person is the dazzling beauty, Dona Inez Ramirez. Dona Inez confesses to the King Bird that she envies the "down-to-earth" femininity of Helena: "A brown-faced cowgirl, with a snub nose, and her hair pulled into a knot behind her head, and a ragged old sombrero on, and a man's overalls. She's real. She's honest." Inez's words point to the essence of the Western heroine found in the majority of Faust's novels: superior to a man in perception, in common sense, and in wit.

Turning now to MOUNTAIN RIDERS, Mr. Ricardo introduces his quotation by saying simply, "Consider the meeting of two men" and begins with this excerpt:

Derry went down to the creek and filled the pot with water. As he came back, he was walking slowly, for it seemed to him that he had entered a new life—that everything he had done before that had been as nothing, and that he never before had found a real man—not even that hardy Yankee skipper, so handy with fists and tongue.

As he reached the fire, he suddenly extended his hand. Rainey took it with an almost hesitant gesture and, looking up, smiled into the face of Derry. And Rainey had the look, at that moment, of a very happy but rather guilty boy.

To understand fully the meaning of this passage one must understand, first of all, that this is not the first meeting of these two men nor is the attraction of Derry founded in anything erotic. MOUNTAIN RIDERS is the "Jim Silver" novel in which Barry Christian escapes the hangman. How is this accomplished? By the use of someone unknown to the area's lawmen. How is this new man, Derry, tricked into aiding Christian? Through the deceptive friendship of one of Christian's henchmen, Rainey.

Derry has just arrived from the Pacific. The captain of his freighter had been a harsh, brutal drunkard. Yet it was in defending himself from that man's beatings that Derry had learned how to fight. Further, until his previous three encounters with Rainey, Derry had never met a human who possessed even one virtue. The novel begins with a description of Derry:

Tom Derry was not a handsome man. He was rather tall and very lean, and the narrows of his waist ran up almost to his shoulders, and one had to look twice to see where his hips appeared. But his appearance was deceptive, for his leanness was twisted about with muscles like hard fingers of wisteria that intertwined around the trunk of an old tree.

His face was no better-looking than his scrawny body. He had a nose, but that was about all one could say for it. He had plenty of mouth.

Neither is Rainey noticeably attractive: "He was a man of fifty, perhaps, with a face heavily but pleasantly lined, a long-legged fellow with a rather studious humping of the shoulders." But what motivates Derry's friendship with Rainey is his admiration of Rainey's bravery, loyalty, and self-effacement. Three times before the meeting quoted by Mr. Ricardo, Rainey has saved Derry's life: first, from a maddened bull by a single, small rifle shot from over three hundred yards' distance; then from a posse pursuing Derry, a rescue in which Rainey is wounded; and, finally, a refusal to abandon Derry, even though Rainey has a far fleeter horse. Yet the reader is made aware that Rainey, from the very first moment, is intent upon deceiving Derry as to his true character, so that Christian can be set free. Thus Rainey pretends to mourn for the men he had killed in previous gun battles or shrugs off his wound with a show of bravado. Through such clever deceitfulness, he has now succeeded in making Derry think that Jim Silver is the villain and Barry Christian the innocent victim. And this is why Rainey playacts with the "hesitant gesture" and smile and why he "had the look, at that moment, of a very happy but rather guilty boy"—a Tom Sawyer figure who once again had tricked a Ben Rogers into the task of whitewashing. Lastly, only four pages after Mr. Ricardo's quoted passage, Derry falls in love with Maria Carey. He immediately makes her his "share" in the $25,000 transaction with the Carey clan.

From context of novels I turn to the context of the letter in which Faust wrote: "Six years ago, summering at an Italian beach, I was staggered by the physical splendor of the Italian men." But this is not the complete sentence. Mr. Ricardo omits the second half that explains why Faust recalls that earlier impression: ". . . and wondered why they never won the Olympic games." Faust was planning to revisit Greece and Olympia that spring; presently he was watching the Italian track and field team in Florence train themselves without proper coaching; he saw that Italy certainly would again perform miserably in the 1936 Berlin Games to come. But Faust, with his strong competitive spirit and his empathy with Italy as his second home, knew well "the best coach in the world," Boyd Comstock. In this letter Faust is writing to his literary agent and financial adviser, Carl Brandt. He asks Brandt to keep an account of $1,000 secret from Dorothy to finance Comstock's coaching of the Italian team. Now Brandt always sought to curb Faust's endless financial gifts. Hence Faust wishes to convince Brandt that this particular outlay of money will not be wasted— that the Italian runners and jumpers have indeed a true potential, despite their past record. But what of the impression made six years earlier, "staggered by the physical splendor"? To me, Faust's "physical" connotes athletic fitness, muscle coordination, ease in movement. I do not find Faust's impression a necessarily homosexual one, for heterosexuals can note these qualities in others, too. Faust, in fact, was always an admirer of physical prowess, whether in a boxer, a sports car, or a racing horse.

The root causes of why Faust took pleasure in barroom drinking and barroom company during his university years, his Pacific wanderings, and his Army days—and why he continued this in middle age—are too complex and varied to be discussed adequately in this short reply. Of course, in such an analysis one surface element would be a commonsense recognition that most men of Faust's generation (a pre-TV era) took a similar deep pleasure in the talk and laughter of barroom company; many drank too much too often. But it was in such surroundings that Faust conversed with many of those "down-and-outers" whom he was able to help so generously. If they happened to be struggling writers (as he once had been), he was just as generous with literary advice and contacts with editors. The fact that most of those whom he helped were men is not surprising.

Jack Ricardo has written a challenging article, one that causes us to reexamine texts and be as objective as we can be.

II

William F. Nolan

In the previous issue Jack Ricardo made a case for his theory that Faust's writing revealed a hidden homosexual (or bisexual) side to his personality. It *is* true that Max Brand often lovingly described his super-masculine heroes (as well as villains) frequently to the near-exclusion of the heroine. But it must be remembered that he was writing for a specific pulp market (mainly *Western Story Magazine*), a market that idealized its men (as heroes) and relegated its women to the roles of romantic "stage dressing." You just didn't waste description on a female. As Faust once declared (in relation to writing Western pulp fiction): "There has to be a woman, but not much of a one."

If we are to judge Faust's sexual nature by the number of lengthy, sensually detailed descriptions in his work, then the case becomes clear: he must have harbored a secret desire to bed a horse! Faust's great (and near mythical) wonder horses, story for story, garner much more descriptive space than do his heroes and are delineated in much more loving detail. Great shoulders, great fetlocks, dark, liquid eyes, deep chests . . . on and on.

There is absolutely no evidence in his private life or in his life as a writer to indicate that Frederick Faust was homosexual or bisexual. On the contrary, he was a known "womanizer"—and Robert Easton's biography states that Faust had numerous affairs with women. These affairs seriously damaged his marriage, but did not destroy it; Faust was, in the end, emotionally loyal to his wife, Dorothy.

Mr. Richardo's theory is totally without factual basis and can be dismissed as nothing more than unfounded conjecture.

III

Ed Gorman

While Jack Ricardo's argument about the "true" sexual nature of Brand is interesting, I'm skeptical about all attempts to submit authors to Freudian theories. I'm also not sure that it matters. If Brand is more interesting to Jack as a homosexual or bisexual writer, fine. I guess I hadn't wondered about Brand's "real" sexual nature before and probably wouldn't have if Jack hadn't brought it up. It's a legitimate inquiry, I suppose, but what would it prove even if we knew the definitive answer? While Jack's quotes are titillating, I also think they're irrelevant. As John D. MacDonald once replied in a similar circumstance, all men are a little bit women and *vice versa*. And I guess that's how I choose to read Brand. I'm not saying Jack's wrong; I'm not saying I'm right. I'm just saying that the Freudian stuff gets overdone, especially when the critic makes the mistake of confusing the author with his characters. But thanks, Jack, for a thoughtful and interesting article.

SHAKESPEARE'S PRESENCE IN FAUST'S WESTERNS

Leo A. Hetzler

This article first appeared in Singing Guns.

Faust had a special admiration and affection for Shakespeare. William Nolan has noted that by the end of high school Faust had already memorized some 25,000 lines. His daughter Jane remembers how the family would gather after a candlelit dinner to read one of Shakespeare's plays, each member taking a role: "Pop explained lines, shouted over the good ones, taught us the difference between the best and the poorest passages, and in all ways formed our taste."

It is not surprising, then, that Faust made references to Shakespeare's plays in his Westerns. Indeed, he expected the reader to know the particular context and to discern the point he was making. For example, in BORDER GUNS Dr. Watts, in attempting to convey to Lew Weldon the character of General O'Mallock, explains: " 'When the flush of his youth was ended, then he turned his mind to other affairs than mere danger and fighting. Though, to the end, danger was his bright goddess, as she was to Harry Hotspur.' " This simile is quite evocative, for the reader forms a mental image of the fiery son of the Earl of Northumberland ("Henry IV," Part I). When we first meet Hotspur, his uncle is trying to quiet him from publicly voicing his rebellion against the king:

Worcester: I'll read you matter deep and dangerous,
As full of peril and adventurous spirit
As to o'er walk a current roaring loud,
On the unsteadfast footing of a spear.

Hotspur:	If he fall in, good night! Sink or swim:
	Send danger from the east unto the west,
	So honour cross it from north to south,
	And let them grapple.

Dr. Watts continues his character description of the general:

"Now, as the years went by, he determined to marry. He was nearly fifty, then. He found a girl who loved his great, brave past, and who loved him because of it. As Desdemona loved Othello, Mr. Weldon. Quite that way!"
    "This O' Mallock was a half-breed then?" asked Weldon a little sharply.

Even before Othello is mentioned, the reader (and Weldon) are thinking of the Moor; a general "determined to marry" and "nearly fifty." Further, a reader would recall Desdemona's explanation to the Doge of Venice and his Senate why she, a young aristocrat, married the fearsome, middle-aged Othello (I.iii):

> That I did love the moor, to live with him,
> My down-right violence and storm of Fortune
> May trumpet to the world. My heart's subdued
> Even to the very quality of my lord:
> I saw Othello's visage in my mind,
> And to his honours and his valiant parts,
> Did I end my soul and fortunes consecrate.

By "quality," "visage," and "parts," Desdemona means Othello's career (his "great, brave past") as a gifted professional general. There is another point: Lew Weldon's question was placed there by Faust to show that this gunman not only knew the play but remembered the context for that particular speech: she was defying the racial prejudice of her father, her relatives, and her friends in marrying a non-European.
    Faust will sometimes transfer an incident from these Elizabethan plains to the Old West. Once again he expects the reader to recognize the incident and thus enjoy a double pleasure. For instance in "Cayenne Charlie," Charlie greets the self-inflated gunman, Bud Vincent, with these words:

"Why, if it ain't little ol' Buddie Vincent, that regular man-killin' 'puncher! If it ain't ol' Buddie, the riot gun and sharpshooter. Him that kills linnets on the wing at a hundred yards, and shoots the eyelashes off a wolf at a half a mile. Why, doggone me, Buddie, how many men you murdered since I last seen you?"

Here Faust combines two passages from "Henry IV," Part I. The first is Prince Hal's mocking words on the exaggerated exploits of the Scottish rebel, Douglas (II.iv):

Falstaff:	. . . that sprightly Scot of Scots, Douglas, that runs o'horseback up a hill perpendicular.
Prince Hal:	He that rides at high speed and with his pistol kills a sparrow flying.
Falstaff:	You have hit it.
Prince Hal:	So did he never the sparrow.

The second passage is again Prince Hal's derisive words, but this time about Hotspur's reputation: "'. . . the Hotspur of the North: he that kills some six or seven dozens of Scots at a breakfast, washes his hands, and says to his wife, 'Fie upon this quiet life! I want work.' '' (II.iv) Thus the reader, with these references in mind, knows that Bud Vincent's boasting is mere bluster.

In MAX BRAND: THE BIG "WESTERNER" (University of Oklahoma Press, 1970) Robert Easton describes Faust's intense and lifelong love of literature, particularly Shakespeare: reading the plays aloud with family and friends, his personal identification with the playwright's rise from rural obscurity to become the master of an age, his treasured facsimile of the 1632 edition of the bard's works, how characters leaped from the plays to a new life in Faust's fiction, how Faust in his conversation could make Shakespeare "come alive." According to Easton, Faust admired the "values of remoteness and timeliness" to be found in "Hamlet" and other plays, as well as in other classics. Faust's own works are, of course, imbued with the same values and dimensions.

In THE IRON TRAIL Faust makes both humorous and serious use of the balcony scene from "Romeo and Juliet," where the two first profess their love for one another. In this novel it is Eddie Larned who seeks out Dolly Exeter on her balcony to see whether or not they are in love. Eddie had been planning a move against her household, to steal the Exeter jewels. But now he confesses his love for her and tells her he must see her father to reveal who he really is. Dolly, before this scene, had been the only one suspicious of him. But now she declares her trusting love for him. The humorous aspect is the eavesdropper, the villainous Dandy Dick Pritchard, who has been blackmailing Eddie into stealing the jewels. Surprisingly, however, Pritchard proves to be a romantic; he is deeply disappointed that these Western lovers voice their love without his beloved Old World flourishes: "Mr. Pritchard could hardly believe that the matter had ended in this fashion. Was there to be *no* concession to romance? No panting voices? No echoes of poetry?" However, Pritchard realizes that beneath the Westerners' plain words true love is all too apparent:

No, nothing in the world could be farther from Romeo and Juliet, and yet Mr. Pritchard felt that he had overheard a love scene just as decisive as more famous and more wordy ones—some of his own included! There was no doubt about anything. Eddie Clewes was in love. And by that last speech of Dolly Exeter, she had confessed her love for Eddie as clearly as though she had promised in definite words to marry him.

In JIM CURRY'S TEST the murderer, Charlie Mark, has a nightmare in which he sees once more all the men he has slain:

He stood in heaven to be judged, and one by one the witnesses against him filed past him and looked him in the face—all those who had fallen under his gun in the terrible two months of his masquerade as the outlaw. One by one they went past and searched his face with eager eyes, but each was baffled. They had never seen the face beneath the mask when he killed them; they could not brand him now. But at length a square-bearded man halted in the very act of passing, turned and grasped the fob which dangled outside of his watch pocket. "It is he!" said the man in the vision, and a voice asked: "Are you the man?"

This nightmare, of course, is one that Richard III has on the eve of the fatal battle at Bosworth. Eleven ghosts file by his bed, each accusing him and predicting his end. Later a warning is given that part of his army has been bought by his rival, the Earl of Richmond. Faust has constructed an even more dramatic scene. Charlie's victims cannot accuse him because of the mask he had worn. But, as in Macbeth's vision of Birnam Wood and a man-not-of-woman-born, there is a foretelling of what will happen in the latter part of Charlie's dream: that enigmatic watch fob will be the means of his later defeat.

In BROTHER OF THE CHEYENNES there are two probable influences from "Othello": the essential characteristics of Iago are to be found in Major Marston and the handkerchief as proof of non-love appears as a green scarab. Major Marston is undoubtedly the most loathsome of all the villains in Faust's Westerns (in contrast, for example, to the soulless evil of Barry Christian or the pragmatic evil of Chester Bent). Marston outwardly plays the role of the concerned friend, but inwardly he sadistically takes pleasure in the mental and emotional anguish his lies inflict. His chief victims are Rusty Sabin (Red Hawk) and Mairsy Lester. For instance, when Marston finally ensnares Rusty in his prison, he dissuades Mairsy from visiting him but tells her that Rusty has asked for the return of the scarab he had given her as a pledge of his love. Mairsy protests:

"But he couldn't have done that! . . . You were in the room, Arthur, when he gave it to me. You heard him tell me never to send it to him unless I wanted to be rid of him."

"Well, that's true . . . I remember the scene perfectly well," answered Marston. "I wonder if that's really in his mind? I never thought of that. I wonder if he really wants to be free from you again? . . . I suppose it's the wild life calling him back."

Is this not a portrait enriched by Faust's acquaintance with Iago? Marston then describes to Rusty how Mairsy had begged that he not be set free, pleading: "I never want to see him again!" Then, as proof, Marston hands Rusty the scarab. And like Iago, he enjoys Rusty's suffering: "At the sight of it, a keen thrill of pleasure ran through Marston's heart." Of course, these few quotations cannot convey the subtle meaning of Marston, just as a few quotations from "Othello" would similarly fail to convey Iago's.

A final instance of Shakespeare's possible influence may be found in another villain, Chester Bent in DESTRY RIDES AGAIN, and once more the Shakespearean character is Richard III. Like Bent, Richard delights in the intricacies of the plots he weaves to entrap his enemies. And like Bent and the later Iago, Richard gloats over his own cleverness. For example, in the following soliloquy Richard, who has been urging Edward IV to execute their brother, George, the Duke of Clarence, is now on his way to wed Ann, the widow of Henry VI's son, Prince Edward. Richard speaks first of his sick brother, Edward IV (I.i):

> He cannot live, I hope; and must not die
> Till George be pack'd with post-haste up to heaven.
> I'll in, to urge his hatred more to Clarence,
> With lies well steel'd with weighty arguments;
> Clarence hath not another day to live;
> Which done, God take King Edward to his mercy.
> And leave the world for me to bustle in!
> For then I'll marry Warwick's youngest daughter.
> What though I kill'd her husband and her father . . .
> But yet I run before my horse to market:
> Clarence still breathes; Edward still lives and reigns:
> When they are gone, then must I count my gains.

Similarly, Bent gives a gloating summary of his plottings. At the beginning of Chapter Thirty-Three he has just come from having deceived Charlie that his own latest murder was the work of Destry (he had carefully left Destry's knife in the corpse) and has persuaded her to arrange a secret meeting with Destry, a rendezvous Bent will later turn into a death-trap. Bent, once alone, feels "a happy glow of achievement" already possessing his body. "What fascinated him was the intricacy of his plan, the width of the end which he aimed at, the skill with which his purposes were so dovetailed together that where the one plan ended, and the other began would have been hard to tell." Then in the next four paragraphs, and in the same tone Richard uses, he lists his plots that had become "desirable" for their "excitement." Further, the final moments of Richard and Bent have certain similarities. The horse imagery (lines 2 and 11) that runs through the play is noticeable in the above passage from "Richard III." It culminates on Bosworth field, where Richard is unhorsed but yet drives relentlessly on foot toward his arch-foe, the Earl of Richmond. Similarly, Bent is unhorsed but yet charges toward Destry.

These examples, then, help to illustrate what one would expect to find in Faust's Westerns, the presence of the writer he admired and loved the most. Let us recognize, too, that Faust himself was Shakespeare's Prospero, creating and peopling a world ''such as dreams are made on,'' and by ''this rough magic'' acting out what pleased his imagination (''The Tempest,'' IV.i):

> Spirits, which by mine art
> I have from their confines call'd to enact
> My present fancies.

THE MAKING OF A MEDICAL MAN: MAX BRAND'S YOUNG DR. KILDARE

Susan L. Zodin

What follows is a compilation of a series of articles that first appeared in
Singing Guns.

With the publication of "Internes Can't Take Money" by Hearst's *Cosmopolitan* magazine, Max Brand introduced the world in 1936 to Dr. James Kildare. A second story, "Whiskey Sour" (1938), continued the depiction of a "gangster" atmosphere surrounding the young doctor as he cared for East Side street toughs and local political bosses while defying his hospital superiors. It was not until later that same year that Brand drastically altered Kildare's personality to fit Metro-Goldwyn-Mayer's idea for a new movie series. The final result became the image of Kildare which most readers and movie/television viewers identify with today.

In YOUNG DR. KILDARE Brand presents us with a young and idealistic, yet intelligent and dedicated, Kildare, just graduated from medical school and torn between his duty (as expected by others) to work in a rural practice with his father and his dream of being an interne in New York's Dupont General Hospital (changed to Blair for the movies). In addition to this conflict, his hometown sweetheart wants to marry him and settle down, but Kildare is not ready for marriage, being devoted wholly to medical practice. He chooses to leave his family and search for an answer in the big city. This problem is familiar in fiction—the protagonist, having raised himself from humble beginnings by education and hard work, finds himself upset at cutting his ties to home but is inevitably drawn to a new life and future. Brand handles this conflict carefully, having Kildare's family express support and love rather than bitterness.

Arriving in New York, Kildare becomes surrounded by Ivy League fellow internes and discovers the difference between his rural education and their urban background. This creates misunderstandings later in the plot when Kildare's shyness and single-minded dedication to research are mistaken by his roommates for arrogance. But the biggest problem arrives with the appearance of Dr. Leonard Gillespie, Blair's famous diagnostician. Brand's invention of the Gillespie character is vastly more important than that of Kildare. Any good writer could create a young hero, but to rise above the typical he would need a special literary foil—a person who embodied the trials and tribulations to be overcome by the leading character in order to reach his goals. Gillespie is not only a character and medical master; his presence in the stories is a spur to the rest of the hospital staff. He is a harsh critic of "sloppy" medicine and a yardstick of talent for colleagues to measure up to. Certainly Kildare had heard of Gillespie before their first meeting—young medical students for decades have studied an older doctor's work—but Brand's molding of personality for Kildare makes the young interne's attraction to Gillespie one of honest admiration and reverence, much as Gillespie himself probably had for Lister, Welch, and Halsted.

To Kildare, Gillespie is "almost God," the perfect physician. But, as fate or fictional irony would have it, the relationship between the two begins with disaster: Gillespie is dying from cancer and has only a year or so left, which puts a stronger-than-ever emphasis on his twenty-five year quest to find an assistant worthy of carrying on his work. (In subsequent books Gillespie is confined to a wheelchair, supposedly due to his illness but in reality based on the fact that the M-G-M role was portrayed by the crippled actor, Lionel Barrymore.) In the welcoming ceremony of the internes by chief-of-staff Walter Carew, Gillespie examines the young doctors for medical insight and character. Kildare's diagnostic eye notices the skin tumor on Gillespie's hand and comprehends its fatal meaning; however, Gillespie, surprised by the young man's intelligence, hides his true feelings and belittles Kildare's abilities.

Kildare finds himself in trouble from the first day of his hospital practice. Assigned to ambulance duty, he meets veteran orderly, Joe Weyman, who considers Kildare just another "know-it-all" kid doctor, but, when an apparent drunk turns out to be a coronary case and dies for lack of proper care, Kildare takes the blame for Weyman and wins a devoted friend—and bodyguard. As Brand more and more rushed Kildare into places where no one would *ever* dream of treading, Weyman's strong-arm presence saves the doctor from physical harm as he pursues his investigations.

Another problem for Kildare is the suicide attempt by heiress Barbara Chanler. Ashamed of having smoked marijuana at a society party, she becomes emotionally distraught, convincing the majority of older physicians that she is going insane. Kildare wins her confidence by simple kindness and understanding instead of complicated psychotherapy treatments, and he promises her that he will straighten everything out. Carew, head psychiatrist Lane Porteus, and Gillespie berate Kildare for keeping the girl's confession confidential and threaten him with dismissal, but Kildare's medical oath and personal beliefs lead him into accepting charges of insubordination and improper behavior rather than violating the patient's confidence. Brand never lets Kildare be actually contemptuous of authority, depicting him instead as the martyr or scapegoat protecting the patient's welfare against the established rules. With the axe about to fall on his career plans, Kildare finds the man who was Barbara's date at the party and learns the truth of her frightened behavior—after some bluffing intimidation. Returning to the hospital, he assures Barbara of her innocence and reunites her with her parents and fiancé.

The book concludes with Kildare's despairing for his lost chance to remain in New York. Carew has the hospital board of directors assembled to expel the young interne; Kildare's sweetheart is in the city to bring him back home, and he seems resigned to a small rural practice; Gillespie apparently has no interest in teaching him. Indeed, throughout most of the book, Gillespie has constantly criticized Kildare's diagnostic abilities and independent thinking. Interested readers, having suffered along with Kildare through an intriguing and suspenseful plot, find themselves at a loss at this point. Surely Kildare won't be restricted to a mediocre practice, and Gillespie's hope for a successor won't remain unfulfilled. Of course not—there is a happy ending for all, due in part to M-G-M's decision to produce several more cinema sequels because of the popularity of the characters. Listening to Carew lecturing on discipline and hospital rules, Kildare sees no apparent hope, when suddenly a phone call from Dr. Porteus announces Barbara Chanler's cure and Kildare's "amazing" work.

While Carew and members of the board are momentarily speechless, Gillespie tells Kildare that he wants him as his assistant. Gillespie's criticisms and gruff behavior turn out to have been only a test of Kildare's determination, honesty, and medical talents; after twenty-five years of searching for the right man, and with the cancer giving him a time limit on his future, Gillespie had to make sure that Kildare was finally what he wanted. Thus begins one of the most famous partnerships in medical fiction, one that has lasted over fifty years.

The success of the Kildare stories is due to the excellent writing skills of Max Brand. He describes the personalities of the characters so well that the reader quickly finds them familiar and believable. This accuracy also extends to his settings, giving a comfortable "at home" quality to the story, allowing the reader to feel at ease in the East Side neighborhoods and in Kildare's rural New England home. Brand's friendship with physicians and scientific writers enabled him to include accurate accounts of hospital surgery, laboratory procedures, and mental therapy—accounts that inform the reader without becoming overly technical. Many of the stories have a crime or disaster as background action, and Brand's talent at creating suspense keeps readers involved with the plot until the absolute conclusion.

Finally, Brand tied his fictional world to the real one with references to the 1939 World's Fair in New York, to developments in 1940's research with sulfa drugs, and to the beginning of World War II.

For readers of Max Brand's Dr. Kildare books one certainty always appears in the plots: the young doctor will find himself in trouble with a capital T. I would like to discuss three stories in which Kildare's honesty, compassion, and determination are tested by the legal and medical codes as he fights for his patients' rights.

CALLING DR. KILDARE (1939) was the second M-G-M project in the motion-picture series, starring Lew Ayres, Lionel Barrymore, and Laraine Day. In it, Brand depicts the trials of the young interne as he begins work under the famous Dr. Gillespie. The story opens with the dedicated student in the middle of yet another all-night work session. Many of his friends have mistakenly blamed Gillespie for being a slave-driver; Joe Weyman suggests that Kildare "slap the old goat down," but, in reality, Kildare's toil is self-imposed. Afraid of wasting the short time left in which to learn from the fatally ill internist, he is attempting to force-feed information into his brain at the cost of sleep, proper food—and other things. One of these costs is Kildare's personal concern for the patients' humanity. Gillespie, angry at two missed diagnoses, accuses the interne of being a "machine" more like a bookworm and laboratory fiend than a sympathetic human being and drives him out of the office. This is the *first* firing of Kildare by his mentor, followed by many more in the series, but Brand's later plot developments show that all is not lost.

An example of this is Gillespie's continuing regard for the interne's welfare. Planning to give Kildare more human insight and maturity, he has Carew assign the young man to an outpatient dispensary and, with Head Nurse Molly Byrd's help, chooses student nurse Mary Lamont (Miss Day) to assist—and spy on— Kildare. Gillespie's wish to expand Kildare's horizons is soon granted—more than he wants. Answering an emergency call outside the clinic, Kildare finds a young man (Nick) hiding in an abandoned cellar; Nick has been shot in a fight fatal to his opponent, "Bowler" Smith. The interne's first impulse is to call for an ambulance, but Nick fears the police. The appearance of Nick's sister, Rosalie, doesn't help Kildare's dilemma; red-haired, glamorous, and city-sophisticated, Rosalie (Lana Turner) uses her romantic appeal and talent for creating sympathy to lead the naive interne into secretly treating her injured brother.

Unable to obtain blood transfusion equipment from the hospital, Kildare scrapes up odds and ends from the clinic and, finding that his own blood matches Nick's, performs a crude transfusion and removes the bullet. This unselfish act, based on Kildare's inner judgment that Nick is honest and deserves a break in life, makes a deep impression on the witnesses. Nick believes that Kildare's blood will almost magically change his life for the better, and he appreciates the interne's faith in his innocence.

Driven back to the hospital by Rosalie, Kildare immediately is called on the carpet by Carew for returning late to duty and not being able to explain his absence from the clinic. The interne also finds out at Sullivan's Saloon (the local cafe) that the police are searching the neighborhood for Nick, and, to add to these problems, Mary, reporting the day's events to Gillespie, mentions seeing Kildare and Rosalie together in the hospital's parking area.

Gillespie, talking later to Mike Ryan and Weyman at Sullivan's, learns about the murder of Smith, the manhunt for Nick, and Rosalie's golddigger reputation in the district. Resolving to champion the "innocence" of Kildare, he phones Jimmy's parents in Connecticut, asking them to invite their son home for a few days. Soon after receiving his father's note, Kildare goes to Carew for permission to be absent from duty but finds his office closed for the night—leaving only Gillespie with the proper authority. The internist expresses bitter words against certain kinds of women, informs Kildare that Carew is unhappy about his recent behavior (which, of course, makes no difference to Gillespie), and ends by berating the young man for throwing away his great chances for "a thug and a shoddy little light of love." Kildare is calm throughout this tirade until Gillespie, exasperated, remarks: "Take all the leave you want. You have my leave to go. You have my leave never to come back."

The reader, having seen Gillespie's interest in Kildare's affairs, can understand his *real* affection for the interne despite his gruff manner and his amazement and amusement at someone who actually dares to oppose him rather than be intimidated. Brand does an excellent job in this scene, revealing the respect, admiration, and love between the two men by using criticism and disagreements instead of open affection, lending more depth and interest to their personalities.

In Dartford, Kildare assists his father in solving a problem case, tactfully letting the older man make the final diagnosis and giving "country medicine" a small victory over "city ways." However, more serious is the break-up between Jimmy and his sweetheart, Beatrice Raymond, who has been feeling guilty for forcing Kildare into a long-distance engagement while he is so involved in his hospital work. They part as friends, though both regret that fate has driven them apart. Back home, his mother, realizing that he must face his New York problems, sends him back to the city. Going immediately upon arrival to see Nick, Kildare is interrupted by the appearance of a police detective. Saved temporarily from jail by the good reputation of the hospital, Kildare learns from Nick that a friend, "Happy" Leeman, had started the dispute between Smith and himself. Visiting Leeman to hint at his responsibility for the disagreement, Kildare is attacked by the angry thug but saved by the appearance of Weyman, who had followed the interne into trouble. Meanwhile, Gillespie has called Rosalie into his office to discuss Kildare's future. She shows her honest love for him but wants him in a lucrative private practice (presumably to help pay for her "classy" tastes). Gillespie, through a combination of put-on dramatics and sincere feelings, tells her of his fatal illness and the need for someone to inherit his work. She admits that Kildare's biggest wish in life is to be like Gillespie and sorrowfully agrees to give him up.

When Kildare returns from delivering the real criminal to jail, Rosalie tells him she only pretended to love him so that he would take care of Nick. This lie hurts both of them, but they realize it is for their mutual good. Carew drops all charges against the interne, and Gillespie brusquely orders him back to work, sending Mary Lamont to help him and serve as a better romantic interest.

In this novel the great use of suspense and dramatic dialogue regarding Kildare's secret treatments, the search for the real killer, and Gillespie's undercover work makes it one of the best books in the series. Kildare's change from a statistical, impersonal physician to the caring "friend of the needy" enables him to fulfill Gillespie's image of his proper behavior and to be rewarded by a second chance at his dreams, an opportunity more precious than his first, enriched by Gillespie's continuing faith and pride even in times of trouble.

DR. KILDARE'S SEARCH—M-G-M's DR. KILDARE'S STRANGE CASE—contains not only dramatic medical techniques but also a love triangle which causes problems for the young interne as he decides the course of his future. As the story begins, Dr. Gillespie, ever testing the intelligence of his assistant, lets Kildare take first charge in the examination of an outside-referred patient, much to the annoyance of the original physician. Surprisingly, the older doctor disagrees with the interne's decision, but Kildare sticks to his beliefs and is proved correct. Gillespie, in one of Brand's most emotional passages of dialogue, admits his fallibility as a mortal but urges Kildare always to remember that every doctor faces times when an instant decision may determine the life or death of a patient and that, if he is certain he is right, he needs to be able to stand by his opinion against all opposition. These "passing on of wisdom" conversations are common in the Kildare stories, as Brand illustrates the characters' striving for perfection in medicine.

Gillespie is worried about Mary Lamont's increasing interest in wealthy neurosurgeon, Gregory Lane. In a plan to improve Kildare's appeal to the nurse, he asks his assistant to accompany him to the new medical research center founded by millionaire Paul Messenger. Kildare had saved the life of Messenger's daughter—in THE SECRET OF DR. KILDARE—and the philanthropist here offers the talented interne the position of director at the complex. Gillespie urges the young man to accept, citing the large salary, furnished house, and great professional reputation awaiting him and Mary for the future, although it would be an indescribable blow to the senior doctor. Mary's jubilation, however, is short-lived, as Kildare tells her that he has decided to decline the offer. "There are two bids, and I sold out to the higher one. Messenger means an easy life . . . a home, and all that. It even means having you. Gillespie means a hard grind, but he's stored up a thousand years of things I must know. It's no sacrifice." But it is a sacrifice to Mary, in a way. Her love for Kildare is mixed with frustration at not being able to have material wealth in married life.

Gillespie, meanwhile, assuming that Kildare wouldn't dare lose this chance of a lifetime, is packing up the dozens of notebooks the young man has used in his studies, all the while muttering about " 'going back to the old days with no damned foreign interference.' " Overjoyed—and saddened—by Kildare's decision to stay at the hospital with his small salary, Gillespie decides to assign him to assist Dr. Lane, since the neurosurgeon has had problems with patient fatalities. This also gives Kildare a chance to compete for Mary's attentions.

After watching Lane at work, Kildare is unable to find fault with his technique and feels that his only problem is bad luck. This appears to be true, as an emergency case, Henry Thornton, is brought in exhibiting extremely psychotic behavior. Insisting that he will miss an important appointment on Friday, three days in the future, Thornton refuses the needed immediate operation but falls unconscious—leaving Lane with the dilemma of deciding for surgery against the legal and medical codes requiring the patient's permission. Kildare repeats Gillespie's words on having the courage of one's convictions, and Lane goes ahead with treatment. Thornton's continuing schizophrenic conduct after surgery leads Carew to accuse Lane of incompetence and malpractice, although Kildare attempts to persuade the administrator that the surgical procedure was not at fault. This seems to be a perfect opportunity for Kildare to eliminate a serious romantic rival, but the interne's inherent honesty and concern for others leads him to oppose Carew and the board in his support for Lane.

Finding the address of Thornton, Kildare and Weyman break in and find evidence that the patient was separated from his wife, hoping to be reconciled with her in a meeting on Friday. However, they have no clue as to her whereabouts. Kildare plans to use a highly dangerous and controversial treatment, insulin shock—first used in Austria in 1933, only seven years before Brand was writing about it—to bring Thornton back to sanity and perhaps to save his marriage.

Late on Thursday night, Kildare and Mary administer the drug, which causes violent convulsions and sub-normal body temperatures. The young nurse, afraid they have killed Thornton, is even more panicked upon the unexpected entrance of Carew, who is outraged at the interne's actions and promises to add him to the malpractice inquiry by the board. Thornton, however, is cured by the treatment, much to the relief of Carew and Lane. Kildare, finding out that Mrs. Thornton is in a small Colorado town awaiting news from her husband, borrows money from his father and travels by plane, bus, and—finally—muleback to reach her and bring her back to New York. Brand's characterization of the interne's dedication is here again illustrated: having given money out of his pocket, having given the blood out of his body—in CALLING DR. KILDARE—and in this case having traveled across the country to fulfill a patient's wish, Kildare can appeal to the public as a true hero.

Gillespie, finding Kildare AWOL and angry over Carew's threats against the younger man, accuses the chief of staff of committing ''intellectual murder.'' Upon Kildare's return and the happy reunion of the Thorntons, the senior doctor is relieved when everything ends well, but he warns Kildare not to gamble with his future. Dr. Lane is found innocent of malpractice and admits to Mary that Kildare's inner wealth is more important for her future than any financial security he could give her. Realizing the depth of sacrifice Kildare was willing to make in rejecting Messenger's job offer and in risking his reputation if Thornton had died during surgery, Mary resolves to wait as long as necessary to be able to marry the man she loves.

This story, although almost as dramatic in plot as CALLING DR. KILDARE,

is a good example of Max Brand's talent in creating "quiet" depth in personalities. Kildare, as usual, is honest, noble, and dedicated; his character is the
constant for Dr. Lane and Mary Lamont as they measure their personal needs
and desires against his spiritual and ethical riches. Gillespie also, through his
stubborn determination to provide Kildare a chance at material wealth, experiences the strength of the interne's devotion to the work of the older interests in
lieu of any earthly rewards. All the characters have found contentment at the
conclusion and are made stronger by the trials they have faced and beaten.

The last Brand-written Kildare movie, THE PEOPLE VS. DR. KILDARE,
was based on his novel, DR. KILDARE'S TRIAL. Shorter than his other novels,
it still has much suspense and dramatic action as the young doctor, now a
resident, fights for his medical reputation in a court of law. Kildare, usually
purposely finding trouble in his crusades, has it come to him this time unexpectedly—and unwelcomely. Arriving at the scene of a traffic accident, he finds
himself in charge of two critical cases. A young boy, Tommy, has a fractured
spine and mustn't be carelessly moved, and Estelle Courcy, later revealed as a
dancer and a model, has a compound leg fracture and severe abdominal bleeding. Believing death to be only minutes away, Kildare prepares to perform an
emergency operation, but Estelle hysterically refuses treatment before falling
unconscious. (This situation is identical to Dr. Lane's experience with Thornton
in DR. KILDARE'S SEARCH, and Kildare uses the same reasoning to justify
his actions here, despite the serious outcome.) Ignoring a traffic cop's insistence
on obtaining the patient's permission, Kildare sets to work and removes the
hemorrhaging spleen. In enough trouble by performing unauthorized surgery,
Kildare finds even more as he examines an irregular growth on the pancreas.
Arguing with his conscience on ethics, he finally decides to excise the tissue.

Back at the hospital Kildare's woes grow no less, as Tommy, fearing permanent paralysis, begs the doctor for anesthesia. Kildare agrees, only to relive
the dangerous nervous stress, and assigns Mary to work with the boy in therapy.
Gillespie also unwittingly causes trouble for his assistant, when, not knowing
about the emergency street operation, he criticizes the poor care of Miss Courcy's leg.

Later, accidentally hearing about Gillespie's comments, Estelle decides to sue
Kildare and the hospital for malpractice, her scarred leg ruining her future dancing and modeling career. Her fiancé tells Mary of his deep concern for Estelle's
health, and Mary in turn tells Kildare, hoping that the woman can be given
every chance for recovery. Gillespie, hearing of this, rebukes her, saying: " 'He
never does anything but his best. You've made the idiot emotional. You've made
this case into a great test for him.' "

The pressure increases as Kildare, examining the pancreatic tissue, finds cancer cells. Bound by honor and concern for Estelle's future, he refuses to reveal
this to Gillespie, Carew, and the hospital lawyer—effectively ruining his own
case for the welfare of the patient. Kildare is confronted by the District Attorney,
and, reacting to a hospital clerk's question about when he expected to be back,

Kildare replies, his black humor barely concealing his martyrdom: "Why, I don't know. As a matter of fact, I suppose it might be years."

In the courtroom, Kildare's future grows more and more bleak. Street witnesses describe his "brutality" and "rudeness" while administering to the victims. The District Attorney brings Estelle to the stand in a stereotypic victim pose—fainting, innocent, helpless, and outraged—describing how her future has been destroyed by a crooked leg. Even Kildare's character witnesses hurt more than help his case; Carew's praise of Kildare's talents is countered by his admission of the interne's prior disciplinary problems. At last, Kildare himself is on the stand, but he "chooses not to remember" the surgical details regarding the pancreatic cancer.

All seems lost as the young resident faces not only a jail term and the permanent loss of his medical license, but marriage to Mary and the opportunity to work further with Gillespie have also been jeopardized. Then the senior diagnostician is called as the last witness. This scene is another dramatic highlight in the Kildare series, as Brand makes Gillespie an outstanding orator and champion of medicine in his defense of Kildare. Beginning with a demonstration of what a "born" doctor is—the all-seeing eye, caring heart and instinctive brain—Gillespie discusses his search for a successor to his work: "After nearly a century, I found myself looking around for someone into whose hands I could pour what I'd learned . . . but it wasn't easy. At last I found him. I found that he could work day and night, and that, what he learned, he held onto like a bulldog. We began to work together, and he has never failed me from that day to this."

In this one declaration Brand shows the real affection of Gillespie for Kildare, making up for all the criticisms and problems the young man had suffered in his trial-by-fire training. The internist then refutes all of the prosecution's charges: Kildare, accused of performing the dramatic surgery for profit and publicity, has given up chances for wealth and power (Messenger, et al.) to remain on hospital salary; the "brutal" doctor and Mary helped Tommy Long move his limbs again; and, even though Jimmy had broken legal rules before, he has never been wrong from the viewpoint of sound medicine and God Almighty. Gillespie tells the court that doctors can't give specific odds for life and death in a split-second decision, but Kildare made his best guess and did what his conscience told him—saving Estelle's life at the cost of her leg. Estelle, moved by this oration, suddenly jumps to her feet—despite her "crippled" leg—and begs Kildare to forgive her. The court drops all charges, and the young doctor has been saved once again by his mentor for a future as a medical leader.

I would like to discuss now three stories in which personal problems and family worries threaten the young hero's work and future dreams and yet increase his inner qualities of charity and idealism. The first example of this category, and my personal favorite, THE SECRET OF DR. KILDARE, is the young doctor's attempt to protect the quickly failing health of his mentor, Dr. Leonard Gillespie, who has exhausted himself by fanatical dedication to his work despite age and physical weakness. A serious collapse of the senior physician leads Kildare to an agonizing decision—to leave his job with Gillespie and force the old man to take a complete rest from work, unable to continue without an assistant.

Max Brand often used outside conflicts such as legal problems to jeopardize the young doctor's career, but here he lets Kildare take a hand in his own future—walking voluntarily, as it were, out of "paradise," although the resultant troubles affect everyone concerned—even himself. But how best to have an excuse for quitting a chance-in-a-lifetime position so hard won and cherished? In past novels Brand had already established Kildare's rural background and personal penury; here, emphasizing these "drawbacks" even more, he finds an apparent answer in the person of millionaire, Paul Messenger, whose need for a family physician can offer Kildare a chance for material wealth and future career glory. Messenger's daughter, Nancy, whose sudden, portentous change of personality has upset her family and fiancé, fears the mention of illness and physicians, so Dr. Carew assigns Kildare as an "undercover" diagnostician to discover her problems without her knowledge of his true identity.

As Kildare prepares to move into the Park Avenue atmosphere of the Messenger social circle, his friends, especially Mary Lamont and Gillespie, are shocked at his unexplained and ostensible abandonment of the senior physician for a greedy chance at monetary rewards—not knowing that the only actual reason for his conduct is to preserve Gillespie's waning strength and perhaps even to save his life. The moment of teacher-student separation is highlighted by excellent dialogue and the strong emotional characterization of the participants. Gillespie's mood as the unwitting "victim" changes from confusion and the attempted appeasement of Kildare's youthful impatience with poverty to angry bitterness at the "betrayal" and heartache. Kildare, acquiescing with this last emotion, still believes a greater good is being served by the breakup.

Away from the hospital Kildare tries to forget his personal problems as he works on the important outside case. In his conversations with Nancy Messenger he begins to realize that her terrible fear of illness is connected to a childhood memory of her mother's death from a brain tumor. This neurosis, augmented by a visit to a quack medical friend of her old nanny's and by arguments with Nancy's fiancé, causes a hysterical mental reaction which leaves the young girl blind. Kildare, unable to find a pathological explanation for the condition, goes to Staten Island where Gillespie, having quit his research, is on a vacation. Angrily refusing to discuss the case with his interne, he drives him away, saying: " 'You don't need me any longer, young Dr. Kildare. You found your way into the long green that means so much to you. Don't come with your whining questions to me again as long as you live!' " In spite of depicting here what seems to me to be a heartfelt sentiment, Brand shows the power of true friendship over outward emotion as the next scene finds the old man returning to the hospital as an informal consultant on Nancy's treatment. Still confused and upset over Kildare's behavior, Gillespie nevertheless feels affection for the young man and his concern and interest in solving a problem case.

With the help of Paul Messenger, Nancy's fiancé, and the senior staff physicians, Kildare is able to calm Nancy's fears of a brain tumor and then to restore her sight. Her grateful father offers him a check for $20,000, but Kildare, in refusing it, gives Mary an insight into his true motives regarding Gillespie. The senior diagnostician, deeply touched by Kildare's self-martyrdom, accepts the interne back as his assistant and plans a more moderate work rate for the future research.

A second instance of personal difficulties for the young doctor occurs when, faced with a serious illness afflicting Mary Lamont's brother, Douglas, in DR. KILDARE'S CRISIS, Kildare finds that his and Mary's future wedding plans and subsequent life together are threatened. Douglas Lamont, an idealistic economist, comes to New York with great plans to organize a system of fresh-air farms for the overworked and poor urban classes—much like President Roosevelt's New Deal programs. This use of plot elements that are recognizably similar to real-life events is an excellent example of Max Brand's talents with popular fiction—adding to his accuracy and honesty in storytelling those plausible contemporary circumstances that both attract the reader's attention and facilitate an understanding of the action.

Attempting to aid Douglas's project by introducing him to Paul Messenger and other wealthy and influential businessmen, Kildare becomes troubled by the physical signs of a manic-depressive condition in the young man—bursts of strong bodily and mental activity followed by exhaustion. Diagnosing epilepsy, Kildare tries to make Lamont slow down his pace, but Douglas insists on pushing his work through in order to gain financial support for his ideas. Disobeying his medical prescriptions, Douglas attends a meeting with Messenger but suffers a dramatic collapse with serious convulsions. Mary, torn between her sisterly devotion to Douglas and her love for Jimmy, decides to leave the hospital and dedicate her nursing skills to her brother's care. Kildare, confused by her reaction, is also divided between understanding her duty to Douglas and his own need for her attention. In the midst of these sacrificial resolutions Gillespie steps in with his usual common sense and quick action to save the day. Bullying his way onto the ship on which the Lamonts have booked passage out of New York, he takes them back to the hospital, sees to the care of Douglas, and reunites Mary and Kildare.

DR. KILDARE'S CRISIS was one of the shorter novels of the series, dealing mainly with non-hospital action. Gillespie's input is limited, for the most part, to the beginning and the end of the drama, as Brand lets Kildare ''enjoy'' his resident-physician independence. However, a serious flaw appears toward the end, concerning ambulance man, Joe Weyman, a regular ''sidekick'' participant in Kildare's medical adventures. After Mary leaves with Douglas en route to the ship, Weyman, sent by Gillespie to search for her, is in a fatal traffic accident. The character doesn't appear in the next installment, DR. KILDARE'S TRIAL, but does appear two years later in Brand's last two short novels in the series, ''Dr. Kildare's Hardest Case'' and ''Dr. Kildare's Dilemma.'' Weyman also stays alive as a character in the Lew Ayres/Van Johnson M-G-M movie series which ended in 1947. This "resurrection," unexplained to readers, proved necessary for continued sub-plot action through the rest of Brand's stories on the subject.

The last family-related Kildare story is DR. KILDARE TAKES CHARGE—M-G-M's DR. KILDARE GOES HOME. It has two strong plots which involve the young resident in trouble both at home (Dartford, Connecticut) and in the hospital. In Jimmy's hometown old Stephen Kildare is overworked because of a rural epidemic. Jimmy Kildare, facing the permanent loss of his hospital work because of his duty to his father, prepares to remain in Dartford to help, but with Gillespie's assistance he manages to recruit several young physicians unable to succeed in private practice, who form a country clinic.

Risking what little income and professional reputation they have, Kildare and the others try to inaugurate a campaign of preventive medicine and public health insurance, but the stubborn New England "Yankee" town rejects the "new-fangled city ways." Brand again introduces here a relationship between the financial world and real life with a discussion on proper diets, sanitation, vaccination, and other preventive health care ideas as well as the "co-op" insurance system supported by taxing per capita in the community. Both of these ideas were relatively new in the 1930s and 1940s as FDR's New Deal programs and research in nutrition and hygiene came forth to help the public. Faced with failure for the clinic staff as well as resigning himself to a rural practice, Kildare is intrigued by the pathological symptoms of Geoffrey Winslow, the town leader, and—despite initial angry protests—insists on treating the serious condition. Cured by the determination and humanistic concern of Kildare, Winslow addresses the community at a town meeting and pledges money and support for the clinic.

Freed by the success of his friends who aid his father's practice, Kildare returns to Blair General and Gillespie only to find trouble there as well. Young William Carew and his sweetheart, Marguerite, are deeply in love, but they are unable to obtain support for their marriage from Dr. Carew, who believes them too immature and foolish to have a serious relationship. This generation-gap misunderstanding, common to many families, almost leads to tragedy as William and Marguerite decide on a suicide pact to demonstrate their true love despite all worldly opposition. Kildare and Mary frantically search for the two teenagers through their usual New York neighborhood haunts as the senior Carew, realizing that his authoritative "father-knows-best" attitude and previous disregard of home life in favor of hospital responsibilities has led to disaster, despairs over the possible death of his son and the girl. Finally, Kildare finds the two lovers as they prepare to jump into the harbor. He brings them back to the hospital where Walter Carew, overjoyed at his second chance to deal with his son, promises the young couple that he will help them with their wedding plans and future life.

In this story, as in DR. KILDARE'S CRISIS, Kildare is older and more responsible for independent actions than he had been as an interne. He can relate to Dr. Carew as a fellow staff physician and as a man in advising him on William's and Marguerite's viewpoints on life, and he organizes his peers into a clinic practice—dealing not only with personal concerns but also with money problems, town politics, and medical equipment needs. Allowing his characters to mature and expand their talents, Max Brand still shows their strong personal affection and loyalty, observed by the strengthening of the Gillespie-Kildare-Lamont relationship and benefits to Kildare's family and friends resulting from his actions.

With the increasing development of the Kildare/Mary Lamont romance throughout the Kildare film series, the movie-going public waited eagerly for the medical pair's wedding to take place. Unfortunately, Laraine Day's decision to give up that role in favor of new opportunities forced scriptwriters, Willis Goldbeck and Harry Ruskin, to kill off the young nurse in a street accident in DR. KILDARE'S WEDDING DAY. Thus a main focus of the film deals with Kildare's emotional shock at the tragedy, his helplessness in saving the girl he loves, and his consequent apathy toward resuming his medical work. A great deal of fascinating background (never discussed in the books) is presented concerning Gillespie's own student days and a similar disaster in his life when his sweetheart suddenly died. By sharing his memories and spiritual views, Gillespie, with kind encouragement, is able to bring the young doctor back to his duty.

Lew Ayres's last film in the series (due to conflicts with the studio over his controversial publicity as a conscientious objector during the U.S. draft in World War II) was DR. KILDARE'S VICTORY, released in November 1941. Following up on the tragedy of the previous plot, the film has Kildare, in deep mourning for Mary, seemingly determined permanently to forgo romantic love in the future. However, the studio decided (for some inexplicable reason, since the character was to be dropped in the later series of ''Gillespie'' films) to introduce a new love interest for the young physician in the person of debutante Cynthia Charles on whom Kildare performs an emergency heart operation. Along with dealing with her embarrassing exclamations of affection for him, the internist also saves two friends, an interne and a nurse, from disciplinary problems over hospital regulations on ambulance response zoning.

During the time that DR. KILDARE'S VICTORY was in production, Brand was working on the novelette ''Dr. Kildare's Hardest Case.'' A role similar to Cynthia Charles's character was created in Sylvia Harned, a wealthy but spoiled society girl, who is involved with a hospital therapy treatment. Opening with a look at war construction at the New York Naval Yard, the story shows how a top officer, Lt. Commander Jervis, is injured in an accident and brought to Kildare and Gillespie at Blair. The young doctor, believing Jervis's slow recovery to be partially due to emotional upset, discovers the officer's past romance with Sylvia and persuades her (by belittling her haughty and selfish attitude) to face her inner thoughts and past concerns for the sick man. With Gillespie's help and Sylvia's emotional support for Jervis, Kildare is able to diagnose and cure the mysterious illness—once again bringing the medical part of the story to a successful end. However, he finds himself in an awkward position when Sylvia, touched by his compassionate and dedicated nature, transfers her attentions to him and vows to win his love.

This situation seems to be a great solution to "shock" Jimmy back to a normal life—freed from the constant regrets and unhappiness over Mary and ready for a brighter future. But, as stated before, it didn't matter one way or another, since the loss of Ayres led to the termination of the Kildare character in the remaining six films. The issue is further complicated by the "resurrection" of Mary in the book version of "Dr. Kildare's Hardest Case" published with "Dr. Kildare's Girl"—a year after the magazine story supporting her death on screen! Actually, Mary doesn't take part in the book's action, but Gillespie refers to her on the last page in a conversation with Sylvia over Kildare's future. (Joe Weyman, who died at the end of DR. KILDARE'S CRISIS, also is "reborn" as a soldier at the Naval base who helps the doctor with Jervis's treatment.) A possible answer to these perplexing contradictions is that Brand and the studio might have had different concepts of time frames for plot developments. This can be seen when comparing the book action and film action on a fictional calendrical basis. Gillespie's "last year of life" established in YOUNG DR. KILDARE actually covered *nine* years (1938–47) because of the film sequels; Kildare's one-year internship lasted through five screen stories; and it took four installments from "Dr. Kildare Goes Home" to cover about two months' book action to the September 1 wedding day. The problem arises in this particular situation when the magazine and book versions of DR. KILDARE'S SEARCH are compared to other stories in the series and their time frame of action. *Cosmopolitan's* version has the story set several months after Mary's death, but the book's reference implies that the wedding is *far in the future,* putting this plot even before DR. KILDARE'S TRIAL, which is known to be thirty days before the ceremony. However, the trial events (of August 1941) do not agree with the December war projects of DR. KILDARE'S HARDEST CASE, if the latter story's book version fate for Mary is true. It is hard, however, to fit the story in a proper plot sequence with the other books in the series.

Possibly, if there had been no problems with Ayres's draft status, the studio might have assigned another female star to DR. KILDARE'S WEDDING DAY and planned future plots showing his children, his work in the practice after Gillespie's death, etc. Then Brand's book story of DR. KILDARE'S SEARCH would have been a chance for the Mary Lamont character to carry on in new stories. However, this idea never came to fruition as Brand continued the Sylvia Harned romance in his last work on the subject, a four-chapter, unfinished story entitled "Dr. Kildare's Dilemma." [Editors' note: Faust himself wished the Mary Lamont character to be kept alive, evident in the restored version of this fragment found elsewhere in THE MAX BRAND COMPANION.] Written probably in late 1942 or early 1943, "Dr. Kildare's Dilemma" was published in two parts (February 1971 and January 1973) in *The Faust Collector,* a Los Angeles fanzine edited by William Clark.

After DR. KILDARE'S VICTORY, the Gillespie character (Lionel Barrymore) was presented in CALLING DR. GILLESPIE (with Philip Dorn), DR. GILLESPIE'S NEW ASSISTANT, DR. GILLESPIE'S CRIMINAL CASE, THREE MEN IN WHITE, BETWEEN TWO WOMEN (all four with Van Johnson and Keye Luke), and DARK DELUSION (with James Craig). Ayres and Barrymore were reunited in the WMGM radio show, ''The Story of Dr. Kildare'' (1949–51), and new fans were introduced to the characters in the NBC television series, ''Dr. Kildare'' (1961–66), starring Richard Chamberlain and Raymond Massey. All in all Max Brand's vision of medical heroes for the public has lasted over fifty years and is still rewarding for those who share it.

THOUGHTS ON MAX BRAND'S *THE GARDEN OF EDEN*

Leo A. Hetzler

This essay first appeared in Singing Guns.

THE GARDEN OF EDEN is one of those instances in which Frederick Schiller Faust, as early as 1922, expanded the Western story as a genre in which the deepest and most basic questions that confront a human being could be explored. Yet, at the same time, Faust makes the book a highly entertaining and richly colorful one. In a sense THE GARDEN OF EDEN, in its setting and action, stands outside the corpus of Faust's Westerns, just as do the series of Whistling Dan Barry stories. Its action does not revolve around gun play, pursuits, and archvillains; rather, Faust explores the interplay of religion and myth within the human psyche. Indeed, the closest contemporary counterpart would be Peter Shaffer's drama, ''Equus,'' with its theme that an imperfect myth that nevertheless gives some explanation of, and purpose to, life is preferable to no myth at all. But Faust goes beyond this and, in the final chapter, gives testimony to the one and true myth.

The novel's central concept engages the reader's curiosity, and it is quite original: four men, disgruntled with the imperfections of this world, create their own religion and withdraw to a hidden, sealed-off valley to make their own Eden. Order and perfection are imposed on every facet of this valley's life and most successfully in the strictly controlled breeding of an exceptionally fine group of Arabian gray horses—even the slightest imperfection in a colt or yearling results in its elimination as unfit. To provide an heir to preserve and enforce their holy commandments among the Negro servant class, the Four Founders kidnap a male baby with instructions that he someday choose a wife from outside the valley.

A deep and complex tension reverberates throughout the novel, arising from the dual nature of the religion that was created by the Four Founders. On the one hand, an Eden of prosperity, peace, and order has emerged from a set of Commandments and a Voice that speaks intuitively in the Room of Silence to the Leader. Faust uses all his skills as a creative writer to portray what is right and moral in this mythic system. Its end product, David, is honest, just, noble, and poetic-minded. In his disputations with Ben Connor, it is his arguments and principles that are the right and valid ones. Again, when the Voice speaks to him, its messages are always true; for instance, its reply to David's question whether Ben is to be trusted or not: "His soul is good, but his words are a temptation" (Ben's soul will ultimately be proven to be good).

Equally sound is the revelation that the Voice will continue to communicate with David until he loves someone more than he loves God. Then, too, prophecies of the old blind seer, Abraham, all come true. Further, constant echoes from the Old Testament and the words of Christ are in the very air of this Eden; for example, David says to Ben (as God said to Adam): "We will walk together in the cool of the morning," and David courts Ruth in the words of the Song of Solomon. And, of course, this Eden is invaded by a serpent, who works through a woman to bring about its fall: Ben, with his apple-fragranced lure and the snake-god ornament that promises power.

However, there is another side to this Eden's mystic religion. It was born out of a disdain for, and a rejection of, human imperfections and failings. Its laws are narrowly rationalistic, finding no room for love, forgiveness, and the yearnings of the heart. Thus David punishes mistakes by flogging. And, despite Elijah's fears and pleas, he condemns to death Elijah's beloved colt, Timeh, because it has an almost indiscernible imperfection.

Before we discuss how David will reach a reconciliation with the Four Founders through a New Enlightenment, let us turn to the serpent. Faust was faced with a writer's problem: the choice of a character to fulfill a functional but necessary role, and to do so plausibly, and, if possible, to invent one who would go beyond this—to be a significant participant in the novel's final resolution.

Faust's solution fulfills these requirements admirably. He brings to the West a homesick New York City racetrack gambler and an expert on horses. Ben Connor lives only for money; his only god is Fortuna, emblemized by the good-luck charm on the cane he flourishes in the opening paragraph. These given traits will "hook," or lead into, first, his meeting the "Eve" of the plot, Ruth Manning, and second, his invading the Garden of Eden. He befriends Ruth, a telegraph operator, when he "listens in" on the latest games Fortuna is playing in New York with horses, boxers, and investors. Ruth, too, thinks of everything in terms of luck; for instance: "Isn't that the luck?" she asks in reference to the latest vogue for a style of hat that is unbecoming to her. And later she remarks to Ben: "Luck! That's all there is running things!" Then, at a local horse race, amid many splendid mounts, only Ben recognizes the good points in a small, thin mare—an Eden gray—but he declines betting on her (and winning) when he discovers that the little horse will be bearing a rider weighing two hundred pounds and that the horse is eight years old. Ben's whole being is now concentrated on getting his hands on a prime Eden gray, no matter what means he has to use.

Faust also employs Ben to bring an effective light touch of humor to the serious tone of the story. Ben himself is totally unaware, of course, that any of his remarks are humorous, except for the one instance of a grumpy wit, when, in the opening, he replies to the question of the non-stop conversationalist, Jack Townsend, about why he came west: "I've come here for the silence. . . ." But what often causes the reader to smile is Ben's utter incomprehension of the ways of romantic love. Thus Ben is appalled by David's poetic phrases in court-ing Ruth, for he is sure that such nonsense will drive her away. In fact, when Ruth enters the next morning smiling and singing, Ben is grateful that she could so easily forget David's silly drivel of the night before. And Ben, thinking how he had phrased the only marriage proposal he had ever made in his life, advises David to talk to Ruth only about himself: "That's what I most generally do with a girl."

Ruth Manning is a typical Faustian woman: clever, independent, and level-headed. But she does succumb to Ben's temptation to lure David out of Eden. However, Faust is careful to stress that Ben's most telling argument is not the promise of wealth for herself but rather of bringing about what is best for David. Even this would not have been enough to win her, if there had not been other factors: for this orphan, Ben is her first and only male friend; she is at that moment bored, tired, and overworked; and, what finally wins her consent, Shakra lovingly nuzzles her. Thus, in this lengthy temptation scene, Faust keeps the reader from thinking ill of her acceptance to play the role of deceiver.

Fittingly, the Biblical Ruth, a Moabite, entered Israel as an outsider. She allowed Boaz, a rich landowner, to admire her, and she woke him at night with words that were almost a marriage proposal. She became the great-grandmother of David and hence an ancestor of Christ, who would preach (what is also the novel's theme) the benefits of self-knowledge and sacrificial love.

The concluding movement of THE GARDEN OF EDEN reminds one of the Greek playwright, Æschylus: a final enlightenment, a healing, and a new syn-thesis. The movement begins with Ruth's attack on Ben's belief in the superi-ority of his worldly wisdom over David's naiveté: "At least, he's had the courage and the faith to believe it. What faith have we? I know your heaven, Ben Connor. It's paved with dollar bills. And mine, too." But David lacks a spirit of forgiveness and expels Ruth. Yet that act rouses an enlightenment in Ben, who then strives to open David's eyes. He tells him that Ruth had thought she had acted for his own good. Even more significantly he points out that the Founders were nothing more than tragic victims who, tiring of this world, showed that they were more caring for their individual souls than for the world. Ben then hurls away the lucky charm that symbolized his own former, equally false faith. As a final movement in Ben's redemption, he tells Ruth that the one thing he really regretted was causing her sorrow.

David in his pride thinks that the servants will stay in the valley, out of love for him. When they depart because of a greater love for distant families, David thinks the Eden grays will be company enough for him. But they, too, leave. At last, the sight of the depression that Ruth's head had made upon her pillow breaks his stubborn pride, and he prays, "not the proud prayers of the old days when David talked as equal to the Voice, but that most ancient prayer of sinners: 'O Lord, I believe. Help thou mine unbelief!' " Love answers love, and Glani, alone of all the horses, comes back to him, and David weeps. He is now filled with forgiveness: "Timeh shall live. I, who have judged others so often, have been myself judged and found wanting. Timeh shall live. What am I that I should speak of the life or the death of so much as the least bird in the trees?" Then he finds Ruth waiting at the gate, and he thinks on the providence of God: "Through a thief He has taught me wisdom; through a horse He has taught me faith; and you, oh my love, are the key with which He has unlocked my heart."

Of all the elements in THE GARDEN OF EDEN, Faust's highest achievement lies in his creation of an array of styles or "voices" to convey the story's moods and tones—and to make what happens believable. Dialogue crafted to definite character had always been one of Faust's strengths, and so it is here. Thus Ben lives vividly on the page because of the words Faust gives him, both before and after his enlightenment. But the new challenge for Faust in THE GARDEN OF EDEN was to create a language for David, for the Holy Book of Matthew, and for the Negro servants. This he does supremely well. The Book for instance, has the phrasing, the rhythms, and the wording of the New Testament: thus it opens: "In the beginning there was a man whose name was John." Again, John enlists his three followers as Christ had His Apostles: "Follow me." And what David wrote in the Book of his joy in having found Ruth was expressed in the same simple phrasing yet so sublime that it brings her enlightenment to its final phase. Then, too, the story's final sentence is rich in spiritual symbolism. "And they began to climb the mountain"—the ascent is not only a progression in conjugal love, it is the archetypal image for the progression in growing closer to God.

To the Negros Faust pays the straightforward compliment of recognizing that they are all diverse individuals; thus Abraham is perceptive and wise, Joseph impetuous and weak, Zacharias noble and calm, and Elijah compassionate and emotional. In fact, in this novel whose mystery (of the valley's history) is not revealed until the final pages, an early clue is Abraham's one startling moment of unconscious relapse into slave dialect: "Mah ol' Marse Johnnie Cracker," a phrase so unlike his and the others' stately speech. Further, at the end Faust ennobles them not only in their desire to be reunited with their lost families, but in their motivation as revealed in the ballad they sing with deep fervency: "Oh, Jo, come back from the cold and the stars." Just as the family in the ballad mourns because death has taken away little Jo, so their families must have mourned at their sudden disappearance more than a generation before.

One final remark: all the elements in the novel, separated here for purposes of discussion, are actually closely intertwined, reinforcing one another. A further point: throughout THE GARDEN OF EDEN Faust is far more subtle in characterization and in clarifying motivation (at every juncture) than I have been able to suggest. In Faust's artistic process he had begun with a central idea—a few charcoal strokes as the focus for his canvas—then created further strokes, and finally, drawing upon his mastery with words, brought all to life with rich color, blending and shading characterization, incidents, and dialogue to reveal an Æschylean new vision.

THE FANTASY OF FREDERICK FAUST

Darrell C. Richardson

An earlier version of this essay appeared as "The Fantasy of Frederick Faust" in The Philadelphia Science Fantasy Society News.

Faust wrote practically all types of stories. The keynote of most of them was action. It is no wonder that he turned occasionally to the field of fantasy. Many of his stories, such as THE UNTAMED, have a definite suggestion of fantasy. However, I am reviewing here only those of his works that are definitely fantastic.

"John Ovington Returns" first appeared in *All-Story Weekly.* The story concerns the return of John Ovington to his old ancestral home as owner and heir. Shown the old library by the servant, he discovers among the portraits one that seems to be a likeness of himself. It turns out to be his own great-grandfather of the same name—John Ovington. He finds the man's diary and reads it. Then the balance of the story concerns John Ovington's helplessly repeating his ancestor's history—even down to the final tragic ending.

He meets a beautiful girl, the closest neighbor, who is the great-granddaughter (with the same name) of the first John Ovington's sweetheart. Even the letters he passes back and forth with Beatrice Jerva are almost duplicates of the letters written by the first John Ovington and the first Beatrice Jerva. Their various meetings are similar. And then another man enters the scene—Vincent Colver—the descendant of the man who carried away the first Beatrice from her lover. A queer and brooding sense of failure grips the heart of John Ovington as he fights the battle for love. "It is hard to play against fate, and to come into the play with the stage set against me." Later Beatrice writes him a note, and, as expected, it is the same note the other Beatrice wrote the other John four generations before. She is planning to run away with Vincent that very night and will take the Newbory Road. John Ovington waits for them, and then suddenly—and for the first time—the fates are reversed because Ovington, as Vincent pulls a gun, fells him to the ground and rides away with Beatrice in his arms. "Dearest," he says, "after four generations of waiting I have returned for you and won you away from fate."

"Devil Ritter" is another very fine fantastic novelette. It compares with the very best work of Tod Robbins, Phillip M. Fisher, or Homer Eon Flint. There is a brooding sense of the weird about this story. It appeared in the same issue of *All-Story Weekly* as Part One of Giesy's "Palos of the Dog Star Pack." Jim Crawley is intrigued by the terrible fear of a neighbor, Vincent Noyes. Noyes has a beautiful cat named Abdullah, which appears to have a human mind. He is being pursued by a woman named Ires and has been followed all the way from India. Some days later Crawley finds Noyes murdered in a deserted house and the next day apprehends a mysterious woman visitor in the dead man's apartment. It seems that she, too, is in the power of some weird force, and Crawley decides to help her. It develops that she is in the power of Devil Ritter who has developed a force called the "thought wave," a type of mental telepathy. He has the power to steal into another person's mind and use their brain. He can read thoughts across the world through the vibrations of the universe. The girl is Ritter's special "medium" through whom he is attuned to the thoughts of all his victims. Through his hypnotic power Ritter calls the girl back to him after she has fled with Crawley. Crawley finds the address of Ritter's secret house in New York and goes to find her and kill Ritter. Ritter has a huge blond giant named Boone, who guards him. Crawley breaks in on them, conquers even the mighty Boone, and carries the girl away. She is in a strange trance.

The following night Ritter follows them up to New Haven where they have fled and enters their rooms. They are powerless before his will. And then when hope seems gone—the climax comes in a most dramatic way. Abdullah, the cat, is up on the mantel over the fireplace. He is afraid of Devil Ritter, and in moving away from him the cat dislodges a heavy bronze satyr which drops squarely on the Devil's forehead, killing him instantly. They are freed from the spell with his death.

Perhaps the main reason why "That Receding Brow" is quite rare is accounted for by the fact that it appeared in the issue of *All-Story Weekly* which also carried Part One of the famous Merritt serial, "The Conquest of the Moon Pool." The story begins in a zoo where a foolish young man goads a huge orangutan to attack him through the bars. He is saved by a queer old gentleman who seems to be able to speak the language of the ape. The director of the zoo, Olaf Thorwalt, arrives in time to witness the scene. He is strangely attracted to the powerful old gentleman who has a receding brow and bears a marked resemblance to an ape. He goes to visit the old man that night. The balance of the novelette is a tale told by the old man (William Cory) about his experiences in Africa with the famous explorer, Alexander Middleton. Middleton journeyed into the interior of Africa with twenty-five picked adventurers in search of the missing link. Over half of the men die or are killed on the way. After enduring unspeakable hardships, they at last reach the immense hidden valley and find that it is actually inhabited by a race of *Pithecanthropi erecti* (erect apes).

Middleton makes friends with one of the tree dwellers and finds it to be halfway between the higher apes and man in the scale of evolution. As he starts to carry it back to civilization, its mate comes through the trees, calling it. It breaks away to go to its mate, and in desperation Middleton fires, killing the female. The tree-dweller sorrowfully takes its dead mate in its arms and carries it away into the forest, and the greatest scientific discovery of the age is lost forever. According to the voodoo guide, the tree-dweller throws a curse on the party saying: ''All will die but one, and he shall live in death.'' One by one the members of the expedition die on the return trip until only Middleton is left. He finally reaches civilization but is ill of fever for months. As he recovers, he changes and becomes as the tree-dwellers—by implication the famous explorer, Alexander Middleton, and William Cory, the old man with the receding brow, are one and the same.

''The Lost Garden'' appeared in *All-Story Weekly* and was reprinted in the December 1941 issue of *Famous Fantastic Mysteries*. As the title implies, it is the tale of a weird and beautiful garden and of a phantom love. Henry Arsigny, a rich young American, settles down in a little village near Bordeaux and becomes a recluse. The years roll by, and the teller of the story becomes a friend and is invited to dinner one night. The servants are serving the magnificent meal when he arrives. Two guest chairs are apparently empty, and yet the plates are being served as though living people were present. It seems that this is the ''special'' night when Monsieur Arsigny must be alone with his imaginary guests. This night comes but once a year. When Arsigny sees himself intruded upon, he springs to his feet and draws his dagger—but, seeing who it is, he finally invites him to sit down, asking the servants to lay another plate. Then he tells the story of the lost garden of Marie Vivraine, his youthful lover in New Orleans, of that strange man, James Baron, who dreamed of the lost garden of five hundred years ago—and of their second meeting in France. There was an enactment of the tragic event that had been foredoomed five hundred years before when Baron and Marie in a queer flashback to a former existence stepped off the high balcony of the tavern onto the stairs that were not there—and which have not been there for nameless generations. And so Henry Arsigny bought the old Château and restored the lost garden to life and lives with his memories.

Under the pseudonym of George Challis, Faust made an attempt to write a science fiction thriller. This novel, ''The Smoking Land,'' was a six-part serial in *Argosy*. Far to the north of any civilization, locked in the jaws of the glaciers of the Ice Pole region, lies the mysterious unknown island called the Smoking Land. Smoky Cassidy is hunting for it because when his friend, Cleveland Darrell, disappears, he leaves an odd message behind him: ''Bound north of Alaska to the Smoking Land. . . .'' Reaching the land at last, he finds it a strange and terrible place. The people dress in the garb of sixteenth-century England and speak in the archaic tongue. But in the subterranean caverns there are electricity, machines, and scientific progress advanced to an unheard-of degree.

From Sylvia, priestess of the nameless goddess, Smoky learns that the wise men who live in the core of the Flaming Mountain can tell him about Cleve Darrell. She offers to lead him there, past the Fountain of Life, which is nothing more than an open volcanic crater. To save her from spurting lava, Smoky carries her beyond the portal which is forbidden to all priestesses of the goddess. For this, Sylvia is put on trial for her life, and one of the judges is Cleve Darrell—the same Cleve Darrell, except for premature white hair and a haunting fear in his eyes. Showing no recognition of his old friend, Darrell rises and sentences Smoky and the girl to be beheaded.

Later Darrell visits Smoky in his cell and reveals that he was only acting a part and will try to save him. Darrell tells the story of his disappearance and something of the great scientific power of this lost race of people. Smoky and Darrell manage to steal one of the great air ships and escape with Sylvia. However, they have to crash land on an ice floe to elude the silver ships of their pursuers. They are bombed and thought to be dead but are saved by a cave-like opening. After weary months they reach civilization. Their strange story is not told to a skeptical public.

'' 'Sunset' Wins,'' a novelette by George Owen Baxter in *Western Story Magazine* that Faust originally titled "The Dream of Macdonald," is an addition to the sparse list of the Faust tales of fantasy. An off-the-trail yarn—it begins in Scotland with the Macdonald Clan and the Connells of Connell Castle, and traces these clans down into England, and then over to the American Colonies. The prologue brings the clans through the Revolution and the Civil War. We then come down to modern days—a Macdonald marries a Connell in New York City. The story concerns their son, Gordon Macdonald, a huge, powerful, red-headed lad—a throwback to his mighty Scottish ancestors of the past.

Gordon Macdonald's career starts as a lad in New York, but in the first few pages of the novel he has had adventures and scraps in Australia and Bombay, India, traveled across the Himalayas and across Tibet, seen the interior of Russia and Siberia, then to Brazil and South America. He deserts ship in Mexico and rides across the border into Texas, and all this has happened before he is nineteen years old. Many adventures are skipped over lightly and the last few paragraphs of the first chapter cover ten years, during which time "Red" Macdonald has become the most feared fighter in the West.

In Chapter Two he meets the great stallion, Sunset, which is a turning point in his life. The rest of the novel is difficult to describe. Highly fantastic, it is comparable to "John Ovington Returns" in that he seems to be living over again situations from a former existence. He has strange dreams that always turn into reality. On one occasion ghosts of all the men he has killed all over the world come back to taunt him at a banquet table. Macdonald, that magnificent and evil brute, kills each one of them all over again! The pursuit of the red horse, Sunset, leads him on to his death. The tale is a Western tragedy like THE SEVENTH MAN, as the hero goes bravely out to meet fate. Woven into the story is one of the most doomed and tender love affairs to be found in Faust's fiction.

FOREVER UNTAMED: FAUST'S INDIAN FICTION FROM "BEYOND THE OUTPOSTS" TO THE RED HAWK TRILOGY

Edgar L. Chapman

This essay is an expansion of the author's Introduction to THE LEGEND OF THUNDER MOON by Max Brand, published with a restored text by the University of Nebraska Press in fall 1996.

I

Frederick Faust seems to have felt a special sympathy for North American Indians, especially the Plains tribes, and his fiction about them constitutes a subgenre in itself as Robert and Jane Easton have observed in THE COLLECTED STORIES OF MAX BRAND. No doubt Faust's identification with native Americans grew out of his own sense of deprivation and dispossession and his general alienation from the American myths of progress and prosperity. Having experienced poverty and rejection in his youth in the San Joaquin Valley, Faust could imaginatively project himself into the experience of the Indian peoples who had been shoved aside in the nation's rush to fulfill its "manifest destiny."

Faust's fiction about Indians began rather tentatively, but, as Robert Easton noted in a letter to me dated, January 23, 1995, he gradually acquired a considerable library of books about native American cultures, and he began to describe the Indian presence in the American West more confidently. In the process of writing numerous stories with Indian characters, his understanding deepened, and his fascination with Plains Indian mythology, especially that of the Cheyennes, grew. In addition to making the Indians' traditional culture more accessible to his readers, Faust's work gradually moves away from many conventional attitudes about the Indians. By the end of his career in writing Western stories, Faust's work had transcended stereotypes and undoubtedly created much sympathy for his Indian characters while demonstrating many evils of white racism.

It is notable that his writing on this theme quickly grew independent of formulaic compromises and encouraged his readers to identify with native American and "white Indian" characters who view the claims of white civilization with skepticism. Near the close of Faust's career as a pulp author he developed one of his most memorable creations, the white Indian, Rusty Sabin, who becomes deeply estranged from both white society and the tribal life of the Cheyennes at the end of the trilogy of novels devoted to him.

Rusty's alienation mirrors the ambivalence that Faust felt about North American society throughout his career. In Faust's debut as a Western writer he produced a mythic figure, Dan Barry, who cannot abandon the wilderness and accept accommodation to the "civilized world." As he came to the end of his career as a Western writer, Faust produced three memorable heroes of his stature—Silvertip, the Montana Kid, and Rusty Sabin—all of whom seem unable to accommodate themselves to society and progress. Each of the three embodies some of the values Faust had celebrated in THE UNTAMED. It should surely be no surprise that Faust's white Indian characters also provide a symbolic means of expressing some of Faust's alienation.

It has been observed that the Indian has been alternately demonized and eulogized as a noble savage throughout American history. Today the process seems to continue in the attitudes of "political correctness" and "multi-culturalism" where the Indian is once again being lauded not as a person but as a symbol of pastoral tranquillity and reverence for nature. The history of this process is described in Robert Berkhofer's THE WHITE MAN'S INDIAN (Knopf, 1978) where we learn that, after the Puritans used the imagery of demonism to portray Indians, Enlightenment thinkers like Benjamin Franklin and Philip Freneau turned toward the myth of the noble savage as a way of opposing primitive virtue to the bigotry and chicanery of "civilization." Such alternating attitudes were to continue to flourish both among intellectuals and in the world of popular culture throughout the nineteenth century and in the early twentieth century when Faust began writing.

In the era of American Romanticism (roughly 1815–1865) writers like James Fenimore Cooper, Washington Irving, and Henry W. Longfellow and such painters as George Catlin and Karl Bodmer were depicting Indians as noble hunters and warriors while lamenting their imminent eclipse by white civilization. Yet this was also the age of Indian removal west of the Mississippi and the tragic "Trail of Tears" walked by the Five Civilized Tribes of the Southeast when social and political leaders like Andrew Jackson, who had little use for Indians and their culture, were forcibly dispossessing many Indian nations of their ancestral lands.

Indian resistance to westward expansion reached its climax in the post–Civil War era of the 1870s and 1880s when the Apaches, the Plains Indians, and major mountain tribes such as the Utes and Nez Percés became embroiled in bitter wars before being forced to accept confinement to reservation life. This era was accompanied by a harsh transformation of the image of the Indian from benevolent savage to destructive menace. While a few intellectuals such as Helen Hunt Jackson spoke out against the nation's policies of shameful dealing with the Indians, which she documented in A CENTURY OF DISHONOR (1881), more belligerent attitudes prevailed among the noisy majority, especially during the era of the strongest Indian resistance. This was demonstrated in the last chapter of the tragic story of Indian resistance in the mixture of white fear and bloodlust aroused during the Ghost Dance period (1889–1890). When a Paiute shaman used the Ghost Dance ritual to spread his vision of a return to the freedom and plenty in the days of the buffalo, his message found ardent support. But, just as messianic dreams tend to stir hopes in defeated peoples, they produce guilt and apprehension in the conquerors. The result was a series of white and Indian confrontations, culminating in the tragic massacre of the Sioux at Wounded Knee in 1890. This event, which marked the end of organized Indian resistance to the "manifest destiny" of the United States, was hailed as a heroic victory by many popular newspapers in the dominant culture. Indeed, such oracles of popular opinion as *The Police Gazette* rejoiced in the result, as though it were a triumph comparable to the defeat of the Sioux nation under Crazy Horse instead of a mishandled police action.[1] The U.S. government apparently agreed, for, as Peter Matthiessen noted in IN THE SPIRIT OF CRAZY HORSE (Viking, 1983), the soldiers involved in the Wounded Knee massacre were given decorations despite the scorn of hardened officers like General Nelson Miles.

Meanwhile, the dime novel Western and the nineteenth-century stage contributed to thoughtless popular views by depicting the Indian as a bloodthirsty fiend or convenient antagonist for the noble Western hero, though, of course, these fiction writers would occasionally throw in a sympathetic Indian as an occasional friend of the white man.[2] Early twentieth-century fiction about the frontier West was more literate but scarcely kinder in attitude. Owen Wister's overpraised THE VIRGINIAN (Macmillan, 1902) brings in some Indians who have left the reservation to make trouble in 1890s' Wyoming as stage props to demonstrate the Virginian's skill with a six-gun and allow him to sustain a wound from which Molly Stark Wood can conveniently nurse him back to health.

Other writers in what has been considered the Sentimental Age (1900–1920) of the Western novel were not much different. Frederic Remington made use of a white Indian motif in JOHN ERMINE OF THE YELLOWSTONE (Macmillan, 1902), but his hero is obliged to struggle for acceptance and must die tragically. In general, the writers of Western novels of this era, including Harold Bell Wright, Rex Beach, Emerson Hough, William MacLeod Raine, Clarence E. Mulford, and B. M. Bower, preferred to write about the ranching life in the West after the Indian wars or to use Indians as mere antagonists for the hero. Their readers seldom were expected to feel much interest about Indian culture or sympathy for the Indian point of view.

The chief exception here is Zane Grey whose experiences with Navajos in

Arizona and Utah had created admiration and empathy. In THE RAINBOW TRAIL (Harper, 1915) Grey attempts in one digressive chapter to give a poetic rendering of the Navajo's daily life style, and he returned to this theme in THE VANISHING AMERICAN (Harper, 1925) when he described a tragic romance between a Navajo and a white woman from the East.[3] Such surprisingly imaginative sympathy for the Indian found an echo in an even more unexpected source, a pair of novels by another adventure writer, Edgar Rice Burroughs, which may have been written because of the publication of Grey's work and because of Faust's early Indian novels. Both THE WAR CHIEF (A.C. McClurg, 1927) and APACHE DEVIL (Burroughs, 1933) depict vigorously the exploits of a daring white Indian who is the adopted son of the Apache chieftain, Geronimo, scarcely the most popular Indian leader in white legend. A man who admired a heroic and "primitive" life style, Burroughs had some experience as a cavalry soldier in Arizona campaigns against maverick Apaches, and there he apparently came to admire rather than detest his antagonists.[4]

By 1925 Frederick Faust seems to have become increasingly interested in the tribal culture and vanished world of the Indians, and during the next decade he regularly produced novels and stories with Indians as major and minor characters. Unlike Grey and Burroughs, who drew on personal experience, however limited, Faust had enjoyed few opportunities to learn about Indian culture first-hand (especially the Plains Indian culture, since Faust grew up in northern California in 1892–1914 and then resided in New York and Italy for much of his adult life). He was obliged to turn for information and inspiration to scholarly books.

II

There were numerous books on the Indians and the Great Plains in Faust's personal library (now owned by the Easton family), including what must be considered three major sources on Plains Indian life. These comprise several books by George Bird Grinnell and important works by George Catlin and James Willard Schultz.[5] Although Grinnell was by far the most important source for Faust, as he was for some later authors, each of these sources made important contributions to Faust's work.

Catlin's LETTERS AND NOTES ON THE MANNERS, CUSTOMS, AND CONDITIONS OF THE NORTH AMERICAN INDIANS, WRITTEN DURING EIGHT YEARS TRAVEL (1832–1839), AMONGST THE WILDEST TRIBES OF INDIANS OF NORTH AMERICA (1841), the earliest of the books, was a significant resource for a number of reasons. NORTH AMERICAN INDIANS—to shorten its title somewhat—records Catlin's observations and experiences of several Indian tribes during a period where they flourished as lords of the plains, living handsomely off the buffalo they hunted on horseback. Several of Faust's stories are set in the time of Catlin's westward journeys, or shortly thereafter, and the presence of numerous illustrative sketches and color plates in the fine edition Faust owned must have been invaluable to him.

The somewhat Byronic Catlin (1796–1872) was an energetic painter who came of age during the era of the Romantic movement in America. When, like many other painters of his time, Catlin turned from portraiture to landscape and Indian subjects, he suddenly found his calling and pursued this vocation with zeal. Though self-taught rather than formally trained as a painter, Catlin made numerous trips to the Great Plains and the upper reaches of the Missouri, sketching and painting Indians of many nations. At the same time he shrewdly recorded his observations and impressions. His letters, journals, and notes were eventually published as a massive record of his wanderings. Although Catlin was an ambitious entrepreneur who intended to profit handsomely and become a celebrity in New York and Europe (as indeed he did), he was also genuinely fascinated by his subjects and probably less affected by the mythology of the noble savage than many painters of his generation. Although, as Brian Dippie indicated in CATLIN AND HIS CONTEMPORARIES (University of Nebraska Press, 1990), Catlin often sought government patronage for his work, in fact Congress and Presidents who were constantly squabbling over slavery, Indian removal, and manifest destiny had little time or money to spend on American art or ethnography. However, Catlin's writing about the Indian peoples he met in the as yet unfenced Great Plains is extremely valuable, and, indeed, Catlin's NORTH AMERICAN INDIANS has been cited as one of three major ethnographic works dealing with the Plains Indians prior to the Civil War. It is clear that Faust drew on Catlin for his portraits of Plains Indian life in THE STONE THAT SHINES (Five Star Westerns, 1997), the Thunder Moon novels, and VENGEANCE TRAIL.

Faust's second major resource was the pioneering work in ethnography by George Bird Grinnell (1849–1938). Though Grinnell was trained as a zoologist in a time when anthropology was in its early stages, he traveled widely in the West, even accompanying General Custer on his fateful Black Hills expedition of 1874. In later years Grinnell devoted his summers to the collection of Indian folklore and observation of Indian cultures, including the Blackfeet, the Pawnees, and most significantly the Cheyennes. Eventually Grinnell would publish the fruits of his years of careful study in THE FIGHTING CHEYENNES (Scribner, 1915) and THE CHEYENNE INDIANS (Yale, 1923). These massive works are now considered classics of ethnographic research and brought Grinnell enormous respect (including an honorary degree from Yale, his alma mater). Grinnell's influence on Faust's novels, especially those dealing with Cheyenne life, is immense and clearly obvious from the beginning in the first Cheyenne magazine serial, "The Squaw Boy," published in book form as LOST WOLF.[6]

Finally, the third important source for Faust was the work of James Willard Schultz, especially his memorable MY LIFE AS AN INDIAN (Doubleday, Page, 1907). Schultz (1859–1947) was a nonconformist with interesting parallels to Faust. According to his biographer, Warren L. Hanna, Schultz as a youth had fled from a conventional life at a military academy in New York state following the death of his father, going first to St. Louis in 1877 and then to the upper Missouri River country and Fort Benton in Montana, as the mountain men had once done. Before long, as Hanna relates in his THE LIFE AND TIMES OF JAMES WILLARD SCHULTZ (University of Oklahoma Press, 1986), Schultz began living with the Piegan Blackfeet where he learned the language and culture, after a time acquiring the name of Apikuni and marrying a Blackfoot woman. Eventually Schultz separated himself from tribal life, but he always tended to reside in remote wilderness areas. After the turn of the century Schultz began publishing articles about his life as a white Indian in various popular magazines. These helped to solidify his friendship with Grinnell, who encouraged Schultz's writing, and the result was the publication of MY LIFE AS AN INDIAN which imposes fictional patterns on autobiographical fact. Other books followed, including some avowed fiction, books that inspired a good deal of controversy. Schultz championed Indians and became involved in conservation enterprises, especially the establishment of Glacier National Park. To many in his time he seemed abrasive, unconventional, and iconoclastic, though he always had a staunch defender in Grinnell, a major influence on his work.

William Bloodworth is of the view that Faust first became aware of Schultz's MY LIFE AS AN INDIAN in 1926. Although Faust only occasionally uses the Blackfeet culture in his fiction (notably in MOUNTAIN GUNS and the important late story, "Outcast Breed"), Schultz's book probably did exert an important influence on his earlier work. It was valuable not only in describing everyday Indian life but also in demonstrating how the consciousness of a white Indian operates in a man who has deliberately moved outside his native culture. Knowledge of Schultz's work probably gave Faust greater confidence in dealing with this theme in his own stories.

Although how closely Faust read his sources must remain a matter of conjecture, study of his works dealing with Indians of varied background suggests that eventually he became an authority on Plains Indian culture and rather deeply attracted to Cheyenne mythology as depicted both in Grinnell's major works and in his collections of folk tales. It also is possible that for a number of reasons, commercial as well as personal, Faust tended to avoid the tragic drama of the decline of Indian culture, even if, like Catlin, he was strongly drawn to the world of freedom and heroic action that he associated with the Plains Indians before they became ensnared in their final wars with the advancing white civilization.

Faust's Westerns using Indians as important characters began to appear in 1925, starting with the serial, "Beyond the Outposts." His reasons for turning to this theme were complex, but surely the era of Indian independence and nomadic freedom appealed strongly to his imagination. From the beginning Faust had tended to reject, emotionally and imaginatively, the myth of progress involved in the conquest of the West as the Dan Barry trilogy demonstrates vividly. In fact, despite his concession to convention in the happy endings of his novels, Faust differs sharply from the writers of the Sentimental Age of the Western story (Wister, Grey, Bower, Raine, Hough, and so on) in being strongly alienated from the dominant middle-class American values that they espoused. Faust, somewhat like Cooper in THE PRAIRIE (1827) and Catlin nearly a century earlier, felt drawn to the "golden age" of the Plains Indians, before their free and nomadic life style was destroyed by the historical process.

We should also note here that until about 1925 Faust's novels generally appear to be set somewhat vaguely in the period 1890–1914, when the West was already largely settled and the frontier had supposedly been closed officially by the government (1890). This was an age of railroads, cattle barons, and outlaws like Butch Cassidy's wild bunch and the Dalton gang who, as earlier gangs, followed a tradition of lawlessness. Yet there was also an atmosphere of the fading of the lawless or "untamed" West, a mood found in Stephen Crane's anti-heroic Western stories like "The Bride Comes to Yellow Sky." Learned minds were reflecting on the importance of the fading frontier in the American past, as reflected in historian Frederick Jackson Turner's famous essay. This period was also the age of Faust's childhood, youth, and college years (1892–1915). Despite the appearance of the telephone and the occasional automobile, the West remained a challenging physical setting and a region of the mind where mythic conflicts could exist. Though the herds of buffalo and Indians in nomadic state belonged to an earlier generation and had receded into legend, the Western era between 1890 and World War I was available as a region of the imagination, as a continuing arena for traditional conflicts and tests of manhood.

By the middle twenties, however, with the triumph of the automobile and post–World War I technology, it was much harder for a writer to pretend that the untamed West was actually a contemporary fact. Faust turned to what was clearly an earlier and legendary time in his Westerns dealing with Indians. It is not surprising that he should have turned to the high point of the Plains Indians' culture for imaginative release—when the combination of the horse, the buffalo hunt, and effective weapons created a sense of extraordinary freedom. Nor is it surprising that he would employ white Indian figures in his fiction, since they permitted the same imaginative identification as his mythic hero, Dan Barry, a character strongly allied with the "untamed" wilderness.

In his first Indian novel-length story, "Beyond the Outposts," it almost seems enough for the main characters to break away from white civilization to find the boundless prairies. This episodic story is narrated by Lew Dorset, an aged frontiersman, recalling his youth. This narrator is also the hero, though he begins inauspiciously as the son of a reckless Southern feudist, a man whose killing of some members of a rival clan make him an outlaw. Initially Lew goes westward, not from wanderlust but to find his fugitive father who has escaped hanging by flight to the territory "beyond the outposts."[7] As the title suggests, the setting is the era of Catlin, when the West was a seemingly boundless expanse of Indians and buffalo. Somewhere near Council Bluffs Lew is hired by a train of freighters, after one of the leaders, Chris Hudson, befriends him. But Lew also antagonizes a handsome young frontiersman, Chuck Morris. After a brief period of mutual enmity they fight, gain respect for each other, and become friends. Together they work as hunters for the wagon train of freighters. Though Dorset is slightly better skilled with rifle and revolver than Morris, Lew defers to Morris's superior charm and education until he learns that Morris lacks moral discernment. In this the two show a resemblance to Tom Sawyer and Huckleberry Finn.

Although the plot unfolds in episodic and picaresque fashion, it eventually involves the Sioux and Pawnees in a series of events of questionable credibility. While Dorset and Morris are hunting, their companions in the wagon train are massacred by Cheyennes whom Dorset forever after condemns as murderers— a surprising circumstance, given Faust's persistent preference for the Cheyennes in later novels. Dorset and Morris set off for revenge and attack the party of drunken Cheyennes, killing several. To escape pursuit, they take refuge in a Sioux village ruled by a powerful chief, Standing Bear, and become friendly with the chief's brother, Three Buck Elk. In the ensuing action the pair become heroes for the Sioux when they help defend their village against the Pawnees. Both white men are allowed to join the tribe and spend several years with the Sioux who are consistently depicted as admirable, though Faust provides little detail about their culture. If ''Beyond the Outposts'' may demonstrate that Faust could do a suspenseful serial about Indians living on the plains, it is marred by clichés of plot, and its treatment of Indians is superficial. Though Faust presents his narrator/hero as a man who learns high and honorable values from the Sioux, little attention is given to Sioux culture or mythology. In future stories he would seldom mention the Sioux.

When he produced LOST WOLF as a serial and its sequel, THE WHITE CHEYENNE, Faust turned to a portrayal of the Cheyennes, and this time he chose to exploit the white Indian theme by narrating the adventures of a white warrior reared from childhood by the Cheyennes. Though the treatment of Cheyenne tribal life is more superficial than in later stories, Faust's sympathy for the Cheyennes and their world is already apparent. Here, Faust's depiction of the Cheyenne world is knowledgeable enough to suggest that he had already discovered Grinnell's books. Though William Bloodworth in his MAX BRAND has implied that they did not influence him until later, internal evidence, such as Faust's insistence on the chastity of Cheyenne women and the Cheyennes' high standard of honor, courage, and cleverness, argues otherwise.

However, both LOST WOLF and THE WHITE CHEYENNE are novels about a white Indian rather than depictions of Cheyenne life. Their spirited hero is Glanvil Tucker whose parents are killed while traveling in an emigrant train by a raiding party of Cheyennes. After capture the boy is adopted by the Cheyennes, and over the next seven years he acquires a thoroughly Cheyenne consciousness as well as tribal renown. Though the lad, known as White Badger, learns self-reliance and becomes a Cheyenne trickster as well as a famous warrior, he is renamed Lost Wolf by the Pawnees, traditional enemies of the Cheyennes, and eventually finds himself in a limbo between white and red cultures. After capture by the Pawnees he is saved from death by a mountain man, Danny Croyden, who purchases Lone Wolf from a Pawnee leader. Croyden becomes Lost Wolf's new mentor, teaching him the rudiments of white civilization during a five-year sojourn in the mountains. But neither the white world nor the Cheyenne world are fully able to contain the boy's energy and exuberance; at times he seems a force of nature, like Dan Barry, Faust's archetypal Western hero. The novel thus ends with the question of Lost Wolf's psychological orientation unresolved.

In attempting to portray a white hero with a Cheyenne mind, Faust clearly fails to develop the possibilities of this theme in LOST WOLF or THE WHITE CHEYENNE, but they do provide foreshadowings of future works. In the latter novel time has elapsed, and a minister's daughter, Peggy Gleason, is a great beauty who wins the hearts of many swains in Zander City, including the first-person narrator, a scapegrace gambler of a respected family in Charleston, South Carolina. This narrator's comments about Indians, despite some limitations, reveal a fair-minded spirit in contrast to the conventional frontier attitudes of Zander City. Though some think the Cheyennes must be "red devils" and that no one should keep faith with the Cheyennes, the narrator believes otherwise:

Taking them first to last, I suppose the Cheyenne was the finest fighting man among the Indians of North America. They were big strapping fellows; they felt that, man for man, they were the heroes of the world. They carried the impress of this self-confidence in their faces.

Running Deer was an exception among an exceptional lot. He was made like a Greek athlete of the youthful type. He looked like his name, composed specifically for grace and speed, and he had a handsome face. Change the color of his skin, and any white mother would have been glad to have him as one of her children.

Moreover, the narrator deplores the bitter feeling between Indians and whites on the frontier, finding both races to blame. Commenting on Zander City's reaction to Running Deer and the Indian's contempt for his white captors, Faust's narrator observes that: "The longer you looked the more you could see the horrible antipathy of race for race, with a million years which would have to be unlived before the two could understand one another. The whites looked upon the Cheyenne as if he were a brute fashioned in the shape of a man more or less by accident. The Cheyenne, behind his mask of indifference, regarded the whites as snakes whose fangs it would be a virtuous act to draw." Despite this mutual antipathy, Lost Wolf sends a messenger to begin negotiations for an exchange of prisoners between whites and Cheyennes; Lost Wolf offers a frontier bully named The Doctor in exchange for his friend, Running Deer. While listening to the good citizens of Zander City debate the matter, the gambler/narrator is appalled to learn how easily some can suggest a treacherous plan to get The Doctor back while keeping Running Deer and trying him for murder.

While denying that he supports the Indians, Faust's narrator concludes that "the conduct of the people of Zander was very scoundrelly on this occasion."

Whatever one thinks of Faust's presentation of the conflict between Indian and white, it is obvious that the author does not subscribe to conventional views of white and Indian relationships. Quoting a speech by the minister, Bloodworth condemns THE WHITE CHEYENNE for perpetuating stereotypes about native Americans, but this speech does not represent either the narrator's views or the dominant theme of the book. It can only be justified on grounds of realistic characterization: the minister is a moral man but somewhat obtuse about certain issues. In the event this novel is diverted from a conflict over Cheyenne rights between Lost Wolf and the frontiersmen of Zander City by what is essentially a Western "taming of the shrew" motif. Seeing Peggy, Lost Wolf, who has come to town to free his Cheyenne blood brother from white captivity, loses his heart. At the novel's close Lost Wolf appears ready to leave the Cheyenne world for the difficult business of adjusting to white culture. Though he now has a powerful motivation for accepting white culture in his desire to marry Peggy Gleason, his future may remain problematical. Faust shrugs off the difficulties of the white Indian's acceptance of a more authoritarian civilization through suggesting that Lost Wolf's talent for role-playing will be equal to any difficulties. The last words of summing up about Lost Wolf belong to his former mentor, Danny Croydon, who says: "What he doesn't know by teaching, he knows by instinct. I think that lad will find a way to get on with the whites when he bends his mind to it." In the Red Hawk novels of ten years later Faust would offer a more tragic point of view.

III

After this spirited pair of novels about Lost Wolf, Faust might have been expected to return to fictional treatments of the Cheyennes the following year. But, while he continued to use the first-person point of view in his next serial of the Plains Indians, "The Trail of the Stone-That-Shines," this tale offers something different: a portrayal of life among the Mandans. The result is an unusual and somewhat more realistic story. "The Trail of the Stone-That-Shines" is again set in the Catlin era of the Plains tribes, and more than any other Faust novel it reflects the influence of Catlin's observations. Among accounts of his time only Catlin gives detailed descriptions of the tribal life of the Mandans, a people later destroyed by disease and warfare with other Indians. Friendly to Lewis and Clark, the Mandans were a light-skinned nation who lived in semi-permanent wooden "earth lodges" along the Missouri River and engaged in rudimentary agriculture. Although the plot of the story deals mainly with the search of two white adventurers for treasure, their life among the Mandans affords Faust the opportunity to describe daily tribal life more authentically than before.

In the description of the Mandan "city" his narrator comments on the crowding and smoke usually found in an earth lodge at night, the constant noise of dogs and crying infants that white visitors noted in Indian villages, and the importance of shamans and their visions, sacred "medicine pouches," and sacramental objects. All this is observed during the sojourn of Faust's white adventurer among the Mandans. Although the plot relies on familiar conventions, Faust's characterizations are sharply and often amusingly drawn. The narrator is Christy Deever, another Huck Finn type, a fatherless lad from Georgia who has been employed as a servant and companion by a Virginia gentleman called The Colonel. The Colonel, a genuinely honest and fearless man but unfortunately an inveterate romantic fond of grandiloquent speech and impulsive quixotic gestures, gains Christy's affection but also provides a ready target for his barbed wit. At times the pair may remind us of a frontier Don Quixote and Sancho Panza, though here it is the Sancho Panza figure who narrates the story.

The serial opens on a note of farcical romanticism. As Christy is about to enter adolescence, The Colonel's fondness for cards, together with bad judgment in playing them, has depleted his fortunes and frustrated his plan to wed the beautiful but tart-tongued belle, Martha Farnsworth. Miss Farnsworth, who clearly loves The Colonel despite his obvious flaws, sends her improvident swain westward in the hope that he can make enough money to mend his fortunes. Traveling on the Great Plains without any specific plan, The Colonel and Christy befriend a Mandan who takes them to live with his tribe. After helping the Mandans during a thunderstorm and later coming to their aid against their traditional enemies, the Sioux, The Colonel wins the trust of the tribe because of his kindness, courage, and simplicity. Still seeking wealth, The Colonel decides, on Christy's advice, to try to find the source of the quartz which provides a medicine stone for a warrior and shaman known as Stone-That-Shines. (This visionary, by the way, is treated with more sympathy than Faust usually shows toward Indian "medicine men": in many of the early Indian stories Faust tends to assume the conventional white attitude that Indian shamans are pious frauds. Stone-That-Shines, in fact, is a faint early sketch for Red Hawk, the hero of Faust's final white Indian trilogy.) The Colonel is more interested in the metal in Stone-That-Shines's medicine stone than in his visions. Both The Colonel and Christy realize that, if they can find the mother lode from which it was taken, The Colonel may be able to find the wealth he seeks. After they set out to follow the shaman's ambiguous directions to the source of the stone, they encounter difficulties when the Colonel, rejecting Christy's wiser judgment, is friendly to The Quail, the most beautiful maiden in the village. Her infatuation with The Colonel, which he has innocently encouraged, causes her to steal horses and weapons and abandon the tribe to follow them. Unfortunately her love for the Colonel has aroused the jealous ire of the war chief, who is determined to win The Quail. Thus her involvement in the story produces its share of melodramatic complications before Christy and The Colonel are free to return home with their wealth.

"The Trail of the Stone-That-Shines" offers Faust's readers a fresh and deeper understanding of Plains Indian culture. Faust's dramatization of the importance of the sacred or symbolic object, the stone-that-shines, would be echoed in later novels. Moreover, despite the tendency of his Indian stories to portray shamans as frauds, this serial demonstrates Faust's growing interest in Plains Indian mythology.[8]

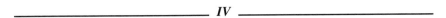

IV

In THE BORDER BANDIT Faust featured Indian characters in a divergence from the white Indian motif: he turned to the theme of masculine bonding, or a close relationship between the white hero and an Indian warrior. To be sure, Faust had touched this convention lightly in "Beyond the Outposts," but he exploited the idea more thoroughly in THE BORDER BANDIT and a number of subsequent novels. In the wide-ranging saga of THE BORDER BANDIT Faust describes the transformation of a sentimental New England gentleman into a defiant Western outlaw. One feature of this metamorphosis involves the hero's winning both a deadly enemy and a close friend in a nearby Indian nation, this time the Comanches who roam the southern Texas border. Because of a foolish insult to a Comanche chief strolling the street of the border town of Siddon Flat, the haughty Oliver Tay finds himself kidnapped and sold into servitude in a Mexican silver mine (the setting is roughly the Santa Anna era when convict labor was routinely used in Mexican mines). Surviving this ordeal and transformed from an Eastern milksop into a formidable hero, Oliver later gains the grudging friendship of Yellow Wolf, a Comanche warrior.

Hereafter Faust was to adopt the practice of establishing a close relationship between the hero and at least one admirable native American in a number of succeeding stories. In SAWDUST AND SIXGUNS Anthony Castracane, a circus athlete who is insulted and turned into an outlaw on the post–Civil War frontier, befriends an Osage warrior in a fight against the Pawnees. The Osage friend becomes almost his only supporter as "Mad" Anthony fights to win back his honor. In THE RESCUE OF BROKEN ARROW Faust returned to a variation of the white Indian motif when an Irish rascal named Bandon Cashel is expelled from a wagon train heading to Oregon, once again set in the Catlin era. Soon Cashel becomes a guest of the Cheyennes and eventually a hero of the tribe after leading them in a daring rescue of Broken Arrow, a chief who has been captured by the Pawnees. In another version of this plot, VENGEANCE TRAIL, Faust produced a splendid adventure for young adults. Here Johnnie Tanner, the son of an impoverished woman who manages a New York boarding house, goes westward to follow a thief who has stolen his father's Navy Colt. Again the period is the Catlin era, and Johnnie, traveling down the Ohio River in a steamboat, joins forces with a mountain man, Hank Raney. The two follow the trail of the thief to the Great Plains where, "beyond the outposts," they sojourn with a Cheyenne tribe. Eventually Johnnie becomes a hero of the Cheyennes when he aids them in their ongoing war against the Pawnees.

In the process he recovers his father's revolver—which is a kind of talisman representing Johnnie's self-esteem. It had been stolen by a noted thief, Pawnee Harry, a white man who frequently lives with the Pawnees. Faust developed a similar plot on a more adult level in TAMER OF THE WILD, but this time the outcast hero, Rory Michel, befriends an Apache tribe and helps them in crucial situations. Faust's command of the dominant images and concepts of Apache culture is less extensive than his understanding of the Plains Indians. But it is notable that Faust chose to treat the Apaches sympathetically at a time when only a few Western writers seemed willing to risk championing a nation that had fought so fiercely against the U.S. cavalry.[9]

In the last three novels to be mentioned here, Faust took the theme of masculine bonding beyond a simple brotherly relationship between a white hero and an admirable Indian warrior. In each case Faust's hero leaves the white world under the cloud of a questionable moral status but finds honor and self-respect in an Indian tribal world. Even the theme of masculine bonding could be used to support the hero's quest for status, as it is in the fine adventure tale, LUCKY LARRIBEE. Here Larribee, another of Faust's disenchanted heroes, wins honor and fame through his epic pursuit of a legendary stallion, Sky Blue. On his long quest in pursuit of this magnificent horse, Larribee finds his main ally in a Cheyenne chief, Shouting Thunder, whom Larribee aids in his battles with the Pawnees and the Crows. (The Pawnees, by the way, are always honorable enemies but nevertheless the perennial antagonists of the Cheyennes, just as they are portrayed in Grinnell's books.) Larribee is never completely accepted into Shouting Thunder's tribe and must find recognition as a man of stature in the white world. LUCKY LARRIBEE is probably one of Faust's more realistic treatments of the relationship between white North Americans and the Cheyennes.

V

More interesting than the masculine bonding stories are Faust's later treatments of the white Indian motif, especially when the white protagonist is reared in an Indian tribe. Technically, of course, any adult white male in Faust's stories who voluntarily accepts Indian tribal life could be called a "white Indian," but such a person's consciousness has been greatly influenced by an upbringing in Anglo-Saxon culture. In the Lost Wolf stories Faust experimented with a hero who has been entirely raised by the Cheyennes and who is psychologically more Indian than white. In 1927–1928 he returned to the Cheyenne material and the white Indian theme to describe more vividly a hero with an Indian consciousness. This series of stories comprises the saga of Thunder Moon who is a white man reared as a Cheyenne. Thunder Moon, actually William Sutton, is kidnapped as a small baby by a Cheyenne, Big Hard Face, a warrior who can find no woman to marry him but who desires to have a son to raise. Hence, Thunder Moon grows up with a Cheyenne vision of the world.

This series is again set in what is roughly the Catlin antebellum era, and, since the dominance of the Plains tribes is contested only by other Indians, Faust is able to treat his material mainly in the spirit of rollicking comedy. Much of the humor of the saga arises from Thunder Moon's return to his ancestral Southern plantation only to find a rigidly stratified society of slaves, poor whites, and country gentlemen, a world much too constricting for his tastes. We should note that the Thunder Moon novels are somewhat episodic in their development, since they were originally published partly as full-length serials and partly as novelettes in *Far West Illustrated* and *Western Story Magazine.* Although later Dodd, Mead split them awkwardly into a three-book sequence, a more faithful publication has been undertaken by the University of Nebraska Press: THE LEGEND OF THUNDER MOON, RED WIND AND THUNDER MOON, THUNDER MOON AND THE SKY PEOPLE, and FAREWELL, THUNDER MOON.[10]

In the first Thunder Moon novel Faust describes Big Hard Face's theft of the infant William Sutton and Thunder Moon's childhood and youth among the "Suhtai," another name for the Cheyennes in their pastoral existence on the Great Plains, although according to Grinnell in THE CHEYENNE INDIANS it had originally been the name of another tribe absorbed by the Cheyennes. During Thunder Moon's maturation, he becomes immersed in the Cheyenne vision of life, accepting a mythology in which the world is influenced by the "sky people" and other spirits. Thunder Moon also becomes an able rider and hunter. Although he is something of a prankster, he grows to feel an authentic love for his adopted father, Big Hard Face, a luckless warrior who despite his valor has had trouble acquiring wealth as well as a wife. Despite his great size and athletic ability, Thunder Moon refuses to undergo the ordeal of the sundance ritual, impeded by inhibitions which Faust—in an unusually dubious point of view— attributes to his white heritage. Eventually Thunder Moon overcomes the stigma of refusing this ritual by leading some young warriors on a successful raid against the Comanches, resulting in the acquisition of many horses. This event makes Thunder Moon and his foster father wealthy, in Cheyenne terms, and creates an impressive reputation for Thunder Moon.

In the second novel in the series, RED WIND AND THUNDER MOON, Faust complicates matters by introducing an attractive Cheyenne maiden, Red Wind, who clearly intends to win Thunder Moon's love. Nevertheless, the luckless young woman is not allowed to succeed in her designs, and, in fact, Thunder Moon never seems to realize that she loves him. Instead Thunder Moon goes eastward to find his white parents and assume his white identity.

In THUNDER MOON AND THE SKY PEOPLE, though it's not very credible that Thunder Moon should be easily able to find the very plantation from which he was stolen, he does so and is recognized as William Sutton, the missing heir to the Sutton lands. What follows is at first light-hearted comedy, as the Sutton family accepts Thunder Moon as their lost son only to have him collide with the social prejudices of some of the Suttons and the neighboring planters. On his side Thunder Moon views the Sutton life style with the same irreverence as that which archetypal outsider, Huckleberry Finn, usually feels toward the social pretensions of genteel Southern aristocrats in Mark Twain's classic. To be precise, Thunder Moon's attitude toward the world of the Suttons often resembles Huck's view of the Grangerford clan and their feud over a point of honor. Thunder Moon, with a mind shaped by Cheyenne myths with their sense of cosmic forces ruling life, finds the Sutton concern over aristocratic style both touching and laughable, although his attraction to Charlotte Keene, a young white woman, develops into a passion that will ultimately lead him to abandon his Indian identity.

The tone of this novel alters somewhat when Red Wind and Big Hard Face arrive to remind Thunder Moon of his place in the Cheyenne world. The introduction of these Indians into the Sutton world of wealthy planters reveals that world's implicit racism toward native Americans. Big Hard Face is jailed on a flimsy pretext, and Thunder Moon learns with a shock that his actual father is willing to have his foster father imprisoned or murdered. Rescuing Big Hard Face, Thunder Moon flees with Red Wind and Standing Antelope, a young protégé of Thunder Moon's, apparently repudiating the aristocratic world of the Suttons. In their flight Big Hard Face is killed by a bullet from the pursuing posse, a death that provides a kind of ironic justice for his original crime of abducting William Sutton.

It is clear that Thunder Moon cannot easily reject his Cheyenne acculturation, or accept a white outlook, for he finds the Southern planter's way of life boring and ridiculous, at least after its novelty wears off. But the discovery of his genetic parents and the adventure with the Suttons also alienate Thunder Moon to some degree from his Indian upbringing, as becomes clear in the final novella of the saga, FAREWELL, THUNDER MOON (originally published in *Western Story Magazine* under the revealing title, ''Thunder Moon Goes White''). Thunder Moon eventually decides to leave the Cheyennes when, shocked to discover that there is jealousy toward him in the tribe, he chooses marriage with Charlotte, the white woman he fell in love with at the Sutton estate. His preference of Charlotte over Red Wind symbolizes his choice of the white man's road instead of the Indian vision of life. Clearly the Thunder Moon saga shows a deepening of Faust's understanding of the power of Cheyenne culture and the Cheyenne world-view. Although these stories have a good deal of rousing action, they do not add much to the sympathetic treatment of Indian life and culture that Faust had been developing in earlier novels.

VI

A more important and memorable treatment of the white Indian motif appears in the Red Hawk trilogy near the end of Faust's career as a pulp Western writer. In these novels, published in hardcovers as CALL OF THE BLOOD, BROTHER OF THE CHEYENNES, and CHEYENNE GOLD, Faust describes the way the Cheyenne vision of life influences and shapes the mind of Rusty

Sabin, a white boy adopted by the Cheyennes and raised as Red Hawk. Practically all the earlier Indian stories seem to be mere blueprints or sketches for this surprising trilogy. Whereas Lost Wolf and Thunder Moon were white lads who grew up to become formidable Cheyenne warriors, they remain primarily tricksters, despite their Cheyenne mental outlooks; but Rusty Sabin is both a warrior and a young man who becomes a visionary and a shaman. The Red Hawk novels show that the Cheyenne mythology, as described by Grinnell, by now had sunken deeper roots in Faust's imagination. Although Thunder Moon had been governed by the "sky people," Rusty actively seeks solitude and visions; in fact, he grows up to enjoy a spiritual communion with Sweet Medicine, the legendary Cheyenne culture hero. Though Rusty Sabin eventually meets his white father and learns to live in a white frontier settlement, he never relinquishes his Indian consciousness. At the end of the saga he remains more Red Hawk than Rusty Sabin.

I have treated the three novels to an extensive discussion in "The Image of the Indian in Max Brand's Pulp Western Novels" in *Heritage of Kansas* (spring 1978), but a few significant themes deserve comment here. The first novel in the trilogy, CALL OF THE BLOOD, describes the formation and growth of Rusty's Cheyenne consciousness, though we are also shown that as a tiny child he is aware of the murder of his white mother, which occurs in a scene that Faust portrays with extraordinary emotional power. In its central actions this novel depicts Rusty's fascination with the mythic vision of Cheyenne culture and his response to his own inner vision, the eye of his imagination prompted by the spirit of Sweet Medicine. Rusty's long pursuit of the legendary stallion, the White Horse, is not necessarily a logical course to follow, but he undertakes it successfully, driven by his vision of the horse's power and grace. His success affirms his reputation as a warrior who possesses "medicine," or spiritual power. In this respect the novel recapitulates motifs but with more psychological credibility than Faust had used before in his white Indian novels.

The story comes to a dramatic climax with Rusty's reunion with his biological father, Marshall Sabin, whose lifelong hatred of Indians has created his reputation as the Wind Walker, a nemesis of the red man. Again, Rusty has the opportunity to kill the dreaded foe, and common sense or the white man's logic would dictate that he fire when he has Marshall Sabin in his rifle sights. But his decision, prompted by intuition and a Cheyenne code of honor, to confront Marshall Sabin in a hand-to-hand combat leads to Marshall's discovery that Rusty, "a damned white-skinned red-hearted murderer of a Cheyenne," is indeed his lost son.

Faust's portrait of Rusty's Cheyenne consciousness remains consistent. Despite his reunion with his father, whom he admires as a warrior, Rusty continues to think as Red Hawk, his Cheyenne self, who recognizes that, while he and his father are both splendid warriors, they share little else in common. In fact, they will never be close or find real understanding between each other, as Rusty suggests when he says: "My skin is white, and you are my father . . . but all my life the Cheyennes are my people.'' Though Marshall Sabin appears again at the beginning of BLOOD OF THE CHEYENNES, the second Red Hawk novel, he soon departs for another part of the West to carry on his scouting and his long vendetta against the Indians. His departure is appropriate, because BLOOD OF THE CHEYENNES contains Faust's most realistic treatment of the bitter conflict between white culture and the Cheyenne mind. Though BLOOD OF THE CHEYENNES has the secondary theme of a romance that develops between Rusty and Maisry Lester, it is primarily focused on Rusty's encounter with white culture and the contrasting effects that Rusty has on two white men, Bill Tenney, a professional thief and rascal, and Major Marston, an ambitious Army officer. Tenney, whose response to the white world has been to turn to a Darwinian or Hobbsian role as a robber and predator, learns the nature of honor and integrity from Rusty's innocence and vision of a higher order. By contrast, Marston, who has a privileged place in the white world as the commander of a fort, becomes jealous of everything Rusty possesses, from the love of Maisry Lester to his reputation as a man of principle.

Before Marston meets his comeuppance in the climactic fight at the end of the novel, he demonstrates a capacity to lie, steal, and plot the massacre of the Cheyenne village where Rusty has grown up. Though he is essentially a larger-than-life melodramatic villain, Marston is an impressive indictment of white racism. Moreover, Marston does nothing that at one time or another has not been attributed to Custer or other white officers of the U.S. Army. Marston's attempt to attack and destroy a peaceful Cheyenne village, though thwarted, resembles, for instance, Custer's actual destruction of the slumbering village of Black Kettle on the Washita, or for that matter Colonel Chivington's infamous massacre of the Cheyennes at Sand Creek (see SON OF THE MORNING STAR [North Point Press, 1984] by Evan S. Connell). In most respects Marston represents an extreme embodiment of white racism, dying with hatred of Rusty on his lips (''a damned . . . a white Indian . . .''). Part of his malice results from his contempt for the Cheyenne vision of life. When Tenney tells Marston that Tenney would like to nurse the dying major back to life so that Rusty ''could kill you all over again . . . ,'' the major acknowledges the sentiment. ''You and I could understand each other,'' the major gasps, although Rusty's innocence and view of life baffles him. ''But that red-headed fool on the ground there . . . nobody could understand him. He's a cross between a baby and an old man with a lot of the fool mixed in all the way. . . .'' Tenney agrees with his kinship to the major but ascribes Rusty's strength to a different source from that understood by whites. To the major's final query: ''Where did he get his strength?'' Tenney replies simply: ''Out of the sky. . . .'' Indeed, Marston is not alone in regarding Rusty as foolish by the pragmatic standards of the white world; the entire novel suggests that, while Rusty will not abandon his Cheyenne ideals, he will remain an enigma to most in white civilization.

In the final novel of the trilogy, CHEYENNE GOLD, Rusty's devotion to the sources of his Cheyenne spiritual power is reaffirmed. Yet in this book he becomes estranged not only from the white world but also from the Cheyenne nation. Leaving the tribe to meditate in the hallowed Sacred Valley, Rusty becomes increasingly solitary in his orientation to the cosmos, while his passage through the Sacred Valley invites interpretation in terms of Jungian symbolism of initiation into spiritual enlightenment.[11] There is a semblance of a conventional plot here: Rusty is torn between his love for Maisry Lester and his interest in the Cheyenne woman, Blue Bird; and he must discover the valley's gold and preserve the secret from curious whites who would violate the holy ground of the Cheyennes and destroy their culture. But, despite his involvement in such actions, Rusty finally chooses to leave the Cheyennes and go westward to the mountains. Neither white civilization nor red culture can completely accommodate a white man with an Indian vision of life, just as much of white America found itself uncomfortable with the disconcerting opinions of an actual white Indian, James Willard Schultz.

Rusty's alienation from both cultures is symbolized by his inability to make a final choice between the two women who love him. Choosing either would require a commitment to one culture or the other, a decision Rusty is unable to make at the close of the novel. Unlike in earlier Faust Indian stories the conflict between Cheyenne values and white culture is not resolved according to conventional formula. Moreover, a certain tragic aura hangs over the novel's treatment of the discovery of gold. Although the intruding whites are temporarily prevented from learning about the mineral wealth and rushing in to exploit the Cheyenne homelands, the knowledgeable reader will realize that Custer's fateful expedition to the Black Hills in 1874 produced a discovery of gold that led to the violation of the sacred territory and the final tragic war between the Sioux and Cheyennes and the U.S. cavalry. The Red Hawk trilogy remains a memorable achievement.

VII

Although the question seems moot at this late date, we may ask how serious Faust was in treating the condition of the Indians in his Western fiction. A partial answer may be found not only by looking at a study of the Red Hawk novels, but by a glance at a neglected short novel, "Outcast Breed," which has recently been given a new prominence by Robert and Jane Easton in THE COLLECTED STORIES OF MAX BRAND. This short novel concerns the plight of a man, John Cameron, who is by genetic heritage one-quarter Blackfoot. Known to most of the white world as "Mark Wayland's breed," he is rejected by whites and Blackfeet alike after the murder of his foster father.

Thrown on his own resources, Cameron manages to clear his name of suspicion of murder and capture the real murderer, an arrogant white man who cannot for long accept the frustration of his desires. But the reader is likely to find the story most memorable when it depicts the undisguised racism of the white man's West. "Outcast Breed" is an impressive criticism of racism, but it also offers a memorable portrait of a hero caught between two worlds, neither of which is willing to welcome him. Faust clearly understood Cameron's spiritual limbo, which is similar to that of Indians raised on the reservations and exposed to white culture and education. Neither returns to the traditional tribal world nor assimilates the dominant culture, and there seems to be no formulaic convention to offer escape from the dilemma. Faust recognized this tragic situation when he introduced Walking Thunder, a wise Cheyenne who had attended the Carlisle school, to offer advice to the embittered white hero of BLOOD ON THE TRAIL. This lonely Cheyenne, a rueful beneficiary of the white world's education and a man who has gained wisdom through the crucible of experience, is one of those characters in the later novels (such as Lanky in DEAD OR ALIVE) who probably speaks for the mature Faust. Walking Thunder lives as a recluse in the mountains, like a latter-day Thoreau, but surprisingly he gives Dave Reagan, whose chief friend is a tamed wolf, a counsel of wisdom, emphasizing both stoicism and personal responsibility. Life in the mountains appears free, Walking Thunder says, but the appearance is an illusion: to live alone still requires responsible action and even the right to live alone is not given to all. In fact, Walking Thunder tells Dave bluntly: "... you haven't earned the right to live alone." As for Dave's resentment against social injustices, Walking Thunder reminds Dave that others must also bear the burden of society's unfairness: "I am a man with a red skin and I live in a nation of white people. ... What is your curse compared to mine?" Knowledgeable readers of Faust's fiction know such statements are a consistent thread in his writing, demonstrating a clear rejection of not only social injustice but of racism and all it entails. John Clute, an English critic, has perceptively observed in a recent assessment in THE SCIENCE FICTION ENCYCLOPEDIA (St. Martin's, 1993) edited by John Clute and Peter Nicholls: "Throughout MB's work, illuminating the most pulp-like plots, can be discerned the voice of a slyly civilized writer." Faust's use of the white Indian motif may appear to be a commercial subterfuge, but it anticipated by several decades a current trend in Western fiction, films, and television. In such films as the Michael Mann version of THE LAST OF THE MOHICANS (20th-Fox, 1992) and in the popular CBS series "Dr. Quinn, Medicine Woman" and even in the frequently maligned "Walker, Texas Ranger," the protagonists are white men who have acquired an Indian vision of life. Through these characters and their native American mentors, a viewing audience beguiled by a technological civilization is offered the benefits of insights from an older cultural tradition created by people who lived in a closer relationship to the earth and its wilderness. Similarly in the later Indian stories Faust, the latter-day romantic poet and "slyly civilized writer," moves beyond stereotypes and seeks to initiate his readers into an understanding of the spiritual value of the Cheyenne myths and vision of the world.

AN ENDURING FASCINATION: MAX BRAND'S MEXICAN NOVELS

Edgar L. Chapman

The following essay was especially written for inclusion here.

---------------------------- *I* ----------------------------

"Mexico is a foreign country" for Americans, or so a sequence of poems by Robert Warren in the 1940s tells us.[1] Warren was only one of many English and American writers who for various ideological or cultural reasons showed an interest in Mexico and its people in the uncertain period from World War I through World War II. Warren's poems were only a late entry in this tradition, as were Graham Greene's famous novel, THE POWER AND THE GLORY (Viking, 1940), and the fine Elia Kazan film, VIVA ZAPATA! (20th-Fox, 1952), based on an excellent screenplay by John Steinbeck. Despite being "foreign" to most North Americans, Mexico was also a country capable of winning their hearts, and the nation and its people play a surprisingly large role in Frederick Faust's Western fiction. As the world of Faust's Western fiction unfolds, Mexico is gradually transformed over the years from an ambiguous and exotic world of adventure, somewhat like Edmund Spenser's land of "Faerie," into a more human and historically credible setting with a vital Latin culture and a people with enormous zest for living.

Mexico and the country along the border between Mexico and the United States are the setting for many of Faust's novels and short novels, while Mexican-American characters appear in certain other novels set north of the border, such as THE BLACK SIGNAL. Since the Max Brand Westerns so frequently depict outlawry in a romantic light, Faust uses the border as a romantic motif in several stories—most obviously in THE BORDER BANDIT. However, adventures set inside "foreign" Mexico required Faust to go beyond the usual stereotypes in popular fiction in order to maintain credibility. When successful, his work represents the harvest of a sustained and laborious interest in "things Mexican." Faust's use of Mexico should not surprise us since Faust had a wide-ranging mind, and an author who produced around 300 books that might be classified as Westerns would require a variety of settings. Faust also wrote numerous stories set on the Great Plains as well as in Canada and Alaska. This was so despite the often-voiced opinion—which has some validity—that Faust's Westerns are set in a mythic West, but Canada and Alaska do not have the importance in Faust's work given to Mexico.

II

On the whole, Faust probably gave more prominence to Mexicans and Mexican-Americans than did any other Western writer prior to the sixties, when "political correctness" became prominent. Mexican-Americans tend to be either stereotyped, sketchily characterized, or ignored in the work of many other successful Western writers, with a few notable exceptions. The chief of these exceptions is Eugene Cunningham, who introduced Chihuahua Joe as a sympathetic Mexican-American gunman and sidekick into his action-filled RIDERS OF THE NIGHT (Houghton Mifflin, 1932) who also appears in other novels he wrote.[2] In a later generation Frank O'Rourke was among those authors who notably portrayed the Mexican culture of New Mexico in sympathetic detail in several Westerns. Cunningham was virtually a contemporary of Faust while O'Rourke once dedicated a book to Max Brand, though Ernest Haycox and Luke Short were probably stronger influences.[3]

The portrayal of Mexicans or Mexican-Americans as villains has had a long history, the classic case being Clarence E. Mulford's HOPALONG CASSIDY (A.C. McClurg, 1910) in which the treatment of Antonio, a Mexican horse wrangler, is downright xenophobic. In Mulford's novel Antonio is depicted as "a Mexican of little courage, much avarice, and great capacity for hatred. Crafty, filled with cunning of the coyote kind, shifty-eyed, gloomy, taciturn, and scowling, he was well fitted for the part he had elected to play in the range dispute between his ranch and the Bar-20. He was absolutely without mercy or conscience; indeed, one might aptly say that his conscience, if he had ever known one, had been pulled out by the roots and its place filled with viciousness. Cold-blooded in his ferocity, easily angered and quick to commit murder if the risk was small, he embraced within his husk of soul the putrescence of all that was evil."[4]

GRINGO GUNS (Morrow, 1935) by Peter Field (Francis Thayer Hobson) uses a bank robbery in Colorado by a group of Mexican and Mexican-American outlaws as the igniting spark of the plot, which involves the heroes' pursuit of the gang southward into the towns of Spanish New Mexico. Harsh, negative caricatures of the Mexican or Mexican-American are not the only offense today's readers may perceive in some older Westerns. In "WHIP" RYDER'S

WAY (Lippincott, 1935) by Grant Taylor, set in New Mexico and contemporary with Faust's late Westerns, we find that the hero and his two partners do more than change clothes when they disguise themselves as Mexicans: "They had changed personalities, which lends more a disguise than clothing. Temperamentally, they were no longer Anglo-Saxons of the ambitious, toiling race, but *mañana* people who look on the world as a place to travel through leisurely and pleasantly, and with as little labor and discomfort as possible." It is disappointing to encounter such generalizations, even though Taylor's action-oriented novel is fairly sympathetic to Mexican-Americans and ultimately portrays a Villa-like bandit, General Sacobota, in an understanding spirit. In general, Faust avoids such stereotypes in his middle or later books, though in the relatively early serialized novel from 1924, TRAIN'S TRUST, he develops a contrast between the Spanish town section of San Lorenzo and the Anglo section in terms that are somewhat similar, though with more ambivalence than Taylor.[5] Another dubious aspect of some earlier Westerns is the generous use of ethnic slurs, the most offensive synonym for Mexican or Mexican-American in many pre-World War II Westerns being "greaser." Field's GRINGO GUNS is again a regrettable offender here. To be sure, the Max Brand Westerns sometimes employed this conventional ethnic slur, "greaser," but Jon Tuska has obtained the manuscript versions of Faust's fiction for *Western Story Magazine* and learned that Frank Blackwell, the editor, was responsible for this sort of thing in Faust's fiction.[6]

In general, American movies in Faust's time were as bad as or worse than pulp fiction according to Helen Delpar in THE ENORMOUS VOGUE OF THINGS MEXICAN, 1920–1935 (University of Alabama Press, 1992), which maintains that even supposedly enlightened intellectuals saw Mexico through glasses shaped by ideologues, either by Marxists analyzing Mexico's revolution in terms of rigid theory or by latter-day romantics seeing a mystic salvation in Mexico's suppressed Indian culture. Faust made Mexico the setting for numerous stories, and Mexicans and Mexican-Americans figure strongly in what many have considered some of his most entertaining fiction.

III

Faust, like John Steinbeck, was acquainted with Mexican-Americans in the San Joaquin Valley. When Faust was at the University of California, he was absorbed in the Mexican Revolution like the rest of the radicals. Later in El Paso in 1919 he was still intrigued by the changing fortunes in Mexico; in fact, he expressed interest in meeting the bandit-turned-revolutionary, Pancho Villa. In the process of researching Mexico, Faust amassed a number of books on the subject, including Prescott's history of Cortez's conquest, which he read to his children; Hubert Howe Bancroft's history of the conquest; a book on travels in Mexico by the poet and translator Bayard Taylor; a biography of Porfírio Díaz; and VIVA MEXICO! (Appleton, 1910), a sardonic book describing travel in

Mexico by Charles Macomb Flandrau, published on the eve of the revolution against Díaz. Finally, Faust is known to have owned a 1933 biography of Pancho Villa, VIVA VILLA! by Edgcumb Pinchon. Pinchon's subtitle, "A Recovery of the Real Pancho Villa, Peon, Bandit, Soldier, Patriot," provides little doubt where this author's sympathies lay. Faust also developed an extensive research file on Mexican culture and history. Among other interests, the file shows concern for the differences between the upper and lower classes. Moreover, as with Faust's Westerns in general, his writing about this land and culture deepened and matured over the years. Early Westerns about Mexico, such as SEVEN TRAILS, provide only a hint of what he would accomplish in the Montana Kid trilogy.

IV

At first Faust seemed to turn to Mexican settings as another exotic backdrop for adventure. The outlaw hero in SEVEN TRAILS, Peter Quince (a name slyly lifted from Shakespeare), takes refuge in Mexico after a series of romances in the United States. Like many of Faust's early heroes, Quince is temperamentally alienated from the world of the workaday West. A handsome rebel, Quince's major crimes consist of daring exploits and a series of six romances with beauties named Mary rather than any very serious anti-social actions. Since Quince's father, the legendary John Quincey, had disappeared into Mexico during Quince's childhood, Quince's descent into Mexico becomes reminiscent of classical heroes and their mythic journeys to the underworld to discover the true identity or nature of the father. This novel appears to be set in prerevolutionary Mexico, although time is unimportant because the novel becomes increasingly dreamlike in its Mexican scenes. Quince romances the seventh Mary, the supposed daughter of a *hidalgo*, Señor Monterey. Hired by Monterey to confront the mysterious outlaw, El Tigre, Quince wins Mary's love, while meeting and becoming reconciled to his father, John Quincey, who turns out to be El Tigre. Although Quincey has been accused of kidnapping Mary, Señor Monterey took the girl in infancy from her North American parents. This unexpected revelation frees Mary to accept the love of Quince and restores a certain aura of innocence to the outlaw father, John Quincey. Yet the novel shows only a casual interest in Mexico as a semifeudal state.

The same claims could be made about several other early novels set in Mexico. THE TRAIL TO SAN TRISTE, for instance, deals with the search for a missing treasure in the Mexican mountains. Nevertheless, some aspects of this novel are eerily fascinating. THE GENTLE GUNMAN takes place in Argentina, a country Faust never visited but makes credible. THE BELLS OF SAN FILIPO returns to Mexico and the lost treasure motif, this time with a hero whose skill with a gun earns him the name of The Doctor. Faust handles the setting with great assurance, and some of his characters are vividly sketched. But a much important use of Mexico appears in THE BORDER BANDIT, another serial from 1926. This saga is an exuberant adventure placed roughly in the 1840s, and Faust displays an intensified sense of the historical past in a long opening sequence where he portrays Oliver Tay as a sentimental gentleman of his era. Much of this novel employs a favorite Faust theme, the transformation of an ordinary man, or even a lazy dreamer, into a dynamic hero. Tay is kidnapped and sold as a slave laborer to the owner of a Mexican silver mine. There Oliver learns how to survive and develops the strength and will to escape, forming a strong friendship with a couple of Mexican cutthroats. Later Oliver learns to use the new Colt revolvers and becomes a leader of his friends' outlaw gang.

After THE BORDER BANDIT, Faust continued to use Mexican and border outlawry in other Westerns. Numerous novels from Faust's middle period (roughly 1925–1931) play on the theme of outlawry in Mexico, or make use of Mexican-American characters. We shall make note of many but treat only three in detail here, "The City in the Sky," SOUTH OF RIO GRANDE, and TWENTY NOTCHES.

"The City in the Sky" should occupy a special place in the canon of Max Brand Westerns. This novel about the heroic exploits of an untried youth, Leicester Tarron, exemplifies the ideal of Frank Blackwell, Street & Smith's editor of *Western Story Magazine*. Essentially Blackwell wanted adventure fiction set in the West, and he preferred plots based on chase, pursuit, and relentless action with, of course, plenty of gun play, daring riding, and a strong element of suspense. "The City in the Sky" ought to have satisfied him on all counts. At the same time the serial is one Faust's most poetic Westerns: it makes young Tarron's journey into the mountains of Mexico not only a rite of passage from youth into manhood but something like a neo-medieval allegory of the search for the meaning of life. In fact, the dreamlike and allegorical mood of the story is so pronounced at times that the original magazine title is far more apt than that of the later Dodd, Mead abridgment in book form, FLAMING IRONS. It has many of Faust's most successful motifs in the action. Tarron, introduced as the indolent youngest son of a hard-working rancher, is a mythic hero waiting for his opportunity. His father and brothers scorn Tarron for avoiding the daily and brutal ranch work, but Tarron's dexterity, his skill with guns and horses, and his ability to interpret trail signs are exactly the qualities needed in a larger-than-life hero. His name is also taken from two of Faust's favorite reservoirs of romantic story, with "Leicester" evoking the age of Elizabethan free-booting and "Tarron" coming directly from the world of Celtic myth, in this case the Mabinogion, which also was to provide Faust with Caradac and Rhiannon for one of his most popular novels, SINGING GUNS.

The story begins with a group of gunfighters pursuing a fugitive named Dorn and Tarron, astonishing them by deducing a great deal about Dorn from some horse tracks. Later Tarron assumes the job of assisting Dorn on a journey to take a mysterious message to a wealthy Mexican family. Dorn's pursuers seem to have an endless number of men and resources, and eventually Dorn is murdered, but not before Tarron learns that he is to take the message on to the city of La Paz, should Dorn be killed. Although Tarron crosses the border successfully and enters the mountains of Mexico, he discovers that his job will be harder than he thought, since hardly anyone knows where the city of La Paz is. An elderly Mexican mountaineer suggests that perhaps Tarron is searching for the "city of peace" which exists only in the sky—in other words, Tarron is searching for the realm St. Augustine called the City of God and to which John Bunyan gave the name of the Celestial City. Though Faust eventually abandons the obvious symbolic overtones of his story, they linger in the mind long after it is revealed that La Paz is the older name of Santa Maria, a town where Tarron must elude the forces of the ruthless North American millionaire, Robert Langhorne. When Tarron reaches La Paz, he rescues Señor Lopez, a captive in Langhorne's hacienda, and brings him safely to the Casa Alvarado where Lopez decodes Dorn's message to reveal the whereabouts of a lost mine. Tarron's ordeal, which brings him from youth to manhood, at times seems a quest for the heavenly city, even though it is finally transmuted into a search for fortune and a happy marriage. But this ending is undercut a few years later by the return of Ingram, the gunman who had been Langhorne's chief agent. Defeated by Tarron in his work for Langhorne, Ingram must finally test Tarron's skill with a gun. An early morning duel at the crossroads outside of town produces the final defeat—death for Ingram—and Tarron's happiness is apparently secure. Yet this encounter has an ironic touch: it reminds the reader that only in the "city in the sky" will Tarron find true peace.

Not only does this neo-medieval romance stand almost in a class by itself among Faust's Westerns, but it is to his great credit that the Mexican characters tend to be memorable, even poetic. A mountaineer of ninety befriends Tarron and suggests that La Paz might well be the city in the sky. For such a man, a fount of arcane wisdom, money is less important than the truths of experience and the record of integrity one leaves behind. His middle-aged daughter, bitter over the grinding poverty in which they live, betrays Tarron to his enemies for a small bribe, but both her father and the reader tend to forgive the woman for her action, or at least to feel compassion for her. After all, in the face of hunger, what meaning can Tarron and his strange quest have for her?

By contrast with "The City in the Sky," SOUTH OF RIO GRANDE seems almost like Steinbeckian realism. This novel was once made into an indifferent black-and-white Western film with Robert Preston, Robert Stack, and Mickey Rooney, MY OUTLAW BROTHER (Eagle-Lion, 1951). One of its virtues is Faust's use of two protagonists who are flawed rather than the warriors of extraordinary talents and skills—Peter Quince, Oliver Tay, Tarron—that Faust had sent to Mexico in earlier serials. Dennis MacMore is an untried youth in search of his brother, and Joe Warder, an experienced U.S. marshal, is like many of Faust's lawmen, a reformed jailbird. Both are courageous, but neither is a mythic gunfighter. Faust made such characterizations a common practice around the time of SINGING GUNS with the partnership of Caradac and Rhiannon or the pairing off a brave tenderfoot or untried youth with an older and more experienced mentor. Warder provides an effective narrative point of view, telling his story in a tough, anti-heroic manner comparable to the hard-boiled style developed in detective stories by Dashiell Hammett. Reluctantly accepting the perilous mission of finding the elusive outlaw, El Tigre, Warder establishes himself as one of Faust's more credible heroes. A capable man with a gun, Warder describes himself as forty-two, too old for marriage; he leaves the romantic escapades to the daring Dennis MacMore, who wins the Mexican beauty, Carmel. MacMore, who goes to Mexico to find his missing brother, Patrick, is full of the daredevil romanticism of Faust's heroes with Celtic heritages.

Besides this heightened realism of character in SOUTH OF RIO GRANDE, there is a surprisingly detailed realism of setting. The action takes place around the city of San Clemente, a provincial town in the mountains. Here Faust's extensive research appears in his sketches of the social life of San Clemente, including evening band concerts in the central plaza. The mythic aspects emerge in the treatment of the villain, El Tigre, a mysterious outlaw leader who raids north of the Rio Grande and retreats into the Mexican mountains. In reality, El Tigre is not a Mexican but a fictional identity created by Patrick MacMore, the missing brother, a myth supposedly more bestial than human in order to increase the terror inspired by his band and to mask his own importance in their crimes. The dual identity of MacMore and El Tigre does more than serve the purpose of the plot. The mythic El Tigre represents a symbol of the bestial savage, the regression into the Hobbesian ''natural man'' that Patrick MacMore has become in Mexico. In his final appearance, disguised as the savage El Tigre, Patrick is consumed by a savage fury to kill. But in his last moments, when he attacks Dennis MacMore and Warder, a semblance of humane feeling surfaces—though wearing a false scar and brandishing an axe, El Tigre recognizes and avoids killing his brother. Something rational and human prevents Patrick MacMore from descending completely into savagery and fratricide. While El Tigre is hardly a pulp magazine version of Conrad's Kurtz, he is the dominant presence in SOUTH OF RIO GRANDE and is obviously a Jungian shadow symbol, representing the bestial or darker side of humanity, the reverse of Faust's mythic hero figures. For whatever reasons, Mexico liberated some of Faust's most mythic conceptions, whether of heroism or villainy.

Though set in the mountains of New Mexico, the same Mexican atmosphere pervades the middle sections of TWENTY NOTCHES, the third highly original novel from this period. There are a number of nominally credible North American settings in TWENTY NOTCHES, but the novel's relationship to history and geography becomes irrelevant. The novel's plot seems to draw both hero and reader into a realm of dreamlike adventure. This curious work is as anomalous among Faust's Westerns as his eccentric early tale, THE GARDEN OF EDEN. TWENTY NOTCHES appears to be modeled consciously on some well-known fairy tale, such as ''Jack the Giant Killer'' or ''Jack and the Beanstalk.'' Faust's pulp fiction provided a kingdom that liberated his imagination from the literary restraints he accepted for poetry, yet at times the pressure to turn to a realm of imaginative dreaming was clearly overriding, as Faust once confessed to Grace Flandrau.

TWENTY NOTCHES seems to reflect the pressures and the need to create a definitive fairy tale in the form of a Western adventure. It begins with three tramps riding in an empty boxcar in the Southwest, watching the hills go by. As in fairy tales that begin with three brothers, the tramps are a representative trio, an aged sage, a middle-aged cynic, and a young loafer of unrealized potential called simply The Sleeper. As the train passes a ranch located near a shaded oasis, the eldest tramp turns the conversation to the owner who, according to legend, owns a magic gun with twenty notches, an old Colt that cannot miss. Challenged by the middle-aged cynic to check the truth of this tale, The Sleeper jumps off the train to visit the home of Trot Enderby, the owner of the Colt. Enderby turns out to be a cruel and arrogant man who, like a fairy tale ogre, imprisons The Sleeper under the guard of two large dogs and forces him to chop wood on short rations and limited sleep. Eventually The Sleeper, roused to a fury by injustice, manages to kill the savage dogs and avenges himself on Enderby by stealing clothes, a horse, and the magic gun. Thus armed with a supposedly fabulous weapon, The Sleeper visits the town of Alcalde, where he astonishes everyone by displaying his prize publicly. Believing in his invincibility, he humiliates the dreaded Enderby when the rancher arrives to protest. Now acclaimed as a hero, The Sleeper is challenged by a local hotel owner to go into the mountains and recover Ironwood, a fine stallion belonging to a crippled cowboy that was stolen by the legendary outlaw, Parmenter. The Sleeper's meeting with the cowboy's beautiful daughter creates an additional incentive. When The Sleeper arrives at Parmenter's mountain stronghold, the Mexican-American town of Guadalupe, he finds acceptance from the bandit. Thus the narrative parallels the exploits of a pluck hero going to the land of a fairy tale giant, and, as in such tales, The Sleeper steals the giant's treasure— Parmenter's stolen stallion—and returns it to its owner. Finally, in a climactic scene, The Sleeper kills Parmenter and his best gunman, though appropriately enough he performs this deed with an ordinary gun rather than the supposedly magic six-shooter. In the end it is The Sleeper's confidence and courage that provide the real magic.

Though it exists on the borderline of fantasy, TWENTY NOTCHES avoids the use of overt magic, and The Sleeper's actions are made credible because of his worldly experience and considerable talents. His experiences have made him shrewd; he has learned to accept no story at face value and to be constantly on the alert for treachery. These realistic touches merely support Faust's grand design: a Western adventure constructed entirely on the pattern of a mythic fairy tale. This novel is worthy of admiration for its sheer audacity. And, once again, the presence of a Mexican town at the center of a lawless kingdom in the mountains is used to create the dreamlike atmosphere of the story.

Faust made use either of Mexico or Mexican characters in a number of other books through the late twenties and early thirties. The presence of the border and the clash of the two cultures, Anglo and Mexican, provides exotic local color or mystery in several stories: THE BLACK SIGNAL, which realistically depicts a family of Mexican-Americans, though the necessities of plot oblige the daughter to lose the hero to a North American lady; THE BORDER KID, a story of imposture and the discovery of honor that at times resembles an Arabian Nights tale; BORDER GUNS, a twentieth-century story about smuggling; THE RETURN OF THE RANCHER, where a crucial point of the story depends on the hero's recovery of his old friendship with the Mexican gunfighter, Gaspar Sental; VALLEY VULTURES, which offers the rare case of a Mexican-American villain in Faust's fiction; OUTLAW'S CODE, where a North American outlaw is persuaded to search for a missing man south of the border, a story that seems vaguely suggested by the disappearance of Ambrose Bierce; GUNMAN'S GOLD, where Shannigan, an adventurer for hire, lives on the border and clearly seems to prefer the Mexican culture; SMUGGLERS' TRAIL, which combines the lawless atmosphere of border outlawry with the unpleasant business of smuggling Chinese; and the short novels, "Chip Champions a Lady," involving one of Faust's plucky serial characters in a Mexican-American setting, and "The Best Bandit" which shows another North American gunman besting some of Mexico's worst badmen. It also is easy to overlook, in such a rapid survey, the fact that two of the Silvertip novels, SILVERTIP and SIL-VERTIP'S SEARCH, can also be placed in this group, since the first involves Silvertip's championing a number of Mexican-Americans and the second takes Silvertip on an adventure into Mexico in which the redoubtable hero must masquerade as a Mexican *vaquero*.

The final half-dozen stories cited above were all composed in Faust's final years as a Western writer and show him at the height of his powers as an author. They also suggest an intensification of Faust's interest in Mexican culture, which was to bear fruit in his final trilogy. In fact, these stories might be even more highly rated were it not for their being overshadowed by Faust's other achievements of those years.

Faust's determination to treat Mexico and Mexicans fairly and with respect appears in an interesting way in his serial DEAD OR ALIVE. This story of a young cowboy whose loyalty draws him into a world of banditry and revenge contains one of Faust's most despicable villains, an oddly credible demagogue named Reginald Channing Carter. To redeem their names, the narrator and his mentor, Lanky, Faust's real hero, join the terrifying gang of Don Pedro, a supposedly ruthless Mexican who has escaped from indescribable horrors in Mexico. But Lanky immediately realizes that because the gang is mainly made up of North Americans, the mysterious Mexican leader is a myth created in order to exploit ethnic fears. After capturing Carter, Lanky reveals that Carter, the originator of the myth, has escaped from the legendary Valle Nacional in Yucatán, where convicts were sent to prison labor camps to work until they succumbed to disease or malnutrition. Thus Carter's fictitious monster, a terrifying Mexican bandit evoking terrible xenophobic fears while disguising the North

American membership of the gang, has been created as an act of revenge for Carter's horrifying imprisonment. To explain why the legend of the Valle Nacional should have evoked such terror, we need look no farther than Porfirio Díaz's Mexico, the setting for Faust's Montana Kid trilogy.

V

Of Faust's final group of Westerns (1932–1936) the Montana Kid trilogy usually ranks among his most memorable stories. Though serialized in the pulps, these novels were written for Cass Canfield, the fine editor at Harper & Bros., to whom Faust and his agent, Carl Brandt, hoped to sell more ambitious work during the years when Faust was striving to make his mark as a historical novelist. Faust was never able to complete his historical novel about the Civil War to Canfield's satisfaction, but the first Montana Kid novel was sufficiently strong to require a new byline. This was Evan Evans, the name of one of Faust's doctors. Harper was, of course, capitalizing on the "vogue for things Mexican," and the new name was even supported by a somewhat romanticized biographical sketch. The creation of the Evans name also indicated that Harper considered these novels superior to Faust's prior work for the pulps. After the three Montana Kid stories were published, Harper, wanting to continue to profit from the Evans name after Faust had been killed in World War II, went on to publish a few of the better pulp novels. Generally these later Evan Evans novels have a strong historical or literary flavor but suffer from careless development.

In the Montana Kid novels Faust achieved a happy combination of the mythic and the historical, making full use of his research on Porfirio Díaz's Mexico as it existed in the first decade of the twentieth century prior to the Mexican Revolution. Díaz was a skillful dictator who ruled Mexico for a third of a century (1877–1911), though pretending to observe democratic forms. Ironically enough, Díaz did not come from a peninsular Spanish background but was mostly descended from an Indian heritage, rising to eminence as the supposed heir to the tradition of Mexico's native people and their political messiah, Benito Juarez. Yet Díaz gradually gathered most of the power of the nation into his own hands, skillfully manipulating the newspapers and benefiting from able advisers and administrators. Though Díaz labored to create the image of a modern and orderly Mexico, with a capital whose public architectural style was modeled on Paris, his success was largely achieved through an influx of capital from the United States and the wealthy nations of Western Europe, which aimed to exploit Mexico's resources (see THE COURSE OF MEXICO [Oxford, 1995] by Michael C. Meyer and William L. Sherman).

Díaz was able to identify potential rivals in the military early and buy them off with governorships. It was assumed that provincial governors would take bribes and plunder the politically impotent in their jurisdiction. This system was supported by the fierce national police, the *Rurales,* who gained a reputation of getting their man and sometimes shooting him while he was "trying to escape."

Troublemakers and dissidents, if poor, along with Indians and convicted felons were usually transported to the Valle Nacional in Yucatán, where they became virtual conscripts in slave labor. Díaz's regime favored the foreign-born and the Creole class of Mexicans, especially the rich or landed. In fact, the government perpetuated the "hacienda class" of large landowners who were taxed but lightly and often given much of the local political power. One such aristocratic family was the legendary Terrazas, who ruled a vast domain in northern Mexico, exercising extraordinary power over the debt-ridden peons. Díaz's Mexico was a neo-medieval realm masquerading as a modern country supposedly modeled, ironically, on nineteenth-century France. Europeans and North Americans were often taken in by the imposture, particularly if they paid little attention to the sufferings of the lower class, the enormous *barrios* around Mexico City, or the terrible poverty of the Indians. Because of government censorship, the shame of the Valle Nacional and its convict labor were a reasonably well-guarded secret. Such a nation with its history of repression eventually inspired bandit leaders like Pancho Villa to instigate a revolution. This revolution in turn made heroes not only out of "social bandits" like Villa but also the populist, Emiliano Zapata. Though Díaz's government boasted that it had introduced a stable order and technological advances, it also produced enormous discontent among the poor, many of whom would have sympathized with such a flamboyant populist bandit as Faust's Mateo Rubriz.

On the eve of the revolution some of the crimes of Díaz's dictatorship began to emerge for public view. Most dramatically, starting with a series of articles for *The American Magazine* in 1910, the American muckraking journalist, John Kenneth Turner, set out to reveal the sordid truth about Mexico's injustices. Though this series was soon discontinued, Turner's work caused a sensation among the intelligentsia. Exiled Mexican liberals, such as Francisco Madero and his allies who assailed the Díaz regime from the safety of St. Louis, hailed Turner's revelations as confirmations of their own claims about Mexico's injustices. Despite the effort to stymie their publication, Turner's articles were soon brought out as a book, BARBAROUS MEXICO (C. H. Kerr, 1911). One early chapter of this volume is called "In the Valley of Death," a variation of the Valley of the Dead, the name used in Faust's second Montana Kid novel for the infamous Valle Nacional. It is likely that Faust was aware of Turner's revelations, particularly since the Mexican Revolution was a fashionable cause during much of the time of Faust's attendance at the University of California. Moreover, Juan-Silva, who manages a plantation in MONTANA RIDES AGAIN, hopes to return in triumph to Spain and buy a castle on the hill where he was a sheepherder as a boy. Turner had noted that some of those who administered the plantations in the Valle National were actually Spaniards. Clearly Faust did his research well for these novels.

A close study of the trilogy reveals two predominant themes: first, there are the hero's enduring alienation and enormous guile. Montana not only has great skill with weapons, horses, and a poker deck but dislikes conventional society as much as Faust's first mythic hero, Dan Barry, did, Secondly, there is the reliance on elaborate plots of daring exploit and escape, followed by pursuit. Larger-than-life heroes are one reason that readers remember successful authors of Western stories. Wister's The Virginian, Zane Grey's Lassiter, Mulford's Cassidy, and Max Brand's Dan Barry are four examples of mythic heroes who have intrigued both readers and scholars. Knowledgeable readers of Faust would add others, such as Destry, Caradac and Rhiannon, and Silvertip. Surely Faust's the Montana Kid is one of his most memorable creations, representing a character type he had been developing since the creation of Destry: a hero who adds cleverness and subtlety to his gifts of physical strength and competence. As we have observed, Montana recognizes the boredom and hypocrisy of conventional middle-class society as well as any Faust character; but he does not foolishly throw his life away on revenge, as Faust's Dan Barry did in THE SEVENTH MAN. Montana combines the qualities of strength and guile that Northrop Frye has identified as essential to the heroes of romance and found most clearly in Odysseus (see Frye's THE SECULAR SCRIPTURE [Harvard, 1976]).

Montana may also be contrasted with Faust's other popular mythic hero of the middle thirties, Silvertip. Whereas Silvertip is noted for his extraordinary generosity and idealism, he equals Montana in his alienation from society. Silvertip's chief occupation, when not engaged in fighting some act of injustice, is living as a recluse in the wilderness. By contrast, Montana is more human and sociable; his interests in gambling and women ensure that he will travel in the world of society, if only along its fringes. The Montana Kid may also be considered an imaginative revision of the legend of Billy the Kid, the charming bandit who was, according to Walter Noble Burns, a hero to Latin Americans. Indeed, Faust is known to have owned a copy of Burns's book.

At the beginning of the tale Montana is an impudent, cynical, and streetwise youth. His past resembles the legendary youth of Billy the Kid as it appears in Burns's treatment (though frequently dubious, this is very likely the version that Faust knew, nor does it matter that Burns's version was largely fictional, as Jon Tuska pointed out in BILLY THE KID: HIS LIFE AND LEGEND [Greenwood Press, 1994]). The Montana Kid is an heroic character, rather than a mere criminal or psychopath, and presented as the kind of man Billy the Kid should have been, rather than what he actually was. The youthful past of the Montana Kid also reveals similarities with Faust's. Both, for instance, were orphaned around the age of thirteen and both forced to learn in the school of experience. But neither is a thorough cynic: like Faust, the Kid is something of a romantic, and he is attracted to the challenge posing as the Lavery heir. At the same time Faust demonstrates that the Kid feels contempt for his second-rate confederates.

While sources in Faust's biography and the history of the West may be suggested as origins for the Montana Kid, we should not forget Faust's love of classical myths and of heroic medieval and Renaissance literature. Much has been made of the mythic origins of Dan Barry in THE UNTAMED since Faust called attention to them in his first chapter, and these classical antecedents are important. But scant notice, if any, has been given to the mythic origins of the Montana Kid who clearly is a descendant of Homer's Odysseus, the trickster who combined physical skill and prowess with an undying wanderlust. Although the legend of Robin Hood, a supporter of King Richard, the monarch whom Faust presents with admiration in THE GOLDEN KNIGHT, is also an important precursor, it is clear that Odysseus, whose wanderings even take him to the Underworld, is a strong mythic influence in the creation of the Montana Kid. This mythic tradition helps to explain why the trilogy begins with the proposal of an enormous trick, the Kid's imposture as the missing heir to the Lavery cattle kingdom in the Big Bend of Texas.

MONTANA RIDES!, like its successors, is constructed around one of Faust's favorite motifs: pursuit, capture, rescue, and escape. But in the interwoven adventures of the three novels, the importance of cleverness and guile, as well as of physical talents, plays a major role. This pattern, in fact, emerges in the Kid's successful impersonation of the missing Lavery heir and recurs in later episodes of MONTANA RIDES! particularly in the scene where the Kid impersonates a vagabond from Chihuahua City, successfully deceiving Rubriz and many of his gang. The initial imposture in which the Kid plays the role of the missing Lavery heir takes up half the book and is cleverly developed, but once the challenge of winning this game is over, the Kid predictably becomes bored with his victory. This is not surprising, for the Kid's favorite drug appears to be adrenaline, produced in response to challenging situations.

Faust's command of a sophisticated moral awareness is demonstrated in his depiction of the Kid's ethical growth. In a subtle and ironic way Montana becomes a prisoner of his own success. Winning the respect and affection of the Lavery family (especially Mrs. Lavery and Ruth) and their ranch hands does not free him to enjoy their affection and wealth; instead it seems to confine him to a social role that he does not want and to create a burden of personal obligation. As Montana comes to realize, only a man without principle and humane feeling could continue to play the impostor's role and live on unmerited wealth and undeserved affections. Faust's novel shows the Kid moving beyond the mere enjoyment of a dangerous game to the recognition of the demands of conscience. This developing moral awareness in Montana parallels Destry's discovery of humility at the end of DESTRY RIDES AGAIN. At first, the Kid believes that he can be freed from his violation of the trust of the Lavery family by telling the truth and by performing a selfless act of heroism, restoring to them the son they think they have found. But as the action shifts to Mexico and the Kid's rescue of "Tonio," the real Richard Lavery, Montana's moral awareness deepens, and he learns to feel empathy for others. Not knowing of his biological parents, Tonio has been happy as the presumed son of Mateo Rubriz. Montana's revelation of Tonio's true parentage destroys the latter's assumptions about his world and raises the ancient question of who should take precedence: one's birth parents or one's foster parents. The Kid's rescue of Tonio creates its own moral ambivalence. This is a key insight developed in the trilogy, a theme that helps the three novels transcend the limitations of formula adventure: no action, however, heroic, is performed entirely in a moral vacuum. Virtually every effort, however noble, exacts an emotional or moral sacrifice (to say nothing of a physical risk) requiring emotional costs for others. The point is illustrated again in Faust's surprisingly complex characterization of Mateo Rubriz.

Rubriz appears initially to be the familiar Mexican bandit chief of popular literature and cinema, but Faust's characterization transcends the stereotype and frequently surprises us. To begin with, readers are prepared to dislike Rubriz because of his raising the kidnapped Lavery baby as his son, but Faust creates sympathy for the bandit by revealing that Rubriz had been publicly flogged by the elder Richard Lavery in the streets of Bentonville. Though Rubriz is depicted as a man of enormous gusto, he never becomes a Falstaffian buffoon. Faust constantly reminds us of Rubriz's courage, his skill with weapons, his cunning, his dominance over his band, his independent spirit, and his fierce pride, not only in himself but in Mexico. Indeed, Rubriz's hatred of *gringos* stems from the insults heaped by North Americans on Mexico. Ultimately Rubriz's love for his ''son'' has transformed the boy from a *gringo* into a fearless and independent bandit. But his love so dominates Rubriz that he casually plots the murder of the senior Lavery and Ruth. In the second half of the novel Rubriz's relentless pursuit demonstrates the strength of his love for Tonio. Tonio's response to the discovery that he is an Anglo North American also reveals Faust's narrative skill. Tonio's psychological dilemma is very contemporary, for Tonio's decision to go north with Montana to see his biological parents is hardly more dramatic than his emotional struggle.

Though the second half of MONTANA RIDES! is primarily a tale of pursuit, it concludes with two scenes that deepen the characters of Rubriz and Ruth Lavery. In Montana's room, Rubriz's character is humanized and expanded far beyond the limits of stereotyped Mexican outlaws. Armed with a shotgun, he stealthily enters the Lavery ranch house where Tonio and Montana are recuperating from their ordeal. Yet Rubriz abandons his revenge because of his love for Tonio and his admiration for Montana. Reinforcing the bonding between Montana and Tonio, this scene is important for Rubriz for two reasons. First, although his pride is wounded and his honor and reputation somewhat diminished by Montana's successful kidnapping of Tonio, Rubriz feels a genuine love for his foster son. Second, though Rubriz has circumvented the security of the Lavery ranch, he recognizes Montana as an antagonist—and a North American worthy of his respect. At this point Rubriz has been enlarged in stature from a savage antagonist for Montana into the robust Rabelaisian figure of the second and third novels.

In the remarkable final scene of the novel Ruth Lavery follows Montana to the slope where he expects to hop on a freight train, but she persuades him to stay to marry her. Though this ending will not resolve Montana's conflict with conventional society, it is presented effectively in a tone that is restrained or ''hard-boiled'' rather than sentimental. The scene also deepens the characterization of Ruth Lavery, no longer the romantic ingenue. Her daring and resolution, foreshadowed earlier, move her beyond the conventional boundaries of her role.

The central theme of the second half of MONTANA RIDES!, the journey into an underworld to rescue a person, recapitulates the mythic journeys of many classical heroes, including Hercules's rescue of Alcestis and the voyage of Odysseus to Hades in "The Odyssey." It also repeats the central action of Dionysus in Faust's own mythological verse epic. In fact, Dionysus's journey to the Underworld shaped the plot of many of Faust's Westerns in the period 1929–34. Yet, if MONTANA RIDES! is a novel that frequently surprises as an early reviewer noted in the *Saturday Review of Literature,* regrettably the slow-moving film, BRANDED (Paramount, 1950), which attempts to translate Faust's vision to the screen, is a disappointment despite the presence of Alan Ladd and Charles Bickford. Ladd lacks the flamboyance of the Kid, and the film's Mexican sequence is extremely ponderous. The production also suffers from the increasing emphasis on surface realism in Western films under the influence of Luke Short's *Saturday Evening Post* serials and the Westerns of John Ford, Howard Hawks, and other legendary directors.

VI

A similar theme of a journey into a dangerous underworld dominates the second Montana Kid novel. In MONTANA RIDES AGAIN Mexico is no longer simply the perilous realm of MONTANA RIDES! but the arena of Montana's finest heroism. This novel recounts Montana's dramatic recovery of the emerald crown of Our Lady of Guadalupe, symbolizing both a sacred object and a talisman, a Jungian mandala, defining the achievement of Rubriz and Montana and even the honor and integrity of Mexico itself. In recovering the sacred icon, Rubriz, an admirer of Benito Juarez, takes center stage and consolidates his position as a heroic figure equal to Montana. More than a worthy antagonist for the Kid he reveals his self-awareness and guile, his zest for life, and gains the status of an authentic Mexican hero. But in his capture and imprisonment, he also embodies the long suffering of the underprivileged.

The quality of Faust's imagination is also revealed in two other memorable Mexican characters: Brother Pascual, the friar, a gentle giant and serious moralist, and Rosita, the *cantina* dancer who aspires to wealth and fame but settles for a life of adventure with Montana. Far from stereotypes both are endowed with a buoyant vitality. Pascual's urge to commit violence frequently struggles with his Christian beliefs; and Rosita, proud and clever, plays against the role of conventional Mexican spitfire for her own purposes. Here, and throughout the saga, the more spirited of Faust's characters surprise readers and reverse their expectations, perhaps explaining why Faust's better novels remain more popular than those of most of his contemporaries which have faded from view.

Yet more important than characterization is the development of Faust's themes. Like the recent film, RAIDERS OF THE LOST ARK (Paramount, 1981) and its sequels, MONTANA RIDES AGAIN is a sophisticated adventure tale with deep mythic resonance. The story of the stolen crown of Our Lady of Guadalupe is more than a conventional tale of daring theft; this numinous object is a potent icon like the Ark of the Covenant or the Holy Grail. The stolen crown becomes a mythic force, as both the goal of Montana's quest and a symbol of the honor of Mexico. While fulfilling both roles, the icon may also represent Montana's attainment of selfhood.[7] Since it has been plundered by a rapacious provincial governor, the crown must be restored by a daring theft, which only the bandit, Rubriz, is willing to undertake. The central action of the novel follows that of the Mexican Revolution and makes Rubriz a social bandit, a Robin Hood embodying the aspirations of the repressed class. Yet this mythic motif is not the only structural principle of MONTANA RIDES AGAIN, which is also dominated by the theme of rescue and liberation. In the beginning Rubriz's scheme to provoke a gunfight between Montana and Jack Lascar rescues Montana from a conventional marriage to Ruth. Later, in Mexico, Montana's courtship liberates Rosita from being the mistress of a wealthy man. And, of course, both Rubriz and Montana try to free the emerald crown from the general who, in stealing it, has violated the sanctity of the church. But the most impressive act of liberation is the Montana Kid's rescue of Rubriz from the Valley of the Dead in Yucatán. Here the heroic exploit of journeying to the Underworld and bringing back the person apparently lost dramatizes a major obsession of Faust's work. According to Robert Easton, Faust's own life was a constant effort to escape from some ''valley of the dead,'' whether the poverty and obscurity of his childhood and youth in the San Joaquin Valley, or the consequences of leaving Berkeley without a degree, or his later life as a pulp fiction writer. The liberation of a comrade appears in Faust's more serious non-Western fiction in this period: Blondel's efforts in Faust's best historical novel, THE GOLDEN KNIGHT, are concerned with liberation of Richard the Lion-Hearted from his Austrian prison; and Anthony Hamilton's most daring achievement in SPY MEETS SPY is the rescue of Louise, his fellow agent, from the Soviet prison on the island of Solovki. The Kid not only frees Rubriz from a virtual death sentence but destroys the legend that there is no escape from the Valle Nacional. A symbol of this victory is the heart failure of Juan-Silva, the aged Pluto of this Hades. Ironically, the liberation of Rubriz also enables the Kid to recover the second half of the emerald crown, which Rubriz and the Kid had divided in their effort to escape from the governor's fortress.

MONTANA RIDES AGAIN may well be Faust's most enjoyable Western adventure novel. It ends with Pascual's reply to Rubriz's wry complaint that Montana has not only brought back the crown but appears to be purloining the women of Mexico in the person of Rosita: ''Does the *gringo* dog come down here to steal our girls away from us?'' Pascual replies earnestly: ''And our hearts, brother.'' To this Rubriz offers a grudging assent.

Montana's heroics aside, Faust's Mexican characters, especially Rubriz,

Brother Pascual, and Rosita, have won the hearts of many of Faust's readers. They return, along with Montana, in the final novel of the trilogy, THE SONG OF THE WHIP, which has been admired for its stirring action and affirmation of human rights. Will Cuppy, the perceptive reviewer for *Books,* hailed the hardcover edition of the novel as the appearance of a work "so well-written, so exciting, and so thoroughly readable that we advise even non-Western fans to go for it—it's the literate brand and won't disgrace you one bit."[8] (Cuppy was perhaps aware that Evan Evans, the imputed author, was actually Max Brand, and his reference to the "literate brand" is probably a clever inside joke.) The writing sustains a high level of interest and displays Faust's strengths of characterization. The novel's demonstration of Faust's growing admiration for Mexican culture, particularly that of the lower class, has also been noted.[9] Although Faust does not center the plot around a mythic event such as a rescue from the Valley of the Dead, he continues to employ his motif of rescue and escape. Whereas MONTANA RIDES AGAIN might be considered a fable about the recovery of an object sacred to Mexico, THE SONG OF THE WHIP is clearly about a series of acts to establish human rights.

Most of the action centers around the power of the Lerrazas family in northern Mexico, mainly in Chihuahua. The Lerrazas are mentioned in the peons' grimly defiant folk song, "The Song of the Whip," which Faust composed for the novel. Clearly this landed baronial family recalls the aristocratic family of the Terrazas who dominated much of northern Mexico with the tacit support of Díaz. The Terrazas not only managed to gain ownership over a cattle barony of nearly seven million acres but also were able to amass great wealth in other forms as well. With wealth came privilege and power in the administration of provinces and in the dispersing of "justice" in local and regional courts. The Terrazas controlled the lives of thousands of members of the lower class on the eve of the revolution. The peons who were perpetually in debt to the great landowners had become much poorer than their ancestors a century before and at least twelve times poorer than their North American counterparts.

THE SONG OF THE WHIP begins with twin episodes of social tyranny. A Texan named Riley, a responsible citizen of the town where Montana is sojourning, discreetly suggests that the Kid move on. Yet a more overt act of tyranny is being performed across the river where a Lerraza foreman routinely flogs a peon named Julio Mercado. Such an open and obvious display of ruthless power tends to offend North Americans, including even the careful Mr. Riley, although his role in the story is to express the town's social disapproval of the Montana Kid, whose chief fault is described as the need to " 'go around singing the Declaration of Independence every day of your life.' " Both forms of social oppression have unexpected results. Although Mercado has not been rebellious until the flogging, his courageous defiance of his oppressors emerges in his singing of "The Song of the Whip," which encourages Montana to rescue him and punish his oppressors, thereby setting off a series of events that unsettle much of northern Mexico.

In the ensuing action the Kid frees Mercado, boldly captures the foreman, and whips him. News of this dramatic act reunites the Kid with Rubriz's gang who are now presented as "social bandits" whose freedom mocks the tyranny of the government regime and of the Lerrazas. Soon they are joined by Brother Pascual and by Rosita. To consolidate further the novel's central social group, "Tonio Rubriz," the Lavery son from MONTANA RIDES!, returns to Mexico to join the gang for one last adventure. This fellowship becomes reminiscent of other legendary groups of social bandits like that of Robin Hood's whose defiance of authority developed into a political cause. Much of the action illustrates banditry with a social purpose, for Montana's audacity and defiance of the Lerrazas, supported by Rubriz's band, undermines the credibility of the great hacienda owners. When the Lerrazas set a trap for Montana, using Mercado's aged mother as bait, the Kid not only responds with an extraordinary Houdini-like escape but takes refuge in the apartment of Dorotea Lerraza, the beautiful heiress to this hacienda. Here the Kid not only wins her heart, wooing her with a sophisticated detachment, but gains her loyalty. After he has compromised Dorotea's reputation, he also steals El Capitán, the most formidable horse belonging to the Lerrazas. Other events in the novel show the implicit support of the Mexican government for the Lerrazas. Benito Jalisca, a *Rurale,* is allowed to make the pursuit of the Montana Kid his personal obsession, although finally Montana has to shoot him. Concern about what is happening in the kingdom of the Lerrazas also arouses interest in Mexico City. But there are also divisions within the fellowship of resistance fighters. Tonio falls in love with Rosita, but her only passion is for Montana. As a result Tonio betrays the gang by conspiring with the authorities in the hope that the Kid will be killed or captured. Seemingly invincible for a season, Montana, Rubriz, and their band appear to be on the verge of annihilation until they are saved by courageous actions on the part of Rosita and Dorotea. Forced to disguise herself, Dorotea cuts off her long hair, an action that symbolizes her transformation from aristocratic boredom to concern for social justice. In the concluding sequence the Kid, Rubriz, and their companions are rescued, but their heroic status is shown to be limited. Like all other heroes they are human and mortal, after all. Besides, the conflicts within that have brought the free fellowship of the outlaw band to near annihilation remain unresolved. Has Tonio's jealousy of Montana ended? What is the resolution of the romantic triangle involving Montana, Rosita, and Dorotea, since both of the women clearly love the Kid? The fellowship has been imperiled more by inner rivalries and psychological conflicts than by the power of the Lerrazas.

In Brother Pascual's closing speech to the Kid the Friar, the novel's voice of moral wisdom, emphasizes the changes in the lives of those in the group who have gathered around Montana and questions whether these changes have been beneficial. Montana is last seen as a departing figure, his horse drifting northward toward the Rio Grande and the United States. This ending may be read as an expression of moral ambiguity, and, if it appeared in a more obviously literary

context, it might well have garnered praise as an aesthetically satisfying conclusion. In judging this ending we should note that like Faust's original hero,
Dan Barry, the Kid is occasionally associated with the flight of wild geese, and
his departure northward may be read as a return to his original uncommitted
state. But no sympathetic reader can doubt that the lives of the major characters
have been changed by their actions, and very likely they have grown in self-
knowledge.

VII

The chief political and social effect of the defiance of the Lerrazas under
Kid's leadership is largely symbolic. Montana and Rubriz are not ready to set
out, like the rebels commanded by Pancho Villa and Emiliano Zapata, on a
revolution to establish social justice in Mexico. At some point in his career the
"social bandit" may choose outlawry and political revolution, but this is not
the fate envisioned by Faust for Montana and Rubriz. Yet the acts of defiance
by the Kid and Rubriz create a changed consciousness and bring about revolutions. Such acts help to define the existential nature of tyranny and demonstrate
that it can be successfully defied. In the context of the darkening international
scene of the mid-1930s the Montana Kid trilogy, like Faust's spy novels of that
time, take on significant social importance. These novels indirectly celebrate the
human will to defy and defeat tyrannical regimes. Porfirio Díaz's Mexico may
be considered a symbol of both the fascist and Soviet regimes of Europe. Like
the classic film, THE ADVENTURES OF ROBIN HOOD (Warner's, 1938),
these novels are devoted to the exploits of adventurers and rogues who defy
repressive regimes with a touch of humor.

Although the Montana Kid trilogy is conceived and developed on a deeper
level than Faust's earlier adventure novels about Mexico, it must be admitted
that they are adventure novels with strong elements of violent action. This com-
ponent will never allow them to be acceptable to some. Describing with some
realism the harsh world of Díaz's Mexico on the eve of the revolution, and
foregrounding the spirit of populist bandits, the novels could scarcely avoid
episodes of violent action, but perhaps the age when critics could fashionably
deplore the violence in traditional Westerns is past. When an admired contemporary detective series such as Robert B. Parker's Spenser novels often seems
to treat modern Massachusetts as a stage for violent conflict resembling HIGH
NOON (United Artists, 1952) and portrays its hero as a man from Laramie,
Wyoming, then it is obvious that conventional attitudes toward the violence in
Western novels and films need revision. Of course, in an era when American
society appears to be deteriorating and growing increasingly violent, it becomes
hard not to make sweeping condemnations of the violence in fiction and films.
But as such films as THE TREASURE OF THE SIERRA MADRE (Warner's,
1948)—and the B. Traven novel on which it is based—remind us, violent works
set in Mexico may have the purpose of illuminating human motives and char-

acter. Similarly, Faust's Montana Kid novels, though less ironic, help to clarify political and social issues. We need to be reminded that sophisticated adventure novels and films, such as Steven Spielberg's RAIDERS OF THE LOST ARK and INDIANA JONES AND THE LAST CRUSADE (Paramount, 1989), may do more than entertain audiences for a couple of hours. They also may offer vivid reminders of how a thorough social and political tyranny operates and how much it depends on ideology. In THE LAST CRUSADE the scene in Berlin, where troops march while the Nazis burn books, shows us something of the essence of the fascist spirit.

In the process such works may also offer the exhilaration of liberation. Jane Tompkins in her book, WEST OF EVERYTHING: THE INNER LIFE OF WESTERNS (Oxford, 1992), has testified to the enormous emotional power of Louis L'Amour's novel, LAST OF THE BREED (Bantam, 1987), and has commented that experiencing the ordeal of the hero of this novel brings a kind of psychological liberation: ''To be a prisoner of adventure in this way is to be free—free of the present moment with the burden of consciousness it holds.'' The corollary of this discovery is the realization that we may return to the present moment with a renewed consciousness of potential for living. Many of Faust's sympathetic readers, such as William F. Nolan, have felt that one of the chief values of his best work is to provide a titanic sense of release or liberation from the humdrum restrictions of life. Even Bloodworth, the most moderate of Faust's critics, seems to suggest this response when he quotes with approval Rubriz's exuberant statement to Montana: ''What a wonderful thing it is that in such a little world there should be two such men as you and I.'' Perhaps when there are no more social injustices or tyrannical governments, there will be no more heroes and adventure novels. Until then, the sophisticated ones continue to have relevance.

NOTES

FOREVER UNTAMED: FAUST'S INDIAN FICTION FROM "BEYOND THE OUTPOSTS" TO THE RED HAWK TRILOGY

1. *The Police Gazette* of January 17, 1891, reprinted in THE POLICE GAZETTE (Simon & Schuster, 1972) edited by Gene Smith and Jayne Barry Smith, p. 127. While this was clearly a lowbrow and rabble rousing publication, its attitudes were widely shared. A number of hostile and racist comments toward the Sioux which appeared in more respectable newspapers are reprinted as chapter headings by Douglas C. Jones in his novel, A CREEK CALLED WOUNDED KNEE (Scribner, 1978), a historical novel dealing with the Wounded Knee tragedy, and a book which has been praised by Elliott Arnold and other knowledgeable readers.

2. Daryl Jones in THE DIME NOVEL WESTERN (Bowling Green University Popular Press, 1978) argues persuasively, pp. 26–119, that the dime novel hero began as a vengeance-seeking Indian killer, but that this hero became more noble and chivalric in the later years of the nineteenth century. Thus the occasional noble savage might appear to soften the treatment of native Americans in pale imitation of Cooper; but there was no dramatic alteration of their image in popular fiction. On this point, see Berkhofer's THE WHITE MAN'S INDIAN (Knopf, 1978), pp. 97–99.

3. Grey had described the conflicts between Indians and white settlers on the Ohio frontier as extremely savage in his early Ohio River trilogy (1903–1909), making the Indian-hater, Lew Wetzel, one of his heroes. But Grey's fiction is never without sympathy for Indians, and this feeling was intensified after he became acquainted with Navajos in his hunting trip (1907) with Buffalo Jones. However, it should be noted that Nophaie, the hero of THE VANISHING AMERICAN, is a Navajo who received the white culture's education before choosing to return to the reservation. Moreover, the novel does not take place in a period of warfare between whites and Indians but is set in the early twentieth century. Nophaie is made more sympathetic by serving admirably in the Allied cause in World War I, as did many native Americans and a major reason why some

were granted U.S. citizenship in 1924. Yet, according to a 1982 Foreword by Grey's son, Loren Grey, to a reprint from Pocket Books, the author was obliged by the publishers to change the ending so that Nophaie died rather than marry his white sweetheart, Marian.

4. This phase of Burroughs's life is treated by Richard A. Lupoff in EDGAR RICE BURROUGHS: MASTER OF ADVENTURE, Revised Edition (Ace, 1968), pp. 38–41. The Apache novels are briefly assessed on pp. 138–139, and again on p. 281, where Lupoff, one of the first to take Burroughs seriously as a writer, offers an argument that THE WAR CHIEF is one of the best of Burroughs's novels.

5. In his MAX BRAND: THE BIG "WESTERNER" (University of Oklahoma, 1970), p. 169, Robert Easton does not mention Catlin, instead ascribing to Grinnell and Schultz the main sources of Faust's knowledge of Indian life. More recently Easton has commented on the importance of Catlin in Faust's work: Faust owned a fine two-volume first edition of Catlin with "marvelous color plates." Since Catlin painted his Indians in the 1830s and 1840s, his art was no doubt quite stimulating to Faust's imagination for the majority of his Plains Indian novels, which are set in that period. In his January 24, 1995, letter Easton also lists six books by Grinnell, including THE FIGHTING CHEY-ENNES and re-tellings of Pawnee and Blackfoot folk tales. Oddly enough, no copy of Grinnell's THE CHEYENNE INDIANS has turned up, but it is hard to believe that Faust did not have some acquaintance with it. Easton also lists four books by Schultz, including MY LIFE AS AN INDIAN, as part of Faust's surviving library, as well as books dealing with Indian life by General O. O. Howard, Douglas Branch, Bleasdell Cameron, Randall Parrish, James McLaughlin, Thomas Marquis, Frederick Paxson, Clark Wissler, William Christie Macleod, and Paul Radin whose fame as an anthropologist is well known.

6. The treatment of Cheyenne life is much more confident and knowledgeable in LOST WOLF than in Faust's only previous story about Indians, "Beyond the Outposts," where the Cheyennes appear as villainous in contrast to the Sioux. It is therefore easy to suspect that Faust may have begun reading Grinnell between the composition of these two novels. The influence of Grinnell is obvious in nearly all the Plains Indian stories thereafter, and it grows and deepens. Incidentally, in my 1978 essay on Faust's treatment of Indians in his fiction I did not have access to editions of either "Beyond the Out-posts," which remains substantially different in magazine form from the Putnam edition, or LOST WOLF. Hence, I erroneously assumed that THE WHITE CHEYENNE, the sequel to LOST WOLF, was Faust's first novel treating Indian life.

7. The missing father or the ambiguous father figure is a particularly strong theme in the early Westerns (1918–1926), as in "Black Jack," where the hero must try to live down his father's reputation as an outlaw. But the motif remains persistent throughout the canon, although from the time of SINGING GUNS, many of the heroes begin to find surrogate father figures. The biographical reasons for Faust's concern with this theme are described by Easton in MAX BRAND: THE BIG "WESTERNER," pp. 3–27.

8. This serial is now scheduled for first book publication as THE STONE THAT SHINES (Five Star Westerns, 1997).

9. The Apaches, because of the fierceness of their resistance to the white advance, probably had fewer sympathetic treatments than other Indian nations in Western fiction prior to the end of World War II and before Elliott Arnold's BLOOD BROTHER (Duell, 1947) which eventually inspired the important film, BROKEN ARROW (Twentieth-Fox, 1950) with its sympathetic treatment of Cochise. However, in addition to the Burroughs books already mentioned, Will Levington Comfort published a biographical novel of Mangas Coloradas called APACHE (Dutton, 1931), practically contemporary with

Faust's TAMER OF THE WILD. It should be noted that Hollywood's film treatment of the Apaches had also been harsh. For instance, they are the dreaded menace in John Ford's STAGECOACH (United Artists, 1939), though here they are at least treated with more respect than the Sioux receive in Cecil B. DeMille's wretched epic, THE PLAINS-MAN (Paramount, 1936).

10. In order to avoid confusion here, we should note that the first Thunder Moon novel did not appear in hardcover form until 1969. The sequels, including the serial ''Thunder Moon, Squawman'' and some novelettes, were first published as 60,000-word books by Dodd, Mead in 1982, under the titles THUNDER MOON'S CHALLENGE and THUNDER MOON STRIKES. Since these hardcover editions had not appeared at the time of my 1978 essay, I was unable to discuss them, though I was aware Faust had written continuations of the Thunder Moon stories. The series has now been published as a four-volume series by the University of Nebraska Press, and this new edition restores the integrity of ''Thunder Moon, Squawman'' as a complete novel (the third in the series); its title, however, has been changed to the more appropriate THUNDER MOON AND THE SKY PEOPLE. The first entry is THE LEGEND OF THUNDER MOON, followed by RED WIND AND THUNDER MOON and the final volume entitled FARE-WELL, THUNDER MOON.

11. Jon Tuska offers a Jungian interpretation of Faust's Indian novels in his ''Frederick Faust's Western Fiction: An Overview'' (elsewhere in THE MAX BRAND COM-PANION). I find Jungian interpretations of Faust's fiction helpful and suggestive, and it seems to me that the Red Hawk trilogy in particular is inviting to such readings. However, in this essay, I am more concerned with the social and cultural implications of Faust's fiction dealing with Indians.

AN ENDURING FASCINATION: MAX BRAND'S MEXICAN NOVELS

1. Subtitled ''Five Studies in Naturalism,'' Warren's sequence appeared in his first volume of SELECTED POEMS: 1923–1943 published in 1944.

2. Chihuahua Joe is a daredevil, a dandy, and a first-rate gunfighter, though he is given comic and ungrammatical English with, of course, a few Spanish words thrown in. Although the character may have been intended to counteract negative stereotypes, he, or his type, appeared as a sidekick in several later stories and films, such as Dan Cushman's pulp stories about a Texas gunman called The Pecos Kid, and a B Western movie series featuring Tim Holt, who was helped by a brave but comic Mexican-American sidekick played by Richard Martin.

3. O'Rourke described the world of Mexican-Americans in the Rio Arriba region of New Mexico in several novels, including SEGUNDO (Dell, 1956) and THE BRAVA-DOS (Dell, 1957). THUNDER IN THE SUN (Ballantine, 1954) treated the Mexican Revolution sympathetically, and O'Rourke returned to this theme in A MULE FOR THE MARQUESA (Morrow, 1964) which became Richard Brooks's fine film, THE PRO-FESSIONALS (Columbia, 1966).

4. This quotation comes from the fifties Dell paperback reprint of Mulford's story. It was originally published in 1910 by A. C. McClurg of Chicago. Not surprisingly, a more recent reprint, probably prompted by the publication of Louis L'Amour's four Hopalong Cassidy novels, cosmetically cleans up the ethnic slurs in the passage.

5. It must be acknowledged that Faust depicted an unsavory Mexican in the early novel, ALCATRAZ (Putnam, 1923); this fellow mistreats the stallion so shamefully that Alcatraz is driven to escape to the hills and becomes an "outlaw," thereby emulating some of Faust's human heroes. Will James had described a similar pattern in his novel, SMOKY (Scribner, 1926).

6. This information is provided in Tuska's essay on Faust's Western fiction already cited.

7. Seeing the crown as a metaphor of the self would be a Jungian interpretation of this story. We should note, incidentally, that there is an authentic crown of Our Lady of Guadalupe—containing emeralds and other stones—at the shrine dedicated to the Virgin of Guadalupe near Mexico City. The brown-skinned, or Indian, Virgin was first seen in a vision by Juan Diego, a humble Indian, in 1531 (about a decade after Cortez's conquest of Mexico) and is generally viewed as a model of the way that an imported religion may be adapted to the national and psychological needs of an indigenous native population. A replica of the original crown also resides today in Notre Dame Cathedral in Paris—a gift of Mexican Catholics—but this could not have been the source of Faust's symbol, since it was not bestowed on Notre Dame until 1949. (This information comes from a letter of Guy Lalier, Intendant of Notre Dame de Paris, to Edgar L. Chapman, August 23, 1995.)

8. Cuppy's review appears on page 12 in the June 7, 1936, issue. The reviews of the trilogy in several publications are unusually positive; the favorable response in the *Saturday Review of Literature,* mentioned earlier, appeared in the July 1, 1933, issue. An able and veteran reviewer, Cuppy may have based his allusion to the "literate Brand" on his recognition of Faust's style, since he had reviewed some of Faust's Dodd, Mead books published under the Max Brand name.

9. Christine Bold, on the evidence of publication dates, erroneously believes that THE SONG OF THE WHIP is Faust's final Western. This is incorrect: though the novel was published in 1936, it was actually sold earlier than THE STREAK and consequently written before that novel, as the research of such Faust scholars as Jon Tuska has established (letter to E.L.C., November 17, 1994). Bold finds it tempting to read the ending of THE SONG OF THE WHIP as a disillusioned farewell to the Western; but this interpretation ignores the characters and theme that Faust develops in the novel, not to mention Faust's artistry.

INDEX

ABOUT THE EDITORS AND CONTRIBUTORS

JON TUSKA and VICKI PIEKARSKI are authors or editors of numerous works about the American West, including Piekarski's WESTWARD THE WOMEN (Doubleday, 1983) and Tuska's BILLY THE KID: HIS LIFE AND LEGEND (Greenwood, 1994). Together they are co-editors-in-chief of the ENCYCLO-PEDIA OF FRONTIER AND WESTERN FICTION (McGraw-Hill, 1983), which is now being prepared in its second edition. Together they were the co-founders of Golden West Literary Agency and the first Westerners in the history of the Western story to co-edit and co-publish twenty-six new hardcover Western fiction books a year in two prestigious series, the Five Star Westerns and the Circle Ⓥ Westerns.

MARTHA BACON was an associate editor of *The Atlantic Monthly*, poet, and novelist.

ADRIANA FAUST BIANCHI is the daughter of Faust's younger daughter, Judy, and makes her home in Florence, Italy, where Faust lived for many years.

WILLIAM A. BLOODWORTH, JR. is president of Augusta College in Georgia, author of MAX BRAND (Twayne Publishers, 1993), and is currently editing a collection of Frederick Faust's letters with biographical commentary.

CARL BRANDT, of the Brandt and Brandt Literary Agency in New York City, was Faust's literary agent and longtime friend.

EDGAR L. CHAPMAN is professor of English at Bradley University, Peoria, Illinois, and author of numerous articles about Frederick Faust's fiction.

CHESTER D. CUTHBERT is a Canadian collector of Faust's fiction and has contributed several articles about this author to various publications.

EDWARD H. DODD, JR., of the publishing firm, Dodd, Mead & Company, published Faust's works in book form for many years.

JANE FAUST EASTON is the elder daughter of Frederick Faust. She lives in Santa Barbara, California.

ROBERT EASTON is a distinguished author whose first novel, THE HAPPY MAN (Viking, 1943), is regarded as a classic of the Western story. He is the author of MAX BRAND: THE BIG "WESTERNER" (University of Oklahoma Press, 1970). His highly acclaimed Saga of California series is now appearing in mass merchandise paperback editions. The third volume in this saga, BLOOD AND MONEY, will appear as a Five Star Western.

STEVE FISHER was the author of some twenty novels, mostly crime fiction, and contributed as well to seventy-five film scripts and twice that many teleplays.

DAVID L. FOX is the editor and publisher of *Singing Guns,* a fanzine devoted to the life and work of Frederick Faust.

ED GORMAN is the author of several crime novels and a number of Western stories. He is the editor of the magazine *Mystery Scene* and is at work on a new Five Star Western about Cedar Rapids policewoman Anna Tolan.

WALTER MORRIS HART was professor of English at the University of California, Berkeley, first Faust's teacher and then longtime friend.

LEO A. HETZLER is professor of English at St. John Fisher College, Rochester, New York. He is the author of numerous essays on Max Brand.

GILBERT J. MCLENNAN, who later became a rancher in the Colorado Rockies, knew Faust in the American Legion in Canada in 1916.

DWIGHT BENNETT NEWTON is a prolific Western novelist and short story writer, currently at work on his seventy-first novel for Five Star Westerns.

WILLIAM F. NOLAN is a highly successful author of numerous novels and short stories, teleplays, and biographies. He has long been an indefatigable researcher of details about Faust's life and work and edited MAX BRAND: WESTERN GIANT (Bowling Green University Popular Press, 1986). He is currently preparing for publication a collection of Max Brand Western stories and another collection of Max Brand's crime fiction.

SAMUEL A. PEEPLES is the author of a number of Western novels, under his own name and as Brad Ward, the most familiar of which is FRONTIER STREET (Macmillan, 1958), a novel expanded from the short story originally adapted as LAWLESS STREET (Columbia, 1955) starring Randolph Scott.

JACK RICARDO is a full-time freelance writer who discovered Max Brand Westerns and became an avid collector. His article, ''Max Brand and the Homoerotic Novel,'' appeared in *Inches*.

DARRELL C. RICHARDSON was the first critic and commentator to take Frederick Faust's fiction seriously. For years he supplied the materials for book editions of Faust's work published by Dodd, Mead and Harper & Bros., was the editor and publisher of the first fanzine devoted entirely to Frederick Faust and his work, and was the author and editor of the first book about Frederick Faust. He served as the consulting editor for THE MAX BRAND COMPANION.

HARVEY RONEY was Faust's classmate at the University of California, Berkeley, and later a businessman in Los Angeles.

JOHN SCHOOLCRAFT was Faust's college mate who later collaborated with Faust on a novel and published stories on his own.

HERBERT WADOPIAN, lieutenant, was Faust's platoon leader during the Second World War.

SUSAN L. ZODIN holds a degree in medical history and is doing research into the role of fictional physicians in American medicine.